FEMINIST THOUGHT

THIRD EDITION

FEMINIST THOUGHT

A MORE COMPREHENSIVE INTRODUCTION

Rosemarie Tong

University of North Carolina, Charlotte

A Member of the Perseus Books Group

Copyright © 2009 by Westview Press
Published by Westview Press,
A Member of the Perseus Books Group

Westview Press books are available at special discounts for bulk purchases in the United
States by corporations, institutions, and other organizations. For more information,
please contact the Special Markets Department at the Perseus Books Group, 2300
Chestnut Street, Philadelphia, PA, or call (800) 810-4145, extension 5000,
or e-mail special.markets@perseusbooks.com.

A CIP catalog record for this book is available from the Library of Congress

ISBN: 978-0-8133-4375-4
10 9 8 7 6 5 4

Contents

Preface

Oftentimes, a new edition of a book, particularly a third edition, amounts to little more than some added references and updates. But I can assure readers that this new edition of *Feminist Thought: A More Comprehensive Introduction,* constitutes a major overhaul: eighteen months of drafting and redrafting. Chapters that remain substantially the same are the chapters on liberal feminism, radical feminism, and ecofeminism, though even these have significant revisions. Substantially reformulated chapters are the ones on psychoanalytic feminism and Marxist/socialist feminism. I have reassigned some feminist thinkers I previously classified as postmodern feminists to the psychoanalytic feminist fold, and I have amplified my discussion of socialist feminism in ways that better clarify the differences between it and Marxist feminism. In addition, although Chapter 6, "Multicultural, Global, and Postcolonial Feminism," includes ideas from the second edition, I have thoroughly revised the section on multicultural feminism, offering new interpretations of this mode of feminist thinking. Further enhancing this chapter, which is now one of my favorite chapters, is a serious effort to address the differences between multicultural, global, and postcolonial feminism. New or expanded discussions of Susan Okin, Martha Nussbaum, Chila Bulbeck, Linda Martin Alcoff, and Adrian Piper are featured. Another chapter that blends a bit of old material with much new material is Chapter 8, "Postmodern and Third-Wave Feminism." Among the feminist thinkers now showcased are Hélène Cixous, Judith Butler, Leslie Heywood, Jennifer Drake, and Rebecca Walker. Finally, a new chapter makes its debut in this third edition. Although Chapter 5, "Care-Focused Feminism," includes previous discussions of Carol Gilligan and Nel Noddings, equally long discussions of Virginia Held and Eva Feder Kittay have been added.

As I reflect on this third edition of *Feminist Thought,* I realize how quickly and richly feminist thinking has developed. I applaud the creative and scholarly abilities of the feminists whose work I try to summarize, interpret, and share with as wide and diverse an audience as possible. Feminist thinking has energized the academy and challenged it to reject the limits that had been previously imposed on it by a "white/male/exclusionary" modality of thought. Just as importantly—indeed more importantly—feminist thinking has motivated feminist action. The world is more fair, just, and caring thanks to the ideas not only of the feminist thinkers featured in this book but also the many feminist thinkers who, for lack of pen perhaps, have not been able to write down, let alone widely publicize their ideas. It is to this group of feminist thinkers I dedicate this book.

Acknowledgments

As anyone who has ever written a book knows, it is not a solo project. Rather, it is a collaborative effort. My only fear is that I will fail to say a public thank-you to one of the persons who helped me bring this book to completion.

First, I want to thank Lisa Singleton for the long hours she spent researching for me and the even longer hours she spent typing draft after draft of a book that seemed without end. Without Lisa's cheerful commitment to this project, it would not have seen the light of day. There is no way that I can thank this gifted woman enough.

Second, I want to thank Karl Yambert, my editor. His patience is that of Job. Due to life's unpredictable and sometimes sad detours, it took me far longer to complete this book than I hoped. Rather than chastising me, Karl made things easy for me. Had I had a less understanding editor, I would have probably abandoned this third edition.

Third, I want to thank my diligent copyeditor, Patty Boyd, for perfecting my manuscript and the anonymous reviewers who motivated me to improve it. Their behind-the-scenes work is most appreciated.

I also want to thank Laura Stine, my project editor, for getting this edition of *Feminist Thought* to press.

Finally, I thank all feminist thinkers for building a body of thought that is moving us closer to being a more just and compassionate world. I am grateful to be a part of this effort and hope to remain a part of it until the day I die.

Introduction:
The Diversity of Feminist Thinking

Since writing my first introduction to feminist thought nearly two decades ago, I have become increasingly convinced that feminist thought resists categorization into tidy schools of thought. Interdisciplinary, intersectional, and interlocking are the kind of adjectives that best describe the way we feminists think. There is a certain breathlessness in the way we move from one topic to the next, revising our thoughts in midstream. Yet despite the very real problems that come with trying to categorize the thought of an incredibly diverse and large array of feminist thinkers as "x" or "y" or "z," feminist thought is old enough to have a history complete with a set of labels: liberal, radical, Marxist/socialist, psychoanalytic, care-focused, multicultural/global/colonial, ecofeminist, and postmodern/third wave. To be sure, this list of labels is incomplete and highly contestable. Indeed, it may ultimately prove to be entirely unreflective of feminism's intellectual and political commitments to women. For now, however, feminist thought's old labels still remain serviceable. They signal to the public that feminism is not a monolithic ideology and that all feminists do not think alike. The labels also help mark the range of different approaches, perspectives, and frameworks a variety of feminists have used to shape both their explanations for women's oppression and their proposed solutions for its elimination.

Because so much of contemporary feminist theory defines itself in reaction against traditional liberal feminism, liberalism is as good a place as any to begin a survey of feminist thought. This perspective received its classic formulation in Mary Wollstonecraft's *A Vindication of the Rights of Women,*[1] in John Stuart Mill's "The Subjection of Women,"[2] and in the nineteenth-century women's suffrage movement. Its main thrust, an emphasis still felt in contemporary groups such as the National Organization of Women (NOW), is that female subordination is rooted in a set of customary and legal constraints that blocks women's entrance to and success in the so-called public world. To the extent that society holds the false belief that women are, by nature, less intellectually and physically capable than men, it tends to discriminate against women in the academy, the forum, and the marketplace. As liberal feminists see it, this discrimination against women is unfair. Women should have as much chance to succeed in the public realm as men do. Gender justice, insist liberal feminists, requires us, first, to make the rules of the game fair and, second, to make certain that none of the runners in the race for society's goods and services is systematically disadvantaged.

But is the liberal feminist program drastic and dramatic enough to completely undo women's oppression? Radical feminists think not. They claim the patriarchal system is characterized by power, dominance, hierarchy, and competition. It cannot be reformed but only ripped out root and branch. It is not just patriarchy's legal and political structures that must be overturned on the way to women's liberation. Its social and cultural institutions (especially the family and organized religion) must also be uprooted.

As in the past, I remain impressed by the diverse modalities of thinking that count as "radical feminist thought." Although all radical feminists focus on sex, gender, and reproduction as the locus for the development of feminist thought,[3] some of them favor so-called androgyny, stress the pleasures of sex (be it heterosexual, lesbian, or autoerotic), and view as unalloyed blessings for women not only the old reproduction-controlling technologies but also the new reproduction-assisting technologies. In contrast, other radical feminists reject androgyny; emphasize the dangers of sex, especially heterosexual sex; and regard as harmful to women the new reproduction-assisting technologies and, for the most part, the old reproduction-controlling technologies. As in the second edition of my book, I sort this varied array of radical feminist thinkers into two groups: "radical-libertarian feminists" and "radical-cultural feminists."[4]

With respect to gender-related issues, radical-libertarian feminists usually reason that if, to their own detriment, men are required to exhibit masculine characteristics only, and if, to their own detriment, women are required to exhibit feminine characteristics only, then the solution to this harmful state of affairs is to *permit* all human beings to be androgynous—to exhibit a full range of masculine *and* feminine qualities. Men should be permitted to explore their feminine dimensions, and women their masculine ones. No human being should be forbidden the sense of wholeness that comes from combining his or her masculine and feminine sides.

Disagreeing with radical-libertarian feminists that a turn to androgyny is a liberation strategy for women, radical-cultural feminists argue against this move in one of three ways. Some anti-androgynists maintain the problem is not femininity in and of itself, but rather the low value that patriarchy assigns to feminine qualities such as "gentleness, modesty, humility, supportiveness, empathy, compassionateness, tenderness, nurturance, intuitiveness, sensitivity, unselfishness," and the high value it assigns to masculine qualities such as "assertiveness, aggressiveness, hardiness, rationality or the ability to think logically, abstractly and analytically, ability to control emotion."[5] They claim that if society can learn to value "feminine" traits as much as "masculine" traits, women's oppression will be a bad memory. Other anti-androgynists object, insisting femininity *is* the problem because it has been constructed by men for patriarchal purposes. In order to be liberated, women must reject femininity as it has been constructed for them and give it an entirely new meaning. Femininity should no longer be understood as those traits that deviate from masculinity. On the contrary, femininity should be understood as a way of being that needs no reference point external to it. Still other anti-androgynists, reverting to a "nature theory," argue that despite patriarchy's imposition of a false, or inauthentic, *feminine* nature upon women, many women have nonetheless rebelled against it, unearthing their true, or authentic, *female* nature instead. Full personal freedom for a woman consists, then, in her ability to renounce her false feminine self in favor of her true female self.

As difficult as it is to fully reflect the range of radical feminist thought on gender, it is even more difficult to do so with respect to sexuality. Radical-libertarian feminists argue that no specific kind of sexual experience should be prescribed as *the* best kind for women.[6] Every woman should be encouraged to experiment sexually with herself, with other women, and with men. Although heterosexuality can be dangerous for women within a patriarchal society, women must nonetheless feel free to follow the lead of their own desires, embracing men if that is their choice.

Radical-cultural feminists disagree. They stress that through pornography, prostitution, sexual harassment, rape, and woman battering,[7] through foot binding, suttee, purdah, clitoridectormy, witch burning, and gynecology,[8] men have controlled women's sexuality for male pleasure. Thus, in order to be liberated, women must escape the confines of heterosexuality and create an exclusively female sexuality through celibacy, autoeroticism, or lesbianism.[9] Only alone, or with other women, can women discover the true pleasure of sex.

Radical feminist thought is as diverse on issues related to reproduction as it is on matters related to sexuality. Radical-libertarian feminists claim biological motherhood drains women physically and psychologically.[10] Women should be free, they say, to use the old reproduction-controlling technologies and the new reproduction-assisting technologies on their own terms—to prevent or terminate unwanted pregnancies or, alternatively, so that women can have children when they want them (premenopausally or postmenopausally), how they want them (in their own womb or that of another woman), and with whom they want them (a man, a woman, or alone). Some radical-libertarian feminists go farther than this, however. They look forward to the day when ectogenesis (extracorporeal gestation in an artificial placenta) entirely replaces the natural process of pregnancy. In contrast to radical-libertarian feminists, radical-cultural feminists claim biological mother-hood is the ultimate source of woman's power.[11] It is women who determine whether the human species continues—whether there is life or no life. Women must guard and celebrate this life-giving power, for without it, men will have even less respect and use for women than they have now.[12]

Somewhat unconvinced by the liberal and radical feminist agendas for women's liberation, Marxist and socialist feminists claim it is impossible for anyone, especially women, to achieve true freedom in a class-based society, where the wealth produced by the powerless many ends up in the hands of the powerful few. With Friedrich Engels,[13] Marxist and socialist feminists insist women's oppression originated in the introduction of private property, an institution that obliterated whatever equality of community humans had previously enjoyed. Private ownership of the means of production by relatively few persons, originally all male, inaugurated a class system whose contemporary manifestations are corporate capitalism and imperialism. Reflection on this state of affairs suggests that capitalism itself, not just the larger social rules that privilege men over women, is the cause of women's oppression. If all women—rather than just the "exceptional" ones—are ever to be liberated, the capitalist system must be replaced by a socialist system in which the means of production belong to everyone. No longer economically dependent on men, women will be just as free as men.

Socialist feminists agree with Marxist feminists that *capitalism* is the source of women's oppression, and with radical feminists that *patriarchy* is the source of women's oppression. Therefore, the way to end women's oppression, in socialist feminists' estimation, is to kill the two-headed beast of capitalist patriarchy or patriarchal capitalism (take your pick). Motivated by this goal, socialist feminists seek to develop theories that explain the relationship between capitalism and patriarchy.

During the first stage of theory development, socialist feminists offered several "two-system" explanations of women's oppression. Among these two-system theories were those forwarded by Juliet Mitchell and Alison Jaggar. In

Women's Estate, Mitchell claimed that women's condition is determined not only by the structures of production (as Marxist feminists think), but also by the structures of reproduction and sexuality (as radical feminists believe), and the socialization of children (as liberal feminists argue).[14] She stressed that women's status and function in all of these structures must change if women are to achieve full liberation. Still, in the final analysis, Mitchell gave the edge to capitalism over patriarchy as women's worst enemy.

Like Mitchell, Alison Jaggar attempted to achieve a synthesis between Marxist and radical feminist thought. Acknowledging that all feminist perspectives recognize the conflicting demands made on women as wives, mothers, daughters, lovers, and workers,[15] Jaggar insisted that socialist feminism is unique because of its concerted effort to interrelate the myriad forms of women's oppression. She used the unifying concept of alienation to explain how, under capitalism, everything (work, sex, play) and everyone (family members and friends) that could be a source of women's integration as persons becomes instead a cause of their disintegration. Together with Mitchell, Jaggar insisted there are only complex explanations for women's subordination. Yet, in contrast to Mitchell, she named patriarchy rather than capitalism as the worst evil visited on women.

After Mitchell and Jaggar, another group of socialist feminists aimed to develop new explanations of women's oppression that did not in any way pinpoint capitalism or patriarchy as the *primary* source of women's limited well-being and freedom. Iris Marion Young, Heidi Hartmann, and Sylvia Walby constructed explanations for women's oppression that viewed capitalism and patriarchy as interactive to the point of full symbiosis. To a greater or lesser extent, these thinkers addressed the question of whether capitalism could survive the death of patriarchy, or vice versa. Although the nuances of their theories were difficult to grasp, Young, Hartmann, and Walby—like their predecessors Mitchell and Jaggar—pushed feminists to address issues related to women's unpaid, underpaid, or disvalued work.

To the degree that liberal, radical, and Marxist-socialist feminists focus on the macrocosm (patriarchy or capitalism) in their respective explanations of women's oppression, psychoanalytic feminists are most at home in the microcosm of the individual. They claim the roots of women's oppression are embedded deep in the female psyche. Initially, psychoanalytic feminists focused on Sigmund Freud's work, looking within it for a better understanding of sexuality's role in the oppression of women. According to Freud, in the so-called pre-Oedipal stage, all infants are symbiotically attached to their mothers, whom they perceive as omnipotent. The mother-infant relationship is an ambivalent one, however: sometimes mothers give too much—their presence is overwhelming—but other times mothers give too little—their absence disappoints.

The pre-Oedipal stage ends with the so-called Oedipal complex, the process by which the boy gives up his first love object, the mother, in order to escape castration at the hands of the father. As a result of submitting his id (desires) to the superego (collective social conscience), the boy is fully integrated into culture. Together with his father, he will rule over nature and woman, both of whom supposedly contain a similarly irrational power. In contrast to the boy, the girl, who has no penis to lose, separates slowly from her first love object, the mother. As a result, the girl's integration into culture is incomplete. She exists at the periphery, or margin, of culture as the one who does not rule but is ruled, largely because, as Dorothy Dinnerstein suggested, she fears her own power.[16]

Because the Oedipus complex is the root of male rule, or patriarchy, some psychoanalytic feminists speculate that the complex is nothing more than the product of men's imagination—a psychic trap that everyone, especially women, should try to escape. Others object that unless we are prepared for reentry into a chaotic state of nature, we must accept some version of the Oedipus complex as the experience that integrates the individual into society. In accepting *some* version of the Oedipus complex, Sherry Ortner noted, we need not accept the *Freudian* version, according to which the qualities of authority, autonomy, and universalism are labeled male, whereas love, dependence, and particularism are labeled female.[17] These labels, meant to privilege that which is male over that which is female, are not essential to the Oedipus complex. Rather, they are simply the consequences of a child's actual experience with men and women. As Ortner saw it, dual parenting (as recommended also by Dorothy Dinnerstein and Nancy Chodorow) and dual participation in the workforce would change the gender valences of the Oedipus complex.[18] Authority, autonomy, and universalism would no longer be the exclusive property of men; love, dependence, and particularism would no longer be the exclusive property of women.

Not sure that dual parenting and dual participation in the workforce were up to changing the gender valences of the Oedipal complex, a new generation of psychoanalytic feminists turned to theorists like Jacques Lacan for more insights into the psychosexual dramas that produce "man" and "woman," the "feminine" and the "masculine," the "heterosexual" and the "lesbian," and so forth. Formidable theorists like Luce Irigaray and Julia Kristeva claimed that feminists had spent too much time focusing on the Oedipal realm and not nearly enough time on the prelinguistic, pre-Oedipal domain. This domain, often referred to as the Imaginary, is the domain infants are supposed to leave behind so they can enter the Symbolic order, the realm of language, rules, and regimes: civilization. But, asked Irigaray and Kristeva, why should women abandon the Imaginary so they can be oppressed, suppressed, and repressed in patriarchy's Symbolic order? Why not instead stay in the Imaginary, and relish the joy of being different from men? Why not remain identified with one's first love, the mother, and develop with her new ways of speaking and writing, of constituting one's subjectivity, that do not lead to women's oppression? Why lead life on men's terms at all?

In earlier editions of this book, I had included theorists like Carol Gilligan and Nel Noddings with psychoanalytic feminists because of their interest in women's psychology. But I now realize that Gilligan and Noddings are not the same kind of thinkers as those I currently classify as psychoanalytic feminists. What distinguishes Gilligan and Noddings from psychoanalytic feminists, and what links them to feminists thinkers like Sara Ruddick, Virginia Held, and Eva Feder Kittay, is their focus on the nature and practice of care. More than any other group of feminist thinkers, care-focused feminists are interested in understanding why, to a greater or lesser degree, women are usually associated with the emotions and the body, and men with reason and the mind. On a related note, care-focused feminists seek to understand why women as a group are usually linked with interdependence, community, and connection, whereas men as a group are usually linked with independence, selfhood, and autonomy. These thinkers offer a variety of explanations for *why* societies divide realities into things "feminine" and things "masculine." But whatever their explanation for men's and women's differing gender identities and behaviors, care-focused feminists regard women's hypothetically greater capacities for care as a human strength, so much so that they tend to privilege feminist approaches to an ethics of care over the reigning ethics of justice in the Western world. In addition, care-focused feminists provide excellent explanations for why women as a group disproportionately shoulder the burden of care in virtually all societies, and why men as a group do not routinely engage in caring practices. Finally, care-focused feminists provide plans and policies for reducing women's burden of care so that women have as much time and energy as men have to develop themselves as full persons.

Like all the feminists who preceded them and now overlap with them, multicultural, global, and postcolonial feminists focus on the causes of and explanations for women's subordination to men worldwide. However, these groups' main contribution to feminist thought is their strong commitment to highlighting the differences that exist among women and identifying ways that diverse kinds of women can work together. Unafraid of the challenges that women's differences sometimes present to women's alleged solidarity, multicultural, global, and postcolonial feminists courageously address the ways in which race, ethnicity, sexual identity, gender identity, age, religion, level of education, occupation/profession, marital status, health condition, and so on, may separate one group of women from another. They aim to reveal how contextual factors shape women's self-understanding as being oppressed or not oppressed. They also seek to help feminists reject both female essentialism (the view that all women are, down deep, exactly alike) and female chauvinism (the view that privileged women should take it upon themselves to speak on behalf of all women).

Although the terms "multicultural," "global," and "postcolonial" are often used interchangeably to describe feminists who focus on women's varying social, cultural, economic, and political contexts, I reserve the term "multicultural" to denote feminists who focus on the differences that exist among women who live within the boundaries of one nation-state or geographical area. In turn, I use the terms "global" or "postcolonial" to denote feminists who focus on the ways in which most women's lives in most developing nations are generally worse off than most women's lives in most developed nations. These feminists challenge women in developed nations to acknowledge that many of their privileges are bought at the expense of the well-being of women in developing nations. Regrettably, the harmful effects of nineteenth- and twentieth-century colonization campaigns are still felt in the so-called Third World.

As attentive as multicultural, global, and postcolonial feminists are to the complexities of human beings' relationships to each other, they do not focus, as ecofeminists do, on human beings' relationships to the nonhuman world—that is, to nature itself. In many ways, ecofeminists offer the broadest and also the most demanding conception of the self's relationship to the other. According to ecofeminists, we are connected not only to each other but also to the non-human world: animal and even vegetative. Unfortunately, we do not always acknowledge our responsibilities to each other, let alone to the nonhuman world. As a result, we deplete the world's natural resources with our machines, pollute the environment with our toxic fumes, and stockpile arms centers with tools of total destruction. In so doing, we delude ourselves that we are controlling nature and enhancing ourselves. In point of fact, said ecofeminist Ynestra King, nature is already rebelling, and each day the human self is impoverished as yet another forest is "detreed" and yet another animal species is extinguished.[19] The only way not to destroy ourselves, insist ecofeminists, is to strengthen our relationships not only with each other but also with the nonhuman world.

Challenging all the versions of feminism that have preceded them, postmodern and third-wave feminists push feminist thought to new limits. Although postmodern feminists' insistence that women are in no way "one" poses problems for feminist theory and action (if women do not exist as a class or group or collectivity, it is difficult to fight against women's oppression), this insistence also adds needed fuel to the feminist fires of plurality, multiplicity, and difference. Moreover, postmodern feminists' rejection of in-the-box thinking helps feminists speak and write in ways that overcome the binary oppositions of traditional patriarchal thought. Postmodern feminists erase the lines between masculine and feminine, sex and gender, male and female. They seek to break down the conceptual grids that have prevented women from defining themselves in their own terms rather than through men's terms.

Third-wave feminists, eager to shape a new-millennium feminism, push just as hard as postmodern feminists do to rethink the category "woman/women." For third-wave feminists, difference is the way the world is. Conflict and even self-contradiction are the name of the game as women seek new identities for themselves and stir up what Judith Butler termed "gender trouble."[20] Yet for all their differences from first-wave and second-wave feminists, third-wave feminists have no intentions of thinking, speaking, or writing themselves and other women out of existence. Instead, they aim to answer the "woman question"—Who is she and what does she want?—in ways that it has never been answered before.

Clearly, it is a major challenge to contemporary feminism to reconcile the pressures for diversity and difference with those for integration and commonality. Fortunately, contemporary feminists do not shrink from this challenge. It seems that each year, we better understand the reasons why women worldwide are the "second sex" and how to change this state of affairs. In this third edition of my book, I have tried to discuss the weaknesses as well as the strengths of each of the feminist perspectives presented here. In so doing, I have aimed not so much at *neutrality* as I have at *respect,* since each feminist perspective has made a rich and lasting contribution to feminist thought. At the end of this book, readers looking for one winning view, a champion left standing after an intellectual free-for-all, will be disappointed. Although all feminist perspectives cannot be equally correct, there is no need here for a definitive final say. Instead there is always room for growth, improvement, reconsideration, and expansion for true feminist thinkers. And this breathing space helps keep us free from the authoritarian trap of having to know it all.

As I revised each chapter of this book and decided to delete some old chapters and add some new ones, I became increasingly convinced that I write out of a specific background of experience, as do we all. Thus, I have tried very hard to avoid either accepting or rejecting an analysis simply because it resonates or fails to resonate with my own ideas and experiences. Whether I have largely succeeded or mostly failed in this attempt is something I must leave up to you, my thoughtful readers.

1

Liberal Feminism

Liberalism, the school of political thought from which liberal feminism has evolved, is in the process of reconceptualizing, reconsidering, and restructuring itself.[1] Because this transformation is well under way, it is difficult to determine the precise status of liberal feminist thought. Therefore, if we wish to gauge the accuracy of Susan Wendell's provocative claim that liberal feminism has largely outgrown its original base,[2] we must first understand the assumptions of both classical and welfare liberalism. It may turn out that liberal feminists are "liberal" only in some ways.

Conceptual Roots of Liberal Feminist Thought and Action

In *Feminist Politics and Human Nature*,[3] Alison Jaggar observed that liberal political thought generally locates our uniqueness as human persons in our capacity for rationality. The belief that reason distinguishes us from other animals is, however, relatively uninformative, so liberals have attempted to define reason in various ways, stressing either its *moral* aspects or its *prudential* aspects. When reason is defined as the ability to comprehend the rational principles of morality, then the value of individual autonomy is stressed. In contrast, when reason is defined as the ability to determine the best means to achieve some desired end, then the value of self-fulfillment is stressed.[4]

Whether liberals define reason largely in moral or prudential terms, they nevertheless concur that a just society allows individuals to exercise their autonomy and to fulfill themselves. Liberals claim that the "right" must be given priority over the "good."[5] In other words, our entire system of individual rights is justified because these rights constitute a framework within which we can all choose our own separate goods, provided we do not deprive others of theirs. Such a priority defends religious freedom, for example, neither on the grounds that it will increase the general welfare nor on the grounds that a godly life is inherently worthier than a godless one, but simply on the grounds that people have a right to practice their own brand of spirituality. The same holds for all those rights we generally identify as fundamental.

The proviso that the right takes priority over the good complicates the construction of a just society. For if it is true, as most liberals claim, that resources are limited and each individual, even when restrained by altruism,[6] has an interest in securing as many available resources as possible, then it will be a challenge to create political, economic, and social institutions that maximize the individual's freedom without jeopardizing the community's welfare.

When it comes to state interventions in the private sphere (family or domestic society),[7] liberals agree that the less we see of Big Brother in our bedrooms, bathrooms, kitchens, recreation rooms, and nurseries, the better. We all need places where we can, among family and friends, shed our public personae and be our "real" selves. When it comes to state intervention in the public sphere (civil or political society),[8] however, a difference of opinion emerges between so-called classical, or libertarian, liberals on the one hand, and so-called welfare, or egalitarian, liberals on the other.[9]

Classical liberals think the state should confine itself to protecting civil liberties (e.g., property rights, voting rights, freedom of speech, freedom of religion, freedom of association). They also think that, instead of interfering with the free market, the state should simply provide everyone with an equal opportunity to determine his or her own accumulations within that market. In contrast, welfare liberals believe the state should focus on economic disparities as well as civil liberties. As they see it, individuals enter the market with differences based on initial advantage, inherent talent, and sheer luck. At times, these differences are so great that some individuals cannot take their fair share of what the market has to offer unless some adjustments are made to offset their liabilities. Because of this perceived state of affairs, welfare liberals call for government interventions in the economy such as legal services, school loans, food stamps, low-cost housing, Medicaid, Medicare, Social Security, and Aid to Families with Dependent Children so that the market does not perpetuate or otherwise solidify huge inequalities.

Although both classical-liberal and welfare-liberal streams of thought appear in liberal feminist thought, most contemporary liberal feminists seem to favor welfare liberalism. In fact, when Susan Wendell (not herself a liberal feminist) described contemporary liberal feminist thought, she stressed it is "committed to major economic re-organization and considerable redistribution of wealth, since one of the modern political goals most closely associated with liberal feminism is equality of opportunity, which would undoubtedly require and lead to both."[10] Very few, if any, contemporary liberal feminists favor the elimination of government-funded safety nets for society's most vulnerable members.

Since it is nearly impossible to discuss all liberal feminist thinkers, movements, and organizations in a single book, I have decided to focus only on Mary Wollstonecraft, John Stuart Mill, Harriet Taylor (Mill), the woman's suffrage movement in the United States, Betty Friedan, and the National Organization for Women. My aim is to construct a convincing argument that, for all its shortcomings, the overall goal of liberal feminism is the worthy one of creating "a just and compassionate society in which freedom flourishes."[11] Only in such a society can women and men thrive equally.

Eighteenth-Century Thought: Equal Education

Mary Wollstonecraft wrote at a time (1759–1799) when the economic and social position of European women was in decline. Up until the eighteenth century, productive work (work that generated an income from which a family could live) had been done in and around the family home by women as well as men. But then the forces of industrial capitalism began to draw labor out of the private home and into the public workplace. At first, this industrialization moved slowly and unevenly, making its strongest impact on married, bourgeois women. These women were the first to find themselves left at home with little productive work to do. Married to relatively wealthy professional and entrepreneurial men, these women had no incentive to work outside the home or, if they had several servants, even inside it.[12]

In reading Wollstonecraft's *A Vindication of the Rights of Woman*,[13] we see how affluence worked against these eighteenth-century, married, bourgeois women. Wollstonecraft compared such "privileged" women (whom she hoped to inspire to a fully human mode of existence) to members of "the feathered race," birds that are confined to cages and that have nothing to do but preen themselves and "stalk with mock majesty from perch to perch."[14] Middle-class ladies were, in Wollstonecraft's estimation, "kept" women who sacrificed health, liberty, and virtue for whatever prestige, pleasure, and power their husbands could provide. Because these women were not allowed to exercise outdoors lest they tan their lily-white skin, they lacked healthy bodies. Because they were not permitted to make their own decisions, they lacked liberty. And because they were discouraged from developing their powers of reason—given that a great premium was placed on indulging self and gratifying others, especially men and children—they lacked virtue.

Although Wollstonecraft did not use terms such as "socially constructed gender roles," she denied that women are, by nature, more pleasure seeking and pleasure giving than men. She reasoned that if they were confined to the same cages that trap women, men would develop the same flawed characters.[15] Denied the chance to develop their rational powers, to become moral persons with concerns, causes, and commitments beyond personal pleasure, men, like women, would become overly "emotional," a term Wollstonecraft tended to associate with hypersensitivity, extreme narcissism, and excessive self-indulgence.

Given her generally negative assessment of emotion and the extraordinarily high premium she placed on reason as the capacity distinguishing human beings from animals, it is no wonder Wollstonecraft abhorred Jean-Jacques Rousseau's *Emile*.[16] In this classic of educational philosophy, Rousseau portrayed the development of rationality as the most important educational goal for boys, but not for girls. Rousseau was committed to sexual dimorphism, the view that "rational man" is the perfect complement for "emotional woman," and vice versa.[17] As he saw it, men should be educated in virtues such as courage, temperance, justice, and fortitude, whereas women should be educated in virtues such as patience, docility, good humor, and flexibility. Thus, Rousseau's ideal male student, Emile, studies the humanities, the social sciences, and the natural sciences, whereas Rousseau's ideal female student, Sophie, dabbles in music, art, fiction, and poetry while refining her homemaking skills. Rousseau hoped sharpening Emile's mental capacities and limiting Sophie's would make Emile a self-governing citizen and a dutiful paterfamilias and Sophie an understanding, responsive wife and a caring, loving mother.

Wollstonecraft agreed with Rousseau's projections for Emile but not with his projections for Sophie. Drawing upon her familiarity with middle-class ladies, she predicted that, fed a steady diet of "novels, music, poetry, and gallantry," Sophie would become a detriment rather than a complement to her husband, a creature of bad sensibility rather than good sense.[18] Her hormones surging, her passions erupting, her emotions churning, Sophie would show no practical sense in performing her wifely and, especially, motherly duties.

Wollstonecraft's cure for Sophie was to provide her, like Emile, with the kind of education that permits people to develop their rational and moral capacities, their full human potential. At times, Wollstonecraft constructed her argument in favor of educational parity in utilitarian terms. She claimed that unlike emotional and dependent women, who routinely shirk their domestic duties and indulge their carnal desires, rational and independent women will tend to be "observant daughters," "affectionate sisters," "faithful wives," and "reasonable mothers."[19] The truly educated woman will be a major contributor to society's welfare. Rather than wasting her time and energy on idle entertainments, she will manage her household—especially her children—"properly."[20] But it would be a mistake to think that most of Wollstonecraft's arguments for educational parity were utilitarian. On the contrary, her overall line of reasoning in *A Vindication of the Rights of Woman* was remarkably similar to Immanuel Kant's overall line of reasoning in the *Groundwork of the Metaphysic of Morals*—namely, that unless a person acts autonomously, he or she acts as less than a fully human person.[21] Wollstonecraft insisted if rationality is the capacity distinguishing human beings from animals, then unless females are mere animals (a description most men refuse to apply to their own mothers, wives, and daughters), women as well as men have this capacity. Thus, society owes girls the same education that it owes boys, simply because all human beings deserve an equal chance to develop their rational and moral capacities so they can achieve full personhood.

Repeatedly, Wollstonecraft celebrated reason, usually at the expense of emotion. As Jane Roland Martin said, "In making her case for the rights of women . . . [Wollstonecraft] presents us with an ideal of female education that gives pride of place to traits traditionally associated with males at the expense of others traditionally associated with females."[22] It did not occur to Wollstonecraft to question the value of these traditional male traits. Nor did it occur to her to blame children's lack of virtue on their absentee fathers, who should be summoned, in her view, only when "chastisement" is necessary.[23] On the contrary, she simply assumed traditional male traits were "good," and women—not men—were the ones who were rationally and morally deficient.

Throughout the pages of *A Vindication of the Rights of Woman,* Wollstonecraft urged women to become autonomous decision makers; but beyond insisting that the path to autonomy goes through the academy, she provided women with little concrete guidance.[24] Although Wollstonecraft toyed with the idea that women's autonomy might depend on women's economic and political independence from men, in the end she decided *well-educated* women did not need to be economically self-sufficient or politically active in order to be autonomous. In fact, Wollstonecraft dismissed the woman's suffrage movement as a waste of time, since in her estimation, the whole system of legal representation was merely a "convenient handle for despotism."[25]

Despite the limitations of her analysis, Wollstonecraft did present a vision of a woman strong in mind and body, a person who is not a slave to her passions, her husband, or her children. For Wollstonecraft, the ideal woman is less interested in fulfilling herself—if by self-fulfillment is meant any sort of pandering to duty-distracting desires—than in exercising self-control.[26] In order to liberate herself from the oppressive roles of emotional cripple, petty shrew, and narcissistic sex object, a woman must obey the commands of reason and discharge her wifely and motherly duties faithfully.

What Wollstonecraft most wanted for women is personhood. She claimed that a woman should not be reduced to the "toy of man, his rattle," which "must jingle in his ears whenever, dismissing reason, he chooses to be amused."[27] In other words, a woman is not a "mere means," or instrument, to one or more man's pleasure or happiness. Rather, she is an "end-in-herself," a rational agent whose dignity consists in having the capacity for self-determination.[28] To treat someone as a mere means is to treat her as less than a person, as someone who exists not for herself but as an appendage to someone else. So, for example, if a husband treats his wife as no more than a pretty indoor plant, he treats her as an object that he nurtures merely as a means to his own delight. Similarly, if a woman lets herself so be treated, she lets herself be treated in ways that do not accord with her status as a full human person. Rather than assuming responsibility for her own development and growing into a mighty redwood, she forsakes her freedom and lets others shape her into a stunted bonsai tree. No woman, insisted Wollstonecraft, should permit such violence to be done to her.

Nineteenth-Century Thought: Equal Liberty

Writing approximately one hundred years later, John Stuart Mill and Harriet Taylor (Mill) joined Wollstonecraft in celebrating rationality. But they conceived of rationality not only morally, as autonomous decision making, but also prudentially, as calculative reason, or using your head to get what you want. That their understanding of rationality should differ from that of Wollstonecraft is not surprising. Unlike Wollstonecraft, both Mill and Taylor claimed the ordinary way to maximize aggregate utility (happiness/pleasure) is to permit individuals to pursue their desires, provided the individuals do not hinder or obstruct each other in the process. Mill and Taylor also departed from Wollstonecraft in insisting that if society is to achieve sexual equality, or gender justice, then society must provide women with the same political rights and economic opportunities as well as the same education that men enjoy.

Like Mary Wollstonecraft, who twice attempted suicide, refused marriage until late in life, and had a child out of wedlock, John Stuart Mill and Harriet Taylor led fairly unconventional lives. They met in 1830, when Harriet Taylor was already married to John Taylor and was the mother of two sons (a third child, Helen, would be born later). Harriet Taylor and Mill were immediately attracted to each other, both intellectually and emotionally. They carried on a close, supposedly platonic relationship for twenty years, until the death of John Taylor, whereupon they married. During the years before John Taylor's death, Harriet Taylor and Mill routinely saw each other for dinner and frequently spent weekends together along the English coast. John Taylor agreed to this arrangement in return for the "external formality" of Harriet's residing "as his wife in his house."[29]

Due to their unorthodox bargain with John Taylor, Harriet Taylor and Mill found the time to author, separately and conjointly, several essays on sexual equality. Scholars generally agree that Taylor and Mill coauthored "Early Essays on Marriage and Divorce" (1832), that Taylor wrote the "Enfranchisement of Women" (1851), and that Mill wrote "The Subjection of Women" (1869). The question of these works' authorship is significant because Taylor's views sometimes diverged from Mill's.

Given their personal situation, Mill and Taylor's focus on topics such as marriage and divorce is not surprising. Confident in their relationship, Mill and Taylor did not feel they had to agree with each other about how to serve women's and children's best interests. Because she accepted the traditional view that maternal ties are stronger than paternal ties, Taylor simply assumed the mother would be the one to rear the children to adulthood in the event of divorce. Thus, she cautioned women to have few children. In contrast, Mill urged couples to marry late, have children late, and live in extended families or communelike situations so as to minimize divorce's disrupting effects on children's lives.[30] Apparently, Mill envisioned that divorced men as well as divorced women would play a role in their children's lives.

Although Taylor, unlike Mill, did not contest traditional assumptions about male and female child-rearing roles, she did contest traditional assumptions about women's supposed preference for marriage and motherhood over a career or occupation. Mill contended that even after women were fully educated and totally enfranchised, most of them would *choose* to remain in the private realm, where their primary function would be to "adorn and beautify" rather than to "support" life.[31] In contrast, in "Enfranchisement of Women," Taylor argued that women needed to do more than read books and cast ballots; they also needed to be *partners* with men "in the labors and gains, risks and remunerations of productive industry."[32] Thus, Taylor predicted that if society gave women a bona fide choice between devoting their lives "to one *animal* function and its consequence"[33] on the one hand, and writing great books, discovering new worlds, and building mighty empires on the other, many women would be only too happy to leave "home, sweet home" behind them.

Whereas the foregoing passages from "Enfranchisement" suggest Taylor believed a woman had to choose between housewifery and mothering on the one hand and working outside the home on the other, some other passages indicate she believed a woman had a third option: namely, adding a career or an occupation to her domestic and maternal roles and responsibilities. In fact, Taylor claimed a married woman cannot be her husband's true equal unless she has the confidence and sense of entitlement that come from contributing "materially to the support of the family."[34] Decidedly unimpressed by Mill's 1832 argument that women's economic equality would depress the economy and subsequently lower wages,[35] Taylor wrote instead: "Even if every woman, as matters now stand, had a claim on some man for support, how infinitely preferable is it that part of the income should be of the woman's earning, even if the aggregate sum were but little increased by it, rather than that she should be compelled to stand aside in order that men may be the sole earners, and the sole dispensers of what is earned."[36] In short, in order to be partners rather than servants of their husbands, wives must earn an income outside the home.

In further explaining her view that married as well as single women should work, Taylor betrayed her class bias. Insisting that women cannot both work full-time outside the home and be devoted wives and mothers without running themselves ragged, Taylor claimed that working wives with children would need a "panoply of domestic servants" to help ease their burdens.[37] In critic Zillah Eisenstein's estimation, Taylor's words revealed her privileged status. Circa 1850, only upper-middle-class women like Taylor could afford to hire a slew of household workers.[38] Thus, Taylor, a product of class privilege, offered rich women a way to "have it all" without offering poor women the same. Never did she wonder who would be taking care of the families of rich women's hired female help.

Like Wollstonecraft, Taylor wrote not so much to *all* women as to a certain privileged class of married women. Nonetheless, her writings helped smooth the entrance of many poor as well as rich women into the public world. So, too, did Mill's. He argued in "The Subjection of Women" that if women's rational powers were recognized as equal to men's, then society would reap significant benefits: public-spirited citizens for society itself, intellectually stimulating spouses for husbands, a doubling of the "mass of mental faculties available for the higher service of humanity," and a multitude of very happy women.[39] Although Mill's case for the liberation of women did not depend on his ability to prove that *all* women can do anything men can do, it did depend on his ability to demonstrate that *some* women can do anything men can do.[40] Unlike Wollstonecraft, who put no "great stress on the example of a few women who, from having received a masculine education, have acquired courage and resolution,"[41] Mill used the life stories of exceptional women to strengthen his claim that male-female differences are not absolute but instead are differences of average. The average woman's inability to do something the average man can do, said Mill, does not justify a law or taboo barring all women from attempting that thing.[42]

Mill also made the point that even *if* all women are worse than all men at something, this still does not justify forbidding women from trying to do that thing, for "what women by nature cannot do, it is quite superfluous to forbid them from doing. What they can do, but not so well as the men who are their competitors, competition suffices to exclude them from."[43] Although Mill believed women would fare quite well in any competitions with men, he conceded that occasionally a biological sex difference might tip the scales in favor of male competitors. Like Wollstonecraft, however, he denied the existence of general intellectual or moral differences between men and women: "I do not know a more signal instance of the blindness with which the world, including the herd of studious men, ignore and pass over all the influences of social circumstances, than their silly depreciation of the intellectual, and silly panegyrics on the moral, nature of women."[44]

Also like Wollstonecraft earlier, Mill claimed that society's *ethical* double standard hurts women. He thought many of the "virtues" extolled in women are, in fact, character traits that impede women's progress toward personhood. This is as true for an ostensibly negative trait (helplessness) as for an ostensibly positive trait (unselfishness). Mill suggested that because women's concerns were confined to the private realm, women were preoccupied with their own interests and those of their immediate families. As a result of this state of affairs, women's unselfishness tended to take the form of extended egoism. Women's charity typically began and ended at home. They spared no effort to further the interests of their loved ones, but they showed scant regard for the common weal.

As described above, women's family-oriented unselfishness was not the humanitarian unselfishness Mill espoused. He treasured the unselfishness that motivates people to take into account the good of society as well as the good of the individual person or small family unit. Mill believed that if women were given the same liberties men enjoy, and if women were taught to value the good of the whole, then women would develop genuine unselfishness. This belief explains Mill's passionate pleas for women's suffrage. He thought that when citizens vote, they feel obligated to cast their ballots in a way that benefits all of society and not just themselves and their loved ones.[45] Whether Mill was naive to think that citizens are inherently public-spirited is, of course, debatable.

Overall, Mill went further than Wollstonecraft did in challenging men's alleged intellectual superiority. Stressing that men's and women's intellectual abilities are of the same *kind,* Wollstonecraft nonetheless entertained the thought that women might not be able to attain the same *degree* of knowledge that men could attain.[46] Mill expressed no such reservation. He insisted intellectual achievement gaps between men and women were simply the result of men's more thorough education and privileged position. In fact, Mill was so eager to establish that men are not intellectually superior to women that he tended to err in the opposite direction, by valorizing women's attention to details, use of concrete examples, and intuitiveness as a superior form of knowledge not often found in men.[47]

Unlike Taylor, and despite his high regard for women's intellectual abilities, Mill assumed most women would continue to choose family over career even under ideal circumstances—with marriage a free contract between real equals, legal separation and divorce easily available to wives, and jobs open to women living outside the husband-wife relationship. He also assumed that women's choice of family over career was entirely voluntary and that such a choice involved women consenting to put their other interests in life on the back burner until their children were adults: "Like a man when he chooses a profession, so, when a woman marries, it may in general be understood that she makes choice of the management of a household, and the bringing up of a family, as the first call upon her exertions, during as many years of her life as may be required for the purpose; and that she renounces not all other objects and occupations, but all which are not consistent with the requirements of this."[48] Mill's words attested to his apparent belief that ultimately, women, more than men, are responsible for maintaining family life. However enlightened his general views about women were, Mill could not overcome the belief that she who bears the children is the person best suited to rear them.

As noted, Taylor disagreed with Mill that truly liberated women would be willing to stay at home to rear their children to adulthood. Yet, like Mill, Taylor was fundamentally a reformist, not a revolutionary. To be sure, by inviting married women with children as well as single women to work outside the home, Taylor did challenge the traditional division of labor within the family, where the man earns the money and the woman manages its use. But Taylor's challenge to this aspect of the status quo did not go far enough. For example, it did not occur to her that if husbands were to parent alongside their wives and if domestic duties were equally divided, then both husbands and wives could work outside the home on a full-time basis, and working wives with children would not have to work a "double day" or hire a "panoply" of female servants to do *their* housework and childcare.

Nineteenth-Century Action: The Suffrage

Both John Stuart Mill and Harriet Taylor Mill believed women needed suffrage in order to become men's equals. They claimed the vote gives people the power not only to express their own political views but also to change those systems, structures, and attitudes that contribute to their own and/or others' oppression. Thus, it is not surprising that the nineteenth-century U.S. women's rights movement, including the woman suffrage movement, was tied to the abolitionist movement, though not always in ways that successfully married gender and race concerns.[49]

When white men and women began to work in earnest for the abolition of slavery, it soon became clear to female abolitionists that male abolitionists were reluctant to link the women's rights movement with the slaves' rights movement. Noting it was difficult for whites (or was it simply white *men?*) to view women (or was it simply *white* women?) as an oppressed group, male abolitionists persuaded female abolitionists to disassociate women's liberty struggles from blacks' liberty struggles. Indeed, male abolitionists even convinced famed feminist orator Lucy Stone to lecture on abolition instead of women's rights whenever her audience size was noticeably large.[50]

Convinced their male colleagues would reward them for being team players, the U.S. women who attended the 1840 World Anti-Slavery Convention in London thought that women would play a major role at the meeting. Nothing could have proved less true. Not even Lucretia Mott and Elizabeth Cady Stanton, two of the most prominent leaders of the U.S. women's rights movement, were allowed to speak at the meeting. Angered by the way in which the men at the convention had silenced women, Mott and Stanton vowed to hold a women's rights convention upon their return to the United States. Eight years later, in 1848, three hundred women and men met in Seneca Falls, New York, and produced a Declaration of Sentiments and twelve resolutions. Modeled on the Declaration of Independence, the Declaration of Sentiments stressed the issues Mill and Taylor had emphasized in England, particularly the need for reforms in marriage, divorce, property, and child custody laws. The twelve resolutions emphasized women's rights to express themselves in public—to speak out on the burning issues of the day, especially "in regard to the great subjects of morals and religion," which women were supposedly more qualified to address than men.[51] The only one of these resolutions the Seneca Falls Convention did not unanimously endorse was Resolution 9, Susan B. Anthony's Woman's Suffrage Resolution: "Resolved, that it is the duty of the women of this country to secure to themselves their sacred right to the franchise."[52] Many convention delegates were reluctant to press such an "extreme" demand for fear that all of their demands would be rejected. Still, with the help of abolitionist Frederick Douglass, Resolution 9 did manage to pass.

Assessing the Seneca Falls Convention from the vantage point of the twentieth century, critics observe that, with the exception of Lucretia Mott's hastily added resolution to secure for women "an equal participation with men in the various trades, professions, and commerce,"[53] the nineteenth-century meeting failed to address class concerns such as those that troubled underpaid white female mill and factory workers. Moreover, the convention rendered black women nearly invisible. In the same way that the abolitionist movement had focused on the rights of black *men*, the nineteenth-century women's rights movement focused on the rights of mostly privileged *white* women. Neither white women nor white men seemed to notice much about black women.

Yet, many working-class white women and black women did contribute to the nineteenth-century women's rights movement. In fact, some black women were exceptionally gifted feminist orators. For example, Sojourner Truth delivered her often quoted speech on behalf of women at an 1851 women's rights convention in Akron, Ohio. Responding to a group of male hecklers, who taunted that it was ludicrous for (white) women to desire the vote since they could not even step over a puddle or get into a horse carriage without male assistance, Sojourner Truth pointed out that no man had ever extended such help to her. Demanding the audience look at her black body, Sojourner Truth proclaimed that her "womanhood," her "female nature," had never prevented her from working, acting, and yes, speaking like a man: "I have ploughed, and planted, and gathered into barns and no man could head me! And ain't I a woman? I could work as much and eat as much as a man—when I could get it—and bear the lash as well! And ain't I a woman? I have borne thirteen children and seen them most all sold off to slavery, and when I cried out with my mother's grief, none but Jesus heard me! And ain't I a woman?"[54]

As the fates would have it, the Civil War began just as the women's rights movement was gaining momentum. Seeing in this tragic war their best opportunity to free the slaves, male abolitionists again asked feminists to put women's causes on the back burner, which they reluctantly did. But the end of the Civil War did not bring women's liberation with it, and feminists increasingly found themselves at odds with recently emancipated black men. Concerned that women's rights would again be lost in the struggle to secure black (men's) rights, the male as well as female delegates to an 1866 national women's rights convention decided to establish an Equal Rights Association.

Co-chaired by Frederick Douglass and Elizabeth Cady Stanton, the association had as its announced purpose the unification of the black (men's) and woman suffrage struggles. There is considerable evidence, however, that Stanton and some of her co-workers actually "perceived the organization as a means to ensure that Black men would not receive the franchise unless and until white women were also its recipients."[55] Unmoved by Douglass's and Truth's observation that on account of their extreme vulnerability, black men needed the vote even more than women did, Anthony and Stanton were among those who successfully argued for the dissolution of the Equal Rights Association for fear that the association might indeed endorse the passage of the Fifteenth Amendment, which enfranchised black men but not women.

Upon the dissolution of the Equal Rights Association, Anthony and Stanton established the National Woman Suffrage Association. At approximately the same time, Lucy Stone, who had some serious philosophical disagreements with Stanton and especially Anthony about the role of organized religion in women's oppression, founded the American Woman Suffrage Association. Henceforward, the U.S. women's rights movement would be split in two.

In the main, the National Woman Suffrage Association forwarded a revolutionary feminist agenda for women, whereas the American Woman Suffrage Association pushed a reformist feminist agenda. Most American women gravitated toward the more moderate American Woman Suffrage Association. By the time these two associations merged in 1890 to form the National American Woman Suffrage Association, the wide-ranging, vociferous women's rights movement of the early nineteenth century had transformed into the single-issue, relatively tame woman's suffrage movement of the late nineteenth century. From 1890 until 1920, when the Nineteenth Amendment was passed, the National American Woman Suffrage Association confined almost all of its activities to gaining the vote for women. Victorious after fifty-two years of concerted struggle, many of the exhausted suffragists chose to believe that simply by gaining the vote, women had indeed become men's equals.[56]

Twentieth-Century Action: Equal Rights

For nearly forty years after the passage of the Nineteenth Amendment, feminists went about their work relatively quietly in the United States. Then, around 1960, a rebellious generation of feminists loudly proclaimed as fact what the suffragists Stanton and Anthony had always suspected: In order to be fully liberated, women need economic opportunities and sexual freedoms as well as civil liberties. Like their grandmothers, some of these young women pushed a reformist, liberal agenda, whereas others forwarded a more revolutionary, radical program of action.

By the mid-1960s, most liberal feminists had joined an emerging women's *rights* group, such as the National Organization for Women (NOW), the National Women's Political Caucus (NWPC), or the Women's Equity Action League (WEAL). The general purpose of these groups was to improve women's status "by applying legal, social, and other pressures upon institutions ranging from the Bell Telephone Company to television networks to the major political parties."[57] In contrast, most radical feminists had banded together in one or another women's *liberation* groups. Much smaller and more personally focused than the liberal women's rights groups, these radical women's liberation groups aimed to increase women's consciousness about women's oppression. The groups' spirit was that of the revolutionary new left, whose goal was not to *reform* what they regarded as an elitist, capitalistic, competitive, individualistic system, but to *replace* it with an egalitarian, socialistic, cooperative, communitarian, sisterhood-is-powerful system. Among the largest of these radical women's liberation groups were the Women's International Terrorist Conspiracy from Hell (WITCH), the Redstockings, the Feminists, and the New York Radical Feminists. Although Maren Lockwood Carden correctly noted in her 1974 book, *The New Feminist Movement,* that the ideological contrasts between the women's rights and women's liberation groups of the 1960s had blurred by the mid-1970s,[58] women's rights groups still remained less revolutionary than women's liberation groups.

Because this chapter is about *liberal* feminists, I reserve discussion of radical women's liberation groups to Chapter 2. Here I appropriately concentrate on the history of twentieth-century liberal *women's rights* groups and their activities, most of which have been in the area of legislation. Between the passage of the Nineteenth Amendment and the advent of the second wave of U.S. feminism during the 1960s, only two official feminist groups—the National Woman's Party and the National Federation of Business and Professional Women's Clubs (BPW)—promulgated women's rights. Despite their efforts, however, discrimination against women did not end, largely because the importance of women's rights had not yet been impressed on the consciousness (and conscience) of the bulk of the U.S. population. This state of affairs changed with the eruption of the civil rights movement. Sensitized to the myriad ways in which U.S. systems, structures, and laws oppressed blacks, those active in or at least sympathetic toward the civil rights movement were able to see analogies between discrimination against blacks and discrimination against women. In 1961, President John F. Kennedy established the Commission on the Status of Women, which produced much new data about women and resulted in the formation of the Citizens' Advisory Council, various state commissions on the status of women, and the passage of the Equal Pay Act. When Congress passed the 1964 Civil Rights Act—amended with the Title VII provision to prohibit discrimination on the basis of *sex* as well as race, color, religion, or national origin by private employers, employment agencies, and unions—a woman shouted from the congressional gallery: "We made it! God bless America!"[59] Unfortunately, this woman's jubilation and that of women in general was short-lived; the courts were reluctant to enforce Title VII's "sex amendment." Feeling betrayed by the system, women's joy turned to anger, an anger that feminist activists used to mobilize women to fight for their civil rights with the same passion blacks had fought for theirs.

Among these feminist activists was Betty Friedan, one of the founders and first president of the National Organization for Women (NOW). Friedan reflected on how she and some of her associates had reacted to the courts' refusal to take Title VII's "sex amendment" seriously: "The absolute necessity for a civil rights movement for women had reached such a point of subterranean explosive urgency by 1966, that it only took a few of us to get together to ignite the spark—and it spread like a nuclear chain reaction."[60]

The "spark" to which Friedan pointed was the formation of NOW, the first explicitly feminist group in the United States in the twentieth century to challenge sex discrimination in all spheres of life: social, political, economic, and personal. After considerable behind-the-scenes maneuvering, Friedan—then viewed as a home-breaker because of her controversial book, *The Feminine Mystique* (see the next section for discussion)—was elected NOW's first president in 1966 by its three hundred charter members, male and female.

Although NOW's first members included radical and conservative feminists as well as liberal feminists, it quickly became clear that NOW's essential identity and agenda were fundamentally liberal. For example, the aim of NOW's 1967 Bill of Rights for Women was to secure for women the same rights men have. NOW demanded the following for women:

I. That the U.S. Congress immediately pass the Equal Rights Amendment to the Constitution to provide that "Equality of rights under the law shall not be denied or abridged by the United States or by any State on account of sex," and that such then be immediately ratified by the several States.

II. That equal employment opportunity be guaranteed to all women, as well as men, by insisting that the Equal Employment Opportunity Commission enforces the prohibitions against racial discrimination.

III. That women be protected by law to ensure their rights to return to their jobs within a reasonable time after childbirth without the loss of seniority or other accrued benefits, and be paid maternity leave as a form of social security and/or employee benefit.

IV. Immediate revision of tax laws to permit the deduction of home and child-care expenses for working parents.

V. That child-care facilities be established by law on the same basis as parks, libraries, and public schools, adequate to the needs of children from the pre-school years through adolescence, as a community resource to be used by all citizens from all income levels.

VI. That the right of women to be educated to their full potential equally with men be secured by Federal and State legislation, eliminating all discrimination and segregation by sex, written and unwritten, at all levels of education, including colleges, graduate and professional schools, loans and fellowships, and Federal and State training programs such as the Job Corps.

VII. The right of women in poverty to secure job training, housing, and family allowances on equal terms with men, but without prejudice to a parent's right to remain at home to care for his or her children; revision of welfare legislation and poverty programs which deny women dignity, privacy, and self-respect.

VIII. The right of women to control their own reproductive lives by removing from the penal code laws limiting access to contraceptive information and devices, and by repealing penal laws governing abortion.[61]

NOW's list of demands pleased the organization's liberal members but made both its conservative and radical members angry, albeit for different reasons. Whereas conservative members objected to the push for permissive contraception and abortion laws, radical members were angered by NOW's failure to support women's sexual rights, particularly the right to choose between heterosexual, bisexual, and lesbian lifestyles. Missing from NOW's 1967 Bill of Rights was any mention of important women's issues such as domestic violence, rape, sexual harassment, and pornography.[62]

Although Friedan acknowledged that "the sex-role debate . . . cannot be avoided if equal opportunity in employment, education and civil rights are ever to mean more than paper rights,"[63] she still insisted "that the gut issues of this revolution involve employment and education and new social institutions and not sexual fantasy."[64] Worried that NOW would change its traditional liberal focus to a more radical one, Friedan was among those who most strongly opposed public support of lesbianism by NOW. Allegedly, she termed NOW's lesbian members a "lavender menace,"[65] since, as she saw it, they alienated mainstream society from feminists in general.

Friedan's concerns about the "lavender menace" notwithstanding, NOW eventually endorsed four resolutions forwarded by "the lavender menace," the Gay Liberation Front Women and Radical Lesbians. The resolutions, presented at NOW's 1970 Congress to Unite Women, read:

1. Women's Liberation is a lesbian plot.
2. Whenever the label lesbian is used against the movement collectively or against women individually, it is to be affirmed, not denied.
3. In all discussions of birth control, homosexuality must be included as a legitimate method of contraception.
4. All sex education curricula must include lesbianism as a valid, legitimate form of sexual expression and love.[66]

Moreover, NOW began to stress that its aim was to serve not only the women most likely to survive and thrive in the system but any woman who believes women's rights should be equal to men's. Beginning with the 1971 presidency of Arlein Hernandez, a Hispanic woman, a diverse array of minority and lesbian women (including Patricia Ireland, president of NOW from 1993 to 2001) assumed leadership as well as membership roles in NOW.[67] The organization's greater attention to women's differences meant its members could no longer claim to know what *all* women want but only what *specific groups* of women want. Increasingly, the intellectual energies of NOW as well as other women's rights groups became focused on the implications of the so-called sameness-difference debate: Is gender equality best achieved by stressing women's oneness as a gender or their diversity as individuals, the similarities between women and men or the differences between them? To this day, the many answers to this question continue to shape and reshape NOW's political agenda.

Twentieth-Century Thought: Sameness Versus Difference

It is instructive to reflect upon Betty Friedan's career as a writer not only because of her identification with NOW but also because of her own evolution as a thinker who first took it for granted that all women are the same and who then came to quite a different conclusion. Like most contemporary liberal feminists, Friedan gradually accepted both the *radical* feminist critique that liberal feminists are prone to co-optation by the "male establishment" and the *conservative* feminist critique that liberal feminists are out of touch with the bulk of U.S. women who hold the institutions of marriage, motherhood, and the family in high regard. When she wrote her 1963 classic, *The*

Feminine Mystique,[68] Friedan seemed oblivious to any other perspectives than those of white, middle-class, heterosexual, educated women who found the traditional roles of wife and mother unsatisfying. She wrote that in lieu of more meaningful goals, these women spent too much time cleaning their already tidy homes, improving their already attractive appearances, and indulging their already spoiled children.[69] Focusing on this unappealing picture of family life in affluent U.S. suburbs, Friedan concluded that contemporary women needed to find meaningful work in the full-time, public workforce. Wives' and mothers' partial absence from home would enable husbands and children to become more self-sufficient people, capable of cooking their own meals and doing their own laundry.[70]

Although Friedan had little patience for obsequious wives and doting mothers, she did not, as some critics thought, demand women *sacrifice* marriage and motherhood for a high-powered career. On the contrary, she believed a woman could have a loving family as well: "The assumption of your own identity, equality, and even political power does not mean you stop needing to love, and be loved by, a man, or that you stop caring for your own kids."[71] In Friedan's estimation, the error in the feminine mystique was not that it *valued* marriage and motherhood but that it *overvalued* these two institutions. To think that a woman who is a wife and mother has no time for a full-time, professional career is to limit her development as a full human person, said Friedan. As soon as a woman sees housework for what it is—something to get out of the way, to be done "quickly and efficiently"—and sees marriage and motherhood for what it is, a part of her life but not all of it, she will find plenty of time and energy to develop her total self in "creative work" outside the home.[72] With just a bit of help, any woman, like any man, can meet all of her personal obligations and thereby become free to assume significant roles and responsibilities in the public world, reasoned Friedan.

In critics' estimation, *The Feminine Mystique* explained well enough why marriage and motherhood are not enough for a certain kind of woman. But as the critics saw it, the book failed to address a host of issues deeper than "the problem that has no name"—Friedan's tag for the dissatisfaction supposedly felt by suburban, white, educated, middle-class, heterosexual housewives in the United States. In particular, *The Feminine Mystique* misjudged just how difficult it would be for even privileged women to combine a career with marriage and motherhood unless major structural changes were made both within and outside the family. Like Wollstonecraft, Taylor, and Mill before her, Friedan sent women out into the public realm without summoning men into the private domain to pick up their fair share of the slack.

By the time she wrote *The Second Stage*,[73] about twenty years after *The Feminine Mystique*, Friedan had come to see that her critics were right. Often it is very difficult for a woman to combine marriage, motherhood, and full-time work outside the home. Observing the ways in which some members of her daughter's generation ran themselves ragged in the name of feminism—trying to be full-time career women as well as full-time housewives and mothers— Friedan concluded that 1980s "superwomen" were no less oppressed (albeit for different reasons) than their 1960s "stay-at-home" mothers had been. Increasingly, she urged feminists to ask themselves whether women either can or should try to meet not simply one but two standards of perfection: the one set in the workplace by traditional men, who had wives to take care of all their non-workplace needs, and the one set in the home by traditional women, whose whole sense of worth, power, and mastery came from being ideal housewives and mothers.[74]

Friedan's own answer to the question she posed was that women needed to stop trying both to "do it all" and to "be it all." She insisted, however, that the proper cure for the superwoman syndrome was not simply to renounce love in favor of work, or vice versa. On the contrary, said Friedan, women who chose either work or love often told her they regretted their decision. For example, one woman who renounced marriage and motherhood for a full-time career confessed to Friedan: "I was the first woman in management here. I gave everything to the job. It was exciting at first, breaking in where women never were before. Now it's just a job. But it's the devastating loneliness that's the worst. I can't *stand* coming back to this apartment alone every night. I'd like a house, maybe a garden. Maybe I should have a kid, even without a father. At least then I'd have a family. There has to be some better way to live."[75] Another woman who made the opposite choice, forsaking job for family, admitted to Friedan:

> It makes me mad—makes me feel like a child—when I have to ask my husband for money. My mother was always dependent on my father and so fearful of life. She is lost now without him. It frightens me, the thought of being dependent like my mother, though I have a very happy marriage. I get so upset, listening to battered wives on television, women with no options. It improves your sense of self-worth when you don't depend on your husband for everything good in life, when you can get it for yourself. I'm trying so hard to treat my daughter equally with my son. I don't want her to have the fears that paralyzed my mother and that I've always had to fight. I want her to have real options.[76]

Rather than despairing over these and other women's choices, Friedan used them as talking points to convince 1980s feminists to move from what she termed first-stage feminism to what she labeled second-stage feminism. She noted this new form of feminism would require women to work with men to escape the excesses of the *feminist* mystique, "which denied the core of women's personhood that is fulfilled through love, nurture, home" as well as the excesses of the *feminine* mystique, "which defined women solely in terms of their relation to men as wives, mothers and homemakers."[77] Together, women and men might be able to develop the kind of social values, leadership styles, and institutional structures needed to permit both sexes to achieve fulfillment in the public and private world alike.

Friedan's program for reigniting the women's movement was, as we shall see, vulnerable to several attacks. For example, it inadequately challenged the assumption that women are "responsible for the private life of their family members."[78] Zillah Eisenstein criticized Friedan's support of so-called flextime (an arrangement that permits employees to set their starting and leaving hours): "It is never clear whether this arrangement is supposed to ease women's double burden (of family and work) or significantly restructure *who* is responsible for childcare and *how* this responsibility is carried out."[79] Suspecting that women rather than men would use flextime to mesh their workday with their children's school day, Eisenstein worried that flextime would give employers yet another reason to devalue female employees as less committed to their work than male employees.

In all fairness to Friedan, however, she did explicitly mention in *The Second Stage* (written after Eisenstein's critique of Friedan) that when an arrangement like flextime is described as a structural change permitting mothers to better care for their children, the wrongheaded idea that home and family are *women's* sole responsibility rather than *women's and men's* joint responsibility is reinforced.[80] Unlike the Friedan of *The Feminine Mystique,* the Friedan of *The Second Stage* seemed quite aware that unless women's assimilation into the public world is coupled with the simultaneous assimilation of men into the private world, women will always have to work harder than men. Although Friedan conceded that most men might not be ready, willing, or able to embrace the "househusband" role, she nonetheless insisted it is just as important for men to develop their private and personal selves as it is for women to develop their public and social selves. Men who realize this also realize women's liberation is men's liberation. A man does not have to be "just a breadwinner"[81] or just a runner in the rat race. Like his wife, he, too, can be an active participant in the thick web of familial and friendship relationships he and she weave together.[82]

In some ways, the difference between the Friedan of *The Feminine Mystique* and the Friedan of *The Second Stage* is the difference between a feminist who believes women need to be the *same* as men in order to be equal to men and a feminist who believes women can be men's equals, provided society values the "feminine" as much as the "masculine." The overall message of *The Feminine Mystique* was that women's liberation hinged on women becoming like men. Friedan peppered the pages of *The Feminine Mystique* with comments such as: "If an able American woman does not use her human energy and ability in some meaningful pursuit (which necessarily means competition, for there is competition in every serious pursuit of our society), she will fritter away her energy in neurotic symptoms, or unproductive exercise, or destructive 'love,'" and "Perhaps men may live longer in America when women carry more of the burden of the battle with the world instead of being a burden themselves. I think their wasted energy will continue to be destructive to their husbands, to their children, and to themselves until it is used in their own battle with the world."[83] To be a full human being is, in short, to think and act like a man.

Eighteen years after the publication of *The Feminine Mystique,* Friedan's message to women had substantially changed. In *The Second Stage,* she described as *culturally feminine* the so-called beta styles of thinking and acting, which emphasize "fluidity, flexibility and interpersonal sensitivity," and as *culturally masculine* the so-called alpha styles of thinking and acting, which stress "hierarchical, authoritarian, strictly task-oriented leadership based on instrumental, technological rationality."[84] Rather than offering 1980s women the same advice she had offered 1960s women—namely, minimize your feminine, beta tendencies and maximize your masculine, alpha tendencies—Friedan counseled 1980s women to embrace feminine, beta styles. Having convinced herself that women did not need to deny their differences from men to achieve equality with men, Friedan urged 1980s women to stop "aping the accepted dominant Alpha mode of established movements and organizations" and start using their "Beta intuitions" to solve the social, political, and economic problems that threaten humankind.[85] The challenge of the second stage of feminism, insisted Friedan, was for women (and men) to replace the "win-or-lose, do-or-die method of the hunter or the warrior" with the kind of thinking "women developed in the past as they dealt on a day-to-day basis with small problems and relationships in the family, mostly without thinking about it in the abstract."[86] Only then would the world's citizens realize their very survival depends on replacing competitive strategies with cooperative initiatives.

Given the foregoing analysis, it is not surprising that Friedan later claimed gender-specific laws rather than general-neutral laws are better able to secure equality between the sexes. In 1986, she joined a coalition supporting a California law requiring employers to grant as much as four months' unpaid leave to women disabled by pregnancy or childbirth. In taking this stand, she alienated the NOW members who believed that to treat men and women equally should mean to treat them in the same way. If men should not receive special treatment on account of their sex, then neither should women. According to Friedan, this line of reasoning, which she herself pressed in the 1960s, is misguided. It asks the law to treat women as "male clones," when in fact "there has to be a concept of equality that takes into account that women are the ones who have the babies."[87]

If the Friedan of the 1980s is right, then the task of liberal feminists is to determine not what liberty and equality are for abstract, rational persons but what liberty and equality are for concrete men and women. To be sure, this is a difficult task. Among others, Rosalind Rosenberg advised liberal feminists: "If women as a group are allowed special benefits, you open up the group to charges that it is inferior. But, if we deny all differences, as the women's movement has so often done, you deflect attention from the disadvantages women labor under."[88] Rosenberg's cautionary words raise many questions. Is there really a way to treat women and men both *differently* and *equally* without falling into some version of the pernicious separate-but-equal approach that characterized race relations in the United States until the early 1960s? Or, should liberal feminists work toward the elimination of male-female differences as the first step toward true equality? If so, should women become like men in order to be equal with men? Or should men become like women in order to be equal with women? Or finally, should both men and women become androgynous, each person combining the same "correct" blend of positive masculine and feminine characteristics in order to be equal with every other person?

To the degree that *The Feminine Mystique* advised women to become like men, *The Second Stage* urged women to be like women. But *The Second Stage* did more than this. It also encouraged men and women alike to work toward an androgynous future in which all human beings manifest both traditionally masculine and traditionally feminine traits. Once she decided that androgyny was in all human beings' best interests, Friedan stayed committed to her vision. Indeed, she devoted many pages of her third major book, *The Fountain of Age*, to singing androgyny's praises. Specifically, she urged aging alpha men to develop their passive, nurturing, or contemplative feminine qualities, and aging beta women to develop their bold, assertive, commanding, or adventurous masculine qualities.[89] Insisting that people over fifty should explore their "other side"—whether masculine or feminine—Friedan noted that women over fifty who go back to school or work or who become actively engaged in the public world report the fifty-plus years as being the best ones of their lives. Similarly, men over fifty who start focusing on the quality of their personal relationships and interior lives report a similar kind of satisfaction in older age. Unfortunately, added Friedan, the number of men who age well is far smaller than the number of women who age well. In our society, there are simply more opportunities for older women to develop their masculine traits than there are for older men to develop their feminine traits. If a man has neglected his wife and children for years because he has made work his first priority, by the time he is ready to attend to his personal relationships, these relationships may be extremely troubled. As a result, he may decide to seek a new wife with whom to have a second family—*repeating* the activities of his youth in the hope of "getting it right" this time. Worried about the left-behind "old wife" and "first family," Friedan urged aging men to find ways of loving and working that *differed* from the ways they loved and worked as twenty-, thirty-, or forty-year-olds.

The overall message of *The Fountain of Age* is that the people most likely to grow, change, and become more fully themselves as they age are precisely those people who move beyond polarized sex roles and creatively develop whichever side of themselves they neglected to develop as young men and women. In short, the happiest and most vital old men and women are androgynous persons.

The more she focused on the idea of androgyny, the more Friedan seemed to move toward humanism and away from feminism, however. Increasingly, she described *feminist* "sexual politics" as the "no-win battle of women as a whole sex, oppressed victims, against men as a whole sex, the oppressors."[90] In addition, she urged women to join with men to create a "new [human] politics that must emerge beyond reaction."[91] Eventually, Friedan claimed that because "human wholeness" is the true "promise of feminism," feminists should move beyond a focus on *women's* issues (issues related to women's reproductive and sexual roles, rights, and responsibilities) in order to work with men on "the concrete, practical, everyday problems of living, working and loving as equal persons."[92]

In a shift that appears to be more than mere coincidence, NOW's focus has also moved in the "human" direction suggested by Friedan, a trend that has brought NOW and its first president under concerted attack by radical feminists in particular. In contrast to Friedan and many liberal members of NOW, radical feminists doubt feminism can move beyond "women's issues" and still remain *feminism*. They claim that as long as our culture's understanding of what it means to be a human being remains androcentric (male-centered), it is premature for feminists to become humanists.

To be sure, Friedan was not the first liberal feminist who found humanism attractive. In their own distinct ways, Wollstonecraft, Taylor, and Mill
each wanted *personhood,* full membership in the human community for
women. The hypothesis that the ends and aims of feminism may, after all, be
identical with those of humanism is a controversial one but worth keeping in
mind as we consider recent trends in liberal feminism.

Contemporary Directions in Liberal Feminism

Betty Friedan is just one of thousands of women who may be classified as liberal
feminists. As Zillah Eisenstein noted, Elizabeth Holtzman, Bella Abzug,
Eleanor Smeal, Pat Schroeder, and Patsy Mink are liberal feminists, as are many
other leaders and members of NOW and the Women's Equity Action League.[93]
Although these women are sometimes divided on specific issues related to
women, they do agree that the single most important goal of women's liberation
is sexual equality, or, as it is sometimes termed, gender justice.

Liberal feminists wish to free women from oppressive gender roles—that
is, from those roles used as excuses or justifications for giving women a lesser
place, or no place at all, in the academy, the forum, and the marketplace.
These feminists stress that patriarchal society conflates *sex* and *gender,*[94]
deeming appropriate for women only those jobs associated with the traditional feminine personality. Thus, in the United States, for example, women
are pushed into jobs like nursing, teaching, and childcare, while they are
steered away from jobs in business, science, technology, engineering, and
mathematics. In addition, legislation specifically barring women from such
"masculine" jobs as mining and firefighting or preventing women from
working the night shift or overtime is not exactly a distant memory. To be
sure, de jure gender discrimination in the workplace is relatively rare nowadays. But de facto gender discrimination in the workplace remains all too
prevalent. Faced with a choice between male or female candidates for certain
jobs, many employers still prefer to hire men for particularly demanding positions on the grounds that women are more likely than men to let their family responsibilities interfere with their job commitment and performance.

It is sometimes argued that men, no less than women, are also the victims of
de facto gender discrimination—that even if the law has always been kind to
men, other vehicles of social control have not. Thus, men's liberation activists
complain about parents who never hire male babysitters and about nursery
schools that prefer to fill their staff positions with women. Although liberal
feminists sympathize with men who find it difficult to pursue child-centered
careers because of de facto gender discrimination, they still think the kind of de

facto gender discrimination men experience is not nearly as systematic as the kind that women experience. Society remains structured in ways that favor men and disfavor women in the competitive race for power, prestige, and money. The fact that, as of 2005, U.S. women still earned only seventy-two cents for every dollar men earned is not an accident.[95] Although women sometimes earn less than men because they freely choose to work less hard or fewer hours than men do, more often, women's salaries are lower than men's because society expects women to make their families their first priority. If a dual-career couple has a child, an aging parent, or an ailing relative in need of care, chances are that the female member of the couple will be the person who slows down or gives up her career to lend a helping hand.

In their discussions of the structural and attitudinal impediments to women's progress, contemporary liberal feminists often disagree about how to handle these hurdles. There are two types of liberal feminists: classical and welfare. Like classical liberals in general, classical liberal feminists favor limited government and a free market. They also view political and legal rights as particularly important. Freedom of expression, religion, and conscience play a major role in the psyches of classical liberal feminists. In contrast, welfare liberal feminists are like welfare liberals in general. Welfare liberals think government should provide citizens, especially underprivileged ones, with housing, education, health care, and social security. Moreover, they think the market should be limited by means of significant taxes and curbs on profits. For welfare liberal feminists, social and economic rights are the condition of possibility for the exercise of political and legal rights.

One way to better understand the difference between classical liberal feminists and welfare liberal feminists is to focus on a concrete issue such as affirmative action policy. Classical liberal feminists believe that after discriminatory laws and policies have been removed from the books, thereby formally enabling women to compete equally with men, not much else can be done about "birds of a feather flocking together"—about male senior professors, for example, being more favorably disposed toward a male candidate for a faculty position than toward an equally qualified female candidate. In contrast, welfare liberal feminists urge society to break up that "old flock (gang) of mine," especially when failure to make feathers fly results in asymmetrical gender ratios such as the one that characterized Harvard University's senior arts and sciences faculty in the early 1970s: 483 men, zero women.[96] Specifically, they advocate that female applicants to both schools and jobs either be (1) selected over *equally* qualified white male applicants (so-called affirmative action) or, more controversially, (2) selected over *better* qualified white male applicants, provided the female applicants are still able to perform adequately (so-called preferential treatment).[97] Welfare liberal feminists insist that to the degree such policies are viewed as temporary, they do not constitute reverse discrimination. As soon as men and women have equal social status and economic clout, there will be no need for either affirmative action or preferential treatment policies. Indeed, when women achieve de facto as well as de jure equality with men, policies advantaging women over men would be markedly unfair.

We may think the only meaningful liberal feminist approaches to combating gender discrimination are the classical and welfare approaches, both of which rely heavily on legal remedies. But as noted earlier, in the analysis of Betty Friedan's writings, another approach to combating gender discrimination uses the ideal of androgyny to counteract society's traditional tendency to value masculine traits or men more than feminine traits or women. If society encouraged everyone to develop both positive masculine and positive feminine traits, then no one would have reason to think less of women than of men. Discrimination on the bases of gender and biological sex would cease.

Clearly, discussions of sex differences, gender roles, and androgyny have helped focus liberal feminists' drive toward liberty, equality, and fairness for all. According to Jane English, terms such as *sex roles* and *gender traits* denote "the patterns of behavior which the two sexes are socialized, encouraged, or coerced into adopting, ranging from 'sex-appropriate' personalities to interests and professions."[98] Boys are instructed to be masculine, girls to be feminine. Psychologists, anthropologists, and sociologists tend to define the "masculine" and "feminine" in terms of prevailing cultural stereotypes, which are influenced by racial, class, and ethnic factors. Thus, to be masculine in middle-class, white, Anglo-Saxon, Protestant United States is, among other things, to be rational, ambitious, and independent, and to be feminine is, among other things, to be emotional, nurturant, and dependent. To be sure, even within this segment of the population, exceptions to the rule will be found. Some biological males will manifest feminine gender traits, and some biological females will manifest masculine gender traits. But these individuals will be deemed exceptional or deviant. No matter what group of people (e.g., working-class Italian Catholics) is under scrutiny, then, gender-role stereotyping will limit the individual's possibilities for development as a unique self. The woman who displays characteristics her social group regards as masculine will be viewed as less than a *real* woman; the man who shows so-called feminine traits will be considered less than a *real* man.[99]

In order to liberate women and men from the culturally constructed cages of masculinity and femininity, many liberal feminists besides Betty Friedan advocate the formation of androgynous personalities.[100] Some liberal feminists favor monoandrogyny—the development of an ideal personality type that embodies the best of prevailing masculine and feminine gender traits.[101] According to psychologist Sandra Bem, the monoandrogynous person possesses a full complement of traditional female qualities—nurturance, compassion, tenderness, sensitivity, affiliation, cooperativeness—along with a full complement of traditional male qualities—aggressiveness, leadership, initiative, competitiveness.[102] (Recall that this list of traditional qualities probably needs to be modified, depending on the racial, class, and ethnic characteristics of the group under consideration.) Other liberal feminists resist monoandrogyny and instead advocate polyandrogyny—the development of multiple personality types, some of which are totally masculine, others totally feminine, and still others a mixture.[103] Whether liberal feminists espouse monoandrogyny or polyandrogyny, however, they tend to agree a person's biological sex should not determine his or her psychological and social gender.

Critiques of Liberal Feminism

In recent years, nonliberal feminists have increasingly dismissed liberal feminists. These critics claim that the main tenets of liberal feminist thought (all human persons are rational and free, share fundamental rights, and are equal) do not necessarily advance all women's interests. At best, they advance the interests of only certain kinds of women—namely, privileged women who, because of their privilege, think and act like men. Because the critiques leveled against liberal feminism are quite harsh, we need to carefully assess their merit.

Critique One:
Reason, Freedom, and Autonomy Are Not As Good As They Sound

In *Feminist Politics and Human Nature,* Alison Jaggar formulated a powerful critique of liberal feminism. She claimed that the rational, free, and autonomous self that liberals favor is not neutral between the sexes. On the contrary, it is a "male" self.

Realizing that not everyone would understand why a rational, free, and autonomous self is "male," Jaggar carefully defended her point. She first noted that because liberals, including liberal feminists, locate human beings' "specialness" in human rationality and autonomy, liberals are so-called normative dualists—thinkers committed to the view that the functions and activities of the mind are somehow better than those of the body.[104] Eating, drinking, excreting, sleeping, and reproducing are not, according to this view, quintessential human activities, because members of most other animal species also engage in them. Instead, what sets human beings apart from the rest of animal creation is their capacity to think, reason, calculate, wonder, imagine, and comprehend.

Jaggar then speculated that because of the original sexual division of labor, mental activities and functions were increasingly emphasized over bodily activities and functions in Western liberal thought. Given men's distance from nature, their undemanding reproductive and domestic roles, and the amount of time they were consequently able to spend cultivating the life of the mind, men tended to devalue the body, regarding it as a protective shell whose contours had little to do with their self-definition. In contrast, given women's close ties to nature, their heavy reproductive and domestic roles, and the amount of time they consequently had to spend caring for people's bodies, women tended to value the body, viewing it as essential to their personal identity. Because men took over the field of philosophy early on, observed Jaggar, men's way of seeing themselves came to dominate Western culture's collective pool of ideas about human nature. As a result, all liberals, male or female, nonfeminist or feminist, tend to accept as truth the priority of the mental over the bodily, even when their own daily experiences contradict this belief.

Liberal feminists' adherence to some version of normative dualism is problematic for feminism, according to Jaggar, not only because normative dualism leads to a devaluation of bodily activities and functions but also because it usually leads to both political solipsism and political skepticism. (Political solipsism is the belief that the rational, autonomous person is essentially isolated, with needs and interests separate from, and even in opposition to, those of every other individual. Political skepticism is the belief that the fundamental questions of political philosophy—what constitutes human well-being and fulfillment, and what are the means to attain it?—have no common answer.) Thus, the result of valuing the mind over the body and the independence of the self from others is the creation of a politics that puts an extraordinary premium on liberty—on the rational, autonomous, independent, self-determining, isolated, separated, unique person's ability to think, do, and be whatever he or she deems worthy.[105]

Jaggar criticized political solipsism on empirical grounds, noting it makes little sense to think of individuals as somehow existing prior to the formation of community through some sort of contract. She observed, for example, that any pregnant woman knows a child is related to others (at least to her) even before it is born. The baby does not—indeed could not—exist as a lonely atom prior to subsequent entrance into the human community. Human infants are born helpless and require great care for many years. She explained that because this care cannot be adequately provided by a single adult, humans live in social groups that cooperatively bring offspring to maturity: "Human interdependence is . . . necessitated by human biology, and the assumption of individual self-sufficiency is plausible only if one ignores human biology."[106] Thus, Jaggar insisted, liberal political theorists need to explain not how and why isolated individuals come together but how and why communities dissolve. Competition, not cooperation, is the anomaly.

To add force to her empirical argument, Jaggar observed that political solipsism makes no sense conceptually. Here she invoked Naomi Scheman's point that political solipsism requires belief in abstract individualism.[107] The abstract individual is one whose emotions, beliefs, abilities, and interests can supposedly be articulated and understood without any reference whatsoever to social context. Kant's person is this type of abstract individual—a pure reason unaffected/uninfected by either the empirical-psychological ego or the empirical-biological body. However, Kant's philosophy notwithstanding, said Scheman, we are not *abstract* individuals. We are instead *concrete* individuals able to identify certain of our physiological sensations as ones of sorrow, for example, only because we are "embedded in a social web of interpretation that serves to give meaning"[108] to our twitches and twinges, our moans and groans, our squealing and screaming. Apart from this interpretative grid, we are literally *self-less*—that is, our very identities are determined by our socially constituted wants and desires. We are, fundamentally, the selves our communities create, an observation that challenges the U.S. myth of the self-sufficient individual.

Political skepticism collapses together with political solipsism according to Jaggar, for political skepticism also depends on an overly abstract and individualistic conception of the self. In contrast to the liberals or liberal feminists who insist the state should refrain from privileging any one conception of human well-being over another, Jaggar argued that the state should serve as more than a traffic cop who, without commenting on drivers' stated destinations, merely makes sure their cars do not collide. Whether we like it or not, she said, human biology and psychology dictate a set of basic human needs, and societies that treat these basic needs as optional cannot expect to survive, let alone to thrive. Thus, said Jaggar, the state must do more than keep traffic moving; it must also block off certain roads even if some individuals want to travel down them.

Defenders of liberal feminism challenge Jaggar's and Scheman's critique of liberal feminism on the grounds that the liberalism of liberal *feminists* is not the same as the liberalism of liberal *nonfeminists*. In what she termed a qualified defense of liberal feminism, Susan Wendell stressed that liberal feminists are not fundamentally committed either to separating the rational from the emotional or to valuing the former over the latter. On the contrary, they seem fully aware that reason and emotion, mind and body, are "equally necessary to human survival and the richness of human experience."[109] Indeed, observed Wendell, if liberal feminists lacked a conception of the self as an *integrated* whole, we would be hard pressed to explain their tendency to view androgyny as a positive state of affairs. For the most part, liberal feminists want their sons to develop a wide range of emotional responses and domestic skills as much as they want their daughters to develop an equally wide range of rational capacities and professional talents. Complete human beings are *both* rational and emotional. Thus, Wendell urged critics to read liberal feminist texts more sympathetically, as "a philosophically better kind of liberalism"[110] and to overcome the misconception that "[a] commitment to the value of individuals and their self-development, or even to the ethical priority of individuals over groups," is automatically a commitment "to narcissism or egoism or to the belief that one's own most important characteristics are somehow independent of one's relationships with other people."[111] Just because a woman refuses to spend her whole day nurturing her family does not mean she is more selfish than a man who, in the name of professional duty, may spend no time with his family. A person is selfish only when he or she takes more than his or her fair share of a resource: money, time, or even something intangible like love.

Critique Two:
Women as Men?

Jean Bethke Elshtain, a communitarian political theorist, is even more critical of liberal feminism than Alison Jaggar is. Like Jaggar, Elshtain claimed liberal feminists are wrong to emphasize individual interests, rights, and personal freedom over the common good, obligations, and social commitment, since "there is no way to create real communities out of an aggregate of 'freely' choosing adults."[112] In addition, more so than Jaggar, Elshtain castigated liberal feminists for putting an apparently high premium on so-called male values. She accused the Friedan of the 1960s—and, to a lesser extent, Wollstonecraft, Mill, and Taylor—of equating male being with human being, "manly" virtue with human virtue. In her critique "Why Can't a Woman Be More Like a Man?" Elshtain identified what she considered liberal feminism's three major flaws: (1) its claim women *can* become like men if they set their minds to it; (2) its claim most women *want* to become like men; and (3) its claim all women *should* want to become like men, to aspire to masculine values.

With respect to the first claim, that women *can* become like men, Elshtain pointed to the general liberal feminist belief that male-female differences are the products of culture rather than biology, of nurture rather than nature. She claimed liberal feminists refuse to entertain the possibility that some sex differences are biologically determined, for fear that affirmative answers could be used to justify the repression, suppression, and oppression of women. For this reason, many liberal feminists have, in Elshtain's estimation, become "excessive environmentalists," people who believe that gender identities are the nearly exclusive product of socialization, changeable at society's will.[113]

Although she wanted to avoid both the reactionary position of contemporary sociobiologists, according to whom biology is indeed destiny, and the sentimental speculations of some nineteenth- and twentieth-century feminists—according to whom women are, by nature, morally better than men[114]—Elshtain claimed that society cannot erase long-standing male-female differences without inflicting violence on people. Unless we wish to do what Plato suggested in *The Republic*, namely, banish everyone over the age of twelve and begin an intensive program of centrally controlled and uniform socialization from infancy onward, we cannot hope, said Elshtain, to eliminate gender differences between men and women in just a few generations. In sum, women *cannot* be like men unless we are prepared to commit ourselves to the kind of social engineering and behavior modification that is incompatible with the spirit, if not also the letter, of liberal law.[115]

Liberal feminism also has a tendency, claimed Elshtain, to overestimate the number of women who want to be like men. She dismissed the view that any woman who wants more than anything else to be a wife and mother is a benighted and befuddled victim of patriarchal "false consciousness." Patriarchy, in Elshtain's estimation, is simply not powerful enough to make mush out of millions of women's minds. If it were, feminists would be unable to provide a cogent explanation for the emergence of feminist "true consciousness" out of pervasive patriarchal socialization. Elshtain observed that liberal feminists' attempt to reduce "wifing" and "mothering" to mere "roles" is misguided:

> Mothering is not a "role" on par with being a file clerk, a scientist, or a member of the Air Force. Mothering is a complicated, rich, ambivalent, vexing, joyous activity which is biological, natural, social, symbolic, and emotional. It carries profoundly resonant emotional and sexual imperatives. A tendency to downplay the differences that pertain between, say, mothering and holding a job, not only drains our private relations of much of their significance, but also over-simplifies what can and should be done to alter things for women, who are frequently urged to change roles in order to solve their problems.[116]

If, after investing years of physical and emotional energy in being a wife and mother, a woman is told she made the wrong choice, that she could have done something "significant" with her life instead, her reaction is not likely to be a positive one. It is one thing to tell a person he or she should try a new hairstyle; it is quite another to advise a person to get a more meaningful destiny.

Finally, as Elshtain saw it, liberal feminists are wrong to sing "a paean of praise to what Americans themselves call the 'rat race,'"[117] to tell women they *should* absorb traditional masculine values. Articles written for women about dressing for success, making it in a man's world, being careful not to cry in public, avoiding intimate friendships, being assertive, and playing hardball serve only to erode what may, according to Elshtain, ultimately be the best about women: their learned ability to create and sustain community through involvement with friends and family. Woman ought to resist membership in the "rat race" culture. Rather than encouraging each other to mimic the traditional behavior of successful men, who spend a minimum of time at home and a maximum of time at the office, women ought to work toward the kind of society in which men as well as women have as much time for friends and family as for business associates and professional colleagues.

Although she came close here to forwarding the problematic thesis that every wife and mother is the Virgin Mary in disguise, Elshtain insisted maternal thinking "need not and must not descend into the sentimentalization that vitiated much Suffragist discourse."[118] Fearing that full participation in the public sphere would threaten female virtue, the suffragists reasoned "the vote" was a way for women to reform the evil, deceitful, and ugly public realm without ever having to leave the supposed goodness, truth, and beauty of the private realm. As Elshtain saw it, had the suffragists not constructed a false polarity between male vice and female virtue, between the "evil" public world and the "good" private world, they might have marched into the public world, demanding it absorb the virtues and values of the private world from which they had come.[119]

In assessing Elshtain's critique of liberal feminism, 1990s liberal feminists observed that although Elshtain's critique applied to Friedan's *The Feminine Mystique* (1963), it did not apply to Friedan's *The Second Stage* (1981). More generally, 1990s liberal feminists found several reasons to fault Elshtain's communitarian line of thought. In particular, they saw her as embracing an "overly romanticized view of a traditional community, where the status quo is not only given but often embraced"[120] and where, therefore, women's traditional roles remain largely unchanged even if supposedly more valued by society as a whole. They also saw her as accepting the values of a community without critically examining its exclusionary potentialities or asking what kind of communities constitute an environment in which women can thrive.

Critique Three:
Racism, Classism, and Heterosexism

Feminist critics of liberal feminism fault it not only for espousing a male ontology of self and an individualist politics but also for being only or mainly focused on the interests of white, middle-class, heterosexual women. Although liberal feminists accept this criticism as a just and fair one, they nonetheless note in their own defense that they have come a long way since the nineteenth century when, for example, they largely ignored black women's concerns. Nowadays, the situation is quite different. Liberal feminists are very attentive to how a woman's race affects her views on any number of topics, including fairly mundane ones such as housework.

We will recall that because Friedan addressed a largely white, middle-class, and well-educated group of women in *The Feminist Mystique,* it made sense for her to describe the housewife role as oppressive. After all, her primary audience did suffer from the kind of psychological problems people experience when they are underchallenged and restricted to repeatedly performing the same routine tasks. But as Angela Davis commented, the housewife role tends to be experienced as liberating rather than oppressive by a significant number of black women.[121] Indeed, stressed Davis, many black women, particularly poor ones, would be only too happy to trade their problems for the "problem that has no name." They would embrace white, middle-class, suburban life enthusiastically, happy to have plenty of time to lavish on their families and themselves.

Liberal feminists' increased stress on issues of race has prompted an increasing number of minority women to join and become active in liberal feminist organizations. For example, largely because NOW has allied itself with minority organizations devoted to welfare reform, civil rights, immigration policy, apartheid, and migrant worker and tribal issues, by 1992, minority women constituted 30 percent of NOW's leadership and 10 percent of its staff.[122] Unlike nineteenth-century liberal feminists, today's liberal feminists no longer mistakenly contrast women's rights with blacks' rights, implying that black women are neither "real women" nor "real blacks" but some sort of hybrid creatures whose rights are of little concern to either white women or black men.

In addition to racism, classism previously existed to a marked degree within liberal feminism, largely because the women who initially led the women's rights movement were from the upper middle class. Seemingly

oblivious to the social and economic privileges of the women whom she addressed in *The Feminine Mystique,* Friedan simply assumed all or most
women were supported by men and therefore worked for other than *financial* reasons. Later, when she came into increased contact with single mothers
trying to support their families on meager wages or paltry welfare benefits,
Friedan realized just how hard life can be for a poor urban woman working
in a factory, as opposed to a wealthy suburban woman driving to a PTA
meeting. Thus, in *The Second Stage,* Friedan tried to address some of the economic concerns of working women. Nevertheless, her primary audience
remained the daughters of the housewives she had tried to liberate in the
1960s: well-educated, financially comfortable, working mothers whom she
wished to rescue from the hardships of the so-called double day. In the final
analysis, *The Second Stage* is a book for middle-class professional women
(and men) much more than a text for working-class people. It envisions a
society in which men and women assume equal burdens and experience
equal benefits in both the public and the private worlds. But it fails to ask
whether a capitalist society can afford to develop ideal work and family conditions for *all* of its members or only for the "best and brightest"—that is,
for those professionals and quasi professionals who are already well enough
off to take advantage of joint appointments, parental leaves, the mommy
track, flextime, leaves of absence, and so on.

Similarly, Friedan's *The Fountain of Age* (1993) is directed more toward relatively well-to-do and healthy old people than relatively poor and frail old
people. Although Friedan's anecdotes about people remaking their lives after the
age of sixty are inspiring, they are, as one commentator noted, mostly tales
about "life-long achievers with uncommon financial resources"[123] who are continuing to do in their "golden years" what they did in their younger years. The
experience of this group of people is to be contrasted with U.S. citizens whose
work years have worn them out physically and psychologically and who find it
extremely difficult to survive let alone thrive on a small, fixed income. As such
people age, especially if they are infirm, their main enemy is not "self-image."
On the contrary, it is "unsafe neighborhoods, unmanageable stairs, tight bud-
gets and isolation."[124] To be sure, Friedan noted the plight of aging, infirm U.S.
citizens in *The Fountain of Age* and recommended a variety of concrete ways
(e.g., home care and community support) to ameliorate their situation. Yet she
failed to address society's *general unwillingness* to allocate time, money, and love
to old people who act old and need more than what some consider their fair
share of society's resources. Indeed, by emphasizing the importance of remaining "vital" in old age, Friedan may have inadvertently helped widen the gap
between advantaged and disadvantaged old people.

Finally, in addition to racism and classism, heterosexism has posed problems for liberal feminists. When lesbians working within the women's rights movement decided publicly to avow their sexual identity, the leadership and membership of organizations such as NOW disagreed about how actively and officially the organization should support gay rights. As already described, Friedan was among the feminists who feared that a vocal and visible lesbian constituency might further alienate the public from "women's rights" causes. Friedan's successor in office, Arlein Hernandez, was embarrassed by her predecessor's lukewarm support for lesbians, however. Upon accepting the presidency of NOW in 1970, Hernandez issued a strong statement in support of lesbians: "[NOW does] not prescribe a sexual preference test for applicants. We ask only that those who join NOW commit themselves to work for full equality for women and that they do so in the context that the struggle in which we are engaged is part of the total struggle to free all persons to develop their full humanity. . . . [W]e need to free *all* our sisters from the shackles of a society which insists on viewing us in terms of sex."[125] Lesbians, no less than heterosexual women, insisted Hernandez, have sexual rights.

To be sure, not all of NOW's membership applauded Hernandez's views. Specifically, conservative members complained that "gay rights" was not a bona fide woman's issue. Radical members of NOW countered that if anyone knew what a real *woman's* issue was, it was the lesbian: she who puts women, not men, at the center of her private as well as public life. The battle between these two groups in NOW escalated to such a degree it threatened NOW's existence for a year or so before the organization officially proclaimed lesbian rights as a NOW issue. In 1990, NOW manifested its support of lesbians in a particularly visible way: It elected Patricia Ireland, an open bisexual, as its president. It is important to stress, however, that even today NOW supports lesbianism as a personal sexual preference—as a lifestyle or partner choice some women make—rather than as a political statement about the best way to achieve women's liberation. Liberal feminists do not claim that women must orient all of their sexual desires toward women and away from men or that all women must love women more than they love men. The claim is instead that men as well as women must treat each other as equals, as persons equally worthy of love.

Conclusion

One way to react to the limitations of liberal feminism is to dismiss it as a bourgeois, white movement. In essence, this is precisely what Ellen Willis did in her 1975 article "The Conservatism of *Ms.*," which faulted *Ms.* magazine, the most widely recognized publication of liberal feminism, for imposing a pseudofeminist "party line." After describing this line at length, Willis noted its overall message was a denial of women's pressing need to overthrow patriarchy and capitalism and an affirmation of women's supposed ability to make it in the "system." Whatever *Ms.* has to offer women, insisted Ellis, it is not feminism:

> At best, Ms.'s self-improvement, individual-liberation philosophy is relevant only to an elite; basically it is an updated women's magazine fantasy. Instead of the sexy chick or the perfect homemaker, we now have a new image to live up to: the liberated woman. This fantasy, misrepresented as feminism, misleads some women, convinces others that "women's lib" has nothing to do with them, and plays into the hands of those who oppose any real change in women's condition.[126]

Willis's criticism may have been on target at the time, but *Ms.* has changed since the mid-1970s. Its editors have featured articles that show, for example, how classism, racism, and heterosexism intersect with sexism, thereby doubling, tripling, and even quadrupling the oppression of some women. Moreover, liberal feminists have, with few exceptions,[127] moved away from their traditional belief that any woman who wants to can liberate herself "individually" by "throwing off" her conditioning and "unilaterally" rejecting "femininity."[128] They now believe that achieving even a modest goal such as "creating equal employment opportunity for women" calls for much more than the effort of individual women; it will require the effort of a whole society committed to "giving girls and boys the same early education and ending sex prejudice, which in turn will require major redistribution of resources and vast changes in consciousness."[129] Sexual equality cannot be achieved through individual women's willpower alone. Also necessary are major alterations in people's deepest social and psychological structures.

In a 2002 article entitled "Essentialist Challenges to Liberal Feminism," Ruth E. Groenhout argued that feminists who are not liberal feminists should reconsider their wholesale rejection of liberalism. Specifically, she suggested that, properly interpreted, the liberal view of human nature is not quite as bad as Jaggar and Elshtain portrayed it. As Groenhout understands it, the liberal picture of human nature contains "a crucial aspect of the feminist analysis of the wrongness of sexist oppression."[130]

Sexual oppression, and social systems that perpetuate sexual oppression, are morally evil because they limit or deny women's capacity to reflect on and determine their own lives. Sexism also causes immeasurable harm to people, and its consequences are a part of the evil it causes, but sexism would be wrong even if it did not result in either impoverishment or sexualized violence against women. It is wrong, ultimately, because it treats some humans as less than human and limits their freedom to take responsibility for their own lives.[131]

For all the ways liberal feminism may have gone wrong for women, it did some things very right for women along the way. Women owe to liberal feminists many of the civil, educational, occupational, and reproductive rights they currently enjoy. They also owe to liberal feminists the ability to walk increasingly at ease in the public domain, claiming it as no less their territory than men's. Perhaps enough time has passed for feminists critical of liberal feminism to reconsider their dismissal of it.

2

Radical Feminism:
Libertarian and Cultural Perspectives

As we noted in Chapter 1, the 1960s and 1970s feminists who belonged to women's rights groups such as the National Organization for Women believed they could achieve gender equality by reforming the "system"—by working to eliminate discriminatory educational, legal, and economic policies.[1] Achieving equal rights for women was the paramount goal of these reformers, and the fundamental tenets of liberal political philosophy were a comfortable fit for these reformers. But not all 1960s and 1970s feminists wanted to find a place for women in the "system." The feminists who formed groups such as the Redstockings, the Feminists, and the New York Radical Feminists perceived themselves as revolutionaries rather than reformers. Unlike reformist feminists, who joined fundamentally mainstream women's rights groups, these revolutionary feminists did not become interested in women's issues as a result of working for government agencies, being appointed to commissions on the status of women, or joining women's educational or professional groups. Instead, their desire to improve women's condition emerged in the context of their participation in radical social movements, such as the civil-rights and anti–Vietnam War movements.[2]

Dubbed "radical feminists," these revolutionary feminists introduced into feminist thought the practice of consciousness-raising. Women came together in small groups and shared their personal experiences *as women* with each other. They discovered that their individual experiences were not unique to them but widely shared by many women. According to Valerie Bryson, consciousness-raising showed how the trauma of a woman who had been raped or who had had to resort to an illegal abortion seemed to be linked to the experiences of the wife whose husband refused to do his share of housework, appeared never to have heard of the female orgasm or sulked if she went out for the evening; the secretary whose boss insisted that she wear short skirts, expected her to "be nice" to important clients or failed to acknowledge that she was effectively running his office; and the female student whose teachers expected less of the "girls," refused requests to study female writers or even traded grades for sexual favours.[3]

Empowered by the realization that women's fates were profoundly linked, radical feminists proclaimed that "the personal is political" and that all women are "sisters." They insisted that men's control of both women's sexual and reproductive lives and women's self-identity, self-respect, and self-esteem is the most fundamental of all the oppressions human beings visit on each other.

The claim that women's oppression *as women* is more fundamental than other forms of human oppression is difficult to unpack. According to Alison Jaggar and Paula Rothenberg, it can be interpreted to mean one or more of five things:

1. That women were, historically, the first oppressed group.
2. That women's oppression is the most widespread, existing in virtually every known society.
3. That women's oppression is the hardest form of oppression to eradicate and cannot be removed by other social changes such as the abolition of class society.
4. That women's oppression causes the most suffering to its victims, qualitatively as well as quantitatively, although the suffering may often go unrecognized because of the sexist prejudices of both the oppressors and the victims.
5. That women's oppression . . . provides a conceptual model for understanding all other forms of oppression.[4]

But just because radical feminists agreed in principle that sexism is the first, most widespread, or deepest form of human oppression did not mean they also agreed about the nature and function of this pernicious ism or the best way to eliminate it. On the contrary, radical feminists split into two basic camps—*radical-libertarian feminists* and *radical-cultural feminists*—and depending on their camp, these feminists voiced very different views about how to fight sexism.

Radical-libertarian feminists claimed that an exclusively feminine gender identity is likely to limit women's development as full human persons. Thus, they encouraged women to become androgynous persons, that is, persons who embody both (good) masculine and (good) feminine characteristics or, more controversially, any potpourri of masculine and feminine characteristics, good or bad, that strikes their fancy. Among the first radical-libertarian feminists to celebrate androgynous women was Joreen Freeman. She wrote: "What is disturbing about a Bitch is that she is androgynous. She incorporates within herself qualities defined as 'masculine' as well as 'feminine.' A Bitch is blatant, direct, arrogant, at times egoistic. She has no liking for the indirect, subtle, mysterious ways of the 'eternal feminine.' She disdains the vicarious life deemed natural to women because she wants to live a life of her own."[5] In other words, a "Bitch" does not want to limit herself to being a sweet girl with little in the way of power. Instead, she wants to embrace as part of her gender identity those masculine characteristics that permit her to lead life on her own terms.

Freeman's views did not go unchallenged. Among others, Alice Echols rejected as wrongheaded Freeman's celebration of the Bitch. She said that Freeman's Bitch was far too masculine to constitute a role model for women. Still, Echols credited Freeman for expressing radical-libertarian feminists' desire to free women from the constraints of female biology. Just because a woman is biologically a female does not mean she is destined to exhibit only feminine characteristics. Women can be masculine as well as feminine.[6] They can choose their gender roles and identities, mixing and matching them at will.

Later, after the shock value of Freeman's rhetoric had dissipated, some radical feminists began to have second thoughts about the wisdom of women striving to be androgynous persons. As they saw it, a Bitch was not a full human person but only a woman who had embraced some of the worst features of masculinity. According to Echols, this group of radical feminists, soon labeled radical-cultural feminists, replaced the goal of androgyny with a summons to affirm women's essential "femaleness."[7] Far from believing, as radical-libertarian feminists did, that women should exhibit both masculine and feminine traits and behaviors, radical-cultural feminists expressed the view that it is better for women to be strictly female/feminine. Women, they said, should not try to be like men. On the contrary, they should try to be more like women, emphasizing the values and virtues culturally associated with women ("interdependence, community, connection, sharing, emotion, body, trust, absence of hierarchy, nature, immanence, process, joy, peace and life") and deemphasizing the values and virtues culturally associated with men ("independence, autonomy, intellect, will, wariness, hierarchy, domination, culture, transcendence, product, asceticism, war and death").[8] Moreover, and in the ideal, women should appreciate that, despite cultural variations among themselves, all women share one and the same female nature,[9] and the less influence men have on this nature, the better.[10]

To be certain, like any other conceivable classification of radical feminists, the libertarian-cultural distinction is subject to criticism. Yet, in my estimation, this particular distinction helps explain not only why some radical feminists embrace the concept of androgyny and others eschew it, but also why some radical feminists view both sex and reproduction as oppressive, even dangerous for women and why others view these aspects as liberating, even empowering for women. As we shall see throughout this chapter, radical feminists are not afraid to take exception to each other's views.

Libertarian and Cultural Views on the Sex/Gender System

In order to appreciate radical-libertarian and radical-cultural feminist views on androgyny in greater detail, it is useful first to understand the so-called sex/gender system. According to radical-libertarian feminist Gayle Rubin, the sex/gender system is a "set of arrangements by which a society transforms biological sexuality into products of human activity."[11] So, for example, patriarchal society uses certain facts about male and female biology (chromosomes, anatomy, hormones) as the basis for constructing a set of masculine and feminine gender identities and behaviors that serve to empower men and disempower women. In the process of accomplishing this task, patriarchal society convinces itself its cultural constructions are somehow "natural" and therefore that people's "normality" depends on their ability to display whatever gender identities and behaviors are culturally linked with their biological sex.

Among others, radical-libertarian feminists rejected patriarchal society's assumption there is a necessary connection between one's sex (male or female) and one's gender (masculine or feminine). Instead, they claimed that gender is separable from sex and that patriarchal society uses rigid gender roles to keep women passive ("affectionate, obedient, responsive to sympathy and approval, cheerful, kind and friendly") and men active ("tenacious, aggressive, curious, ambitious, planful, responsible, original and competitive").[12] They claimed the way for women to dispel men's wrongful power over women is for both sexes first to recognize women are no more destined to be passive than men are destined to be active, and then to develop whatever combination of feminine and masculine traits best reflects their individually unique personalities.

Some Libertarian Views on Gender

Millett's Sexual Politics

Among other prominent radical-libertarian feminists, Kate Millett insisted that the roots of women's oppression are buried deep in patriarchy's sex/gender system. In *Sexual Politics* (1970), she claimed the male-female sex relationship is the paradigm for all *power* relationships: "Social caste supersedes all other forms of inegalitarianism: racial, political, or economic, and unless the clinging to male supremacy as a birthright is finally forgone, all systems of oppression will continue to function simply by virtue of their logical and emotional mandate in the primary human situation."[13] Because male control of the public and private worlds maintains patriarchy, male control must be eliminated if women are to be liberated. But this is no easy task. To eliminate male control, men and women have to eliminate gender—specifically, sexual status, role, and temperament—as it has been constructed under patriarchy.

Patriarchal ideology exaggerates biological differences between men and women, making certain that men always have the dominant, or masculine, roles and women always have the subordinate, or feminine, ones. This ideology is so powerful, said Millett, that men are usually able to secure the apparent consent of the very women they oppress. Men do this through institutions such as the academy, the church, and the family, each of which justifies and reinforces women's subordination to men, resulting in most women's internalization of a sense of inferiority to men. Should a woman refuse to accept patriarchal ideology by casting off her femininity—that is, her submissiveness/subordination—men will use coercion to accomplish what conditioning has failed to achieve. Intimidation is everywhere in patriarchy, according to Millet. The streetwise woman realizes that if she wants to survive in patriarchy, she had better act feminine, or else she may be subjected to "a variety of cruelties and barbarities."[14]

Millett stressed that despite men's continual attempts to condition and coerce all women, many women have proved uncontrollable. During the 1800s, for example, U.S. women's resistance to men's power took several forms, including the women's movement inaugurated in 1848 at Seneca Falls, New York. As noted in Chapter 1, this spirited movement helped women gain many important legal, political, and economic liberties and equalities. Nevertheless, the women's movement of the 1800s failed to liberate women fully, because it did not adequately challenge the sex/gender system at its deepest roots. As a result, twentieth-century patriarchal forces regained some of the ground they had lost from nineteenth-century feminist activists.

Millett singled out authors D. H. Lawrence, Henry Miller, and Norman Mailer as some of the most articulate leaders of patriarchy's 1930–1960 assault on feminist ideas. She claimed that because readers typically took Lawrence's, Miller's, and Mailer's *descriptions* of relationships in which women are sexually humiliated and abused by men as *prescriptions* for ideal sexual conduct, women tended to regard themselves as sexual failures, unable to emulate the sexual behavior of the characters in Miller's *Sexus,* for example:

"You never wear any undies do you? You're a slut, do you know it?"
I pulled her dress up and made her sit that way while I finished my coffee.
"Play with it a bit while I finish this."
"You're filthy," she said, but she did as I told her.
"Take your two fingers and open it up. I like the color of it."
. . . With this I reached for a candle on the dresser at my side and I handed it to her.
"Let's see if you can get it in all the way. . . . "
"You can make me do anything, you dirty devil."
"You like it, don't you?"[15]

To the objection that readers of *Sexus* can tell the difference between fiction and reality, Millett replied that pornography often functions in much the same way advertising does. The perfectly slim bodies of the models who grace the covers of *Vogue* become standards for average women. Nobody has to articulate an explicit law, "Thou shalt mold thine lumpen body in the image of Cindy Crawford." Every woman simply knows what is expected of her, what it means to be a beautiful woman. In the same way, every reader of *Sexus* simply knows what is expected of him or her, what it means to be a sexually vital person as opposed to a sexual dud.

In addition to these literary pornographers, Millett identified two other patriarchal groups—neo-Freudian psychologists and Parsonian sociologists—as leading the assault on feminists. Although Sigmund Freud's openness about sexuality, his willingness to talk about what people do or do not do in the bedroom, initially appeared as a progressive step toward better, more various, and more liberating sexual relations, Millett claimed Freud's disciples used his writings to "rationalize the invidious relationship between the sexes, to ratify traditional roles, and to validate temperamental differences."[16] In a similar vein, the followers of Talcott Parsons, an eminent sociologist, used his writings to argue that distinctions between masculine and feminine traits are biological/natural rather than social/cultural, and that without rigid gender dimorphism, society could not function as well as it does now. Convinced that gender identities and behaviors are not "an arbitrary imposition on an infinitely plastic biological base," but rather "an adjustment to the real biological differences between the sexes," Parsons's disciples confidently asserted that women's subordination to men is natural.[17]

Rather than concluding her discussion of patriarchal reactionaries on a despairing note, however, Millett ended it on an optimistic note. In the late 1970s, women were, she believed, regrouping their forces. Aware of their nineteenth-century predecessors' mistakes, these twentieth-century feminists were determined not to repeat history. Millett observed in contemporary feminism a determined effort to destroy the sex/gender system—the basic source of women's oppression—and to create a new society in which men and women are equals at every level of existence.[18]

Although Millett looked forward to an androgynous future, to an integration of separate masculine and feminine subcultures, she insisted this integration must proceed cautiously with a thorough evaluation of all masculine and feminine traits. Obedience, as it has been traditionally exhibited by women, for example, should not be unreflectively celebrated as a desirable human trait, that is, as a trait an androgynous person should recognize as positive and therefore seek to possess. Nor is aggressiveness, as it has been traditionally exhibited by men, to be incorporated into the psyche of the androgynous person as a desirable human trait. Androgyny, speculated Millett, is a worthy ideal only if the feminine and masculine qualities integrated in the androgynous person are separately worthy.[19] After all, if we are told the ideal human combines in herself or himself masculine arrogance and feminine servility, we will be less favorably impressed than if we are told the ideal human combines the strength traditionally associated with men and the compassion traditionally associated with women. Not only is it undesirable to combine in one person the two vices of arrogance and servility—the excess and defect, respectively, of the virtue of self-respect—but it is also impossible, since these two vices are polar opposites. In contrast, it is both possible and desirable to combine in one person the qualities of strength and compassion, since these two virtues are complementary and likely to help a person live well in his or her community.

Firestone's Dialectic of Sex

Like Millett, Shulamith Firestone, another radical-libertarian feminist, claimed the material basis for the sexual/political ideology of female submission and male domination was rooted in the reproductive roles of men and women. Firestone, however, believed Millett's solution to this problem—the elimination of the sexual double standard that permits men but not women to experiment with sex, and the inauguration of a dual-parenting system that gives fathers and mothers equal child-rearing responsibilities—was inadequate. It would, in her estimation, take far more than such modest reforms in the sex/gender system to free women's (and men's) sexuality from the biological imperatives of procreation and to liberate women's (and men's) personalities from the socially constructed, Procrustean prisons of femininity and masculinity. In fact, said Firestone, it would take a major biological and social revolution to effect this kind of human liberation: Artificial (ex utero) reproduction would need to replace natural (in utero) reproduction, and so-called intentional families, whose members *chose* each other for reasons of friendship or even simple convenience, would need to replace the traditional biological family constituted in and through its members' genetic connections to each other.

Firestone maintained that with the end of the biological family would come the breakup of the Oedipal family situation that prohibits, among other things, parent-child incest. No longer would there be concerns about so-called inbreeding as people reverted to their natural "polymorphous perversity"[20] and again delighted in all types of sexual behavior. Genital sex, so important for the purposes of biological sex, would become just one kind of sexual experience—and a relatively unimportant one—as people rediscovered the erotic pleasures of their oral and anal cavities and engaged in sexual relations with members of the same as well as the opposite sex.

Firestone claimed that as soon as both men and women were truly free to engage in polymorphous, perverse sex, it would no longer be necessary for men to display only masculine identities and behaviors and for women to display only feminine ones. Freed from their gender roles at the level of biology (i.e., reproduction), women would no longer have to be passive, receptive, and vulnerable, sending out "signals" to men to dominate, possess, and penetrate them in order to keep the wheels of human procreation spinning. Instead, men and women would be encouraged to mix and match feminine and masculine traits and behaviors in whatever combination they wished. As a result, not only would human beings evolve into androgynous persons, but all of society would also become androgynous. As Firestone saw it, the biological division of the sexes for the purpose of procreation had created not only a false dichotomy between masculinity and femininity but also an invidious cultural split between the sciences and the arts.

Firestone believed we associate science and technology with men and the humanities and the arts with women. Thus, the "masculine response" to reality is the "technological response": "objective, logical, extroverted, realistic, concerned with the conscious mind (the ego), rational, mechanical, pragmatic and down-to-earth, stable."[21] In contrast, the "feminine response" to reality is the "aesthetic response": "subjective, intuitive, introverted, wishful, dreamy or fantastic, concerned with the subconscious (the *id*), emotional, even temperamental (hysterical)."[22] Only when the aforementioned biological revolution eliminates the need for maintaining rigid lines between male and female, masculine and feminine, will we be able to bridge the gap between the sciences and the arts. Androgynous persons will find themselves living in an androgynous society in which the categories of the technological and the aesthetic, together with the categories of the masculine and the feminine, will have disappeared through what Firestone termed "a mutual cancellation—a matter-antimatter explosion, ending with a poof!"[23] At last, claimed Firestone, the male Technological Mode would be able to "produce in actuality what the female Aesthetic Mode had envisioned," namely, a world in which we use our knowledge to create not hell but heaven on earth—a world in which men no longer have to toil by the sweat of their brow to survive and in which women no longer have to bear children in pain and travail.[24]

Clearly, Firestone's version of androgyny is quite different from Millett's. Indeed, we may ask whether it is androgyny in the strict sense of the term, for in the world envisioned by Firestone, men and women as defined by current gender traits and role responsibilities no longer exist. Nevertheless, because Firestone's utopian persons are permitted to combine within themselves a range of characteristics we currently term masculine and feminine, Firestone's version of androgyny might, after all, be situated on the same continuum with Millett's. But for Millett, the ideal androgynous person combines a balance of the *best* masculine and feminine characteristics, whereas for Firestone, there is no *one* way to be androgynous.

Some Cultural Views on Gender

Marilyn French

Because Marilyn French attributes male-female differences more to biology (nature) than to socialization (nurture), and because she seems to think traditional feminine traits are somehow better than traditional masculine traits, I view her as more of a radical-cultural feminist than a radical-libertarian feminist. Like Millett and Firestone fifteen years earlier, French claimed men's oppression of women leads logically to other systems of human domination. If it is possible to justify men's domination of women, it is possible to justify all forms of domination. "Stratification of men above women," wrote French, "leads in time to stratification of classes: an elite rules over people perceived as 'closer to nature,' savage, bestial, animalistic."[25]

Because French believed sexism is the model for all other isms, including racism and classism, she sought to explain the differences between sexism's enslaving ideology of "power-over" others and an alternative, nonsexist liberating ideology of "pleasure-with" others.

Examining the origins of patriarchy, French concluded early humans lived in harmony with nature. They saw themselves as small parts of a larger whole into which they had to fit if they wanted to survive. Considering evidence from primates and the world's remaining "simple societies," French speculated that the first human societies were probably matricentric (mother centered), for it was the mother who more than likely played the primary role in the group's survival-oriented activities of bonding, sharing, and harmonious participation in nature. Nature was friend, and as sustainer of nature and reproducer of life, woman was also friend.[26] French also speculated that as the human population grew, food inevitably became scarce. No longer experiencing nature as a generous mother, humans decided to take matters into their own hands. They developed techniques to free themselves from the whims of nature. They drilled, dug, and plowed nature for the bounty it had decided to hold back from them. The more control humans gained over nature, however, the more they separated themselves from it physically and psychologically. French claimed that because a "distance had opened up between humans and their environment as a result of increasing controls exercised over nature," humans became alienated from nature.[27] Alienation, defined by French as a profound sense of separation, aroused "hostility," which in turn led to "fear" and finally to "enmity." It is not surprising, then, that these negative feelings intensified men's desire to control not only nature but also women, whom they associated with nature on account of their role in reproduction.[28]

Out of men's desire to control the woman/nature dyad was born patriarchy, a hierarchical system that values having power over as many people as possible. Originally developed to ensure the human community's survival, the desire for power over others rapidly became, under patriarchy, a value cultivated simply for the experience of being the person in charge, the lawgiver, the boss, number one in the pecking order. French speculated that untempered by cooperation, patriarchal competition would inevitably lead to unbridled human conflict.[29]

Intent on sparing the world conflict—particularly as it could, in these times, escalate into a nuclear holocaust—French claimed that feminine values must be reintegrated into the masculine society created by a patriarchal ideology. If we want to see the twenty-first century, said French, we must treasure in our lives and actions "love and compassion and sharing and nutritiveness [*sic*] equally with control and structure, possessiveness and status."[30] Were we to take this last assertion at face value, we could easily infer that, for French, the best society is an androgynous one in which both men and

women embrace the historically feminine values of love, compassion, sharing, and nurturance just as eagerly as humans embrace the historically masculine values of control, structure, possessiveness, and status. Yet a closer
reading of French suggests she actually esteemed feminine values *more* than
masculine values and that any time she affirmed a masculine value, she did so
only because she had subjected it to what Joyce Trebilcot termed a "feminist
reconceiving"[31]—that is, a linguistic reinterpretation of a concept that
involves changing its descriptive meaning, the evaluative meaning, or both.[32]
According to French, most of her linguistic reinterpretations of masculine
values involved changing their descriptive rather than evaluative meaning.
For example, French did not claim that the masculine value of so-called
structure is *bad* in and of itself. Instead, she argued that structure, understood as a system or an organization, is *good* provided it serves to connect
rather than disconnect people.[33]

That French's androgyny involved a substantial reinterpretation of
male/masculine values but not of female/feminine values became increasingly clear throughout her *Beyond Power* (1985). Because "humanness" had
been deleteriously identified with a destructive, power-mongering masculine
world in the past, French suggested the term should now be beneficially
identified with a creative, power-sharing feminine world. Guided by the
value of having power over others, the masculine world accommodates only
those thoughts and actions that keep a small group of people in power. This
world has room for "true grit," "doing what you have to do," and "the end
justifying the means," but no room for "knowing when to stop," savoring
the "best things in life" (which, we are told, are "for free"), and reflecting on
process as well as product. Thus, to be a total man, or patriarch, is not to be
a full human being. Rather, it is to be what psychoanalytic feminist Dorothy
Dinnerstein termed a minotaur—"[the] gigantic and eternally infantile offspring of a mother's unnatural lust, [the] male representative of mindless,
greedy power, [who] insatiably devours live human flesh."[34]

In contrast, the feminine world, guided by the value of having pleasure—
by which French meant the ability of one group or person to affirm all others—accommodates many ways of being and doing. French viewed pleasure
as a very broad and deep concept that encompassed all the enriching experiences we believe a full human person should have.[35] It can be derived from
self as well as others, from the mind as well as the body, from the simple and
bucolic as well as the complex and urbane.

Because of her obvious dislike for the *masculine* version of power over others, French claimed the androgynous person must strike a balance between
pleasure with others and a *feminine* version of power over others she labeled

"power-to" do for others. French emphasized it is good for us to have power as well as pleasure in our lives, provided our power manifests itself not as the desire to destroy (power over others) but as the desire to create (power to do for others). Conceding we may never be able to completely eliminate our desire to be "top dog," French nonetheless insisted it is possible for us to curb our competitive drives and to cultivate instead our cooperative capacities.

Mary Daly

More than Millett, Firestone, and even French, radical-cultural feminist Mary Daly denigrated traditional masculine traits. Although Daly began her intellectual journey in *Beyond God the Father: Toward a Philosophy of Women's Liberation* (1973) with a plea for androgyny, she ultimately rejected the terms "masculine" and "feminine" as hopelessly befuddled products of patriarchy. Her term-transforming travels through *Gyn/Ecology* ended in *Pure Lust,* a spirited defense of "wild," "lusty," and "wandering" women—women who no longer desire to be androgynous and who prefer to identify themselves as radical lesbian feminist separatists.

In *Beyond God the Father,* her first major work, Daly focused on God as the paradigm for all patriarchs, arguing that unless he is dethroned from both men's and women's consciousness, women will never be empowered as full persons.[36] She repeatedly claimed that if anyone ever had a power-over-others complex, it is the transcendent God who appears in Judaism, Islam, and especially Christianity. This God is so remote and aloof that he dwells in a place beyond earth, suggesting that power over others inevitably leads to separation from others. A transcendent God, observed Daly, is a God who thinks in terms of I-it, subject-object, or self-other relationships. Furthermore, what is most alien to this transcendent God, this total being, is the natural world he called into existence out of total nothingness. Thus, women, who are associated with nature on account of their reproductive powers, play the role of object/other against both God's and men's role of subject/self.

Because the old transcendent God rejected women, Daly wished to replace him with a new, immanent God. An immanent God thinks in terms of I-thou, subject-subject, or self-self relationships and is thoroughly identified with the natural world in which he/she/it abides, she said. Thus, women are equal to men before this God, whom Daly described as Be-ing.[37]

One of the main ways in which I-it thinking is reflected in patriarchal society, said Daly, is through the institution of rigid masculine and feminine gender roles, polarizing the human community into two groups. Because men collectively perceive and define women as the second sex, each man becomes an I, or a self, and each woman becomes an it, or another. One way, then, to overcome I-it thinking, and the transcendent God who thinks I-it thoughts, is to break down gender dimorphism by constructing an androgynous person who is neither "I" nor "it" but beyond both forms of existence.

Significantly, Daly's concept of androgyny in *Beyond God the Father,* is more akin to French's than either Millett's or Firestone's. She rejected the pluralist model of androgyny, according to which men and women have separate but supposedly equal and complementary traits, and the assimilation model of androgyny, according to which women and men exhibit feminine as well as masculine traits.[38] As she saw it, both of these models of androgyny were deficient because neither of them asked whether the concepts of masculinity and femininity are worth preserving.

Although Daly's concerns about using the terms "masculinity" and "femininity" were similar to those previously raised by French, she proposed to handle these terms in a different way than French had. Whereas French seemed interested in reinterpreting traditional masculine traits, Daly seemed intent on reinterpreting traditional feminine traits. Daly insisted that positive feminine traits such as love, compassion, sharing, and nurturance must be carefully distinguished from their pathological excesses, the sort of masochistic feminine "virtues" for which they are frequently mistaken. For example, loving ordinarily is good, but under patriarchy, loving can become, for women, a form of total self-sacrifice or martyrdom. Thus, Daly argued that the construction of the truly androgynous person cannot and must not begin until women say no to the values of the "morality of victimization." Out of this no, said Daly, will come a yes to the values of the "ethics of personhood."[39] By refusing to be the other, by becoming selves with needs, wants, and interests of their own, women will end the game of man as master and woman as slave.

In *Beyond God the Father,* Daly observed what she described as the Unholy Trinity of Rape, Genocide, and War combining in their one patriarchal person the legions of sexism, racism, and classism. In *Gyn/Ecology: The Metaethics of Radical Feminism,* she articulated this claim more fully, arguing that this Unholy Trinity, this single patriarchal person, has but one essential message: necrophilia, defined as "obsession with and usually erotic attraction toward and stimulation by corpses, typically evidenced by overt acts (as copulation with a corpse)."[40] Whereas Daly emphasized in *Beyond God the Father* that women cannot thrive as long as they subscribe to the morality of victimization, she stressed in *Gyn/Ecology* that women cannot even survive as long as they remain in patriarchy. Not only are men out to twist women's minds, but they are also out to destroy women's bodies through such practices as Hindu suttee, Chinese foot binding, African female circumcision, European witch burning, and Western gynecology.[41]

In *Gyn/Ecology*, Daly decided to reject several terms she had used in *Beyond God the Father*. Among these terms was "androgyny," a term that she now viewed as twisted, as idealizing someone like "John Travolta and Farrah Fawcett-Majors Scotch-taped together."[42] The more she reflected on the traditional concept of femininity, the more Daly was convinced that there is nothing good in this notion for women to pursue. She asserted patriarchy has constructed both the positive feminine qualities of nurturance, compassion, and gentleness and the negative feminine qualities of pettiness, jealousy, and vanity. Thus, she concluded, women should reject the seemingly "good" aspects of femininity as well as the obviously "bad" ones. They are all "man-made constructs" shaped for the purposes of trapping women deep in the prison of patriarchy.[43]

Stripped of their *femininity*, women would be revealed in their original (prepatriarchal) *female* power and beauty, insisted Daly. Daly used Jerzy Kosinski's image of a painted bird to detail the differences between "false femininity" and "true femaleness." Kosinski tells the tale of a keeper who imprisons a natural, plain-looking bird simply by painting its feathers with a glittering color. Eventually, the bird is destroyed by her unpainted "friends," the victim of their jealousy. Reversing Kosinski's image, Daly claimed when it comes to women, it is not the artificial, painted birds (whom Daly looks upon as tamed, domesticated, feminized females), but the natural, plain-looking birds (whom Daly calls "wild females") who suffer. For Daly, painted birds are the women who permit "Daddy" to deck them out in splendor, to "cosmetize" and perfume them, to girdle and corset them. They are the women whom "Daddy" dispatches to destroy real, natural women: that is, the women who refuse to be what the patriarchs want them to be, who insist on being themselves no matter what, and who peel patriarchal paint off their minds and bodies.[44] In Daly's words, the "painted bird functions in the anti-process of double-crossing her sisters, polluting them with poisonous paint."[45] The real, natural woman, in contrast, is "attacked by the mutants of her own kind, the man-made women."[46]

For Daly, flying is the antidote to being painted. The real, natural woman does not take off patriarchal paint only to become vulnerable. Rather, she "takes off." She "sends the paint flying back into the eyes of the soul-slayers"; she "soars . . . out of the circle of Father Time" and flies "off the clock into other dimensions."[47] She flies free of "mutant fembirds," the women who have permitted themselves to be constructed by patriarchy. She also flies free of the power of patriarchal language and therefore patriarchal values.

In many ways, Daly's decision to reject androgyny in *Gyn/Ecology* led her to where Friedrich Nietzsche's transvaluation of values led him: to a redefinition of what is good and what is bad, counter to the prevailing notions of good and bad. In *On the Genealogy of Morals,* Nietzsche contended there are two basic kinds of moralities: master and slave. In the master morality, good and bad are equivalent to noble and despicable, respectively. To be good is to be on top of the world. To be bad is to be repressed, oppressed, suppressed, or otherwise downtrodden. The criteria for goodness articulated in the slave morality are the polar opposites of the criteria for goodness articulated in the master morality: Those who espouse a slave morality extol qualities such as kindness, humility, and sympathy as virtues, and denigrate qualities such as assertiveness, aloofness, and pride as vices. Such thinkers venerate weak and dependent individuals as saints and condemn strong and independent individuals as sinners.

Motivated by the all-consuming resentment (*resentiment*) of the masters, the slaves manifest a negative attitude toward what Nietzsche believed is the most natural drive of a human being: the will to power. As Nietzsche saw it, the slaves lack not only a desire for power but also a desire for life. Fearful of conflict, of challenge, of charting the course of their destinies, the slaves wish to be complacent in their mediocrity. Nietzsche found slaves profoundly boring. He also found them incredibly dangerous, for they seemed intent on clogging Western civilization's arteries with sugarplums, placebos, and the milk of human kindness:

> For this is how things are: the diminution and leveling of European man [sic] constitutes *our* greatest danger, for the sight of him makes us weary. We can see nothing today that wants to grow greater, we suspect that things will continue to go down, down, to become thinner, more good-natured, more prudent, more comfortable, more mediocre, more indifferent, more Chinese, more Christian—there is no doubt that man [sic] is getting "better" all the time.
>
> Here precisely is what has become a fatality for Europe—together with the fear of man [sic] we have also lost our love of him, our reverence for him, our hopes for him, even the will to him. The sight of man [sic] now makes us weary.[48]

In order to stop this will to impotence, mediocrity, and death, Nietzsche mandated a transvaluation of all values that would reassign, for example, "good" values to the category of bad values and "bad" values to the category of good values. He declared war on the accepted slave values of his time, which he identified as the values of Judaism, Christianity, democracy, and socialism—any philosophy or theology that asks the individual to sacrifice himself or herself for the greater good of the community. Because slave morality is, according to Nietzsche, a perversion of the original, natural morality/psychology of the masters, transvaluation must consist in overcoming the slave morality/psychology. Transvaluation begins with the recognition that all the stronger values, or master values, still exist but now go unrecognized under false names such as "cruelty," "injury," "appropriation," "suppression," and "exploitation." These false names, said Nietzsche, do not connote what the masters originally meant, but what the slaves have interpreted them to mean. The process of transvaluation will end, therefore, with the restoration of false names' true meanings.

Like Nietzsche, Daly is a transvaluator of values. She claimed that with respect to women, she whom the patriarch calls evil is in fact good, whereas she whom the patriarch calls good is in fact bad. Providing a dictionary of new language in the last section of *Gyn/Ecology,* Daly invited "hags," "spinsters," and "haggard heretics" to "unspook" traditional language and their old feminine selves by "*spinning*" for themselves a new, unconventional language and new female selves. Daly insisted that *women* should decide who women want to be. For example, if women want to be hags instead of bathing beauties, then so be it. It is for women to decide whether being a hag is good or bad. Explained Daly:

> *Hag* is from an Old English word meaning harpy, witch. Webster's gives as the first and 'archaic' meaning of *hag:* "a female demon: FURY, HARPY." It also formerly meant: "an evil or frightening spirit." (Lest this sound too negative, we should ask the relevant questions: "Evil" by whose definition? "Frightening" to whom?) A third archaic definition of *hag* is "nightmare." (The important question is: Whose nightmare?) *Hag* is also defined as "an ugly or evil-looking old woman." But this, considering the source, may be considered a compliment. For the beauty of strong, creative women is "ugly" by misogynistic standards of "beauty." The look of female-identified women is "evil" to those who fear us. As for "old," ageism is a feature of phallic society. For women who have transvalued this, a Crone is one who should be an example of strength, courage, and wisdom.[49]

By the time she wrote the last page of *Gyn/Ecology,* Daly had completely replaced the ideal of the androgynous person with the ideal of the "wild female" who dwells beyond masculinity and femininity. To become whole, a woman needs to strip away the false identity—femininity—patriarchy has constructed for her. Then and only then will she experience herself as the self she would have been had she lived her life in a matriarchy rather than a patriarchy.

In *Pure Lust: Elemental Feminist Philosophy,* Daly continued her transvalu-ation of values. In this book about woman's power, Daly extended French's analysis of power-to. It is this power men have fed on, making women grow thin, weak, frail, even anorexic. In order to grow strong, women must resist the trap of androgyny. Utterly dependent on their God-given helpmates, pa-triarchs offer women androgyny in a last-ditch effort to keep women by their sides: "Come, join forces with us. Masculinity and femininity together!" Women should not, said Daly, be deceived by these inviting words, which are simply a ploy on the part of men to appropriate for themselves whatever is best about women. Men have gradually realized it is in their own (but not women's) best interests to become androgynous persons, since their maleness has so little to offer them. For example, at the end of the film *Tootsie,* after the lead character's male identity has been disclosed (he had been posing as a female television star named Dorothy), he tells Julie, a woman he had be-friended in his incarnation as Dorothy, that he actually *is* Dorothy. Daly commented: "The message clearly is one of cannibalistic androgynous male-ness. Little Dustin, whom Julie had loved but rejected because she believed he was a woman, incorporates the best of womanhood—like Dionysus and Jesus before him."[50] Men want to be androgynous so that they can subsume or even consume all that is female, draining women's energies into their bod-ies and minds. Instead of submitting to the gynocidal process of androgyny, women must, said Daly, spin new, powerful self-understandings, remaining radically apart from men, reserving their energies for their own pursuits.

What is most impressive about *Pure Lust* is Daly's ability to provide new meanings, simultaneously prescriptive and descriptive, for terms. The term "lust" is a case in point. Daly wrote, "The usual meaning of *lust* within the lecherous state of patriarchy is well known. It means 'sexual desire, especially of a violent self-indulgent character: LECHERY, LASCIVIOUSNESS.'"[51] Lust, then, is evil, said Daly, but only because we live in a society with a slave morality, which resents women. If we lived instead in a nonpatriarchal society, contin-ued Daly, lust would have good meanings such as "vigor," "fertility," "craving," "eagerness," and "enthusiasm."[52] Thus, the lusty women of *Pure Lust* are the wild females of *Gyn/Ecology,* the undomesticated women who refuse to be gov-erned by the rules of men's "sadosociety," which is "formed/framed by statutes of studs, degrees of drones, canons of cocks, fixations of fixers, precepts of prickers, regulations of rakes and rippers . . . bore-ocracy."[53]

The Daly of *Pure Lust* had no use for what she regarded as the petrified lan-guage of patriarchy, referring to it only with the aim of redefining, reinterpret-ing, or reclaiming its terms. *Pure Lust* transvaluated what counts as moral virtue and moral vice for women. In particular, the book showed how patriarchal forces deprived natural women of bona fide passions, substituting for these true passions a collection of "plastic" and "potted" ones: a set of inauthentic, counterfeit emotions created for artificial women.

According to Daly, plastic passions like guilt, anxiety, depression, hostility, bitterness, resentment, frustration, boredom, resignation, and fulfillment are no substitute for genuine passions like love, desire, joy, hate, aversion, sorrow, hope, despair, fear, and anger. Whereas genuine passions spur women to meaningful action, plastic passions enervate women. In Daly's estimation, the plastic passion of fulfillment, for example, is not to be confused with the genuine passion of joy. Fulfillment is simply the "therapeutized perversion" of joy. A fulfilled woman is "filled full," "finished," "fixed" just the way patriarchy likes her. Because she is so "totaled," she cannot live the "e-motion of joy." She lacks the energy to move or act purposely.[54] Fulfillment, said Daly, is just another term for Betty Friedan's "problem that has no name"[55]—having a comfortable home, a successful husband, a wonderful child, but no joy.

Like plastic passions, potted passions are also a poor substitute for genuine passions, in Daly's estimation. Although potted passions are in many ways more real than plastic passions, they are not nearly as grand as genuine passions. To appreciate Daly's point, we may view a genuine passion as a live evergreen out in the woods, a potted passion as a decked-out but cut (and hence, dying) Christmas tree, and a plastic passion as an artificial Christmas tree. The genuine passion of love, for example, is a life-transforming emotion, but when it is either potted or packaged and then sold as "romance," women are duped into settling for love's illusion rather than its reality.[56] There is, of course, something tragic about settling for so little when there is so much to be had. Thus, Daly hoped the words in *Pure Lust* would help women liberate themselves from the pots and plastic molds blocking their volcanic genuine passions.

Sexuality, Male Domination, and Female Subordination

Radical-libertarian and radical-cultural feminists have very different ideas not only about gender but also about sexuality.[57] Among the feminists who have written insightfully on this difference is Ann Ferguson. Unfortunately for my purposes, Ferguson and I use different terms to express what I think are essentially the same ideas. To avoid an unnecessarily confusing discussion of Ferguson's work, I substitute my terms "radical-libertarian" and "radical-cultural" for her terms "libertarian" and "radical."

According to Ferguson, radical-libertarian feminists' views on sexuality are as follows:

1. Heterosexual as well as other sexual practices are characterized by repression. The norms of patriarchal bourgeois sexuality repress the sexual desires and pleasures of everyone by stigmatizing sexual minorities, thereby keeping the majority "pure" and under control.
2. Feminists should repudiate any theoretical analyses, legal restrictions, or moral judgements that stigmatize sexual minorities and thus restrict the freedom of all.
3. As feminists we should reclaim control over female sexuality by demanding the right to practice whatever gives us pleasure and satisfaction.
4. The ideal sexual relationship is between fully consenting, equal partners who negotiate to maximize one another's sexual pleasure and satisfaction by any means they choose.[58]

In contrast, radical-cultural feminists' views on sexuality are as follows:

1. Heterosexual sexual relations generally are characterized by an ideology of sexual objectification (men as subjects/masters; women as objects/slaves) that supports male sexual violence against women.
2. Feminists should repudiate any sexual practice that supports or normalizes male sexual violence.
3. As feminists we should reclaim control over female sexuality by developing a concern with our own sexual priorities, which differ from men's—that is, more concern with intimacy and less with performance.
4. The ideal sexual relationship is between full consenting, equal partners who are emotionally involved and do not participate in polarized roles.[59]

Radical-libertarian feminists challenged theories of sexuality that separated supposedly good, normal, legitimate, healthy sexual practices from supposedly bad, abnormal, illegitimate, unhealthy sexual practices.[60] These feminists urged women to experiment with different kinds of sex and not to confine themselves to a limited range of sexual experiences.[61]

Among the most forceful and articulate spokespersons for radical-libertarian-feminist ideology was Gayle Rubin. She claimed that contemporary society remains uncomfortable with any form of sex that is not between married, heterosexual couples intent on procreating children.[62] It represses—indeed punishes—to a greater or lesser extent unmarried heterosexuals who engage in casual sex for pleasure, bisexuals, homosexuals, lesbians, transsexuals, transvestites, fetishists, sadomasochists, sex workers, and "those whose eroticism crosses transgenerational boundaries."[63] As a result of this state of affairs, many people deny themselves the joys of sex, said Rubin. Wanting to let people have a good time, so to speak, Rubin urged feminists to lead a campaign to stop viewing sex in terms "of sins, disease, neurosis, pathology, decadence, pollution or the decline and fall of empires."[64] For Rubin, all sex was good; no judgments should be made about the rightness or wrongness of any form of sex.

Not surprisingly, radical-libertarian feminists' views on sexuality were not uniformly accepted by one and all. Rejecting Rubin's celebration of all forms of sexuality, radical-cultural feminists insisted that, in a patriarchal society, it was feminists' responsibility to make judgments about one form of sexuality in particular: namely, sex between men and women.

Radical-cultural feminists equated heterosexuality as they experienced it with "male sexuality," that is, "driven, irresponsible, genitally-oriented and potentially lethal"[65] sexuality. They contrasted this "male sexuality" with "female sexuality," that is "muted, diffuse, interpersonally-oriented, and benign"[66] sexuality. In radical-cultural feminists' estimation, because men want "power and orgasm" in sex and women want "reciprocity and intimacy" in sex,[67] the only kind of sex that is *unambiguously good* for women is monogamous lesbianism.[68] Women must understand, they said, that patriarchal heterosexuality is an institution bent on sapping women's emotional energies and keeping women perpetually dissatisfied with themselves:

> Only women can give each other a new sense of self. That identity we have to develop with reference to ourselves, and not in relation to men. This consciousness is the revolutionary force from which all else will follow, for ours is an organic revolution. For this we must be available and supportive to one another, give our commitment and our love, give the emotional support necessary to sustain this movement. Our energies must flow toward our sisters, not backwards towards our oppressors. As long as women's liberation tries to free women without facing the basic heterosexual structure that binds us in one-to-one relationships with our oppressors, tremendous energies will continue to flow into trying to straighten up each particular relationship with a man, how to get better sex, how to turn his head around—into trying to make the "new man" out of him, in the delusion that this will allow us to be the "new woman." This obviously splits our energies and commitments, leaving us unable to be committed to the construction of the new patterns which will liberate us.[69]

In sum, patriarchal heterosexuality is beyond repair. It must be destroyed so that women can fully live, according to radical-cultural feminists.

The Pornography Debate

Women's different reactions to pornography, or their use of it in their lives, dramatically highlight the general differences between radical-libertarian feminists and radical-cultural feminists on sexual matters. Radical-libertarian feminists urged women to use pornography to overcome their fears about sex, to arouse sexual desires, and to generate sexual fantasies.[70] These feminists claimed that women should feel free to view and enjoy all sorts of pornography, including violent pornography. Some radical-libertarian feminists even invited women to engage in rape fantasies in which men "had their way" with women in bed. There is a difference between an actual rape and a rape fantasy, insisted the most "libertarian" members of the radical-libertarian feminist camp. The same woman who derives sexual pleasure from *playing* Scarlett O'Hara–Rhett Butler sex games with her boyfriend would protest loudly were he *actually* to attempt to rape her. Just because a woman wants to explore whether power games are part of what makes sex "sexy" for her does not mean she wants to serve as an object for male violence in real life.[71] Rather than stubbornly insisting that pornographic representations of men sexually dominating women somehow harm women in real life, said radical-libertarian feminists, feminists should engage in an entirely open-minded and nondefensive examination of pornography, saving their venom for real rapists.

Ironically, radical-libertarian feminists' defense of pornography served to increase, not decrease, radical-cultural feminists' opposition to it. Radical-cultural feminists stressed that sexuality and gender *are* the products of the same oppressive social forces. There is no difference between gender discrimination against women in the boardroom and the sexual objectification of women in the bedroom. In both instances, the harm done to women is about men's power over women. Pornography is nothing more than patriarchal propaganda about women's "proper" role as man's servant, helpmate, caretaker, and plaything, according to radical-cultural feminists. Whereas men exist for themselves, women exist for men. Men are subjects; women are objects, they said.

Radical-cultural feminists insisted that with rare exception, pornography harms women. First, it encourages men to behave in sexually harmful ways toward women (e.g., sexual harassment, rape, domestic violence). Second, it defames women as persons who have so little regard for themselves they actively seek or passively accept sexual abuse. And third, it leads men not only to think less of women as human beings but also to treat them as second-class citizens unworthy of the same due process and equal treatment men enjoy.

Unable to prove that exposure to pornographic representations directly causes men either to harm women's bodies or to defame women's characters, radical-cultural feminists sought protection for women in antidiscrimination laws. They followed the lead of Andrea Dworkin and Catharine MacKinnon, who defined pornography as "the graphic sexually explicit subordination of women through pictures or words that also includes women dehumanized as sexual objects, things, or commodities; enjoying pain or humiliation or rape; being tied up, cut up, mutilated, bruised, or physically hurt; in postures of sexual submission or servility or display; reduced to body parts, penetrated by objects or animals, or presented in scenarios of degradation, injury, torture; shown as filthy or inferior; bleeding, bruised, or hurt in a context that makes these conditions sexual."[72]

Radical-cultural feminists claimed that sexuality is the primary locus of male power in which women-harming gender relations are constructed.[73] They also claimed that because pornographers systematically depict women as less fully human and, therefore, less deserving of respect and good treatment than men, pornographers can and ought to be viewed as agents of sexual discrimination, guilty of violating women's civil rights. For this reason, any woman—or man, child, or transsexual used in the place of a woman—should be granted a legal cause of action against a particular pornographer or pornographic business if she is coerced into a pornographic performance, has pornography forced on her, or has been assaulted or attacked because of a particular piece of pornography. Further, any woman should be able to bring civil suit against traffickers in pornography on behalf of all women.[74] Emptying the pockets of pornographers is the best way for feminists to fight the misogynistic ideology pornographers willingly spread.

Although radical-cultural feminists, under the leadership of MacKinnon and Dworkin, were initially successful in their attempt to have antipornography ordinances passed in Minneapolis and Indianapolis, a coalition of radical-libertarian and liberal feminists called the Feminist Anti-Censorship Taskforce (FACT) joined nonfeminist free-speech advocates to work against MacKinnon and Dworkin's 1980s legislation. Largely because of FACT's efforts, the U.S. Supreme Court eventually declared the Minneapolis and Indianapolis antipornography ordinances unconstitutional.[75] During the period that FACT worked to defeat MacKinnon and Dworkin's legislation, its membership insisted phrases such as "sexually explicit subordination of women" have no context-free, fixed meaning.[76]

FACT referred to the film *Swept Away* to show just how difficult it is to decide whether a particular scene or set of scenes depicts the sexually explicit subordination of women. In the movie, an attractive, upper-class woman and a brawny, working-class man are shown, during the first half of the film, as *class* antagonists and then, during the second half of the film, as *sexual* antagonists when they are stranded on an island and the man exacts his revenge on the woman by repeatedly raping her. Initially, she resists him, but gradually she falls in love with him, and eventually, he with her.

Because scenes in *Swept Away* clearly present the woman character as enjoying her own sexual humiliation, the film falls under a radical-cultural feminist definition of pornography and could have been suppressed, pending the outcome of a civil suit brought against its creators, manufacturers, and distributors. According to FACT, however, such suppression would have represented censorship of the worst sort because the film challenged viewers to think seriously about precisely what does and does not constitute the sexually explicit subordination of women. Critical and popular opinion of the film varied, ranging from admiration to repulsion. Whereas the reviewer for *Ms.* wrote that "'Swept Away' comes to grips with the 'war' between the sexes better than anything" she had ever read or seen, the reviewer for the *Progressive* stated he did not know what was "more distasteful about the film—its slavish adherence to the barroom credo that what all women really want is to be beaten, to be shown who's boss, or the readiness with which it has been accepted by the critics."[77] FACT emphasized if two film critics can see the images and hear the words of *Swept Away* so differently, then contextual factors, such as the critics' own sexual fantasies and erotic impulses, must ultimately explain their divergent interpretations. What looks like the sexually explicit subordination of a woman to a radical-cultural feminist may, as far as the woman herself is concerned, be the height of sexual pleasure.

Shocked by radical-libertarian feminists' seeming acceptance of women's sexual abuse, radical-cultural feminists accused radical-libertarian feminists of false consciousness, of buying the "bill of goods" men are only too eager to sell women. Bitter debates about sexuality broke out between radical-libertarian and radical-cultural feminists, reaching fever pitch at the 1982 Barnard College sexuality conference. A coalition of radical-libertarian feminists, including lesbian practitioners of sadomasochism and butch-femme relationships, bisexuals, workers in the sex industry (prostitutes, porn models, exotic dancers), and heterosexual women eager to defend the pleasures of sex between consenting men and women, accused radical-cultural feminists of prudery. To this charge, radical-cultural feminists responded they were not prudes. On the contrary, they were *truly* free women who could tell the difference between "erotica," where the term denotes sexually explicit depictions and descriptions of women being integrated, constituted, or focused during loving or at least life-affirming sexual encounters, and "thanatica," where the term denotes sexually explicit depictions and descriptions of women being disintegrated, dismembered, or disoriented during hate-filled or even death-driven sexual encounters.

Radical-libertarian feminists faulted radical-cultural feminists for present-ing "vanilla" sex—gentle, touchy-feely, side-by-side (no one on the top or the bottom) sex—as the only kind of sex that is good for women. Why, asked radical-libertarian feminists, should we limit women, or men for that matter, to a particular "flavor" of sex? If women are given free rein, some may choose vanilla sex, but others may prefer "rocky-road" sex—encounters where pain punctuates pleasure, for example. No woman should be told that if she wants to be a *true* feminist, then she must limit herself to only certain sorts of sex-ual encounters. After all, if women's sexuality is as "absent" as Catharine MacKinnon herself has claimed,[78] then it is premature for anyone, including radical-cultural feminists, to fill the vacuum with only their own ideas. Bet-ter that all sorts of women offer diverse descriptions of what they find truly pleasurable. To this line of reasoning, radical-cultural feminists again retorted that radical-libertarian feminists were not *true* feminists but deluded pawns of patriarchy who had willfully closed their ears to pornography's women-hating message. Before too long, the Barnard conference collapsed, as the gulf between radical-libertarian and radical-cultural feminists widened.

The Lesbianism Controversy

Another topic that divided radical-libertarian feminists from radical-cultural feminists was lesbianism, particularly "separatist" lesbianism. Lesbianism fully surfaced as an issue within the women's movement during the 1970s. Ironically, at the Second Congress to Unite Women, a group of women wearing T-shirts emblazoned with the label "lavender menace" staged a protest. The organizers of the conference had anticipated trouble due to the publication of Ann Koedt's provocative essay "The Myth of the Vaginal Orgasm." In this essay, Koedt claimed many women believe the orgasms they feel during heterosexual intercourse are vaginally caused when in fact they are clitorally stimulated. Koedt also claimed that many men fear "be-com[ing] sexually expendable if the clitoris is substituted for the vagina as the center of pleasure for women."[79] Viewing men's fear of "sexual expend-ability" as alarmist, Koedt noted that even if all women recognized they did not *need* men as sexual partners for *physiological* reasons, many women would still select men as sexual partners for *psychological* reasons.[80]

Radical-libertarian feminists interpreted Koedt as justifying women's engagement in noncompulsory (freely chosen) heterosexuality. Since a woman does not *need* a male body to achieve sexual pleasure, she does not have to engage in sexual relations with a man unless *she* wants to. In contrast to radical-libertarian feminists, radical-cultural feminists interpreted Koedt as implying that since there is no physiological reason for a woman to have sex with a man, there is no *feminist* psychological reason for a woman to *want* to have sex with a man. Indeed, there are only *nonfeminist* psychological reasons for a woman to want to have sex with a man, the kind of bad reasons Adrienne Rich discussed in her essay on compulsory heterosexuality.[81] Therefore, if a woman wants to be a *true* feminist, she must become a lesbian. She must do what comes "naturally," thereby freeing her own consciousness from the false idea that she is deviant, abnormal, sick, crazy, or bad because she enjoys sex with women, not with men.

For a time, the radical-cultural feminists' interpretation of Koedt's essay predominated in feminist circles, so much so that many heterosexual feminists felt deviant, abnormal, sick, crazy, or bad if they wanted to have sex with men. Deirdre English, a radical-libertarian feminist, reported she found it "fascinating and almost funny"[82] that so many heterosexual feminists "seemed to accept the idea that heterosexuality meant cooperating in their own oppression and that there was something wrong with being sexually turned on to men. How many times have I heard this? 'Well, unfortunately, I'm not a lesbian but I wish I was, maybe I will be.'"[83] The so-called political lesbian was born: she who did not find herself erotically attracted to women but who tried as hard as possible to reorient her sexual impulses toward women and away from men.

Radical-libertarian feminists agreed with radical-cultural feminists that heterosexuality is a flawed institution that has harmed many women. Still, radical libertarians insisted it would be just as wrong for radical-cultural feminists to impose lesbianism on women as it had been for patriarchy to impose heterosexuality on women.[84] Men having sex with women is not, in and of itself, bad for women, in radical-libertarian feminists' estimation. Rather, what is bad for women is men having sex with women in a particular way: "fucking for a minute and a half and pulling out."[85] Women can and do find pleasure in sex with men when men make women's sexual satisfaction just as important as their own sexual satisfaction, said radical-libertarian feminists.

Radical-libertarian feminists also stressed that individual men, as bad as they could be, were not women's primary oppressors. On the contrary, women's main enemy was the patriarchal system, the product of centuries of male privilege, priority, and prerogative. Thus, unlike those radical-cultural feminists who urged women to stop relating to men on all levels beginning with the *sexual,* radical-libertarian feminists did not press for a separatist agenda. On the contrary, radical-libertarian feminists urged women to confront individual men about their chauvinistic attitudes and behaviors in an effort to get men freely to renounce the unfair privileges patriarchy had bestowed upon them.[86] These feminists recalled that even WITCH, one of the most militant feminist groups in the 1960s, had not urged women to renounce men or heterosexuality entirely but to relate to men only on gynocentric terms:

Witches have always been women who dared to be: groovy, courageous, aggressive, intelligent, nonconformist, explorative, curious, independent, sexually liberated, revolutionary. (This possibly explains why nine million of them have been burned.) Witches were the first Friendly Heads and Dealers, the first birth-control practitioners and abortionists, the first alchemists (turn dross into gold and you devalue the whole idea of money!). They bowed to no man, being the living remnants of the oldest culture of all—one in which men and women were equal sharers in a truly cooperative society, before the death-dealing sexual, economic, and spiritual repression of the Imperialist Phallic Society took over and began to destroy nature and human society.

WITCH lives and laughs in every woman. She is the free part of each of us, beneath the shy smiles, the acquiescence to absurd male domination, the make-up or flesh-suffocating clothing our sick society demands. There is no "joining" WITCH. If you are a woman and dare to look within yourself, you are a Witch. You make your own rules. You are free and beautiful. You can be invisible or evident in how you choose to make your witch-self known. You can form your own Coven of sister Witches (thirteen is a cozy number for a group) and do your own actions.

You are pledged to free our brothers from oppression and stereotyped sexual roles (whether they like it or not) as well as ourselves. You are a Witch by saying aloud, "I am a Witch" three times, and *thinking about that.* You are a Witch by being female, untamed, angry, joyous, and immortal.[87]

Thus, women in the 2000s, like women in the 1960s, do not have to live together on the fringes of society or to have sex only with each other in order to be liberated, according to today's radical-libertarian feminists. Freedom comes to women as the result of women's giving each other the power of self-definition and the energy to rebel continually against any individual man, group of men, or patriarchal institution seeking to disempower or otherwise weaken women.

Reproduction, Men, and Women

Not only do radical-libertarian and radical-cultural feminists have different views about sex, but they also have different ideas about reproduction.

Whereas radical-libertarian feminists believe women should substitute artificial for natural modes of reproduction, radical-cultural feminists believe it is in women's best interests to procreate naturally. As we shall see, radical-libertarian feminists are convinced the less women are involved in reproduction, the more time and energy women will have to engage in society's productive processes. In contrast, radical-cultural feminists are convinced the ultimate source of women's power rests in their power to gestate new life. To take this power from a woman is to take away her trump card and to leave her with an empty hand, entirely vulnerable to men's power.

Natural Reproduction: The Site of Women's Oppression

Firestone's *The Dialectic of Sex.* In *The Dialectic of Sex,* Shulamith Firestone claimed that patriarchy, the systematic subordination of women, is rooted in the biological inequality of the sexes. Firestone's reflections on women's reproductive role led her to a feminist revision of the materialist theory of history offered by Karl Marx and Friedrich Engels. Although Marx and Engels correctly focused on class struggle as the driving forces of history, they paid scant attention to what she termed "sex class." Firestone proposed to make up for this oversight by developing a feminist version of historical materialism in which sex class, rather than economic class, is the central concept.

To appreciate Firestone's co-optation of Marxist method, we have only to contrast her definition of historical materialism with Engels's definition of historical materialism, which is "that view of the course of history which seeks the ultimate cause and great moving power of all historical events in the economic development of society, in the changes of the modes of production and exchange, in the consequent division of society into distinct classes, and in the struggles of these classes against one another."[88] Firestone reformulated his definition as follows:

> Historical materialism is that view of the course of history which seeks the ultimate cause and the great moving power of all historical events in the dialectic of sex: the division of society into two distinct biological classes for procreative reproduction, and the struggles of these classes with one another; in the changes in the modes of marriage, reproduction and child care created by these struggles; in the connected development of other physically-differentiated classes (castes); and in the first division of labor based on sex which developed into the (economic-cultural) class system.[89]

In other words, for Firestone, relations of reproduction rather than of production are the driving forces in history. The original class distinction is rooted in men's and women's differing reproductive roles; economic and racial class differences are derivatives of sex class differences.

In much the same way that Marx concluded workers' liberation requires an economic revolution, Firestone concluded women's liberation requires a biological revolution.[90] Like the proletariat who must seize the means of *production* to eliminate the economic class system, women must seize control of the means of *reproduction* to eliminate the sexual class system. Just as the ultimate goal of the communist revolution is, in a classless society, to obliterate class distinctions, the ultimate goal of the feminist revolution is, in an androgynous society, to obliterate sexual distinctions. As soon as technology overcomes the biological limits of natural reproduction, said Firestone, the biological fact that some persons have wombs and others have penises will "no longer matter culturally."[91] Sexual intercourse will no longer be necessary for human reproduction. Eggs and sperm will be combined in vitro, and embryos will be gestated outside of women's bodies.

No matter how much educational, legal, and political equality women achieve and no matter how many women enter public industry, Firestone insisted that nothing fundamental will change for women as long as natural reproduction remains the rule and artificial or assisted reproduction the exception. Natural reproduction is neither in women's best interests nor in those of the children so reproduced. The joy of giving birth—invoked so frequently in this society—is a patriarchal myth. In fact, pregnancy is "barbaric," and natural childbirth is "at best necessary and tolerable" and at worst "like shitting a pumpkin."[92] Moreover, said Firestone, natural reproduction is the root of further evils, especially the vice of possessiveness that generates feelings of hostility and jealousy among human beings. Engels's *Origin of the Family, Private Property, and the State* was incomplete not so much because he failed adequately to explain why men became the producers of surplus value, said Firestone, but because he failed adequately to explain *why* men wish so intensely to pass *their* property on to *their* biological children. The vice of possessiveness—the favoring of one child over another on account of the child's being the product of one's own ovum or sperm—is precisely what must be overcome if humans are to put an end to divisive hierarchies.

Piercy's *Woman on the Edge of Time*. Firestone's last point was developed by Marge Piercy in her science fiction novel *Woman on the Edge of Time*.[93] Piercy set the story of her utopia within the tale of Connie Ramos's tragic life. Connie is a late-twentieth-century, middle-aged, lower-class Chicana with a history of what society describes as "mental illness" and "violent behavior." Connie has been trying desperately to support herself and her daughter, Angelina, on a pittance. One day, when she is near the point of exhaustion, Connie loses her temper and hits Angelina too hard. As a result of this one outburst, the courts judge Connie an unfit mother and take her beloved daughter away from her. Depressed and despondent, angry and agitated, Connie is committed by her family to a mental hospital, where she is selected as a human research subject for brain-control experiments. Just when things can get no worse, Connie is psychically transported by a woman named Luciente to a future world called Mattapoisett—a world in which women are not defined in terms of reproductive functions and in which both men and women delight in rearing children. In Mattapoisett, there are neither men nor women; rather, everyone is a "per" (short for *person*).

What makes Piercy's future world imaginable is artificial reproduction. In Mattapoisett, babies are born from the "brooder." Female ova, fertilized in vitro with male sperm selected for a full range of racial, ethnic, and personality types, are gestated in an artificial placenta. Unable to comprehend why Mattapoisett women have rejected the experience that meant the most to her—physically gestating, birthing, and nursing an offspring—Connie is initially repelled by the brooder. She sees the embryos "all in a sluggish row . . . like fish in the aquarium."[94] Not only does she regard these embryos as less than human, she pities them because no woman loves them enough to carry them in her own womb and, bleeding and sweating, bring them into the world.

Eventually, Connie learns from Luciente that the women of Mattapoisett did not easily give up natural reproduction for artificial reproduction. They did so only when they realized natural reproduction was the ultimate cause of all isms, including sexism: "It was part of women's long revolution. When we were breaking all the old hierarchies. Finally there was the one thing we had to give up too, the only power we ever had, in return for no power for anyone. The original production: the power to give birth. Cause as long as we were biologically enchained, we'd never be equal. And males never would be humanized to be loving and tender. So we all became mothers. Every child has three. To break the nuclear bonding."[95] Thus, as a result of women's giving up their monopoly on the power to give birth, the original paradigm for power relations was destroyed, and all residents of Mattapoisett found themselves in a position to reconstitute human relationships in ways that defied the hierarchical ideas of better-worse, higher-lower, stronger-weaker, and especially dominant-submissive.

Piercy's utopia is more radical than a Marxist utopia because the family is eliminated as a biological as well as an economic unit. Individuals possess neither private property nor private children. No one has his or her own genetic child. Children are not the possessions of their biological mothers and fathers, to be brought into this world in their parents' image and likeness and reared according to their idiosyncratic values. Rather, children are precious human resources for the entire community, to be treasured on account of their uniqueness. Each child is reared by three co-mothers (one man and two women or two men and one woman), who are assisted by "kidbinders," a group of individuals who excel at mothering Mattapoisett's children. Child-rearing is a communal effort, with each child having access to large-group experiences at childcare centers and small-group experiences in the separate dwellings of each of his or her co-mothers.[96]

Connie initially doubts that Mattapoisett's system for begetting, bearing, and rearing children is all it is touted to be. She wonders whether co-mothers and kidbinders really love the children they rear. But gradually, she decides a biological relationship is not essential to good parenting. Indeed, she eventually agrees that artificial reproduction is superior to natural reproduction because it results in a truly nurturing and unselfish mode of mothering, totally separated from ambivalent feelings of resentment and guilt and always freely chosen.

Natural Reproduction: The Site of Women's Liberation

Marge Piercy Critiqued. As nicely as Piercy reformulated some of Firestone's more controversial ideas, radical-cultural feminists nonetheless challenged her views as well as Firestone's. Claiming that most women continue to view their life-giving abilities as empowering and enjoyable, radical-cultural feminists dismissed Mattapoisett as a social ideal that is both implausible and unintelligible to today's women. Women should not give up biological motherhood for ex utero gestation, not now, not ever.

Radical-cultural feminists insisted Mattapoisett is an implausible social ideal for today's women because women's oppression is not likely to end if women give up the only source of men's dependence on them: "Technological reproduction," said Azizah al-Hibri, "does not equalize the natural reproductive power structure—it *inverts* it. It appropriates the reproductive power from women and places it in the hands of men who now control both the sperm and the reproductive technology that could make it indispensable. . . . It 'liberates' them from their 'humiliating dependency' on women in order to propagate."[97] Far from liberating women, reproductive technology further consolidates men's power over women; it gives them the ability to have children without women's aid.

In addition to being an implausible social ideal for today's women, Mattapoisett is, in the estimation of radical-cultural feminists, also an unintelligible social ideal to today's women. Even though some women use other women's eggs and wombs to procreate and some women adopt other women's children, society continues to define a mother as someone who is genetically, gestationally, and socially related to the children she rears with or without a spouse or partner. Indeed, most women who go to infertility clinics do so because they want Connie's experience of carrying a child nine months "heavy under their hearts," bearing a baby "in blood" and nursing a child.[98] Thus, there is no way for women to decide in the abstract whether they should deprive themselves of a very meaningful present experience for a future experience they might or might not find equally meaningful.

Firestone et al. Critiqued.   Having dismissed Piercy's "utopia" as an implausible and unintelligible world for today's women, radical-cultural feminists proceeded to criticize Firestone's master plan to achieve women's liberation as a blueprint for women's further enslavement. They claimed women's oppression was caused not by female biology in and of itself, but rather by men's jealousy of women's reproductive abilities and subsequent desire to seize control of female biology through scientific and technological means.[99]

Viewing natural reproduction through the lens of male alienation from the gestational process and female immersion in it, radical-cultural feminist Mary O'Brien noted that until the introduction of artificial reproduction, the "reproductive consciousness" of a man differed from that of a woman in at least three ways. First, the woman experienced the process of procreation as one continuous movement taking place *within* her body, whereas the man experienced this same process as a discontinuous movement taking place *outside* his body. After the act of sexual intercourse, through which he impregnated the woman, the man had no other procreative function. Second, the woman, not the man, necessarily performed the fundamental *labor* of reproduction—pregnancy and birthing. At most the man could attend childbirth classes with the woman and try to imagine what being pregnant and giving birth feel like. Third, the woman's connection to her child was certain—she knew, at the moment of birth, the child was flesh of her flesh. In contrast, the man's connection to the child was uncertain; he could never be absolutely sure, even at the moment of birth, whether the child was in fact genetically related to him. For all he knew, the child was the genetic progeny of some other man.[100]

In radical-cultural feminists' estimation, men's alienation from natural reproduction helps explain why men have played a smaller role in the life of the "product" of natural reproduction than women have. It also helps explain why men have sought to limit women's reproductive powers. In *Of Woman Born,* Adrienne Rich noted men realize patriarchy cannot survive unless men are able to control women's power to *bring* or *not bring* life into the world. Rich described how men took the birthing process into their own hands. Male obstetricians replaced female midwives, substituting their "hands of iron" (obstetrical forceps) for midwives' hands of flesh (female hands sensitive to the female anatomy).[101] In addition, Rich cataloged the ways in which male physicians wrote the rules not only for giving birth but also for being pregnant. Male experts told women how to act during pregnancy—when to eat, sleep, exercise, have sex, and the like. In some instances, males even dictated to women how to feel during childbirth. The overall effect of men's intrusion into the birthing process was to confuse women, since men's "rules" for women's pregnancies often clashed with women's "intuitions" about what was best for their bodies, psyches, and babies. For example, when a woman and physician disagreed about whether she needed a cesarean section to deliver her baby, a woman did not know whether to trust the *authority* of her physician or the *experience,* the sensations, of her own body.

To the degree they were deprived of control over their pregnancies, said Rich, women experienced pregnancy as a mere event, as something that simply happened to them. Indeed, confessed Rich, she herself felt out of control and alienated during her pregnancy:

> When I try to return to the body of the young woman of twenty-six, pregnant for the first time, who fled from the physical knowledge of her pregnancy and at the same time from her intellect and vocation, I realize that I was effectively alienated from my real body and my real spirit by the institution—not the fact—of motherhood. This institution—the foundation of human society as we know it—allowed me only certain views, certain expectations, whether embodied in the booklet in my obstetrician's waiting room, the novels I had read, my mother-in-law's approval, my memories of my own mother, the Sistine Madonna or she of the Michelangelo Pietà, the floating notion that a woman pregnant is a woman calm in her fulfillment or, simply, a woman waiting.[102]

Rich concluded that if they reclaimed their pregnancies from the authorities, women would no longer have to sit passively waiting for their physicians to deliver their babies to them. Instead, women would actually direct the childbirth process, experiencing its pleasures as well as its pains. In Rich's estimation, childbirth does not have to feel like "shitting a pumpkin."[103]

On the contrary, it can feel a great deal more exhilarating and certainly far less dehumanizing.

Rich's concerns about the ways in which patriarchal authorities have used medical science to control women's reproductive powers reached new heights in the works of Andrea Dworkin, Margaret Atwood, Genea Corea, and Robyn Rowland. Dworkin claimed infertility experts have joined gynecologists and obstetricians to seize control of women's reproductive powers once and for all. She said artificial reproduction is patriarchy's attempt to guarantee that women's procreative experience is just as alienating as men's.[104] With the introduction of in vitro fertilization and the use of surrogate mothers, a woman's experience of bringing a child into the world becomes discontinuous, especially if her only contribution to this process is the donation of her egg. Moreover, the woman who relies on artificial reproduction to procreate can be no more certain than her male partner that the child born to them is indeed *their* genetic child. For all she knows, the embryo transplanted into her womb is not her and her mate's embryo but the embryo of some other couple. Finally, should scientists develop an artificial placenta, women's "labor" would no longer be needed to complete the procreative process. Speculating that patriarchal society might view a reproductively useless woman as somebody good only for sex work or domestic work, Dworkin urged women to resist the further development of reproductive technology.

Concerns such as Dworkin's are one of the inspirations for Margaret Atwood's *Handmaid's Tale*,[105] a work of feminist science fiction in stark contrast to Marge Piercy's *Woman on the Edge of Time*. In the Republic of Gilead, Atwood's antiutopia, women are reduced to one of four functions. There are the Marthas, or domestics; the Wives, or social secretaries and functionaries; the Jezebels, or sex prostitutes; and the Handmaids, or reproductive prostitutes. One of the most degrading Gileadean practices, from a woman's perspective, is a ritualistic form of sexual intercourse in which the so-called Commander pretends to have sex with his Wife. The Wife, who is infertile, lies down on a bed with her legs spread open. The Wife's Handmaid, one of the few fertile women in Gilead, puts her head between the spread legs of the Wife. Then the Commander engages in sexual intercourse with the Handmaid. If the Handmaid gets pregnant, the Commander and his Wife lay claim to the child she is gestating. Adding to the oddity of this arrangement is the fact that on the day the Handmaid gives birth to the child, the Wife simulates labor pains, as other Wives and Handmaids in Gilead gather round the Wife and her Handmaid in a rare moment of "female bonding."

After one such birth day, the central character, Offred—whose name literally means "to be of Fred"—recalls better times and speaks in her mind to her mother, who had been a feminist leader: "Can you hear me? You wanted a woman's culture. Well, now there is one. It isn't what you meant, but it exists. Be thankful for small mercies."[106] Of course, they are *very* small mercies, for with the exception of birth days—those rare occasions when a Handmaid manages to produce a child—women have little contact with each other. The Marthas, Wives, Jezebels, and Handmaids are segregated from one another, and the contact women do have—even within an assigned class—is largely silent, for women are permitted to speak to each other only when absolutely necessary.

Like Dworkin and Atwood, Genea Corea was suspicious of what the new reproductive technologies and their concomitant social arrangements promise women. Corea claimed if men control the new reproductive technologies, men will use them not to empower women but to further empower themselves. To reinforce her point, she drew provocative analogies between Count Dracula and Robert Edwards, one of the codevelopers of in vitro fertilization. Correa suggested that just as Dracula never had enough blood to drink, Edwards never had enough eggs to use in experiments. Indeed, Edwards routinely attended the hysterectomies his colleagues performed for the sole purpose of collecting the eggs they discarded after the surgeries.[107] Fearing that male infertility experts like Edwards do not have women's best interests at heart, Corea ended her essay "Egg Snatchers" with a series of questions for all women to ask themselves:

> Why are men focusing all this technology on woman's generative organs—the source of her procreative power? Why are they collecting our eggs? Why do they seek to freeze them?
>
> Why do men want to control the production of human beings? Why do they talk so often about producing "perfect" babies?
>
> Why are they splitting the functions of motherhood into smaller parts? Does that reduce the power of the mother and her claim to the child? ("I only gave the egg. I am not the real mother." "I only loaned my uterus. I am not the real mother." "I only raised the child. I am not the real mother.")[108]

Agreeing with Dworkin, Atwood, and Corea that the new reproductive technologies will simply increase men's control over women, Robyn Rowland, another radical-cultural feminist, pointed to the work of microbiologist John Postgate as an example of the form this new power over women might take. In an interview with Rowland, Postgate, who wanted to control the size of the human population, proposed the development of a "manchild pill," which would ensure the conception of boys. Girls would become scarce and the birthrate would inevitably plunge. Postgate conceded that under such circumstances men would probably start to fight each other for the sexual and reproductive services of society's few remaining women. Women would need to be sequestered for their own good while society developed rules for a system of male access to them.[109]

As if a vision of a future world in which the term "trophy wife" denotes an even uglier reality than it does now is not bad enough, Rowland imagined an even worse scenario: a world in which only a few superovulating women are permitted to exist, a world in which eggs are taken from women, frozen, and inseminated in vitro for transfer into artificial placentas. The replacement of women's childbearing capacity by male-controlled technology would, she said, leave women entirely vulnerable, "without a product" with which "to bargain" with men: "For the history of 'mankind' women have been seen in terms of their value as childbearers. We have to ask, if that last power is taken and controlled by men, what role is envisaged for women in the new world?"[110]

Unlike radical-libertarian feminists, radical-cultural feminists urged women not to forsake their power to bring new life into the world. Only oppressive forms of power need to be forsaken, and according to radical-cultural feminists, women's reproductive powers are anything but oppressive. On the contrary, women's life-giving capacities are the paradigm for the ability of people to connect with one another in a caring, supportive relationship.

Libertarian and Cultural Views on Mothering

Although commentators do not always make adequate distinctions between biological and social motherhood, these two dimensions of mothering need to be distinguished. If we accept Alison Jaggar's extension of the term *mothering* to "any relationship in which one individual nurtures and cares for another,"[111] then a person does not need to be a biological mother to be a social mother. Nevertheless, patriarchal society teaches its members that the woman who bears a child is best suited to rear him or her. In viewing this tenet as one that often places unreasonable demands on women's bodies and energies, radical-libertarian feminists have tended to make strong arguments against biological motherhood. Not surprisingly, many radical-cultural feminists have challenged these arguments, insisting no woman should, in an act of unreflective defiance against patriarchy, deprive herself of the satisfaction that comes from not only bearing a child but also playing a major role in his or her personal development. As we shall see, the arguments on both sides of this debate are powerful.

The Case Against Biological Motherhood

There are at least two versions of the radical-libertarian feminist case against biological motherhood: a weaker, more general version offered by Ann Oakley, and a stronger, more specific version offered by Shulamith Firestone. As Oakley saw it, biological motherhood is a myth based on the threefold belief that "all women need to be mothers, all mothers need their children, all children need their mothers."[112]

The first assertion, that all women need to be mothers, gains its credibility, according to Oakley, from the ways in which girls are socialized and from popular psychoanalytic theory that provides "pseudo-scientific backing" for this process of socialization. If parents did not give their daughters dolls; if the schools, the churches, and the media did not stress the wonders of biological motherhood; if psychiatrists, psychologists, and physicians did not do everything in their power to transform "abnormal" girls (i.e., "masculine" girls, who do not want to be mothers) into "normal" girls (i.e., "feminine" girls, who do want to be mothers), then girls would not grow into women who *need* to mother in order to have a sense of self-worth. For Oakley, women's supposed need to mother "owes nothing" to women's "possession of ovaries and wombs" and everything to the way in which women are socially and culturally conditioned to be mothers.[113]

The second assertion, that mothers need their children, is based on the belief that unless a woman's "maternal instinct" is satisfied, she will become increasingly frustrated. In Oakley's view, there is no such thing as maternal instinct. Women do not naturally experience a desire to have a biological child, and there are no hormonally based drives that "irresistibly draw the mother to her child in the tropistic fashion of the moth drawn to the flame"[114] during and after pregnancy. To support her contention that the "instinct" for mothering is learned, Oakley pointed to a study in which 150 first-time mothers were observed. Few of these women knew how to breast-feed, and those who did had seen either their own mother or some other female relative nursing a baby. Additionally, Oakley noted that most women who abuse or neglect their children were themselves abused or neglected as children. Never having seen a woman mothering properly, these women never learned the behavior repertoire society associates with adequate mothering. Mothers, in short, are not born; they are made.[115]

The third assertion, that children need their mothers, is, according to Oakley, the most oppressive feature of the myth of biological motherhood. Oakley noted that this assertion contains three assumptions unnecessarily tying women to children: first, that children's mothering needs are best met by their biological mothers; second, that children, especially young children, need the care of their biological mothers much more than the care of anyone else, including their biological fathers; and third, that children need *one* nurturant caretaker (preferably the biological mother), not many.[116]

As Oakley saw it, each of these three assumptions (in support of the assertion children need their mothers) is false. First, social mothers are just as effective as biological mothers. Studies have shown, claimed Oakley, that adopted children are at least as well adjusted as nonadopted children.[117] Second, children do not need their biological mothers more than children need their biological fathers. Men no less than women can play the major role in their children's upbringing. What children need are adults with whom to establish intimate relationships—trustworthy and dependable persons who provide children with consistent care and discipline. Finally, one-on-one child-rearing is not necessarily better than collective socialization or "multiple mothering." Children reared in Israeli kibbutzim, for example, are just as happy, intelligent, emotionally mature, and socially adept as children reared exclusively by their biological mothers in U.S. suburbs.[118]

In Oakley's estimation, being a biological mother is not a natural need of women any more than being reared by one's biological mother is a natural need of children. Therefore, she concluded biological motherhood is a social construction, a myth with an oppressive purpose. Not wanting to be accused of selfishness and even abnormality, women who would be happier not having children at all become mothers reluctantly; and women who would be happier sharing their child-rearing responsibilities with one or more nurturant adults make of mothering an exclusive and twenty-four-hour-a-day job. No wonder, said Oakley, so many mothers are unhappy—an unhappiness made all the worse because society looks with disfavor on any mother who expresses dissatisfaction with her all-consuming maternal role.

Although Shulamith Firestone's negative assessment of biological motherhood did not substantively differ from Oakley's, it was harsher in tone. In *The Dialectic of Sex,* Firestone suggested the desire to bear and rear children is less the result of an "authentic liking" for children and more a "displacement" of ego-extension needs. For a man, a child is a way to immortalize his name, property, class, and ethnic identification; for a woman, a child is a way to justify her homebound existence as absolutely meaningful. At times, a father's need for immortality or a mother's need for meaning becomes pathological. When this happens, said Firestone, the less-than-perfect child inevitably suffers.[119]

Firestone believed that if adults, especially women, did not feel they had a duty to have children, they might discover in themselves an *authentic* desire to live in close association with children. People do not need to be biological parents to lead child-centered lives, said Firestone. Ten or more adults could agree, for example, to live with three or four children for as long as the children needed a stable family structure. During their years together, the people in this household would relate not as parents and children but as older and younger friends. Firestone did not think adults have a natural desire to be any closer to children than this kind of household arrangement permits. Instead, she believed adults have been socialized to view biological reproduction as life's raison d'être because without this grandiose sense of mission and destiny, the pains of childbearing and the burdens of child-rearing would have proved overwhelming. Now that technology promises to liberate the human species from the burdens of reproductive responsibility, Firestone predicted women will no longer want to bear children in pain and travail or rear children endlessly and self-sacrificially. Rather, women and men will want to spend some, though by no means most, of their time and energy with and on children.[120]

The Case for Biological Motherhood

Although Adrienne Rich agreed with some of Firestone's analysis, she criticized Firestone for condemning biological motherhood "without taking full account of what the experience of biological pregnancy and birth might be in a wholly different political and emotional context."[121] Throughout *Of Woman Born,* Rich sharply distinguished between biological motherhood understood as "the *potential relationship* of any woman to her powers of reproduction and to children" and biological motherhood understood as "the *institution,* which aims at ensuring that that potential—and all women—shall remain under male control."[122] As Rich saw it, there is a world of difference between *women's* deciding who, how, when, and where to mother and *men's* making these decisions for women.

Rich agreed with Firestone that biological motherhood, as it has been institutionalized under patriarchy, is definitely something from which women should be liberated. If success is measured in terms of patriarchy's ability to determine not only women's gender behavior but also their gender identity through "force, direct pressure . . . ritual, tradition, law and language, customs, etiquette, education, and the division of labor," then *institutionalized* biological motherhood is one of patriarchy's overwhelming successes.[123] Men have convinced women that unless a woman is a mother, she is not really a woman, said Rich. Indeed, until relatively recently, the forces of patriarchy convinced most women that mothering is their one and only job. This view of women's role is very restricting. It blocks women's access to the public realm of culture, and it fails to acknowledge women's right to have and to fulfill their own wants and needs. Good mothers are not supposed to have any personal friends or plans unrelated to those of their families. They are supposed to be on the job twenty-four hours a day and love every minute of it. Ironically, observed Rich, it is just this expectation that causes many women to act in anything but "motherly" ways. The constant needs of a child can tax a mother's patience and, with no relief from the child's father or any other adult, make her feel angry, frustrated, and bitter: "I remember being uprooted from already meager sleep to answer a childish nightmare, pull up a blanket, warm a consoling bottle, lead a half-asleep child to the toilet. I remember going back to bed starkly awake, brittle with anger, knowing that my broken sleep would make the next day hell, that there would be more nightmares; more need for consolation, because out of my weariness I would rage at those children for no reason."[124] Rich's point was not that mothers do not love their children but that no person can be expected to remain always cheerful and kind unless the person's own physical and psychological needs are satisfactorily met.

Rich also argued eloquently that the *institution* of biological motherhood prevents women from rearing their children as women think they should be reared. She recounted squabbles with her own husband about the best way to raise their two sons. She also recalled mothering his way even though she knew full well that father did not always know best. Under patriarchy, she wrote, most men have demanded sons for the wrong reasons: "as heirs, field-hands, cannon-fodder, feeders of machinery, images and extensions of themselves; their immortality."[125] What is worse, most husbands have demanded their wives help them raise their sons to be "real men"—that is, "macho" or hyperaggressive and supercompetitive men. Rich happily recalled a seashore vacation she spent with her two boys, but without her husband. While vacationing alone, she and her children lived spontaneously for several weeks, ignoring most of the established rules of patriarchy. They ate the wrong food at the wrong time. They stayed up past the proper bedtime. They wore the wrong clothes. They giggled at silly jokes. Through all of these "trespasses" against the rules of the father, they were enormously happy. Indeed, suggested Rich, were fathers told they do *not* know best, then mothers would find child-rearing energizing rather than enervating, joyful rather than miserable.

As Rich saw it, if women took control of child-rearing as well as child-bearing, more mothers would experience biological motherhood on their own terms. Rich insisted no woman should renounce, in the name of "liberation," what female biology has to offer:

> I have come to believe . . . that female biology—the diffuse, intense sensuality radiating out from clitoris, breasts, uterus, vagina; the lunar cycles of menstruation; the gestation and fruition of life which can take place in the female body—has far more radical implications than we have yet come to appreciate. Patriarchal thought has limited female biology to its own narrow specifications. The feminist vision has recoiled from female biology for these reasons; it will, I believe, come to view our physicality as a resource, rather than a destiny. In order to live a fully human life we require not only control of our bodies (though control is a prerequisite); we must touch the unity and resonance of our physicality, our bond with the natural order, the corporeal ground of our intelligence.[126]

According to Rich, Firestone was wrong to argue that female biology is necessarily limiting and that the only way to liberate women from this limitation is through reproductive technology. In a patriarchal society, the solution to the pains of childbearing is not reproductive technology but rather for a woman to ride with, not against, her body. A woman must not give up on her body before she has had a chance to use it as she thinks best. Likewise, the solution to the impositions of child-rearing in a patriarchal society is not the renunciation of children; the solution is for every woman to rear children with feminist values.

Genetics, Gestational, and Rearing Connections

The attention of radical-cultural feminists and radical-libertarian feminists has recently centered on surrogate, or contracted, motherhood—an arrangement in which a third party is hired and usually paid to bear a child who will be reared by someone else.[127] The birth mother (the woman whose gestational services have been contracted) is either the full biological mother of the child (both the genetic and the gestational mother) or the gestational but not the genetic mother of the child.

In general, radical-cultural feminists oppose contracted motherhood on the grounds it creates destructive divisions among women. One such division is between economically privileged women and economically disadvantaged women. The privileged can hire the disadvantaged to meet the former's reproductive needs, adding gestational services to the child-rearing services poor women traditionally have provided to rich women. The second division is one Genea Corea envisioned, namely, among child-begetters, child-bearers, and child-rearers. According to Corea, reproduction is currently being segmented and specialized as if it were simply a mode of production. In the future, no one woman will beget, bear, and rear a child. Rather, genetically superior women will beget embryos in vitro; strong-bodied women will bear these test-tube babies to term; and sweet-tempered women will rear these newborns from infancy to adulthood.[128] As a result of this division of labor, a dystopia similar to the one Atwood described in *The Handmaid's Tale* could actually come into existence, complete with divisive female-female relationships. No woman was whole in Gilead; all individual women were reduced to parts or aspects of the monolith, Woman.

In addition to lamenting the ways in which contracted motherhood might harm women's relationships to each other and to their children, radical-cultural feminists bemoan its rooting of parental rights either in persons' *genetic* contribution to the procreative process or in persons' professed *intention* to rear children. Basing parental rights exclusively on genetic contribution means if a surrogate mother is genetically unrelated to the child in her womb, she has no parental rights to it after it is born. Only if she is the genetic as well as the gestational mother of the child does she have grounds for claiming parental rights to it—rights that have to be balanced against those of the child's genetic father. In contrast, basing parental rights exclusively on one or more persons' professed intention to rear the child implies that because the surrogate mother has expressed no such intentions, she has no grounds for claiming parental rights to the child even if she is genetically related to the child.

According to radical-cultural feminists, men have reason to base all parental rights on either genes or intentions. After all, until the time a man takes an active part in the rearing of his child, the only kind of relationship he can have with his child is a genetic or an intentional one. Unlike his wife or other female partner, he cannot experience the kind of relationship a pregnant woman can experience with her child. For this reason, observe radical-cultural feminists, patriarchal society unfairly dismisses the gestational relationship as unimportant, as a mere biological event with no special parental meaning. But the truth of the matter, continue radical-cultural feminists, is that the gestational connection is of extraordinary importance. It is the child's gestator who proves through her concrete actions, some of which may cause her inconvenience and even pain, that she is *actually* committed to the child's well-being. As radical-cultural feminists see it, when parental claims are in question, the kind of *lived commitment* a gestational parent has to a child should count at least as much as the kind of *contemplated commitment* a genetic or an intentional parent has to a child.

Radical-libertarian feminists disagree with radical-cultural feminists' assessment of contracted motherhood, arguing that contracted motherhood arrangements, if handled properly, can bring women closer together rather than drive them farther apart. These feminists note some contracted mothers and commissioning couples live near each other so they can *all* share in the rearing of the child whom they have collaboratively reproduced.[129] Thus, contracted motherhood need not be viewed as the male-directed and male-manipulated specialization and segmentation of the female reproductive process but as women getting together (as in the case of the postmenopausal South African mother who carried her daughter's in vitro fetus to term) to achieve, in unison, something they could not achieve without each other's help.[130] As long as women control collaborative-reproduction arrangements, contracted motherhood increases rather than decreases women's reproductive freedom, in radical-libertarian feminists' estimation.

Believing it does women a disservice to overstate the importance of the gestational connection, radical-libertarian feminists object to the radical-cultural feminist position on contracted motherhood for two reasons. First, if women want men to spend as much time caring for children as women now do, then women should not repeatedly remind men of women's *special* connection to infants. Doing so implies that women are more suited to parenting tasks than men are. Second, if women want to protect their bodily integrity from the forces of state coercion, then women should not stress the symbiotic nature of the maternal-fetal connection. Increasingly aware of pregnant women's power to affect the well-being of their fetuses during the gestational process, society is more and more eager to control the pregnancies of "bad gestators." If a pregnant woman harms her fetus by drinking large quantities of alcohol or using illicit drugs, concerned citizens will urge that she be treated, voluntarily or involuntarily, for her addictions. Should treatment fail, many of these same citizens will become more aggressive in their demands; they will recommend that the state punish the "bad gestator" for negligently, recklessly, or intentionally engaging in life-style behavior resulting in serious, largely irreparable damage to her future child. Society will brand such a woman as a "fetal abuser" or "fetal neglecter." For this reason, if no other, radical-libertarian feminists believe the less that women emphasize how "special" the mother-fetus relationship is, the better served will women's interests be.

Critiques of Radical-Libertarian and Radical-Cultural Feminism

In many ways, radical-libertarian and radical-cultural feminists are each other's best critics, but they are certainly not each other's only critics. Nonradical feminists have directed much in the way of criticism against both the "libertarian" and the "cultural" wings of radical feminist thought. These critics have faulted radical-libertarian feminism for the same reason they have faulted liberal feminism—namely, for its insistence on making everything a "choice" when in fact women's ability to choose is enormously constrained in a patriarchal context. In contrast, these same critics have faulted radical-cultural feminism for propounding so-called essentialism, the view that men and women are fundamentally and perhaps irrevocably different because of their natures.

In an effort to avoid redundancy, I direct readers to the critiques of liberal feminism at the end of Chapter 1. That discussion about women's limited ability to choose applies almost as well to radical-libertarian feminist thought as to liberal feminist thought. I do, however, want to add here Jean Bethke Elshtain's critique of radical-cultural feminism. Her views on essentialism merit considerable thought. In addition, I want to describe how both radical-libertarian and radical-cultural feminists sometimes unnecessarily polarize issues related to sex, reproduction, and biological motherhood.

Woman's "Goodness"?

Jean Bethke Elshtain claimed radical-cultural feminists are wrong to suggest males and females are, on either the biological or the ontological level, two kinds of creatures: the men corrupt and the women innocent. Such a biology or ontology denies the unique and fascinating history of individual men and women. It implies that what is most important about individuals is not their specific lives but some sort of abstract a priori essence they share.

Falling into the trap of essentialism—the conviction that men are men and women are women and that there is no way to change either's nature—is both an analytic dead end and a political danger, in Elshtain's estimation. Essentialist claims about what makes certain groups of people the way they are (e.g., women, blacks, Jews) are the political-philosophical constructs of conservatism. The history of essentialist arguments is one of oppressors telling the oppressed to accept their lot in life because "that's just the way it is." Essentialist arguments were used to justify slavery, to resist the Nineteenth Amendment (which gave women the vote), and to sustain colonialism. By presenting women as a priori nurturing and life-giving and men as a priori corrupt and obsessed with death, said Elshtain, radical-cultural feminists fall into the trap of doing unto others that which they do not want done unto themselves and other oppressed groups.[131]

Elshtain urged radical-cultural feminists to overthrow the categories that entrap women (and men) in rigid roles. Roles, she said, are simplistic definitions that make every man an exploiter and oppressor and every woman a victim. The fact is, not every woman is a victim and not every man is an exploiter and oppressor. Elshtain cited Mary Beard's *Women As a Force in History* (a liberal feminist text charting women's role in shaping preindustrial culture)[132] and Sheila Rowbotham's *Women, Resistance and Revolution* (a Marxist feminist text detailing women's involvement in twentieth-century revolutions)[133] to support her view that women have played strong and active roles in social history. She also pointed to examples of men who have supported women in their liberation struggles.[134] According to Elshtain, essentialism in any form has no place in the complex world we live in.

Also at issue in Elshtain's critique is the radical-cultural feminist understanding of patriarchy. Elshtain faulted Mary Daly for implying that no matter when and where it appears, patriarchy, be it in the form of Hindu suttee, Chinese foot binding, African female circumcision, or Western gynecology, is about men's *hating* women. To claim all these various practices boil down to the same thing, said Elshtain, is to show little or no awareness of the rich diversity of different societies.[135] As a Western feminist searching for signs of patriarchy in Asia and Africa, Daly was sometimes unaware of her own cultural baggage. As an outsider, she was not always privy to the contextual meaning certain rituals and customs have for their female participants. Female circumcision is a case in point. For Daly, this practice is about men's depriving women of a wide range of sexual experiences; for the women circumcised, it may mean something different—for example, a rite of passage into a much-coveted womanhood or a means of rebelling against civilized, Christian, colonial powers. To Daly's objection that these women are not ready, willing, or able to see the harm men are doing to them, Elshtain responded it might be Daly's vision rather than these women's that is clouded. Indeed, Daly's failure to acknowledge the possibility that certain African and Asian rituals have *positive,* non-Western meanings suggests a certain ethnocentrism on her part.[136]

Admitting that Daly and other radical-cultural feminists may have wanted to stress the metaphorical rather than the historical meaning of patriarchy, Elshtain conceded that, as a metaphorical term, *patriarchy* carries a certain emotional force and lends direction to women searching for a point of attack. Nevertheless, Elshtain claimed the concept of patriarchy is troubling, even in its strictly metaphorical capacity. To be sure, she said, the term *patriarchy* is a useful analytical tool for women who are just beginning to rethink their political and personal experiences of oppression. But beyond this, patriarchy becomes a blunt instrument. If chanted incessantly, the formula "men *over* women; women *for* men" becomes monotonous and even meaningless. In Elshtain's estimation, the tendency of radical-cultural feminists to view all patriarchies as equally evil (women-hating, misogynistic) contributes to the "broken record effect" characterizing some feminist texts.[137]

Elshtain speculated that the absolute condemnation of patriarchy by radical feminists might be rooted in their fear that women may have certain things—even ugly things—in common with the men. Unable to accept their own "masculine" qualities, radical-cultural feminists project these rejected qualities onto men in order to shield themselves from the more troubling parts of their own personalities. This defensiveness, said Elshtain, then leads radical-cultural feminists toward a utopian vision of an all-women community. Man encompasses evil; woman encompasses good. Because the essence of womanhood is supposedly about the positive force of "power-to" rather than the negative force of "power-over," a world of women will be warm, supportive, nurturing, and full of creativity. It will be a return to the womb. Only men are holding women back.

Elshtain believed if her critique was on target, radical-cultural feminists were in for a grave disappointment. Given that women as well as men are human beings, vice as well as virtue will inevitably appear in an all-women community. Elshtain asked radical-cultural feminists to reconsider the concept of "pure voice"—the idea that the victim, in her status as victim, speaks in a pure voice—"I suffer, therefore I have moral purity."[138] This belief about women's moral purity is exactly what Victorian men used to keep women on pedestals, away from the world of politics and economics; Elshtain was distressed that twentieth-century radical-cultural feminists had not expanded beyond this nineteenth-century male notion.

Beyond Polarization?

In the estimation of socialist feminists such as Ann Ferguson, radical-libertarian and radical-cultural feminists need to heal the split between themselves to avoid unnecessary polarization. As emphasized above, Ferguson stressed that despite their reservations about male-female sexual relationships, radical-libertarian feminists still believed consensual (noncompulsory) heterosexuality could be just as pleasurable for women as for men. In addition to celebrating consensual heterosexuality, radical-libertarian feminists affirmed the "liberated sexuality" of lesbians—a form of sexual expression in which equal partners aim to mutually satisfy each other's sexual needs.

Contrasting radical-libertarian feminists with radical-cultural feminists, Ferguson noted that the latter group not only stressed the dangers of heterosexuality but also implied there is no such thing as consensual heterosexuality—that is, mutually desired sex between men and women who treat each other as equals. Only lesbians are capable of consensual sex in a patriarchal society. Whenever a man and a woman have sex in a patriarchal society, the man will, more or less, use sex as an instrument to control the woman. He will have his way with her, even if it means raping her, beating her, or reducing her to a sex object. In contrast, whenever two women have sex, to the extent their psyches have escaped the norms of patriarchal society, they will experience the "erotic" as that which resides not only in women's physical desire for each other but also in their emotional bonding and connections to each other. Supposedly, female sexuality is essentially about emotional intimacy, whereas male sexuality is essentially about physical pleasure; it is the kind of love that women would have had for each other had not the institution of "compulsory heterosexuality" forced them to redirect their original love for their mothers to men.[139]

According to Ferguson, both the radical-libertarian and the radical-cultural feminist perspectives on sexuality fail on account of their *ahistoricity*. There is, she said, no one universal "function" for human sexuality, whether it is conceived as emotional intimacy or as physical pleasure.[140] Rather, "sexuality is a bodily energy whose objects, meaning and social values are historically constructed."[141] Thus, radical-cultural feminists are wrong to posit an *essential* female sexuality that for all practical purposes amounts to a certain form of lesbian sexuality.

Ferguson used her own sexuality as a case study in the historical construction of human sexuality in general. She observed that her lesbianism is no more based on the fact that her "original," or first, sexual object was her mother than on the fact that her second sexual object was her father. Rather, what explains her current way of loving is "first, the historical and social contexts in my teenage years which allowed me to develop a first physical love relationship with a woman; and, second, the existence of a strong self-identified lesbian-feminist oppositional culture today which allowed me to turn toward women again from an adult life hitherto exclusively heterosexual."[142] Ferguson speculated that had she grown up in a more restricted sexual environment or in a less feminist era, she probably would not have *wanted* to have lesbian lovers. After all, she said, "One's sexual objects are defined by the social contexts in which one's *ongoing* gender identity is constructed in relation to one's peers."[143]

Like radical-cultural feminists, radical-libertarian feminists are guilty of ahis-toricism, in Ferguson's estimation, but in a different way. Radical-libertarian feminists seem to think that a woman is always able to give free or true consent. Thus, radical-libertarian feminist Gayle Rubin claimed if a woman experiences herself *as* consenting to heterosexual or lesbian sadomasochism or bondage and domination, then she *is* consenting to these practices. No one has a right to crit-icize her as a "victim of false consciousness," a person who fails to realize that were she truly a man's equal, she would have nothing to do with any form of sexuality that eroticizes dominance-and-subordination relationships. But in Fer-guson's estimation, depending on this woman's "social context," the woman may in fact be a "victim of false consciousness." The "freedom" of an economi-cally dependent housewife to consent to S/M sex with her husband must be challenged; so, too, must the "freedom" of a teenage prostitute to consent to sex with a man far older and richer than she.[144]

Issues of real versus apparent consent arise just as frequently in the repro-ductive arena as they do in the sexual realm. Radical-libertarian feminists like Firestone and Rubin would probably accept as a *real* choice a woman's deci-sion to sell her gestational services. No doubt they would view such a decision as helping to erode the institution of biological motherhood, which maintains that she who bears a child should rear the child not only because she is best suited for this task but also because she wants to do so. Because a surrogate mother is prepared to walk away from the child she has gestated for the "right price," she debunks the "myth" of biological motherhood. But in Ferguson's estimation, it is debatable whether all surrogate mothers choose money over the product of their gestational labor. Depending on a woman's social circum-stances, her consent to surrender the child she has gestated to the couple who contracted for it may not be truly free. Since most surrogate mothers are less advantaged than their clients, the surrogates might easily be driven to sell one of the few things they have that patriarchal society values: their reproductive services. To say women choose to do this might simply be to say that when women are forced to choose between being poor and being exploited, they may choose being exploited as the lesser of two evils.

Assuming socialist feminists like Ferguson are correct to stress that women's sexual and reproductive desires, needs, behaviors, and identities are largely the product of the time and place that women occupy in history, these feminists are also right to argue that (1) neither heterosexuality nor lesbianism is either inherently pleasurable or inherently dangerous for women; and (2) neither natural reproduction nor artificial reproduction is either inherently empowering or inherently disempowering for women. Socialist feminists urge *all* radical feminists to ask themselves what kind of sexual and reproductive practices people would adopt in a society in which all economic, political, and kinship systems were structured to create equality between men and women and as far as possible between adults and children. In an egalitarian world, would men and women engage in "male breadwinner/female housewife sex prostitution," or would they instead develop forms of egalitarian heterosexuality seldom imagined let alone practiced in our very unequal, patriarchal world? Would some lesbians continue to engage in S/M and butch-femme relationships, or would all lesbians find themselves turned off by such practices? Would there be "man-boy" love or "parent-child" love (incest)? Would women use more or less in the way of contraceptives? Would couples contract for gestational mothers' services, or would they instead prefer to adopt children? Would there be more or fewer children? Would most people choose to reproduce "artificially," or would they instead choose to reproduce the "old-fashioned," natural way?

What is common to the kind of questions just posed, said Ferguson, is that the answers they yield will be lived in the future world that feminists *imagine* and not, for the most part, in the present world feminists *experience*. For now, feminists should seek to develop an approach to sexuality and reproduction that permits women to understand both the pleasures and the dangers of sex, and the liberating and enslaving aspects of reproduction. The dead-end approaches of the past have turned out to be part of the problem of human oppression rather than a remedy for it. The sooner these either-or approaches to sexuality and reproduction are replaced with both-and approaches, the sooner will men and women stop "playing" the destructive game of male domination and female subordination.

Marxist and Socialist Feminism:
Classical and Contemporary

Although it is possible to distinguish between Marxist and socialist feminist thought, it is quite difficult to do so. Over the years, I have become
convinced that the differences between these two schools of thought are
more a matter of emphasis than of substance. Classical Marxist feminists
work within the conceptual terrain laid out by Marx, Engels, Lenin, and
other nineteenth-century thinkers. They regard classism rather than sexism as the fundamental cause of women's oppression. In contrast, socialist
feminists are not certain that classism is women's worst or only enemy.
They write in view of Russia's twentieth-century failure to achieve socialism's ultimate goal—namely, the replacement of class oppression and antagonism with "an association, in which the free development of each is
the condition for the free development of all."[1] Post-1917 Communism
in the Soviet Union and later in the so-called Eastern Bloc was not true
socialism but simply a new form of human exploitation and oppression.
Women's lives under Communism, particularly during the Stalin years
(1929–1953), were not manifestly better than women's lives under capitalism. Women's move into the productive workplace had not made them
men's equals either there or at home. For these reasons and related ones,
socialist feminists decided to move beyond relying on class as the sole category for understanding women's subordination to men. Increasingly,
they tried "to understand women's subordination in a coherent and systematic way that integrates class and sex, as well as other aspects of identity such as race/ethnicity or sexual orientation."[2]

Some Marxist Concepts and Theories

To appreciate the differences between classical Marxist and contemporary socialist feminism, we need to understand the Marxist concept of human nature. As noted in Chapter 1, liberals believe that several characteristics distinguish human beings from other animals. These characteristics include a set of abilities, such as the capacity for rationality and the use of language; a set of practices, such as religion, art, and science; and a set of attitude and behavior patterns, such as competitiveness and the tendency to put oneself over others. Marxists reject the liberal conception of human nature, claiming instead that what makes us different from other animals is our ability to produce our means of subsistence. We are what we are because of what we do—specifically, what we do to meet our basic needs through productive activities such as fishing, farming, and building. Unlike bees, beavers, and ants, whose activities are governed by instinct and who cannot willfully change themselves, we create ourselves in the process of intentionally transforming and manipulating nature.[3]

For the liberal, the ideas, thoughts, and values of individuals account for change over time. For the Marxist, material forces—the production and reproduction of social life—are the prime movers in history. In laying out a full explanation of how change takes place over time, an explanation usually termed *historical materialism,* Marx stated, "The mode of production of material life conditions the general process of social, political, and intellectual life. It is not the consciousness of men that determines their existence, but their social existence that determines their consciousness."[4] In other words, Marx believed a society's total mode of production—that is, its forces of production (the raw materials, tools, and workers that actually produce goods) plus its relations of production (the ways in which production is organized)—generates a superstructure (a layer of legal, political, and social ideas) that in turn reinforces the mode of production. Adding to Marx's point, Richard Schmitt later emphasized that the statement "Human beings create themselves" is not to be read as "Men and women, as *individuals,* make themselves what they are," but instead as "Men and women, through production *collectively,* create a society that, in turn, shapes them."[5] So, for example, people in the United States think in certain ways about liberty, equality, and freedom *because* their mode of production is capitalist.

Like Marxists in general, Marxist and socialist feminists claim that social existence determines consciousness. For them, the observation that "women's work is never done" is more than an aphorism; it is a description of the nature of woman's work. Always on call, women form a conception of themselves they would not have if their roles in the family and the workplace did not keep them socially and economically subordinate to men. Thus, Marxist and socialist feminists believe we need to analyze the links between women's work status and women's self-image in order to understand the unique character of *women's* oppression.[6]

The Marxist Theory of Economics

To the degree Marxist and socialist feminists believe women's work shapes women's thoughts and thus "female nature," these thinkers also believe capitalism is a system of power relations as well as exchange relations. When capitalism is viewed as a system of exchange relations, it is described as a commodity or market society in which everything, including one's own labor power, has a price and all transactions are fundamentally exchange transactions. But when capitalism is viewed instead as a system of power relations, it is described as a society in which every kind of transactional relation is fundamentally exploitative. Thus, depending on one's emphasis, the worker-employer relationship can be looked at as either an exchange relationship in which items of equivalent value are freely traded—labor for wages—or as a workplace struggle in which the employer, who has superior power, takes advantage of workers in any number of ways.

Whereas liberals view capitalism as a system of voluntary exchange relations, Marxists and socialists view capitalism as a system of exploitative power relations. According to Marx, the value of any commodity is determined by the amount of labor, or actual expenditure of human energy and intelligence, necessary to produce it.[7] To be more precise, the value of any commodity is equal to the *direct* labor incorporated in the commodity by workers, plus the *indirect* labor stored in workers' artificial appendages—the tools and machines made by the direct labor of their predecessors.[8] Because all commodities are worth exactly the labor necessary to produce them and because workers' labor power (capacity for work) is a commodity that can be bought and sold, the value of workers' labor power is exactly the cost of whatever it takes (food, clothing, shelter) to maintain them throughout the workday. But there is a difference between what employers pay workers for their mere *capacity* to work (labor power) and the value that workers actually create when they put their work capacity to use in producing commodities.[9] Marx termed this difference "surplus value," and from it employers derive their profits. Thus, capitalism is an exploitative system because employers pay workers only for their labor power, without also paying workers for the human energy they expend and the intelligence they transfer into the commodities they produce.[10]

At this point in an analysis of Marxist economic thought, it seems reasonable to ask how employers get workers to labor for more hours than are necessary to produce the value of their subsistence, especially when workers receive no compensation for this extra work. The answer to this query is, as Marx explained in *Capital,* a simple one: Employers have a monopoly on the means of production, including factories, tools, land, means of transportation, and means of communication. Workers are forced to choose between being exploited and having no work at all. It is a liberal fiction that workers freely sign mutually beneficial contractual agreements with their employers. Capitalism is just as much a system of power relations as it is one of exchange relations. Workers are free to contract with employers only in the sense that employers do not hold a gun to their heads when they sign on the dotted line.

Interestingly, there is another, less discussed reason why employers are able to exploit workers under capitalism. According to Marx, capitalist ideologies lead workers and employers to focus on capitalism's surface structure of exchange relations.[11] As a result of this ideological ploy, which Marx called the *fetishism of commodities,* workers gradually convince themselves that even though their money is very hard earned, there is nothing inherently wrong with the specific exchange relationships into which they have entered, because life, in all its dimensions, is simply one colossal system of exchange relations.

That liberal ideologies, typically spawned in capitalist economics, present practices such as prostitution and surrogate motherhood as contractual exercises of free choice, then, is no accident, according to Marxist and socialist feminists. The liberal ideologies claim that women become prostitutes and surrogate mothers because they *prefer* these jobs over other available jobs. But, as Marxist and socialist feminists see it, when a poor, illiterate, unskilled woman chooses to sell her sexual or reproductive services, chances are her choice is more coerced than free. After all, if one has little else of value to sell besides one's body, one's leverage in the marketplace is quite limited.

The Marxist Theory of Society

Like the Marxist analysis of power, the Marxist analysis of class has provided both Marxist and socialist feminists with some of the conceptual tools necessary to understand women's oppression. Marx observed that every political economy—the primitive communal state, the slave epoch, the precapitalist society, and the bourgeois society—contains the seeds of its own destruction. Thus, according to Marx, there are within capitalism enough internal contradictions to generate a class division dramatic enough to overwhelm the very system that produced it. Specifically, there exist many poor and propertyless workers. These workers live very modestly, receiving subsistence wages for their exhausting labor while their employers live in luxury. When these two groups of people, the haves and the have-nots, both become conscious of themselves *as* classes, said Marx, class struggle ensues and ultimately topples the system that produced these classes.[12] It is important to emphasize the dynamic nature of class. Classes do not simply appear. They are slowly and often painstakingly formed by similarly situated people who share the same wants and needs. According to Marx, people who belong to any class initially have no more unity than "potatoes in a sack of potatoes.[13] But through a long and complex process of struggling together about issues of local and later national interest to them, a group of people gradually becomes a unity, a true class. Because class unity is difficult to achieve, its importance cannot be overstated, said Marx. As soon as a group of people is fully conscious of itself as a class, it has a better chance of achieving its fundamental goals. There is power in group awareness.

Class consciousness is, in the Marxist framework, the opposite of false consciousness, a state of mind that impedes the creation and maintenance of true class unity. False consciousness causes exploited people to believe they are as free to act and speak as their exploiters are. The bourgeoisie is especially adept at fooling the proletariat. For this reason, Marxists discredit egalitarian, or welfare, liberalism, for example, as a ruling-class ideology that tricks workers into believing their employers actually care about them. As Marxists see it, fringe benefits such as generous health-care plans or paid maternity leave are not gifts employers generously bestow on workers, but a means to pull the wool over workers' eyes. Grateful for the benefits their employers give them, workers minimize their own hardships and suffering. Like the ruling class, the workers begin to perceive the status quo as the best possible world for workers and employers alike. The more benefits employers give their workers, the less likely their workers will form a class capable of recognizing their true needs as human beings.

Because Marxist and socialist feminists wish to view women as a collectivity, Marxist teachings on class and class consciousness play a large role in Marxist and socialist feminist thought. Much debate within the Marxist and socialist feminist community has centered on the following question: Do women per se constitute a class? Given that some women are wives, daughters, friends, and lovers of *bourgeois* men, whereas other women are the wives, daughters, friends, and lovers of *proletarian* men, it would appear women do not constitute a single class in the strict Marxist sense. Yet, bourgeois and proletarian women's domestic experiences, for example, may bear enough similarities to motivate unifying struggles such as the 1970s wages-for-housework campaign (see discussion below). Thus, many Marxist and socialist feminists believe women can gain a consciousness of themselves as a *class* of workers by insisting, for example, that domestic work be recognized as real work, that is, productive work. The observation that wives and mothers usually love the people for whom they work does not mean that cooking, cleaning, and childcare are not productive work. At most it means wives' and mothers' working conditions are better than those of people who work for employers they dislike.[14]

By keeping the Marxist conceptions of class and class consciousness in mind, we can understand another concept that often plays a role in Marxist and socialist feminist thought: alienation. Like many Marxist terms, the term *alienation* is extraordinarily difficult to define simply. In *Karl Marx,* Allen Wood suggested we are alienated "if we either experience our lives as meaningless or ourselves as worthless, or else are capable of sustaining a sense of meaning and self-worth only with the help of illusions about ourselves or our condition."[15] Robert Heilbroner added that alienation is a profoundly fragmenting experience. Things or persons who are or should be connected in some significant way are instead viewed as separate. As Heilbroner saw it, this sense of fragmentation and meaninglessness is particularly strong under capitalism.

As a result of invidious class distinctions, as well as the highly specialized and highly segmented nature of the work process, human existence loses its unity and wholeness in four basic ways. First, workers are alienated from the *product* of their labor. Not only do workers have no say in what commodities they will or will not produce, but the fruits of their labor are snatched from them. Therefore, the satisfaction of determining when, where, how, and to whom these commodities will be sold is denied the workers. What should partially express and constitute their being-as-workers confronts them as a thing apart, a thing alien.[16]

Second, workers are alienated from *themselves* because when work is experienced as something unpleasant to be gotten through as quickly as possible, it is deadening. When the potential source of workers' humanization becomes the actual source of their dehumanization, workers may undergo a major psychological crisis. They start feeling like hamsters on a hamster wheel, going nowhere.

Third, workers are alienated from *other human beings* because the structure of the capitalist economy encourages and even forces workers to see each other as competitors for jobs and promotions. When the source of workers' community (other workers experienced as cooperators, friends, people to be with) becomes instead the source of their isolation (other workers experienced as competitors, enemies, people to avoid), workers become disidentified with each other, losing an opportunity to add joy and meaning to their lives.

Fourth, workers are alienated from *nature* because the kind of work they do and the conditions under which they do it make them see nature as an obstacle to their survival. This negative perception of nature sets up an opposition where in fact a connectedness should exist—the connectedness among all elements in nature. The elimination of this type of alienation, entailing a return to a humane kind of work environment, is yet another important justification for the overthrow of capitalism.[17]

Building on the idea that in a capitalist society, human relations take on an alienated nature in which "the individual only feels himself or herself when detached from others,"[18] Ann Foreman claimed this state of affairs is worse for women than it is for men:

> The man exists in the social world of business and industry as well as in the family and therefore is able to express himself in these different spheres. For the woman, however, her place is within the home. Men's objectification within industry, through the expropriation of the product of their labour, takes the form of alienation. But the effect of alienation on the lives and consciousness of women takes an even more oppressive form. Men seek relief from their alienation through their relations with women; for women there is no relief. For these intimate relations are the very ones that are essential structures of her oppression.[19]

As Foreman saw it, women's alienation is profoundly disturbing because women experience themselves not as selves but as others. All too often, said Foreman, a woman's sense of self is entirely dependent on her families' and friends' appreciation of her. If they express loving feelings toward her, she will be happy, but if they fail to give her even a thank-you, she will be sad. Thus, Marxist and socialist feminists aim to create a world in which women can experience themselves as whole persons, as integrated rather than fragmented beings, as people who can be happy even when they are unable to make their families and friends happy.

The Marxist Theory of Politics

Like the Marxist theories of economics and society, the Marxist theory of politics offers Marxist and socialist feminists insights to help liberate women from the forces that oppress them. As noted previously, class struggle takes a certain form within the workplace because the interests of the employers are not those of the workers. Whereas it is in the employers' interests to use whatever tactics may be necessary (harassment, firing, violence) to get workers to work ever more effectively and efficiently for less wages than their work is worth, it is in the workers' interests to use whatever countertactics may be necessary (sick time, coffee breaks, strikes) to limit the extent to which their labor power is used to produce sheer profit for their employers.

The relatively small and everyday class conflicts occurring within the capitalist workplace serve as preliminaries to the full-fledged, large-scale class struggles that Marx envisioned. As noted above, Marx predicted that as workers become increasingly aware of their common exploitation and alienation, they will achieve class consciousness. United, the workers will be able to fight their employers for control over the means of production (e.g., the nation's factories). If the workers manage to win this fight, Marx claimed that a highly committed, politically savvy, well-trained group of revolutionaries would subsequently emerge from the workers' ranks. Marx termed this special group of workers the "vanguard" of the full-scale revolution for which he hoped. More than anything else, Marx desired to replace capitalism with socialism, a nonexploitative, nonalienating political economy through which communism, "the complete and conscious return of man himself as a social, that is, human being,"[20] could come into existence.

Under capitalism, Marx suggested, people are largely free to *do* what they want to do within the confines of the system, but they have little say in determining the confines themselves. "Personality," said Marx, "is conditioned and determined by quite definite class relationships."[21] Decades later, Richard Schmitt elaborated on Marx's powerful quote:

> In as much as persons do certain jobs in society, they tend to acquire certain character traits, interests, habits, and so on. Without such adaptations to the demands of their particular occupations, they would not be able to do a great job. A capitalist who cannot bear to win in competition, or to outsmart someone, will not be a capitalist for long. A worker who is unwilling to take orders will not work very often. In this way we are shaped by the work environment, and this fact limits personal freedom for it limits what we can choose to be.[22]

In contrast to the persons living under capitalism, persons living under communism are free not only to *do* but also to *be* what they want, because they have the power to see clearly and change the system that shapes them.

If we read between these lines, we can appreciate another of Marxism's major appeals to Marxist and socialist feminists. It promises to reconstitute human nature in ways that preclude all the pernicious dichotomies that have made slaves of some and masters of others. Marxism also promises to make people free, a promise women would like to see someone keep. There is, after all, something very liberating about the idea of women and men constructing together the social structures and social roles that will permit both genders to realize their full human potential.

The Marxist Theory of Family Relations

Although the fathers of Marxism did not take women's oppression nearly as seriously as they did workers' oppression, some of them did offer explanations for why women are oppressed qua women. With the apparent blessing of Marx, Engels wrote *The Origin of the Family, Private Property, and the State* (1845), in which he showed how changes in the material conditions of people affect the organization of their family relations. He argued that before the family, or structured conjugal relations, there existed a primitive state of "promiscuous intercourse."[23] In this early state, every woman was fair game for every man, and vice versa. All were essentially married to all. In the process of natural selection, suggested Engels, various kinds of blood relatives were gradually excluded from consideration as eligible marriage partners.[24] As fewer and fewer women in the tribal group became available to any given man, individual men began to put forcible claims on individual women as their possessions. As a result, the pairing family, in which one man is married to one woman, came into existence.

Noting that when a man took a woman, he came to live in *her* household, Engels interpreted this state of affairs as a sign of women's economic power. Because women's work was vital for the tribe's survival and because women produced most of the material goods (e.g., bedding, clothing, cookware, tools) that could be passed on to future generations, Engels concluded that early pairing societies were probably matrilineal, with inheritance and lines of descent traced through the mother.[25] Later, Engels speculated that pairing societies may have been not merely matrilineal societies but also matriarchal societies in which women ruled at the political, social, and economic levels.[26] But his main and less debatable point remained that whatever power women had in past times, it was rooted in their position in the household, at that time the center of production.[27] Only if the site of production changed would women lose their advantaged position.[28] As it turned out, said Engels, a site change did occur. The "domestication of animals and the breeding of herds" outside the household led to an entirely new source of wealth for the human community.[29] Somehow, men gained control of the tribe's animals (Engels did not tell us why or how),[30] and the male-female power balance shifted in favor of men, as men learned to produce more than enough animals to meet the tribe's needs for milk and meat.

Surplus animals constituted an accumulation of wealth men used as a means of exchange between tribes. Possessing more than enough of a valuable socioeconomic good, men found themselves increasingly preoccupied with the issue of property inheritance. Directed through the mother's line, property inheritance was originally a minor matter of the bequest of a "house, clothing, crude ornaments and the tools for obtaining and preparing food—boats, weapons and domestic utensils of the simplest kinds."[31] As production outside the household began to outstrip production within it, the traditional sexual division of labor between men and women, which had supposedly arisen out of the physiological differences between the sexes—specifically, the *sex act*[32]—took on new social meanings. As men's work and production grew in importance, not only did the value of women's work and production decrease, but the status of women within society decreased. Because men now possessed things more valuable than the things women possessed and because men, for some unexplained reason, suddenly wanted *their own* biological children to get *their* possessions, men exerted enormous pressure to convert society from a matrilineal one into a patrilineal one. As Engels phrased it, mother right had "to be overthrown, and overthrown it was."[33]

Engels presented the "overthrow of mother right" as "*the world-historic defeat of the female sex.*"[34] Having produced and staked a claim to wealth, men took control of the household, reducing women to the "slaves" of men's carnal desire and "mere instrument[s] for the production of [men's] children."[35] In this new familial order, said Engels, the husband ruled by virtue of his economic power: "He is the bourgeois and the wife represents the proletariat."[36] Engels believed men's power over women is rooted in the fact that men, not women, control private property. The oppression of women will cease only with the dissolution of the institution of private property.

The emergence of private property and the shift to patrilineage also explained, for Engels, the transition to the monogamous family. Before the advent of technologies such as in vitro fertilization (see Chapter 2), it was always possible to identify the biological mother of a child. If the child came out of a woman's body, the child was the biological product of her egg and some man's sperm. In contrast, before the development of DNA testing to establish biological paternity, the identity of a biological father was uncertain because a woman could have been impregnated by a man other than her husband. Thus, to secure their wives' marital fidelity, men imposed the institution of heterosexual monogamy on women, the purpose of which was, according to Engels, to provide a vehicle for the guaranteed transfer of a father's private property to his biological children. Male dominance, in the forms of patrilineage and patriarchy, is simply the result of the class division between the propertied man and the propertyless woman. Engels commented that monogamy was "the first form of the family to be based not on natural but on economic conditions."[37] In his estimation, the monogamous family is the product not of love and commitment but of power plays and economic exigencies.

Because Engels viewed monogamous marriage as an economic institution that has nothing to do with love and everything to do with the transfer of private property, he insisted that if wives are to be emancipated from their husbands, women must first become economically independent of men. He stressed that the first presupposition for the emancipation of women is "the reintroduction of the entire female sex into public industry," and the second is the socialization of housework and child-rearing.[38] Remarkably, Engels believed that proletarian women experience less oppression than do bourgeois women. As he saw it, the bourgeois family consists of a relationship between a husband and a wife in which the husband agrees to support his wife provided that she promises to remain sexually faithful to him and to reproduce only his legitimate heirs. "This marriage of convenience," observed Engels, "often enough turns into the crassest prostitution—sometimes on both sides, but much more generally on the part of the wife, who differs from the ordinary courtesan only in that she does not hire out her body, like a wageworker, on piecework, but sells it into slavery once and for all."[39]

In contrast to the bourgeois marriage, the proletarian marriage is not, in Engels's estimation, a mode of prostitution, because the material conditions of the proletarian family differ substantially from those of the bourgeois family. Not only is the proletariat's lack of private property significant in removing the primary male incentive for monogamy—namely, the reproduction of legitimate heirs for one's property—but the general employment of proletarian women as workers outside the home also leads to a measure of equality between husband and wife. This equality, according to Engels, provides the foundation of true "sex-love." In addition to these differences, the household authority of the proletarian husband, unlike that of the bourgeois husband, is not likely to receive the full support of the legal establishment. For all these reasons, Engels concluded that with the exception of "residual brutality" (spouse abuse), all "the material foundations of male dominance had ceased to exist" in the proletarian home.[40]

Classical Marxist Feminism: General Reflections

Affirming the ideas of Marx and Engels, classical Marxist feminists tried to use a class analysis rather than a gender analysis to explain women's oppression. A particularly good example of classical Marxist feminism appeared in

Evelyn Reed's "Women: Caste, Class, or Oppressed Sex?"[41] Stressing that the same capitalist economic forces and social relations that "brought about the oppression of one class by another, one race by another, and one nation by another"[42] also brought about the oppression of one sex by another, Reed resisted the view that women's oppression *as women* is the worst kind of oppression for *all* women. Although Reed agreed that relative to men, women occupy a subordinate position in a patriarchal or male-dominated society, she did not think that all women were equally oppressed by men or that no women were guilty of oppressing other women. On the contrary, she thought bourgeoisie women were capable of oppressing both proletarian men and women. In a capitalist system, money is most often power.

Not found in Reed is any manifesto urging all women to band together to wage a "caste war" against all men.[43] Rather, she encourages oppressed women to join oppressed men in a "class war" against their common capitalist oppressors, female and male. Reed thought it was misguided to insist that all women, simply by virtue of possessing two X chromosomes, belong to the same class. On the contrary, she maintained that *"women, like men are a multiclass sex."*[44] Specifically, proletarian women have little in common with bourgeoisie women, who are the economic, social, and political as well as sexual partners of the bourgeoisie men to whom they are linked. Bourgeoisie women are not united with proletarian women but with bourgeoisie men "in defense of private property, profiteering, militarism, racism—and the exploitation of other women."[45]

Clearly, Reed believed that the primary enemy of at least proletarian women is not patriarchy, but first and foremost, capitalism. Optimistic about male-female relations in a postcapitalist society, Reed maintained that "[f]ar from being eternal, woman's subjection and the bitter hostility between the sexes are no more than a few thousand years old. They were produced by the drastic social changes which brought the family, private property, and the state into existence."[46] With the end of capitalist male-female relationships, both sexes will thrive in a communist society that enables all its members to cooperate with each other in communities of care.

Women's Labor After the 1917 Communist Revolution in Russia

During the 1917 Communist Revolution and for several years afterward, Reed's brand of optimism seemed well-founded. Women were invited to enter the productive workforce to supposedly find in it the beginnings of their full human liberation. With economic independence would come the possibility of women's developing self-confidence and viewing themselves as makers of meaningful human history. Unfortunately, things did not turn out so well for postrevolution Soviet women. On the contrary! Rather than finding in the workplace meaningful, high-waged work, most women found drone-like, exhausting work that was typically less valued than men's work.[47] Not wanting to jeopardize Communist plans to totally destroy capitalism, most Marxist feminists kept quiet about their workplace situation in public. However, in private they complained about such workplace disadvantages as (1) the relegation of most women to low-status "women's work" (i.e., secretarial work; rote factory work; and service work, including jobs related to cooking, cleaning, and caring for the basic needs of the young, the old, and the infirm); (2) the creation of "female professions" and "male professions"; (3) the payment of lower wages to women than the wages paid to men; and (4) the treatment of women as a "colossal reserve of labor forces" to use or not use, depending on the state's need for workers.[48]

Unable to find in strict Marxist theory an explanation for why, on the average, socialist women were not faring as well as socialist men in the productive workforce, some Marxist feminists turned their attention to the work women did in the domestic realm—work that men typically did not do. Trying to explain why socialist women were saddled with their families' domestic work, whether or not the women worked in the productive workforce, Margaret Benston defined women as that class of people "responsible for the production of simple use-values in those activities associated with the house and family."[49] As she saw it, women must break out of this class to be liberated, but they cannot do so unless their domestic labor is socialized:

> Women, particularly married women with children, who work outside the home simply do two jobs; their participation in the labor force is only allowed if they continue to fulfill their first responsibility in the home. . . . Equal access to jobs outside the home, while one of the preconditions for women's liberation, will not in itself be sufficient to give equality for women; as long as work in the home remains a matter of private production and is the responsibility of women, they will simply carry a double work-load.[50]

To bring women into the productive workforce without simultaneously socializing the jobs of cooking, cleaning, and childcare is to make women's oppressed condition even worse, claimed Benston. To be sure, she conceded, the socialization of domestic work might lead to women's doing the same sorts of "female" work outside the home as they do inside the home. But the simple fact that women will be doing this "female" work *outside* their own home for wages over which they have control can be viewed as an advancement for women, insisted Benston.

The Wages-for-Housework Campaign

Agreeing with Benston that in a socialist society, it might be necessary to socialize domestic work to achieve full liberation for women, Maria Dalla Costa and Selma James nonetheless argued that in a capitalist society, the best way (or at least the quickest way) for women to achieve economic parity with men might not be for women to enter the productive workforce and for domestic labor to be socialized, but instead for women to stay at home and demand wages for the "real work"—that is, productive work— they did there. Unlike most classical Marxist feminist thinkers, Dalla Costa and James claimed that women's work *inside* the home generates surplus value.[51] They reasoned that women's domestic work is the necessary condition for all other labor, from which, in turn, surplus value is extracted. By providing not only food and clothes but also emotional comfort to current (and future) workers, women keep the cogs of the capitalist machine running. Therefore, argued Dalla Costa and James, men's employers should pay women wages for the housework they do.[52] Let housewives get the cash that would otherwise fatten employers' wallets.[53]

Acknowledging that domestic labor could be viewed as productive work, most Marxist feminists nonetheless concluded that paying women wages for housework was neither as feasible nor as desirable as Dalla Costa and James seemed to think. Paying women to do housework was not feasible, in their estimation, for several reasons. First, if employers were required to pay housewives wages for housework, the employers would probably pay housewives' husbands lower wages. Under such circumstances, the total capitalist profit margin would remain high, and the material conditions of workers would not improve. Second, not all or not even most women in advanced capitalist economies are stay-at-home domestic workers. Many married women as well as married men work outside the home as do many single men and women. Would employers be required to pay all their workers' wages for their at-home domestic work? If so, would employers have any way to monitor the quantity and quality of their workers' domestic labor? Third, if small companies as well as major corporations were required to pay all their workers for domestic work, most small companies would probably go out of business. Back in 1972, the height of the wages-for-housework campaign, the Chase Manhattan Bank estimated that "for her average 100-hour workweek, the housewife should be paid $257.53."[54] In that same year, noted Ann C. Scott, "white males had average incomes of $172 a week;

white females had average incomes of $108 a week."[55] By 2005, over thirty years later, annual median earnings in the United States for women are $32,168, and for men are $41,965.[56] Add to these median wages the wages for domestic labor done by employees in their own homes, and there is no question that most small or even large companies could not sustain such a hit. Indeed, even if wages for domestic labor were paid at the rate of only the minimum wage of $5.85 per hour for, say, a fifty-six-hour domestic work week, each employee's salary would need to be topped off with over $17,000 annually.[57]

Clearly, it does not seem feasible to pay anyone, including wives, girlfriends, mothers, and daughters, wages for housework. But even if it were feasible to do so, would it be desirable? Many Marxist and other feminists in the 1970s were not confident that wages for housework would liberate women. Carol Lopate, among others, argued that paying women for housework would have the net effect of keeping women isolated in their own homes with few opportunities to do anything other than routinized and repetitious work:

> The decrease in house size and the mechanization of housework have meant that the housewife is potentially left with much greater leisure time; however, she is often kept busy buying, using, and repairing the devices and their attachments which are theoretically geared toward saving her time. Moreover, the trivial, manufactured tasks which many of these technological aids perform are hardly a source of satisfaction for housewives. Max-Pacs may give "perfect coffee every time," but even a compliment about her coffee can offer little more than fleeting satisfaction to the housewife. Finally, schools, nurseries, day care, and television have taken from mothers much of their responsibility for the socialization of their children.[58]

Moreover, and even more important, paying women wages for domestic work would give women little impetus to work outside the household. As a result, the traditional sexual division of labor would be strengthened. Men would feel no pressure to do "women's work," and women would have no incentive to do "men's work."[59]

Contemporary Socialist Feminism: General Reflections

The more Marxist feminists realized that, like everyone else, they had unreflectively assumed that domestic work is *women's* work, the more it concerned them that the advent of Communist/socialist societies had not resulted in the socialization of this work. Rather than there being an approximately equal number of men and women doing domestic work for wages, it was business as usual. That is, women continued to do domestic work in the home "for free," whether or not they had a paid job outside the home. Unable to explain in exclusively economic terms why domestic work is viewed as women's work in socialist as well as capitalist societies, many Marxist feminists concluded that domestic work is assigned to women in all societies simply because all women belong to the same sex class—namely, the second (female) sex, which exists to serve the first (male) sex.

The Marxist feminists who decided that women's sex class as well as economic class plays a role in women's oppression began to refer to themselves as socialist feminists or materialist feminists. One of the initial goals of this evolving group of feminist theorists was to develop a theory powerful enough to explain the complex ways in which capitalism and patriarchy allied to oppress women. The result of this effort was, as might be predicted, not a unitary theory, but a variety of theories that sorted themselves into two types: (1) two-system explanations of women's oppression and (2) interactive-system explanations of women's oppression.

Two-System Explanations of Women's Oppression

Two-system explanations of women's oppression typically combine a Marxist feminist account of class power with a radical feminist account of sex power.[60] Some two-system explanations adhere to the Marxist base-superstructure model that views economics as "the fundamental motor of social relations"[61] shaping the form of society, including its ideologies and psychologies. These explanations claim that, at root, women have more to fear from capitalist forces than from patriarchal forces.[62] In contrast, other two-system explanations are less committed to the Marxist base-superstructure model. They imply that patriarchy, not capitalism, may be women's ultimate worst enemy.

Juliet Mitchell. In the early 1970s, Juliet Mitchell sketched a plausible two-system explanation of women's oppression. In *Woman's Estate,* she abandoned the classical Marxist feminist position according to which a woman's condition is simply a function of her relation to capital, of whether she is part of the productive workforce. In place of this monocausal explanation for women's oppression, she suggested women's status and function are multiply determined by their role in not only production but also reproduction, the socialization of children, and sexuality. "The error of the old Marxist way," she said, "was to see the other three elements as reducible to the economic; hence the call for the entry into production was accompanied by the purely abstract slogan of the abolition of the family. Economic demands are still *primary*, but must be accompanied by coherent policies for the other three elements (reproduction, sexuality and socialization), policies which at particular junctures may take over the primary role in immediate action."[63]

In attempting to determine which of these elements most oppressed 1970s U.S. women, Mitchell concluded that U.S. women had not made enough progress in the areas of production, reproduction, and the socialization of children. She noted that even though women are just as physically and psychologically qualified for high-paying, prestigious jobs as men are, employers continued to confine women to low-paying, low-status jobs.[64] Moreover, said Mitchell, despite the widespread availability of safe, effective, and inexpensive reproduction-controlling technologies, women often failed or refused to use them. As a result, the causal chain of "maternity—family— absence from production and public life—sexual inequality" continued to bind women to their subordinate status. Furthermore, although 1970s U.S. women had far fewer children than U.S. women did at the turn of the century, the modern women spent no less time socializing them.[65] In fact, the pressures to be a perfect mother, always attentive to every physical and psychological need of her children, seemed to be increasing.

Interestingly, like radical-libertarian feminists, Mitchell thought 1970s U.S. women had made major progress in the area of sexuality. She claimed that unlike previous generations, 1970s U.S. women felt free to express their sexual desires publicly and to present themselves as sexual beings. Still, Mitchell acknowledged that pushed to its extreme, women's newly won sexual liberation could mutate into a form of sexual oppression. Whereas turn-of-the-century U.S. society condemned sexually active women as "wanton whores," 1970s U.S. society tended to celebrate them as "sex experimenters" or healthy role models for sexually repressed women to emulate. Commenting on this state of affairs, Mitchell observed that too much sex, like too little sex, can be oppressive.[66] Women can be made to feel that something is wrong with them if they are not sexually active or sexually preoccupied.

Mitchell speculated that patriarchal ideology, which views women as lovers, wives, and mothers rather than as workers, is *almost* as responsible for women's position in society as capitalist economics is. She claimed that even if a Marxist revolution destroyed the family as an economic unit, it would not thereby make women men's equals *automatically*. Because of the ways in which patriarchal ideology has constructed men's and women's psyches, women would probably continue to remain subordinate to men until their minds and men's minds had been liberated from the idea that women are somehow less valuable than men.

Alison Jaggar. Like Mitchell, Alison Jaggar provided a two-system explanations of women's oppression. But in the final analysis, instead of identifying capitalism as the primary cause of women's low status, she reserved this "honor" for patriarchy. Capitalism oppresses women as *workers,* but patriarchy oppresses women as *women,* an oppression that affects women's identity as well as activity. A woman is always a woman, even when she is not working. Rejecting the classical Marxist doctrine that a person has to participate directly in the capitalist relations of production to be considered truly alienated, Jaggar claimed, as did Foreman above, that all women, no matter their work role, are alienated in ways that men are not.[67]

Jaggar organized her discussion of women's alienation under the headings of sexuality, motherhood, and intellectuality. In the same way wageworkers may be alienated from the product(s) on which they work, women, viewed simply as women, may be alienated from the "product(s)" on which they typically work—their bodies. Women may insist that they diet, exercise, and dress only to please themselves, but in reality they most likely shape and adorn their flesh primarily for the pleasure of men. Moreover, women do not have final or total say about when, where, how, or by whom their bodies will be used, because their bodies can be suddenly appropriated from them through acts ranging from the "male gaze" to sexual harassment to rape. Likewise, to the same degree that wageworkers can be gradually alienated from themselves—their bodies beginning to feel like things, mere machines from which labor power is extracted—women can be gradually alienated from themselves. To the degree that women work on their bodies—shaving their underarms, slimming their thighs and augmenting their breasts, painting their nails and coloring their hair—they may start to experience their bodies as objects or commodities. Finally, just as many wageworkers are in competition with each other for their employers' approbation and rewards, many women are in competition with each other for men's approbation and reward.[68]

Motherhood, continued Jaggar, may also be an alienating experience for women, especially when mostly or exclusively men decide the policies and laws that regulate women's reproductive choices. For example, in societies that use children's labor power nearly as much as adults' labor power, women may be pressured to bear as many children as physically possible. In contrast, in societies that view children as an economic burden for parents to support, women may be discouraged from having large families. Indeed, women may be pressured or even forced to use contraception, be sterilized, or have an abortion.[69]

In the same way that women may be alienated from the *product* of their reproductive labor, said Jaggar, women may be alienated from the *process* of their reproductive labor. Obstetricians may try to take control of the birthing process, performing medically unnecessary cesarean sections or anesthetizing women about to deliver against their wishes. Moreover, as the new reproductive technologies develop, an increasing number of women may be alienated from both the product and the process of reproduction in even more dramatic ways. For instance, as noted in Chapter 2, in vitro fertilization makes possible gestational surrogacy. With this technology, a woman can have one or more of her eggs surgically removed, fertilized in vitro with her partner's sperm, and then transferred into the womb of another woman for gestation. The woman who gestates the child contracts to return the child to the couple for rearing. Raising the same type of concerns that some radical-cultural feminists raised about gestational surrogacy in Chapter 2, Jaggar claimed that such arrangements do not do full justice to the gestational mother in particular. By virtue of her reproductive work, the embryo is shaped into a viable human infant to which she may be emotionally as well as physically bonded. Should not this circumstance give her some parental claim to the child, even though she did not provide the "raw material," the egg, for the child?[70]

Child-rearing, like childbearing, may also be an alienating experience for women when scientific experts (most of whom are men) take charge of it, stressed Jaggar.[71] As she saw it, the pressures on mothers are enormous because, with virtually no assistance, they are supposed to execute every edict issued by child-rearing authorities, some of whom have never experienced the daily demands of child rearing. Echoing the thoughts of Adrienne Rich in *Of Woman Born* (see Chapter 2), Jaggar explained how contemporary child-rearing practices may ultimately alienate or estrange mothers from their children: The extreme mutual dependence of mother and child encourages the mother to define the child primarily with reference to her own needs for meaning, love, and social recognition. She sees the child as her product, as something that should improve her life and that often instead stands against her, as something of supreme value, that is held cheap by society. The social relations of contemporary motherhood make it impossible for her to see the child as a whole person, part of a larger community to which both mother and child belong.[72]

One of the saddest features of a mother's possible alienation from her children, then, is that her inability to see her children as persons may be matched only by their inability to see her as a person. Alluding to Dorothy Dinnerstein and some other psychoanalytic feminists, Jaggar described how some children turn on their mothers, blaming them for everything that goes wrong in their lives: "I'm a failure because you, my mother, loved me too much/too little." In addition to separating mothers from their children, the conditions of contemporary motherhood can drive wedges between mothers and fathers, said Jaggar. All too often, a domestic dispute begins with a father's laying down the law for the kids and a mother's defying its terms. Furthermore, the standards governing proper mothering sometimes impede the growth of genuine friendships between women, as mothers compete to rear the "perfect child"[73]—that is, the well-mannered, multitalented, physically attractive, achievement-oriented boy or girl whose photograph appears on every other page of the yearbook.

Finally, said Jaggar, not only may many women be alienated from their own sexuality and from the product and process of motherhood, but they may also be alienated from their own intellectual capacities. Many women feel so unsure of themselves that they hesitate to express their ideas in public, for fear their thoughts are not worth expressing; they remain silent when they should loudly voice their opinion. Worse, when women do express their thoughts forcefully and with passion, their ideas are often rejected as irrational or the product of mere emotion. To the extent men set the terms of thought and discourse, suggested Jaggar, women cannot be at ease in the world of theory.[74]

Jaggar concluded that although the overthrow of capitalism might end women's as well as men's exploitation in the productive workforce, it would not end women's alienation from everything and everyone, especially themselves.[75] Only the overthrow of patriarchy would enable women to become full persons.

Interactive-System Explanations of Women's Oppression

In contrast to two-system explanations, which, as we have just noted, tended to identify either class or sex as the primary source of women's oppression, interactive-system explanations strove to present capitalism and patriarchy as two equal partners colluding in a variety of ways to oppress women. Interactive-system thinkers included Iris Marion Young, Heidi Hartmann, and Sylvia Walby. To a greater or lesser extent, these contemporary socialist feminists used terms like "capitalist patriarchy" or "patriarchal capitalism" in their work. Trying hard never to view one system as more fundamental to women's oppression than the other system, these feminists wanted to stress the interdependency of capitalism and patriarchy.

Iris Marion Young. According to Iris Marion Young, as long as classical Marxist feminists try to use class as their central category of analysis, they will not be able to explain why women in socialist countries are often just as oppressed as women in capitalist countries. Precisely because class is a gender-blind category, said Young, it cannot provide an adequate explanation for women's specific oppression. Only a gender-sighted category such as the "sexual division of labor" has the conceptual power to do this.

Young reasoned that whereas class analysis looks at the system of production as a whole, focusing on the means and relations of production in the most general terms possible, a sexual division-of-labor analysis pays attention to the characteristics of the individual people who do the producing in society. In other words, a class analysis calls only for a general discussion of the respective roles of the bourgeoisie and the proletariat, whereas a sexual division-of-labor analysis requires a detailed discussion of who gives the orders and who takes them, who does the stimulating work and who does the drudge work, who works more hours and who works less hours, and who gets paid relatively high wages and who gets paid relatively low wages. Therefore, as compared with a class analysis, a sexual division-of-labor analysis can better explain why women usually take the orders, do the drudge jobs, work part-time, and get paid relatively low wages, whereas men usually give the orders, do the stimulating jobs, work full-time, and get paid relatively high wages.

Because she believed that capitalism and patriarchy are necessarily linked, Young insisted that a sexual division-of-labor analysis is a total substitute for, not a mere supplement to, class analysis. We do not need one theory (Marxism) to explain *gender-neutral capitalism* and another theory (feminism) to explain *gender-biased patriarchy,* said Young. Rather, we need a single theory—a socialist feminist theory—able to explain *gender-biased* (i.e., *patriarchal*) *capitalism.* "My thesis," wrote Young, "is that marginalization of women and thereby our functioning as a secondary labor force is an essential and fundamental characteristic of capitalism."[76]

Young's thesis is a controversial one, a major departure from the more traditional Marxist view that workers, be they male or female, are interchangeable. She argued that capitalism is very much aware of its workers' gender and, I may add, race and ethnicity. Because a large reserve of unemployed workers is necessary to keep wages low and to meet unanticipated demands for increased supplies of goods and services, capitalism has both implicit and explicit criteria for determining who will constitute its primary, employed workforce and who will act as its secondary, unemployed workforce. For a variety of reasons, not the least being a well-entrenched gender division of labor, capitalism's criteria identify men as "primary" workforce material and women as "secondary." Because women are needed at home in a way men are not—or so *patriarchy* believes—men are freer to work outside the home than women are.

Under capitalism as it exists today, women experience patriarchy as unequal wages for equal work, sexual harassment on the job, uncompensated domestic work, and the pernicious dynamics of the public-private split. Earlier generations of women also experienced patriarchy, but they lived it differently, depending on the dynamics of the reigning economic system. As with class society, reasoned Young, patriarchy should not be considered a system *separate* from capitalism just because it existed *first*. In fact, class and gender structures are so intertwined that neither one actually precedes the other. A feudal system of gender relations accompanied a feudal system of class arrangements, and the social relations of class and gender grew up together and evolved over time into the forms we now know (e.g., the capitalist nuclear family). To say gender relations are independent of class relations is to ignore how history works.

Heidi Hartmann.   Reinforcing Young's analysis, Heidi Hartmann noted that a strict class analysis leaves largely unexplained why women rather than men play the subordinate and submissive roles in both the workplace and the home. To understand not only workers' relation to capital but also women's relation to men, said Hartmann, a feminist analysis of patriarchy must be integrated with a Marxist analysis of capitalism. In her estimation, the partnership between patriarchy and capitalism is complex because patriarchy's interests in women are not always the same as capitalism's interests in women. In the nineteenth century, for example, proletarian men wanted proletarian women to stay at home, where women could "personally service" men.[77] In contrast, bourgeoisie men wanted proletarian women to work for next to nothing in the productive workforce. The bourgeoisie presented this option to proletarian women as an opportunity to earn "pin money" to supplement their men's puny take-home pay. Only if all men—be they proletarian or bourgeoisie—could find some mutually agreeable way to handle this particular "woman question" could the interests of patriarchy and capitalism be harmonized.

To some degree, this harmony was achieved when bourgeoisie men agreed to pay proletarian men a family wage large enough to permit them to keep their wives and children at home, said Hartmann. Bourgeoisie men struck this bargain with proletarian men because the bourgeoisie decided that, all things considered, (1) stay-at-home housewives would produce and maintain healthier, happier, and therefore more productive male workers than working wives would, and (2) women and children could always be persuaded at a later date to enter the workforce for low wages should male workers demand high wages. For a time, this arrangement worked well enough, but over time, the size of the family wage shrank and many proletarian men could no longer pay all their family's bills. Consequently, many proletarian women decided to enter the workforce not to earn "pin money," but to earn enough money to help their male partners support the family's true living costs.[78] Regrettably, these women typically came home to male partners who had little or no interest in helping with domestic work. Hartmann concluded that women were in a no-win situation when it came to work-related issues. Everywhere women turned, the sexual division of labor disadvantaged them. The only possible hope for women was to fight capitalism and patriarchy simultaneously. These two systems are simply two heads of the same beast: capitalist patriarchy.

Sylvia Walby.   Like Young and Hartmann, Sylvia Walby conceptualized patriarchy and capitalism as developing in tandem. As she saw it, patriarchy is located in six somewhat independent structures: unpaid domestic work, waged labor, culture, sexuality, male violence, and the state.[79] These structures, and their relative importance, vary from one historical era to another. Walby noted, for example, that patriarchy oppressed women mostly in the private sphere of domestic production during the nineteenth century, and mostly in the public sphere of waged labor and the state in the twentieth century.

Focusing on workplace gender inequity in the United Kingdom in particular, Walby observed that in 1992, the British government made full employment for both men and women one of its main goals. As a result of this development in government policy, more women than ever entered the productive workforce, where they gained not only economic clout but also a strong political voice. Their collective power grew so much that the traditional British "strong male breadwinner logic" no longer made much sense. The British government became convinced that to compete successfully in the European Union, the nation needed to provide women workers with hours that were more flexible, ample childcare, and decent minimum wages. More optimistic than some of the socialist feminists who preceded her, Walby claimed that at least in the United Kingdom, "the modernization of the gender regime is creating a new political constituency of working women who are vocalizing their perceived interests in policies to assist combining home and work."[80]

Women's Labor Issues

The preceding discussion suggests that the distinctions some socialist feminists make between two-system explanations and interactive-system explanations for women's oppression are somewhat forced and probably of more theoretical than practical interest to the average woman. Yet the relevance of contemporary socialist feminism's overall message for women cannot be overstated. Worldwide, women's oppression is strongly related to the fact that women's work, be it at home or outside the home, is still unpaid, underpaid, or disvalued, a state of affairs that largely explains women's lower status and power nearly everywhere.

Although much more could be said about women's domestic work than we have discussed, suffice it to say that according to 1995 calculations of the International Labour Organization (ILO), "if the household duties performed by women were calculated as productive activity in the various systems of national accounting, the value of the world's GDP (gross domestic product) would increase by 25 to 30 percent."[81] Whether they live in developing or developed nations, socialist or capitalist nations, women still do the majority of unpaid work in the home, even when they also do full-time or part-time paid work outside the home. The "double day" alluded to several times in our general discussion of socialist feminist thought is a very hard day. Many women would be far more physically and psychologically happy if they worked only a "single day." Yet women are likely to continue to work double shifts, so to speak, as long as domestic work is viewed as women's work.

Although contemporary socialist feminists continue to bemoan the fact that women do too much work for free in the home, they have increasingly turned their attention to how little women are paid for the work they do outside the home. In particular, contemporary socialist feminists have focused on the gender pay gap and the often oppressive nature of women's work in the so-called global factory. To ignore these issues in this chapter would be to play into the unfortunate impression that just because "communism" has failed, and the old Soviet Union has been dismantled, all types of Marxist and socialist feminism are dead. On the contrary, said Nancy Holmstrom:

Today, the socialist feminist project is more pressing than ever. . . . The brutal economic realities of globalization impact everyone across the globe—but women are affected disproportionately. Displaced by economic changes, women bear a greater burden of labor throughout the world as social services have been cut, whether in response to structural adjustment plans in the third world or to so-called welfare reform in the United States. Women have been forced to migrate, are subject to trafficking, and are the proletarians of the newly industrializing countries. On top of all this they continue to be subject to sexual violence and in much of the world are not allowed to control their own processes of reproduction. How should we understand these phenomena and, more importantly, how do we go about changing them? Feminist theory that is lost in theoretical abstractions or that depreciates economic realities will be useless for this purpose. Feminism that speaks of women's oppression and its injustice but fails to address capitalism will be of little help in ending women's oppression. Marxism's analysis of history, of capitalism, and of social change is certainly relevant to understanding these economic changes, but if its categories of analysis are understood in a gender- or race-neutral way it will be unable to do justice to them. Socialist feminism is the approach with the greatest capacity to illuminate the exploitation and oppression of most of the women of the world.[82]

Gender Pay Gap

Most, though not all, nations have gender pay gaps, in the estimation of Shawn Meghan Burn. Japan has a particularly egregious one. Japanese women earn only 51 percent of Japanese men's wages.[83] However, the situation is dramatically different in Sri Lanka, where women earn 96 percent of men's wages.[84] In the United States, women earned 81.7 percent of men's wages in 2006.[85] There is, however, data to support the claim that U.S. women's most recent wage gains are in some measure the result of U.S. men's wage losses.[86]

Some of the most frequently cited reasons for the gender pay gap are (1) the concentration of women in low-paying, female-dominated jobs; (2) the high percentage of women who work part-time rather than full-time; and (3) outright wage discrimination against women. Worldwide, women tend to engage in service work (teaching, nursing, childcare), clerical work, agricultural work (picking fruit), and light industrial work (producing clothes, shoes, toys, and electronic devices), while men tend to engage in heavy industrial work, transportation work, management, administration, and policy work.[87]

Although U.S. women have gained some access to high-paying, male-dominated jobs like construction and trucking in recent years, their numbers in these occupations remain relatively small. A January 2006 report from the Bureau of Labor Statistics, for example, shows that there are 6.9 million men and only 172,000 women in the construction and extraction occupations. Similarly, whereas there are 2.7 million men in the category "driver/sales workers and truck drivers," there are only 113,000 women in this category.[88] Also worrisome is that despite a significant increase in the number of women in such major professions as business, health care, and legal services, women in these professions continue to hit the "glass ceiling," that is, "the invisible but effective barrier which prevents women from moving beyond a certain point on the promotion ladder."[89] For example, in the United States, women chief executive officers, especially in the *Fortune* 500 companies, are relatively few, whereas the number of women in less lucrative and prestigious jobs such as human resources and accounting are legion.[90] Similarly, it is no accident that there are 370,000 male physicians and surgeons in the United States, but only 188,000 female physicians and surgeons. Nor is it an accident that female registered nurses outnumber male registered nurses 1.7 million to 185,000 in the United States.[91] Another notable statistic, this time in the area of legal services, reveals that U.S. women are more likely to be paralegals than are U.S. men. Indeed, in the United States, there are only 34,000 male paralegals and legal assistants, compared with 267,000 female paralegals and legal assistants.[92] Add to all these statistics the fact that there are 2.2 million men in computer and mathematical occupations, compared with 756,000 women, and 2.2 million male engineers compared with 364,000 female engineers,[93] and one must conclude that women's *access* to high-paying, high-status occupations and professions in the United States remains limited.

Beyond U.S. women's relative lack of access to certain high-paying jobs,[94] another explanation for the gender pay gap is women's tendency to limit the time they devote to work in the productive workforce. Far more women than men work part-time,[95] and far more women than men leave the productive workforce for months or even years to tend to family matters.[96] Thus, over time, women earn less than men, simply because women work fewer hours and years than men typically do.

As tempting as it may be to explain part of the current gender pay gap in terms of women's decision to work less hours or years in the paid workforce, this explanation does not address the question contemporary socialist feminists have since forcefully ask: Namely, *why* is it that *women* limit their paid work outside the home in ways that men do not? Is it because women do not want to work long hours outside the home? Or is it because women view the money they earn as luxury money they can forsake? Or is it because women think it is their responsibility rather than men's to take time off work to rear their children properly or to take care of their sick relatives and aging parents, or to do both?

One of the most disturbing aspects of the gender pay gap is that even when women work full-time, stay in the workforce, and do the same jobs that men do, women's wages often lag behind men's.[97] Clearly, this state of affairs requires not only a "capitalist" explanation (women are paid less because their wages are viewed as secondary wages), but also a "patriarchal" explanation: Women are paid less simply because they are *women,* a very disturbing thought to say the least.

In addition to not answering the question why women, rather than men, limit their time in the workforce, the human-capital approach does not explain why many employers prefer to hire women as part-timers. Could it be that female part-time workers, who, by the way, are usually not entitled to employer-paid benefit packages, can be easily motivated to work longer hours than they should? Acculturated to help out in a pinch, women who work part-time may work longer and harder than their contract specifies, simply because they do not want to let other people down.

Feminist solutions to the gender pay gap are various, depending on which aspects of the gap are put under the microscope or require the most attention. Liberal feminists prefer the remedy of equal pay for equal work. They invoke legislation such as the U.S. 1963 Pay Act, which mandates that women's pay should be equal to men's when their positions are equal.[98] Although the Equal Pay Act sounds like an ideal tool for U.S. women to use, it may not be. Equal Pay Act civil suits put the burden of proof on the shoulders of the plaintiff. She has to prove that her work position is the same as that of a comparable male employee. Such proof might be relatively easy to secure in some lines of work such as mail carrier or flight attendant, but it is far harder to secure in a profession such as law, where different labels such as "associate," "assistant," and "partner" can be used to make two virtually identical positions sound quite different.[99] Moreover, the usefulness of the Equal Pay Act as a reference point for gender-based civil suits seems predicated on women's gaining access to slots in male-dominated jobs or professions. The act does little, if anything, to question the sexual division of labor per se, that is, to question why the kind of work men typically do tends to be valued more than the kind of work women typically do.

Viewing liberal feminists' preference for an equal-pay-for-equal-work remedy for the gender pay gap as a capitulation to the view that women have to be like men (in this instance, work like men) to be valued like men, many contemporary socialist feminists have joined with many radical-cultural feminists to endorse a comparable-worth remedy for the gender pay gap. As they see it, a comparable-worth remedy for the gender pay gap is an opportunity not only to secure better wages for women but also to force society to reconsider why it pays some people so much and others so little.[100]

Many social scientists are convinced that as long as women remain in traditionally female-dominated jobs and, more significantly, as long as society continues to assign less value to female-dominated jobs than to male-dominated jobs, the gender pay gap is likely to persist. Society needs to ask itself why in the United States, registered nurses, 91.9 percent female, earned an average of $971 weekly in 2006, whereas airplane pilots and flight engineers, 71 percent male, earned $1,419 weekly; childcare workers, 78 percent female, earned $345 weekly, whereas construction managers, 12 percent male, earned $1,145 weekly.[101] Do such pay differentials exist because, for example, flying planes is so much more physically, psychologically, and intellectually demanding than, for example, nursing? Or do they exist simply because most airplane pilots are men and most nurses are women?

Convinced that gender considerations factor into how much or how little workers are paid, comparable-worth advocates demand that employers evaluate their employees *objectively* by assigning "worth points" to the four components found in most jobs: (1) "knowledge and skills," or the total amount of information or dexterity needed to perform the job; (2) "mental demands," or the extent to which the job requires decision making; (3) "accountability," or the amount of supervision the job entails; and (4) "working conditions," such as how physically safe the job is.[102] When Norman D. Willis and Associates used this index to establish the worth points for various jobs performed in the state of Washington in the 1980s, they found the following disparities: "A Food Service I, at 93 points, earned an average salary of $472 per month, while a Delivery Truck Driver I, at 94 points, earned $792; a Clerical Supervisor III, at 305 points, earned an average of $794. A Nurse Practitioner II, at 385 points, had average earnings of $832, the same as those of a Boiler Operator, with only 144 points. A Homemaker I, with 198 points and an average salary of $462, had the lowest earnings of all evaluated jobs."[103] After reflecting on the Willis and Associates study, a federal court judge in Tacoma ruled that the state was in violation of Title VII of the 1964 Civil Rights Act, which prohibits discrimination by type of employment and level of compensation, and should eliminate pay gaps within its systems.[104]

On the average, contemporary socialist feminists support a comparable-worth approach to further reducing the gender wage pay gap, for two reasons—one having to do with addressing the feminization of poverty, and the other with addressing the valuation of different kinds of work. Because 61 percent of all poor families are headed by single women[105] and because women are the primary recipients of food stamps, legal aid, and Medicaid, if wage-earning women in female-dominated jobs were paid what their jobs are worth, these women might be able to support themselves and their families adequately without being forced, in one way or another, to attach themselves to men as a source of desperately needed income. In addition to seeing comparable worth as a way to alleviate women's poverty, contemporary socialist feminists see it as a way to highlight the arbitrariness of societal determinations about what kind of work counts as "worthy" work. According to Teresa Amott and Julie Matthaei, for example, we need to ask ourselves questions such as the following one:

Why should those whose jobs give them the most opportunity to develop and use their abilities also be paid the most? The traditional argument—that higher pay must be offered as an incentive for workers to gain skills and training—is contradicted by the fact that our highly paid jobs attract many more workers than employers demand. And given unequal access to education and training, a hierarchical pay scheme becomes a mechanism for the intergenerational transmission of wealth privilege, with its historically-linked racism, sexism, and classism.[106]

Clearly, the comparable-worth remedy for the gender pay gap has more potential to destabilize capitalist forces than does the equal-pay-for-equal-work remedy for the gender pay gap. The question is whether consumerism writ large has made it all too difficult for a sufficient number of people to challenge the status quo.

Women's Work in the Global Market

In recent years, contemporary socialist feminists have sought to move beyond analyzing the gender pay gap in developed nations to discussing the working conditions of women in developing nations. The forces of so-called globalization—described by the World Bank as the "growing integration of economies and societies around the world"[107]—have resulted in the creation of very large, profit-driven multinational corporations. Most of these multinationals have as their point of origin one or more developed nations and as their point of destination one or more developing nations. Interestingly, multinationals in developing nations prefer to hire women not only because so many women need work but also because their manual dexterity and docility make them ideal sweatshop workers.

To better understand how much profit, say, a U.S. multinational may make by moving its plants to a developing nation, we need read only some late 1990s statistics compiled by Shawn Meghan Burn:

The *maquiladoras* of Mexico's border towns are but one example of women in the global factory.

There, over 2,000 multinational corporations have drawn over a half million workers, two-thirds of them women, who get paid between $3.75 and $4.50 a day. In El Salvador, women employees of the Taiwanese *maquilador* Mandarin are forced to work shifts of 12 to 21 hours during which they are seldom allowed bathroom breaks; they are paid about 18 cents per shirt, which is later sold for $20 each. Mandarin makes clothes for the Gap, J. Crew, and Eddie Bauer.

In Haiti, women sewing clothing at Disney's contract plants are paid 6 cents for every $19.99 *101 Dalmatians* outfit they sew; they make 33 cents an hour. Meanwhile, Disney makes record profits and could easily pay workers a living wage for less than one half of 1 percent of the sales price of one outfit. In Vietnam, 90 percent of Nike's workers are females between the ages of 15 and 28. Nike's labor for a pair of basketball shoes (which retail for $149.50) costs Nike $1.50, 1 percent of the retail price.[108]

The executives of U.S. multinationals defend such low wages on the grounds that the wages are higher than those the workers would otherwise receive. Another argument is that the wages the multinationals pay are, at least, a living wage—that is, a wage sufficient to meet the subsistence needs of a family. But such claims, particularly the second one, are not always true. Other statistics compiled by Burn revealed, for example, that in the 1990s, Nicaraguan sweatshop workers earned in the range of $55 to $75 a month— less than half of the $165 a month their families needed to meet their most basic needs.[109] To be sure, some multinationals do pay their workers— female and male—living wages, but such multinationals seem to be more the exception rather than the rule.

Disturbed by the situation just described, contemporary socialist feminists have recently taken a lead in trying to improve not only pay but working conditions in sweatshops. Some of the strategies they have used involve the unionization of workers (even more difficult to achieve in today's developing nations than it was in the early days of union organizing in the United States) and consumer boycotts of sweatshop imports.[110]

Critiques of Marxist and Socialist Feminism

Given women's distinctly unprivileged position in the workplace, it is somewhat difficult to understand why, beginning in the 1970s, many feminists, including some Marxist feminists, abandoned *materialist* explanations of women's oppression. They turned instead to *psychological* explanations for women's oppression, explanations that could answer the question why women's status remains low irrespective of the political and economic character of the society in which they live. For example, the same Juliet Mitchell who wrote *Women's Estate* in 1971 wrote *Psychoanalysis and Feminism* several years later.[111] In the later book, Mitchell claimed that the causes of women's oppression are ultimately buried deep in the human psyche.

Mitchell rejected liberal feminists' claim that social reforms aimed at giving women more educational and occupational opportunities will make women men's equals. Women's suffrage, coeducational studies, and affirmative action policies might change the way "femininity" is expressed, but these practices could not, in her view, significantly change the overall status of women. Likewise, Mitchell rejected the claim of radical-cultural feminists that reproductive technology is the key to women's liberation, because, as she saw it, a purely biological solution cannot resolve an essentially psychological problem. Finally, Mitchell rejected the claim of classic Marxist feminists that an economic revolution aimed at overthrowing capitalism will make men and women full partners. Just because women enter the productive workforce to labor side by side with men does not mean women will return home in the evening arm in arm with men. Mitchell observed that even Mao Zedong admitted that "despite collective work, egalitarian legislation, social care of children, etc., it was too soon for the Chinese really, deeply and irrevocably to have changed their *attitudes* towards women."[112] As Mitchell saw it, attitudes toward women will never really change as long as both female and male psychology are dominated by the phallic symbol. Thus, patriarchy and capitalism must be overthrown if society is to be truly humanized.[113]

Interestingly, the publication of *Psychoanalysis and Feminism* coincided with the first few issues of *m/f*, devoted to questioning the bipolar opposition between masculinity and femininity. Launched in 1978, the first editorial of this British journal provided a strong statement of both dissatisfaction with classical Marxist models and the move toward cultural analysis. The editors placed themselves firmly within Marxism, expressing a wish to engage with class politics, but were explicitly critical of *materialist* explanations of women's oppression. Psychoanalysis was seen by the editors as essential to an understanding of gendered subjectivity. So too was discourse, the language used to interpret women's identity and activity. Their next editorial questioned the very category "women," suggesting that there is no unity to "women," or to "women's oppression," and that differing discourses simply constructed varying definitions of "women."[114] Thus began the deconstruction of "women" and the ascendancy of postmodern feminism, a type of feminism we will consider in Chapter 8.

Conclusion

As understandable as it was for many feminists to look under materialist surfaces to find deeper cultural explanations for women's oppression, it was probably a mistake for them to reject materialist explanations outright. Stevi

Jackson recently made a plea for a return to materialism—a plea that may rescue contemporary socialist feminism from undeserved neglect:

> A materialist analysis is as relevant now as it ever was. While accepting that traditional Marxists had little to say about gender divisions, that one theory cannot explain the whole of human life, the method of analysis Marx left us remains useful. There are good reasons why materialist perspectives remain necessary to grapple with the complexities of a postcolonial world, with the intersections of gender, ethnicity, and nationality. It seems evident that the material foundations and consequences of institutionalized racism, the heritage of centuries of slavery, colonialism and imperialism and the continued international division of labour are at least as important as culturally constituted difference. We live our lives now within a global system characterised by extremely stark material inequalities. Even within Western nations the material oppression suffered by women has not gone away, and for many women the situation is worsening as a result of unemployment and cuts in welfare provision. Intersections between class, gender, and racism are clearly important here, too, and need to be pursued in terms of structural patterning of inequality as well as multilayered identities. The continued vitality of approaches which deal with such inequalities is crucial for feminist politics and theory.[115]

However exciting it may be for contemporary socialist feminists to probe women's psyche from time to time, the fundamental goal of these feminists needs to remain constant: to encourage women everywhere to unite in whatever ways they can to oppose structures of oppression, inequality, and injustice.

4

Psychoanalytic Feminism

Each school of feminist thought we have considered so far has offered explanations and solutions for women's oppression that are rooted either in society's political and economic structures or in human beings' sexual and reproductive relationships, roles, and practices. Liberal feminists claimed that providing women with the same rights and opportunities men enjoy may be enough to eliminate gender inequity. Radical feminists thought otherwise. They insisted that if gender equity is our goal, we must first examine men's and women's sexual and reproductive rights and responsibilities. Only then will we understand fully why systems that foster male domination and female subordination are so persistent and prevalent. Radical-libertarian feminists claimed that women need to be liberated not only from the burdens of natural reproduction and biological motherhood but also from the restrictions of a sexual double standard that gives men sexual freedoms women are typically denied. Radical-cultural feminists disagreed. They claimed that the source of women's power is rooted in women's unique reproductive role. All children are born of women; without women *no* children would be born. Radical-cultural feminists also stressed that male sexual behavior is not worthy of women's emulation, because men frequently use sex as an instrument of control and domination rather than of love and bonding. Finally, Marxist and socialist feminists hypothesized that unless capitalist economic structures are destroyed, people will continue to be divided into two oppositional classes—the haves and the have-nots—and because of the ways in which capitalism and patriarchy reinforce each other, women, more than men, will find themselves in the ranks of the have-nots.

In contrast to liberal, radical (libertarian and cultural), and Marxist/socialist feminists, psychoanalytic feminists maintain that the fundamental explanation for women's way of acting is rooted deep in women's psyche, specifically, in women's way of thinking about themselves as women. Relying on Freudian constructs such as the pre-Oedipal stage and the Oedipal stage (explained below) and/or on Lacanian constructs such as the Symbolic order (also explained below), they claim that gender identity and hence gender inequity is rooted in a series of infantile and early childhood experiences. These experiences, most of which are accessible to us only through psychoanalysis, are, in the estimation of psychoanalytic feminists, the cause of individuals' viewing themselves in masculine or feminine terms, of thinking of themselves as boys or girls. Moreover, these same experiences are the cause of society's privileging things "masculine" over things "feminine." Hypothesizing that in a nonpatriarchal society, masculinity and femininity would be both differently constructed and valued, psychoanalytic feminists recommend that we work toward such a society by altering our early infantile childhood experiences or, more radically, transforming the linguistic structures that cause us to think of ourselves as men or women.

Sigmund Freud

By no means was Sigmund Freud a feminist, yet psychoanalytic feminists have found in his writings clues about how to better understand the causes and consequences of women's oppression. Freud's theories about psychosexual development disturbed his late-nineteenth-century Viennese contemporaries not so much because he addressed traditionally taboo topics (e.g., homosexuality, sadism, masochism, and oral and anal sex), but because he theorized that all sexual "aberrations," "variations," and "perversions" are simply stages in the development of *normal* human sexuality.[1] According to Freud, children go through distinct psychosexual developmental stages, and their gender identity as adults is the result of how well or badly they have weathered this process. Masculinity and femininity are, in other words, the product of sexual maturation. If boys develop "normally" (i.e., typically), they will end up as men who display expected masculine traits; if women develop "normally," they will end up as women who display expected feminine traits.

The theoretical bases for Freud's views on the relationship between sex and gender are found in *Three Contributions to the Theory of Sexuality*. In this work, Freud laid out his theory of psychosexual development in detail. Because adults in Freud's time equated sexual activity with reproductive genital sexuality (heterosexual intercourse), adults thought children were sexless. Dismissing this view of children's sexualities as naive, Freud argued that far from being without sexual interests, children engage in all sorts of sexual behavior. He claimed that children's sexuality is "polymorphous perverse"—that insofar as the infant is concerned, her or his entire body, especially its orifices and appendages, is sexual terrain. The infant moves from this type of "perverse" sexuality to "normal" heterosexual genital sexuality by passing through several stages. During the *oral* stage, the infant receives pleasure from sucking her or his mother's breast or her or his own thumb. During the *anal* stage, the two- or three-year-old child enjoys the sensations associated with controlling the expulsion of her or his feces. During the *phallic* stage, the three- or four-year-old child discovers that the genitals are a source of pleasure, and either resolves or fails to resolve the so-called Oedipus complex. Around age six, the child ceases to display overt sexuality and begins a period of latency that ends around puberty, when the young person enters the *genital* stage characterized by a resurgence of sexual impulses. If all goes normally during this stage, the young person's libido (defined by Freud as undifferentiated sexual energy) will be directed outward, away from autoerotic and homoerotic stimulation and toward a member of the opposite sex.

Freud stressed that the critical moment in the psychosexual drama described above occurs when the child tries to successfully resolve the Oedipus complex. He claimed that the fact that only boys have penises fundamentally affects the way in which boys and girls undergo psychosexual development. The boy's Oedipus complex stems from his natural attachment to his mother, for it is she who nurtures him. Because of the boy's feelings toward his mother, he wants to possess her—to have sexual intercourse with her—and to kill his father, the rival for his mother's attentions. Freud added, however, that the boy's hatred of his father is modulated by his coexisting love for his father. Because the boy wants his father to love him, he competes with his mother for his father's affections, experiencing increased antagonism toward her. Nevertheless, despite his increased antagonism toward his mother, the boy still wishes to possess her and would attempt to take her from his father were it not for his fear of being punished by his father. Supposedly, having seen either his mother or some other female naked, the boy speculates that these creatures without penises must have been castrated, by his father, no less. Shaken by this thought, the boy fears his father will castrate him, too, should he dare to act on his desire for his mother. Therefore, the boy distances himself from his mother, a painful process that propels him into a period of sexual latency that will not surface again until the time of puberty.[2]

During the period of sexual latency, the boy begins to develop what Freud called a superego. To the degree the superego is the son's internalization of his father's values, it is a patriarchal, social conscience. The boy who successfully resolves the Oedipus complex develops a particularly strong superego. In the course of giving up mother love (albeit out of fear of castration), he learns how to defer to the authority of his father. The boy waits his turn for his own woman, temporarily subordinating his id (instincts) to his superego (the voice of social constraints). Were it not for the trauma of the Oedipus complex and his fear of castration, the boy would fail to mature into a man ready, willing, and able at the appropriate time to claim the torch of civilization from his father.

The female experience of the Oedipus complex is dramatically different from the male experience, in Freud's estimation. Like the boy, the girl's first love object is her mother. But unlike the typical boy, whose love object will supposedly remain a woman throughout his life, the typical girl has to switch from desiring a woman to desiring a man—at first her father and later other men who take the place of the father. According to Freud, the transition from a female to a male love object begins when the girl realizes she does not have a penis, that she is castrated: "They [girls] notice the penis of a brother or play-mate, strikingly visible and of large proportions, at once recognize it as the superior counterpart of their own small and inconspicuous organ (the cli-toris), and from that time forward they fall a victim to envy for the penis."[3]

Preoccupied by her deficiency, the girl somehow discovers her mother also lacks a penis. Distraught by the sight of her mother, the girl looks to her father to make good the deficiency she shares with her mother. She does not turn away from her mother without feeling an incredible sense of loss, however. Freud claimed that like any person who loses a love object, the girl will somehow try to become the abandoned love object. Thus, the girl tries to take her mother's place with her father. As a result, the girl comes to hate her mother not only because of her mother's supposedly inferior state of being but also because her mother is a rival for the father's affections. At first the girl desires to have her father's penis, but gradually she begins to desire something even more precious—a baby, which for her is the ultimate penis substitute.[4]

Freud theorized that it is much more difficult for the girl than the boy to achieve normal adult sexuality, precisely because the girl has to stop loving a woman (her mother)[5] and start loving a man (her father). This total switch in love object requires the girl to derive sexual pleasure from the "feminine" vagina instead of the "masculine" clitoris.[6] Freud further theorized that before the phallic stage, the girl has active sexual aims. Like the boy, she wants to take sexual possession of her mother, but with her clitoris. If the girl goes through the phallic stage successfully, said Freud, she will enter the stage of latency without this desire, and when genital sensitivity reappears at puberty, she will no longer long use her clitoris actively. Instead, the girl will be content to use it passively for autoerotic masturbation or as a part of fore-play preparatory to heterosexual intercourse. But because the clitoris is not easy to desensitize, continued Freud, there is always the possibility the girl will either regress into the active clitoral stage or, exhausted from suppressing her clitoris, give up on sexuality altogether.

The long-term negative consequences of penis envy and rejection of the mother go beyond possible frigidity for the girl. Freud thought the girl's difficult passage through the Oedipus complex scars her with several undesirable gender traits as she grows toward womanhood. First, she becomes *narcissistic* as she switches from active to passive sexual aims. Girls, said Freud, seek not so much to love as to be loved; the more beautiful a girl is, the more she expects and demands to be loved. Second, she becomes *vain*. As a compensation for her original lack of a penis, the girl focuses on her total physical appearance, as if her general "good looks" could somehow make up for her penile deficiency. Finally, the girl becomes a victim of an exaggerated sense of *shame*. It is, said Freud, not uncommon for girls to be so embarrassed by the sight of their "castrated" bodies that they insist on dressing and undressing under their bedsheets.[7]

As bad as female narcissism, vanity, and shame are, Freud suggested these character flaws in women are small in comparison to those that most account for women's inferiority as a sex. As discussed earlier, the boy's fear of castration enables him to resolve his Oedipus complex successfully, to submit himself fully to the father's law. In contrast, because the girl has no such fear—since she literally has nothing to lose—she moves through the Oedipus complex slowly, resisting the father's laws indefinitely.[8] That the girl is spared the threat of castration is, said Freud, a mixed blessing, for only by being pushed, albeit out of fear, to fully internalize the father's values can an individual develop a strong superego, which holds in check the animalistic urges of the id, the force that rules one's unconscious. Because women remain resistant to the father's laws, women are supposedly less obedient than men to the civilizing forces of the superego. Speculating in this fashion, Freud concluded:

> For women the level of what is ethically normal is different from what it is in men. Their super-ego is never so inexorable, so impersonal, so independent of its emotional origins as we require it to be in men. Character traits which critics of every epoch have brought up against women—that they show less sense of justice than men, that they are less ready to submit to the great necessities of life, that they are more influenced in their judgements by feelings of affection or hostility—all these would be amply accounted for by the modification of their super-ego which we have already inferred.[9]

In other words, female moral inferiority is traceable to girls' lack of a penis. Because they do not have to worry about being castrated, girls are not nearly as motivated as boys supposedly are to become obedient rule followers whose "heads" control their "hearts."

Feminist Critiques of Freud

Because penis envy and related ideas paint such an unflattering portrait of women, many feminists were and still are angered by traditional Freudian theory. In the 1970s, feminists with otherwise widely different agendas—for example, Betty Friedan, Shulamith Firestone, and Kate Millett—made Freud a common target. They argued women's social position and powerlessness relative to men had little to do with female biology and much to do with the social construction of femininity.

Betty Friedan

According to Betty Friedan, Freud's ideas were shaped by his culture, which she described as Victorian, even though Freud wrote many of his most influential essays about female sexuality in the 1920s and 1930s. What most disturbed Friedan about Freud, however, was his supposed biological determinism. As she interpreted it, Freud's aphorism "Anatomy is destiny"[10] means a woman's reproductive role, gender identity, and sexual preference are determined by her lack of a penis, and any woman who does not follow the course nature sets for her is in some way "abnormal."[11]

Not only did Friedan reject Freud's methodology, but she also rejected what she regarded as his fixation on sex. By encouraging women to think female discontent and dissatisfaction have their roots in women's lack of the penis per se rather than in the privileged socioeconomic and cultural status its possession confers on men, Freud led women to believe, falsely, that women are defective. Moreover, by suggesting to women that in lieu of possessing the penis, they can instead have a baby, Freud lured women into the trap of the feminine mystique. Thus, Friedan faulted Freud for making a specific sexual experience she termed "vaginalism" the be-all and end-all of women's existence. In particular, she condemned him for encouraging women to be receptive, passive, dependent, and ever ready for the supposed "final goal" of their sexual life: impregnation.[12]

Shulamith Firestone

Blaming neo-Freudian therapists even more than she blamed Freud for justifying female subordination, Shulamith Firestone claimed that women's sexual passivity is not natural but simply the social result of women's physical, economic, or emotional dependence on men.[13] Rather than "helping" depressed women and children adjust to the status quo, said Firestone, neo-Freudian therapists should encourage them to rebel against it.[14] In particular, neo-Freudian therapists should not use their considerable skills to "fit" rebellious women and children into the patriarchal structure known as the nuclear family. Rather, the therapists should challenge men's abuse of women and children within the confines of "home, sweet home."[15]

The more she reflected on the causes of women's and children's oppression, the more Firestone became convinced that human beings should abolish the nuclear family and, with it, the incest taboo, "the root cause of the Oedipus complex."[16] No longer having to resolve the Oedipus complex, children would not be forced to distinguish between "bad," *sexual* feelings for their parents and "good," *loving* feelings for their parents. Were children permitted to combine their sexual and loving feelings for their parents, said Firestone, the power dynamics between men and women as well as parents and children would be fundamentally altered. Just as importantly, no particular form of sexuality would be proclaimed "normal." Gay men, lesbians, bisexuals, and transsexuals would be regarded as just as normal as heterosexuals.

Kate Millet

Like Firestone, Millett directed her critique of Freudianism more against neo-Freudian therapists than against Freud himself. In particular, she faulted neo-Freudian therapists for claiming that male sexual aggression is rooted in the "biological . . . necessity for overcoming the resistance of the sexual object."[17] She observed that in their attempt to prove this claim, neo-Freudian therapists sometimes went to ridiculous extremes, looking for male aggression everywhere, including in such unlikely species as the prehistoric cichlid fish. Supposedly, the males of this species of fish are able to impregnate the females of their species only because the latter respond to their aggressive advances with "awe." Millett used this example to show, as Friedan might, that there is little sound evidence to support the theory that nature has determined men play first fiddle simply because they have a penis.[18]

Decidedly resistant to all types of biological determinism, Millett found the concept of penis envy a transparent instance of male egocentrism. Instead of celebrating woman's power to give birth, said Millett, neo-Freudian therapists interpret it as a pathetic attempt to possess a substitute penis: "Freudian logic has succeeded in converting childbirth, an impressive female accomplishment . . . into nothing more than a hunt for a male organ."[19] Had Freud made the clitoris, not the penis, the center of his analysis of female sexuality, mused Millett, he might have been better able to understand, for example, the problems that truly ailed his eighteen-year-old "hysterical" patient, Dora.

A bright and intelligent woman, Dora was a member of a typical Viennese middle-class family: father, mother, son, daughter. From Freud's point of view, Dora's family exhibited all the classic signs of "Oedipal behavior," with father and daughter aligned against mother and son. To make matters even worse, Dora's father had a lover, a longtime family friend, Frau K., whose husband, Herr K., had had sexual designs on Dora from the time she was fourteen. Although Dora had a close relationship with Frau K.—indeed, the girl found in the woman the affectionate mother her biological mother had never been—Dora terminated this relationship as soon as she realized Frau K. was her father's lover and Herr K. had sexual designs on her. When she confronted her father about his infidelity and Herr K.'s lechery, he denied everything and attributed his daughter's "fantasies" to her being "hysterical." When she was brought to Freud for treatment, Freud believed Dora's account of her father's adulterous behavior and Herr K.'s lecherous advances. Nevertheless, he failed to reassure Dora that the bad behavior of these two men was the cause of her "hysteria." Instead, Freud told Dora her *real* problems were her sexual jealousy of Frau K. and her inability to be sexually aroused by Herr K.'s advances. Apparently unimpressed by Freud's diagnosis, Dora terminated treatment with him after three months, announcing she would rather be dead than married. Freud interpreted her abrupt termination of treatment as an instance of transference, causing Dora to shift her negative feelings toward her father and Herr K. to Freud himself. Supposedly, she sought revenge on all men by rejecting Freud.[20]

Maintaining that Freud's treatment of Dora was unacceptable, Millett claimed that Dora's so-called hysteria was a clear case of justifiable anger. A feminist psychotherapist would regard Dora's reasons for not wishing to get married as quite rational, given the emotional wringer through which she had been squeezed. At the very least, a feminist psychotherapist would tell Dora she had every right to accuse her father of adultery and Herr K. of a form of sexual harassment akin to rape.[21] Told that Freud suspected Herr K. and Dora's father were in cahoots, a feminist psychotherapist would conclude Freud failed to serve the best interests of his patient, precisely because Freud belonged to Herr K.'s and Dora's father's patriarchal club.

Early Feminist Appropriations of Freud

As it so happens, several early twentieth-century psychoanalysts, including Alfred Adler, Karen Horney, and Clara Thompson, largely agreed with the points made by feminist critics of Freud. Like Friedan, Firestone, and Millett, they believed that women's (and men's) gender identity, gender behavior, and sexual orientation are not the result of biological facts. Rather, these facets of a human being are the product of social values. Although Alder, Horney, and Thompson did not refer to themselves as psychoanalytic feminists, their work is quite feminist in spirit and content. They helped reinterpret Freud's work to demonstrate that women's lack of a penis is important only because patriarchal society privileges men over women.

Alfred Adler

According to Adler, men and women are fundamentally the same because all human beings are born helpless. Our infantile experience of powerlessness is the source of our lifelong struggle to overcome feelings of impotency. Adler insisted that our biology, specifically the mere fact some of us have penises and others of us have vaginas, does not determine our destiny. On the contrary, our so-called creative selves have the power to shape our lives in any direction we want. Indeed, our creative selves have the power to interpret our biological givens, for example, as positively or negatively as we choose.[22] Thus, women's lack of a penis in and of itself is no better or worse than men's lack of a vagina or uterus. The value of the presence or absence of these organs depends on the value individuals assign to having a penis or a vagina.

Given his views about the powers of the creative self, Adler was able to provide nondeterministic explanations for why so-called neurotic women suffer from a sense of inferiority and are plagued by "masculinity complexes." Acknowledging that Western society is a patriarchal one in which women "are determined and maintained by privileged males for the glory of male domination,"[23] Adler hypothesized that as long as patriarchy exists, so-called neurotic women will exist. A "neurotic" woman is simply a woman thwarted by patriarchy in her struggle to overcome her feelings of infantile helplessness. By recognizing that all human beings, be they women or men, have creative selves and desire to empower themselves through thought and action, Adler provided "neurotic" women with the rationale to heal themselves: Not they but patriarchal society is sick.

Karen Horney

Like Adler, Karen Horney emphasized the role environment plays in a person's growth as a person. A medical school student in turn-of-the-century Berlin, Horney experienced firsthand how patriarchal society constricts women's creative development. She claimed women's feelings of inferiority originated not in women's recognition of their castration but in women's realization of their social subordination. Although Horney conceded women are symbolically castrated in that they have been denied the power the penis represents, she refused to accept that ordinary women are radically defective beings simply because they lack penises. She instead argued that patriarchal culture first forces women to be feminine (passive, masochistic, narcissistic) and then tries to convince women they *like* being feminine. In this light, women who want what society considers truly valuable—namely, masculine things—will be labeled "sick," as suffering from a "masculinity complex," or as "flying from womanhood."[24] Refusing to consider women who want to play a major role in society as mentally ill, Horney instead described them as persons struggling to achieve a balance between three pulls in their character: the self-effacing pull, the resigned pull, and the expansive pull. Not content with their powerless status in society, their behind-the-scenes role, women who choose to move beyond "femininity" are creating an ideal self that will include masculine as well as feminine traits. Far from being mentally ill, such women are psychologically healthy to an amazing degree. In other words, these women know that society, not biology, has caused them to be the way they are. They theorize that as soon as they learn how to view *themselves* as men's equals, society will have little, if any power over women's destiny.[25]

Clara Thompson

Clara Thompson sided with Adler and Horney in portraying human development as a process of growth away from one's biology and toward mastery of one's environment. Working within the framework of interpersonal psychology—which views people's relationships with others as crucial to their development and well-being—Thompson explained female passivity as the product of a set of asymmetrical male-female relationships in which constant deferral to male authority causes women to have weaker egos than men do. Female and male identities do not emanate from unchanging female and male biologies, in Thompson's estimation. Rather, they emerge from ever-changing social ideas about what it means to be male or female. Along with Adler and Horney, Thompson believed women's guilt, inferiority, and self-hatred are grounded not in mere biological facts but in society's interpretation of these facts. Thus, the transformation of the legal, political, economic, and social institutions that shape society is a necessary step in the transformation of women's psychology.[26]

In reinterpreting Freud's observations, Adler, Horney, and Thompson moved beyond Freud. First, they spoke of masculine bias and male dominance and offered a political as well as psychoanalytic analysis of women's situation, something Freud did not do. Second, they proposed a unitary theory of human development that did not set men and women traveling down separate developmental tracks toward separate developmental goals. Instead, Adler, Horney, and Thompson insisted that all human beings—men *and* women—want the same thing, the opportunity to shape their own destiny creatively and actively. Third, and perhaps most important, these early feminist psychoanalysts all insisted that the self is an identity that develops uniquely and individually in each person, growing out of the interface between nature and culture. For Adler, Horney, and Thompson, there is not *one* universally healthy, normal, and natural male self for men and *another* universally healthy, normal, and natural female self for women. Rather, there are as many human selves as there are individual people.[27]

Later Feminist Appropriations of Freud

Later psychoanalytic feminists such as Dorothy Dinnerstein and Nancy Chodorow also worked to reinterpret Freud's texts. These theorists maintained that by focusing less on the Oedipal stage and more on the pre-Oedipal stage of psychosexual development, they could provide a better explanation of how patriarchal society constructs sexuality and gender. Many of society's views about women's inferiority and men's superiority, said Dinnerstein and Chodorow, are traceable to women's doing all or most of the mothering work in society. Were men to mother just as much as women do, boys and girls would grow up differently. They would realize that neither sex is inferior or superior to the other, and that both sexes merit equal respect.

Dorothy Dinnerstein:
The Mermaid and the Minotaur

According to Dinnerstein, our culture's gender arrangements strongly influence how men and women conceive of themselves and each other, and the resulting portrait is not pretty. In it, women are depicted as "mermaids" and men as "minotaurs." Dinnerstein wrote: "The treacherous mermaid, seductive and impenetrable female representative of the dark and magic underwater world from which our life comes and in which we cannot live, lures voyagers to their doom. The fearsome minotaur, gigantic and eternally infantile offspring of a mother's unnatural lust, male representative of mindless, greedy power, insatiably devours live human flesh."[28]

Because Dinnerstein found this portrait ugly, she sought to explain why we continue to paint it over and over again, albeit in different hues. The answer to our pathological need to make monsters of ourselves is buried, she speculated, deep in our psychosexual development, in the pre-Oedipal stage. The infant's relationship with her or his mother is profoundly symbiotic because the infant is initially incapable of distinguishing between herself or himself and the mother. Because the maternal body is the infant's first encounter with the material or physical universe, the infant experiences the mother's body as a symbol of an unreliable and unpredictable universe. The mother is the source of pleasure and pain for the infant, who is never certain whether the mother will meet his or her physical and psychological needs. As a result, the infant grows up feeling very ambivalent toward mother figures (women) and what they represent (the material/physical universe, or nature).

Not wanting to reexperience utter dependence on an all-powerful force, men seek to control both women and nature, to exert power over them. Fearing the power of the mother within themselves, women concomitantly seek to be controlled by men. Men's need to control women and women's need to be controlled by men tragically leads, said Dinnerstein, to a *mis*shapen set of six gender arrangements, which together constitute a paradigm for destructive human relations in general.

Dinnerstein pointed to men's greater sexual possessiveness as the first characteristic of currently skewed gender relationships. Men hope to overcome their past inability to totally control their mothers by trying to totally control their wives or girlfriends. Given men's intense desire to control women, when a woman is unfaithful to a man, the man feels the same despair he felt upon realizing his mother had a self separate from his own, a self whose will often conflicted with his. This refelt sense of despair, said Dinnerstein, explains men's violent reactions to their wives' or girlfriends' "infidelities," ranging from extramarital affairs with male lovers to pajama parties with female friends.

Curiously, although many women accept men's sexual possessiveness of women as some sort of right, women do not generally claim the same right for themselves. Dinnerstein explained this asymmetry as follows: Because a woman fears the power of the mother within herself, she is always in search of a man who can control her. But because a man does not represent "mother" to her in the way she represents "mother" to him, she needs him less than he needs her. No matter how deep the symbiosis she achieves with him, it will not equal the kind of symbiosis she had with her mother in the past or that she could have with another woman/mother now or in the future. Consequently, if a man leaves a woman, she will not feel the same intensity of grief she felt when her original mother left her.[29]

Muted female erotic impulsivity is the second mark of current gender arrangements, according to Dinnerstein. A muted female eroticism is one oriented exclusively toward male pleasure. Through sexual intercourse, the woman seeks to satisfy the man, and whatever pleasure she experiences is experienced vicariously as delight in his satisfaction. Her own sexual wants and needs must go unattended, for were she to insist on their fulfillment, she and the man would be in for a shock. They would both reexperience the rage they felt as infants when they first recognized their mothers as independent selves who had lives and interests of their own. Moreover, were she to let her partner totally satisfy her, the woman would feel enormous guilt for having abandoned her primary love object (mother and women) for a secondary love object (father and men). Better to deprive herself of sexual pleasure, she senses, than suffer the pangs of conscience.[30]

This guilt on the part of women contributes to the third feature of the current gender relations identified by Dinnerstein: the idea that sexual excitement and personal sentiment must be tied together for women but not for men. Because of the guilt she feels about abandoning her mother, a woman refuses to allow herself even vicarious pleasure in sex unless the relationship is infused with the same type of all-encompassing love that existed between her and her mother. In order to feel good about a sexual liaison, a woman must believe the relationship underlying it is like the one she initially had with her mother: deep, binding, and strong. Only such a sexual liaison can possibly justify her rejection of her mother. To forsake total symbiosis with her mother for a one-night stand with a man, for example, is to settle for a superficial intimacy that cannot approximate the deep intimacy of the mother-child relationship.

In contrast to women, men are notorious for their ability to separate sex from intense emotional commitment. This ability is also rooted in the mother-infant relationship, especially in the loss of the illusion of infant omnipotence. In the male-female sexual relationship, the man feels especially vulnerable because a woman "can reinvoke in him the unqualified, boundless, helpless passion of infancy."[31] Depending on how much a man needs to be in charge of his destiny, he will be threatened by the overwhelming powers of sexual passion. Once again, he will fear being overwhelmed by a woman able to shatter his ego by withdrawing herself from him. Thus, he will seek to remain in control of the sexual act, distancing himself from the woman with whom he is being intimate.

Dinnerstein claimed the fourth hallmark of current gender arrangements is that a woman is viewed as an "it," whereas a man is seen as an "I." Because the child encounters a woman before the child is able to distinguish an "I" (center of self-interested sentience and perception) from an "it" (an impersonal force of nature), Dinnerstein speculated that the child initially perceives its mother not as a person but as an object. In contrast, because the father usually plays a small role in an infant's upbringing, taking on a larger part in his child's life only after the child has made the I-it distinction, the child has less difficulty recognizing him as an "I," not an "it." Apparently, children perceive their fathers, but not their mothers, as persons with lives of their own. Dinnerstein also hypothesized that human beings fear the power of an "it" more than the power of an "I." In her estimation, this state of affairs explains why "it-like" female power, in the private or public realm, is ultimately more threatening to both men and women than male power. Thus, not only do men feel a need to control women but women also feel a need to be controlled by men.[32]

The fifth characteristic of current gender arrangements is rooted in our general ambivalence toward the flesh, according to Dinnerstein. We hate the flesh because it limits our control and because we know it will ultimately die, yet we love it because it gives us pleasure. Our general ambivalence toward the body is, however, intensified in the case of women. On the one hand, women's bodies are powerful because they represent the forces of life; on the other hand, women's bodies are disgusting because they bleed and ooze. Because men's bodies do not carry as much symbolic baggage as women's do, men can imagine their own bodies to be largely free of the impurities and problems associated with women's bodies. Rather unfairly, men dispel any remaining ambivalence they may have about the male body by displacing their fears of the flesh onto the female body. The denigration of the female body as dirty, foul, and sinful causes women to deny their bodily core of self-respect, which then deprives women of the ability to reject confidently the negative feelings projected onto their bodies. As a result, many women come to hate their bodies and to punish them in many ways.[33] Bulimia, anorexia, and overeating may at least in part be attributed to women's "flesh" problems.

Dinnerstein observed that the final characteristic of current gender arrangements is the tacit agreement between men and women that men should go out into the public sphere and women should stay behind within the private sphere. Women funnel their energies into symbiosis and personal relationships, eschewing enterprise for fear of putting power back into the hands of women, while men make enterprise their be all and end all, avoiding symbiosis and personal relationships for fear of losing control. Regrettably, the terms of this bargain permit both men and women to remain perpetual children, said Dinnerstein. Rather than taking responsibility for themselves and their world, men and women continue to play the kind of sex and gender games they should have stopped playing generations ago.

As Dinnerstein saw it, our destructive gender arrangements are the direct result of women's role in child-rearing and our subsequent tendency to blame women for everything wrong about ourselves, especially that we are limited beings destined to err, decay, and die. We blame mother/woman for our limitations, speculated Dinnerstein, because it is mother/woman who most likely presides when we skin our knees, break our toys, get the flu, and flunk our exams. Dinnerstein insisted we must stop blaming mother/women for the human condition if we want to overcome our destructive gender arrangements—a set of relationships symptomatic of our increasing inability to deal with each other and our world. Dinnerstein's solution to the scape-goating of women was to propose a dual-parenting system. She believed that such a system would have four positive consequences.

First, said Dinnerstein, dual parenting would enable us to stop projecting our ambivalence about carnality and mortality onto one parent, the female. Because both parents would be involved in the parenting process from the infant's birth onward, we would no longer associate our bodily limitations with the female parent only. It would not even occur to us to blame our car-nality and mortality on women. Thus, we would all be forced to deal with the human condition as a given, rather than mother's fault.

Second, in Dinnerstein's estimation, dual parenting would enable us to overcome our ambivalence about growing up. We remain childish because we approach life as if it were a drama in which women are assigned one role to play and men another. Women play the nurturant mother-goddess role, while men play the mighty world-builder role. Yet both sexes not only doubt whether they can perform these roles satisfactorily, but also wish to break free of them. With the institution of dual parenting, these roles would no longer be split along gender lines. As a result, women would no longer feel totally responsible for nurturing, and men would no longer feel totally responsible for making the world go round. When men as well as women engage in mothering and women as well as men engage in enterprise, the roles of mother goddess and of world builder would be divested of their destructive mystique.

Third, Dinnerstein insisted that dual parenting would help us overcome our ambivalence toward the existence of other separate beings. In the present situa-tion, we do not fully acknowledge each other as autonomous agents. We tend to view other people as means toward an end—the end of making ourselves feel better about ourselves—rather than as separate beings, each of whom is an end unto himself or herself. With the inception of dual parenting, we would not require others to validate our existence. In other words, once we are free to choose whatever combination of nurturing and enterprising activities we prefer, we would no longer need from each other as much confirmation and reinforcement that our actions are valuable and necessary.

Finally, Dinnerstein believed that dual parenting would help us overcome our ambivalence about enterprise. All people, but especially men, tend to use world building as a defense against death. Indeed, the wonders of civilization can be read as the tragic testimony of a species that strives to achieve the good, the true, and the beautiful, knowing full well everyone and everything are doomed to disintegration. Given his traditional role as world builder, society has not permitted man to express reservations about the ultimate worth of his worldly projects. But because of her traditional role as mother goddess—the "wise one" who is not easily deceived by the pomp and circumstance of civilization—society has given woman some license to articulate her misgivings about civilization. Indeed, said Dinnerstein, women often play the role of court jesters, poking fun at the games men play; women's irreverence serves to release the tension that ripples through the world of enterprise. As a result, things never seem bad enough for us to change the course of history dramatically. But, observed Dinnerstein, dual world building and dual child-rearing would enable all of us to see just how bad the world situation is. Because men and women would have an *equal* role in world building as well as child-rearing, women would no longer be able to play the role of court jesters. With nowhere to hide, not even in laughter, both sexes would be required to put aside their games to reshape a fundamentally misshapen world.[34]

Nancy Chodorow:
The Reproduction of Mothering

Less interested in sexual relationships than Dinnerstein, Nancy Chodorow wondered why women *want* to mother even when they do not have to do so.[35] Rejecting Freud's idea that for women babies are substitutes for penises, Chodorow found the answer to her question in a reconsideration of the pre-Oedipal stage of human psychosexual development. She pointed to the different "object-relational" experiences infants have with their mothers. According to Chodorow, the infant boy's pre-Oedipal relationship with his mother is sexually charged in a way that it is not for the infant girl. Feeling a sexual current between himself and his mother, the infant boy senses his mother's body is not like his body. As he enters the Oedipal stage, the growing boy senses how much of a problem his mother's otherness is. He cannot remain attached to her (i.e., overwhelmingly in love with her) without risking his father's wrath. Not willing to take this risk, the son separates from his mother. What makes this process of separation less painful for the son than it might otherwise be is his dawning realization that power and prestige are to be had through identification with men—in this case, the father. The boy's increasing contempt for women supposedly helps him define himself in opposition to the female sex his mother represents.[36]

In contrast to the mother-son pre-Oedipal relationship, the mother-daughter pre-Oedipal relationship is characterized by what Chodorow termed "prolonged symbiosis" and "narcissistic over-identification." Because both the daughter and the mother are female, the infant girl's sense of gender and self is continuous with that of her mother. During the Oedipal stage, however, the mother-daughter symbiosis is weakened as the growing girl begins to desire what her father symbolizes: the autonomy and independence that characterizes a subjectivity, or an "I," on the one hand and the ability to sexually satisfy a woman—in this case, her mother—on the other. Thus, as Chodorow interpreted it, penis envy arises for the girl both because the penis symbolizes male power *and* because it is the sexual organ that apparently satisfies her mother: "Every step of the way . . . a girl develops her relationship to her father while looking back at her mother—to see if her mother is envious, to make sure she is in fact separate, to see if she is really independent. Her turn to her father is both an attack on her mother and an expression of love for her."[37]

Although most girls do finally transfer their primary love from a female to a male object, Chodorow suggested this transfer of love is never complete. Whether a girl develops into a heterosexual woman or not, she will probably find her strongest emotional connections with other women. Thus the pre-Oedipal mother-daughter relationship provides a reference point for female friendships and lesbian relationships: The original mother-daughter symbiosis is never totally severed.[38]

Chodorow theorized that the psychosexual development of boys and girls has several social implications. The boy's separateness from his mother is the cause of his limited ability to relate deeply to others; this emotional deficiency, however, prepares him well for work in the public sphere, which values single-minded efficiency, a "survival-of-the-fittest" mentality, and the ability to distance oneself from others so as to assess them objectively and dispassionately.[39] In contrast, the girl's connectedness to her mother is the cause of her ability to relate to others, to weave intimate and intricate human connections—the kind of relationships that hold the private sphere together. Unfortunately, this very ability is also what makes it difficult for a girl to create a place for herself in the public world. Precisely because women develop permeable ego boundaries, women will tend to merge their own interests with the interests of others, making the identification and pursuit of any independent interests discomfiting.

Because of her view that women's capacity for relatedness is overdeveloped and men's underdeveloped and that men's capacity for separateness is overdeveloped and women's underdeveloped, Chodorow, like Dinnerstein, hypothesized that a dual-parenting system would eliminate these asymmetries. Were children reared by both their mothers and their fathers, boys and girls would grow up equally capable of merging and separating, of valuing their relationships with others and taking pride in their autonomy. More specifically, dual-parented children would realize both men and women are self-interested as well as other-directed.[40] Finally, dual-parented children would no longer view the home as women's domain and the workplace as men's domain. On the contrary, they would grow up thinking that all human beings should spend some of their time out in the world working and the rest of it at home with their families and friends.

Dinnerstein Versus Chodorow

Common to both Chodorow and Dinnerstein is the conviction that the oppression of *women* originates in the female monopoly on mothering. Explanations of female subordination that focus on differences in physical strength, on the workings of capital, or on the laws of society miss this crucial point. Despite this agreement, differences of substance as well as style characterize Dinnerstein's and Chodorow's respective analyses.

Dinnerstein drew a stark picture of current gender relations, accentuating some of the sadder moments in our psychosexual development. Because our experience of being mothered has been so overwhelming and even terrifying, Dinnerstein described human beings' transition from infancy to adulthood as the slow and painful process of rejecting the mother, of devaluing women and all things female. On account of his sexual *dissimilarity* to his mother, a boy can make this break completely, thereby realizing his desire for independence, for omnipotence. On account of her sexual *similarity* to her mother, however, a girl can never totally break from her mother. A woman, precisely because she is a woman, will remain less than autonomous as long as the experience of self-definition is understood largely as the process of maternal and therefore female rejection.

In contrast, Chodorow painted a portrait of mothering less preoccupied with the image of the omnipotent mother who must be controlled, if not by domination, then by rejection. As Chodorow saw it, the infant's connection with his or her mother is not precipitously shattered, with all of the rage and vindictiveness such a sharp break entails. Instead, the connection is gradually eroded, especially for girls. This more temperate approach suggests that for Chodorow, the measure of difference between males and females is *how connected* they are to their mothers, whereas for Dinnerstein it is *how separate* they are from their mothers.

In the main, Chodorow's and Dinnerstein's differences from each other are more a matter of emphasis than substance. Dinnerstein focused on men's *and* women's inability to overcome in adulthood the sense of powerlessness they felt as infants, when their lives depended on the seemingly capricious will of their mothers. Chodorow emphasized men and women's unconscious need as adults to re-create their infantile experience of symbiosis with their mothers. On the whole, Dinnerstein tended to present the mother-child relationship as basically pathological, whereas Chodorow tended to present it as fundamentally healthy.

Whatever their differences, both Dinnerstein and Chodorow were, as noted, equally insistent that dual parenting is the key solution to the state of affairs caused by nearly exclusively female mothering. Mothering must become *parenting*, if women are to cease being the scapegoats of wailing infants and raging men. Men must become equal parents with women in order to free women from the *sole* responsibility for loving and men from the *sole* responsibility for working. Dual parenting would, in the estimation of both Dinnerstein and Chodorow, break down the sexual division of labor completely. Men would be required to spend as much time fathering as women spend mothering, and women would be expected to work alongside men in the workaday world. As a result of this new arrangement, both men and women would develop into autonomous, nurturant people who are equally comfortable in both the private and the public domains.

Critiques of Dinnerstein and Chodorow

Feminists critics challenged Dinnerstein and Chodorow for three reasons. First, they faulted these two theorists for claiming that the root causes of women's oppression are psychological rather than social.[41] According to Dinnerstein and Chodorow, our legal, political, economic, and cultural systems would be dramatically different if women did not want or need to mother. Women are not mothers because law, politics, economics, or culture has forced them to be mothers; rather, women are mothers because they want or need to be mothers. Feminist critics of Dinnerstein and Chodorow countered that woman's want or need to mother is caused not by psychological states of mind but by material conditions—that is, by specific social conditions such as men's typically higher pay in the public labor force. In a society that gives far greater economic rewards to men than to women, it makes sense for women to convince themselves they *like* staying at home with their children. Women would stop wanting and needing to mother if social conditions were such that women were paid as much as or more than men in the public labor force, for example.

Second, feminist critics objected to what they perceived as both Dinnerstein's and Chodorow's failure to appreciate the diverse forms family structure takes. In particular, they faulted Dinnerstein and Chodorow for explaining the pre-Oedipal and Oedipal stages solely in terms of the structures of the two-parent, heterosexual family and for failing to explain it in terms of differently-structured families. There are, after all, many sorts of family structures, ranging from single-parent structures to blended-family and extended-family structures. Moreover, sometimes a child's parents are both female, as when a lesbian couple rears the child; or sometimes a child's parents are both male, as when a gay couple rears him or her. If the Oedipus complex is indeed universal, richer accounts of how it plays out in different family structures must be provided. By focusing on the two-parent, heterosexual family structure, Dinnerstein and Chodorow missed an opportunity to formulate a *fully* feminist psychoanalytic theory.

Third, feminist critics objected to Dinnerstein's and Chodorow's preferred solution for women's oppression, the creation and maintenance of a dual-parenting system. Jean Bethke Elshtain, for example, singled out Dinnerstein for especially strong words. Dinnerstein, said Elshtain, believed women have less of a need to control things and people than men have. As a result of their special symbiotic relationships to their mothers, girls supposedly grow up to be nurturant, affectionate, and caring persons who are "less avid than men as hunters and killers, as penetrators of Mother Nature's secrets, plunderers of her treasure, outwitters of her constraints."[42] If this observation indeed applies to how women's psychology is shaped, asked Elshtain, what will happen to women's positive qualities when women spend as much time in the public realm as men currently do? Absolutely nothing, responded Dinnerstein. Women will remain caring, compassionate, and considerate, "even as they gain public roles, authority, power."[43] Not satisfied by Dinnerstein's response, Elshtain asked why we should assume that men are capable of developing good feminine qualities in the private realm, but not also assume that women are capable of developing bad masculine qualities in the public realm? If men can become more nurturant by taking care of their babies, then it seems women can become more aggressive by doing battle in the nation's boardrooms, courtrooms, and hospitals. In sum, observed Elshtain,

Dinnerstein failed to ask herself what will be lost as well as gained for men and women in a dual-parenting/dual-working system.

Whereas Elshtain singled out Dinnerstein for special criticism, another critic, Alice Rossi, targeted Chodorow. Rossi claimed that Chodorow failed to take seriously the possibility that, in the end, allowing men to care for infants may prove disastrous.[44] She claimed women's biology as well as psychology equips women to perceive their infants' needs so as to better serve the children. Men's biology and psychology does not. Thus, Rossi speculated that the traditional caricature of the bumbling father pinning the diaper on his baby may have some basis in biosocial fact.[45]

Rossi also faulted Chodorow for thinking that girls reared in a dual-parent family will have no more difficulty separating from their mothers than boys will. Again appealing to women's biology and psychology, Rossi emphasized that the girl's *female body* will always cause her to identify with her mother in a way that the boy, with his *male body,* cannot. Even if men and women mothered, their bodily differences would still exist. It is, for example, women's breasts, not men's, that swell with milk. Still, conceded Rossi, entrusting babies to men—giving dual parenting a try—is preferable to parents' handing their babies over to institutionalized childcare, where the biological ties currently holding human beings together are further weakened.[46]

Another feminist critic, Janice Raymond, offered a critique of dual parenting that applied equally well to Dinnerstein and Chodorow. Raymond observed that dual parenting *seems* like a reasonable way to transform distorted gender relations. After all, if Dinnerstein is right that "male absence from child rearing" is leading the world to nuclear war and ecological chaos, then by all means let fathers spend as much time in the nursery as mothers do. However, warned Raymond, to insist dual parenting is *the* solution to the human malaise is to elevate men again to the status of "saviors." Men's rapid insertion into the nursery, unaccompanied by women's rapid promotion in the work world, threatens to give men even more power than they now have—personal and psychic power within the family as well as political and economic power outside the family. Additionally, to present dual parenting as the solution to all our gender woes is again to neglect "gyn-affection," or woman-to-woman attraction and interaction.[47] Specifically, dual parenting, as presented by Dinnerstein and Chodorow, does not in any way compare and contrast lesbian households in which one women stays at home and the other goes to work with lesbian households in which neither woman is the primary parent or primary worker.

As Raymond saw it, that *women* mainly mother is not the problem. Rather, the real problem is that women mother when, where, and how *men* want them to. Girls are taught to direct their love away from women and toward men. Girls see their mothers loving their fathers in a special way—so special that girls surmise men must be worthy of a love that women themselves do not deserve. Raymond speculated that were girls to see their mothers loving other women in an equally special way, girls would grow up with more positive feelings about themselves and other women. Despite their mutual claim that female bonds are stronger and deeper than male bonds, observed Raymond, neither Dinnerstein nor Chodorow envisioned powerful and strong women joining together in communities of care—communities supportive enough to give women as well as children the kind of love they would not otherwise find.[48] Women do not need men to help them mother.

Adding force to Raymond's critique of Dinnerstein and Chodorow were the words of Adrienne Rich. Rich observed that both Dinnerstein and Chodorow accepted without question the assumption that men are the appropriate object of women's sexual love and emotional energy. Specifically, she commented that both Dinnerstein and Chodorow are "stuck . . . trying to reform a man-made institution—compulsory heterosexuality—as if, despite profound emotional impulses and complementarities drawing women toward women, there is a mystical/biological heterosexual inclination, a 'preference' or 'choice' that draws women toward men."[49] Rich found it particularly puzzling that neither Dinnerstein nor Chodorow, both of whom focused on the pre-Oedipal stage, where mother love reigns supreme, thought to reject the institution of compulsory heterosexuality. Lesbianism rather than heterosexuality would seem to be "normal" for women. Why on earth, then, do girls decide to trade the fulfilling intensity of pre-Oedipal mother love for Oedipal father love? That seems the appropriate question for feminists to ask.

Juliet Mitchell: Psychoanalysis and Feminism

Although Juliet Mitchell did not share Dinnerstein's and Chodorow's interest in dual parenting, she, too, sought to use the feminist ideas buried in Freud's views on the unconscious.[50] As Mitchell understood Freud's theory, it is not some simpleminded enunciation of the slogan "Biology is destiny." On the contrary, his theory demonstrates how social beings emerge from merely biological ones. Psychosexual development is a process of the "social interpretation" of biology, *not* the inexorable manifestation of biological destiny.[51] Although Freud studied psychosexual development among a specific group of people (the petite bourgeoisie of nineteenth-century Vienna), said

Mitchell, his analysis is applicable to psychosexual development among any group of people. However, continued Mitchell, it is important to separate the particular emphases of Freud's analysis, its incidental features, from its general parameters, its essence. There are, after all, certain things about nineteenth-century Viennese, petit bourgeois psychosexual development that are unique to it—that do not apply, for example, to twenty-first-century American, working-class psychosexual development, or to twenty-first-century Chinese, upper-class psychosexual development. Still, contemporary American and Chinese biological families, like the Viennese biological family, seem to play out the family drama Freud names the Oedipal situation.[52]

When Mitchell agreed with Freud that the Oedipal situation is universal, she meant that without some sort of prohibition on incest, human society is an impossibility. According to anthropologist Claude Lévi-Strauss, on whose work Mitchell relied, if sexual relations are permitted within the biological family, there will be no impetus for the biological family to form reproductive alliances between itself and other biological families to create the expanded network we call "society"[53] and to add to the genetic diversity of humankind.

As Lévi-Strauss explained, the incest taboo is the impetus that, by forbidding sexual relations within the biological family, forces people to form other, larger, social organizations. Of course, a mere ban on sexual intercourse within biological families is not enough. There must also be some way to facilitate sexual intercourse between biological families. Lévi-Strauss claimed this facilitation takes the form of an exchange system between biological families—specifically, the exchange of women from one group of men to another.[54] Because a woman is forbidden by the incest taboo from marrying her brother or father, the men in her biological family will push her to marry a man they select outside of the biological family. According to Lévi-Strauss, this male-controlled exchange of women constitutes humans' "decisive break" with the beasts. Moreover, added Mitchell, men's exchange of women rather than vice versa accounts for the *patriarchal* character of human society.[55]

Feminist Critiques of Mitchell

Mitchell's feminist critics found much of her analysis useful, but they remain unconvinced by it. They asked Mitchell why *women* rather than *men* are exchanged and why the *father* rather than the *mother* has power over the family. Mitchell sought the answers to these questions in Freud's *Totem and Taboo*, in which he described the primal murder of an original mythical father. The totem is the symbol of the father, and associated with it are two taboos, one against destruction of the totem and one against incest. In the myth, a group of brothers bands together to kill the feared and envied father—feared because of his power, envied because of his harem of women. After their act of patricide, the brothers, feeling very guilty about what they have done and not knowing quite what to substitute for the law of the father, eventually reestablish the father's two taboos. Freud commented that whereas the brothers' reinscription of the *totem* taboo is "founded wholly on emotional motives," their reinscription of the *incest* taboo is founded on a practical as well as an emotional basis.

> Sexual desires do not unite men but divide them. Though the brothers had banded together in order to overcome their father, they were all one another's rivals in regard to the women. Each of them would have wished, like his father, to have all women to himself. The new organization would have collapsed in a struggle of all against all, for none of them was of such overmastering strength as to be able to take on his father's part with success. Thus the brothers had no alternative, if they were to live together, but—not, perhaps, until they had passed through many dangerous crises—to institute the law against incest, by which they all alike renounced the women whom they desired and who had been their chief motive for dispatching their father.[56]

In sum, the brothers must refrain from incest; only then can patriarchy, in which they have a vested interest, thrive.

Although Mitchell's feminist critics dismissed the myth of the primal crime as a mere *myth,* Mitchell countered that the myth is an extraordinarily powerful one that speaks loudly to the collective human unconscious. The figure of the father stands for the desire of human beings to be transcendent, to assert their will, to be somehow in control of their lives. The father (and here Mitchell was borrowing from Jacques Lacan, discussed below) is "he who is ultimately capable of saying 'I am who I am.'"[57] The father represents success in the so-called Symbolic order. He is disentangled from confusions and struggles. He is clear-thinking, farseeing, and powerful. Because he can say, "I am who I am," he can name things for what he wants them to be. Yet, however seductive the image of the transcendent father and the omnipotent patriarch may be, the image is also the source of women's oppression, conceded Mitchell. To the degree that the successful resolution of the Oedipus complex leads to patriarchy as well as civilization, continued Mitchell, it needs to be reinterpreted. There must be some way to explain psychosexual development that does not purchase civilization at women's expense.[58]

Responding in part to Mitchell's challenge, Sherry Ortner, a noted feminist anthropologist and theorist, made the following observation: "The

Oedipus complex is part of a theory of the development of the person. It is powerful, and significantly, an eminently dialectical theory: the person evolves through a process of struggle with and ultimate supersession . . . of symbolic figures of love, desire, and authority. As a general structure (without gender valences attached to the particular figures), there seems no need to dispose of (and . . . probably no possibility of disposing of) this process."[59] Ortner theorized that because gender valences are historical accretions, they can be changed, and with their change, the Oedipal process can be freed from its current patriarchal agenda.[60] In other words, according to Ortner, there is no law that "maleness" and "femaleness" must be understood in only one way, or that "maleness" must be privileged over "femaleness."

In developing her argument, Ortner insisted that labeling authority, autonomy, and universalism as "male" and love, dependence, and particularism as "female" is not essential to the Oedipus complex. Gender valences are simply the consequences of a child's experiences with men and women. A society changes children's *ideas* about "maleness" and "femaleness" by changing children's experiences with men and women. Does this mean, then, that the implementation of Dinnerstein's and Chodorow's system of dual parenting would, after all, be enough to effect a different telling of the Oedipal tale? Or must society undergo a more radical social transformation than this one to eliminate the gender valences that favor one sex over the other? Must we, for example, enter Marge Piercy's Mattapoisett, a fictional world in which children are gestated ex utero and reared by three co-mothers (two men and one woman, or two women and one man)?[61] The possibilities for social transformation in general and for family structure in particular would seem to be many, each one requiring a different telling of the Oedipal tale.

Psychoanalytic Feminism: General Reflections

With greater or lesser success, Chodorow, Dinnerstein, and Mitchell challenged a strict Freudian account of psychosocial development. They tried to provide explanations for psychosexual development that would help rather then hinder women's liberation. Still, this trio of later psychoanalytic feminists did not go far enough. They did not emphasize, as some other later psychoanalytic feminists would, that to understand why we construct men/maleness/masculinity and women/femaleness/femininity the way we do, we may not simply take as gospel a general theory of the psyche. Commented Chris Weedon:

If we assume that subjectivity is discursively produced in social institutions and processes, there is no pre-given reason why we should privilege sexual relations above other forms of social relations as constitutive of identity. There may, of course, be historically specific reasons for doing this in a particular analysis, but they will not be universal. Furthermore, if we are concerned specifically with the question of sexual identity, then psychoanalysis itself must be looked at as one discourse among many which has been influential in constituting inherently patriarchal norms of sexuality.[62]

Weedon's point is this: If we think, for example, that we can change current psychosocial identity by instituting a practice such as dual parenting, then we can also change current psychosexual identity, albeit differently, by instituting an alternative practice such as single parenting. As Weedon stated it, "discourse constitutes rather than reflects meaning."[63] Everyday practice precedes the formulation of general theory.

Observations such as Weedon's partly explain why, in recent years, a new generation of psychoanalytic feminists, including Luce Irigaray and Julia Kristeva, have found French psychoanalyst Jacques Lacan's reinterpretation of Freud so useful. For Lacan, anatomy is not destiny; rather, language is destiny. Therefore, to the degree that language can be changed, destiny can be changed.

Jacques Lacan's Thought

Building upon structural anthropologist Claude Lévi-Strauss's contention that every society is regulated by a series of interrelated signs, roles, and rituals, Jacques Lacan termed this series the "Symbolic order."[64] For a child to function adequately within society, he or she must be incorporated into the Symbolic order by undergoing three stages of psychosexual development.[65] In the first, or pre-Oedipal, phase—termed the "Imaginary" by Lacan—an infant is completely unaware of her or his own ego boundaries. In fact, the infant has no sense of where the mother's body ends and her or his own body begins. As far as the infant is concerned, he or she and the mother are one. Moreover, during this stage of development, the infant is neither feminine nor masculine but possibly either because the infant has yet to acquire language.

In the second, or mirror, phase (also part of the Imaginary), the infant thinks the image of herself or himself, as reflected through the "mirror" of the mother's gaze, is her or his real self. According to Lacan, this is a normal stage in self-development. Before the infant can see itself as a self, the infant must see itself as seen by the mother—that is, as another.[66] Lacan claimed that the process of infantile self-discovery serves as a paradigm for all subsequent relations; the self always discovers more about itself through the eyes of the other.

The third, or Oedipal, phase, in Lacan's scheme of things, includes a period of growing estrangement between the mother and the maturing child. Unlike the infant, the child does not view herself or himself as a unity; rather, the child regards the mother as the other—someone to whom the child must communicate his or her wishes and, therefore, someone who, due to the limitations of language, can never truly fulfill those wishes. During the Oedipal phase proper, the already weakened mother-child relationship is further eroded by the intervention of the father.[67] Fearing *symbolic* castration, the child separates from the mother in return for a medium (language) through which the child can maintain some connection with the mother—the original, never-to-be-had-again source of total gratification.[68]

Like Freud, Lacan maintained that boys experience the splitting from the mother differently than do girls. In the Oedipal phase, the boy rejects identification with his mother, eschewing the undifferentiated and silent state of the womb, and bonds with his anatomically similar father, who represents the Symbolic order, the word. Through identification with his father, the boy not only enters into subjecthood and individuality, but also internalizes the dominant order, the rules of society. In contrast, because of her anatomy, the girl cannot wholly identify with her father in the psychosexual drama. Nor can she totally dis-identify with her mother. As a result, the girl cannot fully accept and internalize the Symbolic order.

From this situation, we can draw one of two conclusions. On the one hand, we can conclude that women are virtually excluded from the Symbolic order. On the other hand, we can conclude that women are repressed within the Symbolic order, forced into it unwillingly. A man with a predilection for contradictions, Lacan seemed to draw both of these conclusions. He thought that because women cannot totally internalize the "law of the father," this law must be imposed on them from the outside. Women are given the same words men are given: masculine words. These words cannot express what women *feel*, however; masculine words can express only what men *think* women feel. Lacking feminine words, women must either babble outside the Symbolic order or remain silent within it.

Thus far, it seems Lacan was not any more able than Freud was to find a comfortable place for women within his framework. Because women cannot completely resolve the Oedipal complex, they remain strangers in the Symbolic order, largely unknown because of their phallic wordlessness. Lacan speculated that were society to try to do the impossible—to know women—society would have to begin its inquiry at the pre-Oedipal level of feminine sexual pleasure (*jouissance*). But like women, *jouissance* cannot be known, because it can be neither thought nor spoken in the phallic language of the fathers. It leads a repressed existence at the margins of the Symbolic order, seeking a nonphallic language capable of thinking and speaking it. Were *jouissance* to find the words to express itself, it would burst the Symbolic order and the order's major prop, patriarchy.

Feminist Appropriations of Lacan's Thought

Luce Irigaray. Although French psychoanalyst Luce Irigaray found much of value in Lacanian (and, for that matter, Freudian) thought, her overall aim was to liberate what she termed "feminine" philosophical thought from what she termed "masculine" philosophical thought. We will recall that, in Lacan, the Imaginary is the pre-linguistic, pre-Oedipal domain in which the child initially mistakes herself or himself for her or his own mirror image. When the child realizes that the mirror image is distinct from his or her own real self, the child enters the Symbolic order. In this realm, the child is able to assert herself or himself as an "I" in language, a distinct subjectivity, separate from other subjectivities. Like Lacan, Irigaray drew contrasts between the Imaginary and the Symbolic order, but unlike Lacan, Irigaray claimed there is *within* the Imaginary a male/masculine imaginary and a female/feminine imaginary.[69] In other words, for Irigaray, the psyche is never bisexual, but always either male/masculine or female/feminine.

For Lacan, the Imaginary is a prison within which the infant is the captive of illusory images. After successfully completing the Oedipal phase, boys are liberated from the Imaginary and enter the Symbolic order, the realm of language and selfhood. Because they never completely resolve the Oedipal phase, however, girls either remain behind in the Imaginary or they enter the Symbolic order mute. In opposition to Lacan, Irigaray refused to bemoan this state of affairs. Instead, she viewed women's total existence in the Imaginary or wordlessness in the Symbolic order as two situations full of untapped possibilities for both women and society.

Irigaray noted that, at present, anything we know about the Imaginary and women, including women's sexual desire, we know from a male point of view. In other words, the only kind of woman we know is the "masculine feminine," the phallic feminine, woman as man sees her. But, said Irigaray, there is another kind of woman to know, the "feminine feminine," woman as women see her.[70] This woman must not be defined, however, through any statement definitively asserting what the true "feminine" is. Defining "woman" in any one way will recreate the phallic feminine: "To claim that the feminine can be expressed in the form of a concept is to allow oneself to be caught up again in a system of 'masculine' representations, in which women are trapped in a system or meaning which serves the auto-affection of the (masculine) subject."[71] What obstructs the progression of women's thought out of the Imaginary is the concept of sameness, the thought product of masculine narcissism and singularity.

Irigaray used the word *speculum* (a concave mirroring medical instrument used in vaginal examinations) to capture the nature and function of the idea of sameness in Western philosophy and psychoanalysis. "Specularization," commented Toril Moi, "suggests not only the mirror-image that comes from the visual penetration of the speculum inside the vagina," but also "the necessity of postulating a subject that is capable of reflecting on its own being."[72] Because of narcissistic philosophical "specularization"— which is epitomized in the medieval description of God as thought thinking thought—masculine discourse has never been able to understand woman, or the feminine, as anything other than a reflection of man, or the masculine. Therefore, it is impossible to think the "feminine feminine" within the structures of patriarchal thought. When men look at women, they see not women but reflections of the image and likeness of men.

In her study of Western philosophy and psychoanalysis, Irigaray found sameness everywhere. Her analysis of sameness in Freud's theory was particularly important because she used it to criticize his theory of female sexuality. Freud saw the little girl as a deficiency or negativity, as a "little man" without a penis. He suppressed the notion of difference, characterizing the feminine as a lack. Woman is a reflection of man, the same as a man except in her sexuality. Female sexuality, because it does not mirror male sexuality, is an absence, or lack, of the male's sexuality. Where woman does not reflect man, she does not exist and, stressed Irigaray, will never exist until the Oedipus complex is exploded.[73]

Irigaray claimed that if women want to experience themselves as something other than "waste" or "excess" in the little structured margins of man's world, they should take three steps of action.[74] First, women should create a female language, eschewing gender-neutral language as forcefully as they eschew male language. Not only is the search for "neutrality" pointless (because no one is really neutral about anything), claimed Irigaray, but it is also morally misguided. Trying to hide the identity of the speaker from the reader/listener is cowardly. Stressing that women will not find liberation in objectivity, Irigaray noted that "neither *I* nor *you,* nor *we* appears in the language of science."[75] Science forbids the "subjective," often because it wishes to mask the identities of its agents. Distressed by the unwillingness of science—and, for that matter, traditional Western philosophy and psychoanalysis—to take responsibility for its own words and deeds, Irigaray urged women to find the courage to speak in the active voice, avoiding at all costs the false security and ultimate inauthenticity of the passive voice.

Second, women should create a female sexuality. Irigaray contrasted the singularity that the male sexual organ implies with the multiplicity the female sexual organs imply. In particular, she localized the feminine voice in the labia, "two lips" that reveal woman to be neither one nor two. Woman is not two, because the labia belong to a single woman's body, "which keeps woman in touch with herself, but without any possibility of distinguishing what is touching from what is touched."[76] However, woman is not one, either, because the labia represent a woman's multiple and diffuse (nonphallic) sexuality: "So woman does not have a sex organ? She has at least two of them, but they are not identifiable as ones. Indeed, she has many more. Her sexuality is always at least double, goes even further; it is plural."[77]

Irigaray did not simply contrast the plural, circular, and aimless vaginal/clitoral libidinal economy of women with the singular, linear, and teleological phallic libidinal economy of men. She also argued that the expression of these libidinal economies is not restricted to sexuality but instead extends to all forms of human expression, including social structures. Just as the penetration of the penis prevents the lips from touching, so the phallic unity of the Symbolic order represses the multiplicity of female sexuality. Thus, patriarchy is the social manifestation of masculine libidinal economy and will remain the order of the day until the repressed "feminine feminine" is set free. Women can unshackle this potentiality, however, through lesbian and autoerotic practice. As women explore the multifaceted terrain of the female body, they can learn to think thoughts, speak words, and do deeds powerful enough to displace the phallus.

Third, in their efforts to be themselves, women should mime the mimes men have imposed on women. Women should take men's images of women and reflect them back to men in magnified proportions. Through miming, women can "*undo* the effects of phallocentric discourse simply by *overdoing* them."[78] For example, if men view women as sex objects, fetishizing women's breasts in particular, then women should pump up their breasts as big as possible and walk into church on Sunday, their breasts fully exposed in all their naked glory, as if to say, "Here, boys; we know what is on your minds. So look. See if we care." To be sure, conceded Irigaray, miming is not without its perils. The distinction between miming the patriarchal definition of woman in order to subvert it and merely fulfilling this definition is not clear. In their attempts to "overdo" the definition of woman, women may inadvertently be drawn back into it. Nevertheless, despite this risk, women should take every opportunity to raise a ruckus in the Symbolic order.

From the preceding discussion, there is clearly a tension between Irigaray's conviction that we must finally end the process of labeling and categorizing on the one hand, and her competing conviction that we cannot help but engage in this process on the other hand.[79] Because Irigaray dared to express both of these convictions, sometimes in the same breath, her critics described her as self-contradictory. Rather than feeling embarrassed by the ambiguities and ambivalence in her writing, however, Irigaray took increasing pleasure in them. For Irigaray, self-contradiction is a form of rebellion against the logical consistency required by phallocentrism. "'She' is indefinitely other in herself. This is doubtless why she is said to be whimsical, incomprehensible, agitated, capricious . . . not to mention her language, in which 'she' sets off in all directions leaving 'him' unable to discern the coherence of any meaning. Hers are contradictory words, somewhat mad from the standpoint of reason, inaudible for whoever listens to them with ready-made grids, with a fully elaborated code in hand."[80] Refusing to be pinned down even by her own theory, Irigaray vowed to liberate her life from the phallocentric concepts that would squeeze its multiple meanings—its exciting differences—into boring sameness.

Julia Kristeva.   Like Irigaray, psychoanalytic feminist Julia Kristeva relied on Lacan's work. She largely accepted Lacan's identification of the pre-Oedipal stage with the Imaginary (see above). She also largely accepted his identification of the Oedipal and post-Oedipal stages with the Symbolic order. However, Kristeva added to Lacan's account a further complexity. She claimed that a certain modality of language, termed by her the "semiotic," is the exclusive modality of language in the pre-Oedipal period, whereas another modality of language, termed by her the "symbolic," is the dominant, although not exclusive modality of language in the Oedipal and post-Oedipal stages. Furthermore, she associated the semiotic with maternal/poetic language and the symbolic with paternal/logical language. As Kristeva saw it, when the child enters the Symbolic order as described by Lacan, the child brings with himself or herself some of the language of the Imaginary. However, most of the language of the Imaginary is left behind, because it is fundamentally at odds with the Symbolic order. Thus, for Kristeva, the semiotic exists both inside and outside the Symbolic order, whereas for Lacan, it presumably exists only outside the Symbolic order.[81]

Further explaining the semiotic-symbolic distinction, Kristeva claimed that the symbolic modality of language is that aspect of meaning-making that permits us to make rational arguments; it produces linear, rational, objective, and grammatical writing. In contrast to the symbolic modality of language, the semiotic modality of language is that aspect of meaning-making that permits us to express feelings. It is, as Kelly Oliver has noted, "the drives as they make their way into signification."[82] The semiotic produces circular, emotional, subjective, and rule-breaking writing. Kristeva believed that a liberated person is someone able to play not only in the space *between* the pre-Oedipal Imaginary and the post-Oedipal Symbolic order but also in the space between the semiotic and symbolic aspects of meaning-making *inside* the Symbolic order.[83] In other words, she claimed that the liberated person can move freely between the "feminine" and the "masculine," chaos and order, revolution and the status quo.

Unlike Irigaray, Kristeva resisted identification of the "feminine" with biological women and the "masculine" with biological men. She maintained that when the child enters the Symbolic order, he or she may identify with either the mother or the father. Depending on the choice the child makes, the child will be more or less "feminine" or "masculine." Thus, men can exist and write in a "feminine" mode, and women can exist and write in a "masculine" mode. Perhaps most interesting and controversial is Kristeva's claim that the "feminine" writings of men have more revolutionary potential than those of women. Culture is more upset when a man speaks like a woman than when a woman speaks like a man, said Kristeva. As Oliver put it, Kristeva thought that "whereas in males an identification with the maternal semiotic is revolutionary because it breaks with traditional conceptions of sexual difference, for females an identification with the maternal does not break traditional conceptions of sexual difference."[84]

Kristeva's main emphasis was on difference in general rather than *sexual* difference in particular. Rejecting traditional accounts of two binary sexes, of two opposed *gender identities,* Kristeva admitted that there are, nonetheless, male and female *sexual differences.* Like Dinnerstein and Chodorow, Kristeva located the beginnings of sexual difference in the child's relation to the mother; but in Kristeva's version of this relationship, a child's sexual identity is specifically formed through a struggle to separate from the mother's body. The male does this not by rejecting his mother's body but by "abjecting" it, that is, reconceiving it as an object that represents everything that is disgusting about being a human being (excrement, blood, mucous).[85] In contrast, the more the female identifies with her mother's body, the more trouble she has rejecting or abjecting it. To the degree that the rejected or abjected maternal body is associated with women per se, women are grouped with society's "misfits"—the Jews, Gypsies, homosexuals, deformed, diseased—an identification that would, contrary to what Kristeva has said elsewhere, motivate women, far more than men, to be revolutionaries.

Just because Kristeva conceded that men and women have different sexual identities does not mean she believed these identities are manifested in the same way by each "female" or "male." For example, Kristeva maintained that the concept "woman" makes no sense at the ontological level but only at the political level:

> The belief that "one is a woman" is almost as absurd and obscurantist as the belief that "one is a man." I say "almost" because there are still many goals which women can achieve: freedom of abortion and contraception, daycare centers for children, equality on the job, etc. Therefore, we must use "we are women" as an advertisement or slogan for our demands. On a deeper level, however, a woman cannot "be"; it is something which does not even belong in the order of being.[86]

Acknowledging that past feminists successfully invoked the term *woman* to improve the lot of many women, Kristeva nonetheless stressed that today's feminists should invoke the term more judiciously lest the "politics of liberation" become the "politics of exclusion and counterpower."[87] Oliver explained: "Feminists in the United States are struggling with this very issue. The feminist movement has had to realize that it is a white middle class movement that has worked to exclude women whose interests and needs are somehow different. Paradoxically as soon as feminism defines 'woman' it excludes all sorts of women."[88] Thus, Kristeva ultimately endorsed only the aspects of the feminist movement that break down or render ambiguous identity, especially sexual identity.

Conclusion

Like liberal, radical, and Marxist/socialist feminists, psychoanalytic feminists have not provided a totally satisfying explanation for female subordination. Moreover, as critic Dorothy Leland observed, psychoanalytic feminists have not offered women any truly desirable ways to achieve a fuller human life. Dual parenting is not a panacea for all women's woes, and in Leland's estimation, neither are Mitchell's, Irigaray's, and Kristeva's attempts to resolve the Oedipal tale. Indeed, said Leland, Kristeva's resolution of the Oedipal tale is particularly disturbing because it offers women only three "options"—none entirely good—to avoid psychosis.[89]

The first option, which Kristeva considered undesirable for women, is total father-identification. According to Kristeva, Electra, who has her mother, Clytemnestra, killed in order to "avenge her father," is the perfect example of a totally father-identified woman.[90] Clytemnestra must be punished, indeed eliminated, because she has dared to take a lover, thereby exposing to the world her *jouissance* (instinctual pleasure), a *jouissance* that the patriarchal order forbids. By having her mother killed, Electra expresses her hate not only of her mother's *jouissance* but also of her own *jouissance*. Electra's expression of mother-hate/self-hate "perpetuates the patriarchal social/symbolic order," said Leland.[91]

The second option for women, which Kristeva also considered undesirable, is total mother-identification. Because she largely accepted Lacan's view that to become civilized, the child must repress both its *jouissance* and its symbiotic relation to the mother, Kristeva viewed total mother-identification as condemning women to "forever remain in a sulk in the face of history, politics, and social affairs."[92] In other words, the price of total mother-identification is not being permitted to be an adult.

The third option for women, which Kristeva considered desirable, is to avoid both total father-identification and total mother-identification:

> Let us refuse both extremes. Let us know that an ostensibly masculine, paternal identification . . . is necessary in order to have a voice in the chapter of politics and history . . . [But] let us right away be wary of the premium on narcissism that such an integration can carry; let us reject the development of a "homologous" woman [i.e., an Electra], who is finally capable and virile; and let us rather act on the socio-politico-historical stage as her negative: that is, act first with all those who refuse and "swim against the tide"—all who rebel against the existing relations of production and reproduction. But let us not take the role of Revolutionary either, whether male or female: let us on the contrary refuse all roles to summon [a] truth outside time, a truth that is neither true nor false, that cannot be fitted into the order of speech and social symbolism.[93]

By "truth," Kristeva meant the semiotic modality of language, said Leland.[94] Yet Kristeva did not view as desirable the total replacement of the symbolic modality of language in the Symbolic order with the semiotic modality of language. Any attempt to totally substitute the symbolic with the semiotic would, in her estimation, destroy the Symbolic order and, with it, civilization. Everyone would be propelled back into the pre-Oedipal stage, or the Imaginary. Permanent existence in this stage is nothing more or less than psychosis, according to Kristeva. Thus, the specific course of action Kristeva recommended for women who did not want to go crazy was to engage in an "impossible dialectic," a "permanent alienation" between the semiotic ("maternal" *jouissance*) and the Symbolic ("paternal" power or law).[95]

Reflecting on Kristeva's recommendation to women, Leland and many other critics of psychoanalytic feminism cannot help but think that women must have more options than the ones noted above. Some of these critics suggest that gender need not be interpreted in terms of masculinity or femininity only, and that sexuality need not be interpreted in terms of maleness or femaleness only. There are multiple genders and multiple sexualities.[96] Other of these critics suggest instead that psychoanalytic feminists develop an entirely non-Freudian/non-Lacanian account of psychosexual development—an account that permits women as well as men to be civilized without assigning either sex to "second sex" status. The merits of this suggestion are obvious. Unfortunately, psychoanalytic feminists have not been able to find in the Western tradition a more convincing psychosexual tale to tell than some version of the Oedipal tale. Whether there are better psychosexual tales told in non-Western traditions is, therefore, an avenue for feminist speculation and exploration.

5

Care-Focused Feminism

Over the last quarter of a century, many feminist thinkers have reflected on the fact that women are society's primary caregivers worldwide. Women, far more than men, rear children, tend to the needs of the infirm, and take care of the elderly. Moreover, in many societies and certainly in the United States, women as a group are associated with values, virtues, and traits such as "interdependence, community, connection, sharing, emotion, body, trust, absence of hierarchy, nature, imminence, process, joy, peace, and life."[1] In contrast, men as a group are associated with values, virtues, and traits such as "independence, autonomy, intellect, will, wariness, hierarchy, domination, culture, transcendence, product, ascetism, war, and death."[2] Care-focused feminists offer various explanations for *why* societies label some values, virtues, and traits female, or feminine, and others male, or masculine. Some of these explanations focus on men's and women's separate biologies, others on men's and women's diverging psychosexual development paths, and still others on the ways in which societies systematically shape men's and women's distinct identities and behaviors. But whatever their explanation for men's and women's contrasting gender identities, care-focused feminists regard women's capacities for care as a human strength rather than a human weakness. Moreover, care-focused feminists expend considerable energy developing a feminist ethics of care as a complement of, or even a substitute for, a traditional ethics of justice.

In this chapter, we will examine the work of some key care-focused feminists to determine why women shoulder the burden of care in so many societies. We

Portions of this chapter draw from Rosemarie Tong, *Feminine and Feminist Ethics*. Belmont, Calif.: Wadsworth, 1993.

will also consider, albeit to a lesser extent, why men as a group do not routinely engage in caring practices and whether this state of affairs contributes to women's oppression. Finally, we will assess whether it is both feasible and desirable to push the value of care out of the private domain into the public domain.

The Roots of Care-Focused Feminism

Carol Gilligan's Ethics of Care

In her groundbreaking book, *In a Different Voice,* moral psychologist Carol Gilligan noted that men's emphasis on separation and autonomy leads them to develop a style of moral reasoning that stresses justice, fairness, and rights.[3] In contrast, women's emphasis on connections and relationships leads them to develop a style of moral reasoning that stresses the wants, needs, and interests of particular people. In addition to making this point, Gilligan claimed that because most experts in moral development theory have used *male* norms as opposed to *human* norms to measure women's as well as men's moral development, the experts have mistakenly concluded women are less morally developed than men. Deeply disturbed by this negative assessment of women, Gilligan set out to prove that not women, but the standards used to judge women's growth as moral persons, must be changed.[4]

In articulating her position that women are no less morally developed than men, Gilligan singled out her former mentor, Harvard's Lawrence Kohlberg, for particular criticism. According to Kohlberg, moral development consists of a six-stage process through which a child must pass to become a fully functioning moral agent. Stage One is "the punishment and obedience orientation." To avoid the "stick" of punishment or receive the "carrot" of a reward, the young child does as he or she is told. Stage Two is "the instrumental relativist orientation." Based on a limited principle of reciprocity ("you scratch my back and I'll scratch yours"), the young child does what meets others' needs, but only if his or her own needs are thereby met. Stage Three is "the interpersonal concordance or 'good boy-nice girl' orientation." The maturing child conforms to prevailing moral norms in order to secure the approbation of other people. Stage Four is "the 'law and order' orientation." The maturing child begins to do his or her duty, show respect for authority, and maintain the given social order for its own sake. Stage Five is "the social-contract legalistic orientation." The young adult adopts an essentially utilitarian moral point of view according to which individuals are permitted to do as they please, provided they refrain from harming other people in the process. Stage Six is "the universal ethical principle orientation." The adult adopts an essentially Kantian moral point of view that provides a moral perspective universal enough to serve as a critique of any conventional morality. The adult is no longer ruled by self-interest, the opinion of others, or the force of legal convention but by self-legislated and self-imposed universal principles such as justice, reciprocity, and respect for the dignity of human persons.[5]

Gilligan took exception to Kohlberg's sixfold scale not because she regarded it as entirely without merit but because girls and women tested on it rarely got past Stage Three, the good-boy/nice-girl stage. Fearing that people would interpret this test result as confirming Freud's view that women are less moral than men, Gilligan set out to prove that women's low scores on Kohlberg's test were undeserved. She hypothesized that women did poorly on Kohlberg's scale because of its flawed design. It was, in her estimation, a test constructed to measure *men's* method of moral reasoning, as if men's way of moral reasoning was the standard of human moral reasoning. As a result of the scale's faulty construction, women who did not morally reason like men did poorly on it. Gilligan claimed the solution to this state of affairs was not to construct a test to measure *women's* method of moral reasoning, as if women's way of moral reasoning was the standard of human moral reasoning. Rather, the solution was to develop a test that could accurately measure both men's and women's moral development. Neither men nor women should be viewed as the morally inferior sex.

Eager to understand more about how women reason toward a moral decision, Gilligan conducted an empirical study of twenty-nine pregnant women. Each of these women was deciding whether to abort her fetus. Gilligan interviewed these women as they were working through their decision and sometimes after they had done so. She eventually concluded that no matter their age, social class, marital status, or ethnic background, each of these women manifested a way of thinking about moral matters that differed markedly from that of the men tested on Kohlberg's moral development scale. Rather than approaching the abortion decision analytically as if they were scientists trying to determine whose rights weigh more—the fetus's or the woman's— the women in Gilligan's study approached the abortion decision as a human relations problem. They worried about how their decision would affect not only the fetus but also themselves in connection to their partners, parents, friends, and so on, and they moved back and forth between three levels of moral reasoning as they sought to make moral sense of their abortion decision. Gilligan noted that the women who failed to come fully to terms with their abortion decision remained stuck either in Level One moral reasoning, in which the moral agent overemphasizes her own interests, or in Level Two moral reasoning, in which the moral agent overemphasizes others' interests. In contrast, the women who engaged in Level Three moral reasoning, in which the moral agents strike a balance between their own interests and those of others, appeared most at peace with their abortion decision.[6]

The more Gilligan reflected on the words of the twenty-nine women she interviewed, the more able she was to describe the differences between a Level One, a Level Two, and a Level Three mode of moral reasoning. At Level One, she said, the self is the sole object of a woman's concern. This self is a disappointed self that feels very alone in the world. "I must," says this self, "take care of myself because no one else in the world cares about me and my happiness."[7] No wonder, said Gilligan, that the Level One moral reasoners in her study often regarded a baby as a person who would love them, making their lives less bleak. As these women struggled further through their abortion decision, however, many of them started to see that a baby, no less than themselves, is a vulnerable person in need of love. They began, noted Gilligan, to reinterpret their *self-interest* as *selfishness*. So, for example, a seventeen-year-old who wanted a baby to provide herself with companionship ultimately decided it would be wrong for her to have a child exclusively for this reason. She realized that she did not have the means to take care of a baby: "What I want to do is to have the baby, but what I feel I should do, which is what I need to do, is have an abortion right now, because sometimes what you want isn't right. Sometimes what is necessary comes before what you want, because it might not always lead to the right thing."[8]

Making the transition from "wish" to "necessity"—from "the 'selfishness' of willful decision" to "the 'responsibility' of moral choice"—is not easy, said Gilligan. Level Two moral reasoning requires women to reach out to others and recognize the importance of others' interests. But there is a problem with Level Two moral reasoning, according to Gilligan. Women who stop at it are in peril of equating goodness with self-sacrifice and always subjugating their own wants to those of other people.

Gilligan provided the example of a woman in her study whose lover wanted her to have an abortion despite her desire to bring the fetus to term. Because this woman wanted both the baby and her lover's approval, she found herself in a moral "no-win" situation. On the one hand, she felt that aborting the fetus would be "selfish." She would thereby secure one of *her* wants, her lover's approval. On the other hand, she felt that not aborting the fetus would also be "selfish." She would thereby secure another of *her* wants, a baby. The woman reasoned that no matter what she decided to do, she would hurt someone: either her lover or her fetus. In the end, the woman decided to have the abortion, consoling herself it was not really *her* decision but her lover's. Because the woman resented her lover's "decision," however, her resentment gradually turned to anger, souring the very relationship for which she had sacrificed her child.[9]

Carefully reflecting on this woman's abortion decision, Gilligan claimed that in order to avoid becoming a resentful, angry, even hateful person, a woman needs to push beyond Level Two to Level Three moral reasoning. As a woman moves towards Level Three moral reasoning, the decision to abort, for example, becomes a choice she must make about how best to care for the fetus, herself, and anyone else likely to be deeply affected by her decision. One of the women in Gilligan's study explained her decision to have an abortion as just such a choice: "I would not be doing myself or the child or the world any kind of favor having this child. I don't need to pay off my imaginary debts to the world through this child, and I don't think that it is right to bring a child into the world and use it for that purpose."[10] Gilligan characterized this woman's transition from Level Two to Level Three moral reasoning as a transition from goodness to truth. A woman moves from simply pleasing others—being the conventionally good, always self-sacrificing woman—to honestly recognizing her own needs as part of any relationship.

It is clear that in Gilligan's estimation women's style of moral reasoning is no better or worse than men's. It is simply different. Moreover, stressed Gilligan, although a woman or a man might, as an individual or as a member of a group, typically engage in a certain style of moral reasoning, fully developed moral agents are likely to display a marked ability to speak the languages of care and justice equally well. Had Gilligan stopped her research on moral development with this observation, we could confidently conclude that, for her, the *morally androgynous* person is the paradigm moral agent. However, after writing *In a Different Voice,* Gilligan hinted that the ideal moral thinker might after all be more inclined to an ethics of care than an ethics of justice. In her anthology *Mapping the Moral Domain,* she expressed concern that a high percentage of today's adolescents "tend[ed] to characterize care-focused solutions or inclusive problem-solving strategies as utopian or outdated."[11] Gilligan worried that because our culture overvalues scientific, objective, and rational thinking, teachers urge students to use only their heads and not also their hearts in moral deliberation. Challenging the wisdom of this pedagogical approach, Gilligan claimed that in many ways, young children who have not been schooled to suppress their feelings seem *more* moral than adults. Precisely because of their strong attachments to family members and friends, young children seem not only really to care about the feelings, wants, needs, and interests of those to whom they are related but also to act upon these sentiments. That girls are more likely than boys to grow into adults who continue to respond to other people's need to be loved and appreciated is probably not a sign of women's moral weakness, then, but of women's moral strength.

Nel Noddings's Ethics of Care

Like Gilligan, care-focused feminist Nel Noddings claimed that women and men speak different moral languages and that our culture favors a "masculine" ethics of justice over a "feminine" ethics of care. Although women can speak the language of justice as well as men can, said Noddings, this language is not women's native moral tongue. Indeed, women seem to enter the moral realm through a "different door" than men do, focusing less on "principles and propositions" and "terms such as justification, fairness, and justice" and more on "human caring and the memory of caring and being cared for."[12] As a result, women's style of moral reasoning is far less abstract and far more concrete than men's. For example, said Noddings, when faced with a decision about further medical treatment for her dying child, a mother is not likely to approach this intensely personal decision as she would approach an extremely difficult math problem. On the contrary, as she struggles to determine what is in her child's best interest, a mother will consult her personal ideals, feelings, and impressions.[13] She will not let her child suffer unnecessary pain for no good reason; she will do what her "heart" tells her "head" to do.

Ethics, insisted Noddings, is about particular relations, where a "relation" means "a set of ordered pairs generated by some rule that describes the affect—or subjective experience—of the members."[14] When all goes well, the cared-for person actively *receives* the caring deeds of the one caring, spontaneously sharing her or his aspirations, appraisals, and accomplishments with the one caring. Caring is not simply a matter of feeling favorably disposed toward humankind in general, of being concerned about people with whom we have no concrete connections. There is, said Noddings, a fundamental difference between the kind of care a mother gives her child and the kind of care a well-off American philanthropist gives a starving Somali child she or he has never met. Real care requires an active encounter with specific individuals; it cannot be accomplished through good intentions alone.

Noddings stressed the universality of the caring attitude underpinning her ethics. Caring is a defining feature of human beings, at least as important as their capacity for rationality. A child's memories of caring, for example, are not memories peculiar to him or her alone, said Noddings. On the contrary, virtually all human beings have such memories. Indeed, Noddings went so far as to claim "that the impulse to act in behalf of the present other is itself innate. It lies latent in each of us, awaiting gradual development in a succession of caring relations."[15]

Because our memories of caring and being cared for can fade, Noddings emphasized that we must use education to enhance our natural tendency to care. She noted our initial experiences of care come easily. We act from a *natural* caring that impels us to help others because we *want* to: "The relation of natural caring will be identified as the human condition that we, consciously or unconsciously, perceive as 'good.' It is that condition toward which we

long and strive, and it is our longing for caring—to be in that special relation—that provides the motivation for us to be moral. We want to be *moral*
in order to remain in the caring relation and to enhance the ideal of ourselves
as one-caring."[16] The little boy helps his exhausted mother fold the laundry
simply because she is his mother, claimed Noddings. He wants to be connected to her and to have her recognize him as her helper. Later, when he is
an adolescent, his childhood memories both of caring *for* his mother and
being cared for *by* his mother flood over him "as a feeling—as an 'I must.'"[17]
In remembrance of his little-boy sentiments, he may choose to be late for a
party so that he can help his mother instead. In such a circumstance, *natural*
caring morphs into *ethical* caring, a deliberate, critical, and reflective extension of *natural* caring.

We should note that Noddings did not describe moral development as the
process of *replacing* natural caring with ethical caring. Although ethical caring requires efforts that natural caring does not, Noddings disagreed with
philosopher Immanuel Kant's view that doing things because we *ought* to do
them is necessarily better than doing things because we *want* to do them. In
contrast to Kant, Noddings argued our "oughts" build on our "wants":

> Recognizing that ethical caring requires an effort that is not needed in
> natural caring does not commit us to a position that elevates ethical car-
> ing over natural caring. Kant has identified the ethical with that which is
> done out of duty and not out of love, and that distinction in itself seems
> right. But an ethic built on caring strives to maintain the caring attitude
> and is thus dependent upon, and not superior to, natural caring. The
> source of ethical behavior is, then, in twin sentiments—one that feels di-
> rectly for the other and one that feels for and with that best self, who
> may accept and sustain the initial feeling rather than reject it.[18]

Morality is not about affirming others' needs through the process of denying one's own interests. Rather, morality is about affirming one's own interests
through the process of affirming others' needs. When we act morally (engage
in ethical caring), we act to fulfill our "fundamental and natural desire to be
and to remain related."[19] We meet others' needs not because inclination
impels us to do so, or because reason forces us to do so, but because we reflec-
tively choose to do so.

In addition to her book on caring, Noddings wrote a book on evil, in
which she claimed women are more capable of withstanding evil than men
are. According to Noddings, women's understanding of evil is concrete,
whereas men's understanding of evil is abstract. For women, an evil event is a

harmful event, something that hurts someone in particular. For men, an evil event is a rule-breaking event—a violation of God's commandments or the state's laws. Wanting to replace the abstract *idea* of evil as sin, guilt, impurity, and fault with the concrete *experience* of evil as "that which harms or threatens harm,"[20] Noddings insisted that eliminating evil is not about punishing sinners. Rather, it is about reducing the kind of pain, separation, and helplessness infants typically feel. Evil is isolation in one's hour of need, and the way to overcome isolation is through relationship.

In her attempt to further elucidate the differences between the "masculine" idea of evil and the "feminine" experience of evil, Noddings interpreted a story Doris Lessing told in *The Diary of a Good Neighbor*. In Lessing's story, Jane, a middle-aged, highly successful novelist and magazine editor, tries to alleviate the suffering of Maudie, a physically unattractive, lower-class, ninety-year-old woman. Several female nurses and nurse aides assist Jane's efforts. In contrast to the male physician, who views Maudie as a "case," these women view Maudie as a unique individual who needs their help to fight the infirmities of old age and the ravages of disease. Reflecting on the women ministering to Maudie, Noddings noted none of them found abstract "meaning" in their patient's suffering. Nor did any of them speak of "God's will," as if Maudie's suffering were the price she had to pay for her "sins." On the contrary, they simply worked "to relieve her pain, alleviate her loneliness, and preserve—as nearly as they [could]—her autonomy." For Maudie's female healers, evil is "the deliberate or negligent failure" to help someone whose body is racked with pain, whose spirit is in anguish, or whose dignity as a person is in jeopardy.[21]

Interwoven among the pages of *Women and Evil* and the pages of *Caring* is a relational ethics, a type of ethics to which Noddings believed women are predisposed. In discussing the evils of poverty, Noddings issued a call to end the kind of nonrelational, dichotomous thinking she believed is the fundamental source of all human conflicts. She specifically rejected the kind of finger-pointing that causes the rich to trace poverty to the sloth, genetic weakness, and lack of ambition of the poor, and, in turn, the poor to trace poverty to the indifference, ruthlessness, and greed of the rich. In either instance, the one-sided nature of such us-versus-them thinking offers a distorted view of the true causes of poverty. The only way to get an accurate picture of the actual causes of poverty, said Noddings, is for mediators to help both the rich and the poor see the lies embedded in their perceptions of each other.

Noddings summoned women to take the lead in bridging the perspectival gap that separates the poor from the rich. Because women have traditionally mediated between squabbling family members, they have learned how to "persuade, plead, appeal and sympathize, interpret, reward, and above all attribute the best possible motive consonant with reality to both parties to [a] dispute." If anyone can improve the vision of both the rich and the poor, it is women, said Noddings. They have the moral skills to reach a loving compromise between people who are not yet each others' equals.[22]

Like poverty, war is another evil whose roots Noddings traced to a morally distorted worldview. With Homer's *Iliad* begins the celebration of the warrior hero, a celebration that paradoxically couples Greek rationality and moderation on the one hand with Greek irrationality and violence on the other. Rather than challenging the warrior hero and his deadly projects, Western philosophy tended to honor him. Indeed, said Noddings, even philosopher William James, who sought for war's "moral equivalent"—that is, for "something heroic that will speak to men as universally as war does"[23]—nonetheless praised the warrior's virtues: his boldness, energy, and valor. Wondering whether it is morally better to be a monk than a soldier, James initially opted for a military ideal as opposed to an ascetic ideal. Only after he managed to reconceive the ascetic life in heroic rather than "effeminate" terms did James produce a convincing argument against war and for peace. Provided that the monk, like the soldier, goes about his business like a *man,* his path is the one to follow since blood is not spilled on it senselessly. In order to feel good about himself, a man supposedly must strive to do his perceived duty no matter what the cost to himself or others. If a man is a warrior, he is to emulate the soldier who fights the hardest. If he is a monk, he is to emulate the martyr who suffers the most: "To reach the extremes by choice, whether of war or pacifism, of poverty or wealth, requires[s] striving, and striving for extremes has been a mark of manhood."[24]

As Noddings saw it, war will not be discarded in favor of peace until concerted caring aimed at uniting people replaces ambitious striving aimed at dividing people by making some individuals winners and other individuals losers. Only when the underappreciated art of relational ethics, of working together to maintain connection, comes into its own will peace have a chance. It is not that women do not strive. They do. It is just that when they strive, they do so not with the unrealistic aim of vanquishing their external foes or internal demons once and for all, but with the realistic goal of continuing as best they can. "A woman knows that she can never win the battle against dust, that she will have to feed family members again and again (and that no meals are likely to go down in history), that she must tend the garden every year, and that she cannot overcome most of its enemies but must treat them with the sort of moderation that encourages harmony," said Noddings.[25] Any woman who realizes her loved ones' survival may someday depend on her having good relations with her opponents also realizes that bad relations—quintessentially, war—are not a genuine solution to the problems underlying the us-versus-them dichotomy.

Caring does not give birth to rivals. Striving to be the best at any cost—the invidious competition hidden within the Greek idea of excellence—does not promote caring. On the contrary, the rivalry prevalent in our society quickly leads to enmity, and enmity leads to disaster. Noddings insisted that in order to avoid war, we must stop trying to be "number one," instead orienting ourselves to the task of creating good human relationships.

Noddings realized we cannot *eliminate* all evil, since it stems foremost from a separation of ourselves from other human beings, from an objectification of those around us. We can only *reduce* evil by accepting and combating our own penchant for it. Suppose, said Noddings, your child was going to be killed in one hour unless you found her, and standing before you was a man who knew where she was but would not tell you. Would you be able and willing to torture the information out of him? Noddings admitted she, for one, would be up to this "challenge."[26] Yet she asked herself whether this one exception to her rule of "do no evil" would lead her to make a series of exceptions, the sum total of which would negate the very rule upon which she had built her own morality.

For an answer to this disturbing question, Noddings turned to a story in Simon Wiesenthal's novel *The Sunflower*. Here, a young Jewish man, who turns out to be Simon himself, comes to the bedside of a dying Nazi named Karl. Guilt ridden because of his role in the Holocaust, Karl beseeches Simon to forgive him. Simon experiences feelings of both pity and repugnance toward Karl. After several minutes pass, however, Simon leaves without saying a word of forgiveness to him. He asks his readers to plumb their own souls and answer the question, "What would you have done in my place?"

In her reflections on Simon's story, Noddings implied that, had she been in Simon's place, she would have forgiven Karl. She claimed that because Simon viewed himself *symbolically*, as a representative of the Jewish people, he could not see the situation that confronted him *relationally*. In other words, Simon could not see the dying Nazi as an individual human being begging his forgiveness. Instead, Simon could see only Nazis in general: they who, as a group, had caused unforgivable harm to Jews in general. Commented Noddings: "Seeing each other and ourselves as symbols, is part of what sustains our capacity to inflict suffering."[27] In Noddings's estimation, Simon added to rather than subtracted from the world's evil when he refused to forgive Karl. She pointed out that even if Simon could only have yelled or screamed at Karl, a relationship of sorts might have been established between them: "Then gradually each might have seen the full horror of their situation. They both might have seen that the possibility of perpetrating unspeakable crimes lay in Simon as well as in Karl and that the possibility and thus the responsibility to resist lay also in both."[28]

When we anesthetize our souls to the cries of other human beings in pain—to men, women, and children who feel separate and helpless—we succumb to evil, concluded Noddings. Evil is not an abstract phenomenon; it is a concrete reality that takes one or more of five forms:

1. Inflicting pain (unless it can be demonstrated that doing so will or is at least likely to spare the victim greater pain in the future)
2. Inducing the pain of separation
3. Neglecting relation so that the pain of separation follows or those separated are thereby dehumanized
4. Deliberately or carelessly causing helplessness
5. Creating elaborate systems of mystification that contribute to the fear of helplessness or to its actual maintenance[29]

These actions, said Noddings, are evil. No higher or better good can ever justify our causing each other pain or rendering each other separate or helpless. Men must learn what women have known for some time, that "one's soul dies as soon as it detaches from the concrete persons who stretch out their hands in need or friendship."[30] Ethics is about overcoming pain, separation, and helplessness—a task that requires human beings to relate to each other as creatures whose goodness requires a sense of community.

Critiques of Gilligan and Noddings

Although many readers of Gilligan and Noddings thought these two women had correctly identified the different ways men and women approach moral issues, by no means was the response to an ethics of care universally favorable. Many thinkers found the work of both Gilligan and Noddings objectionable. In particular, they questioned the wisdom of too closely linking women to an ethics of care.

Critiques of Gilligan.   Much criticism was directed at Gilligan's methodology.[31] Some critics claimed that Gilligan's empirical data was too thin to support the weighty generalizations she made about men's and women's supposedly different moral voices.[32] They emphasized that although most of the women in Gilligan's study made reference to their husbands, boyfriends, lovers, and fathers, Gilligan failed to ask these men about their views on abortion. Had she chosen to interview the men populating the background of her study, said the critics, Gilligan might have produced a more convincing study about men's and women's allegedly different styles of moral reasoning. Then again, continued the critics, she might have instead produced a study showing that men and women actually reason quite *similarly* about matters such as abortion. Such a study result would have had dramatic consequences for Gilligan, however. Indeed, it would have required Gilligan to rethink her views about women's supposed ethics of care and men's supposed ethics of justice.

Other critics of Gilligan's methodology faulted Gilligan for focusing too much on the gender of the diverse women in her study. They claimed she thereby lost many opportunities to consider how race and class shape an individual's morality. Specifically, sociologist Carol Stack stressed the empirical evidence that, in certain circumstances, poor African American men as well as poor African American women favor care reasoning over justice reasoning. Indeed, in a study she herself conducted on poor African Americans migrating from urban environments in the North to rural environments in the South, Stack found that "under conditions of economic deprivation there is a convergence between women and men in their construction of themselves in relationship to others." She further found that "these conditions produce a convergence also in women's and men's vocabulary of rights, morality, and the social good."[33]

As hard as it was for Gilligan to address critics of her methodology, it was even more difficult for her to address critics who claimed that even if women *are* better carers than men (for whatever reasons), it may still be epistemically, ethically, and politically unwise to advertise this state of affairs. Linking women with caring may promote the view that women care by nature, or the view that because women can and have cared, they should always care, no matter the cost to themselves.

Among the critics who worried about the negative consequences of associating women too closely with the values of care was Sandra Lee Bartky. In *Femininity and Domination,* Bartky sought to determine whether women's experience of feeding men's egos and tending men's wounds ultimately disempowers or empowers women. By way of example, she noted that the kind of "emotional work" female flight attendants typically do often leads "to self-estrangement, an inability to identify one's own emotional states, even to drug abuse or alcoholism."[34] To pay a person to be "relentlessly cheerful"[35]—to smile at even the most verbally abusive and unreasonably demanding passengers— means paying a person to feign a certain set of emotions, said Bartky. A person can pretend to be happy only so many times before the person forgets how it feels to be genuinely or authentically happy.

Admitting that the kind of emotional work female flight attendants typically do for passengers is somewhat different from the kind of emotional work wives typically do for their husbands, Bartky noted that many wives find the experience of caring for their husbands empowering. The better caregiver a wife is, the more she may regard herself as the pillar without whom her husband would crumble. But, cautioned Bartky, *subjective feelings* of empowerment are not the same as the *objective reality* of actually having power. Women's androcentric emotional work probably harms women far more than it benefits them in the long run. According to Bartky, caring women reinforce men's status through a variety of "bodily displays," including "the sympathetic cocking of the head; the forward inclination of the body; the frequent smiling; the urging, through appropriate vocalizations, that the man continue his recital, hence, that he may continue to commandeer the woman's time and attention." Men do not accord women similar status, however, and because they do not, said Bartky, women's care of men amounts to "a collective genuflection by women to men, an affirmation of male importance that is unreciprocated."[36]

In Bartky's estimation, the epistemic and ethical consequences of women's unreciprocated care of men is most worrisome. The more emotional support a woman gives a man, the more she will tend to see things as he sees them. She will participate in *his* projects, share *his* friends, rejoice in *his* successes, and feel badly about *his* failures. But women do not need yet another reason to lose their sense of self or to doubt their own vision of reality and version of the truth. Men's and women's interests are not identical in a patriarchal society, and it is important for women to realize this.

As bad as it is, from an epistemic point of view, to know the world only or primarily through someone else's eyes, especially someone who looks down on you, it is even worse, from an ethical point of view, to affirm someone else's morality no matter the goodness or badness of his or her values. Bartky pointed to Teresa Stangl, wife of Fritz Stangl, commandant of Treblinka, as an example. Although her husband's monstrous activities horrified Teresa, she continued to "feed" and "tend" him dutifully, even lovingly. She played footloose and fancy free with her own soul as she helped him deaden his conscience. Quoting a passage from Jill Tweedie's *In the Name of Love*, Bartky observed that one cannot remain silent about evil and expect to keep one's goodness entirely intact: "Behind every great man is a woman, we say, but behind every monster there is a woman too, behind each of those countless men who stood astride their narrow worlds and crushed other human beings, causing them hideous suffering and pain. There she is in the shadows, a vague female silhouette, tenderly wiping blood from their hands."[37] Because horror perpetrated by a loved one is still horror, women need to analyze "the pitfalls and temptations of caregiving itself"[38] before they embrace an ethics of care wholeheartedly.

For reasons related to Bartky's concerns about any ethics of care, philosopher Bill Puka singled out Gilligan's ethics of care for special criticism. He claimed care can be interpreted in two ways: (1) in Gilligan's way, "as a general orientation toward moral problems (interpersonal problems) and a track of moral development"; or (2) in his way, "as a sexist service orientation, prominent in the patriarchal socialization, social conventions, and roles of many cultures."[39] Those who interpret care as Gilligan did will trace women's moral development through the three levels presented earlier in this chapter. In contrast, those who interpret care as Puka did will view these supposed levels of moral development as coping mechanisms women use defensively in a patriarchal world structured to work against their best interests.

Puka developed a persuasive case for his view of care. First, he presented Level One moral reasoning in Gilligan as those strategies of self-protection and self-concern women use to avoid rejection or domination. "I've got to look out for myself" and "If I don't care about myself, no one else will" are statements likely to be uttered by a woman who believes that others are not likely to concern themselves about her needs.[40] On the contrary, others are likely to use her only as long as she pleases them. Thus, she must be prepared for the day she is no longer wanted because she has outlived her usefulness or desirability.

Second, Puka presented Level Two moral reasoning in Gilligan as a resumption of the "conventional slavish approach" that women typically adopt in a patriarchal society.[41] Although Level Two moral reasoning is frequently described as authentically altruistic, as if women truly want to put other people's needs and interests always ahead of their own, in reality such moral reasoning is simply another coping mechanism. Women learn if they make life as easy as possible for others, they will be treated well enough, but if they insist on having things their own way, they will pay dearly for their willfulness.

Finally, Puka presented Level Three moral reasoning in Gilligan as a coping mechanism involving elements of both self-protection and slavishness: "Here a woman learns where she can exercise her strengths, interest, and commitments (within the male power structure) and where she would do better to comply (with that structure). A delicate contextual balance must be struck to be effective here."[42] Insofar as a woman is rationally calculating her chances of surviving and possibly even thriving within a patriarchy, Level Three moral reasoning constitutes a degree of *cognitive* liberation for her. It does not, however, signal *personal* liberation for her. As long as society remains patriarchal, women will not be able to strike a good balance between rights and responsibilities in their moral lives.

Not only was Gilligan criticized for overestimating the value of an ethics of care, she was criticized for underappreciating the value of an ethics of justice. For example, philosopher Brian Barry dismissed Gilligan's ethics of care "as an invitation to dispense with morality and replace it with nepotism, favoritism, and injustice."[43] Indeed, Barry went so far as to claim that care-focused women "would have to be excluded from all public responsibilities [because] it would be impossible to trust them to carry out public duties conscientiously."[44]

Less harsh than Barry's criticism of Gilligan's ethics of care were those criticisms that faulted her simply for not better explaining the relationship between care and justice.[45] For example, philosopher George Sher claimed that Gilligan needed to present care and justice more as fully complementary aspects of morality and less as totally different ways of conceiving morality. No matter how "abstract" and "impartial" ethicists are, they still have to attend to matters of context to determine whether an action does in fact constitute adultery, murder, rape, or arson. Similarly, no matter how "concrete" and "partial" ethicists are, they cannot focus on each element of a moral situation equally without being mired in a swamp of details.[46] Nor can they focus on one person's good in a network of relationships to the exclusion of others' good.

Sher's criticism of Gilligan was developed at greater length by Marilyn Friedman. As Friedman saw it, justice is relevant to care in at least three ways. First, if we view a personal relationship as a "miniature social system which provides valued mutual intimacy, support, and concern for those who are involved,"[47] we will fault relationships in which one person is the main "giver" and the other the main "taker." Regrettably, continued Friedman, many heterosexual relationships are deficient in just such a way. Women often serve men's physical and psychological needs and wants with little or no reciprocation for their caregiving acts. At some point, said Friedman, women must take men to task and demand, as a matter of justice, reciprocation. It is not fair for one person in a relationship to shoulder the lion's portion of the burden of care, while the other lounges in the security of being well cared for.

Second, noted Friedman, personal relationships create "special vulnerabilities to harm."[48] When someone who supposedly cares about us harms us, we may feel especially hurt or violated. An injustice perpetrated in the context of a caring relationship, said Friedman, is in many ways far worse than an injustice perpetrated outside such a context. For example, rape by an acquaintance may inflict deeper psychological wounds than rape by a stranger, because a "date rapist" takes advantage of the victim's trust.

Third, stressed Friedman, if we focus on our closest relationships, especially our familial relationships, we will discover they are fraught with the potential for myriad injustices. Should Mom and Dad give their son privileges they are not willing to give their daughter? Should Mr. and Mrs. Jones pay for their parents' nursing home expenses, or should they instead pay for their children's college education? Should Mr. Smith give up an excellent job so that he can move with Ms. Chang, who has a mediocre job, to a city where she will have an excellent job but he will have only a mediocre one? Unassisted by notions of justice, care cannot adequately address these questions, insisted Friedman. Despite Sher's and Friedman's valid point about the interaction between justice and care, in fairness to Gilligan, they should have properly credited her for also exploring this interaction in several of her writings. Initially, Gilligan offered a care-justice convergence theory. She claimed that, properly practiced, care and justice

> *converge* in the realization that just as inequality adversely affects both parties in an unequal relationship, so too violence is destructive for everyone involved. This dialogue between fairness and care not only provides a better understanding of relations between the sexes but also gives rise to a more comprehensive portrayal of adult work and family relationships.[49]

But later, Gilligan replaced her care-justice convergence theory with a care-justice gestalt theory. Like an ambiguous drawing that may be seen either as a duck or as a rabbit, a moral drama may be framed either in terms of justice or in terms of care, she said. Although these two perspectives never completely and finally converge, they are not usually diametrically opposed polarities, stressed Gilligan. Most individuals are able to interpret a moral drama first from one of these perspectives and then from the other, even if a few individuals lack this perspectival skill. In the same way that some individuals can see only the duck *or* only the rabbit in an ambiguous "duck-rabbit" drawing, some individuals can view moral issues only through the lens of care *or* only through the lens of justice.[50]

Critiques of Noddings.   In some ways, Noddings met with even more criticism than Gilligan did. Although some of the criticisms directed against Noddings echoed those directed against Gilligan, others were unique to Noddings's work. For example, Sarah Lucia Hoagland focused on Noddings's seeming preoccupation with unequal relationships in which one person depends on the other for care.[51] As Hoagland saw it, the overall picture Noddings draws is that of the one-caring consistently giving and the cared-for consistently taking. In fact, said Hoagland, Noddings occasionally implies that the cared-for has *no* obligation to the one-caring over and beyond being a unique self: "The cared-for is free to be more fully himself in the caring relation. Indeed, this being himself, this willing and unselfconscious revealing of self, is his major contribution to the relation. This is his tribute to the one-caring."[52] Such a "tribute" to the one-caring is sad, said Hoagland. A unidirectional mode of caring does little to teach the cared-for about the burdens of the one-caring, and it does even less to teach the one-caring about the legitimacy of her or his own needs.

Hoagland also faulted Noddings for claiming that some type of "ethical diminishment" is almost always the consequence of breaking a relationship, even an abusive one. Hoagland was particularly disturbed by the following passage in Noddings's *Caring:*

> While I must not kill in obedience to law or principle, I may not, either, refuse to kill in obedience to principle. To remain one-caring, I might have to kill. Consider the case of a woman who kills her sleeping husband. Under most circumstances, the one-caring would judge such an act wrong. It violates the very possibility of caring for the husband. But as she hears how the husband abused his wife and children, about the fear with which the woman lived, about the past efforts to solve the problem legally, the one-caring revises her judgment. The jury finds the woman not guilty by reason of an extenuated self-defense. The one-caring finds her ethical, but under the guidance of a sadly diminished ethical ideal. The woman has behaved in the only way she found open to protect herself and her children and, thus, she has behaved in accord with the current vision of herself as one-caring. But what a horrible vision! She is now one-who-has-killed once and who would not kill again, and never again simply one who would not kill.[53]

Angered by Noddings's words, Hoagland asserted that "ethical diminishment" is not the fate of the woman described above. On the contrary, ethical empowerment is her fate. The abused woman has finally found the moral strength to exchange a disempowering and false ethical "ideal" for an empowering and true ethical ideal. An ethics that keeps the one-caring in a destructive relationship is not a *good* ethics, said Hoagland. If a wife is told that ending a relationship with an abusive husband may damage her moral self-image, this woman's guilt, coupled with fear of reprisal on the man's part, may cause her to stay in a relationship that may ultimately destroy her. Unlike

Noddings, Hoagland refused to say anything at all negative about women who end abusive relationships: "I must be able to assess any relationship for abuse/oppression and withdraw if I find it to be so. I feel no guilt, I have grown, I have learned something. I understand my part in the relationship. I separate. I will not be there again. Far from diminishing my ethical self, I am enhancing it."[54] There are times in life when ethics demands we not care, insisted Hoagland.

Reflecting on Noddings's entire ethics of care, Hoagland concluded that it asks far too much in the way of care from the one-caring:

> In direct contrast to eros, which is self-centered, agape is other-centered. The caring of agape always moves away from itself and extends itself unconditionally. Certainly, Nel Noddings's analysis is that caring moves away from itself. However, I would add that since there are not expectations of the cared-for beyond being acknowledged by the one-caring, since my ethical self can emerge only through caring for others, since withdrawal constitutes a diminished ideal, and since there is allegedly no evaluation in receiving the other, the one-caring extends itself virtually unconditionally.[55]

A demand for such a high degree of care on the part of the one-caring, continued Hoagland, evokes the image of the proverbial black Southern mammy who not only obeyed but supposedly loved her master/oppressor. If "motivational displacement is one consequence of enslavement," exclaimed Hoagland, then Noddings's analysis implies that "the care of the caring is successful if the son of a slave owner grows up under the one-caring of the mammy to become a master."[56]

To these objections, Noddings replied that there is a difference between caring for others on the one hand and self-destruction on the other. Simple common sense dictates that "if caring is to be maintained, clearly, the one-caring must be maintained."[57] Yet, continued Noddings, there are a variety of ways to maintain the one-caring, including ones that may permit the person to preserve her or his ethical ideal "undiminished." Not every abusive marital relationship has to terminate with a divorce decree, a prison sentence for the abuser, or an act of preemptive self-defense, claimed Noddings. A bad relationship may yet be salvaged through appropriate and creative forms of intervention:

> Women in abusive relations need others to support them—to care for them. One of the best forms of support would be to surround the abusive husband with loving models who would not tolerate abuse in their presence

and would strongly disapprove of it whenever it occurred in their absence. Such models could support and re-educate the woman as well, helping her to understand her own self-worth. Too often, everyone withdraws from both the abuser and the sufferer.[58]

But, said the critics, even if some flawed relationships can be salvaged, some relationships are so bad they defy redemption and must be ended. In Fyodor Dostoyevsky's *Brother's Karamazov*, there is a terrifying section in which Ivan shrieks that he does not want to dwell in a "heaven" in which a cruelly murdered child, his mother, and his murderer embrace in a hug of cosmic reconciliation. This scene illustrates the assertion by Noddings's critics that there is a final limit on caring. Some things are so evil that they must not be forgiven.

Maternal Ethics and the Ethics of Care

Despite the critics' serious reservations about invoking the mother-infant or parent-child relationship as the paradigm for caring human relationships, care-focused feminists nonetheless continued to claim that the concepts, metaphors, and images associated with such relationships are precisely the ones to use. Among these "maternal thinkers" were Sara Ruddick, Virginia Held, and Eva Kittay. Interestingly, all three of those thinkers viewed caring not only as an other-directed psychological attitude of attentiveness but also as a practice, work, or labor. Caring is about having a certain sort of mind-set, but it is also about assisting those in need of care. Moreover, another thread that tied Ruddick's, Held's, and Kittay's thought together was their insistence that caring practice, work, or labor should be performed in the public domain as well as the private realm.

Sara Ruddick

Sara Ruddick identified the ways in which mothering is both cultural and biological; that is, mothering is an activity that men as well as women *can* do, even though as a result of their historic experiences, women now do it better. Ruddick observed that although biology destines women to bear children, it does not destine women to rear them. Nevertheless, because of a complex interaction between women's childbearing capacities on the one hand and patriarchal society's child-rearing needs on the other, child-rearing became women's work. As a result of this state of affairs, most women, though by no means all women, developed what Ruddick termed "maternal practice."[59]

Ruddick claimed society should not trivialize maternal practice. Like any human practice, it requires special abilities and particular ways of thinking and acting: "The agents of maternal practice, acting in response to demands of their children, acquire a conceptual scheme—a vocabulary and logic of connections—through which they order and express the facts and values of their practice. . . . There is a unity of reflection, judgment, and emotion. This unity I call 'maternal thinking.'" [60]

Ruddick rejected the notion that maternal thinking is merely an emotional, irrational display of love that comes naturally to women; instead she presented it as a type of learned thought. Like all modes of human thinking, maternal thinking has its own logic and interests, specifically, the preservation, growth, and acceptability of one's children. [61]

In some ways, Ruddick's reflections on maternal practice were similar to philosopher Alasdair MacIntyre's ideas about human practices in general. According to MacIntyre, a practice is a cooperative human activity that has its own standards of excellence. These practices include everything from professional activities like healing on the one hand, to personal activities like parenting (MacIntyre's substitute for maternal practice) on the other.

As MacIntyre saw it, no practice can flourish unless its practitioners acknowledge and strive for the goods and satisfaction that the community judges to be essential to the practice. For example, the practice of parenting cannot flourish unless parents *want* to be the best parents possible, that is, the kind of parents whom society regards as worthy of parenthood. Commented MacIntyre: "To enter into a practice is to accept the authority of those standards and the inadequacy of my own performance as judged by them. It is to subject my own attitudes, choices, preferences and tastes to the standards which currently and partially define the practice." [62]

Within the pursuit of any practice, we discover the *good* intrinsic to that kind of endeavor, said MacIntyre. Concomitantly, once we devote ourselves to a practice, we discover and become committed to following the standards of excellence that govern it.

The transformative process of becoming an excellent practitioner of any cooperative activity like parenting is, in MacIntyre's opinion, personally demanding. He claimed that if we are thoroughly engaged in a human practice, we know how hard it is to do *well* what we have chosen to do. We cannot persevere in this demanding process without the kind of virtues that push us forward on the days we would prefer to fall behind:

We have to learn to recognize what is due to whom; we have to be prepared to take whatever self-endangering risks are demanded along the way; and we have to listen carefully to what we are told about our own inadequacies and to reply with the same carefulness for the facts. In others words we have to accept as necessary components of any practice with internal goods and standards of excellence the virtues of justice, courage and honesty.[63]

Unless practitioners are virtuous, insisted MacIntyre, a practice will wither and the values internal to it will disappear.

As *necessary* as virtuous practitioners are for a practice's survival, MacIntyre did not claim that they are *sufficient*. In fact, he maintained that practices and their practitioners cannot act alone. They need institutions—that is, economic, social, and cultural support systems.[64] Although we tend to identify practices like teaching, business, and medicine with institutions like colleges, corporations, and hospitals, we should not do so, said MacIntyre. Practices, characteristically concerned with so-called internal goods like pride in a job well done, are held together by the sealing cement of human cooperation. In contrast, institutions are necessarily concerned with so-called external goods like money, power, and status and are energized by the fragmentary fires of human competition. Yet, observed MacIntyre, we need not automatically reject institutional support, provided that "the ideals and creativity of the practice" do not succumb to "the acquisitiveness of the institution" by our accepting such support.[65] It is simply too hard for us to eschew institutional support in an ever more complex, interrelated, and interdependent world.

Although Ruddick's understanding of a practice largely resonated with MacIntyre's, she took exception to it on several counts. She denied, for example, that the way to achieve the good(s) internal to maternal practice is through compliance with the accumulated wisdom of humankind—especially if humankind turns out to be *mankind*. For women to submit their own attitudes, choices, beliefs, and values about mothering to prevailing norms may be a major mistake, for, as Adrienne Rich noted, our culture conflates the *practice of mothering* with the *institution of motherhood*.[66] In other words, our culture confuses maternal practice as described by Ruddick with a set of social norms according to which mothers need to be female, heterosexual, totally self-sacrificial, and disinterested in any role outside the home. As an institution, motherhood requires mothers to literally live for and through their children. In contrast, as a practice, mothering permits maternal thinkers to realize dimensions of themselves in, with, and beyond their children.

Ruddick's analysis of a practice also differed from MacIntyre's in that she disagreed that honesty, courage, and justice are the three virtues individually necessary and jointly sufficient for the flourishing of all human practices.

Each human practice has its own set of virtues, insisted Ruddick. For example, mothers must cultivate a set of specific virtues (described below), to meet the three fundamental goals of maternal practice: namely, the preservation, growth, and social acceptability of children.[67]

According to Ruddick, preserving the life of a child is the "constitutive maternal act."[68] Infants are totally vulnerable. They simply will not survive unless their caretakers feed, clothe, and shelter them. Ruddick gave the example of Julie, an exhausted young mother with a very demanding infant. Having reached her physical and psychological limits, Julie pictures herself killing her baby daughter. Horrified by her thought, Julie spends the night riding a city bus, her baby in her arms. She reasons that, as long as they remain in the public eye, her baby will be safe.[69]

Ruddick told Julie's story to stress how difficult it is for some mothers to meet their children's basic needs. Not every mother grows so run-down and desperate that she has to take steps to ensure that she will not kill her child. But even under relatively ideal circumstances, most mothers do have days when they find mothering too difficult. To preserve their children on these bad days, said Ruddick, mothers need to cultivate the intellectual virtue of scrutiny and the moral virtues of humility and cheerfulness.

Mothers who possess the virtue of scrutiny survey their children's environment in a careful but not overly cautious way. They do not manufacture nonexistent dangers. Nor do they fail to recognize the real dangers that threaten their children. Mothers with scrutinizing eyes know their children will not die from a face scratching or knee scraping, but also know their children are too vulnerable to fend for themselves. Although children are not as fragile as goldfish, said Ruddick, neither are they as hardy as roaches or weeds.[70] Scrutinizing eyes open and shut when they should.

Closely related to the intellectual virtue of scrutiny, said Ruddick, are the moral virtues of humility and cheerfulness, without which mothers cannot lovingly preserve their children. Humility, said Ruddick, is a way of "preserving and controlling" children in an "exhausting, uncontrollable world."[71] It is the virtue that helps mothers avoid both the *excess* of dominating a child and the *defect* of passively giving in to a child's every demand. Humility also helps mothers understand they cannot protect their children from every evil.

Fortunately, the virtue of cheerfulness, defined by Ruddick as "a matter-of-fact willingness . . . to start and start over again," keeps mothers humble.[72] A humble mother realizes that even if her powers of preservative love are limited, they are *powers* nonetheless. Because the virtue of cheerfulness, like the virtue of scrutiny, also has its excesses and defects, mothers need to guard against despairing glumness on the one hand and an everything-is-wonderful attitude on the other. Mothers should fill their children's heads neither with images of the Big Bad Wolf nor with visions of the Sugar Plum Fairy, but with portraits of fallible and imperfect human beings trying to make the best of things. Cheerfulness, stressed Ruddick, is indeed riding "the bus up and down the nighttime city streets, keeping yourself and your baby safe even though you've imagined murdering her."[73] It is knowing there is usually some way to cope with a truly bad situation.

The second dimension of Ruddick's maternal practice is *fostering* children's growth. A good mother does not impose an already written script on her children. She does not insist her children meet unrealistic standards of abstract perfection. Instead, a good mother tells her children "maternal stories"—that is, realistic, compassionate, and "delightful" stories[74] that help her children reflect on the persons they have been, are, and might someday be. Faced with a stubborn daughter, for example, a mother should help her daughter understand why stubbornness is a character defect and how the girl could transform her stubbornness into the virtue of proper self-determination. A mother should help her children grow not only in physical size and mental intelligence but also in virtue. People become stubborn for reasons. They get tired of having to do things other people's way. Therefore, when they get the opportunity to resist, they fight back by digging in their heels and doing things their own way, no matter how disastrous the consequences may be. Self-awareness of this human tendency can help children understand why a modus operandi of perpetual stubbornness does not make good sense, and why it may be best to do things other people's way from time to time.

The third and final dimension of Ruddick's maternal practice is *training.* Mothers work hard to socialize their children, to transform them into law-abiding citizens who adhere to societal norms. But good mothers do not want their children to become mindless "conformists." Mothers may, for example, refuse to fit their children's vulnerable bodies into military uniforms, or diet them into designer jeans, or dress them for success in the so-called dog-eat-dog world. In a patriarchal society—that is, an overly competitive, hierarchical, and individualistic society—mothers may find themselves caught between the demands of patriarchy on the one hand and their own inner conviction that many of these demands are dehumanizing on the other. If a mother trains her son to be a "winner," he may become both the chief executive officer of a large firm and a very mean-spirited human being. In contrast, if she refuses to teach her son the "ways of the world," he may become both a very nice guy and someone who is labeled a loser. On almost a daily basis mothers must decide, said Ruddick, when and when not to let their own personal values guide their child-rearing practices. Ruddick added that mothers should not make these decisions by themselves; ideally, they should make them together with their children. If children adopt their mothers' values unquestioningly, their "training" will never be completed.[75] External compliance with others' values is an inadequate substitute for learning how to choose one's own values and living in conformity to them.

Clearly, maternal practice is a complex activity. Overall, it is guided by what Ruddick termed the metavirtue of "attentive love." This metavirtue, which is at once cognitive and affective, rational and emotional, enables mothers to "really look" at their children and not be shocked, horrified, or appalled by what they see.[76] Indeed, among the several characteristics that distinguish maternal thinkers from nonmaternal thinkers is the utter realism of maternal thinkers, emphasized Ruddick. A mother who loves her children inattentively lets her fantasies blind her. She does not see her children as they actually are. Rather she sees her children as they could perhaps be: the fulfillment of her dreams. In contrast to these mothers, mothers who love their children attentively accept their children for who they are, working within their physical and psychological limits.

Ruddick's ultimate goal was not simply to develop a phenomenology of maternal practice. Rather, she wanted to demonstrate that anyone, male or female, who engages in maternal practice will come to think like a mother. As it so happens, most of the people who have traditionally engaged in maternal practice have been women. Because women have been excluded from the public realm until relatively recently, *maternal* thinking has not been prevalent enough in government, medicine, law, business, the church, and the academy. Instead, a very *nonmaternal* kind of thinking has dominated the public realm—the kind of thinking that leads to ecological disorder, social injustice, and even war, in Ruddick's estimation. People who do not *think* like mothers, claimed Ruddick, do not *see* like mothers. They do not make a connection, for example, between war in the abstract and war in the concrete. For them, war is about winning, defending one's way of life, and maintaining one's position of power. In contrast, for mothers, war is about destroying the children they have spent years preserving, nurturing, and training: unique human persons who cannot be replaced. In sum, for mothers, war is about death—about canceling out the "products" of maternal practice.

Ruddick did not claim that mothers are absolute pacifists, however. She conceded that "maternal peacefulness"[77] is a myth, since mothers do not always think and act in maternal ways. The scene in the film *The Battle of Algiers* that most haunts me, for example, is one in which several Algerian women shed their veils in order to dress in the style of French women. They then put bombs in their shopping bags, and holding their own children in their arms, they escape scrutiny by the French police as they cross from the Algerian into the French section of town. After all, they look so harmless—the epitome of French motherhood! Having eluded detection, these Algerian women then plant their bombs in an open café, where large numbers of French men, women, and *children* are drinking espresso and licking ice cream cones. The camera focuses on the French children's happy faces and on the Algerian women's stonelike faces. The message is a chilling one: For the cause of Algerian liberation, Algerian women must be prepared to kill not only adults but also children—specifically, French children, who are no less vulnerable and precious than their own children.

Despite scenes like the one I just described and Ruddick's own concession that some mothers will resort to violence if they feel they must, Ruddick's overall claim was that maternal thinking offers "an engaged and visionary stand point from which to criticize the destruction of war and begin to invent peace."78 If mothers look at war through the lens of maternal thinking, they will understand that war simply does not make sense. Only peace makes sense, and if they care about their children, mothers must unite to make peace happen, said Ruddick.

As a first conceptual-political bridge, linking women and peace, Ruddick offered a *women's politics of resistance.*79 When confronted with policies such as stockpiling nuclear weapons—policies that threaten to negate their maternal activities—women may feel moved to protest, picket, and even riot. Although rebellious women sometimes fight alongside sympathetic men, these women often fight alone, *as women,* "invoking their "culture's symbols of femininity": "Women who bring to the public plazas of a police state pictures of their loved ones, like women who put pillowcases, toys, and other artifacts of attachment against the barbed wire fences of missile bases, translate the symbols of mothers into political speech."80

Only thoroughly unsocialized military men will be able to overcome the human sentiments that pictures of "mother love" typically evoke, thought Ruddick. Women who resist should, if necessary, manipulate men's emotions, "woman-handling" men toward peaceful ends.

Conceding that the word *mother* evokes for many feminists sentimentality, even as the word *peacemaker* suggests being an accommodator, Ruddick nonetheless proposed a *feminist politics* as a second way to join women and peace. A feminist politics supports women fighting against all forms of discrimination. Feminists work for women's economic, psychological, and sexual liberation, thereby rendering the lives of *all* women—including mothers— easier. Perhaps most importantly, a feminist politics makes women think about the solidarity among women. The resistance of a women's politics joins with the consciousness-raising of a feminist politics to bring women together against war, claimed Ruddick.

Virginia Held

Approaching maternal practice from a somewhat different perspective than Ruddick, Virginia Held maintained that morality is not unitary. Rather, said Held, there are multiple moral approaches designed to fit certain sets of relationships and activities in the public and private realms. Some of these moral approaches, closely related to the value of justice, are likely to be of particular use in the legal and economic realms. In contrast, other moral approaches are tightly linked to the value of care and are likely to be of special help in the realms of childcare, healthcare, and education. Held insisted each of these two types of moral approaches should be recognized by the other as particularly valuable in its own sphere of influence *and* generally necessary in the other. Society should recognize that the moral approaches designed to govern family disputes are just as socially necessary as the moral approaches fashioned to negotiate international treaties.[81]

Held's point about multiple moral approaches merits careful consideration. At least in the Western world, moral approaches generated in, from, and for private relations have not usually been recognized as fully *moral* approaches. Rather, they have been viewed as merely private matters not warranting serious moral scrutiny. Held pointed out that all too often, traditional ethicists have assumed that bona fide moral issues take root in one sphere only, the public sphere. She claimed this assumption was wrongheaded. Experiences need not unfold in a bustling marketplace or a contentious courtroom to merit moral analysis. On the contrary, they may just as easily arise in a nursery or around the dinner table. In other words, Held maintained that what makes an experience worthy of moral analysis is not *where* it occurs but *how* it occurs. If moral experience is "the experience of consciously choosing, of voluntarily accepting or rejecting, of willingly approving or disapproving, of living with these choices, and above all of acting and of living with these actions and their outcomes,"[82] then such an experience can as easily occur in one's bedroom as in one's office. Therefore, any adequate moral theory must address filial, parental, spousal, and friendship relations as well as physician-patient, lawyer-client, and seller-buyer relations. In the grand scheme of moral concerns, women's struggles and striving in the private realm count as much as do men's struggles in the public realm.

Although Held acknowledged that many women spend as much time in the public realm as they do in the private domain and that nature does not determine women's morality, she nonetheless claimed that a significant gap still exists between women's and men's moral experience. Held faulted traditional ethics not only for discounting *women's* morality but also for presenting *men's* morality as *human persons'* morality. Were traditional ethics truly gender-neutral, said Held, it would not favor paradigms that speak more to men's experience than to women's. Women's caring relationships with their vulnerable infants, aging parents, ailing siblings, and distraught friends—relationships between persons who are not each other's equals—do not fit the model for just transactions between equally informed and equally powerful adults. This does not mean, however, that relationships that arise from the practice of care are any less moral than relationships that arise from the practice of justice. We should not assume, said Held, that how relationships are handled in the public realm should be viewed as more fully moral than how relationships are managed in the private realm. Nor, continued Held, should we believe that the business of the public realm is much more important than the business of the private realm.

Held stressed that traditional ethicists view *contractual* relations as the primary model for human interaction, justifying a human relationship as moral to the degree that it serves the separate interests of individual rational contractors. Yet life is about more than conflict, competition, and controversy—about getting what one wants. It is, as mothering persons know, also about cooperation, consensus, and community—about meeting other people's needs. Held speculated that were the relationship between a mothering person and a child, rather than the relationship between two rational contractors, the paradigm for good human relationships, society might look very different:

> Instead of seeing law and government or the economy as the central and appropriate determinants of society, an ethic of care might see bringing up children and fostering trust between member of the society as the most important concerns of all. Other arrangements might then be evaluated in terms of how well or badly they contribute to the flourishing of children and the health of social relations that would certainly require a radical restructuring of society. Just imagine reversing the salaries of business executives and child care workers.[83]

Held conceded, however, that the kinds of relationships that exist between mothering persons and children can be just as oppressive—indeed, even *more* oppressive—than the relationships that exist between two rational contractors. For example, it is sometimes harder to recognize and handle abuses of power in a parent-child relationship than in an employer-employee relationship.[84]

Moreover, it takes greater moral skill to address questions of justice and rights in the domain of the family than it does in the workplace. One cannot quit a family as easily as one quits a job, nor should one, said Held:

> If a father threatens to disown and permanently sever his ties to a daughter who refuses to marry the man he has chosen to be her husband, she may justifiably see her right to choose her husband as more morally compelling than her tie to her father. If a child is a victim of severe violence in his home, it will be morally better that he lose his ties to his family than that he lose his life. And so on. But these cases of what seem to be the priority of justice are as much failures to care as failures to respect justice. The threat of the father and the injuries of the child make this evident. Where a parent does care well for a child but fails to recognize the child's right (to the extent that these can be separated, which is also questionable), the child morally ought to try to resolve the conflict through discussion and compromise within the network of family relations rather than breaking the relation with the parent altogether.[85]

Like principles, relationships can be evaluated as good, bad, or somewhere between good and bad. Relationships that are entirely bad should be quit, but relationships that have more good dimensions than bad aspects should be given at least a chance to survive. Premature or unreflective severance of them is not warranted.

Unlike some maternal thinkers, Held believed that men as well as women can be mothering persons. Just because men cannot bear children does not mean that they cannot rear children. Men and women can—indeed should—appropriate the moral outlook of caregivers. Leaving caregiving to women alone produces boys with personalities "in which the inclination toward combat is overdeveloped and the capacity to feel for others is stunted."[86] Because bellicose, unfeeling *boys* usually mature into bellicose, unfeeling *men,* Held claimed that human survival may depend on our ability to reorganize the way we parent. For starters, equal parenting, based on men's and women's "equal respect" for each other's "equal rights to choose how to live their lives," should become the order of the day.[87]

Held argued that from a child's point of view, it does not matter who takes care of his or her needs, as long as someone does. Parents should sit down, identify their child's needs, and then divide up the duties between themselves. Achieving an equitable division of labor is not an easy task, however, since parents will be tempted to fall back on the traditional gender roles society has imposed on men and women. Although Held did not claim that all gender differences in parental tasks are inherently oppressive, she warned that parental tasks should not be divided according to the skills a man and woman had when they first married, as these may stem from years of sex-role socialization. As much as possible, a man and a woman should try to perform the same parental tasks, departing from this nontraditional style of parenting only if there are "good reasons, and not merely customs and social pressures" for doing so.[88]

Despite Held's belief that men as well as women can mother, she still indicated that there may be a *qualitative* difference between female mothering and male mothering. The fact that women can *bear* children as well as *rear* children may signal that "women are responsible for the existence of new persons in ways far more fundamental than are men."[89] Men are necessary for conception, but their control over the future of humankind turns out to be limited. It is women who can say a definite yes to life by bringing a pregnancy to term, and it is women who can say a definite no to life through the process of abortion.

By stressing women's ultimate responsibility for bringing (or not bringing) new persons into existence, Held did not intend to negate her previous point that fathers and mothers are obligated to rear children. Because men participate in the inception of life, they should participate in its maintenance. Nevertheless, men's *direct* role in procreation lasts but a few minutes, whereas women's lasts for nine months or more depending on whether breast-feeding is necessary, said Held. The experiences of pregnancy make women especially aware of their procreative role. For example, when a pregnant woman eats, she can focus on the fact that she is "eating for two." If she fails to eat a healthy diet, both she and the fetus will suffer. Likewise, when a pregnant woman finally gives birth, she can say to herself, "Through this pain, I bring life into this world." These kinds of experiences are ones that a man can never have.

Even though the daily toil of rearing a child for eighteen years or more eventually takes a greater toll on a parent than the suffering of giving birth, Held asserted that we should not trivialize the birthing act as if it had no effect whatsoever on subsequent parent-child relationships. In suggesting that biological experiences may differentially influence "the attitudes of the mother and father toward the 'worth' or 'value' of a particular child,"[90] Held wanted to explore the relationship between the kind of *feelings* women and men have for their children on the one hand and the kind of *obligations* the adults have to their children on the other. If ethicists assume that "natural" male tendencies play a role in determining men's moral rights and responsibilities, then the same assumption should apply to "natural" female tendencies:

Traditional moral theories often suppose it is legitimate for individuals to maximize self-interest, or satisfy their preferences, within certain constraints based on the equal rights of others. If it can be shown that the tendency to want to pursue individual self-interest is a stronger tendency among men than among women, this would certainly be relevant to an evaluation of such a theory. And if it could be shown that a tendency to value children and a desire to foster the developing capabilities of the particular others for whom we care is a stronger tendency among women than among men, this too would be relevant in evaluating moral theories.[91]

The fact that Gilligan and Noddings shuddered at the biblical account of Abraham, who was willing to kill his son Isaac to honor God's command, did not surprise Held. Women who birth children—who preserve, nurture, and train them—are not likely to believe that obeying a command, even a command of God, is more valuable than preserving the very lives of their children. To be sure, from the standpoint of traditional ethics, a mother's refusal to subordinate the concrete life of *her* child to the abstract commands of duty or higher law may indicate her "underdevelopment" as a moral agent. Yet, in an age where a blindness to interconnection has led to the destruction of the environment and a perilous buildup of the nuclear arsenal, a focus on connection rather than individualistic rights may, said Held, offer a higher morality without which humankind cannot survive.[92]

The higher morality to which Held referred is an ethics of care. Exploring in depth the relationship between care and justice, Held claimed that care is the condition of possibility for justice rather than vice versa: "Care is probably the most deeply fundamental value. There can be care without justice. There has historically been little justice in the family, but care and life have gone on without it. There can be no justice without care, however, for without care no child would survive and there would be no persons to respect."[93]

So important is care to our world, said Held, that we must, as a society, cultivate the emotions necessary for its practice. Emotions, particularly sensitivity to the feelings of others, are essential to the practice of care. They are part of what makes a relationship good in a particular situation. Held noted that going through the motions of a caring activity "without any of the appropriate feelings" is not actually engaging in the practice of care. People who "are thoroughly unaware of what others are feeling and thinking, and grossly unable to read the moods and intentions of others" cannot truly care, said Held. They must be taught to care. Thus, it is not enough for schools to develop students' rational capacities—their powers of critical thinking. Schools must also develop students' emotional capacities—their powers of sympathy, empathy, and imagination.[94]

Eva Feder Kittay

One of the latest additions to the ranks of care-focused feminists who focus on the mother-child and similar relationships is Eva Feder Kittay. She described herself as among those feminist thinkers who "have begun to formulate a moral theory and a politics grounded in the maternal relation, the paradigm of a relation of care."[95] Yet, because Kittay did not want to be accused of bolstering either the essentialist view that women are by nature mothers or the mythical view that all mothers are good mothers, she used the terms "dependency relations" and "dependency workers" instead of "maternal relations" and "mothers" in her work.

For Kittay, the paradigm dependency worker is a close relative or friend who assumes daily responsibility for a dependent's survival. A dependency worker can be either male or female, according to Kittay, but because of a variety of socioeconomic, cultural, and biological factors, most societies have assigned dependency work to their female members. Kittay theorized that the dependency worker's labor is characterized by intimate and caring connections to the dependent. She also speculated that typically, the dependency worker suffers negative personal or professional consequences, or both, as a result of doing the essential work she or he does.

Closely related to the paradigm case of a dependency worker, said Kittay, is the worker who is paid, often quite modestly, to care for an unrelated person, but who views her job as much more than a mere job. Kittay provided an example of such a dependency worker from her own life: namely, Peggy, the woman who has cared for her severely developmentally disabled daughter, Sesha, for over a quarter of a century and to whom Kittay has distributed many of her motherly tasks. Without Peggy's help, said Kittay, Sesha would not have done nearly as well as she has, and Kittay and her husband would not have done nearly so well in their professional careers. On the contrary, most of their energies, particularly Kittay's, would have been devoted to caring for Sesha.[96]

Unlike the subject of traditional equality theory, Kittay's dependency worker is not an independent, self-interested, and fully autonomous agent. On the contrary, she is, in Kittay's estimation, a transparent self, that is, "a self through whom the needs of another are discerned, a self that, when it looks to its own needs, it first sees the needs of another."[97] As Kittay saw it, to the degree that the dependent needs the help of the dependency worker, to that degree is the dependency worker obligated to the dependent.

Kittay's explanation for the dependency worker's obligations to the dependent resembled the one Robert Goodin offered in his book, *Protecting the Vulnerable*.[98] According to Goodin, "the moral basis of special relations between individuals arises from the vulnerability of one party to the actions of another."[99] For example, a mother has an obligation to care for her infant because she is "*the* individual best situated, or exclusively situated to meet the needs of the dependent."[100] The source of a mother's moral obligation to her infant is not in the *rights* of the dependent as a person, but rather in the *relationship* that exists between one in need and one who is situated to meet the need. The defining characteristic of this largely socially con-structed relationship is that it is not usually *chosen* but already *given* in the ties of family, the dynamics of friendship, or the obligations of employment.

The fact that a relationship is given to the dependency worker, however, does not mean that the dependency worker is necessarily wrong to break the relationship. Kittay disagreed with Goodin when he refused to absolve a slave from his "obligations" to a master who becomes so ill that he cannot survive without the slave's help. The master's fragile condition is the slave's one chance for freedom. Is the slave obligated to stay and take care of his master, who will most likely die if left unattended? Goodin argued yes. As he saw it, if a vulnerability arises in a relationship, the moral worth of the rela-tionship is not relevant to the existence of the obligation.[101] Kittay argued no. As she saw it, the relationship that was given to the slave was a "relation-ship" that society should not have constructed. The relationship's coercive-ness cancels out the obligations that human vulnerability ordinarily creates.

Interestingly, Kittay believed that others' obligations to dependency workers are at least as weighty as dependency workers' obligations to their dependents. Her rationale for this claim was rooted in the image of her mother, who used to sit down to dinner after serving her and her father and proclaim, "After all, *I'm* also a mother's child."[102] Kittay claimed that embedded in this statement is the fundamental source of human equality. Dependency workers and depend-ents exist together in a "nested set of reciprocal relations and obligations."[103] This web of human connections is governed by a principle Kittay termed "doulia," from the Spanish term for a postpartum caregiver (a *doula*) who cares for the mother so that the mother can care for her infant. Thus, because every-one is some mother's child, it is only fair that someone should take care of dependency workers. For society to do anything less than this for dependency workers is not only to wrong dependency workers and their dependents, but also to weaken the entire fabric that binds a people together.

For Kittay, a theory of justice that is not infused with a theory of care will never produce equality. People in John Rawls's hypothetical world subscribe to two principles of justice. The first principle claims that each person is to have an equal right to the most extensive total system of equal basic liberties compatible with a similar system of liberty for all. The second principle argues that social and economic inequalities are to be arranged so that they are both (a) to the greatest benefit of the least advantaged, and (b) attached to offices and positions open to all under conditions of fair and equal opportunity.[104] But people in Kittay's actual world subscribe to more than these two principles of justice. They also call for a third principle of social responsibility for care that Kittay articulates as follows: "To each according to his or her need for care, from each according to his or her capacity for care, and such support from social institutions as to make available resources and opportunities to those providing care, so that all be adequately attended in relations that are sustaining."[105]

Conclusion

Although care-focused feminists have been faulted for being too focused on personal, particularly familial relationships, in fact most care-focused feminists have been quite attentive to professional and public concerns. Both Gilligan and Noddings made strong efforts to demonstrate the relevance of care-focused feminism for education at the primary, secondary, and postsecondary levels. Gilligan stressed that a "central dilemma for American education [is] how to encourage human responsiveness within the framework of a competitive, individualistic culture."[106] As she saw it, unless educators cultivate their students' empathetic skills as well as their reasoning skills, their students may do more harm than good. Physicians, lawyers, and businesspeople, who focus on fighting diseases, winning cases, and increasing profits respectively, may not notice the people they harm along the way to "victory."

Adding to Gilligan's points, Noddings insisted educators must teach citizens how to be globally aware. As she saw it, global citizens care about economic and social justice, protecting the earth, social and cultural diversity, and maintaining world peace. But, said Noddings, it is difficult to teach global citizenship in nations that want to maintain their dominance in the world.[107] One of Noddings's colleagues, Peggy McIntosh, claimed that many U.S. educators are remarkably ambivalent about helping students develop their caregiving skills. These educators see compassionate values as somehow threatening the supposed "manliness" that maintains U.S. world power, said McIntosh:

> The myths of oppositeness and of male superiority require that males be protected from developing attitudes that have been projected onto women. These attributes are seen to undermine, and even to contaminate,

masculinity. Males, especially young males, may have strong competencies in the caring, the relationality, and plural seeing that . . . are essential for global citizenship. What is rewarded in them, however, is solo risk-taking and individualism, and if they are white male, a go-it-alone and "damn-the-torpedoes" kind of bravery without a balanced regard for, or awareness of, the outcomes for other people of one's behaviors.[108]

No wonder it is difficult to educate for global citizenship, said Noddings. For example, U.S. teachers who invite students to consider how the war in Iraq hurts Iraqis may be viewed as unpatriotic or "left loonies," whose insistence on caring for all the world's people challenges the American way of life—a way of life based on the values that have been associated with "white male individualism."[109] And yet, continued Noddings, unless teachers have the courage to teach the practice of care to their male as well as female students, U.S. global awareness will never amount to much. U.S. global policy will amount to no more than temporary disaster relief in the aftermath of a tsunami or the height of a pandemic: a "charity fix" that masks the fact that were it not for a chance event, U.S. society probably would not give a thought to the people upon whom it has decided to lavish temporary attention.

For Gilligan and Noddings, education serves as the conduit from the private realm into the public realm. It is the means by which the ethics of care is exported into the public realm. As these two thinkers saw it, the ethics of care should be the primary ethics used in the professional and public realms. Interestingly, their views on the importance of world peace and general nonviolence within all societies dovetailed well with those of Ruddick explicated above. Gilligan, Noddings, and Ruddick hypothesized that the reason there is so much violence in the world, including the horror of war, is that there is so little care in the world. As Ruddick saw it, maternal thinkers have an obligation to become peace activists. They also have an obligation to become advocates for social justice and a sustainable economy. In other words, maternal thinkers have to enter the public and professional domain in order to shape policies, institutions, and laws that will permit all children and not just their own children to flourish. Maternal thinkers cannot afford to stay at home. Their ethics of care must explode into the professional and public domain.

Further specifying Ruddick's, Gilligan's, and Noddings's views on the public face of care, Held argued that market norms—the norms of efficiency and productivity—must not be allowed to have priority in education, childcare, health care, culture, and environmental protection. She also argued that even realms such as business, where "the individual pursuit of self-interest and the maximization of individual satisfactions are morally permissible," need to "be guided much more than at present by the concerns of care."[110] Somewhat of a realist, however, Held stated that the first task for care thinkers is to resist the expansion of market values into realms where, until recently, these values were considered entirely inappropriate. For example, care thinkers should resist markets in human organs and human gametes (eggs and sperms), as if body parts capable of saving or improving human lives are just commodities worth only as much as the market is prepared to pay for them. Success in resisting the encroachment of market values into areas of human life in which they have traditionally not held sway may later motivate care thinkers to more forcefully push care into realms in which market norms have traditionally been accepted, speculated Held:

> We should not preclude the possibility that economies and corporations themselves could be guided much more than at present by the concerns of care. Economies could produce what people really need in ways that contribute to human flourishing. But long before an economy itself is influenced by the values of caring, persons for whom care is a central value can and should affect the reach of the market.
>
> As a society we ought to be trying to shrink rather than to expand the market, so that other values than market ones can flourish. As we care for our children and their futures, we can become aware of the many values other than market ones we should try to encourage them to appreciate and to need. And we can argue for the kinds of social and economic and other arrangements that will reflect and promote these values.[111]

Clearly, Held did not confine the ethics of care to the private realm. But she wanted first to strengthen care thinking in the private domain so as to have enough men as well as women available to push it full force into a public realm traditionally resistant to it.

Somewhat bolder in her ambitions for an ethics of care, Kittay insisted that society should realize that dependency, the need to care for others, and the need for care for oneself are inescapable parts of the human condition. Theories of justice that are predicated on the myth and value of human independence are likely to result in institutions, practices, and policies that make it difficult or nearly impossible for people to care for each other. Kittay gave the example of the U.S. Personal Responsibility Act of 1996, the goal of which was to motivate (compel) indigent mothers to stop relying on government assistance for their families. Poor women were given only a set amount of time during which they would be eligible for federal funding of their families' basic needs (food, clothing, shelter, and the like). By the end of this time, the women in question were expected to have found some sort of job to support themselves and their families. Absent from this legislation was any acknowledgment that as soon as a poor woman without a spouse or another adult partner went to work outside her home, there would be no one left behind to take care of her children. Unless she could find affordable child-care for her children, the poor woman might be tempted to let her children fend for themselves during her hours away at work.[112]

Kittay contrasted the Personal Responsibility Act of 1996, which, as we just noted, made it very hard for single poor mothers in particular to care for their children, with the U.S. Medical Leave Act of 1993. Kittay noted that, whatever its limits, the 1993 act at least acknowledged the importance of care work. The centerpiece of this act was the provision of *unpaid* work leave to care for a newborn, a newly adopted child, or an ailing family member for a specified amount of time.[113]

Sadly, the 1993 act has not been equally recognized by employers. As a result of ignoring either the letter or the spirit of the act, many employers have met with workers' resistance. Since 1995, about 1,150 lawsuits have been filed in courts. The ground for these suits is the "supposed mistreatment [of workers] on account of family responsibilities—becoming pregnant, needing to care for a sick child or relative."[114] Relying on laws such as Title VII of the 1964 Civil Rights Act, which prohibits "not only overt sex discrimination but also seemingly neutral policies that have a disparate impact on women,"[115] and the 1990 Americans with Disabilities Act, which has been increasingly interpreted to cover people who care for people with disabilities as well as people with disabilities per se, lawyers have won about half of these suits. Employers have been put on guard that public sentiment in favor of making the workplace a hospitable one for caregivers is very strong.

Not only female workers but also male workers want time off work to care for ailing family members. For example, a former Maryland state trooper was the first plaintiff to win significant damages in a sex-discrimination suit that relied on the 1993 Family and Medical Leave Act. The trooper wanted to take four to eight weeks off work—time to which he was entitled per the 1993 act—to care for his wife, whose health had been seriously compromised by a very difficult pregnancy. He was told by his superiors to limit his stay-at-home time to two weeks. They could not afford for him to be gone for any longer. Later, after his wife delivered the baby, the trooper requested thirty days off to help his wife recuperate from the difficult pregnancy and birth. Although Maryland law provides thirty days' unpaid leave to primary caregivers, the trooper's employer denied his request. The personnel manager told the trooper that "unless your wife is in a coma or dead, you can't be primary care provider." He was also told "that God made women to have babies."[116] These sexist remarks came back to haunt the employer. They played a major role in the trooper's winning $375,000 in damages (which were later reduced to $40,000).

As families struggle to combine their personal and professional lives, and as workers from all classes of society start to press their employers to make it easier for them to balance work and personal responsibilities, more space is being carved out for care in the public domain. Although a proliferation of lawsuits is not the ideal way to get employers to transform their workplaces into care-friendly environments, it is still a way to get governments to pass care-friendly laws, laws that help curb the market forces of which Held spoke. For example, as noted by *New York Times* reporter Eyal Press: "In Sweden, parents have the right to work a six-hour day until their children turn 8, at a prorated salary."[117] Even though Sweden's policy and other policies mandating lengthy, paid caregiving leave may constitute a "drag on" an economy, such policies are increasingly the rule in many European nations that have, it would seem, recognized that care is not strictly a private matter.

Clearly, as we have just noted, it is possible to bring care full force into the public domain. In this connection, Fiona Robinson argued that if we focus on making care present in the public realm, there is no reason why the ethics of care cannot be "globalized." Confronted by the horror of world poverty, Robinson claimed that we need a feminist ethics of care, concrete and specific enough, to help privileged people see how their richness makes liars of them if they engage in rights talk without engaging in care action. Robinson conceded that "those who would prefer to cling to the familiar language of rights and duties, justice and reciprocity, and the apparent certainty offered to us by the kind of ethics which 'tells us what to do' and gives us universal standards by which to judge the justice or injustice of all forms of human activity," may not find a feminist ethics of care attractive.[118] These critics, she noted, will very likely continue to dismiss or misunderstand the idea of care "as sentimental, nepotistic, relativistic, paternalistic, and even dangerous."[119] But the fact that critics may snub the ethics of care is not an argument for care-focused feminists to abandon hope of globalizing an ethics of care, said Robinson. Rather, it is a reason for care-focused feminists to push even harder to develop a particularly demanding ethics: an ethics that requires all people and nations to do their fair share of care work so that all of the world's inhabitants can lead lives worth living.

6

Multicultural, Global, and Postcolonial Feminism

Multicultural, global, and postcolonial feminists push feminist thought in the direction of both recognizing women's diversity and acknowledging the challenges it presents. Not all women think and act alike; nor do all women value the same things or aim for the same goals. In short, women are different from each other. For this reason, multicultural, global, and postcolonial feminists challenge female essentialism, the view that the idea of "woman" exists as some sort of Platonic form each flesh-and-blood woman must somehow embody. In addition, they disavow female chauvinism, the tendency of some women, particularly privileged women, to speak on behalf of all women, including women they regard as "other" than themselves.[1]

Yet for all the similarities that link multicultural, global, and postcolonial feminists, these thinkers do have their differences. Multicultural feminists focus on the basic insight that even in one nation—the United States, for instance—all women are not created or constructed equal. Depending on her race and ethnicity but also on her sexual identity, gender identity, age, religion, level of education, occupation or profession, marital status, health condition, and so on, each U.S. woman will experience her identity and status as a woman differently. Expanding on multicultural feminists' basic insight, global and postcolonial feminists stress that depending on whether she is a member of a First World/developed/Northern/Western nation or instead a Third World/developing/Southern/Eastern nation, each woman in the world will be positively or negatively affected in significant ways. Moreover, women living in Eastern/Southern nations that were previously colonized by Western/Northern nations may have particularly complex identities. They may feel a special urgency either to reappropriate their people's precolonial traditions or to resist them with even greater force than their colonizers did.

Multicultural Feminism: General Reflections

Because my experiences are those of a woman living in the United States, it is not surprising that I have chosen the United States as the site to discuss multicultural feminism as it appears within the confines of a single nation's boundaries. Although some nations have fairly homogeneous populations, very few of them have populations as homogeneous as the population of Iceland, for example. In Iceland, marriage with non-Icelanders is extremely rare and most families can trace their genetic heritage back multiple generations to a small cluster of original Icelandic families. In contrast to Iceland, most other nations are multicultural and interracial. Within their historically constructed boundaries is a wide variety of peoples, some of whom are there as a result of migration, immigration, forced resettlement, territory seizure, or enslavement and any of whom may have intermarried. Among these multicultural nations is the United States.

To appreciate the significance of U.S. multicultural feminism, it is important to understand the reasons for its emergence and rapid ascendancy. As we noted in earlier chapters, throughout the 1960s, 1970s, and 1980s, U.S. feminists focused mainly on the gender differences between men and women. Most of these second-wave U.S. feminists, particularly the radical cultural feminists and care-focused feminists among them, stressed the degree to which, in the West, qualities such as autonomy, rationality, physical strength, and fairness or justice are associated with "masculinity," whereas qualities such as connectedness to others, emotionality, physical weakness, and caring were associated with "femininity." These thinkers also debated the extent to which these traits are biological givens or social constructions, and whether masculine traits are better than feminine traits, or vice versa.

Some second-wave U.S. feminists, termed sameness feminists, tried to prove that women had the same intellectual, physical, and moral capacities as men, and that if women were given the same educational and occupational opportunities men had, women could be men's full equals. Like men, women could be chief executive officers of large corporations, army generals, neurosurgeons, and football players. For sameness feminists, the primary enemy of women was sexism—the view that women are unable to do what men do and are appropriately relegated to the domestic sphere. Other second-wave U.S.

feminists, termed difference feminists, countered that it was a mistake for women to try to be like men, because women's ways of knowing, doing, and being were just as good as, if not better than, men's. For difference feminists, the primary enemy was androcentrism—the view that men are the norm for all human beings and that women, because they are not like men, are not fully human.[2]

Importantly, the 1960s–1970s debate between sameness and difference feminists never reached resolution. By the mid-1980s, feminists had moved on to other matters. Marginalized women, particularly women of color and lesbians but also poor, uneducated, and immigrant women, complained that the kind of gender-focused feminism that held sway in the academy was not a feminism for all women. Rather, it was a feminism for a certain group of elite women, namely, white, heterosexual, middle-class, well-educated women. These critics of mainstream feminism said that gender is neither the only nor necessarily the main cause of many women's oppression. For example, just because college-educated homemakers in suburbia may seek release from their domestic duties so they can get jobs in corporate America does not mean that female assembly-line workers do not yearn to be stay-at-home wives and mothers. More generally, just because some women find that matters related to their sexuality and reproductive capacities and responsibilities play the greatest role in their oppression does not mean that all women find this to be the case. For some women, it is not sexism, but racism, ethnocentrism, classism, heterosexism, ableism, or ageism that may be the major contributor(s) to their low status.

Roots of Multicultural Feminism in the United States

Repentant about mainstream feminism's relative neglect of women's differences and its failure to push marginalized women's concerns to the forefront of its agenda, U.S. feminists, the majority of whom were admittedly advantaged in one or more ways, determined to reorder their priorities. Thus was born multicultural feminism, a variety of feminist thought that was rapidly linked to so-called women-of-color feminism in the United States.

To some extent, multicultural feminist thought is related to multicultural thought in general, that is, to a late-twentieth-century ideology that both acknowledged and affirmed that nations like the United States are composed of multiple groups of races and ethnicities. Interestingly, earlier ideologies prevalent in the United States largely rejected the notion of a multicultural society. They maintained that not diversity but unity was the goal of U.S. society. According to historian Arthur M. Schlesinger Jr., early immigrants to the United States wanted to become a new people. For the most part, they did not want to maintain their ethnic identities. On the contrary, said Schlesinger, they *"expected* to become Americans. Their goals were escape, deliverance, assimilation. They saw America as a transforming nation, banishing old loyalties and forging a new national identity based on common political ideals."[3]

Immigrants' desire to be "Americanized" continued during the nineteenth century and into the first half of the twentieth century. Indeed, until the end of World War II, the majority of immigrants to the United States willingly jumped into America's so-called melting pot, first described by Israel Zangwill in a 1909 play:

> There she lies, the great melting pot—listen! Can't you hear the roaring and the bubbling? There gapes her mouth—The harbor where a thousand feeders come from the ends of the world to pour in their human freight. Ah, what a stirring and a seething! Celt and Latin, Slav and Teuton, Greek and Syrian,—black and yellow— . . . East and West, North and South, the palm and the pine, the pole and the equator, the crescent and the cross—how the Great Alchemist melts and fuses them with his purging flame! Here shall they all unite to build the Republic of man and the Kingdom of God. . . . Peace, peace, to all you unborn millions, fated to fill this giant continent.[4]

But, for a variety of reasons, by the 1970s new waves of immigrants began to criticize the Great Alchemist's work. A new *one-divided-into-many* gospel gradually replaced the old *many-united-into-one* gospel. Schlesinger claimed this new gospel rejected the "vision of individuals of all nations melted into a new race."[5] Instead, it favored an opposite vision: a nation of groups, highly visible in their diverse ancestries and distinct identities. Assimilation gave way to a celebration of ethnicity in the 1970s, as "salad bowl" and "quilt" metaphors for the United States increasingly displaced the "melting-pot" metaphor.[6] Multiculturalism, generally defined as a "social-intellectual movement that promotes the value of diversity as a core principle and insists that all cultural groups be treated with respect and as equal," was born.[7] Diversity, not unity, became the immigrants' mantra.

For several years the multicultural movement progressed without much opposition. But during the late 1980s and throughout the 1990s, the movement started to meet with opposition. Of all the arguments raised against multiculturalism, those focusing on its tendency to undermine social solidarity were the strongest. For example, Joseph Raz, himself a supporter of multiculturalism, conceded to his critics: "Without a deep feeling of solidarity, a political society will disintegrate into quarreling factions. Solidarity is required if people are to feel concerned about each other's fortunes and to be willing to make sacrifices for other people. Without such willingness the possibility of a peaceful political society disappears."[8] Critics of multiculturalism insisted labels such as *African American, Asian American, Latin/Hispanic American,* and *Native American* were divisive. These critics longed for the old melting pot and "American Americans."

Defenders of multiculturalism claimed that "we should learn to think of our [society] as consisting not of a majority and minorities but of a plurality of cultural groups."[9] We do not all have to look, act, speak, and think alike to be American, they said. Instead, we need to cultivate mutual tolerance, respect, and knowledge of each other's cultures and to make sure we *all* possess the skills and rights necessary to compete in the economic market and the political arena.[10] An "all-American kid" need not have blue eyes, blond hair, and white skin. Nor need he or she play baseball and love apple pie. On the contrary, an all-American kid may have yellow skin, brown eyes, and black hair. Moreover, he or she may play chess and love Peking/Beijing Duck.

Interlocking Sources of Women's Oppression

Multicultural feminists applaud the new emphasis on people's differences, regretting that second-wave feminist theorists largely ignored women's differences.[11] As noted above, many second-wave feminists wrote as if all women were white, middle-class, heterosexual, and well educated. In *Inessential Woman: Problems of Exclusion in Feminist Thought,* Elizabeth Spelman explained the reasons for this puzzling failure. She said many feminist theorists, particularly liberal feminists, went down the wrong path. In their desire to prove that women are men's full equals, they stressed women's sameness to each other as well as women's sameness to men. These theorists, said Spelman, failed to realize that it is possible to oppress people both by ignoring their differences and by denying their similarities:

> The assertion of differences among women can operate oppressively if one marks the differences and then suggests that one of the groups so differentiated is more important or more human or in some sense better than the other. But on the other hand, to stress the unity of women is no guarantee against hierarchical ranking, if what one says is true or

characteristic of some as a class is only true or characteristic of some women: for then women who cannot be so characterized are in effect not counted as women. When Stanton said that women should get the vote before Africans, Chinese, Germans, and Irish, she obviously was relying on a concept of "woman" that blinded her to the "womanness" of many women.[12]

Spelman urged contemporary feminist theorists to resist the impulse to gloss over women's differences, as if there exists some sort of universal "woman" into whom all of women's autobiographical differences flow and dissolve. In particular, she asked them not to make the mistake historian Kenneth Stampp made when he asserted "that innately Negroes are, after all, only white men with black skins, nothing more, nothing else."[13] Why, asked Spelman, is it that *Negroes* are only white men with black skins, nothing more, nothing else? Why is it not instead that *Caucasians* are only black men with white skins, nothing more, nothing else? If a white man can imagine himself protesting his reduction to a black man with white skin, why does he have trouble imagining a black man protesting his reduction to a white man with black skin? Could it be that whites still think "white" is definitely the best way to be, that is, that white people are somehow the gold standard for all people?

Noting there are many well-intentioned "Stampps" within the ranks of liberal feminists in particular, Spelman observed:

> If, like Stampp, I believe that the woman in every woman is a woman just like me, and if I also assume that there is no difference between being white and being a woman, then seeing another woman "as a woman" will involve seeing her as fundamentally like the woman I am. In other words, the womanness underneath the Black woman's skin is a white woman's, and deep down inside the Latino woman is an Anglo woman waiting to burst through a cultural shroud.[14]

No wonder, said Spelman, that so many women of color reject feminist thought. They regard it as white women's way of thinking. For this very reason, stressed Spelman, feminist thought must take the differences among women seriously; it cannot claim all women are "just like me."

Audre Lorde, bell hooks, and Patricia Hill Collins were among the first U.S. feminists who took the lead in highlighting women's differences. To a greater or lesser extent, each of these feminist thinkers probed the complex identity of so-called women of color and other minority women in the United States, discussing in particular their "multiple jeopardy."[15] Focusing on African American/black women in particular, bell hooks claimed in no uncertain terms that racism, sexism, and classism are not separable in fact, even if they are separable in theory. None of these forms of oppression can be eliminated before the elimination of any other.[16] Oppression is a many-headed beast capable of regenerating any one of the heads temporarily severed from its bloated body. The *whole body* of the beast is the appropriate target for those who wish to end oppression's reign of terror.

Among the many calls hooks issued to black women were calls to resist "White supremacy's" negative sexual stereotypes of black females' bodies. She claimed that white racists who viewed black women as sexually promiscuous animals caused large numbers of black women to react in one of two extreme ways. Some black women became overly modest prudes, obsessed with matters of bodily cleanliness and purity. In contrast, other black women decided to capitalize on their supposed "sexiness." Some black women, hooks commented, "who may have believed themselves to be always the losers in a world of sexist feminine competition based on beauty could see the realm of the sexual as the place where they [could] triumph over white females."[17] She urged black women to expunge from their minds white racists' negative images of them. Unless black women and, for that matter, black men stop internalizing their oppressors' negative view of them, stressed hooks, they will not be free to esteem themselves, that is, to be proud of themselves and joyous about their "blackness."

In a style as direct as bell hooks's style, Audre Lorde noted that "as a forty-nine-year-old Black lesbian feminist socialist, mother of two, including one boy, and a member of an interracial couple," she understood the concept of multiple jeopardy all too well, since she usually found herself a member of some group "defined as other, deviant, inferior, or just plain wrong." The way to overcome one's marginalization, said Lorde, is not "to pluck out some one aspect of [oneself] and present this as [a] meaningful whole," as if one can become a "first-class" member of society simply by fighting racism *or* sexism *or* classism *or* homophobia *or* ableism.[18] (Lorde experienced even more alienation subsequent to a mastectomy.)[19] Rather, the way to overcome one's marginalization is to "integrate all the parts of who I am, openly, allowing power from particular sources of my living to flow back and forth freely through all my different selves, without the restrictions of externally imposed definition."[20] Lorde fought simultaneously against all forms of oppression, including "that piece of the oppressor" within herself.[21] Her priority was to create a society in which everyone is truly equal and where "different" does not mean "inferior" but instead "unique."

Furthering the thought of hooks and Lorde, Patricia Hill Collins wrote that in the United States, black women's oppression is systematized and structured along three interdependent dimensions. First, the *economic* dimension of black women's oppression relegates black women to "ghettoization in service occupations."[22] Second, the *political* dimension denies black women the rights and privileges routinely extended to all white men and many white women, including the very important right to an equal education. Third, the *ideological* dimension imposes a freedom-restricting set of "controlling images" on black women, serving to justify as well as explain white men's and white women's treatment of black women. Reiterating some of hooks's observations, Collins commented that "from the mammies, Jezebels, and breeder women of slavery to the smiling Aunt Jemimas on pancake mix boxes, ubiquitous Black prostitutes, and ever-present welfare mothers of contemporary popular culture, the nexus of negative stereotypical images applied to African-American women has been fundamental to Black women's oppression."[23] Collins theorized the ideological dimension was more powerful in maintaining black women's oppression than either the economic or political dimension. She emphasized that "race, class, and gender oppression could not continue without powerful ideological justification for their existence."[24] For this very reason, Collins urged black feminists to release themselves from demeaning and degrading white stereotypes about them.

Conceptual Challenges for Multicultural Feminism

Although hooks, Lorde, and Collins happened to be African American/black feminists, their thoughts about the multiple sources of oppression of women of color were voiced with equal strength by Latin American/Hispanic feminists (Gloria Anzaldúa, Cherríe Moraga, Ofelia Shutte, Maria Lugones), Asian American feminists (Elaine Kim, Trinh T. Minh-ha, Ronald Takaki), and Native American feminists (Anne Waters, Bonita Lawrence, Donna Hightower Langston).[25] Initially, these so-called women of color sought their liberation in their color—in the fact that their skin color was not white. But later, they began to wonder whether the term "women of color" was really a term of liberation or whether it was, at root, a disguised term of oppression.

One problem some multicultural feminists noted about the concept of women of color was its oppositional nature. They worried that women of noncolor (i.e., women who look white) were the point of reference for women of color (i.e., women who look black, yellow, or red phenotypically).[26] In other words, the theorists feared that, in using the term "women of color" to refer to themselves, women who were African American, Latin American/Hispanic, Asian American, and Native American might "other" themselves and "self" white women.

Among the multicultural feminists who insisted her color did not make her the "Other" was Maria Lugones. Referring to Latin American women as Hispanic women, and writing from the vantage point of an Argentinean woman who has lived in the United States for years, Lugones explained the difference for the respective referents of the terms "we" (i.e., other Hispanic women) and "you" (i.e., white/Anglo women) in some of her writings. She claimed that although Hispanic women in the United States have to participate in the Anglo world, Anglo women in the United States do not have to participate in the Hispanic world. An Anglo woman can go to a Hispanic neighborhood for a church festival, for example, and if she finds the rituals and music overwhelming, she can simply get in her car, drive home, and forget the evening. There is no way, however, that a Hispanic woman can escape Anglo culture so easily, for the dominant white culture sets the basic parameters for her survival as one of its minority members. It is the Hispanic woman who has to live according to the rules of Anglo society, not the Anglo woman who has to live according to the rules of Hispanic society. Another point Lugones made was that a Hispanic woman does not perceive herself as a woman of color in her own home among her family and friends. On the contrary! She perceived herself *as herself*.[27]

Adding to Lugones's thoughts, Audre Lorde reasoned that even if the term "women of color" is set in opposition to the silent term "women of noncolor," this relationship would not in and of itself necessarily make women of color the "Other" and white women the "Self"—not if women of color insisted on defining themselves as the "Self" and white women as the "Other." Tired of explaining her African American/black woman's experience to white audiences, Lorde urged African American women and other women of color to stop explaining their difference from white women, demanding instead that white women start explaining their difference from women of color:

> Traditionally, in American society, it is the members of oppressed, objectified groups who are expected to stretch out and bridge the gap between the actualities of our lives and the consciousness of our oppressor. For in order to survive, those of us for whom oppression is as American as apple pie have always had to be watchers, to become familiar with the language and manners

of the oppressor, even sometimes adopting them for some illusion of protection. Whenever the need for some pretense of communication arises, those who profit from our oppression call upon us to share our knowledge with them. In other words, it is the responsibility of the oppressed to teach the oppressors their mistakes. I am responsible for educating teachers who dismiss my children's culture in school. Black and Third World people are expected to educate white people as to our humanity. Women are expected to educate men. Lesbians and gay men are expected to educate the heterosexual world. The oppressors maintain their position and evade responsibility for their own actions. There is a constant drain of energy which might be better used in redefining ourselves and devising realistic scenarios for altering the present and constructing the future.[28]

Lorde's points are well taken. Yet, questions about other women's differences may be motivated by genuine interest in other women's experiences. Indeed, Lugones pointed out that, provided Anglo and Hispanic women approach each other in the spirit of friends, they can travel between and into each other's worlds and learn from each other.[29]

A second problem some multicultural feminists raised about the concept of women of color was the fact that just because a woman looks white or colored *phenotypically* does not mean she is white or colored *genetically*. Nor does it mean that she thinks of herself as white or as colored. Although many multicultural feminists made this claim eloquently and effectively, Adrian Piper made it particularly poignantly because of her own complex racial and ethnic background. A light-skinned, white-looking person with both "white" and "black" blood flowing through her body, Piper described her complex family genealogy as follows:

Our first European-American ancestor landed in Ipswich, Massachusetts, in 1620 from Sussex; another in Jamestown, Virginia, in 1675 from London; and another in Philadelphia, Pennsylvania, in 1751, from Hamburg. Yet another was the first in our family to graduate from my own graduate institution in 1778. My great-great-grandmother from Madagascar, by way of Louisiana, is the known African ancestor on my father's side, as my great-great-grandfather from the Ibo of Nigeria is the known African ancestor on my mother's, whose family has resided in Jamaica for three centuries.[30]

As someone able to pass for white or black, Piper described her situation as, more often than not, a no-win situation. Many black people were suspicious of her, demanding that she prove her "blackness" to them—a blackness she treasured and happened to claim as her primary and chosen identity. Even worse, some white people castigated her for "fooling" them into thinking that she was *all* white or for using her black genes to her advantage, as she did when she identified herself as African American instead of Caucasian on a demographic form to increase her chances of gaining admission to a prestigious graduate program.

Building on Piper's analysis, but making a different point, Naomi Zack claimed that the "one-drop" rule, according to which a person is black if he or she has any percentage of "black blood" in his or her ancestry, can play itself out in a variety of ways.[31] In a nation like the United States, where, in the past, many white slave-owners had children by black slaves, millions of people who currently regard themselves as white may be black according to the "one-drop" rule. Similarly, many people who look black and identify themselves as black may in fact be genetically more white than black. The category of race, like the categories of gender and class, is not neat and tidy. In fact, it is very messy and increasingly difficult to use coherently.[32]

Taking Piper's and Zack's ideas farther, Linda Martin Alcoff agreed that bodily markings are of a superficial nature and that racial categories have fluid borders. What counts as black in the United States may not count as black in another nation, stressed Alcoff. She noted that "the meanings of both race and such things as skin color or hair texture are mediated by language, religions, nationality, and culture, to produce a racialized identity."[33] Alcoff provided several excellent examples for her observation, including the following:

> In the Dominican Republic, "black" is defined as Haitian, and dark-skinned Dominicans do not self-identify as black but as dark Indians or mestizos. Coming to the United States, Dominicans "become" black by the dominant U.S. standards. Under apartheid in South Africa, numbers of people would petition the government every year to change their official racial classification, resulting in odd official announcements from the Home Affairs Minister that, for example, this year "nine whites became colored, 506 colored became white, two whites became Malay . . . 40 coloreds became black, 666 blacks became colored, 87 coloreds became Indian. . . ."[34]

In providing the above examples, Alcoff's point was not that people often misidentify an individual as black when he or she is in fact white, but that "race does not stand alone."[35] On the contrary, race and ethnicity are socially constructed and deconstructed. Moreover, when it is possible to do so, some individuals choose their race or ethnicity depending on their own priorities and values or those of the society in which they live. It is telling, for example, that in the South African example Alcoff provided, no whites applied to be black.

But just because race and ethnicity are fluid categories, this does not mean that they are meaningless categories. Although all blacks, for example, are not essentially the same, sharing precisely the same "set of characteristics, . . . set of political interests, and . . . historical identity," said Alcoff, it is not accurate to say "that race is no more real than phlogiston or witchcraft."[36] On the contrary, race is very real since it is intensely present in societies like the United States. As Alcoff described it, race "is a structure of contemporary perception, . . . tacit, almost hidden from view, and thus almost [but not quite] immune from critical reflection."[37] This observation is particularly true of people who classify themselves as white but do not reflect on what white identity and white responsibility is.

The truth of Alcoff's observations are ones to which I can testify. Many years ago, I attended a philosophy conference in Los Angeles. The conference was held at a very swanky hotel, and most of the philosophers in attendance were white (and male, for that matter). I decided to take a long walk in a southerly direction. After walking one or so miles from the hotel, I noticed that the neighborhood started to change from mostly white to mostly Latin American/Hispanic to mostly African American. I was surrounded by swirls of color and music of all kinds and rhythms. The smell of one enticing food after another hit my olfactory nerves, as I became increasingly aware of how many people were sitting outside on the curbs for lack of air-conditioning in their own homes. Some of them stared at me. Suddenly, I became self-conscious and then came the realization: I was a spot of white in a sea of color. I was the "Other" and I felt vulnerable. For a moment, I wanted to run back to the hotel—to the safety of my white power and privilege. But somehow, I managed to overcome the urge, embarrassed by my realization that I liked my white privilege and power a bit too much and needed to work harder to divest my interest in maintaining it.

A third factor complicating multicultural feminism, and one closely related to concerns about the concept of women of color, surfaces in the 2000 U.S. census form.[38] The form asks individuals to identify their race/ethnicity as one or more of the following:

1. White
2. Black, African American, or Negro
3. American Indian or Alaska Native
4. Asian Indian

5. Chinese
6. Filipino
7. Japanese
8. Korean
9. Vietnamese
10. Other Asian
11. Native Hawaiian
12. Guamanian or Chamorro
13. Samoan
14. Other Pacific Islander
15. Some other race

The form asks individuals whether they are Spanish/Hispanic/Latino. People are supposed to answer in one of five ways:

1. No, not Spanish/Hispanic/Latino
2. Yes, Mexican, Mexican American, Chicano
3. Yes, Puerto Rican
4. Yes, Cuban
5. Yes, other Spanish/Hispanic/Latino

According to Ella Shohat, as it currently stands, the U.S. census form is very confusing. She stressed that the categories used on the form are clearly "heterotopic" categories, "mingling issues of race (blacks), language (Hispanics), and geography (Asians) as if they were commensurate categories."[39] No wonder, then, that during the 2000 U.S. Census, about seven million people identified themselves as belonging to more than one race or some other race than the racial categories provided on the U.S. Census form.

Increasingly, many U.S. citizens find attempts to categorize individuals racially and ethnically as somewhat off the mark. Specifically, many parents of children whose race or ethnicity, or both, is blended report that their children's self-identity does not rely exclusively or even mainly on racial and ethnic categories. Although personal anecdotes are no substitute for empirical studies, my own two sons, the offspring of an Asian father (he grew up in China) and a Caucasian mother with a Czech ancestry (me), are quite relaxed about their complex racial and ethnic identity. One of my sons describes himself as "nothing in particular, but everything in general . . . American, I guess." The other laughingly categorizes himself as "Chi-Czech." For the most part, neither race nor ethnicity plays a strong role in either of my sons' self-identity. They move between predominantly white and predominantly nonwhite circles with incredible ease, reporting they feel equally at home in both circles of people. For them, a really crucial question to ask is "Are you Goth?"

Yet another factor that complicates multicultural feminism is that as the term "multicultural feminism" is increasingly used, it embraces not only racial or ethnic groups that share a common history or tradition but also groups that feel that something about them—for example, their sexual orientation, class background, or physical condition—is the glue that makes them a "we." For example, one of the earliest and still best expressions of lesbianism as a distinct *culture* appeared in Adrienne Rich's now-classic essay, "Compulsory Heterosexuality and Lesbian Existence."[40] In the essay, Rich was concerned about two matters: (1) why women's love for other women "has been crushed, invalidated, forced into hiding and disguise" by the larger community; and (2) why lesbians' writings have been neglected. According to Rich, any theory, including any feminist theory that "treats lesbian existence as a marginal or less 'natural' phenomenon, as mere 'sexual preference,' or as the mirror image of either heterosexual or male homosexual relations is profoundly weakened thereby." By "lesbian existence" Rich meant "the fact of the historical presence of lesbians and our continuing creation of the meaning of that existence." By "lesbian continuum" Rich meant "a range—through each woman's life and throughout history—of woman-identified experience, not simply the fact that a woman has had or consciously desired genital sexual experience with another woman." For Rich, lesbianism was a culture, no less a culture than any other culture.

Since Rich wrote this article, other groups have identified themselves as cultures, demanding that their voices be heard and that their identities be respected. Among these cultures is so-called Deaf culture.[41] Many individuals with hearing impairments do not perceive themselves as negatively disabled, as people in need of repair. On the contrary, they present themselves as specially abled, as a group of individuals with a history, tradition, language, and unique ability to communicate with each other. Members of Deaf culture also view themselves as a minority group that has been misunderstood, even oppressed, by the dominant culture, that is, by people without hearing impairments. Some hearing people have faulted nonhearing people for wanting to use sign-language only or for refusing cochlear implants for their children or themselves. Critics have labeled anyone who chooses to remain in Deaf culture, when he or she could instead join non-Deaf culture, as "crazy."

By highlighting lesbian culture and Deaf culture, I do not mean to privilege lesbians and people with hearing impairments over individuals in other self-identified cultures. Rather, I simply want to emphasize that, as it is currently evolving, the concept of multicultural feminism exceeds the boundaries of women-of-color feminism. In other words, multicultural feminism in the United States, as elsewhere, is no longer simply a "politics of chromatic alliance."[42] Instead, it is a movement that embraces a variety of marginalized cultures so that they can, at various moments in their development, coalesce to undermine and ultimately overthrow the power of those individuals who have proclaimed themselves to be the Center.

A final problem with the concept of multicultural feminism is a poor understanding of white culture. If by white culture is meant a group of individuals who, because of their skin color, share a living, breathing, organic tradition that weaves together customs, religious beliefs, musical, artistic and literary works, family stories, and so forth, then white culture does not exist. In contrast, if by white culture is meant a hegemonic power structure that will do whatever it has to do to retain and increase its privilege, then white culture most certainly does exist. As a hegemonic power structure in the United States, white culture evolved from the intersection of two historical situations: (1) the people who for nearly two centuries were the most populous in the United States happened to have white skin, and (2) the people who initially gained control of U.S. society's economic, political, and cultural institutions also happened to have white skin. But today, having white skin is neither a necessary nor a sufficient condition for membership in the U.S. power elite. For example, poor white women surviving on social security checks too paltry to cover both their prescription drug bills and their food costs are not members of the power elite, though well-heeled African American lawyers and Latino(a)/Hispanic business persons probably are. There still is an "us" and a "them," but who the "us" and "them" is in the process of change.

Reflecting back over the points just raised, we can see why theorists like Shohat reasoned as they did. Shohat did not want to "follow a color/racial schema whereby the diverse feminists of color stand in line to represent 'their community.'"[43] She stressed the untidiness of the categories we use to describe ourselves and others, and the increasing difficulty we have using them consistently and coherently. For example, how does one categorize a female bisexual of Indian-African origin? asked Shohat. Such a woman "may be pressured to conform to sexual orientation as defined by U.S. norms, and may be accused of passing herself off as African, a charge carrying an implication of opportunism . . . yet the history of Indian-Tanzanian-Americans, which differs from that of both Africans and Indians who immigrated to the U.S. directly from their respective continents, need not be shorn of their Africanness."[44] Throwing up her hands at those who would stubbornly attempt to neatly categorize this kind of diverse individual, Shohat offered a political definition of multi-cultural feminism:

> Rather than simply a "touchy-feely" sensitivity toward a diffuse aggregate of victims, multicultural feminism animates a multifaceted "plurilogue" among diverse resistant practices: "First World" white-feminism, social-ism, anarchism, "Third World" nationalism, "Fourth World" Indigenism, anti-racist diasporic activism and gay/lesbian/bi/transsexual movements.[45]

As stated, Shohat's definition serves as a perfect bridge to a discussion of global and postcolonial feminism. It also invites the question whether global and postcolonial feminism are simply species of the genus *multicultural femi-nism.* Perhaps they are, but a complete answer to such a difficult conceptual question is, as of yet, not available.

Global and Postcolonial Feminism: General Reflections

Agreeing with multicultural feminists that the definition of feminism must be broadened to include all the factors (race, ethnicity, class, sex-ual identity, age, etc.) that oppress women in any one nation, global and postcolonial feminists emphasize that "the oppression of women in one part of the world is often affected by what happens in another, and that no woman is free until the conditions of oppression of women are eliminated everywhere."[46] Specifically, these thinkers focus on the world's division of nations into so-called First World nations (i.e., heavily industrialized and market-based nations located primarily in the Northern Hemisphere) on the one hand and so-called Third World nations (i.e., economically developing nations located primarily in the Southern Hemisphere) on the other. Global and postcolonial feminists closely examine how this state of affairs disempowers and disadvantages Third World women in particular.

Operating under the assumption that most First World feminists remain primarily interested in gender issues related to sexuality and reproduction, many Third World feminists emphasize that even though gender issues are of concern to them, economic and political issues tend to occupy the center of their stage. They stress that their oppression as members of a Third World people are often greater than their oppression as women per se. For this reason, many Third World women reject the label *feminist.* Instead, they use other terms to describe themselves, including Alice Walker's term "womanist."

Walker defined a womanist as "a Black feminist or woman of color" committed to the "survival and wholeness of entire people, male and female."[47]

Most First World feminists largely accept as justified Third World womanists' critiques of themselves. Joining with many Third World womanists, many First World feminists think of feminism as a dynamic movement rather than as a static school of thought. They seek to reconceive feminism as the process whereby women from all over the world discuss their commonalities and differences as honestly as possible in an effort to secure the following two long-term goals:

1. The right of women to freedom of choice, and the power to control our own lives within and outside of the home. Having control over our lives and our bodies is essential to ensure a sense of dignity and autonomy for every woman.
2. The removal of all forms of inequity and oppression through the creation of a more just social and economic order, nationally and internationally. This means the involvement of women in national liberation struggles, in plans for national development, and in local and global struggles for change.[48]

For global and postcolonial feminists, the personal and the political are one. What goes on in the privacy of one's home, including one's bedroom, affects how men and women relate in the larger social order. Sexual and reproductive freedom should be of no more or less importance to women than economic and political justice. Socialist feminist Emily Woo Yamaski made this point most forcefully: "I cannot be an Asian American on Monday, a woman on Tuesday, a lesbian on Wednesday, a worker/student on Thursday, and a political radical on Friday. I am all these things every day."[49]

Beyond emphasizing the interconnections between the various kinds of oppression each woman faces in her own life, global and postcolonial feminists stress the links between the various kinds of oppression women experience throughout the world. Charlotte Bunch explained the connections between local and global feminism in greater detail:

> To make global feminist consciousness a powerful force in the world demands that we make the local, global and the global, local. Such a movement is not based on international travel and conferences, although these may be useful, but must be centered on a sense of connectedness among women active at the grass roots in various regions. For women in industrialized countries, this connectedness must be based in the authenticity of

our struggles at home, in our need to learn from others, and in our efforts to understand the global implications of our actions, not in liberal guilt, condescending charity, or the false imposition of our models on others. Thus, for example, when we fight to have a birth control device banned in the United States because it is unsafe, we must simultaneously demand that it be destroyed rather than dumped on women in the Third World.[50]

The kind of consciousness that global and postcolonial feminism demands clearly requires great sensitivity to and awareness about the situations of women in nations other than one's own.

Diversity and Commonality

By insisting that women are interconnected, global and postcolonial feminists do not intend to sweep women's differences under the rug. On the contrary. They claim women cannot work together *as true equals* until women recognize and address their differences. According to Audre Lorde, when a feminist walks into a room filled with women from all over the world, she probably wants to minimize her differences from them. It is simply too threatening to her notions about "sisterhood" to focus on women's "manyness," so she strains to focus on women's "oneness." Lorde stressed that it is precisely this type of behavior that explains some feminists' inability to forge the kind of alliances necessary to create a better world:

> Advocating the mere tolerance of difference between women is the grossest reformism. It is a total denial of the creative function of difference in our lives. Difference must not be merely tolerated, but seen as a fund of necessary polarities between which our creativity can spark like a dialectic. Only then does the necessity for interdependency become unthreatening. Only within that interdependency of different strengths, acknowledged and equal, can the power to seek new ways of being in the world generate, as well as the courage and sustenance to act where there are no charters.[51]

Just because a feminist from a privileged background wants to work with women very different from her—women who may, for example, have suffered oppressions far more harmful to body, mind, and spirit than the ones she has suffered—does not mean this feminist should deny who she is or how she has suffered. Nor does it mean she should keep her counsel for fear of offending others. On the contrary, to refuse to reveal one's self to others is to assume that others are not capable of coming to terms with one. It is to say, "Although I think I have what it takes to understand others, I doubt that they share this ability." To think in such a fashion is the height of arrogance in global and postcolonial feminists' view.

Sexual/Reproductive Issues Versus Economic Issues

Among the differences global and postcolonial feminists address is one we noted earlier in passing. Whereas some women focus on sexual and repro-ductive issues, other women focus on economic and political issues. In the estimation of global and postcolonial feminists, however, there is no bound-ary between these two kinds of issues. On the contrary, they co-constitute each other.[52] In this connection, global feminist Angela Gillian quoted a Cape Verdean woman who had invited her to speak to a group of adolescent women about the importance of higher education:

> I want my daughter to take part in what is taking place in this country. If she gets married now, she will never participate in the change. I don't want her to be like me. I am married to a good man. As you know about 40 percent of Cape Verdian men are labourers in Europe, and my husband is in Holland. That house over there that we are building brick by brick right next to this little cabin is being made with the money he sends home. Every two years he gets one month's vacation, and comes home to meet the baby he made the last time, and to make a new one. I don't want that for my daughter. I've heard that it is possi-ble to prevent pregnancy by knowing the calendar. Please teach our girls how to count the days so that they can control pregnancies.[53]

Gillian commented that for this woman, the issue was not *men's* oppres-sion of women but how an inequitable international labor system causes both men and women to construct their family relations in deleterious ways. No wonder, said Gillian, that many Third World women are convinced that "the separation of sexism from the political, economic, *and* racial is a strategy of elites. As such, it becomes a tool to confuse the real issues around which most of world's women struggle."[54]

Focus on Global Reproductive Issues

One global theater in which multiple forms of oppression play is the theater of the reproduction-controlling technologies (e.g., contraception, sterilization, and abortion) and the reproduction-aiding technologies (e.g., intrauterine donor insemination and in vitro fertilization). Reflecting on the myriad ways in which government authorities seek to manipulate and control women's reproductive powers worldwide, global and postcolonial feminists note that most First World feminists believe that in order to achieve equality with men, women must be able to control their reproductive destiny by having access to safe and effective contraceptives and abortions, for example. They assume that it is in the best interests of a woman to have only as many children as she can nurture without jeopardizing her health and her ability to work outside the home. The problem with this First World assumption, say global and postcolonial feminists, is that it does not necessarily apply to all women in the Third World. In fact, it does not even apply to all women in the First World.

In the first place, there are women who want large families, despite the fact that being responsible for the care of many children may preclude or limit a woman's participation in the paid workforce. Some women may measure their worth largely in terms of being good mothers and may have no desire to be anything other than good mothers. Other women may reason that because their society—or, on a moral personal level, their husbands—value them only to the extent they can produce large numbers of children, it is in their best interests to do so.

Second, even when women want to use contraceptives and their governments make a wide range of contraceptives available, it is not always in women's best interests to use them—not if the contraceptives are unsafe, for example. It is one thing for women to use potentially harmful contraceptives in a nation like the United States, where follow-up medical care is generally available to all classes of women. But it is quite another for women to have access to such contraceptives with no provisions made for follow-up care. Specifically, Shawn Meghan Burn compared the distribution of some hormonal contraceptives in different countries:

> In most Western countries, the Pill is prescribed by a physician, and a woman must have a Pap smear once a year to get her prescription renewed. This permits screening for . . . side effects . . . and for screening out those women for whom the Pill is contraindicated. . . . However in some countries (including Brazil, Mexico, and Bangladesh), the Pill is sold without a prescription in pharmacies and stores. Depo-Provera is sold over the counter in Nigeria and even along the roadside. Long distances to health-care facilities often preclude the monitoring that increases the safety and effectiveness of contraceptive methods. [55]

Burn's observations notwithstanding, it is not clear, for example, that banning over-the-counter sales of the Pill to Mexican women because of its health risks would serve Mexican women's overall well-being. Ideally, all Mexican women—poor as well as rich—should have access to affordable health care. But in the absence of such care, and even with full knowledge that certain contraceptives may be unsafe, many Mexican women may still prefer the convenience, low cost, and privacy of an over-the-counter Pill purchase to a burdensome, relatively expensive, and public visit to a clinic, where health-care givers may chastise them for wanting to practice birth control.[56] Similarly, in many developing African nations, where men seek to control women's reproductive and sexual lives in particularly harsh ways, a woman may gladly risk using a possibly unsafe contraceptive if that contraceptive is one that she can secure and use without her husband's knowledge.[57]

Third, in the same way that having access to contraceptives is not always an unalloyed blessing for women, easy access to sterilization may not always be in women's best interests, either. Whether sterilization is a good option for a woman may have much to do with her race, class, and nationality, according to global and postcolonial feminists. For example, in the United States, the quintessential First World nation, accessible sterilization has generally proved to be a blessing for well-educated, economically privileged, white women but not for poor women, particularly poor women of color. Specifically, in the 1960s gynecologists observed the unofficial "rule of 120," which precluded the sterilization of a woman unless her age times the number of her living children equaled 120 or more.[58] The physicians followed this rule religiously when it came to healthy, white, middle-class, married women. This state of affairs angered liberal feminists in particular. They pressed physicians to adopt more permissive sterilization policies, arguing that competent, adult women had a right to decide when they no longer wanted children. Back then, these liberal feminists failed to realize that the same gynecologists who were reluctant to sterilize relatively privileged white women were only too willing to sterilize relatively unprivileged women of color, particularly those who were dependent on government funding to support themselves and their children. Indeed, in some Southern U.S. states, sterilizations of indigent black women were so common that the procedures were irreverently referred to as "Mississippi appendectomies."[59] More recently, but in the same manner, some U.S. legislators have drafted policies and laws linking women's welfare eligibility to their willingness to use the contraceptive Norplant. In the estimation of these lawmakers, unless women agree to use this long-term contraceptive implant, they and their children should be denied Aid to Families with Dependent Children.[60]

But, of course, coerced sterilizations are not confined to First World situations such as the one just described. All over the world, sterilizations are often less than fully voluntary. For example, during Indira Ghandi's years as prime minister of India, the nation set the world record for vasectomies at 10 million in 1974, largely as a result of government policies that gave material goods to poor, illiterate men in exchange for their agreement to be sterilized. Not only did Indian government authorities fail to secure anything approximating genuine informed consent from most of these men prior to their sterilization, but the authorities also often neglected to give the men the promised materials goods after their sterilizations. When these facts became known, the public lost confidence in Ghandi's government. Indian citizens protested that poor people should not be seduced with prizes such as money, food, clothes, and radios to give up their reproductive rights.[61] Interestingly, the "sterilization scandal" played a key role in Ghandi's overthrow as prime minister. This scandal did not dissuade government authorities in other nations from developing similarly enticing sterilization policies for their people, however. For example, over twenty years later, Bangladesh's sterilization incentive program gave people not only several weeks' wages but also saris (female dresses) for women and lungis (male pants) for men.[62]

Fourth, as with contraception and sterilization, utilization of abortion services is not an unalloyed blessing for women. To be sure, preventing women from having access to safe abortions often has tragic results. Even in nations where contraceptives are available and affordable, women (and men) do not always elect to use them, for any number of reasons. Unwanted pregnancies are sometimes the result of such decisions. Although relatively few nations completely forbid abortion, about 16 percent permit abortion only to save the woman's life, and another 46 percent of nations make it very difficult for women to have access to safe and legal abortions.[63] As a result of this state of affairs, many women who want abortions resort to illegal, usually unsafe abortions. Worldwide, about 70,000 women die as a result of subjecting themselves to an unsafe abortion.[64] The situation for women is particularly perilous in sub-Saharan Africa, Central Asia, Southeast Asia, and Latin America, according to Burn.[65]

Yet abortion is not always in women's overall best interests. According to global and postcolonial feminists, women in the former Soviet Union, for example, have an average of twelve to fourteen abortions during their lifetimes because contraceptives, although legal, are extremely difficult to obtain. Apparently, Russian cost-benefit studies concluded it is less expensive for the government to provide multiple abortions to women than to provide safe, effective, and monitored contraceptives to women. Sadly, the government ignored the toll that multiple abortions take on women's bodies and psyches.[66]

Abortion is also readily available in nations that want to control the size of their populations. But policies such as the one-child policy in China have resulted in women's having multiple abortions to make sure their one child is a boy. In China, most people, especially people who are bound by patriarchal thinking, still prefer boys to girls for several reasons, especially the reason that, traditionally, it is the son who provides care for his aging parents. In the past, Chinese women got pregnant as many times as necessary to produce at least one male offspring. If women produced too many daughters on the way to delivering a son, the mothers sometimes resorted to female infanticide or child abandonment. Nowadays, due to the availability of low-cost, easily accessible sex-selection techniques such as ultrasound, and to a lesser extent amniocentesis, most Chinese prefer to electively abort their female fetuses over facing the trauma of a female-infanticide or female-abandonment decision.

So effective has the increased use of sex-selection techniques been in China, an enormous sex-ratio imbalance has been created there. In fact, the sex-ratio imbalance in China in 2006 was 119 males for every 100 females.[67] Although one might think that a low supply of women in a nation might increase women's status, instead it seems to increases women's vulnerability. In the rural sections of China, for example, men kidnap women and force their victims to marry them. Even worse, some poor families have resorted to selling their prepubescent daughters to men who want a bride.[68] Realizing that they had a serious "bachelor" problem on their hands, Chinese government officials have relaxed the one-child policy and inaugurated a girls-are-as-good-as-boys campaign. They have also outlawed techniques such as ultrasound and amniocentesis for purposes of sex selection.[69]

As in China, permissive abortion, sterilization, and contraceptive policies in India, another nation that prefers male offspring to female offspring, have resulted in a sex-ratio imbalance of 1,000 males for every 927 females.[70] And, as in China, Indian authorities have decided to ban the use of ultrasound and amniocentesis for sex-selection purposes in an effort to correct India's sex-ratio imbalance. The ban, however, has not been uniformly enforced. In addition, many women, particularly in India's rural regions, continue to engage in female infanticide because daughters are costly in India.[71] Girls' parents must provide wedding dowries for their daughters. These dowries are no trivial matter. On the contrary, they can threaten the livelihood of the girls' parents.

Exacerbating the situation is the fact that when it banned ultrasound and amniocentesis for sex-selection purposes, the Indian government did not ban all sex-selection techniques. For this reason, Gametrics, a U.S. company with clinics in many Third World nations, started to heavily market a *preconception* sex-selection technology in India. The technology separates Y chromosomes from X chromosomes. Women who want a baby boy and who can afford the technology are inseminated with androsperm only. Reflecting on this costly technology, Maria Mies commented: "This example show clearly that the sexist and racist ideology is closely interwoven with capitalist profit motives, that the logic of selection and elimination has a definite economic base. Patriarchy and racism are not only ethically rejectable ideologies, they mean *business* indeed."[72]

Focus on Global Production Issues

No less a woman's issue than reproduction is production, according to global and postcolonial feminists. As Robin Morgan noted, "Women are the world's proletariat."[73] Even though it constitutes 60 to 80 percent of most nations' economies, housework continues to suffer from "gross national product invisibility."[74] To deny that women work, stressed Morgan, is absurd. Women constitute almost the totality of the world's food producers and are responsible for most of the world's hand portage of water and fuel. In most nations, handicrafts are largely or solely the products of female labor, and in most nations, women constitute a large portion of tourist industry workers, including the notorious sex tourism industry, which caters to businessmen who pay for the sexual services of women in the countries they visit.[75]

In addition, women are migrant and seasonal workers in agrarian nations and part-time laborers in industrialized nations. A significant percentage of the elder care, childcare, and domestic work done in First World nations is done by Third World women who have left their own families back home to make money to support them. There is, said Arlie Hochschild, a "global heart transplant" at work in the exportation of care from poor, developing nations to wealthy, developed nations.[76]

Also of particular significance in developing nations is the large number of women who work in factories owned by First World multinational companies. Most of the women (and men) who labor in these factories work under sweatshop conditions. Rosemary Radford Ruether noted that these conditions include the following ones: "workers receive less than a living wage, are forced to work long hours (ten to twelve hours a day) without overtime pay, work in unsafe conditions, are harassed on the job, physically and verbally abused, and are prevented from organizing unions and bargaining for better conditions."[77] Examples of the global market at work include Indonesia, where female factory workers receive about $1.25 a day for ten or even more hours of work; Vietnam, where female factory workers get about six cents an hour to assemble the promotional toys U.S. children find in their McDonald's Happy Meal boxes.[78] And there is Mexico, where female workers laboring in factories on the Mexican side of the United States-Mexico border receive far less wages than do female workers laboring in factories on the U.S. side of this same border.[79]

Global and postcolonial feminists debate whether women should work under sweatshop conditions. On the one hand, such work has made some women better off "as members of families who rely on their support, as mothers who want a better standard of living for their children, as young unmarried women who want the status that economic independence sometimes brings."[80] On the other hand, such work has made other women compliant and docile to a fault, unwilling to defend their human rights for fear of losing their jobs. Protest seems in order, said Ruether, as long as a Nike worker in Asia earns less than $2.00 a day and Nike CEO Phil Knight owns $4.5 billion in Nike stock.[81]

Adding to women's total workload is the eight or more hours of unrecognized work (housework, childcare, elder care, sick care) they do every day. When governments and businesses do respond to women's complaints about their "double day" (eight or more hours of recognized work outside the home and eight or more hours of unrecognized work inside the home), the response, more often than not, does not substantially improve women's situations. Governments or businesses tell women to work part time or to get on a "mommy track," strategies that are not feasible for women who need to support their families and that are not desirable for women who want to improve their status and wages at work. Even worse, some governments and businesses fail to understand women's complaints about their "double day" of work at all, recommending sexist solutions. For example, Cuba's Fidel Castro once proposed that "hairdressers remain open during the evening to ease the burden of the woman who is employed during the day but needs to be attractive in her house wifing role at night."[82] Not only did Castro expose his sexism, but he also showed no awareness of the situation of female hairdressers, who might not be able to work night shifts, because of their own family responsibilities.

Reflecting on how hard women work and how little government and business has done to ameliorate women's lot, Morgan concluded this state of affairs obtains because "Big Brother's" interests are not served by providing women the same kind of work and economic security it provides men. Whether Big Brother lives in the First World or Third World, said Morgan, "a marginal female labor force is a highly convenient asset: cheap, always available, easily and callously disposed of."[83]

Women in Development

Global and postcolonial feminists are somewhat critical of developed nations' efforts to improve developing nations' economies in general and women's lot in particular. Specifically, these feminists are skeptical about First World development programs for Third World people. Most Third World nations are located in the Southern Hemisphere, and most share a colonial history; that is, most developing nations were at one time colonized by European nations that exploited them as sources of cheap labor and valuable resources. These European nations also dismissed the cultures and traditions of the native peoples they colonized as less civilized than their own. Oftentimes, they forced native peoples to learn and speak their languages (English, French, German, Spanish, and so forth) and to convert to their dominant religion, Christianity.[84]

After World War II, most colonizers pulled out of the lands they had exploited, viewing these territories as an increasing cost rather than benefit. Sadly, and largely because of what the colonizing nations had done to them, many Asians, Africans, and South Americans found themselves incredibly poor. They were then forced to go to their former colonizers and borrow money from them. In the 1960s, interest rates were relatively low and many developing nations borrowed large amounts of money from developed nations. The developing nations assumed that they could boost their economies relatively quickly and pay back their debt swiftly. Unfortunately, most developing nations found it extraordinarily difficult to catch up to the nations that had previously exploited them. By the time developing nations realized that development is a slow process, interest rates had risen steeply, and the borrowers were unable to pay the interest on their loans.

To prevent the world economic system from crashing, the International Monetary Fund and the World Bank rescheduled the debts of many developing nations. As part of this plan, they required the affected nations to adjust the structure of their economies to ease their integration into the global economic system. According to Ruether, the "formula" for so-called Structural Adjustment was harsh. Among other things, it required "devaluation of local currency . . . the removal of trade barriers that protected local industries and agriculture . . . the privatization of public sector enterprises, such as transportation, energy, telephones, and electricity . . . and the removal of minimum wage laws and state subsidies for basic foods, education, and health services for the poor."[85] Moreover, in order to earn enough foreign currency to finance their rescheduled external debts, developing nations had to export as many inexpensive goods as possible to developed nations or work for large transnational companies located in their boundaries, or do both. As a result of this state of affairs, most developing nations were unable to produce their own consumer goods and were forced to import them from developed nations. Not only did these goods prove to be costly, but they also bore the cultural imprint of the world's developed nations: Nike sneakers, Camel cigarettes, Coca-Cola, Ford automobiles, Levi Strauss blue jeans, and Dell computers. The so-called McDonaldization of the world seemed harmless enough on the surface, yet it signaled the recolonization of the South by the North.

Global and postcolonial feminists claim that women in developing nations, even more than men in developing nations, are used to service what Alison Jaggar termed the "Southern debt."[86] Detailing how the First World's you-can-catch-up-to-us policies serve the interests of the First World far more than the policies serve the interests of the Third World, Maria Mies noted that First World economists make unrealistic promises to Third World people. They tell Third World people that developing nations can attain the same standard of living First World people enjoy. But down deep, these economists doubt the truth of their stories about endless progress and limitless growth.[87] Observing that the world's population will swell to 11 billion after the year 2050, Mies stated: "If of these eleven billion people the per capita energy consumption was similar to that of Americans in the mid–1970s, conventional oil resource would be exhausted in 34–74 years."[88]

Because the First World already finds it difficult to maintain its high standard of living, Mies speculated that whatever the First World gives the Third World in the way of benefits, it extracts in the way of costs. Specifically, she said, the First World passes on to its Third World "partners" the economic, social, and ecological costs the First World cannot pay without dropping from its privileged status to something more akin to Third World status:

> The relationship between colonized and colonizer is based not on any measure of partnership but rather on the latter's coercion and violence in its dealings with the former. This relationship is in fact the secret of unlimited growth in the centers of accumulation. If externalization of all the costs of industrial production were not possible, if they had to be borne by the industrialized countries themselves, that is if they were internalized, an immediate end to unlimited growth would be inevitable.[89]

In sum, stressed Mies, "catching-up development" is not *feasible* for two reasons: (1) There are only so many resources to divide among humankind, and they are currently inequitably distributed and consumed; and (2) to maintain its present power, the existing "colonial world order" needs to maintain the economic gap it promises to eliminate. For example, First World women's overall affluence depends on Third World women's overall poverty:

> Only while women in Asia, Africa, or Latin America can be forced to work for much lower wages than those in affluent societies—and that is made possible through the debt trap—can enough capital be accumulated in the rich countries so that even unemployed women are guaranteed a minimum income; but all unemployed women in the world cannot expect this. Within a world system based on exploitation "some are more equal than others."[90]

In addition to claiming that "catching-up development" schemes are not feasible, Mies noted that, in her estimation, they are also not *desirable*. She observed that the First World's "good life" is actually a very *bad* life insofar as human relationships are concerned. First World people are too busy making money to spend time with each other. They are so strained and stressed they have little sense of selfhood or ultimate meaning. First World people run the rat race, day after day, until the day they die, said Mies. Their children inherit their considerable material goods, and the cycle of meaningless running around until one drops dead continues.

The point of Mies's critique of the First World was not to recommend that because poor people in the Third World had enviable family and friendship relationships and a more appropriate set of life values than those typically displayed by hard-core First World materialists, the poor should stay dirt poor. Rather, it was that because money and power are limited goods, a relentless and single-minded pursuit of them inevitably leads to discord. In this connection, Mies offered an example that focused on First World women and Third World women as each other's competitors:

> It may be in the interest of Third World women working in the garment industry for export, to get higher wages, or even wages equivalent to those paid in the industrialized countries; but if they actually received these wages then the working-class woman in the North could hardly afford to buy those garments, or buy as many of them as she does now. In her interest the price of these garments must remain low. Hence the interests of these two sets of women who are linked through the world market are antagonistic.[91]

As long as the possession of material goods and power is equated with human happiness, said Mies, there will be the kind of competition and antagonism that inevitably leads to conflict and even war. Women will be set against women globally and against their own men nationally.

From the perspective of global and postcolonial feminists, stressed Mies, the First World must abandon its view of the "good life" and substitute for it a view predicated not on the *quantity* of one's possessions and power but on the *quality* of one's relationships. In addition, the First World must confront the material world's limits and vow to live within them. Only then will it be possible to create a new world order, in which divisions such as First World–Third World are incomprehensible. Finally, from the perspective of global and postcolonial feminists, women should take the lead in devising and implementing the systems, structures, policies, and programs needed to effect this transformation.

Knowing When to Respect Women's Culture

That women are different and that they have different priorities is a tenet of global and postcolonial feminism. According to Mies and Shiva, the East-West confrontations that preoccupied us from World War I onward, as well as the North-South tensions that currently confront us ended not only "all socialist dreams and utopias" but also "all universal" ideologies based on the conception of a common human nature.[92] Belief in oneness, they said, is Eurocentric, ego-centric, and phallogocentric. We must deconstruct the "one" so people can be *themselves*—not the other. Moreover, insisted Mies and Vandana Shiva, because natural and cultural diversity is a precondition for the maintenance of life on the planet, thoughtful people must oppose both the "homogenization of culture on the U.S. coca-cola and fast-food model" and the destruction of life forms "according to the demands of profit-oriented industries."[93]

Attracted to the view that the idea of "the many" needs to replace the idea of "the one," global and postcolonial feminists reasoned that ethical relativism, the theory that ethical judgments are applicable only to the time and place in which they arise, needs to replace ethical absolutism, the theory that ethical judgments are applicable to all times and all places. But this is easier said than done from a feminist point of view. Ethical relativism poses a serious threat to feminism. For example, Mies and Shiva noted the total espousal of ethical relativism implies that global feminists "must accept even violence, and such patriarchal and exploitative institutions and customs as dowry, female genital mutilation, India's caste system. . . . Taken to extremes the emphasis on 'difference' could lead to losing sight of all commonalities, making even communication impossible."[94] In other words, if the idea of difference makes it impossible for women in one culture to communicate with women in another culture, global and postcolonial feminists might as well forget their plans to build a new world order. Such an order is neither viable nor welcome if people are so different they cannot even make sense of each other's words.

Among the global and postcolonial feminists who realized that cultures cannot be excused for traditions that wrongfully harm people—in this instance, women and girls—is Uma Narayan, a woman of Indian background who now lives in the United States. In *Dislocating Cultures: Identities, Traditions, and Third World Feminisms,* Narayan observed that Westerners (her term) should acknowledge their role in creating unfavorable representations of the so-called Other as uncivilized, primitive, barbaric, or animalistic, and for letting their negative ideas about the Other be used as conceptual ammunition to defend unjust colonial policies. But, in her opinion, Westerners should not seek forgiveness for their past sins against Eastern people by refusing to engage in moral criticism of them now.[95] Narayan did not want guilt-ridden Westerners to unreflectively venerate her native land, India, as incapable of evil, but to insist with her that the wrongness that characterized U.S. segregation and South African apartheid is the same wrongness that still characterizes the Indian caste system, for example. In addition, Narayan pleaded that when she, Uma Narayan, condemns female genital mutilation, the sale of human organs, or sex-selective abortion, she should not be dismissed by Westerners as, after all, only a "Westernized" Indian woman, unable to speak on behalf of "authentic" Indian women, who presumably endorse every feature of their culture, no matter how harmful to women.[96]

Narayan's conviction that Westerners, but particularly Western feminists, need to apply the same moral standards to all people is not unique to her. Her viewpoint is shared by an increasing number of global and postcolonial feminists who wish to develop a "feminist humanism" that combines "the respect for differences characteristic of progressive movements since the 1960s with the universalistic aspirations of earlier liberatory traditions."[97] For example, the late feminist political theorist Susan Moller Okin claimed that feminists must talk about *women's* needs generically as well as specifically.[98] Conceding that as a group, women do not experience gender inequality to the same extent and degree, Okin nonetheless insisted that all women do experience it in some way or another, for the same reasons, and with the same consequences. Because virtually all societies regard women as the "second sex," as existing to some degree for men's sexual pleasure, reproductive use, and domestic service—and for all of society's care—women throughout the world tend to have not only less sexual freedom and reproductive choice than men have but also worse socioeconomic and health status.

Okin's views and views like hers were voiced beginning in the 1970s at several International Women's Conferences, including ones in Mexico City (1975), Copenhagen (1980), Nairobi (1985), and Beijing (1995). At these conferences, women from both developed and developing nations revealed that their quality of life was diminished simply by virtue of their female sex. They discussed how their respective nations' sex, reproduction, marriage, divorce, child-custody, family-life, and work laws worsened their lot in life, and how women and girls, far more than men and boys, were sexually vulnerable, unhealthy, uneducated, and poor.[99]

Inspired by the conference discussions, many global and postcolonial feminists went home to take action to improve women's condition worldwide as well as in their own nation. In particular, they began a campaign to have women's rights recognized as human rights in international documents such as the United Nations Universal Declaration of Human Rights, the Convention on the Elimination of All Forms of Discrimination Against Women, and the United Nations Declaration on the Elimination of Violence Against Women.[100] But then some global and postcolonial feminists began to have doubts about a women's rights approach to problems.

One reason some of these feminists lacked enthusiasm for women's rights is that they heard within rights talk a lingering tendency to privilege first-generation civil and political rights over second-generation economic and social rights.[101] Typical first-generation rights include freedom from oppression and from governmental interference with liberty of thought and action, whereas typical second-generation rights include the right to food, clothing, shelter, education, health care, work, rest, and reasonable payment.[102] If women's first-generation rights are honored without equal attention to women's second-generation rights, many women will remain at a real disadvantage, said global and postcolonial feminists. For example, a poor woman's right to have an abortion does not mean much if it simply prevents others from interfering with her decision to abort her fetus. She also needs the funds to pay for an abortion. And even if funding is available, her right to have an abortion will mean but little if, as a result of her abortion decision, she is ostracized from her community or rejected, abused, or divorced by a husband on whom she is financially and socially dependent.

Other global and postcolonial feminists rejected rights language not so much for the reason just given, but because they thought some of the rights that get privileged as *universal human rights* are not as universal as their proponents insist. These global and postcolonial feminists claimed that the rights are the creation of Western liberalism. These rights represent only, or primarily, the values and interests that people in nations like the United States favor. Anne Phillips pointed out that the high value placed on autonomy in statements of universal human rights may be "a central preoccupation of Western cultures" and that many women do not value "personal autonomy and mobility over the ties of family or community."[103] They do not want to be "liberated" from either the constraints of tradition or the obligations and limitations that go with belonging to a community. Phillips's observation was reinforced by Australian feminist Chila Bulbeck, who described her reaction to a pro-choice rally she attended in Washington, D.C.:

> I was struck by the anger of many of the speakers and participants. A black and white women's vocal group from Manhattan . . . shouted out the slogan "We are fierce, we are feminist, and we are in your face." Robin Morgan urged us to buy T-shirts proclaiming "Rage plus women equals power." One placard read "Abort Bush Before His Second Term." Angry arguments erupted between the pro-choice women and the pro-life women who had erected a "cemetery of innocents" nearby (representing aborted fetuses . . .). I went to the United States believing I knew it intimately from the flood of films, television programs, and academic books that pervade Australian popular and intellectual culture. Yet I felt battered and cut adrift by the assertiveness and anger, by the incessant refrain of rights and freedoms. This fashion of feminism was unfamiliar to me.[104]

Still other global and postcolonial feminists raised even more basic objections to rights talk. They thought it was a mistake to invoke as normative the concept of rights instead of its arguably correlative concept of responsibilities or duties. As they saw it, my right to at least a subsistence amount of food is dependent on your or someone else's responsibility to provide it for me. One feminist theorist who insisted that rights are best understood in terms of responsibilities was Diane Elson. She presented human rights as claims "to a set of social arrangements—to norms, institutions, laws and an enabling economic environment—that can best secure the enjoyment of these rights."[105] Moreover, she claimed it is wrong for states to stand idly by as charitable organizations and other nongovernment organizations struggle to maintain society's infrastructures so as to prevent its members from harm.

Although talking about responsibilities rather than rights makes it more clear that the realization of individual rights is dependent on others' felt or accepted responsibilities, such talk does not explain why individuals may lay claim to some social arrangements, goods, and services but not to others. Agreeing with

Elson that states must see to it that their citizens' rights are concretized, Martha Nussbaum specified which social arrangements, goods, and services a state must actually provide to the individuals who live within its border. As she saw it, individuals may demand as a matter of "right" from the state only those arrangements, goods, and services that will enable them to develop two sets of functional human capabilities: those that, if left undeveloped, render a life not human at all, and those that, if left undeveloped, render a human life less than a good life.[106]

Nussbaum's list of functional human capabilities included noncontroversial ones such as life, bodily health, and bodily integrity. But her list also included more controversial functional human capabilities such as the capability to play and to relate to nonhuman animals. Thus, it is not surprising that some global and postcolonial feminists viewed Nussbaum's list as reflecting not the needs of all women but the needs of "highly educated, artistically inclined, self-consciously and voluntarily Western women."[107] To this criticism, Nussbaum responded that she did not wish to impose her "good life" on any woman other than herself; she just wanted other women to have the means they need to choose their own version of the good life.

Many global and postcolonial feminists remained skeptical of Nussbaum's response, however. In an attempt to justify their skepticism, they pointed to passages from Nussbaum's writings such as the following one:

> The capabilities approach insists that a woman's affiliation with a certain group or culture should not be taken as normative for her unless, on due consideration, with all the capabilities at her disposal, she makes that norm her own. We should take care to extend to each individual full capabilities to pursue the items on the list and then see whether they want to avail themselves of these opportunities. Usually they do, even when tradition says they should not. Martha Chen's work with [Indian] widows . . . reveals that they are already deeply critical of the cultural norms that determine their life quality. One week at a widows' conference in Bangelore was sufficient to cause these formerly secluded widows to put on forbidden colors and to apply for loans; one elderly woman, "widowed" at the age of seven, danced for the first time in her life, whirling wildly in the center of the floor . . . Why should women cling to a tradition, indeed, when it is usually not their voice that speaks or their interests that are served?[108]

Nussbaum's suggestion that one week at a conference could undo years of enculturation troubled global and postcolonial feminist critics. Although they conceded that Nussbaum's understanding of human rights in terms of capabilities moves from an abstract interpretation to a contextual interpretation of human rights, her critics nonetheless claimed that it ultimately reverts to type—that is, liberalism as constructed in the Western world. Commented Vivienne Jabri of King's College Centre for International Relations, Department of War Studies:

> The practical implication of Nussbaum's approach . . . is the production of subjects whose emancipation is defined in terms of their full participation in the global liberal order. Apart from the banality of the certainties expressed, there is here a form of "epistemic violence" that astounds. In representing her discourse as a baseline for an international feminism, Nussbaum reiterates a late-modern form of colonial mentality that leaves the subject of its discourse shorn of history and complexity. This subject is hence denied a presence. This form of international feminism is ultimately a form of disciplining biopolitics, where the distribution of female bodies is ultimately what can constitute their freedom, as consumers within the global marketplace, where, to use Spivak, "to be" is "to be gainfully employed."[109]

Clearly, it is not an easy task for feminists to strike a balance between universalism and relativism. Yet it is a task that needs to remain high on feminists' to-do lists.

Conclusion

Multicultural, global, and postcolonial feminists present a great challenge to feminism: how to unite women in, through, and despite their differences. In general, these theorists have offered women two ways to achieve unity in diversity. The first consists of working toward sisterhood or friendship. For example, in the introduction to *Sisterhood Is Global,* Robin Morgan stressed that, in the end, women are not really so very different. Provided women ask each other "*sincere* questions about difference," said Morgan, they will see each other as searching for the same thing: namely, a *self* ("self-identity," "an articulation of self-hood," "self-realization," "self-image," "the right to be oneself").[110]

Furthering Morgan's point, Elizabeth Spelman itemized the kind of sincere questions multicultural, global, and postcolonial feminists may ask each other. These questions included the following: "What do I and can I know about women from whom I differ in terms of race, culture, class ethnicity?" "What happens when oppressors want to undo racism or other oppression;

how do they go about acquiring knowledge about others, knowledge whose absence is now regretted?"[111]

Among the many ways to find answers to these questions, said Spelman, is to "read books, take classes, open your eyes and ears or whatever instruments of awareness you might be blessed with, go to conferences planned and produced by the people about whom you wish to learn and manage not to be intrusive."[112] Other ways are to try to imagine what other women's lives are like and to be tolerant of differences, including the off-putting and threatening ones.

Interestingly, Spelman later refined her thought with some subtle distinctions. She said that there is a difference between merely *imagining* another woman's life and actually *perceiving* it. She explained the difference:

> When I am perceiving someone, I must be prepared to receive new information all the time, to adapt my actions accordingly, and to have my feelings develop in response to what the person is doing, whether I like what she is doing or not. When simply imagining her, I can escape from the demands her reality puts on me and instead construct her in my mind in such a way that I can possess her, make her into someone or something who never talks back, who poses no difficulties for me, who conforms to my desires much more than the real person does.[113]

In addition to specifying the difference between acts of imagination and acts of perception, Spelman elucidated a second important distinction between the act of *tolerating* someone's opinion and the act of *welcoming* someone's opinion. She claimed that merely to tolerate a viewpoint is to fail to seek it out "actively" as a *serious* critique of one's own viewpoint. If I am just tolerating you, I am not open to really changing myself. I am not prepared to be your friend; instead, I am simply willing not to be your enemy. In contrast, if I am welcoming you into me, I am exposing myself to the possibility of real change. I am expressing willingness to view my present self as a self in need of improvement, indeed transformation.

In a dialogical essay she coauthored with Maria Lugones, Spelman stressed that to develop an adequate (i.e., multicultural, global, and postcolonial) feminist theory, a wide variety of women would have to formulate it together. Lugones reacted to Spelman's proposal with some challenging points. She wondered whether women who had previously been marginalized by the recognized authorities in feminist thought would now want to join them to create a better feminist theory. Perhaps these once-marginalized women would prefer to do their own theory, in their own voices, without shouldering the burdens that generally accompany collaborative projects.

Lugones was concerned about the motives behind reigning feminist authorities' sudden interest in the views of "Others." Was the motive a self-interested one, in the sense of "self-growth or self expansion, feeding off the rich 'difference' of the other?" Or, just as bad, was the motive a mere sense of duty, understood as an act of noblesse oblige or as an anemic substitute for true love?[114] Lugones then continued that such motives, if present, would make it impossible for white women/First World women to fully partner with women of color/Third World women in theory making. She stressed that the only motive capable of bringing women together to weave a feminist theory strong enough to withstand the challenges of the twenty-first century is the motive of wanting to be friends. Unless one woman wants to be another woman's friend, she will be unable to summon the psychic energy to travel to that woman's world in order to imagine or see the other woman living her life there as a self rather than as an "Other." Therefore, according to Lugones as well as Spelman and Morgan, the chief task of multicultural, global, and postcolonial feminists is to help women learn how to be each other's friends.

Disagreeing with Morgan's, Spelman's, and Lugones's views on the essential goal of multicultural and global feminism are a variety of thinkers, including bell hooks, Audre Lorde, and Iris Young. Although hooks and Lorde sometimes employed the language of sisterhood in their writings, for them sisterhood is a political rather than a personal concept. Women can be sisters in the sense of being political comrades, but only if they are willing to truly confront their differences. Imagining, perceiving, tolerating, and welcoming are fine, insofar as they go, but confronting differences requires far more painful activities, like being enraged and being shamed. There is a difference, hooks emphasized, between "bourgeois-women's-liberation" sisterhood and multicultural, global, and postcolonial feminist sisterhood. The former focuses on women's "supporting" each other, where support serves "as a prop or a foundation for a weak structure" and where women, emphasizing their "shared victimization," give each other "unqualified approval."[115] The latter rejects this sentimental brand of sisterhood and offers instead a type of sisterhood that begins with women's confronting and combating each other's differences and ends with their using these very same differences to "accelerate their positive advance" toward the goals they share. As hooks explained: "Women do not need to eradicate difference to feel solidarity. We do not need to share common oppression to fight equally to end oppression. . . . We can be sisters united by shared interests and beliefs, united in our appreciation for diversity, united in our struggle to end sexist oppression, united in political solidarity."[116] Lorde also stressed the importance of maintaining women's differences rather than trying to transcend them. She claimed, for example, that feminists don't have to love each other in order to work with each other.[117] In the same vein, Young observed that although women should not be enemies, they should not expect to be friends. They should simply be content to be "strangers."[118]

Rejecting the homogenizing, conformist tendencies of the language of community and family, Young argued that feminists should not try to be "sisters" and "friends" with women whose worlds are radically different than their own. As Nancie Caraway noted, for Young, the "insistence on the ideal of shared subjectivity . . . leads to undesirable political implications."[119] Young repeatedly urged feminists to distrust the desire "for reciprocal recognition and identification with others . . . because it denies differences in the concrete sense of making it difficult for people to respect those with whom they do not identify."[120] She claimed, said Caraway, that multicultural, global, and postcolonial feminists should not want to be sisters or friends, because such desires "thwart our principled calls for heterogeneity in feminism."[121]

The choice between the sisterhood of friendship and the sisterhood of political solidarity is an important one. Multicultural, global, and postcolonial feminists might need to make this choice once and for all in the future, but for now the consensus seems to be a combined approach in which political alliances become opportunities for women to form personal friendships. In this connection, Aristotle had some surprisingly good advice for feminists. According to the Greek philosopher, there are three kinds of friendship: friendship between people who are *useful* to each other (e.g., professional colleagues); friendship between people who enjoy the same sorts of pleasures (e.g., drinking buddies and dance partners); and friendship between people who share meaningful goals and tasks (e.g., famine relief workers and women against oppression). To be this last kind of friend, said Aristotle, is to be a "partner in virtue and a friend in action."[122] Perhaps this is precisely the kind of friends multicultural, global, and postcolonial feminists should want to be.

7

Ecofeminism

Like multicultural, postcolonial, and global feminists, ecofeminists highlight the multiple ways in which human beings oppress each other, but these theorists also focus on human beings' domination of the nonhuman world, or nature. Because women are culturally tied to nature, ecofeminists argue there are conceptual, symbolic, and linguistic connections between feminist and ecological issues. According to Karen J. Warren, the Western world's basic beliefs, values, attitudes, and assumptions about itself and its inhabitants have been shaped by an oppressive patriarchal conceptual framework, the purpose of which is to explain, justify, and maintain relationships of domination and subordination in general and men's domination of women in particular. The most significant features of this framework are:

1. value-hierarchical thinking, namely, "up-down" thinking, which places higher value, status, or prestige on what is "up" rather than on what is "down"
2. value dualisms, that is, disjunctive pairs in which the disjuncts are seen as oppositional (rather than as complementary) and exclusive (rather than as inclusive) and that place higher value (status, prestige) on one disjunct rather than the other (e.g., dualisms that give higher value or status to that which has historically been identified as "mind," "reason," and "male" than to that which has historically been identified as "body," "emotion," and "female")
3. logic of domination, that is, a structure of argumentation that leads to a justification of subordination.[1]

Patriarchy's hierarchical, dualistic, and oppressive mode of thinking has harmed both women and nature, in Warren's opinion. Indeed, because women have been "naturalized" and nature has been "feminized," it is difficult to know where the oppression of one ends and the other begins. Warren emphasized women are "naturalized" when they are described in animal terms such as "cows, foxes, chicks, serpents, bitches, beavers, old bats, pussycats, cats, bird-brains, hare-brains."[2] Similarly, nature is "feminized" when "she" is raped, mastered, conquered, controlled, penetrated, subdued, and mined by men, or when "she" is venerated or even worshipped as the grandest mother of all. If man is the lord of nature, if he has been given dominion over it, then he has control not only over nature but also over nature's human analog, woman. Whatever man may do to nature, he may also do to woman.

Similar to the manner in which radical-cultural feminists and radical-libertarian feminists disagree about whether women's association with the work of childbearing and child-rearing is ultimately a source of power or disempowerment for women, "cultural," "nature," or "psychobiologistic" ecofeminists disagree with "social-constructionist" or "social-transformative" ecofeminists about the wisdom of stressing women's association with nature.[3]

Yet despite their sometimes divergent views on women's particular responsibilities to the environment (must we live as simply as possible?), to animals (must we be vegetarians and antivivisectionists?), and to future generations (must we be pacifists and strict population controllers?), all ecofeminists agree with Rosemary Radford Ruether that women's and nature's liberation are a joint project:

> Women must see that there can be no liberation for them and no solution to the ecological aims within a society whose fundamental model of relationships continues to be one of domination. They must unite the demands of the women's movement with those of the ecological movement to envision a radical reshaping of the basic socioeconomic relations and the underlying values of this [modern industrial] society.[4]

Some Roots of Ecofeminism

In her 1962 book, *Silent Spring,* Rachel Carson warned Americans that unless they began to take care of their environment, then "all man's assaults upon the environment [including] the contamination of air, earth, rivers, and sea with dangerous and even lethal materials . . . [will undoubtedly] shatter or alter the very material . . . upon which the shape of the future depends."[5] As ecological concerns about global warming, ozone depletion, waste disposal, animal farming, endangered species, energy conservation, and wilderness preservation grew, an environmental movement took hold in the United States and throughout the world. Though all environmentalists believe human beings should respect nature, and give reasons for doing so, "human-centered" environmentalists provide reasons that are based on furthering human interests, whereas "earth-centered" environmentalists provide reasons that are based on the intrinsic value of the earth itself.

Human-centered environmentalists emphasize that we harm ourselves when we harm the environment. If we exhaust our natural resources or pollute our skies and water, not only we but also our progeny will suffer. If we want to have the material goods and lifestyles that industrialization makes possible, we must devise some means to handle the toxic wastes it produces as a by-product. If we want to have the benefit of bountiful and inexpensive energy, we must harness new sources of energy like the sun and wind, lest we use the entire supply of oil and natural gas currently fueling our economy. If we want to experience the wilderness and see uncultivated vegetation and undomesticated animals, then we must prevent commercial enterprises from transforming every piece of wild land into a Disneyland or Club Med. And if we want to preserve the rich diversity of nature and the treasures it might still hold for us, then we must safeguard all life-forms, refusing to imperil their existence.

Viewing themselves as realistic or pragmatic about environmental concerns, human-centered environmentalists concede that from time to time, we may have to sacrifice the environment in order to serve our interests. In other words, sometimes a forest must be cut down so we can use the trees to build homes; sometimes the air must be polluted so we can continue to drive our automobiles; sometimes a predatory species of wild animals must be eliminated or relegated to our zoos so our domesticated animals can graze safely. In short, the environment's value is *instrumental;* its meaning, significance, and purpose depends on our needs or wants. The environment exists not for itself but for human beings.

It is not surprising that critics of human-centered environmentalism condemn it as "arrogant anthropomorphism," generally faulting the Judeo-Christian tradition as one of the main players in the devaluation of the environment. They point, for example, to the biblical mandate that instructed *men* to "subdue" the earth and "have dominion over the fish of the sea and over the birds of the air and every living thing that moves upon the earth" as promoting the view that nature has instrumental value only.[6] These same critics also stress how the metaphors and models of mechanistic science, which gained sway during the pre-Enlightenment and Enlightenment periods, reinforced the Bible's anthropomorphic view of nature. They claim that prior to the seventeenth century, we thought of nature organically, as a benevolent female or nurturing mother, as someone who gave freely and generously of *her* bounty to us, her children. After the scientific revolution, however, we reconceived nature mechanistically, as an inert, lifeless machine. As a result of this paradigm shift, we found it easier to justify not only our use but also our misuse and abuse of nature. We reasoned that there is nothing morally wrong with treating a mere "object" in whatever way we wish.

René Descartes' philosophy, which privileged mind over matter, further bolstered the mechanistic conception of nature, according to critics of human-centered environmentalism. His belief that our ability to think ("I think, therefore I am") makes us special led to the view that things that think (*res cogitans,* or human beings) are meant to control things that do not think (animals, trees, and rocks). Gradually, we convinced ourselves that human beings are indeed the highest life-form: the center of the universe. As a result of our exalted self-conception, we took it upon ourselves to decide not only when to protect and preserve the environment for our use but also when to sacrifice it for our greater glory and good.

Human-centered, or anthropomorphic, environmentalism, sometimes termed "shallow ecology," remained the order of the day until the late 1940s, when a new generation of environmentalists forwarded an earth-centered environmentalism they termed "deep ecology." This post-Enlightenment view of nature repudiated the modern conception of nature as a machine, reverting to medieval and even ancient conceptions of nature as an organism that has intrinsic as well as instrumental value.

In his much-anthologized essay, "The Land Ethic," Aldo Leopold wrote that we should think about the land as "a fountain of energy flowing though a circuit of soils, plants, and animals."[7] Leopold believed the earth is a life system, an intricately interwoven and interdependent intersection of elements that functions as a whole organism. If one element of this system becomes diseased, the whole system is probably sick, and the only way to heal the system is to treat or cure the diseased part, whether that diseased part is an excessively flooded plain, a severely overpopulated herd of deer (or human beings), or a heavily polluted river. To be sure, a treatment or cure for the diseased element will not always be found, but that is to be expected. In fact, the ecosystem's laws of death and decay *require* that its old elements be extinguished: The patterns of regeneration and life continually provide the space necessary for new elements of the ecosystem. It is not important for each particular *part* to continue, said Leopold, but only for the *whole* to continue.

From nature's perspective, as opposed to what Leopold called man's perspective, flows an environmental ethics best termed "biocentric" or "ecocentric." He claimed "a thing is right when it tends to preserve the integrity, stability, and beauty of the biotic community. It is wrong when it tends to do otherwise."[8] To illustrate his point, Leopold gave the example of a river sandbar, a very particular and small environmental system. Such a system has an identifiable integrity; it is a unity of interdependent elements combining together to make a whole with a unique character. It has a certain stability, not because it does not change but because it changes only gradually. Finally, it has a particular beauty in its harmonious, well-ordered form: a unity in diversity. When envisioned on a larger scale, this small environmental system interlocks with other small environmental systems, together constituting the very large ecosystem of which human beings are simply a part. This, the largest of all ecosystems, is none other than "nature," and morality becomes a matter of conscious (or thinking) beings' preserving its integrity, stability, and beauty.

Leopold's thinking was at the forefront of the conceptual revolution that replaced the anthropomorphism of shallow ecology with the biocentrism of deep ecology. Arne Naess and George Sessions articulated the principal tenets of deep ecology:

1. The well-being and flourishing of human and non-human life on earth have value in themselves (synonyms intrinsic value, inherent value). These values are independent of the usefulness of the non-human world for human purposes.
2. Richness and diversity of life forms contribute to the realization of these values and are also values in themselves.
3. Humans have no right to reduce this richness and diversity except to satisfy vital needs.
4. The flourishing of human life and cultures is compatible with a substantial decrease of the human population. The flourishing of non-human life requires such a decrease.
5. Present human interference with the non-human world is excessive, and the situation is rapidly worsening.
6. Policies must therefore be changed. These policies affect basic economic, technological, and ideological structures. The resulting state of affairs will be deeply different from the present.
7. The ideological change is mainly that of appreciating life quality (dwelling in situations of inherent value) rather than adhering to an increasingly higher standard of living. There will be a profound awareness of the difference between big and great.
8. Those who subscribe to the foregoing points have an obligation directly or indirectly to try to implement the necessary changes.[9]

Critics of deep ecology fault both the theory underlying deep ecology and some of its tactics. They demand to know what the *source* of nature's intrinsic value is, rejecting the mere fact of nature's "is-ness" as an inadequate answer to their question. Just because something exists, they say, does not make it intrinsically valuable. In an effort to persuade these critics that nature is indeed intrinsically valuable, Peter Wenz argued there is something intuitively wrong about destroying an ecosystem when there is no good reason to do so. He claimed that if the last surviving human being after a worldwide disaster had a choice between saving or not saving all the remaining plant and animal life on the earth, it would not be "a matter of moral indifference" whether the person chose to save these life-forms.[10] Although critics of deep ecology agree with Wenz that the earth has value independent of us, they do not agree with the view that the earth's interests are equal to or even more important than ours. For example, critic Luc Ferry vehemently objected to some deep ecologists' proposal that if we fail or refuse to control the size of our population voluntarily, then the government should force us to do so, so that *nonhuman* animals have enough food and space. Does this mean, asked Ferry, that to get the ideal human-nonhuman population ratio,[11] our government should do nothing to stop the kind of "massive human die backs" caused by famine, disease, and war?[12] Are we to be handled like an overpopulated herd of deer?

Ecofeminism:
New Philosophy or Ancient Wisdom?

Ecofeminism is a relatively new variant of ecological ethics. In fact, the term *ecofeminism* first appeared in 1974 in Françoise d'Eaubonne's *Le Féminisme ou la mort*. In this work, she expressed the view that there exists a direct link between the oppression of women and the oppression of nature. She claimed the liberation of one cannot be effected apart from the liberation of the other.[13] A decade or so after Eaubonne coined the term, Karen J. Warren further specified four core assumptions of ecofeminism:

> (1) There are important connections between the oppression of women and the oppression of nature; (2) understanding the nature of these connections is necessary to any adequate understanding of the oppression of women and the oppression of nature; (3) feminist theory and practice must include an ecological perspective; and (4) solutions to ecological problems must include a feminist perspective.[14]

In many ways, ecofeminism resembles deep ecology, yet ecofeminists generally fault deep ecologists for missing one crucial point. According to ecofeminists, deep ecologists mistakenly oppose anthropocentrism in general when the real problem is not so much or only the Western world's *human*-centeredness, but its *male*-centeredness. Androcentrism, not anthropomorphism, is the chief enemy of nature.

Although she praised deep ecologists' "concerted effort . . . to rethink Western metaphysics, epistemology, and ethics," ecofeminist Ariel Kay Salleh nonetheless found their rethinking "deficient."[15] Noting that most of deep ecology's spokespeople are *men,* Salleh accused them of being afraid to confront the sexism as well as naturism causing our current environmental crisis. The "deep ecology movement will not truly happen," she said, "until men are brave enough to rediscover and to love the woman inside themselves."[16] Salleh's thesis, which is shared by many ecofeminists, is "that the hatred of women, which ipso facto brings about that of nature, is one of the principal mechanisms governing the actions of men (of 'males') and, thus, the whole of Western/patriarchal culture."[17]

Tensions in Nature: Ecofeminist Thought

Although ecofeminists agree that the association of women with nature is the root cause of both sexism and naturism, they disagree about whether women's connections to nature are primarily biological and psychological or primarily social and cultural. They also disagree about whether women should de-emphasize, emphasize, or reconceive their connections with nature. According to Ynestra King, "the recognition of the connections between women and nature and of women's bridge-like position between nature and culture poses three possible directions of feminism."[18] The first direction is to *sever* the woman-nature connection by totally integrating women into culture and the realm of production. The second is to *reaffirm* the woman-nature connection, proposing that female nature is not only different from, but also somehow better than, male culture. The third is to transform the woman-nature connection by using it to create "a different kind of culture and politics that would integrate intuitive, spiritual, and rational forms of knowledge . . . and create a free, ecological society."[19] Implicit in King's understanding of transformative ecofeminism is the postmodern feminist belief that ultimately all forms of human oppression are rooted in those dichotomous conceptual schemes that privilege one member of a dyad over another (e.g., male over female, nature over culture, science over magic).

Sever the Woman-Nature Connection

Simone de Beauvoir.   Among the feminists who have pondered women's association with nature is Simone de Beauvoir. She urged women to transcend their links to nature in order to overcome their status as the other, or second, sex. De Beauvoir believed woman's identity as the other is derived partly from her biology—especially her reproductive capacity—and partly from her socially imposed child-rearing responsibilities. De Beauvoir did not view woman's body as woman's friend. On the contrary, she viewed woman's body as fundamentally alienating, as an energy drain leaving women too tired to participate in the kind of creative activity men enjoy.[20]

Following Jean-Paul Sartre, de Beauvoir stressed that human beings are cast in a *pour-soi–en-soi* dialectic. *Pour-soi* (being-for-itself) entails being a self, consciously aware of the possibilities for self-creation that the future presents; *en-soi* (being-in-itself) entails being the other, a thing without a future and therefore without any possibilities for transformation. Although all human beings are both *pour-soi* and *en-soi,* Western culture tends to view men as more likely to be mainly *pour-soi* and women as more likely to be mainly *en-soi.*

Because the conflict between the *pour-soi* and *en-soi* tendencies in people makes them feel anxious, both men and women engage in modes of "bad faith" to ignore that they alone are the creators of their destinies. Men seek refuge from their freedom in the *idea* of women's "it-ness," or *en-soi* immanent nature. In other words, men see in women what they themselves would like to be: persons who simply *are* and who are therefore relieved of the burdensome task of perpetually becoming something new or different or better—persons who are *finished* and thus totally absorbed in their bodies' repetitive, cyclical motion and altogether oblivious of their minds' urges to transcend the present known into the future unknown.

Knowing full well that they are as free as men, women nonetheless engage in bad faith by playing the role of the other. De Beauvoir noted that "along with the ethical urge of each individual to affirm his subjective existence, there is also the temptation to forgo liberty and become a thing."[21] If women are ever to be liberated from the status of the second sex, they must, she said, resist the temptation of the "easy way out." By refusing to be the other—the "it," the *en-soi,* the immanent one, the natural one—women will liberate not only themselves but also men. No longer will men be able to hide from their freedom in the bosom of "woman."

Reflecting on de Beauvoir's suggested program for women's liberation, ecofeminist Val Plumwood reproached de Beauvoir for giving women who care about nature the wrong advice:

For Simone de Beauvoir woman is to become fully human in the same way as man, by joining him in distancing from and in transcending and controlling nature. She opposes male transcendence and conquering of nature to woman's immanence, being identified with and passively immersed in nature and the body. The "full humanity" to be achieved by woman involves becoming part of the superior sphere of the spirit and dominating and transcending nature and physicality, the sphere of freedom and controllability, in contrast to being immersed in nature and in blind uncontrollability. Woman becomes "fully human" by being absorbed in a masculine sphere of freedom and transcendence conceptualized in human-chauvinist terms.[22]

Plumwood feared that by rejecting the *en-soi* realm, the world of immanence, women will gain not true personhood but merely the opportunity to become men's full partners in the campaign to control or dominate nature. The male-female dichotomy will not be bridged or healed into wholeness. Rather, the female member of this long-standing dyad will simply be erased into the male member. Moreover, the culture-nature dichotomy will not be eliminated, but instead will be worsened. Abandoned by woman, nature will find itself utterly defenseless against the forces of culture.

Sherry B. Ortner.   According to another feminist, Sherry B. Ortner, it will not be easy for women to disassociate themselves from nature, since virtually all societies believe women are closer to nature than men are. There are, she said, three reasons for the near universality of this belief. First, women's *physiology* is "more involved more of the time with the 'species of life'; it is woman's body that nurtures humanity's future." Second, women's primary *place* remains the domestic sphere, where "animal-like infants" are slowly transformed into cultural beings and where plant and animal products are shaped into food, clothing, and shelter. Third, women's *psyche*, "appropriately molded to mothering functions by her own socialization," tends toward more relational, concrete, and particular modes of thinking than do men's psyches.[23]

In Ortner's opinion, virtually every society's view of women as somehow existing *between* nature and culture has several consequences, each of them inviting a different interpretation of the term *intermediate*. First, *intermediate* can simply mean that women have a "middle status," lower than men's status but higher than nature's status. Second, it can mean that women "mediate," or perform some set of synthesizing or converting functions between nature and culture—for example, the socialization of children. Unless children are properly socialized, no society can survive; it needs its members to conform to its rules and regulations. For this reason, hypothesized Ortner, societies seek to restrict women's sexual, reproductive, educational, and occupational choices. The more conservative women are, the more rule-following they and their children will be. Third, and finally, the term *intermediate* can mean "of greater symbolic ambiguity." Because society cannot quite understand the nature of women, it is not certain whether to associate women with life or death, good or evil, order or chaos.[24] Do women hold society together, or do they chip away at its margins?

Society's view that women are intermediaries between culture and nature is, said Ortner, the product of women's "social actuality"—that is, women's physiology, domestic role, and feminine psyche. Thus, the way to alter this view of women is to change women's social actuality so that women as well as men are viewed as fully cultural persons capable of determining the course of history. Unfortunately, continued Ortner, women's social actuality cannot change unless society's view of women as intermediaries between culture and nature changes. Women will never escape this circular trap unless their situation is simultaneously attacked from both sides: from the social actuality side (women's reproductively special physiology, domestic role, and feminine psyche) *and* the conceptual or ideological side (women as occupying middle status, as performing mediating functions between nature and culture, as carrying ambiguous symbolic baggage). Explaining her point at some length, Ortner claimed:

> Efforts directed solely at changing the social institutions—through setting quotas on hiring, for example, or through passing equal-pay-for-equal-work laws—cannot have far-reaching effects if cultural language and imagery continue to purvey a relatively devalued view of women. But at the same time efforts directed solely at changing cultural assumptions—through male and female consciousness-raising groups, for example, or through revision of education materials and mass-media imagery—cannot be successful unless the institutional base of the society is changed to support and reinforce the changed cultural view.[25]

Ortner believed that the effect of this two-pronged attack on women's situation would be to involve both men and women equally "in projects of creativity and transcendence." At last, women as well as men would be seen as "cultural," and women no less than men would participate "in culture's ongoing dialectic with nature."[26]

Like de Beauvoir's line of reasoning, Ortner's led to the conclusion that women can be liberated without nature's being liberated. Had Ortner thought otherwise, she would have argued not only that women are just as "cultural" as men but also that men are just as "natural" as women. In other words, she would have aimed to change men's societal actuality and the ideology that supports it as much as she aimed to change women's. If society needs to bridge women's "distance" from culture by involving women in "creative" and "transcendent" tasks, then it also needs to bridge men's distance from nature by involving men in "repetitive" and "immanent" tasks.

Reaffirm the Woman-Nature Connection

Mary Daly: *Gyn/Ecology.* In general, ecofeminists with a radical-cultural feminist background seek to strengthen rather than weaken women's connections to nature. Unlike de Beauvoir and Ortner, nature ecofeminists like Mary Daly believe the traits traditionally associated with women—such as caring, nurturing, and intuitiveness—are not so much the result of social constructions as the product of women's actual biological and psychological experiences. The problem is not that women have a closer relationship with nature than men do, but that this relationship is undervalued. Nature ecofeminists reject the assumed inferiority of both women and nature as well as the assumed superiority of both men and culture. Instead, they insist nature/woman is at least equal to and perhaps even better than culture/man, implying that traditional female virtues, not traditional male virtues, can foster improved social relations and less aggressive, more sustainable ways of life.

As Mary Daly moved toward a lesbian separatist feminism perspective, she began to reject male culture as evil and to embrace female culture as good. She speculated that before the establishment of patriarchy, there existed an original matriarchy. In this gynocentric world, women flourished. They controlled their own lives, bonded with each other and with the non-human world of animals and nature, and lived both freely and happily. Thus, Daly saw the process of women's liberation as putting women back in touch with women's original "wild" and "lusty" natural world and freeing them from men's "domesticating" and "dispiriting" cultural world.[27]

Daly contrasted women's life-giving powers with men's death-dealing powers. She claimed women have the capacity for a fully human life, a vigorous life lived in dynamic communion with animals, earth, and stars. Men, she maintained, lack this capacity. They are, she said, parasites who feed off women's energy to fuel their destructive activities and constricting thoughts. Because they cannot bring life into the world and are incapable of bonding with nature, men substitute artificial life for flesh-and-blood life and, in acts of envious rage directed against women, seek not only to control and destroy women but also to control and destroy all that is natural. Male culture is everything female nature is not; it is about disease and death rather than health and life, said Daly:

The products of necrophilic Apollonian male mating are of course the technological "offspring" which pollute the heavens and the earth. Since the passion of necrophiliacs is for the destruction of life and since their attraction is to all that is dead, dying, and purely mechanical, the fathers' fetishized "fetuses" (reproductions/replicas of themselves), with which they passionately identify, are fatal for the future of this planet. Nuclear reactors and the poisons they produce, stockpiles of atomic bombs, ozone-destroying aerosol spray propellants, oil tankers "designed" to self-destruct in the ocean, iatrogenic medications and carcinogenic food additives, refined sugar, mind pollutants of all kinds—these are the multiple fetuses/feces of stale male-mates in love with a dead world that is ultimately co-equal and consubstantial with themselves. The excrement of Exxon is everywhere. It is ominously omnipresent.[28]

Daly linked men's pollution of nature with men's "pollution" of women, contrasting men's *gynecology* with women's *gyn/ecology*. Men's gynecology is about segmenting and specializing reproduction as if it was just another mode of production; it is about substituting the fake for the real, the artificial for the natural; it is about cutting whole into parts. In contrast, women's gyn/ecology is about "dis-covering, de-veloping the complex web of living/loving relationships *of our own kind*. It is about *women* living, loving, creating our Selves, our cosmos."[29] Whereas men's gynecology depends upon "fixation and dismemberment," women's gyn/ecology affirms everything is connected.[30] According to Daly, women must work hard to stop the patriarchal forces of necrophilia—that is, of death. Most women, she claimed, have been seduced into cooperating with the "phallocentric" system of "necrophilia"; they have become men's "fembots," permitting themselves to be drained of their life forces.[31] In the days of matriarchy, Daly said, women reproduced through parthenogenesis, their eggs dividing and developing independently of sperm. Now, in the days of patriarchy, men have persuaded women to exchange natural reproduction for artificial reproduction. Men have invited women to enter a world in which *male* gynecologists snatch women's eggs from women's wombs in order to hatch them in technology's wombs, or artificial placentae. With this "advance" in science, said Daly, men move closer to achieving what they really seek—death—and unless women refuse to become men's "fembots," men will consume them together with nature.[32]

Susan Griffin.   Although Susan Griffin did not claim there are *biological* connections between women and nature, she did claim there are *ontological* connections between women and nature.[33] Specifically, Griffin wrote: "We know ourselves to be made from this earth. We know this earth is made from our bodies. For we see ourselves. And we are nature. We are nature seeing nature. We are nature with a concept of nature. Nature weeping. Nature speaking of nature to nature."[34] In addition to implying women have a special way of knowing and perceiving reality because of their special connections to nature, Griffin suggested it is women who must help human beings escape the false and destructive dualistic world into which men, particularly male Western philosophers, have led us.

In particular, Griffin used poetry to challenge dualistic thinking, instrumental rationality, and unbridled technology. She countered the objective, dispassionate, and disembodied voice of male culture with the subjective, passionate, embodied voice of female culture. If men can identify with machines and wonder whether machines (e.g., computers and robots) have feelings as well as thoughts, then women can identify with animals and wonder whether animals have thoughts as well as feelings. In *Woman and Nature,* Griffin often spoke through the voice of an animal:

He says that woman speaks with nature. That she hears voices from under the earth. That wind blows in her ears and trees whisper to her. That the dead sing through her mouth and the cries of infants are clear to her. But for him this dialogue is over. He says he is not part of this world, that he was set on this world as a stranger. He sets himself apart from woman and nature.

And so it is Goldilocks who goes to the home of the three bears, Little Red Riding Hood who converses with the wolf, Dorothy who befriends a lion, Snow White who talks to the birds, Cinderella with mice as her allies, the Mermaid who is half fish, Thumbelina courted by a mole. *(And when we hear in the Navaho chant of the mountain that a grown man sits and smokes with bears and follows directions given to him by squirrels, we are surprised. We had thought only little girls spoke with animals.)*

We are the bird's eggs. Bird's eggs, flowers, butterflies, rabbits, cows, sheep; we are caterpillars; we are leaves of ivy and sprigs of wallflower. We are women. We rise from the wave. We are gazelle and doe, elephant and whale, lilies and roses and peach, we are air, we are flame, we are oyster and pearl, we are girls. We are woman and nature. And he says he cannot hear us speak.

But we hear.[35]

Griffin sought to overcome dualism by providing what David Maccauley has termed an "antidote to Plato's epistemological hierarchy." In his *Republic,* Plato led Western man out of what the philosopher regarded as an inferior sensory realm, the world of appearances, into what he regarded as a superior intellectual realm, the world of forms. In this latter world, *ideas* such as beauty, truth, and goodness supposedly reside. However, in book 1 of *Woman and Nature,* Griffin suggested Plato led us astray by his incorrectly insisting that spirit is superior to matter and by prompting us to view man as mind and woman as body. Plato's dualistic hierarchy, stressed Griffin, is behind Western's society's view that women are men's inferiors.[36]

Emphasizing the links between men's ideas about nature and their attitudes toward women, Griffin saw similarities between men's domestication of animals and domestication of women. She also noted ways in which women have either actively participated in or passively accepted their own "taming." For example, in a chapter entitled "Cows: The Way We Yield," Griffin suggested that the words used to describe a cow can be used equally well to describe a woman:

> She is a great cow. She stands in the midst of her own soft flesh, her thighs great wide arches, round columns, her hips wide enough for calving, sturdy, rounded, swaying, stupefied mass, a cradle, a waving field of nipples, her udder brushing the grass, a great cow, who thinks nothing, who waits to be milked, year after year, who delivers up calves, who stands ready for the bull, who is faithful, always there, yielding at the same hour, day after day, that warm substance, the milk white of her eye, staring, trusting, sluggish, bucolic, inert, bovine mind dozing and dreaming, who lays open her flesh, like a drone, for the use of the world.[37]

Asked why she chose to describe women in terms of domestic rather than wild animals, Griffin responded that her two-year experience as a housebound wife and mother caused her to identify with domestic animals, whom she viewed as well taken care of but decidedly unfree.[38]

Viewing Western thought's decision to privilege culture (man) over nature (woman) as a disastrous one, Griffin proceeded in book 2 of *Woman and Nature* to discuss all the conceptual rifts that Platonic philosophy generated: mind-body, intellect-emotion, city-wilderness, knower-known. She also critiqued scientific knowledge, ridiculing the importance men attach to numbers, in particular how men quantify everything in the universe and in their possession. Everything is reducible to a sum, a statistic, a cost-benefit ratio, said Griffin. Horrified by the thought of a world ruled by and reduced to numbers, Griffin urged women to journey out of culture—the labyrinth of dualistic thinking—back into nature, the cave where matter and spirit merge into one, the true habitat of human beings who are more than mere "ideas."

Finally, in the third and fourth books of *Woman and Nature,* Griffin claimed we can overcome the kind of thinking that belittles nature, materiality, the body, and women, but only if women learn to speak for themselves and for the natural world. She insisted we need to replace "his certainty"— quantity, probability, and gravity—with (her?) "possibility"; his "land" and "timber" with "this earth" and "the forest"; and his reason with her emotion:

They said that in order to discover truth, they must find ways to separate feeling from thought *Because we were less* That measurements and criteria must be established free from emotional bias *Because they said our brains were smaller* That these measurements can be computed *Because we were built closer to the ground* according to universal laws *Because according to their tests we think more slowly, because according to their criteria our bodies are more like the bodies of animals, because according to their calculations we can lift less weight, work longer hours, suffer more pain, they said,* constitute objectivity *because we are more emotional than they are* and based they said only on what *because our behavior is observed to be like the behavior of children* is observably true *because we lack the capacity to be reasonable* and emotions they said must be distrusted *because we are filled with rage* that where emotions color thought *because we cry out* thought is no longer objective *because we are shaking* and therefore no longer describes what is real *shaking in our rage because we are shaking in our rage and we are no longer reasonable.*[39]

Nature has a value that cannot be reduced to its usefulness to culture, and woman has a value that cannot be reduced to her usefulness to man.

In some of her later work, Griffin revisited the nature-culture dichotomy, depicting pornography as culture's revenge against nature as well as men's revenge against women. "We will see," said Griffin, "that the bodies of women in pornography, mastered, bound, silenced, beaten, even murdered, are symbols for natural feeling and the powers of nature which the pornographic mind hates and fears."[40] Commenting on Griffin's analysis of the pornographic mind, David Maccauley urged us to ask ourselves,

Whether there now exists . . . a kind of earth pornography, since the gendered planet, the "mother of life" or "our nurse" as Plato referred to it, is not only violated literally by strip mining, deforestation, and radioactive waste but subjected increasingly to the circulation of a voyeuristic media—as the image of a bounded, blue sphere is re-placed (away from natural context) on billboards or commercials in order to sell computers, hamburgers, or candidate's positions."[41]

Just as women's violated bodies are used to sell all sorts of commodities, such as cars, boats, and designer jeans, so, too, is nature's violated "body" similarly used. Women, implied Griffin, must refuse to let themselves and nature be exploited in such ways. Reform, indeed revolution, begins with saying no to what *is* in order to seek what *might be.*

Spiritual Ecofeminism

Closely allied to radical-cultural ecofeminists are a variety of so-called spiritual ecofeminists.[42] Inspired by Mary Daly's *Gyn/Ecology* and Rosemary Radford Ruether's *New Woman, New Earth,* they insist that no matter which theology, religion, or spirituality women adopt, it must be an embodied rather than a disembodied way of relating to the ultimate source or deepest wellspring of meaning. Implicit in the thought of most spiritual ecofeminists is the view that unless patriarchal religions such as Judaism and Christianity can purge themselves of the idea of an omnipotent, disembodied male spirit, women should abandon the oppressive confines of their synagogues and churches and run to the open spaces of nature, where they can practice any one of several earth-based spiritualities.

Although spiritual ecofeminists draw strength from a variety of earth-based spiritualities, these thinkers tend to gravitate toward ancient goddess worship and nature-oriented Native American ritual. They believe that cultures that view the female body as sacred also view nature as sacred, honoring its cycles and rhythms. Spiritual ecofeminists often draw an analogy between the role of women in biological production and the role of an archetypal "Earth Mother" or "birthmother" (usually referred to as "Gaia") in giving life and creating all that exists.[43] Because women's role is analogous to Gaia's role, women's relationship to nature is privileged over men's relationship to nature, according to spiritual ecofeminists.

Starhawk

Among the best-known spiritual ecofeminists who stress the woman-nature link is Starhawk, a Wiccan priestess, social activist, and psychotherapist. In one of her poems, she wrote that nature's and women's work are one and the same:

> Out of the bone, ash
> Out of the ash, pain
> Out of the pain, the swelling
> Out of the swelling, the opening
> Out of the opening, the labor
> Out of the labor, the birth
> Out of the birth, the turning
> wheel the turning tide.[44]

Through their uniquely female bodily experiences—their monthly menses, the demanding symbiosis of pregnancy, the pain of childbirth, and the pleasure of breast-feeding their infants—women supposedly come to know, in a way men cannot, that human beings are one with nature.

Starhawk claimed that the kind of earth-based spirituality she practices as a witch—that is, a woman charged with the task and possessing the skill to "bend" and "reshape" Western culture—provides a good deal of the energy still left in the feminist movement.[45] In her estimation, earth-based spirituality has three core concepts. The first is *immanence*. The Goddess is *in* the living world, in the human, animal, plant, and mineral communities. Therefore, each being has value, and each conscious being also has power. Understood not as power over but as power from within, this power is "the inherent ability . . . to become what we are meant to be—as a seed has within it the inherent power to root, grow, flower, and fruit."[46] We grow in this kind of creative power, claimed Starhawk, when we take on responsibility for everyone and everything to which we are related and also when we strive to achieve personal integrity by prioritizing our needs and those of our entire relational network. Spirituality is not an "opiate"; it is an energizer and stimulus to action. She explained: "When what's going on is the poisoning and destruction of the earth, our own personal development requires that we grapple with that and do something to stop it, to turn the tide and heal the planet."[47]

The second feature of earth-based spirituality is *interconnection* and the expanded view of self it encourages. Not only are our bodies natural, but so, too, are our minds. Starhawk stressed: "Our human capacities of loyalty and love, rage and humor, lust, intuition, intellect, and compassion are as much a part of nature as the lizards and the redwood forests."[48] The more we understand that we are nature, she wrote, the more we will understand our oneness with all that exists: human beings, natural cycles and processes, animals, and plants. We will make the mistake neither of allying ourselves with human beings against nature nor of allying ourselves with nature against human beings, as some environmentalists do when they engage in extreme forms of so-called ecoterrorism. Killing animal-research scientists in the name of animal liberation is no better than killing animals to find cures for the diseases threatening human beings. There is, implied Starhawk, almost always a way to serve the interests of one and all. Our own interests "are linked to black people in South Africa as well as to forest-dwellers in the Amazon, and . . . their interests in turn are not separate from those of the eagle, the whale, and the grizzly bear."[49]

The third and probably most important feature of earth-based spirituality is the kind of *compassionate lifestyle* many women lead. Starhawk claimed that unless all people adopt this type of lifestyle, which requires them to care for each other, we can forget about "reweaving the world" or "healing the wounds." Thus, she faulted deep ecologist Daniel Connor for suggesting "the AIDS virus may be Gaia's tailor-made answer to human overpopulation," as well as deep ecologist Dave Foreman for opposing the provision of famine relief to starving African nations: "When environmentalists applaud the demise of Africans and homosexuals, they ally themselves with the same interests that are killing people of color, gay people, women, and other vulnerable groups. Those same interests are destroying the earth's ecosystems and raping the wilderness."[50] According to Starhawk, spiritual ecofeminists—especially those who regard themselves as witches—bring to the environmental movement a compassionate perspective that permits them "to identify powerlessness and the structures that perpetuate it as the root cause of famine, of overpopulation, of the callous destruction of the natural environment."[51]

The nature-culture dichotomy, indeed all dichotomies, must be dissolved so we can appreciate the "oneness" of reality. Starhawk implied, however, that it is not a matter of indifference how this oneness is achieved. Culture ought to be subsumed into nature rather than vice versa, for unless we all live more simply, masses of people will not be able to live at all. Like Ruether (quoted below), Starhawk viewed the present distribution of the world's wealth among people as shockingly unjust:

> The 225 richest people in the world have a combined wealth of over $1 trillion, equal to the annual income of the poorest 50 percent of humanity or 2.5 billion people, while the richest three people have assets that exceed that of the forty-eight poorest nations. This means, in terms of absolute levels of poverty, that in 1999 almost half of the world's population was living on less than $2 a day, and more than 20 percent of the world, 1.2 billion people, on less than $1 a day, according to World Bank figures.[52]

In view of such statistics, Starhawk urged people committed to world justice and ecological sustainability to engage in direct action movements such as the massive anti–World Trade Organization protests that started in Seattle in November 1999. She also recommended that social justice activists use the communication media, in particular the Internet and cell phones, to make visible and audible to people the sights and sounds of human poverty.

Starhawk had an ambitious program for achieving social justice. She insisted that, starting in their own local communities, activists must take the five following steps to achieve a sustainable economy: (1) They must shift away from oil and coal to renewable, clean forms of energy (solar and wind); (2) they must stop relying on machines to do their work for them and start relying on their own muscle power; (3) they must get serious about recycling the waste side of consumption and production; (4) they must resist the forces of "monoculture," instead affirming and strengthening different cultures; (5) and they must learn to do more with less resources.[53]

Starhawk admitted that, initially, it would be difficult for people to forsake the creative comforts and luxuries of today's high-end, unsustainable economies. Still, she believed that as people started to lead simpler lives, they would discover there is more to life than possessing things. Starhawk urged women to take the lead in the save-the-earth movement, bringing as many men into it as possible:

> The labor is hard, the night is long
> We are midwives, and men who tend
> the birth and bond with the child.
> We are birthing, and being born
> We are trying to perform an act of
> magic—
> To pull a living child out of a near-corpse of the mother we are
> Simultaneously poisoning, who is ourselves.[54]

With Mary Daly, Starhawk declared her absolute opposition to the forces of death (necrophilia) and her wholehearted affirmation of life.

Carol Christ

Like Starhawk, Carol Christ is a "pagan" spiritual ecofeminist. Christ consistently sought to replace the God of patriarchy (omniscient, omnipotent, and immutable) with a Goddess of humanity (learning, fallible, and constantly changing). She wanted people to practice Goddess religion, that is, the effort to imaginatively reconstruct the egalitarian harmony between humans and nature that existed in supposedly nonhierarchical, prepatriarchal times. For Christ, hierarchical thinking and its alienating dualisms have been our undoing. By tapping into the power of the Goddess in ourselves—a "Goddess" she defined as the lure to goodness—we can help each other overcome the alienated and hostile relations that characterize our power-hungry world.

Interestingly, Christ did not guarantee us success in our efforts to become more egalitarian and loving. She saw the web of good human relationships, including good human relationships with nature, as a fragile one in continual need of repair. But rather than despairing at the thought of people endlessly trying to fix faltering human relationships, Christ embraced this thought as providing us with our meaning and purpose. She suggested we rise each morning with the following greeting to the sun: "As this day dawns in beauty, we pledge ourselves to repair the web."[55]

Like spiritual ecofeminists in general, Christ believed that by connecting to nature—its beauty, mystery, complexity—we can be inspired to be better (i.e., more loving) people. We do not need an all-powerful rule giver, armed with laws and punishments for rule breakers, to force us to be good. On the contrary. We need only the Goddess—that is, the energy of human creativity and transformation within themselves—to want to be good.

Transformative Ecofeminism

Unlike nature ecofeminists and spiritual ecofeminists, social-constructionist ecofeminists sought to transform the nature-woman connection. They claimed that women's connection to nature is socially constructed and ideologically reinforced. Because this is so, women can help transform the meaning of their connection to both nature and culture.

Dorothy Dinnerstein

Western dichotomous thought, said Dorothy Dinnerstein, must be exploded if there is to be an end to the oppression of everyone and everything currently devalued. This explosion must begin with the deconstruction of the male-female dichotomy, for it is the fundamental source of "the silent hatred of Mother Earth which breathes side by side with our love for her, and which, like the hate we feel for our human mothers, poisons our attachment to life."[56] Dinnerstein claimed that as a result of our nearly exclusively female practice of mothering, all infants (be they male or female) come to view women as responsible for both their most positive *and* their most negative feelings. At times, mothers meet their children's needs immediately and completely, totally satisfying and soothing their offspring. At other times, however, mothers fail to meet their children's needs, thereby discomforting, frustrating, or angering the children. As it is with mothers—that is, women—so it is with nature, the realm of reality with which women are identified. Mother Nature can bestow blessings on human beings, but she can also mete out harms and hardships to them: hurricanes, volcanoes, floods, fires, famines, disease, death. Thus, the only way for human beings—especially men, who do not bodily resemble the mother in the ways women do—to deal with "the mother" or "nature" is to seek to control her, to separate her from all that is male or identified as masculine, including culture.

Dinnerstein asserted, however, that the attempt to exclude women and nature from men and culture has caused us (she includes women as complicit in this psychopathological arrangement) not only to *maim and exploit women, and stunt and deform men* but also to proceed *"toward the final matricide—the rageful, greedy murder of the planet that spawned us."*[57] Borrowing an idea from Lewis Mumford, she observed that most of us are firm believers in the "megamachine" myth. This myth espouses the view that human beings can use their minds and tools not only to extend control over nature and everything identified with nature—woman, the body, life, death, and so on—but also to make huge monetary profits in doing so. According to Dinnerstein, this myth will continue to rule our thoughts and actions unless we end the present division of the world into male and female (culture and nature) and the assignments of women to nature (child-rearing as well as childbearing) and men to culture (world building). Women must bring nature into culture (by entering the public world), and men must bring culture into nature (by entering the private world). Then and only then will we see that men and women (culture and nature) are *one* and that it is counterproductive for half of reality to try to dominate the other half. A reality, divided and at war with itself, cannot and will not survive. Thus, Dinnerstein proclaimed, "The core meaning of feminism . . . lies, at this point, in its relations to earthly life's survival."[58] Unless men and women get their act together and start behaving like adults instead of infants, the human species can expect a rapid demise.

Karen J. Warren

Like Dinnerstein, Karen J. Warren emphasized that the dualisms threatening to destroy us are social constructions. In a capitalist, patriarchal society, women and nature, men and culture, have certain meanings, but these meanings are far from necessary. They would be very different in a socialist, nonpatriarchal society. For example, they would be very different in the kind of society Marge Piercy posited in *Woman on the Edge of Time,* a work of fiction in which people rejected all dualisms, beginning with the male-female dichotomy (see Chapter 2). In Mattapoisett, Piercy's utopia that we described earlier, babies are born from brooders and raised by three co-mothers (of both sexes). Since both men and women mother—the men even lactate and nurse—both men and women also work. Piercy's society is also one in which the line between nature and culture is largely nonexistent. Although Mattapoisett is agriculturally oriented, it is also technologically advanced. Almost totally mechanized factories do the society's drudge work and heavy labor, producing the tools and commodities necessary to sustain a system of military *defense* (not offense), agricultural production, a limited (nonpolluting) transportation system, and a comfortable lifestyle for everyone. People's work is both socially useful and personally rewarding, and there is nothing that resembles a sexual division of labor. Work is based entirely on people's abilities and proclivities, with a modicum of unpleasant work (e.g., waste disposal) equally distributed to all people. As the result of serious efforts to control the size of the population, Mattapoisett's communities are small, self-sufficient, and very democratic. People have time for play as well as work. Indeed, inhabitants of Mattapoisett are anything but workaholics. They enjoy both the serenity of the natural world and the excitement of the "holies," a highly developed cinematic/multisensory experience. Persons are both masculine and feminine; society is both natural and cultural.[59]

Wanting very much to reconceptualize nature and culture as well as man and woman, Warren claimed feminists must be ecofeminists—without insisting, as Piercy did, that women must forsake their special role in biological reproduction.[60] Warren argued that, *logically*, feminism is just as much a movement to end naturism as it is a movement to end sexism:

(C1) Feminism is a movement to end sexism.
(C2) But sexism is conceptually linked with naturism (through an oppressive conceptual framework characterized by a logic of domination).
(C3) Thus, feminism is (also) a movement to end naturism.[61]

All forms of oppression are interlocked and intertwined. Oppression is a many-headed beast that will continue to exist and regenerate itself until human beings manage *completely* to behead it.

Focusing on the kind of ethics currently informing environmentalism, Warren noted there are within it many sexist elements, or male biases, that undermine its ability to "save the earth." Only an ecofeminist ethics—an ethics free of androcentric as well as anthropocentric distortions—can overcome naturism once and for all. Such an ethics, said Warren, must be a "care-sensitive ethics."[62]

In elaborating her preferred ecofeminist ethics, Warren claimed it had eight "necessary" or "boundary" conditions. First, an ecofeminist ethics is a theory-in-process that evolves together with people. Second, an ecofeminist ethics is entirely "opposed to any 'ism' that presupposes or advances a logic of domination."[63] No thread of sexism, racism, classism, naturism, or other ism may be woven into the ecofeminist quilt. Third, and very importantly, an ecofeminist ethics is a contextualist ethics that invites people to narrate their relationships: to specify *how* they relate to humans, nonhuman animals, and nature. Fourth, if it is anything, said Warren, an ecofeminist ethics is an inclusivist ethics that acknowledges, respects, and welcomes difference. Unlike an exclusivist ethics, an inclusivist ethics is empirically unbiased; that is, it passes the "R-4 test" for *good* generalizations about different sorts of human beings, nonhuman animals, and nature.[64] By making sure that its empirical claims are based on data that is (1) representative, (2) random, (3) the right size, and (4) replicable, continued Warren, an inclusivist ethics avoids the biases that characterize an exclusivist ethics. Fifth, an ecofeminist ethics does not aim to be "objective," even though, as we just noted, it does aim to be unbiased.[65] To be unbiased is not to be neutral. Rather, it is to be eager to incorporate all perspectives, particularly perspectives that might otherwise not get voiced, into its consciousness. Sixth, an ecofeminist ethics, according to Warren, views the values of care, love, friendship, and appropriate trust as the core values of all ethics. Seventh, an ecofeminist ethics aims to redefine both what it means to be a truly human person and what it means to make a decision ethically. Eighth, and most importantly, an ecofeminist ethics is not based on reason to the exclusion of emotion but on an *intelligence* that requires reason and emotion to work together and to be recognized as equally important in ethical decision making.[66]

By working within the framework of the kind of ethics just described, claimed Warren, ecofeminists can learn to relate to nonhumans in ways that overcome the nature-culture split. In one example, intended to illustrate this type of overcoming, Warren contrasted rock climbers who climb in order to conquer mountains and rock climbers who climb in order to know mountains (and therefore themselves) in new ways. When an ecofeminist climbs a mountain, said Warren, the climber assumes he or she has a genuine *relationship* to it. The person's concern is not in showing the mountain who is boss by conquering it but in becoming its friend, someone who cares about it. Thus, an ecofeminist does not look at the mountain with an "arrogant eye," viewing it as a hunk of inert matter trying to exhaust, and thereby get the best of her or him. Rather, an ecofeminist sees it with a "loving eye," viewing it as a unique reality with much to tell the climber about his or her strengths and weaknesses.[67]

In another example, Warren told the story of a young Sioux boy sent by his father to learn "the old Indian ways" from his grandfather. Among other things, the boy's grandfather taught him how to hunt by instructing him

to shoot your four-legged brother in his hind area, slowing it down but not killing it. Then, take the four-legged's head in your hands, and look into his eyes. The eyes are where all the suffering is. Look into your brother's eyes and feel his pain. Then, take your knife and cut the four-legged under his chin, here, on his neck, so that he dies quickly. And as you do, ask your brother, the four-legged, for forgiveness for what you do. Offer also a prayer of thanks to your four-legged kin for offering his body to you just now, when you need food to eat and clothing to wear. And promise the four-legged that you will put yourself back into the

earth when you die, to become nourishment for the earth, and for the sister flowers, and for the brother deer. It is appropriate that you should offer this blessing for the four-legged and, in due time, reciprocate in turn
with your body in this way, as the four-legged gives life to you for your
survival.[68]

The lesson the Sioux grandfather taught his grandson about hunting is
clearly far more ecofeminist (antinaturist and antisexist) than the lesson the
typical "great white hunter" would teach his grandson about hunting for the
fun or sport of it, for the pleasure of the kill. The Sioux hunting lesson is one
that informs us how people whose conceptual schemes are not oppositional
see themselves in *relationship* to nonhuman nature. Nevertheless, the Sioux
hunting lesson is not fully ecofeminist, for it does not proceed from a gender
analysis. Moreover, it arose in a culture that treats women as less than men's
equals. This last observation suggests, contrary to what Warren asserts, that
even in a culture where women are no more identified with nature than men
are, sexism might still exist.

According to Warren, of the four major schools of traditional feminist
thought (liberal, Marxist, radical, and socialist), the socialist comes closest to
providing the theoretical basis from which to launch transformative ecofeminist
practices.[69] Liberal feminism is deficient, in Warren's estimation, because it
maintains dualisms such as culture-nature, mind-body, and rational-emotional.
Like liberalism, liberal feminism emphasizes the value of individualism and
independence as opposed to the importance of weblike relationships and the
connectedness of all forms of life and natural resources.[70] Thus, liberal feminism
is not particularly compatible with ecology; indeed, its theoretical basis seems to
be at odds with ecology.

Marxist feminism is inadequate for very different reasons, thought Warren. Marxist feminists, like Marxists, believe physical labor is the essential
human activity that transforms natural, material resources into products for
human exchange and consumption. This theoretical approach allows little if
any room for concerns about nature, since Marxists and Marxist feminists
place liberated "men and women, as one class, over and against nature."[71]
Moreover, in setting the human world over and against the nonhuman
world, Marxist feminism fails to appreciate just how closely women's oppression is linked with nature's oppression. To set women in opposition to nature
is to set women in opposition to themselves in a profound way.[72]

Finally, claimed Warren, radical feminism is inadequate because it unwit-
tingly "assumes the very nature-culture split that ecofeminism denies" by
requiring women either to embrace (radical-cultural feminists) or to reject

(radical-libertarian feminists) their biological connections to nature.[73] Stressing that women's interests are served neither by identifying nor by disidentifying women with nature, Warren insisted ecofeminism must view both men and women as equally "natural" and equally "cultural."

Although Warren recognized that socialist feminism is fundamentally anti-individualist, she faulted it for largely overlooking the human-nonhuman dichotomy.[74] Warren thought socialist feminism failed to red-flag the extent to which the oppression of women by men is linked to the oppression of non-humans by humans. For this reason, Warren called for a feminism even more comprehensive than socialist feminism, a feminism she termed "transformative feminism."[75]

According to Warren, transformative feminism has six features. First, it recognizes and makes explicit the interconnections between all systems of oppression. Second, it stresses the diversity of women's experiences, forsaking the search for "woman" and her unitary experience. Third, it rejects the logic of domination. Fourth, it rethinks what it means to be a human being, courageously reconsidering whether humans should view "consciousness" (and rationality) as not only that which distinguishes them from nonhumans but somehow makes them better than nonhumans. Fifth, it relies on an ethic that stresses those traditional feminine virtues that tend to weave, interconnect, and unite people. Finally, it maintains science and technology be used only to the extent they preserve the earth.[76] Given Warren's analysis of transformative feminism, it would seem to constitute a "thinking space" where men and women from all over the world can gather together to mix and match multiple feminist insights.

Global Ecofeminism

Among the ecofeminists who have adopted a global perspective are Maria Mies, a sociologist known for her work on development economics, and Vandana Shiva, a physicist known for her interests in spirituality. Mies and Shiva stressed that because women, more than men, are engaged in the work of sustaining daily *life*, women, more than men, are concerned about the elements: air, water, earth, fire. In order to bear and rear healthy children and to provide their families with nourishing food, adequate clothing, and sturdy housing, women need fertile soil, lush plant life, fresh water, and clean air. In addition, like many multicultural, global, and postcolonial feminists, Mies and Shiva lamented Western culture's obsession with the idea of "sameness"—the universal "I," the overarching "one." Capitalism and patriarchy, they observed, are systems that stamp out difference, doggedly cloning themselves, their ideas, and their salable goods wherever they go. Finally, like many Marxist and socialist feminists, Mies and Shiva observed how people in capitalist patriarchies tend to be alienated from everything: the products of their labor, nature, each other, and even themselves. As a result, human beings in capitalist patriarchies often engage in some fairly bizarre behavior in order to reduce their alienation.

In an essay entitled "White Man's Dilemma: His Search for What He Has Destroyed," Mies described in detail some of the mind-boggling ways all people, but particularly white men in capitalist patriarchies, aim to con-nect with nature—the very nature that their lifestyle and patterns of con-sumption threaten to destroy.[77] First, she said, white man attempts to run away from the confines of his urban office "into 'Nature,' the 'wilderness,' the 'underdeveloped' countries of the South, to areas where White Man . . . has not yet 'penetrated.'" Tourist agents in the First World promote Third World excursions with trip descriptions such as the following one: "Euro-pean tourists can live in villages in close contact with the 'natives' in African-style huts with minimum comfort, African food, no running water and where European and African children play together. The 'real' Africa to be touched!" Second, continued Mies, rather than trying to unite with the "mundane" nature right in his backyard, white man seeks to experience a more "exotic" type of nature: nature as "colony, backward, exotic, distant and dangerous, the nature of Asia, Africa, South America." Those who yearn for this kind of nature do not desire to relate to it productively by working on it or tending to it but rather by absorbing it or consuming it— by locking it in the chambers of their cameras or by marketing it to others as souvenirs. Third, she says, white man longs for yet another kind of na-ture, the space known as woman's body. It, too, is wild terrain, the "dark continent," so white man relates to woman's body as he relates to nature: as object of his gaze, as commodity, as to work a form of play to liberate him, if only for a moment, from his relentless workday:

> The growing sex-obsessing apparent in all industrial societies is . . . a direct consequence of alienation from nature, the absence of a sensual interacting with nature in people's work life. Sexuality is supposed to be the totally "other" from work, sexuality should not interfere with work, should be strictly separated from the work life. Sexuality is the "transcendence" of work, the "heaven" after the "valley of tears and sweat" of work, the real essence of leisure. . . . The tragedy is, however, that this "heaven" is also a commodity, to be bought like any other. And like the acquisition of other consumer goods, ultimately, it disappoints. . . . Therefore, the constantly disappointed striving to attain this "heaven" transforms need into an addiction.[78]

Reflecting on Mies's comments, we may find it easy to view her and her coauthor, Shiva, as socialist-*transformative* ecofeminists. Shiva as well as Mies believed there are enough similarities among women to motivate women to work together against capitalist patriarchy and the destructive isms it spawns. As evidence that all women share similar interests in preserving nature, Mies and Shiva provided numerous examples of Third World and First World women struggling against ecological destruction and deterioration. Women, they noted, have led the battle to preserve the bases of life wherever and whenever military and industrial interests have threatened them.

Among the case studies Shiva presented to demonstrate why trees, for example, are a feminist issue and not simply an ecological issue was the 1974 protest of twenty-seven northern Indian women to stop the felling of their homeland's small, indigenous trees.[79] These women intended to cling physically to the trees if lumberjacks attempted to cut down the trees. The women's protest, known as the *chipko* (a Hindi word meaning "to hug") movement, saved thousands of square kilometers of sensitive watershed. Because wood is inextricably connected to their rural and household economies, providing food, fuel, fodder, products for the home, and income, the *chipko* women were willing to die to keep the indigenous trees from being replaced by imported trees too large for them to fell. According to outsiders, it was in the best interests of northern Indians to plant "income-generating" eucalyptus trees, which produce a marketable fiber. But even if it was in the interests of some northern Indian men to switch their "allegiance" to the eucalyptus, it was not in the best interests of northern Indian women to do so, said Shiva. The women and their families needed and wanted trees for all sorts of purposes: to use as fence poles; to provide materials for baskets, dyes, medicines, and decorations; for shade; for food; and most important, to symbolize who the people of northern India are and stand for as a unique people. Shiva used poetic words to express the *chipko* women's intense feelings about their trees:

A fight for truth has begun
At Sinsyaru Khala
A fight for rights has begun
In Malkot Thano
Sister, it is a fight to protect
Our mountains and forests
They give us life
Embrace the life of the living trees
And streams to your hearts
Resist the digging of mountains

Which kills our forests and streams
A fight for life has begun at
Sinsyaru Khala.[80]

If life is a theme for socialist-transformative ecofeminists, so, too, is free-dom. The freedom to which Mies and Shiva referred is not the kind of Marx-ist freedom that requires man to master nature and therefore woman's body. Rather, it is the kind of freedom that asks all of us to recognize and accept our naturalness, our physicality and materiality, our carnality and mortality. Because nature is an exhaustible good, we must learn to conserve it by living as simply as possible and by consuming as little as possible. If we care about our descendants' lives, we must develop a so-called subsistence perspective.

It is not surprising that Mies and Shiva proposed a subsistence perspective as the key to dissolving all the practices and systems that threaten to destroy the earth. These women are, after all, *socialist*-transformative ecofeminists for whom transformation must be material as well as spiritual. Mies claimed people in capitalist patriarchies need to take ten steps if they are serious about developing a subsistence lifestyle:

1. People should produce only enough to satisfy fundamental human *needs,* resisting the urge to produce "an ever-growing mountain of commodities and money (wages or profit)" in a futile attempt to still people's endless and insatiable wants.
2. People should use only as much of nature as they need to, treating it as a reality with "her own subjectivity;" and people should use each other not to make money but to create communities capable of meeting people's fundamental needs, especially their need for intimacy.
3. People should replace representative democracy with participatory democracy so each man and woman has the opportunity to express his or her concerns to everyone else.
4. People should develop "multidimensional or synergic" problem-solving approaches, since the problems of contemporary society are interrelated.
5. People should combine contemporary science, technologies, and knowledge with ancient wisdom, traditions, and even magic.
6. People should break down the boundaries between work and play, the sciences and the arts, spirit and matter.
7. People should view water, air, earth, and all natural resources as com-munity goods rather than as private possessions.
8. Men as well as women should adopt the socialist-transformative ecofeminist view, the subsistence perspective. Specifically, men must

stop focusing on making as much money as possible and focus instead on making their families as loving as possible.

9. Men as well as women should cultivate traditional feminine virtues (caring, compassion, nurturance) and engage in subsistence production, for "only a society based on a subsistence perspective can afford to live in peace with nature, and uphold peace between nations, generations and men and women."

10. Most important, people should realize that in order for each person to have enough, no person can "have it all."[81]

Kamla Bhasin, an Indian feminist, captured the essences of the "sustainable development" model well:

The standard of living of the North's affluent societies cannot be generalized. This was already clear to Mahatma Gandhi 60 years ago, who, when asked by a British journalist whether he would like India to have the same standard of living as Britain, replied: "To have its standard of living a tiny country like Britain had to exploit half the globe. How many globes will India need to exploit to have the same standard of living?" From an ecological and feminist perspective, moreover, even if there were more globes to be exploited, it is not even desirable that this development paradigm and standard of living was generalized, because it has failed to fulfill its promises of happiness, freedom, dignity and peace, even for those who have profited from it.[82]

Critiques of Ecofeminism

Nature Ecofeminism

Because there are so many varieties of ecofeminism, no general critique is applicable. As noted above, the critiques raised against nature ecofeminism are similar to those raised against radical-cultural feminism. In the estimation of Janet Biehl, nature ecofeminists erred when they "biologize(d) women as presumably uniquely ecological beings" who are able to relate to and understand nature in ways men simply cannot, and who are caring and nurturing in ways men, try as they might, can never be.[83] There is, said Biehl, too much willingness among nature ecofeminists either to reduce women into mere bodies or to limit women's potentialities and abilities to those associated with their supposedly "caring nature." As Biehl saw it, nature ecofeminism is reactionary rather than revolutionary. Quoting Simone de Beauvoir, from whom many nature ecofeminists borrowed their basic concept of women's and nature's otherness, Biehl stressed that women celebrate the nature-woman connection at their own peril, for "that's the formula used to try and keep women quiet."[84] Biehl insisted that nature ecofeminists like Mary Daly misled women by suggesting women can by fiat "reclaim" the meaning of the nature-woman connection as an entirely positive one. In reality, insisted Biehl, the nature-woman connection has been "enormously debasing to women," and centuries of negative cultural baggage cannot be cast off by passionate "reclaiming" alone.[85]

Spiritual Ecofeminism

Critics on the left fault spiritual ecofeminists for substituting religion for politics and for spending too much time dancing in the moonlight, casting "magic" spells, chanting mantras, doing yoga, "mindfully" meditating, and giving each other massages. Defenders of spiritual ecofeminism concede that some spiritual ecofeminists might have mistaken New Age or "spa" spirituality for genuine ecofeminist spirituality, but they insist such mistakes were the exception, not the rule. Goddess worship is not, said Mies and Shiva, "luxury spirituality," "the idealist icing on top of the material cake of the West's standard of living."[86] It is not about turning the East's spiritual and cultural treasures into commodities for sale as exotica to privileged and pampered Western people who lack "meaning." Rather, Goddess worship is an attempt to break the culturally constructed dichotomy between spirituality and materiality and to recognize everything and everyone as worthy and deserving of respect. Spiritual ecofeminists, observed Ynestra King, are not otherworldly dreamers; they are this-worldly activists. Spiritual ecofeminists use such "community-building techniques" as performance art, kinesthetic observations (dancing and chanting), and ritual to enable people "to establish and maintain community with one another in contentious and difficult situations of political engagement in the public world."[87] Some spiritual ecofeminists may indeed choose to restrict their political activities to their local communities, insisting "theirs is the politics of everyday life, the transformation of fundamental relationships, even if that takes place only in small communities."[88] They claim so-called everyday politics is "much more effective than countering the power games of men with similar games."[89] But just because some spiritual ecofeminists refuse to play power games with men does not mean these feminists should be dismissed as crystal gazers. Not everyone who cares about the earth and works to safeguard it needs to move to the Women's Peace Camp at Greenham Commons in England; there is work to be done in one's own backyard as well as in faraway places.

Transformative Ecofeminism

As noted above, like all transformative ecofeminists, social-constructionist ecofeminists deny that women are naturally caring and nurturing. Instead they claim that women's feminine characteristics are the products of enculturation or socialization. For example, Carolyn Merchant repeatedly emphasized that "any analysis that times women's supposed special qualities to a biological destiny thwarts the possibility of liberation. A politics grounded in women's culture, experience, and values can be seen as reactionary."[90] Women are no more "natural" than they are "cultural." But critics of social-constructionist ecofeminism point out that it may be a mistake to delink women and nature.

De-emphasizing the connections between women's and nature's life-giving capacities may, they said, "somewhat diminish the original ecofeminist passion to reclaim 'nature' in an organic sense—certainly when it comes to women's biology."[91] They further claimed that an ecofeminism grounded in women's traditional feminine virtues, maternal roles, and special relationship to nature need not be "reactionary." Such an ecofeminism can be "revolutionary"; it can motivate women to get engaged in political action. For example, Ynestra King, a critic of cultural (nature) ecofeminism, noted that throughout her entire pregnancy, she kept thinking that in the time it took her to gestate one precious human being, eight thousand children in the Persian Gulf had starved to death or died of causes directly attributable to the weapons used by U.S. forces during the Gulf War of 1990–1991. Overwhelmed by this thought, she realized that "thinking like an ecofeminist" requires one to make "abstract connections concrete."[92]

Although they find the perspective of all transformative ecofeminists compelling, critics suspect its demands are too challenging for relatively affluent people to accept. In particular, the critics think the degree of activism and lifestyle change that transformative-socialist ecofeminism requires are commitments that comfortable and complacent citizens are unlikely to embrace. Most people, including most feminists, do not want to radically change the way they live. For example, they do not want to become "card-carrying" vegetarians or pacifists.

In response to this objection, some socialist and transformative ecofeminists simply comment that people's reluctance to make lifestyle changes is not a moral justification for their not doing so. Altruism requires a certain measure of self-sacrifice. Other socialist and transformative ecofeminists soften this response by conceding that moral progress is often incremental. Even if a person is not willing to forsake eating meat altogether, for example, he or she can at least refuse to eat animals that have been factory-farmed or grown under extremely cruel conditions.

Likewise, even if a person is not willing to devote the bulk of his or her time working for environmental causes or feels overwhelmed by them, there is *always* some positive difference, however small, he or she can make. Doretta Zemp, creator of the satirical comic strip *Roseanna of the Planet,* commented:

> Too often the environmental issues are bigger than we are, and we feel helpless in the face of their enormity, such as the greenhouse effect, the rape of the rain forests, and the Bhopal pesticide leak, which killed 2500 people and permanently injured 17,000 more. What can we do about that? But Roseanna, my character, is down to our size. She and her best friend, stuffy old Egmont, wax in passion over concerns that are on our scale: chemicals in the home, neighborhood pollution, and the malathion spraying against our will. They disagree on everything except where to go for solutions. He uses ivory tower rhetoric and blind faith. I see Roseanna as every woman, and I see Egmont as exemplifying conventional wisdom, government, and big business.[93]

While Egmont stands idly by, trusting that Big Brother will save everyone from environmental doom, Roseanna is busy throwing out the ozone-damaging deodorants in her bathroom, the poisonous bug sprays under her kitchen sink, and the herbicide-laden cosmetics on her bureau. There is, she insists, always something one can do.

Finally, even if a person is not a pacifist, he or she can be antimilitary. To be opposed to the waging of wars—the intention of which is domination by means of destruction of life—is not the same as being opposed to participating in any act of violence whatsoever. Self-defense and wars waged for the purpose of liberating oneself and one's people from the forces of death are not incompatible with socialist and transformative ecofeminist ideals. To be sure, socialist and transformative ecofeminists will try to resolve conflicts creatively (i.e., nonviolently) and peacefully (i.e., through rational destruction). But when they realize their voices will not be heard and the destruction of everything and everyone (especially their children) precious to them will continue, even the most peaceful ecofeminists will fight for *life*.

Conclusion

No matter the differences that exist between social-constructionist and nature ecofeminists or between socialist and spiritual ecofeminists, all ecofeminists believe human beings are connected to one another and to the nonhuman world: animal, plant, and inert. Unfortunately, we do not always acknowledge our relationships to and responsibilities for other people, let alone those we have to the nonhuman world. As a result, we do violence to each other and to nature, congratulating ourselves on protecting our self-interests. Meanwhile, each day, we kill ourselves by killing our brothers and sisters and by laying waste to the earth from which we originate and to which we will return.

Given the state of human affairs just described, ecofeminists wonder what it will take for the majority of human beings to realize how irrational as well as unfeeling human systems of oppression and domination are. These systems bring in their wake hate, anger, destruction, and death, yet we humans cling to our social constructs. Is the solution to this pathological state of affairs to create a culture in which we honor women and nature as some sort of saviors? Or is it instead to follow Dinnerstein's instructions and insist that men and women alike assume equal responsibility for both child-rearing and world building? What will it take for us to stop thinking dichotomously, to realize we are our own worst enemies? Are we wasting time waiting for the saving grace of some Godot when we should instead be using our own heads and hearts to stop destroying what we in fact are: an interdependent whole, a unity that exists in and through, and not despite, its diversity? Ecofeminists, especially transformative-socialist ecofeminists, have already made their decision. They stopped waiting for the revolution, the transformation, the miracle to happen a long time ago. They are busy at work (and play) doing what they can to eliminate the blights that brown the earth and kill the human spirit.[94] The question remains, however, whether the rest of us are set to join them. Hopefully, this new millennium will bring the right answer.

8

Postmodern and Third-Wave Feminism

Feminist thought has increased in diversity during the last quarter century. It is no longer in its adolescence; indeed it is adult in its intellectual maturity. But like flesh-and-blood human adults, feminist thought is in the throes of a midlife crisis. Among the many identity challenges it faces are the emergence and growing popularity of postmodern feminism and third-wave feminism.

Because the relationship between postmodernism and feminism is an uneasy one, feminists who classify themselves as postmodern feminists often have difficulty explaining how they can be both postmodern and feminist. Like all postmodernists, postmodern feminists reject phallogocentric thought, that is, ideas ordered around an absolute word (logos) that is "male" in style (hence the reference to the phallus). In addition, postmodern feminists reject any mode of feminist thought that aims to provide a single explanation for why women are oppressed or *the* ten or so steps *all* women must take to achieve liberation. Indeed, some postmodern feminists are so mistrustful of traditional feminist thought that they eschew it altogether. For example, Hélène Cixous wanted nothing to do with terms such as *feminist* and *lesbian*. She claimed these words are parasitic on phallogocentric thought because they connote "deviation from a norm instead of a free sexual option or a place of solidarity with women."[1] It is better, she said, for women seeking liberation to avoid such terms, because they signal a unity that blocks difference. Although postmodern feminists' refusal to develop one overarching explanation and solution for women's oppression poses major problems for feminist theory, this refusal also adds needed fuel to the feminist fires of plurality, multiplicity, and difference. Postmodern feminists invite each woman who reflects on their writings to become the kind of feminist she wants to be. There is, in their estimation, no single formula for being a "good feminist."

Agreeing with the view that there is no one way to be a good feminist—or, for that matter, a woman—third-wave feminists push just as hard as postmodern feminists to take feminist thought in new directions. According to Beverly Guy-Sheftall, third-wave feminists are members of

the so-called third phase of the U.S. women's movement, the first phase being primarily the nineteenth-century woman suffrage movement, followed by the second phase, which began in the mid-1960s and was catalyzed primarily by the Civil Rights movement; and the third wave, referring to a younger generation of women in the 1990s who were certainly influenced by their feminist foremothers but who would define feminism differently, and in some ways reject what they perceived to be the doctrinaire aspects of an ideology, mainstream feminism, that they both respect and find limiting.[2]

Third-wave feminists are more than willing to accommodate diversity and change. They are particularly eager to understand the ways in which gender oppression and other kinds of human oppression co-create and co-maintain each other. For third-wave feminists, difference is the way things are. Their world is the Heraclitean world, not the Parmedian world. Moreover, third-wave feminists expect and even welcome conflict and contradiction, including self-contradiction, as Leslie Heywood and Jennifer Drake explained:

Even as different strains of feminism and activism sometimes directly contradict each other, they are all part of our third-wave lives, our thinking, and our praxes: we are products of all the contradictory definitions of and differences within feminism, beasts of such a hybrid kind that perhaps we need a different name altogether.[3]

But what might be this new name for feminism? Should it be named at all?

Initially, a noticeable number of feminists who shaped second-wave feminist thought did not know what to make of postmodern and third-wave feminism. They rejected postmodern feminism as mere jargon, as elitist babble, and they reacted to third-wave feminism as "back talk" from their rebellious daughters. But as a result of listening more closely to the voices of postmodern and third-wave feminists, many second-wave feminists began to hear some of themselves in these other thinkers. Before long, postmodern and third-wave feminism did not seem so alien to second-wave feminists. Thus, feminism at the beginning of the twenty-first century is in some ways very different from feminism in the 1970s or at the turn of the century, yet in other ways, it remains very much the same, seeking women's best interests diligently.

Postmodernism/Postmodern Feminism: Keynotes

In a moment of exasperation, Judith Butler (discussed in more detail later) said that she was tired of thinkers who include in the category "postmodern" any type of philosophical thought that is not modern ("modern" usually means the kind of philosophical thought that characterized the eighteenth-century European Enlightenment or Age of Reason):

> A number of positions are ascribed to postmodernism, as if it were the kind of thing that could be the bearer of a set of positions. . . . These characterizations are variously imputed to postmodernism or poststructuralism, which are conflated with each other and sometimes conflated with deconstruction, and sometimes understood as an indiscriminate assemblage of French feminism, deconstruction, Lacanian psychoanalysis, Foucaultian analysis, Rorty's conversationalism and cultural studies.[4]

Butler's point was that many critics of postmodernism/postmodern feminism are guilty of not doing their homework. They try to "colonize and domesticate" a wide variety of emerging modes of philosophical thought under what she termed the "sign of the same."[5] Rather than actually reading the writings of postmodernists/postmodern feminists closely, these critics prefer to dismiss them as variations on the same theme.

Butler's point is well taken. Yet, despite the diversity in postmodern/postmodern feminist thought, it is still possible to claim that a large number of postmodern feminists take their intellectual cues from psychoanalysts like Jacques Lacan, existentialists like Simone de Beauvoir, deconstructionists like Jacques Derrida, and poststructuralists like Michel Foucault. A case in point is Luce Irigaray and Julia Kristeva, whom I presented as psychoanalytic feminists in Chapter 4 because of their reliance on Jacques Lacan's thought.

Although I could have discussed any number of postmodern feminists in this chapter, I ultimately selected only two for detailed discussion.[6] First, I focus on Hélène Cixous and the influence of Jacques Derrida's writings on her thought. Second, I focus on Judith Butler and the influence of Michel Foucault's theories on her thought. To be sure, Cixous and Butler are simply representative postmodern feminists, which is a very large and eclectic class. My decision to focus on these two thinkers is mainly a matter of preference, but it is also part of a plan to identify points of resonance between them. It may, after all, be useful to maintain the category "postmodern feminism," if only to begin a useful discussion with other schools of feminist thought.

Before launching into a discussion of Jacques Derrida and Hélène Cixous, we need to look at postmodernism's position on the general map of Western philosophy. Perhaps the easiest way to understand postmodernism is to list the modernist (Enlightenment) beliefs it rejects. Jane Flax has provided a particularly good summary of the Enlightenment's main tenets, including the following:

1. There is a "stable, coherent self" that can know how and why it thinks the way it does.
2. Through its rational powers (reason), the self can gain "objective, reliable, and universal knowledge."
3. The knowledge that reason acquires is true; that is, it "represent[s] something real and unchanging (universal) about our minds and the structure of the natural world."
4. Reason has "transcendental and universal qualities"; that is, somehow reason exists independently of us viewed as historical beings situated in specific times and places.
5. Reason, freedom, and autonomy are interconnected in very complex ways. For example, if I am fully free, I will voluntarily obey the laws reason imposes on me. I will not rebel against the laws that bind me and all rational beings.
6. Power does not trump reason. On the contrary. Claims to power (authority) are grounded in reason. Therefore, when truth conflicts with power, reason steps in and decides the controversy in favor of truth.
7. The exemplar for all true knowledge is science understood as the "right use of reason." Science is neutral and objective in its methodology, and because this is so, it can utilize the laws of nature for our benefit.
8. Language, the tool we use to communicate the knowledge science produces, represents the real world that our rational minds observe. There is an isomorphic correspondence between word and thing. For example, the word "dog" corresponds to the entity, dog. Objects are not constructed by means of words or social conventions. Once perceived by our rational minds, objects are simply acknowledged by us through words.[7]

Enlightenment (modern) thought as summarized by Flax remains the kind of thought that is still operative in most people's everyday lives. But, as postmodernists see it, most people are living in a state of denial. The "Enlightenment world" is a figment of people's imagination. There is neither a stable self nor rational powers capable of yielding universal knowledge. Truth is whatever power proclaims it to be. Freedom is the power to do as one pleases, however irrational or nonbeneficial one's actions may be judged. Science is no more objective than politics or ethics, both of which are subjective, contextual, historical, contingent, and almost always deployed to serve self-interest. And language does not represent reality, because there is no reality for it to signify. On the contrary, language constructs reality—a reality that depends on words for its existence.

Jacques Derrida

Like Jacques Lacan, whose work we discussed in Chapter 4, Jacques Derrida focused much of his work on the mechanisms of the Symbolic order, that is, the series of interrelated signs, roles, and rituals a child must internalize in order to function adequately in society. The more a child submits to the linguistic rules of society, the more those rules will be inscribed in his or her unconscious. In other words, the Symbolic order regulates society through the regulation of individuals; as long as individuals speak the language of the Symbolic order—internalizing its gender, race, and class roles—society reproduces itself in fairly constant forms.

Derrida sought to liberate thinking from the assumption of singularity—that is, the view that one single truth or essence, a "transcendental signifier," exists, in and of itself, as a giver of meaning. He did this by using the techniques of a philosophical method often referred to as "deconstruction." Deconstruction is a deliberate attempt to open or subject a literary, philosophical, or political text to several interpretations, some of which may contradict each other. According to Derrida, our understanding of any word—say, cat—does not depend on the "metaphysical presence" (existence/reality) of either any particular cat or the idea of cat/catness in general. Rather it depends on other words—on a very long chain of "signifiers" that refer to nothing over and beyond themselves.[8]

In an attempt to explain Derrida's deconstruction, most commentators focus on his concept of difference (which he spells *différance* instead of *différence,* the ordinary French spelling of the English word difference). Prior to the emergence of postmodern thought, structuralists insisted that so-called binary oppositions produce meaning in language. In other words, structuralists claimed that the way we understand the term "masculine," for example, depends on our understanding of the term "feminine," and vice versa. Derrida disagreed with this reigning view. As he saw it, language is achieved through the free play of myriad signifiers. Bipolar thought must be resisted whenever it manifests itself.

Toril Moi clarified Derrida's understanding of "playful" signifiers by pointing to structuralist Ferdinand Saussure's concept of the *phoneme* "defined as the smallest differential—and therefore signifying—unit in language."[9] No one phoneme, say, *b,* has any meaning in and of itself, said Moi. On the contrary, the only reason *b* signifies anything is that it is different from *h* and numerous other phonemes. Likewise, the only reason the word *bat* means anything in English is that it can be contrasted with words like *cat, hat,* and the myriad other words that constitute the English language. The word *bat* achieves its meaning by continually deferring its meaning to other English words. It never gets to rest safe and secure in the comfort of an actual bat or the idea of batness-in-itself. Nor does it come into permanent existence by virtue of the intent of some particular author who defines its meaning once and for all. Rather the word *bat* becomes temporarily meaningful only when an author lets it come to the fore by suppressing other words that may, in turn, be selected over it by other authors. No phoneme, word, sentence, paragraph, article, book, has a final meaning. Thus, thinking is nothing more than continually producing new readings of texts.[10] Language and reality are variable and shifting, missing each other in a Heraclitean flux of words, according to Derrida. Words do not stand for things, for pieces of reality. Rather, reality eludes language, and language refuses to be pinned down or limited by reality.

Hélène Cixous

Although no single thinker is *behind* Hélène Cixous's complex thought, she found Derrida's concept of *différance* (defined by Moi as the "open-ended play between the presence of one signifier and the absence of others")[11] and his rejection of binary thought very useful. Cixous is primarily a novelist experimenting with literary style. In applying Derrida's notion of *différance* to writing, she contrasted feminine writing (*l'écriture féminine*) with masculine writing (*littérature*). Viewed within a psychoanalytic framework, masculine writing is rooted in a man's genital and libidinal economy, which is emblemized by the phallus. For a variety of sociocultural reasons, masculine writing has reigned supreme over feminine writing. In the words of Ann Rosalind Jones, man (white, European, and ruling class) has claimed, "I am the unified, self-controlled center of the universe. The rest of the world, which I define as the Other, has meaning only in relation to me, as man/father, possessor of the phallus."[12]

Cixous has objected to masculine writing and thinking because they are cast in binary oppositions. Man has unnecessarily segmented reality by coupling concepts and terms in pairs of polar opposites, one of which is always privileged over the other. In her essay "Sorties," Cixous listed some of these dichotomous pairs:

Activity/Passivity
Sun/Moon
Culture/Nature
Day/Night
Thought has always worked through opposition.
Speaking/Writing
Parole/Ecriture
High/Low
Through dual, hierarchical oppositions.[13]

According to Cixous, each of these dichotomies finds its inspiration in the dyad man-woman. Man is associated with all that is active, cultural, light, high, or generally positive, whereas woman is associated with all that is passive, natural, dark, low, or generally negative. Moreover, the first term in the dyad man-woman is the term from which the second departs or deviates. Man is the self; woman is the other. Thus, woman exists in man's world on his terms. She is either the other for man, or she is unthought. After man is done thinking about woman, "what is left of her is unthinkable, unthought."[14]

Cixous challenged women to write themselves out of the world *men* constructed for women. She urged women to put themselves—the unthinkable/ unthought—into words. The kind of writing Cixous identified as woman's own—marking, scratching, scribbling, jotting down—connotes movements that, once again, bring to mind Heraclitus' ever-changing river. In contrast, the kind of writing Cixous associated with man composes the bulk of the so-called accumulated wisdom of humankind. Stamped with the official seal of social approval, masculine writing is too weighted down to move or change.

For Cixous, feminine writing is not merely a new style of writing; it is "the very possibility of change, the space that can serve as a springboard for subversive thought, the precursory movement of a transformation of social and cultural standards."[15] By developing feminine writing, women can, she insisted, change the way the Western world thinks, speaks, and acts. This is no easy task, however. Trying to write the nonexistent into existence, to "foresee the unforeseeable," may, after all, strain women writers to the breaking point.[16]

In further distinguishing woman's writing from man's, Cixous drew many connections between male sexuality and masculine writing and female sexuality and feminine writing. Male sexuality, which centers on what Cixous called the "big dick," is ultimately boring in its pointedness and singularity.[17] Like male sexuality, masculine writing, which Cixous usually termed phallogocentric writing, is also ultimately boring. Men write the same old things with their "little pocket signifier"—the trio of penis/phallus/pen.[18] Fearing the multiplicity and chaos that exist outside their Symbolic order, men always write in black ink, carefully containing their thoughts in a sharply defined and rigidly imposed structure.

In contrast, female sexuality is anything but boring, Cixous said in no uncertain terms:

> Almost everything is yet to be written by women about femininity: about their sexuality, that is, its infinite and mobile complexity; about their eroticization, sudden turn-ons of a certain minuscule-immense area of their bodies; not about destiny, but about the adventure of such and such a drive, about trips, crossings, trudges, abrupt and gradual awakenings, discoveries of a zone at once timorous and soon to be forthright.[19]

Like female sexuality, feminine writing is open and multiple, varied and rhythmic, full of pleasures and, more important, full of possibilities. When a woman writes, said Cixous, she writes in "white ink," letting her words flow freely where she wishes them to go: "Her writing can only keep going, without ever inscribing or discerning contours. . . . She lets the other language speak—the language of 1,000 tongues which knows neither enclosure nor death. . . . Her language does not contain, it carries; it does not hold back, it makes possible."[20]

Running through Cixous's writing are an optimism and a joy lacking in both Derrida, for whom logocentrism is inevitable, and Lacan, for whom the phallus will always dominate. Cixous insisted women writers have the ability to lead the Western world out of the dichotomous conceptual order that causes it to think, speak, and act in terms of someone who is dominant and someone else who is submissive. If woman explores her body "with its thousand and one thresholds of order," said Cixous, she "will make the old single-grooved mother tongue reverberate with more than one language."[21] The id, implied Cixous, is the source of all desires. "Oral drive, anal drive, vocal drive—all these drives are our strengths, and among them is the gestation drive—just like the desire to write: a desire to live self from within, a desire for the swollen body, for language, for blood."[22]

Michel Foucault

Michel Foucault agreed with Derrida and Cixous that "we should not view the subject as the knowing, willing, autonomous, self-critical or 'transcendental'

subject of Kantian discourse."[23] Rather, we should understand the subject—
that is, the individual person—as the product or effect of a variety of power
relations manifested through a plurality of discourses. Understanding what
Foucault means by power and power relations is no easy task, however, when
one reads his observations about power: "Power is not an institution, and not a
structure; neither is it a certain strength we are endowed with; [rather] it is the
name that one attributes to a complex strategical situation in a particular society."[24] Seeking to further elucidate Foucault's understanding of power, Philip
Barker claimed that power has the following features:

1. Power is coextensive with the social body;
2. relations of power are interwoven with other kinds of relations: production, kinship, family, sexuality;
3. power does not take the sole form of prohibition and punishment, but
   is multiple in form;
4. interconnections of power delineate general conditions of domination
   organized in a more or less coherent and unitary strategy;
5. power relations serve because they are capable of being utilised in a
   wide range of strategies;
6. there are no relations of power without possible resistances.[25]

We find ourselves the objects of multiple power relations and social discourses about sanity, sexuality, and violence, for example, and we experience
ourselves as being controlled by these relations and discourses, as having to
be obedient to them.

As indicated above, discourse about sexuality is a primary site of power in
contemporary society, according to Foucault. What society says about legitimate and taboo types of sexuality shapes the sexual behavior of individual persons.[26] We are, said Foucault, literally "policed" by society's discourse about
sexuality.[27] Policed, I confess my sexual fantasies and hang-ups to my psychia-
trist; I seek forgiveness for my sexual sins by exposing them to my priest; I
report my whereabouts to my parole officer if I bear the label of "sexual pred-
ator"; I reveal my sexual fantasies to my lover. In turn, these authorities judge
me in one way or another. I take their judgments to heart, internalize them,
and then regulate myself in terms of them. Madan Sarup commented that in
Foucault's view, "complex differential power relationships extend to every
aspect of our social, cultural, and political lives, involving all manner of (often
contradictory) 'subject-positions,' and securing our assent not so much by the
threat of punitive measures as by persuading us to internalize the norms and
values that prevail within the social order."[28]

Foucault frequently claimed that as sexual subjects, we are the object of a set of intersecting power relations and discourses that inscribe themselves on our bodies and cause us to recognize ourselves in certain ways. Often, we are unaware of the social forces that have constituted our sexual subjectivity. For this reason, we operate on the unquestioning assumption that our subjectivity is our own. Thus, it is the role of critical thinkers to help us challenge the ways in which power relations and discourses have constituted our subjectivity, particularly our sexual subjectivity so that we can somehow reconstitute it.[29] Foucault claimed that he did not conduct his analyses "in order to say: this is how things are, look how trapped you are."[30] Rather, he conducted them to permit others to help us transform our realities.

To better appreciate how power relations and discourses shape our subjectivities, sexualities, and bodies, we will look at a specific example. A variety of feminist thinkers, including many postmodern feminist thinkers, have expressed disapproval of cosmetic surgery for the purpose of women's beautification. In particular, Kathryn Pauly Morgan, Naomi Wolf, and Debra Gimlin, for example, have argued that cosmetic surgery is a negative and harmful aspect of Western culture and is something that generally runs counter to the feminist stance on the female body. For Morgan, cosmetic surgery is "primarily self-imposed surveillance of the body under patriarchal power . . . a form of colonization of women's bodies."[31] She claimed that cosmetic surgery is required for women in ways that it is not required for men:

As cosmetic surgery becomes increasingly normalized through the concept of female "make over" that is translated into columns and articles in the print media or made into nationwide television shows directed at female viewers, as the "success stories" are invited on the talk shows along with their "makers," and as surgically transformed women enter the Miss America pageants, women who refuse to submit to the knives and to the needles, to the anesthetics and the bandages, will come to be seen as deviant in one way or another. Women who refuse to use these technologies are already becoming stigmatized as "unliberated," not caring about their appearance (a sign of disturbed gender identity and low self-esteem according to various health-care professionals), as "refusing to be all that they could be" or as "granola-heads."[32]

If this is not discourse at work, then what is?

Like Morgan, Wolf claimed that cosmetic surgery is an example of "institutionalized forms of power working in concert to force women into extreme beauty practices."[33] Wolf postulated that women's desire to be beautiful (and the forms that this desire takes) is "the result of nothing more exalted than the need in today's power structure, economy, and culture to mount a counter-offensive against women." Women's beauty, said Wolf, serves as the foundation of women's identity and leaves them "vulnerable to outside approval." Regarding cosmetic surgery in particular, Wolf claimed that a market for it has been created for surgeons to make money, but, more generally, for the powers-that-be to keep women politically, economically, and socially stagnated. Because women are forced to focus on their perceived flaws, their supposed ugliness, they have little time to focus on far more important issues.[34]

Adding yet more force to Morgan's and Wolf's essentially Foucaultian analysis of cosmetic surgery, Debra Gimlin observed that "cosmetic surgery is not about controlling one's own body but is instead an activity so extreme, so invasive that it can only be interpreted as subjugation."[35] On a more general note, discussing women's overall beauty regime in the United States, Sandra Lee Bartky made these observations:

> Women are no longer required to be chaste or modest, to restrict their sphere of activity to the home, or even to realize their properly feminine destiny in maternity. Normative femininity [that is, the rules for being a good woman] is coming more and more to be centered on women's body—not its duties and obligations or even its capacity to bear children, but its sexuality, more precisely, its presumed heterosexuality and its appearance. . . . The woman who checks her makeup half a dozen times a day to see if her foundation has caked or her mascara has run, who worries that the wind or the rain may spoil her hairdo, who looks frequently to see if her stockings have bagged at the ankle, or who, feeling fat, monitors everything she eats, has become, just as surely as the inmate of Panopticon, a self-policing subject, a self committed to a relentless self-surveillance. This self-surveillance is a form of obedience to patriarchy.[36]

The question then becomes one of resistance. How can women disobey the "rule of the Father"? By refusing to submit to the knife? By using cosmetic surgery to deliberately make themselves ugly rather than beautiful?

Judith Butler

Although Judith Butler is influenced by many thinkers, she is certainly influenced by Freud, Derrida, and Foucault. In *Gender Trouble*, Butler challenged the general view that sex, gender, and sexuality constitute a seamless web such that if a person is biologically female (XX chromosomes), she will display feminine traits and desire men as her sexual partners. Instead, Butler claimed that there is no necessary connection between a person's sex and a person's gender. Indeed, she went further than this. Butler said that "sex by definition, will be shown to have been gender all along."[37] She agreed with Simone de Beauvoir that one is not born a woman; one becomes a woman.[38]

But what does it mean to become a woman? Do I choose to become a woman? Or do the kind of discursive powers about which Foucault spoke determine that I become a woman? Butler claimed that there is no preexisting "I" that chooses its gender. Rather, in Foucaultian fashion, she stated that "to choose a gender is to interpret received gender norms in a way that organizes them anew. Less a radical act of creation, gender is a tacit project to renew one's cultural history in one's own terms. This is not a prescriptive task we must endeavor to do, but one in which we have been endeavoring all along."[39] Within the discursive territory of heterosexuality, said Butler, not only is gender constructed, but so too is sex constructed. I find myself in the territory of heterosexuality and start constructing both my sexual and gender identity through my actions.

Although most feminists have always thought *gender* is constructed, until relatively recently, few have also thought *sex* is constructed. But then Butler, among others, started to reflect on the identities of hermaphrodites. Their sex is ambiguous and may be oriented in either male or female directions. Gender and sex, said Butler, are more like verbs than nouns. But my actions are limited. I am not permitted to construct my gender and sex willy-nilly, according to Butler. I am controlled by the scripts society writes about people's sex and gender. It takes considerable imagination and fortitude to alter these scripts.

In an attempt to rewrite the scripts that control them, many readers of Butler focused on her discussion of gender and sex as identities one chooses to perform. They mistakenly understood her to mean that gender and sex were wide-open categories and that individual subjects were free to choose any "sex" or "gender" they chose to enact. These readers failed to realize how limited their options were. Sarah Salin attempted to explain these limitations:

In Butler's scheme of things, if you decided to ignore the expectations and the constraints imposed by your peers, colleagues, etc. by "putting on a gender," which for some reason would upset those people who have authority over you or whose approval you require, you could not simply reinvent your metaphorical gender wardrobe or acquire an entirely new one (and even if you could do that, you would obviously be limited by what was available in the shops). Rather, you would have to alter the clothes you already have in order to signal that you are not wearing them in a "conventional" way—by ripping them or sewing sequins on them or wearing them back to front or upside-down. In other words, your choice of gender is curtailed, as is your choice of subversion—which might make it seem as though, what you are doing is not "choosing" or "subverting" your gender at all.[40]

I can cross-dress, I can undergo a sex change operation, I can act on my primary homosexual desire. But I remain in society's boy-girl grid, no matter what.

Realizing that many of her readers were not understanding the nuances of her thought, Butler sought to distinguish between her concept of *performance* and her concept of *performativity*. She relied on the work of analytic philosopher John Austin to help her. Austin made a distinction between constative utterances or perlocutionary acts on the one hand and performative utterances or illuctionary acts on the other.[41] Constative utterances or perlocutionary acts simply report and describe something, whereas performative utterances or illuctionary acts actually make what is being said happen. For example, a perlocutionary statement or act is an observational statement like "Today is a windy day" or "My dress is blue." In contrast, an illuctionary statement or act is a power statement like "I take you to be my wife" in the context of a wedding ceremony. Saying these words literally makes you a husband. Similarly, commented Salin, in Butler's scheme of things: "When the doctor or nurse declares 'It's a girl/boy,' they are not simply reporting on what they see . . . , they are actually assigning a sex and a gender to a body that can have no existence outside discourse."[42] In other words, in order to be in this world, one must fit into one of these categories. There would need to be a whole other way of classifying individuals to get out of the girl-boy game entirely. To get her point across, Butler referred to a cartoon strip in which an infant is proclaimed to be neither a boy nor a girl but a lesbian. She did this, said Salin, to introduce the idea that it might "be possible to designate or confer identity on the basis of an alternative set of discursively constituted attributes."[43] But a "possibility" is just that. Most interpreters of Butler think that her bottom line is pessimistic: that, at least in our lifetimes, it is highly unlikely that we will be liberated from the gender games that preoccupy us and the hierarchical systems that entrap us.

Butler's penultimate pessimism about transforming society prompted critic Martha Nussbaum to observe:

Thus the one place for agency in a world constrained by hierarchy is in the small opportunities we have to oppose gender roles every time they take shape. When I find myself doing femaleness, I can turn it around, poke fun at it, do it a little bit differently. Such reactive and parodic performances in Butler's view, never destabilize the larger system. . . . Just as actors with a bad script can subvert it by delivering the bad lines oddly, so too with gender: the script remains bad, but the actors have a tiny bit of freedom.[44]

In the end, gender seems to be more trouble for us than we for it.

Critique of Postmodern Feminism

Some critics reject all postmodern feminism as "feminism for academicians." As they see it, postmodern feminists are deliberately opaque, viewing clarity as one of the seven deadly sins of the phallogocentric order. These critics tend to dismiss postmodern feminists as contemporary Epicureans who withdraw from real revolutionary struggle—marches, campaigns, boycotts, protests—into a garden of intellectual delights. Surrounded by friends, by people who share their philosophical perspective, postmodern feminists "use language and ideas in such a specific way that no one else can understand what they are doing."[45] Rarely do they leave their blissful surroundings, and as time passes, their sayings become increasingly irrelevant to the majority of women.

Convinced that Butler's thought in particular is no more than jargon for an elite group of feminists and other social critics, Nussbaum trivialized Butler's ideas about resistance. She claimed that Butler's advice to feminists—namely, that the best they can do is to make fun of the institution of sex-gender that constrains women (and men)—is akin to someone's advising abolitionists that the best they can do is to roll their eyes at the master-slave hierarchy that weakens slaves' bodies and crushes slaves' spirits.[46] But, continued Nussbaum, in the nineteenth century, U.S. abolitionists did far more than roll their eyes at slavery. They fought with every ounce of their energy to achieve freedom for the slaves. Resistance to injustice is not a matter of personal sniping. It is a matter of public outrage.

Nussbaum's main disagreement with Butler is that Butler seems to reduce resistance to "jabbing" at one's oppressors. Indeed, in Nussbaum's estimation, Butler delights in the role of being oppressed. Specifically, Nussbaum claimed that the central thesis of Butler's book *The Psychic Life of Power* is "that we all eroticize the power structures that oppress us, and can thus find sexual pleasure only within their confines."[47] In other words, real social change "would so uproot our psyches that it would make sexual satisfaction impossible."[48] We would be forced to give up our sexual pacifiers if we were to engage in bona fide social revolution, and, above all, we do not want to lose what personally "turns us on." Nussbaum found this conclusion about ourselves truly sad. She asserted that personal sexual pleasure is not our raison d'être. Rather, doing good for others is the purpose of our lives: "Life . . . offers many scripts for resistance that do not focus narcissistically on personal self-preservation. Such scripts involve feminists (and others of course) in building laws and institutions without much concern for how a woman displays her own body and its gendered nature: in short, they involve working for others who are suffering."[49]

Written in 1999, Nussbaum's critique of Butler was very harsh and conceivably based on some misunderstanding of Butler's full views on matters related to social resistance and personal satisfaction. In her 1994 book, *Undoing Gender*, Butler insisted that she does not think "theory is sufficient for social and political transformation."[50] In fact, she claimed,

[Something] besides theory must take place, such as interventions at social and political levels that involve actions, sustained labor, and institutionalized practice, which are not quite the same as exercise of theory. I would add, however, that in all of these practices, theory is presupposed. We are all, in the very act of social transformation, lay philosophers, presupposing a vision of the world, of what is right, of what is just, of what is abhorrent, of what human action is and can be, of what constitutes the necessary and sufficient conditions of life.[51]

Butler may have indeed believed this all along, but it may have taken the strong words of critics like Nussbaum to prompt her to develop her thought in more applied and accessible directions. Such developments in Butler's thinking are a testimony to the resilience of feminist thought, an encouraging sign that it is far from stopping dead in its tracks.

Third-Wave Feminism

If third-wave feminists share any characteristics, it is their willingness to accommodate diversity and change. They seem to be feminist sponges, willing and able to absorb some aspects of all the modes of feminist thought that preceded the third wave's emergence on the scene. Third-wave feminists are particularly eager to understand how gender oppression and other kinds of human oppression co-create and co-maintain each other. For third-wave feminists, difference is the way things are. Moreover, contradiction, including self-contradiction, is expected and even willingly welcomed by third-wave feminists. So too is conflict. In fact, two leading third-wave feminists, Leslie Heywood and Jennifer Drake, commented that "Even as different strains of feminism and activism sometimes directly contradict each other, they are all part of our third-wave lives, our thinking, and our praxes: we are products of all the contradictory definitions of and differences within feminism, beasts of such a hybrid kind that perhaps we need a different name altogether."[52]

As part of their study of interlocking forms of oppression, third-wave feminists engage in research and writing that attends to the lives and problems of specific groups of women. Like multicultural, postcolonial, and global feminists, third-wave feminists stress that women and feminists come in many colors, ethnicities, nationalities, religions, and cultural backgrounds. Thus, a typical third-wave feminist text will include articles about women who represent a wide variety of multicultural perspectives: Hispanic American, African American, Asian American, Native American, and so on. Indeed, one would be hard-pressed to find any third-wave feminist article that is not heavily "hyphenated."

Third-wave feminists' nuanced attention to women's difference is on the right track of contemporary feminist thought, but it is also empirically and conceptually challenging. It is extraordinarily difficult to write an essay on the views of Hispanic American women, for example. For one thing, as we noted in Chapter 6, the category "Hispanic" is a 1970 creation of the U.S. Census Bureau. Not quite knowing how to label a variety of persons of "Spanish origin" living in the United States, government officials decided to label them all "Hispanic." Unlike other Census Bureau designations, the term "Hispanic" denotes neither race nor color, and a Hispanic woman may be white, black, or American Indian. Moreover, a Hispanic woman may be Mexican American, Puerto Rican, or Cuban. She may prefer to be referred to as a Chicana or a Latina, eschewing the label "Hispanic" as the creation of "Anglos" interested in obscuring her true identity.[53] Thus, third-wave feminists do not presume to speak for Hispanic American women in particular, let alone women in general.

Interestingly, precisely because they have had fears about misrepresenting the identities and issues of particular groups of women, third-wave feminists have managed to hear what women different from themselves are actually saying. More than other group of feminists so far, third-wave feminists have brought more different kinds of women, particularly women of color, to the feminist table. A hopeful sign that feminism is well on its way to finally overcoming its "whiteness" is the publication of books like *Colonize This! Young Women of Color on Today's Feminism,* by Daisy Hernandez and Bushra Rehman.[54] Hernandez and Rehman claimed their primary goal is to "introduce some of the ideas of women of color feminists to women who have thought that feminism is just a philosophy about white men and women and has nothing to do with our communities."[55] They viewed their book as enabling women of color to forge their own unique brands of feminism through directly addressing their differences and, *if possible,* overcoming them.

Hernandez and Rehman's book, among others, has gone a long way to correct in part what multicultural, postcolonial, and global feminists have identified as the foremost failing of the second-wave women's movement, namely, the imposed invisibility of women of color (see Chapter 6). Third-wave books let women of color speak for themselves about the gender issues they face and how these issues interlock with other issues they face, some of which these women may view as their main problems. For example, being a woman is not necessarily a black woman's worst problem. Her "blackness," more than her "womanness," may be her paramount enemy.

Aware of the contemporary scene—indeed, full participants in it—third-wave feminists emphasize that soon people of color will not constitute a minority group in the United States. On the contrary: Not white people, but people of color will constitute the majority of the U.S. population. Significantly, third-wave feminists note that, in general, U.S. society is already increasingly comfortable with people who are multiracial and multiethnic—who have transcended the boundaries of any one race or one ethnicity. They also observe that parents of children whose race or ethnicity is blended are starting to report that their children find white/nonwhite oppositions of little meaning or concern to them. In a *New York Times* article, one mother of three multiracial and diversely ethnic sons commented: "Race takes a backseat to what they listen to on their CD players, what movies they see. . . . One is into Japanese anime. Another is immersed in rap. Basically it's the ghetto culture, but ghetto doesn't mean poor or deprived, but hip."[56] The same mother noted that one of her sons has a "hip-hop persona" and has friends whose skin color ranges from very white to very black.

Clearly, being a third-wave feminist in a society where a growing number of young people choose their racial or ethnic classification is different from being a feminist in second-wave feminist days, when racial and ethnic identities were largely imposed and worked against anyone who was nonwhite. Moreover, doing feminism as a third-wave feminist is very challenging in a global context, where women in developing nations interact with women in developed nations. According to third-wave feminist Chila Bulbeck, women in developing nations lead a particularly complex life because their world, the Third World, has two, contradictory identities. Bulbeck noted that the term "Third World" is "double valenced."[57] The Third World can be understood either negatively as a backward, poor, and bad place to live, or positively as "a subversive, immense repressed voice about to burst into centre stage of the globe."[58]

But even though the Third World has positive potential, its negative actuality still works against the women who live in it, in Bulbeck's estimation. Most Third World women are disadvantaged, as are women in the "Fourth World" (that is, the world in which indigenous people in settler societies live—for example, the world of Native American women in the United States).[59] Also disadvantaged are women in the "Fifth World" (i.e., the world of migrants and immigrants who have left their native lands either because they wanted to or because they had to—for example, African women in the United Kingdom).[60] Thus, third-wave feminists realize just how difficult it is to recognize, let alone to meet, diverse women's needs.

In addition to being open to women's different social, economic, political, and cultural differences, third-wave feminists are open to women's sexual differences. In the 1970s, feminists debated whether a woman, to be a real feminist, had to be a lesbian or at least reside on the "lesbian continuum" (which, as we noted in Chapter 6, ranged from women who simply supported women's concerns to women living in long-term, intimate relationships with other women). These earlier feminists also discussed whether sex between heterosexuals or lesbians had to be "vanilla," "touchy-feely," and utterly devoid of all pain and power games, or whether it could sometimes be "rocky road," mechanical, rough, violent, and even manifestly sadomasochistic. Even more specifically, they wondered about the appropriateness of women working in the sex industry as porn models, call girls, lap dancers, exotic dancers, and prostitutes. These earlier feminists asked if these women were the victims of sexual objectification or dire economic conditions, or if they instead were cagey entrepreneurs who realized they could make far more money selling their sexual services than working as waitresses at local diners. Although some second-wave feminists applauded women who used their sexuality in ways that served their self-reported best interests, most second-wave feminists continued to believe that the dangers of sex were greater than its pleasures and that women had best avoid catering to men's sexual desires, commercializing their own bodies, and enjoying violent sex.

In contrast to most second-wave feminists, third-wave feminists are less prescriptive about what counts as good sex for women. They are also more comfortable about women enhancing their bodies to suit social norms and cultural expectations about what counts as beautiful. If a woman wants to wear makeup, have cosmetic surgery, wear sexually provocative clothes, sell her sexual services, then, as far as many third-wave feminists are concerned, she should feel free to do so, provided she feels empowered by her actions and not somehow demeaned, diminished, or otherwise objectified by them. Unlike second-wave feminists, third-wave feminists do not think, for example, that a woman's choice to work as a porn model or a prostitute is necessarily the product of economic desperation, a history of past sexual abuse, or some sort of false consciousness that makes her *think* she likes using her body to make money when she really does not. On the contrary, third-wave feminists maintain that a woman can be both a feminist and a porn queen. The apparent contradiction, *feminist* porn queen, does not seem to bother third-wave feminists.

For these reasons, third-wave feminists are shaping a new kind of feminism that is not so much interested in getting women to want what they *should want,* as in responding to what women say they want and not second-guessing or judging whether their wants are authentic or inauthentic. Third-wave feminists describe the context in which they practice feminism as one of "lived messiness."[61] According to third-wave feminists Heywood and Drake, part of this messiness includes "girls who want to be boys, boys who want to be girls . . . blacks who want to or refuse to be white, people who are white and black, gay and straight, masculine and feminine."[62] Similarly, another third-wave feminist, Rebecca Walker, speculated that because many third-wave feminists grew up "transgender, bisexual, interracial, and knowing and loving people who are racist, sexist, and otherwise afflicted," they are not as judgmental as their second-wave feminist mothers were. Walker stressed that because "the lines between Us and Them are often blurred," third-wave feminists seek to create identities that "accommodate ambiguity" and "multiple positionalities."[63]

The nonjudgmental, nonprescriptive stance of third-wave feminism is further explained by Amy Richards: "I don't think these women are saying 'I'm going to be female, going to be objectified, going to wear sexy clothes and so on and be part of the backlash against feminism.' I think they're saying, 'I'm going to do all these things because I want to embrace my femininity.'"[64] Although many second-wave feminists take issue with third-wave feminists playing up their "femininity," some do not. For example, second-wave feminist Anne Braithwaite reacted to third-wave feminists' overt "sexiness" more sympathetically, commenting that this is the year 2007, not 1967:

> An engagement with . . . practices of seemingly traditional feminin-
> ity does not necessarily carry the same meanings for young women
> today or for the culture they live in than they might have to earlier
> feminist periods, and thus cannot be the point upon which to write
> off specific cultural practices as somehow apolitical and therefore
> "post"- or "anti"-feminist.[65]

For second-wave feminist Cathryn Bailey, the fact that younger feminists
are focusing on their femininity is "a wake-up call for older feminists that
what appears, from one perspective, to be conformist, may from another perspective have subversive potential."[66]

Critique of Third-Wave Feminism

Because they enthusiastically embrace the idea that there is no all-encompassing
single feminist idea, third-wave feminists seem better equipped than their second-wave mothers to deal with women's differences. But it is not as if third-
wave feminism is without faults of its own. At times, the home of third-wave
feminism is so "messy" that not enough pots and pans can be found within it to
cook a decent feminist meal. Not only is the essentialist notion "Woman" gone,
but the category of gender has been broken into so many pieces that third-wave
feminists cannot seem to get a grip on it. The home of third-wave feminists
seems to be inhabited by a collection of strongly individual women, expressing
each other's different feelings to each other and leaving it at that. As Allison
Howry and Julia Wood put it, "many young women today wear their 'feminism
lightly.'"[67]

According to feminist critics of third-wave feminism, this new form of
feminist thought needs a list of core values—an agenda that rallies women to
ally themselves with a goal that goes beyond just being oneself, doing what
one wants to do, or being a person whose identity is almost overwhelmingly
hyphenated and multicultural. Whereas the challenge for second-wave feminism was to learn to recognize and use women's differences productively so as
to overcome the idea that all women are necessarily victims or victims in the
same sort of way, the challenge for third-wave feminists, say their critics, is to
recognize that to have feminism, one has to believe that women constitute
some sort of class or social group, and that just because some women feel
empowered does not mean all women feel this way.[68]

Critics of third-wave feminism are particularly disturbed by its tendency to
describe second-wave feminism as "victim feminism" and third-wave feminism
as "power feminism." In the hands of third-wave feminists like Heywood,

Drake, and Walker, power feminism seems inviting enough, but in the hands of other thinkers, best labeled third-wave *postfeminists*, "power feminism" gets very mean-spirited. Writers like Katie Roiphe, Camille Paglia, and René Denfield insist that nowadays, women are free to be whoever they want to be and to do whatever they want to do.[69] Women's only possible enemy is themselves, these writers imply. According to critics of third-wave feminism, however, Roiphe, Paglia, and Denfield fail to recognize the vulnerability and victimization of women far less advantaged than they are. Women in the United States and many other developed nations may be more equal and free than they were fifty or even twenty-five years ago. But women in other nations, particularly developing nations, live in conditions more oppressive than even those conditions that challenged first-wave U.S. feminists at the turn of the nineteenth century.

Conclusion

Despite the criticisms raised against postmodern feminism and third-wave feminism, these two schools of thought remain two of the most exciting developments in contemporary feminist thought. Although today's feminists have distinctively different agendas, these thinkers share certain tendencies. One such tendency is a common desire to think nonbinary, nonoppositional thoughts, the kind of thoughts that may have existed before Adam was given the power to name the animals, to determine the beginnings and ends of things: "And out of the ground the Lord God formed every beast of the field, and every fowl of the air; and brought them unto Adam to see what he would call them—and whatsoever Adam called every living creature, that was the name thereof."[70] We can imagine this original state prior to Adam's intrusion as a Taoist undifferentiated "uncarved block," waiting to be carved into realities by the subjectivities of people situated in different times and places.[71]

Whether postmodern and third-wave feminists can, by carving the block and by speaking and writing, help overcome binary opposition, phallocentrism, and logocentrism, is not certain. What is certain, however, is that the time has come for a new conceptual order. Bent upon achieving unity, we human beings have excluded, ostracized, and alienated so-called abnormal, deviant, and marginal people. As a result of this policy of exclusion, the human community has been impoverished. It seems, then, that men as well as women have much to gain by joining a variety of postmodern and third-wave feminists in their attempts to shape a feminism that meets people's needs in the new millennium.

Still, today's feminists may have something to lose in the delight of living their own unique feminisms. They may lose themselves as women. Christine di Stephano responded to some current feminist attempts to destroy all categories, including the category *women*:

> Gender is basic in ways that we have yet to fully understand, . . . it functions as "a difference that makes a difference," even as it can no longer claim the legitimating mantle of *the* difference. The figure of the shrinking woman may perhaps be best appreciated and utilized as an aporia within contemporary theory: as a recurring paradox, question, dead end, or blind spot to which we must repeatedly return, because to ignore her altogether is to risk forgetting and thereby losing what is left of her.[72]

Third-wave feminism is probably not the last wave of feminism we will see. The "woman question" has yet to be fully answered.

Notes

Introduction

1. Mary Wollstonecraft, *A Vindication of the Rights of Women,* ed. Carol H. Hoston (New York: W. W. Norton, 1975).

2. John Stuart Mill, "The Subjection of Women," in John Stuart Mill and Harriet Taylor Mill, *Essays on Sex Equality,* ed. Alice S. Rossi (Chicago: University of Chicago Press, 1970), pp. 184–185.

3. Catharine A. MacKinnon elaborated upon the sex/gender system in "Feminism, Marxism, Method, and the State: An Agenda for Theory," *Signs: Journal of Women in Culture and Society* 7, no. 3 (spring 1982): 515–516.

4. Linda Alcoff, "Culture Feminism Versus Poststructuralism: The Identity Crisis in Feminist Theory," *Signs: Journal of Women in Culture and Society* 13, no. 31 (1988): 408; Ann Ferguson, "The Sex Debate in the Women's Movement: A Socialist-Feminist View," *Against the Current* (September/October 1983): 10–16; Alice Echols, "The New Feminism of Yin and Yang," in *Powers of Desire: The Politics of Sexuality,* ed. Ann Snitow, Christine Stansell, and Sharon Thompson (New York: Monthly Review Press, 1983), p. 445 .

5. See Mary Vetterling-Braggin, ed., *"Femininity," "Masculinity,"and "Androgyny"* (Totowa, N.J.: Rowman & Littlefield, 1982), p. 6.

6. Carol S. Vance, ed., *Pleasure and Danger: Exploring Female Sexuality* (Boston: Routledge & Kegan Paul, 1984).

7. Rosemarie Tong, *Women, Sex and the Law* (Totowa, N.J.: Rowman & Littlefield, 1984).

8. Mary Daly, *Gyn/Ecology: The Metaethics of Radical Feminism* (Boston: Beacon Press, 1978).

9. Charlotte Bunch, "Lesbians in Revolt," in *Women and Values,* ed. Marilyn Pearsall (Belmont, Calif.: Wadsworth, 1986), pp. 128–132.

10. Shulamith Firestone, *The Dialectic of Sex* (New York: Bantam Books, 1970).

11. Adrienne Rich, *Of Woman Born* (New York: W. W. Norton, 1976); Sara Ruddick, "Maternal Thinking," in *Mothering: Essays in Feminist Theory,* ed. Joyce Trebilcot (Totowa, N.J.: Rowman & Allanheld, 1984).

12. See, for example, Gena Corea, *The Mother Machine: Reproductive Technologies from Artificial Insemination to Artificial Wombs* (New York: Harper & Row, 1985).

13. Friedrich Engels, *The Origin of the Family, Private Property, and the State* (New York: International Publishers, 1972), p. 103.

14. Juliet Mitchell, *Woman's Estate* (New York: Pantheon Books, 1971).

15. Alison M. Jaggar, *Feminist Politics and Human Nature* (Totowa, N.J.: Rowman & Allanheld, 1983), pp. 316–317.

16. Dorothy Dinnerstein, *The Mermaid and the Minotaur: Sexual Arrangements and Human Malaise* (New York: Harper Colophon Books, 1977), p. 161.

17. Sherry B. Ortner, "Oedipal Father, Mother's Brother, and the Penis: A Review of Juliet Mitchell's *Psychoanalysis and Feminism,*" Feminist Studies 2, nos. 2–3 (1975): 179.

18. Nancy Chodorow, *The Reproduction of Mothering* (Berkeley: University of California Press, 1978).

19. Ynestra King, "Healing the Wounds: Feminism, Ecology, and Nature/Culture Dualism," in *Feminism and Philosophy,* ed. Nancy Tuana and Rosemarie Tong (Boulder, Colo.: Westview Press, 1995).

20. Judith Butler, *Gender Trouble: Feminism and the Subversion of Identity* (New York: Routledge, 1990).

Chapter One

1. Douglas MacLean and Claudia Mills, eds., *Liberalism Reconsidered* (Totowa, N.J.: Rowman & Allanheld, 1983).

2. Susan Wendell, "A (Qualified) Defense of Liberal Feminism," *Hypatia* 2, no. 2 (summer 1987): 65–94.

3. Alison M. Jaggar, *Feminist Politics and Human Nature* (Totowa, N.J.: Rowman & Allanheld, 1983).

4. Ibid., p. 33.

5. Michael J. Sandel, ed., *Liberalism and Its Critics* (New York: New York University Press, 1984), p. 4. I owe this reference to Michael Weber, who also clarified for me the distinction between the "right" and the "good."

6. Jaggar, *Feminist Politics and Human Nature,* p. 31.

7. According to Carole Pateman, the private world is one "of particularism, of subjection, inequality, nature, emotion, love and partiality" (Carole Pateman, *The Problem of Political Obligation: A Critique of Liberal Theory* [Berkeley: University of California Press, 1979], p. 190).

8. Again according to Pateman, the public world is one "of the individual, or universalism, of impartial rules and laws, of freedom, equality, rights, property, contract, self-interest, justice—and political obligation" (ibid., p. 198).

9. Sandel employed this terminology in *Liberalism and Its Critics,* p. 4.

10. Wendell, "A (Qualified) Defense of Liberal Feminism," p. 66.

11. Ibid., p. 90.

12. Zillah Eisenstein, *The Radical Future of Liberal Feminism* (Boston: Northeastern University Press, 1986), pp. 96–99.

13. Mary Wollstonecraft, *A Vindication of the Rights of Woman,* ed. Carol H. Poston (New York: W. W. Norton, 1975).

14. Ibid., p. 56.

15. Ibid., p. 23.

16. Jean-Jacques Rousseau, *Emile,* trans. Allan Bloom (New York: Basic Books, 1979).

17. Allan Bloom advanced a contemporary argument in support of sexual dimorphism (Allan Bloom, *The Closing of the American Mind* [New York: Simon & Schuster, 1987], pp. 97–137).

18. Wollstonecraft, *A Vindication of the Rights of Woman,* p. 61.

19. Ibid.

20. Ibid., p. 152.

21. Immanuel Kant, *Groundwork of the Metaphysic of Morals,* trans. H. J. Paton (New York: Harper Torchbooks, 1958).

22. Jane Roland Martin, *Reclaiming a Conversation: The Ideal of the Educated Woman* (New Haven, Conn.: Yale University Press, 1985), p. 76.

23. Wollstonecraft, *A Vindication of the Rights of Woman,* p. 152.

24. Judith A. Sabrosky, *From Rationality to Liberation* (Westport, Conn.: Greenwood Press, 1979), p. 31.

25. Wollstonecraft, *A Vindication of the Rights of Woman,* p. 147.

26. Ironically, Wollstonecraft's personal life was driven by emotions. As Eisenstein, *The Radical Future of Liberal Feminism,* p. 106, described it, Wollstonecraft "tried unsuccessfully to live the life of independence."

27. Wollstonecraft, *A Vindication of the Rights of Woman,* p. 34.

28. Kant, *Groundwork of the Metaphysic of Morals,* pp. 63–64, 79, 95–98.

29. Alice S. Rossi, "Sentiment and Intellect: The Story of John Stuart Mill and Harriet Taylor Mill," in John Stuart Mill and Harriet Taylor Mill, *Essays on Sex Equality,* ed. Alice S. Rossi (Chicago: University of Chicago Press, 1970), p. 28.

30. John Stuart Mill and Harriet Taylor Mill, "Early Essays on Marriage and Divorce," in Mill and Taylor Mill, *Essays on Sex Equality,* , pp. 75, 81, and 86.

31. Ibid., p. 75.

32. Harriet Taylor Mill, "Enfranchisement of Women," in Mill and Taylor Mill, *Essays on Sex Equality,* p. 95.

33. Ibid., p. 104 (emphasis mine).

34. Ibid., p. 105.

35. Mill and Taylor, "Early Essays on Marriage and Divorce," pp. 74–75.

36. Taylor Mill, "Enfranchisement of Women," p. 105.

37. Richard Krouse, "Mill and Marx on Marriage, Divorce, and the Family," *Social Concept* 1, no. 2 (September 1983): 48.

38. Eisenstein, *The Radical Future of Liberal Feminism,* p. 131.

39. John Stuart Mill, "The Subjection of Women," in Mill and Taylor Mill, *Essays on Sex Equality,* p. 221.

40. Susan Moller Okin, *Women in Western Political Thought* (Princeton, N.J.: Princeton University Press, 1979), pp. 197–232.

41. Wollstonecraft, *A Vindication of the Rights of Woman,* p. 77.

42. Mill, "The Subjection of Women," p. 186.

43. Ibid., p. 154.

44. Ibid., p. 213.

45. John Stuart Mill, "Periodical Literature 'Edinburgh Review,'" *Westminster Review* 1, no. 2 (April 1824): 526.

46. Wollstonecraft, *A Vindication of the Rights of Woman,* p. 39.

47. See Mill's description of Harriet Taylor in John Stuart Mill, *Autobiography* (London: Oxford University Press, 1924), pp. 156–160.

48. Mill, "The Subjection of Women," p. 177.

49. Angela Y. Davis, *Women, Race and Class* (New York: Random House, 1981), p. 42.

50. Judith Hole and Ellen Levine, *Rebirth of Feminism* (New York: Quadrangle Books, 1971), p. 3.

51. Ibid., p. 434.

52. Ibid.

53. Ibid., p. 435

54. Quoted in Elizabeth Cady Stanton, Susan B. Anthony, and Matilda Joslyn Gage, *History of Woman Suffrage,* vol. 1 (1848–1861) (New York: Fowler and Wells, 1881), pp. 115–117.

55. Davis, *Women, Race and Class,* p. 75.

56. Hole and Levine, *Rebirth of Feminism,* p. 14.

57. Maren Lockwood Carden, *The New Feminist Movement* (New York: Russell Sage Foundation, 1974), p. 3.

58. Ibid., p. 16.

59. Caroline Bird, *Born Female* (New York: David McKay Company, 1968), p. 1.

60. Betty Friedan, "N.O.W.: How It Began," *Women Speaking,* April 1967, p. 4.

61. "NOW (National Organization for Women) Bill of Rights (Adopted at NOW's first national conference, Washington, D.C., 1967)," in *Sisterhood Is Powerful,* ed. Robin Morgan (New York: Random House, 1970), pp. 513–514.

62. All these issues were addressed in Patricia Tjadens and Nancy Thoenes, *Full Report of the Prevalence, Incidence and Consequences of Violence Against Women* (Washington, D.C.: National Institute of Justice and Centers for Disease Prevention, 2000).

63. Report of the President, Second National Conference of NOW, Washington, D.C., November 18, 1967," cited in Hole and Levine, *Rebirth of Feminism,* p. 6.

64. Betty Friedan, National Organization for Women, Memorandum, September 22, 1969.

65. Carden, *The New Feminist Movement,* p. 113.

66. Alice Echols, *Daring to Be Bad: Radical Feminism in America 1967–1975* (Minneapolis: University of Minnesota Press, 1987), p. 215.

67. Patricia Ireland, "The State of NOW," *Ms.,* July/August 1992, pp. 24–27.

68. Betty Friedan, *The Feminine Mystique* (New York: Dell, 1974).

69. Ibid., pp. 69–70.

70. Ibid., pp. 22–27.

71. Ibid., p. 380.

72. Ibid., p. 330.

73. Betty Friedan, *The Second Stage* (New York: Summit Books, 1981).

74. Ibid., pp. 20–21.

75. Ibid., p. 67.

76. Ibid., p. 28.

77. Ibid., p. 27.

78. Eisenstein, *The Radical Future of Liberal Feminism,* p. 190.

79. Ibid.

80. Friedan, *The Second Stage,* p. 112.

81. Ibid., p. 148.

82. James Sterba, "Feminism Has Not Discriminated Against Men," in *Does Feminism Discriminate Against Men?: A Debate,* ed. Warren Farrell and James P. Sterba (Oxford: Oxford University Press, 2007).

83. Friedan, *The Feminine Mystique,* pp. 362 and 363.

84. See Judith Stacey, "The New Conservative Feminism," *Feminist Studies* 9, no. 3 (fall 1983): 562.

85. Friedan, *The Second Stage,* pp. 248, 249.

86. Ibid., p. 249.

87. Quoted in John Leo, "Are Women 'Male Clones'?" *Time,* August 18, 1986, p. 63.

88. Quoted in ibid., p. 64.

89. Betty Friedan, *The Fountain of Age* (New York: Simon & Schuster, 1993), p. 157.

90. Ibid., p. 638.

91. Friedan, *The Second Stage,* p. 342.

92. Ibid., p. 41

93. Eisenstein, *The Radical Future of Liberal Feminism,* p. 176.

94. For a detailed discussion of the distinction between sex and gender, see Ethel Spector Person, "Sexuality As the Mainstay of Identity: Psychoanalytic Perspectives," *Signs: Journal of Women in Culture and Society* 5, no. 4 (summer 1980): 606.

95. Jean-Marie Navetta, "Gains in Learning, Gaps in Earning," *AAUW Outlook* (spring 2005): 12.

96. Cited in Hunter College Women's Studies Collective, *Women's Realities, Women's Choices: An Introduction to Women's Studies* (New York: Oxford University Press, 1983), p. 521.

97. Not all liberal feminists agree that women and minority male candidates should be viewed as equally disadvantaged. The more *liberal* a liberal feminist is, the more likely she is to view gender and race or ethnic disadvantages as on a par. The more *feminist* a liberal feminist is, the more likely she is to focus her attention exclusively on women.

98. Jane English, "Sex Roles and Gender: Introduction," in *Feminism and Philosophy*, ed. Mary Vetterling-Braggin, Frederick A. Elliston, and Jane English (Totowa, N.J.: Rowman & Littlefield, 1977), p. 39.

99. There is much debate about how factors such as race, class, and ethnicity affect the social construction of gender. See Carol Stack, *All Our Kin* (New York: Harper & Row, 1974).

100. By no means has the interest in androgyny been confined to liberal feminists. Radical feminists have also explored this notion, expressing, however, more reservations about it.

101. Carolyn G. Heilbrun, *Toward the Promise of Androgyny* (New York: Alfred A. Knopf, 1973), pp. x–xi.

102. Sandra L. Bem, "Probing the Promise of Androgyny," in *Beyond Sex-Role Stereotypes: Reading Toward a Psychology of Androgyny*, ed. Alexandra G. Kaplan and Joan P. Bean (Boston: Little, Brown, 1976), pp. 51ff.

103. Although not a liberal feminist, Joyce Trebilcot has forwarded an analysis of androgyny that liberal feminists have found useful. See Joyce Trebilcot, "Two Forms of Androgynism," in *"Femininity," "Masculinity," and "Androgyny,"* ed. Mary Vetterling-Braggin (Totowa, N.J.: Rowman & Littlefield, 1982), pp. 161–170.

104. Jaggar, *Feminist Politics and Human Nature*, p. 28.

105. Ibid., pp. 40–42.

106. Ibid., p. 41.

107. Naomi Scheman, "Individualism and the Objects of Psychology," in *Discovering Reality: Feminist Perspectives on Epistemology, Metaphysics, Methodology, and the Philosophy of Science*, ed. Sandra Harding and Merrill B. Hintikka (Dordrecht, Netherlands: D. Reidel, 1983), pp. 225–244.

108. Ibid., p. 232.

109. Wendell, "A (Qualified) Defense of Liberal Feminism," p. 66.

110. Ibid.

111. Ibid., p. 76.

112. Jean Bethke Elshtain, "Feminism, Family and Community," *Dissent* 29 (fall 1982): 442.

113. Jean Bethke Elshtain, *Public Man, Private Woman* (Princeton, N.J.: Princeton University Press, 1981), p. 252.

114. In the nineteenth century, many of the suffragists waxed eloquently about women's moral superiority. See Ida Husted Harper, ed., *History of Woman Suffrage,* vol. 5 (New York: National American Woman Suffrage Association, 1922), p. 126. See, for example, the section on feminist ethics in Marilyn Pearsall, ed., *Women and Values* (Belmont, Calif.: Wadsworth, 1986), pp. 266–364.

115. Elshtain, *Public Man, Private Woman,* p. 253.

116. Ibid., p. 243.

117. Ibid., p. 251.

118. Ibid., p. 336.

119. Ibid., p. 237.

120. Barbara Arneil, *Politics and Feminism* (Oxford: Blackwell Press, 1999), p. 147.

121. Angela Y. Davis, "Reflections on the Black Woman's Role in the Community of Slaves," *Black Scholar* 3 (1971): 7.

122. Ireland, "The State of NOW," p. 26.

123. Elizabeth Erlich, "Do the Sunset Years Have to Be Gloomy?" *New York Times Book Review,* 1994, p. 18.

124. Ibid.

125. Quoted in Hole and Levine, *Rebirth of Feminism,* p. 94.

126. Ellen Willis, "The Conservatism of *Ms.,*" in *Feminist Revolution,* ed. Redstockings (New York: Random House, 1975), pp. 170–171.

127. One of these exceptions is Janet Radcliffe Richards, *The Skeptical Feminist* (London: Routledge & Kegan Paul, 1980).

128. Willis, "The Conservatism of *Ms.,*" p. 170.

129. Wendell, "A (Qualified) Defense of Liberal Feminism," p. 86.

130. Ruth Groenhout, "Essentialist Challenges to Liberal Feminism," *Social Theory and Practice* 28, no. 1 (January 2002): 57.

131. Ibid.

Chapter Two

1. See Judith Hole and Ellen Levine, *Rebirth of Feminism* (New York: Quadrangle, 1971), p. 108.

2. Ibid.

3. Valerie Bryson, *Feminist Debates: Issues of Theory and Political Practice* (New York: New York University Press, 1999), p. 27.

4. Alison M. Jaggar and Paula S. Rothenberg, eds., *Feminist Frameworks* (New York: McGraw-Hill, 1984), p. 186.

5. Joreen Freeman, as quoted in Anne Koedt, Ellen Levine, and Anita Rapone, eds., *Radical Feminism* (New York: Quadrangle, 1973), p. 52.

6. Alice Echols, "The New Feminism of Yin and Yang," in *Powers of Desire: The Politics of Sexuality,* ed. Ann Snitow, Christine Stansell, and Sharon Thompson (New York: Monthly Review Press, 1983), p. 445.

7. Ibid.

8. Alison M. Jaggar, "Feminist Ethics," in *Encyclopedia of Ethics,* ed. Lawrence Becker with Charlotte Becker (New York: Garland, 1992), p. 364.

9. Echols, "The New Feminism of Yin and Yang," p. 440.

10. Linda Alcoff, "Cultural Feminism Versus Poststructuralism: The Identity Crisis in Feminist Theory," *Signs: Journal of Women in Culture and Society* 13, no. 3 (1988): 408.

11. Gayle Rubin, "The Traffic in Women," in *Toward an Anthropology of Women,* ed. Rayna R. Reiter (New York: Monthly Review Press, 1975), p. 159.

12. Hester Eisenstein, *Contemporary Feminist Thought* (Boston: G. K. Hall, 1983), p. 8.

13. Kate Millett, *Sexual Politics* (Garden City, N.Y.: Doubleday, 1970), p. 25.

14. Ibid., pp. 43–46.

15. Henry Miller, *Sexus* (New York: Grove Press, 1965), pp. 181–182.

16. Millett, *Sexual Politics,* p. 178.

17. Herbert Barry III, Margaret K. Bacon, and Irwin L. Child, "A Cross-Cultural Survey of Some Sex Differences in Socialization," in *Selected Studies in Marriage and the Family,* 2nd ed., ed. Robert F. Winch, Robert McGinnis, and Herbert R. Barringer (New York: Holt, Rinehart and Winston, 1962), p. 267.

18. In the 1970s, Millett asserted that what society needs is a single standard of "sex freedom" for boys and girls and a single standard of parental responsibility for fathers and mothers. Without such unitary standards for sexual and parental behavior, equality between men and women will remain ephemeral (Millett, *Sexual Politics,* p. 62).

19. Ibid.

20. Shulamith Firestone, *The Dialectic of Sex* (New York: Bantam Books, 1970), p. 59.

21. Ibid., p. 175.

22. Ibid.

23. Ibid., p. 190.

24. Ibid., pp. 191 and 242.

25. Marilyn French, *Beyond Power: On Women, Men and Morals* (New York: Summit Books, 1985), p. 72.

26. Ibid., pp. 25–66.

27. Ibid., p. 67.

28. Ibid., p. 69.

29. Ibid., p. 68.

30. Ibid., p. 443.

31. Joyce Trebilcot, "Conceiving Wisdom: Notes on the Logic of Feminism," *Sinister Wisdom* 3 (fall 1979): 46.

32. Alison M. Jaggar, *Feminist Politics and Human Nature* (Totowa, N.J.: Rowman & Allanheld, 1983), p. 252.

33. French, *Beyond Power,* pp. 487–488.

34. Dorothy Dinnerstein, *The Mermaid and the Minotaur: Sexual Arrangements and Human Malaise* (New York: Harper Colophon Books, 1977), p. 5.

35. French, *Beyond Power,* p. 538.

36. Mary Daly, *Beyond God the Father: Toward a Philosophy of Women's Liberation* (Boston: Beacon Press, 1973).

37. Using French's terminology in this context, we may say that an immanent God infuses women with the "power-to-grow" into their own image and likeness rather than be molded into the image and likeness of a transcendent God interested only in expressing his "power-over" others.

38. Alice Rossi, "Sex Equality: The Beginning of Ideology," in *Masculine/Feminine,* ed. Betty Roszak and Theodore Roszak (New York: Harper & Row, 1969), pp. 173–186.

39. Daly, *Beyond God the Father,* p. 105.

40. Mary Daly, *Gyn/Ecology: The Metaethics of Radical Feminism* (Boston: Beacon Press, 1978), p. 59.

41. Ibid., pp. 107–312.

42. Ibid., p. xi.

43. Ibid., p. 68.

44. See Ann-Janine Morey-Gaines, "Metaphor and Radical Feminism: Some Cautionary Comments on Mary Daly's *Gyn/Ecology,*" *Soundings* 65, no. 3 (fall 1982): 347–348.

45. Daly, *Gyn/Ecology,* p. 334.

46. Ibid., p. 336.

47. Ibid., p. 337.

48. Friedrich Wilhelm Nietzsche, *On the Genealogy of Morals,* trans. Walter Kaufmann and R. Hollingdale (New York: Vintage Books, 1969), p. 44.

49. Daly, *Gyn/Ecology,* pp. 14–15.

50. Mary Daly, *Pure Lust: Elemental Feminist Philosophy* (Boston: Beacon Press, 1984), p. 203.

51. Ibid., p. 2.

52. Ibid., pp. 2–3.

53. Ibid., p. 35.

54. Ibid., p. 204.

55. Betty Friedan, *The Feminine Mystique* (New York: Dell, 1974).

56. Daly, *Pure Lust,* p. 206.

57. See Carole S. Vance, "Pleasure and Danger: Toward a Politics of Sexuality," in *Pleasure and Danger: Exploring Female Sexuality,* ed. Carole S. Vance (Boston: Routledge & Kegan Paul, 1984), pp. 1–27.

58. Ann Ferguson, "Sex War: The Debate Between Radical and Liberation Feminists," *Signs: Journal of Women in Culture and Society* 10, no. 1 (autumn 1984): 109.

59. Ibid., p. 108.

60. Ibid.

61. Ibid., p. 109.

62. Gayle Rubin, "Thinking Sex: Notes for a Radical Theory of the Politics of Sexuality," in *Pleasure and Danger: Exploring Female Sexuality,* ed. Carole S. Vance (Boston: Routledge & Kegan Paul, 1984), pp. 275–301.

63. Ibid., p. 275.

64. Ibid., p. 278.

65. Alice Echols, "The Taming of the Id," in *Pleasure and Danger: Exploring Female Sexuality,* ed. Carole S. Vance (Boston: Routledge & Kegan Paul, 1984), p. 59.

66. Ibid.

67. Ibid.

68. Rubin, "Thinking Sex," p. 278.

69. Radicalesbians, "The Woman-Identified-Woman," in *Radical Feminism: A Documentary Reader,* ed. Barbara A. Crow (New York: New York University Press, 2000), p. 236.

70. Deirdre English, Amber Hollibaugh, and Gayle Rubin, "Talking Sex: A Conversation on Sexuality and Feminism," in *Socialist Review* 11, no 4 (July/August 1981): 53.

71. See the debate between Christina Hoff Sommers and Marilyn Friedman in Marilyn Friedman and Jan Narveson, *Political Correctness: For and Against* (Lanham, Md.: Rowman & Littlefield, 1995), pp. 36–37.

72. Catharine A. MacKinnon, "Francis Biddle's Sister: Pornography, Civil Rights, and Speech," in *Feminism Unmodified: Disclosures on Life and Law* (Cambridge, Mass.: Harvard University Press, 1987), p. 176.

73. Catharine A. MacKinnon, "Feminism, Marxism, Method, and the State: An Agenda for Theory," *Signs: Journal of Women in Culture and Society* 7, no. 3 (spring 1982): 533.

74. Appendix I, Minneapolis, Minn., Code of Ordinances, title 7, ch. 139, 1 amending 39.10.

75. Stuart Taylor Jr., "Pornography Foes Lose New Weapons in Supreme Court," *New York Times,* February 25, 1986, p. 1.

76. Nan D. Hunter and Sylvia A. Law, Brief Amici Curiae of Feminist Anti-Censorship Task Force et al. to U.S. Court of Appeals for the Seventh Circuit, *American Booksellers Association, Inc. et al. v. William H. Hudnut III et al.* (April 18, 1985): 9–18.

77. Ibid., p. 11.

78. MacKinnon, "Feminism, Marxism, Method, and the State," p. 533.

79. Ann Koedt, "The Myth of the Vaginal Orgasm," *Notes from the Second Year: Women's Liberation—Major Writings of the Radical Feminists* (April 1970), p. 41.

80. Ibid.

81. Adrienne Rich, "Compulsory Heterosexuality and Lesbian Existence," in *Living with Contradictions: Controversies in Feminist Social Ethics,* ed. Alison M. Jaggar (Boulder, Colo.: Westview Press, 1994), p. 488.

82. Deirdre English, quoted in Hole and Levine, *Rebirth of Feminism,* p. 221.

83. English, Hollibaugh, and Rubin, "Talking Sex," p. 49.

84. See "Redstockings Manifesto," in *Sisterhood Is Powerful,* ed. Robin Morgan (New York: Random House, 1970), p. 534.

85. English, Hollibaugh, and Rubin, "Talking Sex," p. 50.

86. "Redstockings Manifesto," p. 534.

87. "New York Covens' Leaflet," in *Sisterhood Is Powerful,* ed. Robin Morgan (New York: Random House, 1970), pp. 539–540.

88. Friedrich Engels, *Socialism: Utopian or Scientific,* quoted in Firestone, *The Dialectic of Sex,* pp. 1–12.

89. Firestone, *The Dialectic of Sex,* p. 12.

90. Because the claim that biology is the cause of women's oppression sounds similar to the claim that women's biology is their destiny, it is important to stress the difference between these two claims. Whereas conservatives believe that the constraints of nature exist necessarily, radical feminists insist that it is within women's power to overcome the constraints. For some conservative views, see George Gilder, *Sexual Suicide* (New York: Quadrangle, 1973), and Lionel Tiger, *Men in Groups* (New York: Random House, 1969). For some feminist views, see Mary Vetterling-Braggin, ed., *"Femininity," "Masculinity," and "Androgyny"* (Totowa, N.J.: Rowman & Littlefield, 1982).

91. Firestone, *The Dialectic of Sex,* p. 12.

92. Ibid., pp. 198–199.

93. Marge Piercy, *Woman on the Edge of Time* (New York: Fawcett Crest Books, 1976).

94. Ibid., p. 102.

95. Ibid., pp. 105–106.

96. Ibid., p. 183.

97. Azizah al-Hibri, *Research in Philosophy and Technology,* ed. Paul T. Durbin (London: JAL Press, 1984), vol. 7, p. 266.

98. Anne Donchin, "The Future of Mothering: Reproductive Technology and Feminist Theory," *Hypatia* 1, no. 2 (fall 1986): 131.

99. Mary O'Brien, *The Politics of Reproduction* (Boston: Routledge & Kegan Paul, 1981).

100. Ibid., pp. 8, 20ff., and 35–36. See also Sara Ann Ketchum, "New Reproductive Technologies and the Definition of Parenthood: A Feminist Perspective" (photocopy, June 18, 1987). Paper given at the Feminism and Legal Theory Conference at the University of Wisconsin–Madison, summer 1987.

101. Adrienne Rich, *Of Woman Born* (New York: W. W. Norton, 1979), p. 111.

102. Ibid., pp. 38–39.

103. Firestone, *The Dialectic of Sex,* p. 199.

104. Andrea Dworkin, *Right-Wing Women* (New York: Coward-McCann, 1983), pp. 187–188.

105. Margaret Atwood, *The Handmaid's Tale* (New York: Fawcett Crest Books, 1985).

106. Ibid., p. 164.

107. Genea Corea, *The Mother Machine: Reproduction Technologies from Artificial Insemination to Artificial Wombs* (New York: Harper & Row, 1985), pp. 107–119.

108. Genea Corea, "Egg Snatchers," in *Test-Tube Women: What Future for Motherhood?* ed. Rita Arditti, Renate Duelli Klein, and Shelley Minden (London: Pandora Press, 1984), p. 45.

109. Robyn Rowland, "Reproductive Technologies: The Final Solution to the Woman Question," in *Test-Tube Women: What Future for Motherhood?* ed. Rita Arditti, Renate Duelli Klein, and Shelley Minden (London: Pandora Press, 1984), pp. 365–366.

110. Ibid., p. 368.

111. Alison M. Jaggar, *Feminist Politics and Human Nature* (Totowa, N.J.: Rowman & Allanheld, 1983), p. 256.

112. Ann Oakley, *Woman's Work: The Housewife, Past and Present* (New York: Pantheon Books, 1974), p. 186.

113. Ibid., pp. 187, 199.

114. Ibid., p. 201.

115. Ibid., pp. 201–203.

116. Ibid., p. 203.

117. The claim that adopted children fare just as well as biological children is more controversial than Oakley believed. See, for example, Betty Reid Mendell, *Where Are the Children? A Close Analysis of Foster Care and Adoption* (Lexington, Mass.: Lexington Books, 1973).

118. The kibbutzim have come under fire, however. See, for example, "The Pathogenic Commune," *Science News* 122, no. 76 (July 3, 1982): 76.

119. Firestone, *The Dialectic of Sex,* p. 229.

120. Ibid., pp. 228–230.

121. Rich, *Of Woman Born,* p. 174.

122. Ibid., p. 13.

123. Ibid., p. 57.

124. Ibid., p. 13.

125. Ibid., p. 57.

126. Ibid., pp. 31–32.

127. Because the term "surrogate mother" suggests that such a woman is not a real mother but a substitute mother, many feminists prefer the term "contracted mother."

128. Corea, *The Mother Machine,* pp. 213–249.

129. "A Surrogate's Story of Loving and Losing," *U.S. News & World Report,* June 6, 1983, p. 12.

130. *Boston Globe,* October 2, 1987, p. 1.

131. Jean Bethke Elshtain, *Public Man, Private Woman* (Princeton, N.J.: Princeton University Press, 1981), p. 226.

132. Mary R. Beard, *Woman As Force in History* (New York: Collier Books, 1972).

133. Sheila Rowbotham, *Women, Resistance and Revolution* (New York: Vintage Books, 1972).

134. Elshtain, *Public Man, Private Woman,* p. 228.

135. Ibid., p. 213.

136. Audre Lorde, "An Open Letter to Mary Daly," in *This Bridge Called My Back,* ed. Cherríe Moraga and Gloria Anzaldúa (Watertown, Mass.: Persephone Press, 1981), pp. 94–97.

137. Elshtain, *Public Man, Private Woman,* p. 226.

138. Ibid., p. 225.

139. Rich, "Compulsory Heterosexuality and Lesbian Existence," p. 488.

140. Ann Ferguson, "The Sex Debate in the Women's Movement: A Socialist-Feminist View," *Against the Current* (September/October 1983): 12.

141. Ibid.

142. Ibid., p. 13.

143. Ibid. (emphasis mine).

144. Ibid.

Chapter Three

1. Karl Marx, *Capital* (New York: International Publishers, 1967), vol. 3, p. 791.

2. Nancy Holmstrom, "The Socialist Feminist Project," *Monthly Review Press* 54, no. 10 (2002): 1.

3. Richard Schmitt, *Introduction to Marx and Engels* (Boulder, Colo.: Westview Press, 1987), pp. 7–8.

4. Karl Marx, *A Contribution to the Critique of Political Economy* (New York: International Publishers, 1972), pp. 20–21.

5. Schmitt, *Introduction to Marx and Engels,* p. 14.

6. Nancy Holmstrom, "A Marxist Theory of Women's Nature," *Ethics* 94, no. 1 (April 1984): 464.

7. Robert L. Heilbroner, *Marxism: For and Against* (New York: W. W. Norton, 1980), p. 107.

8. Henry Burrows Acton, *What Marx Really Said* (London: MacDonald, 1967), p. 41.

9. Ernest Mandel, *An Introduction to Marxist Economic Theory* (New York: Pathfinder Press, 1970), p. 25.

10. Marx's discussion of surplus value and exploitation is found in his three-volume work *Capital,* particularly volumes 1 and 2. For a more detailed introduction to these concepts, see Wallis Arthur Suchting, *Marx: An Introduction* (New York: New York University Press, 1983).

11. Schmitt, *Introduction to Marx and Engels,* pp. 96–97.

12. For an elaboration of these points, see Mandel, *An Introduction to Marxist Economic Theory.*

13. Karl Marx, *The 18th Brumaire of Louis Bonaparte* (New York: International Publishers, 1968), p. 608.

14. Here the term *class* is being used in a sense that falls short of the technical Marxist sense. As we shall see, it is very debatable that women form a true class. For an excellent discussion of the phrase *bourgeois feminism,* see Marilyn J. Boxer, "Rethinking the Socialist Construction and International Career of the Concept 'Bourgeois Feminism,'" *American Historical Review* 112, no. 1 (February 2007): 131–158.

15. Allen W. Wood, *Karl Marx* (London: Routledge & Kegan Paul, 1981), p. 8.

16. Heilbroner, *Marxism: For and Against,* p. 72.

17. Karl Marx, "Economic and Philosophic Manuscripts," in *Early Writings,* ed. T. B. Bottomore (New York: McGraw-Hill, 1964), p. 122. I owe this reference as well as several good analyses of alienation to Michael Weber.

18. Ann Foreman, *Femininity As Alienation: Women and the Family in Marxism and Psychoanalysis* (London: Pluto Press, 1977), p. 65.

19. Ibid., pp. 101–102.

20. Quoted in David McLellan, *Karl Marx* (New York: Penguin Books, 1975), p. 33.

21. Karl Marx and Friedrich Engels, *The German Ideology,* in *The Marx-Engels Reader,* ed. Robert C. Tucker (New York: W. W. Norton, 1978), p. 199.

22. Schmitt, *Introduction to Marx and Engels,* p. 202.

23. Friedrich Engels, *The Origin of the Family, Private Property and the State* (New York: International Publishers, 1972), p. 103.

24. Ibid.

25. Notions of hunting and gathering as popularized from anthropological studies are often oversimplified. We should be aware, therefore, of the danger of attributing a rigid sexual division of labor to "hunting and gathering" societies, past and present. Women and children may contribute meat to the diet, just as men may contribute root or grain foods. Noticing Engels's dependence on stereotypical ideas of women's and men's work should lead readers to view Engels's account as less-than-accurate history. I owe this reminder to Antje Haussen Lewis.

26. Engels quoted approvingly the controversial thesis of a now largely discredited anthropologist. The thesis was that women in pairing societies wielded considerable political as well as economic power: "The women were the great power among the clans, [gentes], as everywhere else. They did not hesitate, when occasion required 'to knock off the horns,' as it was technically called, from the head of a chief, and send him back to the ranks of the warriors" (Engels, *Origin of the Family,* p. 113). Apparently, it did not strike Engels as odd that a powerful matriarch would let herself be forcibly seized as a wife by a man whose "horns" she could have had "knocked off."

27. Ibid.

28. Lise Vogel, *Marxism and the Oppression of Women: Towards a Unitary Theory* (New Brunswick, N.J.: Rutgers University Press, 1983), p. 82.

29. Engels, *Origin of the Family,* p. 117.

30. Jane Flax asked why a group of matriarchs would have let men control the tribe's animals or use the fact of their control to gain power over women (Jane Flax, "Do Feminists Need Marxism?" in *Building Feminist Theory: Essays from "Quest," a Feminist Quarterly* [New York: Longman, 1981], p. 176).

31. Engels, *Origin of the Family,* p. 117.

32. Marx and Engels, *German Ideology,* p. 201.

33. Engels, *Origin of the Family,* pp. 118–119.

34. Ibid., p. 120.

35. Ibid., p. 121.

36. Ibid., p. 137.

37. Ibid., p. 128.

38. Ibid., pp. 137–139.

39. Ibid., p. 79.

40. Barrett, *Women's Oppression Today: Problems in Marxist Feminist Analysis* (London: Verso, 1980), p. 49.

41. Evelyn Reed, "Women: Caste, Class, or Oppressed Sex?" *International Socialist Review* 31, no. 3 (September 1970): 15–17 and 40–41.

42. Ibid., p. 17.

43. Ibid.

44. Ibid., p. 40.

45. Ibid.

46. Ibid., p. 41.

47. Truth be told, much factory work, for example, turned out to be as meaningless for "socialist" workers as it had been for capitalist workers.

48. Olga Voronina, "Soviet Patriarchy: Past and Present," *Hypatia* 8, no. 4 (fall 1993): 107.

49. Margaret Benston, "The Political Economy of Women's Liberation," *Monthly Review* 21, no. 4 (September 1969): 16.

50. Ibid., p. 21.

51. Mariarosa Dalla Costa and Selma James, "Women and the Subversion of the Community," in *The Power of Women and the Subversion of Community* (Bristol, England: Falling Wall Press, 1972), p. 34.

52. In the final analysis, Dalla Costa and James viewed men as the dupes of capital rather than as the wily oppressors of women. Men, they said, appear to be the sole recipients of domestic services, but in fact "the figure of the boss is concealed behind that of the husband" (ibid., pp. 35–36).

53. Wendy Edmond and Suzie Fleming expressed the same conviction in even more forceful terms: "Housewives keep their families in the cheapest way; they nurse the children under the worst circumstances and all the toiling of thousands of housewives enables the possessing classes to increase their riches, and to get the labour-power of men and children in the most profitable way" (Wendy Edmond and Suzie Fleming, "If Women Were Paid for All They Do," in *All Work and No Pay,* ed.

Wendy Edmond and Suzie Fleming [London: Power of Women Collective and Falling Wall Press, 1975], p. 8).

54. See Ann Crittenden Scott, "The Value of Housework for Love or Money?" *Ms.,* June 1972, pp. 56–58.

55. Ibid.

56. See Bruce H. Webster Jr. and Alemayehu Bishaw, U.S. Census Bureau, "Income, Earnings, and Poverty Data from the 2005 American Community Survey: American Community Survey Reports," ACS-02 (Washington, D.C.: U.S. Government Printing Office, 2006), available at www.census.gov+acs-02.pdf, p. 7. Unless a woman's salary is quite high, it may cost more for her to work outside the home than simply to work within the home. See Barbara Bergmann, *The Economic Emergence of Women* (New York: Basic Books, 1986), p. 212.

57. U.S. Department of Labor, *Employment Standards Administration Wage and Hour Division,* January 1, 2007, available at www.dol.gov/esa/minwage/america.htm# content.

58. Carol Lopate, "Pay for Housework?" *Social Policy* 5, no. 3 (September-October 1974): 28.

59. Ibid., pp. 29–31.

60. Observed in Stevi Jackson, "Marxism and Feminism," in *Marxism and Social Science,* ed. Andrew Gamble, David Marsh, and Tony Tant (Champaign: University of Illinois Press, 1999), p. 17.

61. Chris Beasley, *What Is Feminism?* (London: Sage Publications, 1999), pp. 62–64.

62. Ibid., p. 64.

63. Juliet Mitchell, *Woman's Estate* (New York: Pantheon Books, 1971), pp. 100–101 (emphasis mine).

64. Mitchell was convinced that women's limited role in production cannot be explained solely or even primarily by their supposed physical weakness. In the first place, men have forced women to do "women's work," and "women's work in all its varieties requires much physical strength. Second, even if women are not as physically strong as men, and even if their original, limited role in production can be attributed to their gap in strength, this same gap cannot explain women's current, limited role in production" (ibid., p. 104).

65. Ibid., p. 107.

66. Ibid.

67. Alison M. Jaggar, *Feminist Politics and Human Nature* (Totowa, N.J.: Rowman & Allanheld, 1983), pp. 114–115 and 308.

68. Ibid., pp. 309–310.

69. Ibid., pp. 310–311.

70. Although Jaggar did not make specific points about in vitro fertilization, the points I raise here seem to fit her analysis.

71. "Percentage of women leading medical research studies rises, but still lags behind men." Massachusetts General Hospital news release. July 19, 2006. http://www.massgeneral.org/news/releases/071906jagsi.html

72. Jaggar, *Feminist Politics and Human Nature,* p. 315.

73. Ibid.

74. Ibid., p. 316.

75. Ibid., p. 317.

76. Iris Marion Young, "Beyond the Unhappy Marriage: A Critique of the Dual Systems Theory," in *Women and Revolution,* ed. Lydia Sargent (Boston: South End Press, 1981), p. 58 (emphasis in original).

77. Heidi Hartmann, "The Unhappy Marriage of Marxism and Feminism: Towards a More Progressive Union," in *Women and Revolution,* ed. Lydia Sargent (Boston: South End Press, 1981), p. 428.

78. Ibid., pp. 428–431.

79. Sylvia Walby, "Policy Developments for Workplace Gender Equity in a Global Era: The Importance of the EU in the UK," *Review of Policy Research* 20, no. 1 (spring 2003): 45.

80. Ibid., p. 53.

81. Shawn Meghan Burn, *Women Across Cultures: A Global Perspective* (Mountain View, Calif.: Mayfield Publishing, 2000), p. 100.

82. Nancy Holmstrom, ed., introduction to *The Socialist Feminist Project: A Contemporary Reader in Theory and Politics* (New York: Monthly Review Press, 2003), p. 3.

83. Burn, *Women Across Cultures,* p. 103.

84. Ibid.

85. Molly Hennessy-Fiske, "Gender Pay Gap Narrows—for Unexpected Reasons." *Los Angeles Times,* December 3, 2006, A23.

86. Ibid.

87. For example, a U.S. Census Bureau study found that the occupations that are most segregated by gender include heavy vehicle and mobile equipment service technicians and mechanics (99% men); brickmasons, blockmasons, and stonemasons (98.9% men); bus and truck mechanics and diesel engine specialists (98.8% men); preschool and kindergarten teachers (97.8% women); dental hygienists (97.7% women); and secretaries and administrative assistants (96.5% women) (G. Scott Thomas, "Where the Men, and Women, Work," *American City Business Journals* (April 19, 2004), available at www.bizjournals.com/edit_special/12.html.

88. See U.S. Department of Labor, Bureau of Labor Statistics, "Median Weekly Earnings of Full-Time Wage and Salary Workers by Detailed Occupation and Sex" (January 2006), available at ftp://ftp.bls.gov/pub/special.requests/lf/aat39.txt.

89. Valerie Bryson, *Feminist Debates: Issues of Theory and Political Practice* (New York: New York University, 1999), p. 137.

90. See U.S. Department of Labor, Bureau of Labor Statistics, "Median Weekly Earnings."

91. Ibid.

92. Ibid.

93. A January 2006 report found that there are almost 2.2 million men in the computer and mathematical occupations, compared with 756,000 women. Likewise, there are 2.2 million men versus 364,000 women in the architecture and engineering occupations (ibid.).

94. See, for example, Katherine Bowers, "Ruling OKs Class Action Suit Against Wal-Mart," *WWD: Women's Wear Daily* 193, no. 29 (February 7, 2007): 39.

95. For example, a 2006 study of U.S. law firms showed that of all lawyer types (partners, associates, counsel, staff attorneys, and senior attorneys), the total percentage of employees who worked part-time was 1.7% for men and 76.4% for women. See "Part-Time Help Firms Hold on to Women Lawyers," *Law Office Management & Administration Report* 7, no. 5 (May 2007): 3. A 2006 Bureau of Labor Statistics report showed that there were 12.6 million male part-time employees compared with 19.8 million female part-time employees. See U.S. Department of Labor, Bureau of Labor Statistics, Current Population Survey, "Household Data Annual Averages" (2006), available at www.bls.gov/cps/cpsaat23.pdf.

96. A provocative recent article that suggests that women do not "choose" to leave the paid workforce in droves, but rather are ambivalent at best about this decision or necessity, is E. J. Graff, "The Opt-Out Myth," *Columbia Journalism Review* (March–April 2007), available at www.cjr.org/issues/2007/2/Graff.asp.

97. See, for example, L. M. Sixel, "EEOC Alleges Unequal Pay for Same Work," *Houston Chronicle,* August 23, 2005, p. 94.

98. *Equal Pay Act of 1963* (Pub. L. 88–93) (EPA), as amended, as it appears in volume 29 of the United States Code, at section 206(d).

99. Amy Joyce, "Unusual Job Titles a Sign of the Times," *Merced (Calif.) Sun-Star,* December 23, 2006, p. 1.

100. Roslyn L. Feldberg, "Comparable Worth: Toward Theory and Practice in the United States," *Signs: Journal of Women in Culture and Society* 10, no. 2 (winter 1984): 311–313.

101. U.S. Department of Labor, Bureau of Labor Statistics, "Median Weekly Earnings."

102. Helen Remick, "Major Issues in A Priori Applications," in *Comparable Worth and Wage Discrimination: Technical Possibilities and Political Realities,* ed. Helen Remick (Philadelphia: Temple University Press, 1984), p. 102.

103. Jake Lamar, "A Worthy but Knotty Question," *Time,* February 6, 1984, p. 30.

104. Teresa Amott and Julie Matthaei, "Comparable Worth, Incomparable Pay," *Radical America* 18, no. 5 (September–October 1984): 25.

105. West Coast Poverty Center, "Poor Families with Children, 2005," chart in "Poverty and the American Family," Web page of West Coast Poverty Center,

University of Washington, Seattle, available at http://wcpc.washington.edu/basics/family.shtml.

106. Amott and Matthaei, "Comparable Worth, Incomparable Pay," 25.

107. The World Bank Group, "Globalization" Web page, available at www.world bank.org/globalization+globalization&hl=en&ct=clnk&cd=3&gl=us.

108. Burn, *Women Across Cultures: A Global Perspective,* p. 120.

109. Ibid.

110. Ibid.

111. Juliet Mitchell, *Psychoanalysis and Feminism* (New York: Vintage Books, 1974), p. 412 (see also Mitchell, *Woman's Estate,* pp. 100–101).

112. Mitchell, *Psychoanalysis and Feminism,* p. 416.

113. Although Mitchell's analysis is dated, women still have not come as long a way as they should have by now.

114. Jackson, "Marxism and Feminism," p. 33.

115. Ibid., p. 33.

Chapter Four

1. Sigmund Freud, *Sexuality and the Psychology of Love* (New York: Collier Books, 1968).

2. Sigmund Freud, "Some Psychical Consequences of the Anatomical Distinction Between the Sexes," in *Sexuality and the Psychology of Love* (New York: Collier Books, 1968), p. 192.

3. Ibid., pp. 187–188.

4. Sigmund Freud, "Femininity," in Sigmund Freud, *The Complete Introductory Lectures on Psychoanalysis,* trans. and ed. James Strachey (New York: W. W. Norton, 1966), p. 542.

5. Ibid., pp. 593–596.

6. Some of Freud's arguments seem to run counter to the case for a shift in female erotogenic zones. Freud claimed that male and female sexual organs develop out of the same embryonic structures and that vestiges of the male reproductive structures are found in the female, and vice versa. Thus, human anatomy would seem to be bisexual. Moreover, Freud observed that although femininity is ordinarily associated with passivity and masculinity with activity, this association is misleading because women can be active and men passive in some directions. It is more precise to say that although feminine persons prefer passive aims and masculine persons active aims, considerable activity is required to achieve any aim whatsoever. When it comes to a sexual aim—switching one's erotogenic zone from the clitoris to the vagina, for example—it takes incredible sexual energy or activity (libido) to accomplish the transition (ibid., p. 580).

7. Ibid., p. 596.

8. Freud, "Some Psychical Consequences," p. 191.

9. Ibid., p. 193.

10. Freud, "The Passing of the Oedipus Complex," in *Sexuality and the Psychology of Love* (New York: Collier Books, 1968), p. 181.

11. Betty Friedan, *The Feminine Mystique* (New York: Dell, 1974), pp. 93–94.

12. Ibid., p. 119.

13. Shulamith Firestone, *The Dialectic of Sex* (New York: Bantam Books, 1970), pp. 48–49.

14. Ibid., p. 69.

15. Ibid., pp. 68–69.

16. Ibid., p. 47

17. Viola Klein, *The Feminine Character* (London: Routledge & Kegan Paul, 1971), p. 77.

18. Kate Millett, *Sexual Politics* (Garden City, N.Y.: Doubleday, 1970), p. 109.

19. Ibid., p. 185.

20. Sigmund Freud, *Dora: An Analysis of a Case of Hysteria,* ed. Philip Rieff (New York: Collier Books, 1963), p. 142.

21. Ibid., p. 50.

22. Alfred Adler, *Understanding Human Nature* (New York: Greenberg, 1927).

23. Ibid., p. 123.

24. Karen Horney, "The Flight from Womanhood," in *Feminine Psychology* (New York: W. W. Norton, 1973), pp. 54–70.

25. There has been much debate among feminists in regard to the theories of Karen Horney. In the past, feminists claimed she was more interested in the whole person's sexual development than in woman's sexual development. But recent analyses have penetrated deeper into Horney's ideas and have shown them to have some very positive contributions to feminism. See Susan Rudnick Jacobsohn, "An Ambiguous Legacy," *Women's Review of Books* 5, no. 4 (January 1988): 22.

26. Clara Thompson, "Problems of Womanhood," in *Interpersonal Psychoanalysis: The Selected Papers of Clara Thompson,* ed. M. P. Green (New York: Basic Books, 1964).

27. For a more complete discussion of Adler, Horney, and Thompson, see Juanita Williams, *Psychology of Women: Behavior in a Biosocial Context* (New York: W. W. Norton, 1977), pp. 65–73.

28. Dorothy Dinnerstein, *The Mermaid and the Minotaur: Sexual Arrangements and Human Malaise* (New York: Harper Colophon Books, 1977), p. 5.

29. Ibid., pp. 40–54.

30. Ibid., pp. 59–66.

31. Ibid., p. 66.

32. Given that a man cannot enter a symbiotic relationship with a woman without reinvoking painful memories of his total helplessness before the infinite power of the mother, he will use his power, Dinnerstein theorized, to fulfill his basic needs for security, love, and self-esteem. This bid for omnipotence extends to control over both nature

and women, two forces that must be kept in check lest their presumably uncontrollable powers be unleashed. In contrast to a man, a woman can safely seek symbiosis with a man as a means to attain the ends of security, love, and self-esteem. She can do this because, for her, symbiosis with a man does not conjure up the specter of the omnipotent mother. However, the *idea* of being or becoming an omnipotent mother does terrify her, and this specter may explain woman's discomfort with female power (ibid., p. 61).

33. Ibid., pp. 124–134.

34. Ibid.

35. Nancy Chodorow, *The Reproduction of Mothering: Psychoanalysis and the Sociology of Gender* (Berkeley: University of California Press, 1978), p. 32.

36. Ibid., p. 107.

37. Ibid., p. 126.

38. Ibid., p. 200.

39. Ibid., pp. 135, 187.

40. Ibid., p. 218.

41. Judith Lorber, "On *The Reproduction of Mothering:* A Methodological Debate," *Signs: Journal of Women in Culture and Society* 6, no. 3 (spring 1981): 482–486.

42. Jean Bethke Elshtain, *Public Man, Private Woman* (Princeton, N.J.: Princeton University Press, 1981), p. 288.

43. Ibid., p. 290.

44. Lorber, "On *The Reproduction of Mothering:* A Methodological Debate," pp. 497–500.

45. Of course, this is a *traditional* caricature. Films and television series currently celebrate a new kind of father who initially has a difficult time taking care of his infant or child but soon becomes better at the job than his wife or lover.

46. Critics of Chodorow who did not share Rossi's *biological* concerns argued that although dual parenting is an improvement over women's monopoly on mothering, "parenting . . . not just by biological parents but by communities of interested adults" is to be preferred to dual parenting. These critics insist although men and women have much to gain by engaging equally in parenting, everyone—particularly children—will be better off if human beings stop viewing children as the possessions and responsibilities of their biological parents and start viewing them instead as people for whom society as a whole is responsible. Lorber, "On *The Reproduction of Mothering*" 486.

47. Janice Raymond, "Female Friendship: Contra Chodorow and Dinnerstein," *Hypatia* 1, no. 2 (fall 1986): 44–45.

48. Ibid., p. 37.

49. Adrienne Rich, "Compulsory Heterosexuality and Lesbian Existence," in *The Signs Reader: Women, Gender, and Scholarship,* ed. E. Abel and E. K. Abel (Chicago: University of Chicago Press, 1983), p. 182.

50. Juliet Mitchell, *Women's Estate* (New York: Pantheon Books, 1971), pp. 164–165.

51. Ibid.

52. Ibid., p. 170.

53. Juliet Mitchell, *Psychoanalysis and Feminism* (New York: Vintage Books, 1974), p. 370.

54. Ibid., p. 373.

55. Ibid., p. 375.

56. Sigmund Freud, "Totem and Taboo," in *The Standard Edition of the Complete Psychological Works of Sigmund Freud,* trans. and ed. James Strachey (New York: W. W. Norton, 1966), p. 144.

57. Jacques Lacan, *The Language of the Self* (Baltimore: Johns Hopkins University Press, 1968), p. 271.

58. Mitchell, *Psychoanalysis and Feminism,* p. 415.

59. Sherry B. Ortner, "Oedipal Father, Mother's Brother, and the Penis: A Review of Juliet Mitchell's *Psychoanalysis and Feminism,*" *Feminist Studies* 2, nos. 2–3 (1975): 179.

60. Ibid.

61. Marge Piercy, *Woman on the Edge of Time* (New York: Fawcett Crest, 1976).

62. Chris Weedon, *Feminist Practice & Poststructuralist Theory* (New York: Basil Blackwell, 1987), p. 50.

63. Ibid., p. 51.

64. Jacques Lacan, *Écrits: A Selection,* trans. Alan Sheridan (New York: W. W. Norton, 1977), pp. 64–66.

65. Claire Duchen, *Feminism in France: From May '68 to Mitterrand* (London: Routledge & Kegan Paul, 1986), p. 78.

66. Lacan, *Écrits: A Selection,* p. 2.

67. According to Lacan, the original mother-child unity is in some way a metaphor for truth—for an isomorphic relationship between word and object. Ideally, both mother and child, and word and object, would remain united, but society will not stand for such unity. As a result of the castration complex brought on by the arrival of the father, who represents social power symbolized by the phallus, not only mother and child but also word and object must be split.

68. Lacan, *Écrits: A Selection,* pp. 1–7.

69. Luce Irigaray, *This Sex Which Is Not One,* trans. Catherine Porter (Ithaca, N.Y.: Cornell University Press, 1985), p. 28.

70. According to Claire Duchen, Irigaray believed "that before a 'feminine feminine,' a non-phallic feminine, can even be *thought,* women need to examine the male philosophical and psychoanalytical texts which have contributed to the construction of the 'masculine feminine,' the phallic feminine, in order to locate and identify it" (Duchen, *Feminism in France,* pp. 87–88).

71. Irigaray, *This Sex Which Is Not One,* p. 32.

72. Toril Moi, *Sexual/Textual Politics: Feminist Literary Theory* (New York: Methuen, 1985), p. 132.

73. Irigaray, *This Sex Which Is Not One,* p. 74.

74. Ibid.

75. Luce Irigaray, "Is the Subject of Science Sexed?" trans. Carol Mastrangelo Bové, *Hypatia* 2, no. 3 (fall 1987): 66.

76. Irigaray, *This Sex Which Is Not One,* p. 32.

77. Ibid.

78. Moi, *Sexual/Textual Politics,* p. 140.

79. In an interview, Irigaray stated that there is nothing other than masculine discourse. When the interviewer said, "I don't understand what 'masculine discourse' means," Irigaray retorted, "Of course not, since there is no other" (Irigaray, *This Sex Which Is Not One,* p. 140).

80. Ibid., p. 29.

81. Dorothy Leland, "Lacanian Psychoanalysis and French Feminism: Toward an Adequate Political Psychology," *Hypatia* 3, no. 3 (winter 1989): 90–99.

82. Kelly Oliver, "Julia Kristeva's Feminist Revolutions," *Hypatia* 8, no. 3 (summer 1993): 101.

83. Julia Kristeva, "The Novel As Polylogue," in *Desire in Language,* trans. Leon S. Roudiez, and ed. Thomas Gora, Alice Jardine, and Leon S. Roudiez (New York: Columbia University Press, 1990), pp. 159–209.

84. Oliver, "Julia Kristeva's Feminist Revolutions," p. 98.

85. Julia Kristeva, *Powers of Horror,* trans. Leon Roudiez (New York: Columbia University Press, 1982), pp. 205–206.

86. Julia Kristeva, from an interview with *Tel Quel,* in *New French Feminisms,* ed. Elaine Marks and Isabelle de Courtivron (New York: Schocken Books, 1981), p. 157.

87. Oliver, "Julia Kristeva's Feminist Revolutions," p. 98.

88. Ibid., pp. 98–99.

89. Leland, "Lacanian Psychoanalysis and French Feminism," p. 93.

90. Ibid., p. 94.

91. Ibid.

92. Cited in ibid., p. 95.

93. Ibid.

94. Ibid.

95. Ibid.

96. Judith Butler, *Gender Trouble: Feminism and the Subversion of Identity* (New York: Routledge, 1990).

Chapter Five

1. This list of psychological traits is found in Mary Vetterling-Braggin, ed., *"Femininity," "Masculinity," and "Androgyny"* (Totowa, N.J.: Littlefield, Adams, 1982), pp. 5–6.

2. Ibid.

3. Carol Gilligan, *In a Different Voice* (Cambridge, Mass.: Harvard University Press, 1982).

4. Gilligan, *In a Different Voice,* pp. 2–23.

5. Lawrence Kohlberg, "From Is to Ought: How to Commit the Naturalistic Fallacy and Get Away with It in the Study of Moral Development," in *Cognitive Development and Epistemology,* ed. Theodore Mischel (New York: Academic Press, 1971), pp. 164–165.

6. Gilligan, *In a Different Voice,* pp. 74–75.

7. Ibid., p. 76.

8. Ibid., p. 77.

9. Ibid.

10. Ibid., p. 81.

11. Carol Gilligan, "Adolescent Development Reconsidered," in *Mapping the Moral Domain,* ed. Carol Gilligan, Janie Victoria Ward, and Jill McLean Taylor (Cambridge, Mass.: Harvard University Press, 1988), p. xxii.

12. Nel Noddings, *Caring: A Feminine Approach to Ethics and Moral Education* (Berkeley: University of California Press, 1984), p. 3.

13. Ibid., p. 96.

14. Ibid., pp. 3–4.

15. Ibid., p. 83.

16. Ibid., p. 5.

17. Ibid., p. 79.

18. Ibid., p. 80.

19. Ibid., p. 83.

20. Nel Noddings, *Women and Evil* (Berkeley: University of California Press, 1989), p. 91.

21. Ibid., p. 96.

22. Ibid., pp. 167–168.

23. Ibid., p. 179.

24. Ibid., p. 181.

25. Ibid., p. 182.

26. Ibid., p. 206.

27. Ibid., p. 211.

28. Ibid., p. 213.

29. Ibid., pp. 221–222.

30. Ibid., p. 222.

31. Fiona Robinson, *Globalizing Care: Ethics, Feminist Theory and International Relations* (Boulder, Colo.: Westview Press, 1999), pp. 15–20.

32. Susan Hekman, *Moral Voices, Moral Selves: Carol Gilligan and Feminist Moral Theory* (Cambridge: Polity Press, 1995), p. 1.

33. Carol Stack, "The Culture of Gender: Women and Men of Color," *Signs: Journal of Women in Culture and Society* 11, no. 2 (winter 1986): 322–323.

34. Sandra L. Bartky, *Femininity and Domination* (New York: Routledge, 1990), p. 105.

35. Ibid., p. 104.

36. Ibid., p. 109.

37. Ibid., p. 113.

38. Ibid., p. 118.

39. Bill Puka, "The Liberation of Caring: A Different Voice for Gilligan's 'Different Voice,'" *Hypatia* 5, no. 1 (spring 1990): 59 and 60.

40. Ibid.

41. Ibid.

42. Ibid., p. 62.

43. Quoted in Robinson, *Globalizing Care*, p. 19.

44. Brian Barry, *Justice As Impartiality* (Oxford: Oxford University Press, 1995), pp. 252–256.

45. A related debate emphasizes that Gilligan's readers are frequently left with the impression that a female ethics of care is *better* than a male ethics of justice. Many radical-cultural feminists would gladly applaud Gilligan were she indeed arguing women's moral values are not only different from men's but also better. But Gilligan insisted she was claiming only a difference, not a superiority. Her aim, she stressed, was to ensure that woman's moral voice be taken as seriously as man's. But if Gilligan was not making any superiority claims, then her book may not be normative enough. Critics wonder which is it better to be: just or caring? Should we be like Abraham, who was willing to sacrifice his beloved son Isaac to fulfill God's will? Or should we be like the mother whose baby King Solomon threatened to cut in half? (We will recall that in this biblical story, two women claim to be the same child's mother. When King Solomon threatened to divide the baby in two, he prompted the true mother to forsake her claim in order to secure her child's survival.) Gilligan resisted answering these questions, although she certainly led many of her readers to view Abraham as a religious fanatic and to view the real mother in the Solomon story as a person who has her values properly ordered.

As Gilligan saw it, the question of which is better—an ethics of care or an ethics of justice—is an apples-and-oranges question. Both an ethics of care and an ethics of justice are good. But to insist one kind of morality is the better is to manifest a nearly pathological need for a unitary, absolute, and universal moral standard that can erase our very real moral tensions as with a magic wand. If we are able to achieve moral maturity, Gilligan implied, we must be willing to vacillate between an ethics of care and an ethics of justice. But even if her critics were willing to concede ethical vacillation is morally acceptable, they were not willing to let Gilligan simply describe an ethics of care on the one hand and an ethics of justice on the other without attempting to translate between these two systems. Her critics believe that such attempts at translation would do much to reinforce Gilligan's later claim that the ethics of care and of justice are ultimately compatible. For more details, see Gilligan, *In a Different Voice*, pp. 151–174.

46. George Sher, "Other Voices, Other Rooms? Women's Psychology and Moral Theory," in *Women and Moral Theory,* ed. Eva Feder Kittay and Diana T. Meyers (Totowa, N.J.: Roman & Littlefield, 1987), p. 188.

47. Marilyn Friedman, "Beyond Caring: The De-Moralization of Gender," in *Science, Morality and Feminist Theory,* ed. Marsha Hanen and Kai Nielsen (Calgary: University of Calgary Press, 1987), p. 100.

48. Friedman, "Beyond Caring," 101f.

49. Gilligan, *In a Different Voice,* p. 174.

50. Gilligan, "Moral Orientation and Moral Development," in *Women and Moral Theory,* ed. Eva Feder Kittay and Diana T. Meyers (Totowa, N.J.: Roman & Littlefield, 1987), pp. 25–26.

51. Sarah Lucia Hoagland, "Some Thoughts About *Caring,*" in *Feminist Ethics,* ed. Claudia Card (Lawrence: University Press of Kansas, 1991), p. 251.

52. Noddings, *Caring,* p. 73.

53. Ibid., p. 102.

54. Hoagland, "Some Thoughts About *Caring,*" p. 256.

55. Ibid., p. 257.

56. Ibid., p. 258.

57. Nel Noddings, "A Response," *Hypatia* 5, no. 6 (spring 1990): p. 125.

58. Ibid.

59. Sara Ruddick, "Maternal Thinking," in *Mothering: Essays in Feminist Theory,* ed. Joyce Trebilcot (Totowa, N.J.: Rowman & Allanheld, 1984), p. 214.

60. Ibid.

61. Ibid., p. 215.

62. Alasdair MacIntyre, *After Virtue* (Notre Dame, Ind.: University of Notre Dame Press, 1981), p. 177.

63. Ibid., p. 178.

64. Ibid., p. 181.

65. Ibid.

66. Adrienne Rich, *Of Woman Born* (New York: W. W. Norton, 1979), p. 174.

67. Sara Ruddick, *Maternal Thinking: Toward a Politics of Peace* (Boston: Beacon Press, 1989), p. 17.

68. Ibid., p. 19.

69. Ibid., p. 67.

70. Ibid., p. 71.

71. Ibid., p. 73.

72. Ibid., p. 74.

73. Ibid.

74. Ibid., p. 98.

75. Ibid., p. 118.

76. Ibid., p. 123.

77. Ibid., p. 221.

78. Robinson, *Globalizing Care,* p. 20.

79. Ruddick, *Maternal Thinking,* pp. 222–234.

80. Ibid.

81. Virginia Held, *The Ethics of Care* (Oxford: Oxford University Press, 2006), p. 64.

82. Virginia Held, "Feminism and Moral Theory," in *Women and Moral Theory,* ed. Eva Feder Kittay and Diana Meyers (Savage, Md.: Rowman & Littlefield, 1987), pp. 112–113.

83. Held, *The Ethics of Care,* p. 113.

84. Held, "Feminism and Moral Theory," pp. 116–117.

85. Held, *The Ethics of Care,* pp. 134–135.

86. Virginia Held, "The Obligations of Mothers and Fathers," in *Mothering: Essays in Feminist Theory,* ed. Joyce Trebilcot (Totowa, N.J.: Rowman & Allanheld, 1984), p. 7.

87. Ibid., p. 11.

88. Ibid., p. 18.

89. Held, "Feminism and Moral Theory," p. 121.

90. Ibid., p. 124.

91. Ibid., p. 125.

92. Ibid., p. 126.

93. Held, *The Ethics of Care,* p. 17.

94. Ibid., pp. 53 and 54.

95. Eva Feder Kittay, *Love's Labor: Essays on Women, Equality and Dependency* (New York: Routledge, 1999), p. 19.

96. Ibid., p. 158.

97. Ibid., p. 51.

98. Robert Goodin, *Protecting the Vulnerable* (Chicago: University of Chicago Press, 1985).

99. Kittay, *Love's Labor,* p. 55.

100. Ibid.

101. Ibid., p. 59.

102. Ibid., p. 25.

103. Ibid., p. 68.

104. John Rawls, *A Theory of Justice* (Cambridge, Mass.: Harvard University Press, 1971), pp. 60–65.

105. Kittay, *Love's Labor,* p. 113.

106. Carol Gilligan, Janie Victoria Ward, and Jill McLean Taylor, eds., *Mapping the Moral Domain* (Cambridge, Mass.: Harvard University Press, 1988), p. 291.

107. Nel Noddings, "Global Citizenship: Promises and Problems," in *Educating Citizens for Global Awareness,* ed. Nel Noddings (New York: Teachers College Press, 2005), p. 17.

108. Peggy McIntosh, "Gender Perspectives on Educating for Global Citizenship," in *Educating Citizens for Global Awareness,* ed. Nel Noddings (New York: Teachers College Press, 2005), p. 26.

109. Noddings, "Global Citizenship," p. 17.

110. Virginia Held, "Care and the Extension of Markets," *Hypatia,* 17, no. 2 (spring 2002): 32.

111. Ibid.

112. Kittay, *Love's Labor.*

113. Ibid.

114. Eyal Press, "Do Workers Have a Fundamental Right to Care for Their Families?" *Sunday New York Times* Magazine, July 29, 2007, 38.

115. Ibid.

116. Ibid., p. 39.

117. Ibid.

118. Fiona Robinson, *Globalizing Care,* p. 146.

119. Ibid., p. 147.

Chapter Six

1. Mary Dietz, "Current Controversies in Feminist Theory," *Annual Review of Political Science,* 6 (2003): 408–409.

2. Nancy Fraser, *Justice Interruptus: Critical Reflections on the "Postsocialist" Condition* (New York: Routledge, 1997).

3. Arthur M. Schlesinger Jr., *The Disuniting of America* (Knoxville, Tenn.: Whittle Books, 1990), p. 2.

4. Jung Young Lee, *Marginality: The Key to Multicultural Theology* (Minneapolis: Fortress Press, 1995), p. 35. Lee is citing Israel Zangwill, *The Melting Pot: A Drama in Four Acts.*

5. Schlesinger, *Disuniting of America,* p. 2.

6. See, for example, Angela Y. Davis, "Gender, Class, and Multiculturalism: Rethinking 'Race' Politics," in *Mapping Multiculturalism,* ed. Avery R. Gorden and Christopher Newfield (Minneapolis: University of Minnesota Press, 1996), pp. 40–48.

7. Blaine J. Fowers and Frank C. Richardson, "Why Is Multiculturalism Good?" *American Psychologist* 51, no. 6 (June 1996): 609.

8. Joseph Raz, "Multiculturalism: A Liberal Perspective," *Dissent* (winter 1994): 74.

9. Ibid., p. 78.

10. Ibid., p. 77.

11. "Second-wave feminism" is a term used to refer to the schools of feminist thought that emerged in the 1970s. They tended to focus on the ways in which women are the same.

12. Elizabeth V. Spelman, *Inessential Woman: Problems of Exclusion in Feminist Thought* (Boston: Beacon Press, 1998), pp. 11–12.

13. Ibid., p. 12.

14. Ibid., p. 13.

15. Deborah King, "Multiple Jeopardy: The Context of a Black Feminist Ideology," in *Feminist Frameworks,* 3rd ed., ed. Alison M. Jaggar and Paula S. Rothenberg (New York: McGraw-Hill, 1993), p. 220.

16. bell hooks, *Yearning: Race, Gender and Cultural Politics* (Boston: South End Press, 1990), p. 59.

17. bell hooks, "Naked Without Shame: A Counter-hegemonic Body Politic," in *Talking Visions: Multicultural Feminism in a Transnational Age,* ed. Ella Shohat (Cambridge, Mass.: MIT Press, 1998), p. 69.

18. Audre Lorde, "Age, Race, Class, and Sex: Women Redefining Difference," in *Race, Class, and Gender,* 2nd ed., ed. Margaret L. Andersen and Patricia Hill Collins (Belmont, Calif.: Wadsworth, 1995), pp. 532 and 539.

19. Audre Lorde, *The Cancer Journals* (San Francisco: Spinster/Aunt Lute, 1980).

20. Lorde, "Age, Race, Class, and Sex," p. 539.

21. Ibid.

22. Patricia Hill Collins, *Black Feminist Thought: Knowledge, Consciousness, and the Politics of Empowerment* (Boston: Unwin Hyman, 1990), p. 6.

23. Ibid., p. 7.

24. Ibid., p. 67.

25. Ella Shohat, ed., introduction to *Talking Visions: Multicultural Feminism in a Transitional Age* (Cambridge, Mass.: MIT Press, 1998), pp. 1–13.

26. Jonna Lian Pearson, "Multicultural Feminism and Sisterhood Among Women of Color in Social Change Dialogue," *Howard Journal of Communications* 18 (2007): 88.

27. Maria Lugones and Elizabeth Spelman, "Have We Got a Theory for You! Feminist Theory, Cultural Imperialism, and the Demand for the Woman's Voice," in *Feminist Philosophies,* ed. Janet A. Kourany, James P. Sterba, and Rosemarie Tong (Englewood Cliffs, N.J.: Prentice-Hall, 1992), p. 388.

28. Audre Lorde, "Age, Race, Class, and Sex," pp. 114–115.

29. Lugones and Spelman, "Have We Got a Theory for You!" p. 391.

30. Adrian Piper, "Passing for White, Passing for Black," in *Talking Visions: Multicultural Feminism in a Transnational Age,* ed. Ella Shohat (Cambridge, Mass.: MIT Press, 1998), p. 89.

31. Naomi Zack, "Mixed Black and White Race and Public Policy," *Hypatia* 10, no. 1 (winter 1995): 123–124.

32. Shohat, *Talking Visions,* pp. 7–8.

33. Linda Martin Alcoff, *Visible Identities: Race, Gender, and the Self* (Oxford: Oxford University Press, 2006), p. 269.

34. Ibid.

35. Ibid.

36. Ibid., p. 179.

37. Ibid., pp. 188–189.

38. U.S. Department of Commerce, "United States Census 2000," *Individual Census Report* (December 31, 2000).

39. Shohat, *Talking Visions,* p. 7.

40. Adrienne Rich, "Compulsory Heterosexuality and Lesbian Existence (1980)," in *Blood, Bread, and Poetry: Selected Prose 1979–1985,* (New York: W. W. Norton, 1986). Quotations in this paragraph are from pp. 27 and 51.

41. Bonnie Poitras Tucker, "The ADA and Deaf Culture: Contrasting Precepts, Conflicting Results," *Annals of the American Academy of Political and Social Sciences* 551 (January 1997): 24–36.

42. Pearson, "Multicultural Feminism and Sisterhood," 91.

43. Shohat, *Talking Visions,* p. 7.

44. Ibid., p. 6.

45. Ibid., p. 2.

46. Charlotte Bunch, "Prospects for Global Feminism," in *Feminist Frameworks,* 3rd ed., ed. Alison M. Jaggar and Paula S. Rothenberg (New York: McGraw-Hill, 1993), p. 249.

47. Alice Walker, *In Search of Our Mothers' Gardens* (New York: Harcourt Brace Jovanovich, 1983), p. xi.

48. Bunch, "Prospects for Global Feminism," p. 250.

49. Quoted in Nellie Wong, "Socialist Feminism: Our Bridge to Freedom," in *Third World Women and the Politics of Feminism,* ed. Chandra Talpads Mohanty, Ann Russo, and Lourde Torres (Bloomington, Ind.: Indiana University Press, 1991), p. 293.

50. Bunch, "Prospects for Global Feminism," p. 251.

51. Audre Lorde, *Sister Outsider* (Trumansburg, N.Y.: Crossing Press, 1984), p. 111.

52. Angela Gillian, "Women's Equality and National Liberation," in *Third World Women and the Politics of Feminism,* ed. Chandra Talpads Mohanty, Ann Russo, and Lourde Torres (Bloomington, Ind.: Indiana University Press, 1991), p. 229.

53. Ibid.

54. Ibid.

55. Shawn Meghan Burn, *Women Across Cultures: A Global Perspective* (Mountain View, Calif.: Mayfield Publishing, 2000), p. 73.

56. Noemi Ehrenfeld Lenkiewicz, "Women's Control over Their Bodies," in *Women in the Third World: An Encyclopedia of Contemporary Issues,* ed. Nelly P. Stromquist (New York: Garland Publishing, 1998), pp. 197–199.

57. Burn, *Women Across Cultures,* p. 53.

58. Adele Clark, "Subtle Forms of Sterilization Abuse: A Reproductive Rights Analysis," in *Test-Tube Women: What Future for Motherhood?* ed. Rita Arditti, Renate Duelli Klein, and Shelley Minden (London: Pandora Press, 1985), p. 198.

59. Helen Rodriguez-Treas, "Sterilization Abuse," in *Biological Woman: The Convenient Myth,* ed. Ruth Hubbard, Mary Sue Henifin, and Barbara Fried (Cambridge, Mass.: Schenkman, 1982), p. 150.

60. "Contraceptive Raises Ethical Concerns," *Medical Ethics Advisor* 9, no. 2 (February 1991): 17.

61. David P. Warwick, "Ethics and Population Control in Developing Countries," *Hastings Center Report* 4, no. 3 (June 1974): 3.

62. Barbara Hartmann, *Reproductive Rights and Wrongs: The Global Politics of Population Control* (Boston: South End Press, 1995).

63. Burn, *Women Across Cultures,* p. 69.

64. David A. Grimes, "Unsafe Abortion: The Silent Scourge," *British Medical Bulletin* 67 (2003): 99–113.

65. Friday E. Okonofua, "Abortion and Maternal Mortality in the Developing World," *Journal of Obstetrics and Gynaecology Canada* 28, no. 11 (November 2006): 974–979.

66. Patricia H. David et al., "Women's Reproductive Health Needs in Russia: What Can We Learn from an Intervention to Improve Post-Abortion Care?" *Health Policy and Planning* 22, no. 2 (February 2007): 83–94.

67. Associated Press, "World Briefing, Asia: China—Retreat on Criminalizing Gender Abortions," *New York Times,* June 27, 2006, p. A6.

68. Judith Banister, "Shortage of Girls in China Today: Causes, Consequences, International Comparisons, and Solutions," *Journal of Population Research* (May 2004), available at www.prb.org/presentations/ShortageofGirlsinChina.ppt.

69. Associated Press, "World Briefing, Asia," A6.

70. Sabu M. George, "Millions of Missing Girls: From Fetal Sexing to High Technology Sex Selection in India," *Prenatal Diagnosis* 26, no. 7 (July 2006): 604–609.

71. Swapan Seth, "Sex Selective Feticide in India," *Journal of Assisted Reproduction and Genetics* 24, no. 5 (May 2007): 153–154.

72. Maria Mies, "New Reproductive Technologies: Sexist and Racist Implications," in Maria Mies and Vandana Shiva, *Ecofeminism* (London: Zed, 1993), p. 194.

73. Robin Morgan, *Sisterhood Is Global* (Garden City, N.Y.: Crossing Press, 1984), p. 5.

74. Ibid.

75. Ibid., p. 765.

76. Arlie Russell Hochschild, "Love and Gold," in *Global Economy,* ed. Arlie Russell Hochschild (New York: Henry Holt and Company, 2002).

77. Rosemary Radford Ruether, *Integrating Ecofeminism, Globalization, and World Religions* (Lanham, Md.: Roman & Littlefield, 2005), p. 146.

78. Joann Lim, "Sweatshops Are Us," in *Rethinking Globalization: Teaching for Justice in an Unjust World,* ed. Bill Bigelow and Bob Peterson (Milwaukee: Rethinking Schools Press, 2002), pp. 158–159.

79. A. K. Nauman and M. Hutchison, "The Integration of Women into the Mexican Labor Force since NAFTA," *American Behavioral Scientist* 40 (1997): 950–956.

80. Fauzia Erfan Ahmed, "The Rise of the Bangladesh Garment Industry: Globalization, Women Workers, and Voice," *NWSA Journal* 16, no. 2 (summer 2002): 34–45.

81. Ruether, *Integrating Ecofeminism, Globalization, and World Religions,* p. 146.

82. Morgan, *Sisterhood Is Global,* p. 16.

83. Ibid.

84. Alison Jaggar, "A Feminist Critique of the Alleged Southern Debt," *Hypatia* 17, no. 4 (fall 2002): 119–121.

85. Ruether, *Integrating Ecofeminism, Globalization, and World Religions,* p. 4.

86. Jaggar, "A Feminist Critique," 2002.

87. Maria Mies, "The Myths of Catching-Up Development," in *Ecofeminism,* ed. Maria Mies and Vandana Shiva (London: Zed, 1993), p. 58.

88. Ibid., p. 60.

89. Ibid., p. 59.

90. Ibid., p. 66.

91. Ibid., p. 67.

92. Maria Mies and Vandana Shiva, "The Myths of Catching-up Development," in *Ecofeminism* pp. 10–11.

93. Ibid., p. 11.

94. Ibid., pp. 11–12.

95. Uma Narayan, *Dislocating Cultures: Identities, Traditions, and Third-World Feminisms* (New York: Routledge, 1997), p. 127.

96. Ibid., p. 146.

97. Nancy Holmstrom, "Human Nature," in *A Companion to Feminist Philosophy,* ed. Alison M. Jaggar and Iris Marion Young (Oxford: Blackwell Publishers, 1998), p. 288.

98. Susan Moller Okin, "Inequalities Between Sexes in Different Cultural Contexts," in *Women, Culture, and Development,* ed. Martha Nussbaum and Jonathan Glover (Oxford: Clarendon Press, 1995), p. 294.

99. Susan Moller Okin, "Feminism, Women's Human Rights, and Cultural Differences," *Hypatia* 13, no. 2 (1998): 42.

100. For the first two documents, see Susan Moller Okin, "Recognizing Women's Rights As Human Rights," *APA Newsletters* 97, no. 2 (spring 1998). For the last document, see United Nations Declaration on the Elimination of Violence Against Women, 85th Plenary Meeting, December 20, 1993, A/RES/48/104, available at www.un.org/documents/ga/res/48/a48r104.htm.

101. Spike V. Peterson and Laura Parisi, "Are Women Human? It's Not an Academic Question," in *Human Rights Fifty Years On: A Radical Reappraisal,* ed. Tony Evans (Manchester, UK: Manchester University Press, 1998), pp. 142–153.

102. Seth Faison, "China Turns the Tables, Faulting U.S. on Rights," *New York Times,* March 5, 1997, p. A8.

103. Anne Phillips, "Multiculturalism, Universalism, and the Claims of Democracy," in *Gender, Justice, Development, and Rights,* ed. Maxine Molyneux and Shahra Razavi (Oxford: Oxford University Press, 2002), p. 125.

104. Chila Bulbeck, *Re-Orienting Western Feminisms: Women's Diversity in a Post-colonial World* (Cambridge: Cambridge University Press, 1998), p. 5.

105. Quoted in Maxine Molyneux and Shahra Razavi, eds., introduction to *Gender Justice, Development and Rights* (Oxford: Oxford University Press, 2002), p. 13.

106. Martha Nussbaum, "Women's Capabilities and Social Justice," in *Gender Justice, Development and Rights,* ed. Maxine Molyneux and Shahra Razavi (Oxford: Oxford University Press, 2002), pp. 60–62.

107. Daniel Engster, "Rethinking Care Theory: The Practice of Caring and the Obligation to Care," *Hypatia* 20, no. 3 (summer 2005): 52.

108. Martha Nussbaum, *Sex and Social Justice* (New York: Oxford University Press, 1999).

109. Vivienne Jabri, "Feminist Ethics and Hegemonic Global Politics," *Alternatives* 29 (2004): 275.

110. Morgan, *Sisterhood Is Global,* p. 36.

111. Spelman, *Inessential Woman,* p. 178.

112. Ibid., pp. 178–179.

113. Ibid., p. 181.

114. Lugones and Spelman, "Have We Got a Theory for You!" pp. 388 and 389.

115. bell hooks, *Feminist Theory: From Margin to Center* (Boston: South End Press, 1984), p. 404.

116. Ibid.

117. Audre Lorde, *Sister Outsider,* p. 113.

118. Iris Marion Young, "The Ideal of Community and the Politics of Difference," in *Feminism/Postmodernism,* ed. Linda J. Nicholson (New York: Routledge, 1990), p. 308.

119. Nancie Caraway, *Segregated Sisterhood: Racism and the Politics of American Feminism* (Knoxville: University of Tennessee Press, 1991).

120. Young, "The Ideal of Community and the Politics of Difference," p. 311.

121. Caraway, *Segregated Sisterhood,* p. 206.

122. Aristotle, *Nichomachean Ethics,* in *The Works of Aristotle Translated into English,* ed. W. D. Ross (London: Oxford University Press, 1963).

Chapter Seven

1. Karen J. Warren, ed., "The Power and the Promise of Ecological Feminism," in *Ecological Feminist Philosophies* (Bloomington: Indiana University Press, 1996), p. 20.

2. Karen J. Warren, "Feminism and the Environment: An Overview of the Issues," *APA Newsletter on Feminism and Philosophy* 90, no. 3 (fall 1991): 110–111.

3. The terms "cultural ecofeminists" and "nature ecofeminists" are from Karen J. Warren, "Feminism and Ecology: Making Connections," in *Readings in Ecology and Feminist Theology,* ed. Mary Heather MacKinnon and Marie McIntyre (Kansas City, Kans.: Sheed and Ward, 1995), p. 114. The terms "psychobiologistic ecofeminists"

and "social-constructionist ecofeminist" are from Janet Biehl, *Rethinking Feminist Politics* (Boston: South End Press, 1991), pp. 11 and 17.

4. Rosemary Radford Ruether, *New Woman/New Earth: Sexist Ideologies and Human Liberation* (New York: Seabury Press, 1975), p. 204.

5. Rachel Carson, *Silent Spring* (Boston: Houghton Mifflin, 1962), pp. 16–23.

6. Robert Alter, trans. and comm., *Genesis* (New York: W. W. Norton, 1996).

7. Aldo Leopold, "The Land Ethic," in *Sand County Almanac* (New York: Oxford University Press, 1987).

8. See John Hospers, *Understanding the Arts* (Englewood Cliffs, N.J.: Prentice-Hall, 1982).

9. Arne Naess, "The Deep Ecological Movement: Some Philosophical Aspects," *Philosophical Inquiry* 8 (1986): 10–13.

10. Peter S. Wenz, "Ecology and Morality," in *Ethics and Animals,* ed. Harlan B. Miller and William H. Williams (Clifton, N.J.: Humana Press, 1983), pp. 185–191.

11. The optimum human population would be about 500 million, according to James Lovelock; 100 million, according to Arne Naess. See Luc Ferry, *The New Ecological Order,* trans. Carol Volk (Chicago: University of Chicago Press, 1992), p. 75.

12. William Aiken, "Non-Anthropocentric Ethical Challenges," in *Earthbound: New Introductory Essays in Environmental Ethics,* ed. Tom Regan (New York: Random House, 1984), p. 269.

13. See George Sessions, "The Deep Ecology Movement: A Review," *Environmental Review* 9 (1987): 115.

14. Karen J. Warren, "Feminism and Ecology," *Environmental Review* 9, no. 1 (spring 1987): 3–20.

15. Ariel Kay Salleh, "Deeper Than Deep Ecology: The Ecofeminist Connection," *Environmental Ethics* 6, no. 1 (1984): 339.

16. Ibid.

17. Ferry, *The New Ecological Order,* p. 118.

18. Ynestra King, "The Ecology of Feminism and the Feminism of Ecology," in *Healing the Wounds: The Promise of Ecofeminism,* ed. Judith Plant (Philadelphia: New Society Publishers, 1989), pp. 22–23.

19. Ibid., p. 23.

20. Simone de Beauvoir, *The Second Sex,* trans. and ed. H. M. Parshley (New York: Vintage Books, 1952), pp. 19–29.

21. Ibid., p. xxi.

22. Val Plumwood, "Ecofeminism: An Overview and Discussion of Positions and Arguments," *Australian Journal of Philosophy* 64, supplement (June 1986): 135.

23. Sherry B. Ortner, "Is Female to Male As Nature Is to Culture?" in *Readings in Ecology and Feminist Theory,* ed. Mary Heather MacKinnon and Marie McIntyre (Kansas City, Kans.: Sheed and Ward, 1995), pp. 40–41 and 51.

24. Ibid., pp. 52–53.

25. Ibid., p. 54.

26. Ibid., pp. 54–55.

27. Mary Daly, *Pure Lust* (Boston: Beacon Press, 1984), p. 25.

28. Mary Daly, *Gyn/Ecology* (Boston: Beacon Press, 1978), pp. 63–64.

29. Ibid., pp. 10–11 (emphasis mine).

30. Ibid.

31. Ibid., pp. 12–13.

32. Ibid., p. 21.

33. See David Maccauley, "On Women, Animals and Nature: An Interview with Eco-Feminist Susan Griffin," *APA Newsletter on Feminism* 90, no. 3 (fall 1991): 118.

34. Susan Griffin, *Woman and Nature: The Roaring Inside Her* (New York: Harper & Row, 1978), p. 226.

35. Ibid., p. 1.

36. Ibid., pp. 83–90.

37. Ibid., p. 67.

38. Maccauley, "An Interview with Eco-Feminist Susan Griffin," p. 117.

39. Griffin, *Woman and Nature*, pp. 1 and 117–118.

40. Susan Griffin, *Pornography and Silence: Culture's Revenge Against Nature* (New York: Harper & Row, 1981), p. 2.

41. Maccauley, "An Interview with Eco-Feminist Susan Griffin," p. 117.

42. Deena Metzger, Gloria Orenstein, Dale Colleen Hamilton, Paula Gum Alleo, Margot Adler, Dolores LaChapelle, A. K. Salleh, and Radha Bratt are also considered to be spiritual ecofeminists.

43. Riane Eisler, "The Gaia Tradition and the Partnership Future: An Ecofeminist Manifesto," in *Reweaving the World: The Emergence of Ecofeminism,* ed. Irene Diamond and Gloria Feman Orenstein (San Francisco: Sierra Club Books, 1990), p. 23.

44. Starhawk, "Power, Authority, and Mystery: Ecofeminism and Earth-Based Spirituality," in *Reweaving the World: The Emergence of Ecofeminism,* ed. Irene Diamond and Gloria Feman Orenstein (San Francisco: Sierra Club Books, 1990), p. 86.

45. Starhawk, "Feminist, Earth-based Spirituality and Ecofeminism," in *Healing the Wounds: The Promise of Ecofeminism,* ed. Judith Plant (Philadelphia: New Society Publishers, 1989), p. 176.

46. Ibid., p. 177.

47. Ibid., p. 178.

48. Ibid.

49. Ibid.

50. Ibid., p. 179.

51. Ibid., p. 180.

52. Rosemary Radforth Reuther, *Integrating Ecofeminism, Globalization and World Religions* (Lanham, Md.: Rowman & Littlefield, 2005), p. 8.

53. Starhawk, *Webs of Power: Notes from the Global Uprising* (Gabriol Island, B.C.: New Society Publishers, 2002), pp. 244–245.

54. Starhawk, "A Story of Beginnings," in *Healing the Wounds: The Promise of Ecofeminism,* Plant, ed., p. 115.

55. Carol Christ, *She Who Changes: Re-imagining the Divine in the World* (New York: MacMillan Palgrave, 2003), p. 240.

56. Dorothy Dinnerstein, "Survival on Earth: The Meaning of Feminism," in *Healing the Wounds: The Promise of Ecofeminism,* ed. Judith Plant (Philadelphia: New Society Publishers, 1989), p. 193.

57. Ibid.

58. Ibid., p. 174.

59. Marge Piercy, *Woman on the Edge of Time* (New York: Fawcett Crest, 1976).

60. Ibid., p. 105.

61. Warren, "The Power and the Promise of Ecological Feminism," p. 178.

62. Karen J. Warren, *Ecofeminist Philosophy: A Western Perspective on What It Is and Why It Matters* (Lanham, Md.: Rowman & Littlefield, 2000), p. 97.

63. Ibid., p. 99.

64. Ibid., p. 100.

65. Ibid.

66. Ibid., p. 101.

67. Ibid., pp. 189–190.

68. Ibid., pp. 189–190.

69. Alison M. Jaggar, *Feminist Politics and Human Nature* (Totowa, N.J.: Rowman & Littlefield, 1983). As readers must realize, I no longer accept Jaggar's categories from which she herself has departed in recent years.

70. Warren, "Feminism and Ecology: Making Connections," pp. 109–111.

71. Ibid., p. 113.

72. Ibid., pp. 112–114.

73. Ibid., pp. 114–115.

74. Ibid., p. 116, quoting Alison Jaggar.

75. Ibid., p. 118.

76. Ibid.

77. Maria Mies, "White Man's Dilemma: His Search for What He Has Destroyed," in Maria Mies and Vandana Shiva, *Ecofeminism* (London: Zed, 1993), pp. 132–163.

78. Ibid., pp. 137–138.

79. Karen J. Warren also presented a discussion similar to Shiva's in "Taking Empirical Data Seriously: An Ecofeminist Philosophy Perspective," in *Living with Contradictions: Controversies in Feminist Social Ethics,* ed. Alison M. Jaggar (Boulder, Colo.: Westview Press, 1994), pp. 642–643.

80. Vandana Shiva, "The Chipko-Women's Concept of Freedom," in Maria Mies and Vandana Shiva, *Ecofeminism* (London: Zed, 1993), p. 247.

81. Maria Mies, "The Need for a New Vision: The Subsistence Perspective," in Mies and Shiva, *Ecofeminism,* p. 319–322.

82. Kamla Bhasin, quoted in ibid., p. 322.

83. Biehl, *Rethinking Feminist Politics,* p. 14.

84. Ibid., p. 16 (quoting from Simone de Beauvoir).

85. Ibid.

86. Maria Mies and Vandana Shiva, Introduction to Mies and Shiva, *Ecofeminism,* p. 19.

87. Ynestra King, "Engendering a Peaceful Planet: Ecology, Economy, and Ecofeminism in Contemporary Context," *Women's Studies Quarterly* 23 (fall/winter 1995): 19.

88. Mies and Shiva, Introduction to *Ecofeminism,* p. 18.

89. Ibid.

90. Carolyn Merchant, *Radical Ecology: The Search for a Livable World* (New York: Routledge, 1992).

91. Biehl, *Rethinking Feminist Politics,* p. 19.

92. King, "Engendering a Peaceful Planet," pp. 16–17.

93. Quoted in Judith Auerbach, "The Intersection of Feminism and the Environmental Movement, or What Is Feminist About the Feminist Perspective on the Environment?" *American Behavioral Scientist* 37, no. 8 (August 1994): 1095.

94. Editors of the International Forum on Globalization, "From Bretton Woods to Alternatives," in *Alternatives to Economic Globalization,* ed. the International Forum on Globalization (San Francisco: Berrett-Koehler, 2002), pp. 228–238.

Chapter Eight

1. Cited in Hélène Vivienne Wenzel, "The Text as Body/Politics: An Appreciation of Monique Wittig's Writings in Context," *Feminist Studies* 7, no. 2 (summer 1981): 270–271.

2. Beverly Guy-Sheftall, "Response from a 'Second Waver' to Kimberly Springer's 'Third Wave Black Feminism?'" *Signs: Journal of Women in Culture and Society* 27, no. 4 (2002): 1091.

3. Leslie Heywood and Jennifer Drake, *Third Wave Agenda: Being Feminist, Doing Feminism* (Minneapolis: University of Minnesota Press, 1997), p. 3.

4. Judith Butler, "Contingent Foundations: Feminism and the Question of 'Postmodernism,'" in *Feminists Theorize the Political,* ed. Judith Butler and Joan W. Scott (New York: Routledge, 1992), p. 4.

5. Ibid., p. 5.

6. Anglo-American feminists initially limited the ranks of postmodern feminists to "French feminists" because so many exponents of postmodern feminism were either French nationals or women living in France (especially Paris). In response to this limitation, many directors of women's studies programs in France protested that U.S. academics have a very narrow conception of who counts as a French feminist or as a postmodern feminist. In a review of Claire Duchen's book, *Feminism in France: From May '68 to Mitterrand* (London: Routledge & Kegan Paul, 1986), Elaine Viennot wrote: "To taste the full flavor of these distortions, it is necessary to know that the French feminist movement is, in certain American universities, an object of study (I

assure you right away, you would not recognize it . . .), and that this book has every possibility of being bought by every American library; it is also necessary to know that certain of our compatriots (J. Kristeva, J. Derrida . . .) reign over there as masters of the university enclave" (Eléanor Kuykendall, trans., *Etudes féministes: bulletin national d'information* 1 [fall 1987]: 40). Whether the sentiments of this review, published by the Association pour les études féministes and the Centre lyonnais d'études féministes/Association femmes, féminisme et recherché Rhône Alpes and brought to my attention by Eléanor Kuykendall, are widely shared by French academics is a question for debate. In any event, Viennot's criticisms are not idiosyncratic and merit a careful reading.

7. Jane Flax, "Postmodernism and Gender Relations in Feminist Theory," in *Feminism/Postmodernism,* ed. Linda Nicholson (New York: Routledge, 1990), pp. 41–42.

8. Jacques Derrida, *Writing and Difference,* trans. Alan Bass (Chicago: University of Chicago Press, 1978).

9. Toril Moi, *Sexual/Textual Politics: Feminist Literary Theory* (New York: Routledge, 1985), p. 106.

10. Ibid.

11. Ibid.

12. Ann Rosalind Jones, "Writing the Body: Toward an Understanding of *l-Ecriture Féminine,*" *Feminist Studies* 7, no. 1 (summer 1981): 248.

13. Hélène Cixous and Catherine Clement, "Sorties," in *The Newly Born Woman,* trans. Betsy Wing (Minneapolis: University of Minnesota Press, 1986), pp. 63, 65.

14. Ibid., p. 65.

15. Hélène Cixous, "The Laugh of the Medusa," in *New French Feminisms,* ed. Elaine Marks and Isabelle de Courtviron (New York: Schocken Books, 1981), p. 249.

16. Ibid., p. 245.

17. Ibid., p. 262.

18. Elaine Marks and Isabelle de Courtviron, "Introduction III," in *New French Feminisms,* ed. Elaine Marks and Isabelle de Courtviron (New York: Schocken Books, 1981), p. 36.

19. Cixous, "The Laugh of the Medusa," p. 256.

20. Ibid., pp. 251 and 259–260.

21. Ibid., p. 256.

22. Ibid., pp. 259–260.

23. Madan Sarup, *Post-Structuralism and Postmodernism,* 2nd ed. (Athens: University of Georgia Press, 1993), p. 74.

24. Michel Foucault, *The History of Sexuality,* vol. 1, *An Introduction,* trans. Robert Hurley (London: Allen Lane, 1979), p. 93.

25. Philip Barker, *Michel Foucault: An Introduction* (Edinburgh: Edinburgh University Press, 1998), p. 27.

26. Chris Weedon, *Feminist Practice and Poststructuralist Theory* (New York: Basil Blackwell, 1987), p. 119.

27. Foucault, *The History of Sexuality,* p. 25.

28. Sarup, *Post-Structuralism and Postmodernism,* p. 74.

29. Barker, *Michel Foucault: An Introduction,* p. 32.

30. Michel Foucault, "The Discourse on Power," in *Remarks on Marx,* trans. R. James Goldstein and James Cascaito (New York: Semiotext(e), Columbia University, 1991), p. 1174.

31. Kathryn Pauly Morgan, "Women and the Knife: Cosmetic Surgery and the Colonization of Women's Bodies," *Hypatia* 6, no. 3 (fall 1991): 40.

32. Ibid.

33. Naomi Wolf, *The Beauty Myth: How Images of Beauty Are Used Against Women* (New York: William Morrow, 1991), pp. 13, 14, and 233.

34. Ibid.

35. Debra L. Gimlin, "Cosmetic Surgery: Paying for Your Beauty," in *Body Work: Beauty and Self-Image in American Culture,* ed. Debra L. Gimlin (Berkeley: University of California Press, 2002), p. 95.

36. Sandra Lee Bartky, "Foucault, Femininity, and the Modernization of Patriarchal Power," in *Femininity and Domination: Studies in the Phenomenology of Oppression* (New York: Routledge, 1990), p. 81.

37. Judith Butler, *Gender Trouble: Feminism and the Subversion of Identity* (New York: Routledge, 1990), p. 8.

38. Simone de Beauvoir, *The Second Sex,* trans. and ed. H. M. Parshely (New York: Vintage Books, 1974).

39. Judith Butler, "Variations on Sex and Gender: Beauvoir, Wittig and Foucault," in *Feminism As Critique: Essays on the Politics of Gender in Late-Capitalist Societies,* ed. Seyla Benhabib and Drucilla Cornell (Cambridge: Polity Press, 1987), p. 131.

40. Sara Salin, *Judith Butler* (New York: Routledge, 2002), p. 50.

41. J. L. Austin, *How to Do Things with Words* (Cambridge, Mass.: Harvard University Press, 1962), p. 6.

42. Salin, *Judith Butler,* p. 89.

43. Ibid.

44. Martha C. Nussbaum, "The Professor of Parody," *The New Republic,* February 22, 1999, p. 41.

45. Claire Duchen, *Feminism in France: From May '68 to Mitterrand* (London: Routledge & Regan Paul, 1986), p. 102.

46. Nussbaum, "The Professor of Parody," p. 41.

47. Judith Butler, *The Psychic Life of Power: Theories in Subjection* (Stanford, Calif.: Stanford University Press, 1997).

48. Nussbaum, "The Professor of Parody," p. 43.

49. Ibid., p. 44.

50. Judith Butler, *Gender Trouble* (New York: Routledge, 2004), p. 204.

51. Ibid., pp. 204–205.

52. Leslie Heywood and Jennifer Drake, eds., introduction to *Third Wave Agenda: Being Feminist, Doing Feminism* (Minneapolis: University of Minnesota Press, 1997), p. 3.

53. Mireya Navarro, "Going Beyond Black and White, Hispanics in Census Pick 'Other,'" *New York Times,* November 9, 2003, late edition, East Coast, A1, A21.

54. Daisy Hernandez and Bushra Rehman, *Colonize This! Young Women of Color on Today's Feminism* (New York: Seal Press, 2002).

55. Ibid., p. xxvii.

56. Navarro, "Going beyond Black and White," pp. A1, A21.

57. Chila Bulbeck, *Re-orienting Western Feminisms: Women's Diversity in a Postcolonial World* (New York: Cambridge University Press, 1997), p. 35.

58. Ibid., p. 34.

59. Ibid.

60. Eileen O'Keefe and Martha Chinouya, "Global Migrants, Gendered Tradition, and Human Rights: Africans and HIV in the United Kingdom," in *Feminist Bioethics, Human Rights, and the Developing World: Integrating Global and Local Perspectives,* ed. Susan Dodds, Anne Donchin, and Rosemarie Tong (Lanham, Md.: Roman & Littlefield, 2004).

61. Heywood and Drake, Introduction, p. 8.

62. Ibid.

63. Rebecca Walker, ed., "Being Real: An Introduction," in *To Be Real: Telling the Truth and Changing the Face of Feminism* (New York: Anchor Books, 1995), pp. xxxiii-xxxiv.

64. Quoted in Cathryn Bailey, "Unpacking the Mother/Daughter Baggage: Reassessing Second- and Third-Wave Tensions," *Women's Studies Quarterly* 3 and 4, no. 30 (fall 2002): 144.

65. Ann Braithwaite, "The Personal, the Political, Third-Wave and Postfeminisms," *Feminist Theory* 3, no. 3 (December 2002): 340.

66. Bailey, "Unpacking the Mother/Daughter Baggage," p. 145.

67. Allison L. Howry and Julia T. Wood, "Something Old, Something New, Something Borrowed: Themes in the Voices of a New Generation of Feminists," *Southern Communication Journal* 4, no. 66 (summer 2001): 324.

68. Ann Ferguson, "Sex and Work: Women As a New Revolutionary Class," in *An Anthology of Western Marxism: From Lukacs and Gramsci to Socialist Feminism,* ed. Robert S. Gottlieb (Oxford: Oxford University Press, 1989), p. 352.

69. Katie Roiphe, *The Morning After: Sex, Fear, and Feminism on Campus* (New York: Little & Brown, 1993); Camille Paglia, *Sex, Art, and American Culture: Essays* (New York: Random House, 1992); and René Denfield, *The New Victorians: A Young Woman's Challenges to the Old Feminist Order* (New York: Routledge, 1995).

70. Genesis 2:19.

71. Lao-tzu, "The Tao-te-Ching," in *The Texts of Taoism,* James Legge, ed. (New York: Dover, 1962).

72. Christine di Stephano, "Dilemmas of Difference," in *Feminism/Postmodernism,* ed. Linda J. Nicholson (New York: Routledge, 1990), pp. 63–82.

Bibliography

Chapter One

The Historical Development of Liberal Feminist Thought

Arneil, Barbara. *Politics and Feminism*. Massachusetts: Blackwell, 1999.

Banner, Lois. *Women in Modern America*. New York: Harcourt Brace, 1995.

Bentham, Jeremy. *The Principles of Morals and Legislation*. New York: Hafner, 1965.

Berg, Barbara. *The Remembered Gate: Origins of American Feminism*. New York: Oxford University Press, 1979.

Berlin, Isaiah. *Two Concepts of Liberty*. Oxford: Clarendon Press, 1961.

Bridenthal, Renate, and Claudia Koonz, eds. *Becoming Visible: Women in European History*. Boston: Houghton Mifflin, 1977.

Brockett, L. P. *Woman: Her Rights, Wrongs, Privileges, and Responsibilities*. Freeport, N.Y.: Books for Libraries Press, 1970.

Butler, Judith, and Joan W. Scott. *Feminists Theorize the Political*. New York: Routledge, 1992.

Butler, Melissa A. "Early Liberal Roots of Feminism: John Locke and the Attack on Patriarchy." *American Political Science Review* 72, no. 1, 1978, pp. 135–150.

Carroll, Bernice A., ed. *Liberating Women's History: Theoretical and Critical Essays*. Urbana: University of Illinois Press, 1976.

Dahlberg, Frances, ed. *Woman the Gatherer*. New Haven, CT: Yale University Press, 1981.

Davis, Angela Y. *Women, Race and Class*. New York: Random House, 1981.

DuBois, Ellen Carol, ed. *Elizabeth Cady Stanton, Susan B. Anthony: Correspondence, Writings, Speeches*. New York: Schocken Books, 1981.

Dworkin, Ronald. "Liberalism." In *Public and Private Morality,* ed. Stuart Hampshire. Cambridge: Cambridge University Press, 1978.

_____. *Taking Rights Seriously.* Cambridge, Mass.: Harvard University Press, 1977.

Eisenstein, Zillah. *The Radical Future of Liberal Feminism.* Boston: Northeastern University Press, 1986.

Epstein, Barbara. *The Success and Failures of Feminism.* Indianapolis: Indiana University Press, 2002, pp. 118–125.

Evans, Judith. *Feminist Theory Today: An Introduction to Second-Wave Feminism.* London: Sage, 1995.

Flexner, Eleanor, and Ellen Fitzpatrick. *A Century of Struggle.* Cambridge, Mass.: Harvard University Press, 1996.

Friedan, Betty. *The Feminine Mystique.* New York: Dell, 1974.

_____. *The Fountain of Age.* New York: Simon & Schuster, 1993.

_____. *The Second Stage.* New York: Summit Books, 1981.

Fuller, Margaret. *Woman in the Nineteenth Century.* New York: W. W. Norton, 1971.

Gerson, Gal. "Liberal Feminism: Individuality and Oppositions in Wollstonecraft and Mill." *Political Studies* 50 (2002): 794–810.

Gilman, Charlotte Perkins. *Women and Economics.* New York: Harper & Row, 1966.

Godwin, William. *Memoirs of Mary Wollstonecraft,* ed. W. Clark Durant, ed. New York: Bordon Press, 1972.

Grimke, Sarah. *Letters on "The Equality of the Sexes" and "The Condition of Woman."* New York: Burt Franklin, 1970.

Guttman, Amy. *Liberal Equality.* New York: Cambridge University Press, 1980.

Harper, Ida Husted, ed. *History of Woman Suffrage.* Vol. 5. New York: National American Woman Suffrage Association, 1922.

Hobbes, Thomas. *Leviathan.* New York: E. P. Dutton, 1950.

Hole, Judith, and Ellen Levine. *Rebirth of Feminism.* New York: Quadrangle, 1971.

Jaggar, Alison M. *Feminist Politics and Human Nature.* Totowa, N.J.: Rowman & Allanheld, 1983.

Kant, Immanuel. *Groundwork of the Metaphysic of Morals,* trans. H. J. Paton. New York: Harper Torchbooks, 1958.

Korsmeyer, Carolyn W. "Reasons and Morals in the Early Feminist Movement: Mary Wollstonecraft." *Philosophical Forum* 5, no. 1–2 (fall–winter 1973): 97–111.

Krouse, Richard. "Mill and Marx on Marriage, Divorce, and the Family." *Social Concept* 1, no. 2 (September 1983): 36–75.

_____. "Patriarchal Liberalism and Beyond: From John Stuart Mill to Harriet Taylor." In *The Family in Political Thought,* ed. Jean Bethke Elshtain. Amherst: University of Massachusetts Press, 1981.

Martin, Jane Roland. *Reclaiming a Conversation: The Ideal of the Educated Woman.* New Haven, Conn.: Yale University Press, 1985.

Mill, John Stuart. *Autobiography.* London: Oxford University Press, 1924.

_____. "Periodical Literature 'Edinburgh Review.'" *Westminster Review* 1, no. 2 (April 1824).

_____. "The Subjection of Women." In *Essays on Sex Equality*, ed. Alice S. Rossi. Chicago: University of Chicago Press, 1970.

_____. *Utilitarianism, Liberty, and Representative Government*. New York: E. P. Dutton, 1910.

Okin, Susan Moller. *Justice, Gender, and the Family*. New York: Basic Books, 1989.

Pateman, Carole. *The Problem of Political Obligation: A Critique of Liberal Theory*. Berkeley: University of California Press, 1979.

Pearsall, Marilyn, ed. *Women and Values: Readings in Recent Feminist Philosophy*. Belmont, Calif.: Wadsworth, 1986.

Rawls, John. *A Theory of Justice*. Cambridge, Mass.: Harvard University Press, 1971.

Rendel, Jane. *The Origins of Modern Feminism: Women in Britain, France, and the United States, 1780–1850*. New York: Schocken, 1984.

Rossi, Alice S. *The Feminist Papers: From Adams to De Beauvoir*. New York: Columbia University Press, 1973.

_____. "Sentiment and Intellect: The Story of John Stuart Mill and Harriet Taylor Mill." In *Essays on Sex Equality*, by John Stuart Mill and Harriet Taylor Mill; ed. Alice S. Rossi. Chicago: University of Chicago Press, 1970.

Rousseau, Jean-Jacques. *Emile*, trans. Allan Bloom. New York: Basic Books, 1979.

Sabrosky, Judith A. *From Rationality to Liberation*. Westport, Conn.: Greenwood Press, 1979.

Sandel, Michael J. *Liberalism and Its Critics*. New York: New York University Press, 1984.

_____. *Liberalism and the Limits of Justice*. New York: Cambridge University Press, 1982.

Sapiro, Virginia. *Women in American Society*. 4th ed. Mountain View, Calif.: Mayfield, 1994.

Scott, Joan W. "Feminism's History." *Journal of Women's History* 16, no. 2 (2004): 10–28.

"Seneca Falls Declaration of Sentiments and Resolutions (1848)." In *Feminism: The Essential Historical Writings*, ed. Miriam Schneir. New York: Random House, 1972.

Stafford, William. "Is Mill's 'Liberal' Feminism 'Masculinist'?" *Journal of Political Ideologies* 9, no. 2 (June 2004): 159–179.

Stanton, Anthony Gage. *History of Woman Suffrage*. New York: Arno Press, 1969.

Stanton, Elizabeth Cady, Susan B. Anthony, and Matilda Joslyn Gage. *History of Woman Suffrage*. Vol. 1, *1848–1861*. New York: Fowler and Wells, 1881.

Strauss, Leo. *Liberalism: Ancient and Modern*. New York: Basic Books, 1968.

Wollstonecraft, Mary. *A Vindication of the Rights of Woman*, ed. Carol H. Poston. New York: W. W. Norton, 1975.

Wright, Frances. *Life, Letters and Lectures, 1834/44*. New York: Arno Press, 1972.

Twentieth-Century Liberal Feminist Action

Ackerman, Bruce. "Political Liberalisms." *Journal of Philosophy* 91, no. 7 (1994): 364–386.

Amnesty International. *Human Rights Are Women's Right.* New York: Amnesty International Publications, 1995.

———. *Women in the Front Line.* New York: Amnesty International Publications, 1991.

Bachman, Ronet, and Linda Salzman. *Violence Against Women.* Washington, D.C.: U.S. Department of Justice, Bureau of Justice Statistics, 2001.

Benatar, David. "The Second Sexism." *Social Theory and Practice* 29 (2003): 177–210.

Bird, Caroline. *Born Female.* New York: David McKay Company, 1968.

Boyd, Susan. *Child Custody Law, and Women's Work.* New York: Oxford, 2003.

Brownmiller, Susan. *Against Our Will.* New York: Simon & Schuster, 1975.

Carden, Maren Lockwood. *The New Feminist Movement.* New York: Russell Sage Foundation, 1974.

Crittenden, Ann. *The Price of Motherhood.* New York: Henry Holt, 2001.

Echols, Alice. *Daring to Be Bad: Radical Feminism in America 1967–1975.* Minneapolis: University of Minnesota Press, 1987, p. 215.

Feldman, Gayle. "Women Are Different." *Self,* July 1997, pp. 105–108, 154.

Friedan, Betty. "Betty Friedan Critiques Feminism and Calls for New Directions." *New York Times Magazine,* July 5, 1981.

———. "Feminism Takes a New Turn." *New York Times Magazine,* November 18, 1979.

———. "N.O.W.: How It Began," *Women Speaking,* April 1967.

Gagne, Patricia. *Battered Women's Justice.* New York: Twayne, 1998, p. 41.

Gilbert, Neil. *The Transformation of the Welfare State.* New York: Oxford, 2002.

Gornick, Janet, and Marcia Meyers. *Families That Work.* New York: Russell Sage, 2003.

Hochschild, Arlie. *Second Shift.* Updated edition. New York: Penguin, 2003.

Ireland, Patricia. "The State of NOW." *Ms.,* July/August 1992.

Kanowitz, Lee. *Women and the Law: The Unfinished Revolution.* Albuquerque: University of New Mexico Press, 1969.

Koss, Mary, et al. "The Scope of Rape: Incidence and Prevalence of Sexual Aggression and Victimization in a National Sample of Higher Education Students." *Journal of Counseling and Clinical Psychology* 24 (1988): 68–72.

Lee, Valerie, et al. *The Influence of School Climate on Gender Differences in the Achievement and Engagement of Young Adolescents.* Washington, D.C.: AAUW Educational Foundation, 1996.

Leivick, Sarah. "Use of Battered Woman Syndrome to Defend the Abused and Prosecute the Abuser." *Georgetown Journal of Gender and Law* 6 (2005): 391ff.

Martin, Del. *Battered Wives.* Revised edition. Volcano, Calif.: Volcano, 1981.

Nathanson, C. A. "Sex Differences in Mortality." *Annual Review of Sociology* 10 (1984): 191–213.

Navetta, Jean-Marie. "Gains in Learning, Gaps in Earning." *AAUW Outlook* (spring 2005): 12.

NOW Bill of Rights. In *Sisterhood Is Powerful,* ed. Robin Morgan. New York: Random House, 1970.

Nye, Andrea. *Feminist Theory and the Philosophies of Man.* New York: Routledge, 1989.

Peters, Julia, and Andrea Wolper, eds. *Women's Rights, Human Rights: International Feminist Perspectives.* New York: Routledge, 1995.

Richards, Janet Radcliffe. *The Skeptical Feminist.* London: Routledge & Kegan Paul, 1980.

Rosser, Sue. *Women's Health: Missing from U.S. Medicine.* Bloomington: Indiana University Press, 1994.

Rossi, Alice. "Equality Between the Sexes: An Immodest Proposal." *Daedalus* 93, no. 2 (1964): 607–652.

Schiebinger, Londa. "Women's Health and Clinical Trials." *Journal of Clinical Investigations* 112 (2003): 973–977.

Stacey, Judith. *Brave New Families: Stories of Domestic Upheaval in Late Twentieth Century America.* New York: Basic Books, 1990.

———. "The New Conservative Feminism." *Feminist Studies* 9, no. 3 (fall 1983).

Steinem, Gloria. "Now That It's Reagan." *Ms.*, January 1981, pp. 28–33.

Sterba, James P., and Linda Lemoncheck. *Sexual Harassment: Issues and Answers.* New York: Oxford, 2001.

Sterba, James P. "Feminism Has Not Discriminated Against Men." In *Does Feminism Discriminate Against Men?* ed. Warren Farrell and James P. Sterba. New York: Oxford University Press, 2007.

Straus, Murray. "The Controversy over Domestic Violence by Women." In *Violence and Intimate Relationships,* ed. X. Arriage and S. Oskamp. Thousand Oaks, Calif.: Sage, 1999, p. 29.

Tjadens, P., and N. Thoenes. *Full Report of the Prevalence, Incidence and Consequences of Violence Against Women.* Washington, D.C.: National Institute of Justice and Centers for Disease Prevention, 2000.

Wagner DeCew, Judith. "The Combat Exclusion and the Role of Women in the Military." *Hypatia* 10 (winter 1995): 56–73.

Warrior, Betsy, and Lisa Leghorn. *Houseworker's Handbook.* 3rd expanded ed. Cambridge, Mass.: Women's Center, 1995.

Weisberg, D. Kelly. *Applications of Feminist Legal Theory to Women's Lives: Sex, Violence, Work, and Reproduction.* Philadelphia: Temple University Press, 1996.

Weitzman, Lenore. *Divorce Revolution.* New York: Free Press, 1985.

Contemporary Directions in Liberal Feminism

Baehr, Amy R. "Toward a New Feminist Liberalism: Okin, Rawls, and Habermas." *Hypatia* 11, no. 1 (winter 1996): 49–66.

Bem, Sandra L. "Probing the Promise of Androgyny." In *Beyond Sex-Role Stereotypes: Reading Toward a Psychology of Androgyny,* ed. Alexandra G. Kaplan and Joan P. Bean. Boston: Little, Brown, 1976.

Brooks, Ann. *Post-feminisms: Feminism, Cultural Theory, and Cultural Forms.* New York: Routledge, 1997.

Bryson, Valerie. *Feminist Debates: Issues of Theory and Political Practice.* New York: New York University Press, 1999.

Card, Claudia, ed. *On Feminist Ethics and Politics.* Lawrence: University Press of Kansas, 1999.

Card, Claudia. "The L Word and the F Word." *Hypatia* 21, no. 2 (2006): 223–229.

Code, Lorraine. *What Can She Know? Feminist Theory and the Construction of Knowledge.* Ithaca, N.Y.: Cornell University Press, 1991.

Eisenstein, Zillah R. *The Radical Future of Liberal Feminism.* New York: Longman, 1981.

English, Jane. "Sex Roles and Gender: Introduction." In *Feminism and Philosophy,* ed. Mary Vetterling-Braggin, Frederick A. Elliston, and Jane English. Totowa, N.J.: Rowman & Littlefield, 1977.

Galston, William A. *Liberal Purposes: Goods, Virtues, and Diversity in the Liberal State.* Cambridge: Cambridge University Press, 1991.

Groenhout, Ruth E. "Essentialist Challenges to Liberal Feminism." *Social Theory and Practice* 28, no. 1 (January 2002): 51–75.

Heilbrun, Carolyn G. *Toward the Promise of Androgyny.* New York: Alfred A. Knopf, 1973.

Hunter College Women's Studies Collective. *Women's Realities, Women's Choices: An Introduction to Women's Studies.* New York: Oxford University Press, 1983.

Klausen, Jytte, and Charles S. Maier, eds. *Has Liberalism Failed Women? Assuring Equal Representation in Europe and the United States.* New York: Palgrave, 2001.

Labaton, Vivien, and Dawn Lundy Martin, eds. *The Fire This Time: Young Activists and the New Feminism.* New York: Anchor Books, 2004.

Molyneux, Maxine, and Shahra Razari, eds. *Gender Justice, Development, and Rights.* Oxford: Oxford University Press, 2002.

Okin, Susan Moller. *Women in Western Political Thought.* Princeton, N.J.: Princeton University Press, 1979.

Person, Ethel Spector. "Sexuality As the Mainstay of Identity: Psychoanalytic Perspectives." *Signs: Journal of Women in Culture and Society* 5, no. 4 (summer 1980): 606.

Saul, Jennifer Mather. *Feminism: Issues and Arguments.* Oxford: Oxford University Press, 2003.

Shildrick, Margrit. *Leaky Bodies and Boundaries: Feminism, Postmodernism, and (Bio)ethics.* New York: Routledge, 1997.

Stack, Carol. *All Our Kin.* New York: Harper & Row, 1974.

Steinem, Gloria. *Outrageous Acts and Everyday Rebellions.* New York: Holt, Rinehart and Winston, 1983.

Trebilcot, Joyce. "Two Forms of Androgynism." In *"Femininity," "Masculinity," and "Androgyny,"* ed. Mary Vetterling-Braggin Totowa, N.J.: Rowman & Littlefield, 1982.

Critiques of Liberal Feminism

Arneil, Barbara. *Politics & Feminism.* Oxford: Blackwell Press, 1999, p. 147.

Bolotin, Susan. "Voices from the Post-Feminist Generation." *New York Times Magazine,* October 17, 1982, p. 28.

Brennan, Teresa, and Carole Pateman. "'Mere Auxiliaries to the Commonwealth': Women and the Origins of Liberalism." *Political Studies* 27, no. 2 (June 1979): 183–200.

Card, Claudia. "The L Word and the F Word." *Hypatia* 21, no. 2 (spring 2006): 223–229.

Clark, Lorenne M. B. "Women and Locke: Who Owns the Apples in the Garden of Eden?" In *The Sexism of Social and Political Theory,* ed. Lorenne M. B. Clark and Lydia Lange. Toronto: University of Toronto Press, 1979.

Davis, Angela Y. "Reflections on the Black Woman's Role in the Community of Slaves." *Black Scholar* 3 (1971): 7.

Dowling, Colette. *The Cinderella Syndrome: Women's Hidden Fear of Independence.* New York: Summit Books, 1981.

Elshtain, Jean Bethke. "Feminism, Family and Community." *Dissent* 29 (fall 1982): 442.

_____. *Meditations on Modern Political Thought: Masculine/Feminine Themes from Luther to Prendt.* New York: Praeger, 1986.

_____. *Public Man, Private Woman.* Princeton, N.J.: Princeton University Press, 1981.

Evans, Sara. "The Origins of the Women's Liberation Movement." *Radical America* 9, no. 2 (1975): 3–4.

Ferguson, Kathy E. "Liberalism and Oppression: Emma Goldman and the Anarchist Feminist Alternative." In *Liberalism and the Modern Polity,* ed. Michael C. G. McGrath. New York: Marcel Dekker, 1978.

_____. *Self, Society and Womankind: The Dialectic of Liberation.* Westport, Conn.: Greenwood Press, 1980.

Flammang, Janet Angela. "Feminist Theory: The Question of Power." *Current Perspectives on Social Theory* 4 (1983): 37–83.

_____. "The Political Consciousness of American Women: A Critical Analysis of Liberal Feminism in America." Ph.D. diss., University of California, Los Angeles, 1980.

Frazer, Elizabeth, and Nicola Lacey. *The Politics of Community: A Feminist Critique of the Liberal Communitarian Debate.* Toronto: University of Toronto Press, 1993.

Gibson, Mary. "Rationality." *Philosophy and Public Affairs* 6, no. 3 (spring 1977): 193–225.

Groenhout, Ruth. "Essentialist Challenges to Liberal Feminism," *Social Theory and Practice* 28, no. 1 (January 2002): 57.

Hewlett, Sylvia Ann. *A Lesser Life: The Myth of Women's Liberation in America.* New York: William Morrow, 1986.

Leo, John. "Are Women 'Male Clones'?" *Time,* August 18, 1986.

MacLean, Douglas, and Claudia Mills, eds. *Liberalism Reconsidered.* Totowa, N.J.: Rowman & Allanheld, 1983.

Richards, Janet Radcliffe. *The Skeptical Feminist.* London: Routledge & Kegan Paul, 1980.

Scheman, Naomi. "Individualism and the Objects of Psychology." In *Discovering Reality: Feminist Perspectives on Epistemology, Metaphysics, Methodology, and the Philosophy of Science,* ed. Sandra Harding and Merrill B. Hintikka. Dordrecht, Netherlands: D. Reidel, 1983.

Schwartzman, Lisa H. *Challenging Liberalism: Feminism as Political Critique.* University Park: Pennsylvania State University Press, 2006.

Stopler, Gila. "Gender Construction and the Limits of Liberal Equality." *Texas Journal of Women and the Law* 15 (2005): 44–78.

Thorne, Barrie, and Marilyn Yalom, eds. *Rethinking the Family: Some Feminist Questions.* Boston: Northeastern University Press, 1989.

Wendell, Susan. "A (Qualified) Defense of Liberal Feminism." *Hypatia* 2, no. 2 (summer 1987): 65–93.

Willis, Ellen. "The Conservatism of *Ms.*" In *Feminist Revolution,* ed. Redstockings. New York: Random House, 1975.

Chapter Two

The Distinction Between Radical-Libertarian and Radical-Cultural Feminists

Alcoff, Linda. "Cultural Feminism Versus Poststructuralism: The Identity Crisis in Feminist Theory." *Signs: Journal of Women in Culture and Society* 13, no. 3 (1988): 408.

Bell, Diane, and Renate Klein. *Radically Speaking: Feminism Reclaimed.* North Melbourne, Australia: Spinifex, 1996.

Calhoun, Cheshire. "Taking Seriously Dual Systems and Sex." *Hypatia* 13, no. 1 (1998): 224–231.

Card, Claudia. "Radicalesbianfeminist Theory." *Hypatia* 13, no. 1 (1998): 206–213.

Coote, Anna, and Beatrix Campbell. *Sweet Freedom: The Movement for Women's Liberation.* Boston: Blackwell Publishers, 1987.

Crow, Barbara A. *Radical Feminism: A Documentary Reader.* New York: New York University Press, 2000.

Echols, Alice. "The New Feminism of Yin and Yang." In *Powers of Desire: The Politics of Sexuality,* ed. Ann Snitow, Christine Stansell, and Sharon Thompson. New York: Monthly Review Press, 1983.

Ferguson, Ann. "Sex War: The Debate between Radical and Liberation Feminists." *Signs: Journal of Women in Culture and Society* 10, no. 1 (autumn 1984): 106–135.

Giovanni, Nikki. *My House.* New York: William Morrow, 1972.

Hole, Judith, and Ellen Levine. *Rebirth of Feminism.* New York: Quadrangle, 1971.

Jaggar, Alison M., and Paula S. Rothenberg, eds. *Feminist Frameworks.* New York: McGraw-Hill, 1984.

Klein, Renate, and Deborah Lynn Steinberg. *Radical Voices: A Decade of Feminist Resistance from Women's Studies International Forum.* New York: Pergamon Press, 1989.

Koedt, Anne, Ellen Levine, and Anita Rapone, eds. *Radical Feminism.* New York: Quadrangle, 1973.

Laclau, Ernesto, and Chantal Mouffe. *Hegemony and Socialist Strategy: Towards a Radical Democratic Politics.* London: Verso, 1989.

Mandell, Nancy. *Feminist Issues: Race, Class, and Sexuality.* Scarborough, Ontario: Prentice-Hall, 1995.

Mantilla, Karla. "Backlash and a *Feminism* That Is Contrary to *Feminism.*" *Off Our Backs* 37, no. 1 (2007): 58–61.

Rhodes, Jacqueline. *Radical Feminism, Writing, and Critical Agency.* New York: State University of New York Press, 2005.

Stanton, Elizabeth Cady. *The Woman's Bible.* 2 vols. New York: Arno Press, 1972; originally published 1895 and 1899.

Stein, Arlene. *Shameless: Sexual Dissidence in American Culture.* New York: New York University Press, 2006.

Trebilcot, Joyce. "Conceiving Wisdom: Notes on the Logic of Feminism." *Sinister Wisdom* 3 (fall 1979).

Whittier, Nancy. *Feminist Generations: The Persistence of the Radical Feminist Movement.* Philadelphia: Temple University Press, 1995.

Radical-Libertarian and Radical-Cultural Feminists: Interpreting the Sex/Gender System

Barry, Herbert III, Margaret K. Bacon, and Irwin L. Child. "A Cross-Cultural Survey of Some Sex Differences in Socialization." In *Selected Studies in Marriage and the Family,* ed. Robert F. Winch, Robert McGinnis, and Herbert R. Barringer. 2nd ed. New York: Holt, Rinehart and Winston, 1962.

Bartlett, Katherine T., and Rosanne Kennedy, eds. *Feminist Legal Theory: Readings in Law and Gender.* Oxford: Westview Press, 1991.

Calhoun, Cheshire. "Taking Seriously Dual Systems and Sex." *Hypatia* 13, no. 1 (winter 1998): 224–231.

Daly, Mary. *Beyond God the Father: Toward a Philosophy of Women's Liberation.* Boston: Beacon Press, 1973.

_____. *Gyn/Ecology: The Metaethics of Radical Feminism.* Boston: Beacon Press, 1978.

_____. *Pure Lust: Elemental Feminist Philosophy.* Boston: Beacon Press, 1984.

Dinnerstein, Dorothy. *The Mermaid and the Minotaur: Sexual Arrangements and Human Malaise.* New York: Harper Colophon Books, 1977.

Eisenstein, Hester. *Contemporary Feminist Thought.* Boston: G. K. Hall, 1983.

Firestone, Shulamith. *The Dialectic of Sex.* New York: Bantam Books, 1970.

French, Marilyn. *Beyond Power: On Women, Men and Morals.* New York: Summit Books, 1985.

Friedan, Betty. *The Feminine Mystique.* New York: Dell, 1974.

Gilder, George. *Sexual Suicide.* New York: Quadrangle, 1973.

Jaggar, Alison M. *Feminist Politics and Human Nature.* Totowa, N.J.: Rowman & Allanheld, 1983.

Miller, Henry. *Sexus.* New York: Grove Press, 1965.

Millett, Kate. *Sexual Politics.* Garden City, N.Y.: Doubleday, 1970.

Morey-Gaines, Ann-Janine. "Metaphor and Radical Feminism: Some Cautionary Comments on Mary Daly's *Gyn/Ecology.*" *Soundings* 65, no. 3 (fall 1982): 347–348.

Nietzsche, Friedrich. *On the Genealogy of Morals,* trans. Walter Kaufmann and R. Hollingdale. New York: Vintage Books, 1969.

O'Toole, Laura L., Jessica R. Schiffman, and Margie L. Kiter Edwards, eds. *Gender Violence: Interdisciplinary Perspectives.* New York: New York University Press, 2007.

Rossi, Alice. "Sex Equality: The Beginning of Ideology." In *Masculine/Feminine,* ed. Betty Roszak and Theodore Roszak. New York: Harper & Row, 1969.

Rubin, Gayle. "The Traffic in Women." In *Toward an Anthropology of Women,* ed. Rayna R. Reiter. New York: Monthly Review Press, 1975.

Soper, Kate. "Feminism, Humanism, and Postmodernism." *Radical Philosophy* 55 (summer 1990): 11–17.

Vetterling-Braggin, Mary, ed., *"Femininity," "Masculinity," and "Androgyny."* Totowa, N.J.: Rowman & Littlefield, 1982.

Women, Gender, and Philosophy. Special issue of *Radical Philosophy* 34 (summer 1983).

Analyzing the Oppressive Features of Sexuality
("Male Domination" and "Female Subordination")

Bacchi, Carol Lee. *Same Difference, Feminism and Sexual Difference.* North Sydney: Allen and Unwin, 1990.

Blumstein, Philip, and Pepper Schwartz. *American Couples.* New York: William Morrow, 1983.

Bushnell, Dana E., ed. *'Nagging' Questions: Feminist Ethics in Everyday Life.* Lanham, Md.: Rowman & Littlefield, 1995.

Coward, Rosalind. *Patriarchal Precedents: Sexuality and Social Relations.* London: Routledge and Kegan Paul, 1983.

Dworkin, Andrea. *Our Blood: Prophecies and Discourses on Sexual Politics.* New York: G. P. Putnam, 1981.

_____. *Right-Wing Women.* New York: Coward-McCann, 1983.

_____. *Woman Hating: A Radical Look at Sexuality.* New York: E. P. Dutton, 1974.

_____. *Letters from a War Zone.* Brooklyn: Lawrence Hill Books, 1993.

Echols, Alice. "The Taming of the Id." In *Pleasure and Danger: Exploring Female Sexuality,* ed. Carole S. Vance. Boston: Routledge & Kegan Paul, 1984.

English, Deirdre, Amber Hollibaugh, and Gayle Rubin. "Talking Sex: A Conversation on Sexuality and Feminism." *Socialist Review* 11, no. 4 (July–August 1981): 43–62.

Epstein, Cynthia Fuchs. *A Woman's Place.* Berkeley: University of California Press, 1971.

Fairchilds, Cissie. "Female Sexual Attitudes and the Rise of Illegitimacy: A Case Study." *Journal of Interdisciplinary History* 8, no. 4 (spring 1978): 627–667.

Frye, Marilyn. *The Politics of Reality: Essays in Feminist Theory.* Trumansburg, N.Y.: Crossing Press, 1983.

Lee, Patrick C., and Robert Sussman Stewart, eds. *Sex Differences: Cultural and Developmental Dimensions.* New York: Urizen, 1976.

Linden, Robin Ruth, et al., eds. *Against Sadomasochism: A Radical Feminist Analysis.* East Palo Alto, Calif.: Frog in the Well Press, 1982.

Maccoby, Eleanor, ed. *The Development of Sex Differences.* Stanford, Calif.: Stanford University Press, 1966.

MacKinnon, Catharine A., ed. *Women's Lives, Men's Laws.* Cambridge, Mass.: Belknap Press of Harvard University Press, 2005.

Martin, Del. *Battered Wives.* New York: Pocket Books, 1976.

Parker, Katy, and Lisa Leghorn. *Woman's Worth: Sexual Economics and the World of Women.* London: Routledge & Kegan Paul, 1981.

Redstockings, ed. *Feminist Revolution.* New York: Random House, 1975.

Rubin, Gayle. "Thinking Sex: Notes for a Radical Theory of the Politics of Sexuality." In *Pleasure and Danger: Exploring Female Sexuality,* Carole S. Vance. Boston: Routledge & Kegan Paul, 1984.

Schechter, Susan. *Women and Male Violence.* Boston: South End Press, 1982.

Schulman, Alix Kates. "Sex and Power: Sexual Bases of Radical Feminism." *Signs: Journal of Women in Culture and Society* 5, no. 4 (summer 1980): 590–604.

Shafer, Carolyn M., and Marilyn Frye. "Rape and Respect." In *Women and Values: Readings in Recent Feminist Philosophy,* ed. Marilyn Pearsall. Belmont, Calif.: Wadsworth, 1986.

Smart, Carol, and Barry Smart, eds. *Women, Sexuality, and Social Control.* London: Routledge and Kegan Paul, 1978.

Spender, Dale. *Man Made Language.* Boston: Routledge & Kegan Paul, 1980.

Strossen, Nadine, ed. *Defending Pornography: Free Speech, Sex, and the Fight for Women's Rights.* New York: New York University Press, 2000.

Vance, Carole S., ed. *Pleasure and Danger: Exploring Female Sexuality.* Boston: Routledge & Kegan Paul, 1984.

Wakoski, Diane. *The Motorcycle Betrayal Poems.* New York: Simon & Schuster, 1971.

Weitz, Rose, ed. *The Politics of Women's Bodies: Sexuality, Appearance and Behavior.* New York: Oxford University Press, 1998.

Pornography:
Symptom and Symbol of Male-Controlled Female Sexuality or Opportunity for Female-Controlled Female Sexuality?

Assiter, Alison. *Pornography, Feminism, and the Individual.* London: Pluto Press, 1991.

Attwood, Feona. "Pornography and Objectification." *Feminist Media Studies* 4, no. 1 (March 2004): 7–19.

Berger, Ronald J., Patricia Searles, and Charles E. Cottle. *Feminism and Pornography.* New York: Praeger Publishers, 1991.

Blakely, Mary Kay. "Is One Woman's Sexuality Another Woman's Pornography?" *Ms.*, April 1985, pp. 37–47.

Chancer, Lynn S. *Reconcilable Differences: Confronting Beauty, Pornography, and the Future of Feminism.* Berkeley: University of California Press, 1998.

Ciclitira, Karen. "Pornography, Women and Feminism: Between Pleasure and Politics." *Sexualities* 7, no. 3 (August 2004): 281–301.

Cornell, Drucilla. *Feminism and Pornography.* Oxford: Oxford University Press, 2000.

Diamond, Irene. "Pornography and Repression." *Signs: Journal of Women in Culture and Society* 5 (1980): 686.

Donnerstein, Edward. *The Question of Pornography: Research Findings and Policy Implications.* New York: Free Press, 1987.

Dworkin, Andrea. "'Pornography's Exquisite Volunteers.'" *Ms.*, March 1981.

———. *Pornography: Men Possessing Women.* New York: Perigee Books, 1981.

English, Deirdre. "The Politics of Porn: Can Feminists Walk the Line?" *Mother Jones,* April 1980.

Garry, Ann. "Pornography and Respect for Women." *Social Theory and Practice* 4 (summer 1978): 395.

Griffin, Susan. *Pornography and Silence.* New York: Harper & Row, 1981.

———. *Rape: The Power of Consciousness.* San Francisco: Harper & Row, 1979.

Itzin, Catherine, ed. *Pornography: Women, Violence, and Civil Liberties.* Oxford: Oxford University Press, 1993.

Lederer, Laura, ed. *Take Back the Night: Women on Pornography.* New York: William Morrow, 1980.

MacKinnon, Catharine A. "Feminism, Marxism, Method, and the State: An Agenda for Theory." *Signs: Journal of Women in Culture and Society* 7, no. 3 (spring 1982): 533.

_____. "Francis Biddle's Sister: Pornography, Civil Rights, and Speech." In *Feminism Unmodified: Disclosures on Life and Law.* Cambridge: Harvard University Press, 1987.

Malamuth, Neil, and Edward Donnerstein. *Pornography and Sexual Aggression.* New York: Academic Press, 1984.

McCarthy, Sarah J. "Pornography, Rape, and the Cult of Macho." *Humanist* 40, no. 5 (September–October 1980): 11–20.

Newland, Laura. "Not for Sale: Feminists Resisting Prostitution and Pornography." *Off Our Backs* 35, no. 7 (August 2005): 30.

Rodgerson, Gillian, and Elizabeth Wilson, eds. *Pornography and Feminism: The Case Against Censorship.* London: Lawrence & Wishart, 1991.

Segal, Lynne. *Sex Exposed: Sexuality and the Pornography Debate.* Piscataway, N.J.: Rutgers University Press, 1993.

Soble, Alan. *Pornography: Marxism, Feminism, and the Future of Sexuality.* New Haven, Conn.: Yale University Press, 1986.

_____. *Pornography, Sex, and Feminism.* Amherst, N.Y.: Prometheus Books, 2002.

Strossen, Nadine. *Defending Pornography: Free Speech, Sex, and the Fight for Women's Rights.* New York: New York University Press, 2000.

Taylor, Stuart Jr. "Pornography Foes Lose New Weapons in Supreme Court." *New York Times,* February 25, 1986, p. 1.

Lesbianism:
A Mere Sexual Preference or the Paradigm for Female-Controlled Female Sexuality?

Allen, Jeffner. *Lesbian Philosophy: Explorations.* Palo Alto: Institute of Lesbian Studies, 1986.

Atkinson, Ti Grace. *Amazon Odyssey.* New York: Links, 1974.

_____. "Lesbianism and Feminism." In *Amazon Expedition: A Lesbian-Feminist Anthology,* ed. Phyllis Birkby et al. Washington, N.J.: Times Change Press, 1973.

_____. "Radical Feminism: A Declaration of War." In *Women and Values: Readings in Recent Feminist Philosophy,* ed. Marilyn Pearsall. Belmont, Calif.: Wadsworth, 1986.

Beck, Evelyn Torton, ed. *Nice Jewish Girls: A Lesbian Anthology.* Watertown, Mass.: Persephone Press, 1982.

Bowleg, Lisa. "Triple Jeopardy and Beyond: Multiple Minority Stress and Resilience among Black Lesbians." *Journal of Lesbian Studies* 7, no. 4, (2003): 87.

Brandt, Eric, ed. *Dangerous Liaisons: Blacks, Gays, and the Struggle for Equality.* New York: New Press, 1999.

Bulkin, Elly, Minnie Bruce Pratt, and Barbara Smith. *Yours in Struggle: Three Feminist Perspectives on Anti-Semitism and Racism.* New York: Long Haul Press, 1984.

Califia, Pat. "Feminism and Sadomasochism." *Co-evolution Quarterly* 33 (spring 1981).

_____. *Sapphistry: The Book of Lesbian Sexuality.* Tallahassee, Fl.: Naiad Press, 1983.

Card, Claudia, ed. *Adventures in Lesbian Philosophy.* Bloomington: Indiana University Press, 1994.

_____. "Radicalesbianfeminist Theory." *Hypatia* 13, no. 1 (1998): 206–213.

Ciasullo, Ann M. "Making Her (In)Visible: Cultural Representations of Lesbianism and the Lesbian Body in the 1990s." *Feminist Studies* 27, no. 3 (fall 2001): 577.

Clarke, Cheryl. "Knowing the Danger and Going There Anyway." *Sojourner: The Women's Forum* 16, no. 1 (1990): 14–15.

_____. "Being Pro-Gay and Pro-Lesbian in Straight Institutions." *Journal of Gay and Lesbian Social Services* 3, no. 2. (1995): 95–100.

Cole, Johnnetta Betsch, and Beverly Guy-Sheftall. "Black, Lesbian, and Gay: Speaking the Unspeakable." In *Gender Talk: The Struggle for Women's Equality in African American Communities.* New York: One World Ballantine Books, 2003.

Cuomo, Chris J. "Thoughts on Lesbian Differences." *Hypatia* 13, no. 1 (1998): 198–205.

Daly, Meg. *Surface Tension: Love, Sex, and Politics Between Lesbians and Straight Women.* New York: Simon & Schuster, 1996.

Ettorre, E. M. *Lesbians, Women, and Society.* London: Routledge and Kegan Paul, 1980.

Frye, Marilyn. *Willful Virgin: Essays in Feminism, 1976–1992.* Freedom, Calif.: Crossing Press, 1992.

_____. "Do You Have to Be a Lesbian to Be a Feminist?" *Off Our Backs* 20, no. 8 (September 30): p. 21.

Fuss, Diane, ed. *Inside/Out: Lesbian Theories, Gay Theories.* London: Routledge, 1991.

Goodman, Gerre, et al. *No Turning Back: Lesbian and Gay Liberation for the '80's.* Philadelphia: New Society Publishers, 1983.

Grier, Barbara, and Colette Reid, eds. *The Lavender Herring: Lesbian Essays from "The Ladder."* Baltimore, Md.: Diana Press, 1976.

Harne, Lynne, and Elaine Miller, eds., *All the Rage: Reasserting Radical Lesbian Feminism.* London: Women's Press, 1996.

Harris, Laura, and Elizabeth Crocker, eds. *Femme: Feminists, Lesbians, and Bad Girls.* New York: Routledge, 1997.

Hawthorne, Susan. "The Depoliticising of Lesbian Culture." *Hecate* 29, no. 2 (2003): 235.

Heller, Dana, ed. *Cross-Purposes: Lesbians, Feminists, and the Limits of Alliance.* Bloomington: Indiana University Press, 1997.

Jeffreys, Sheila. *The Lesbian Heresy: A Feminist Perspective on the Lesbian Sexual Revolution.* North Melbourne, Australia: Spinifex, 1993.

Johnston, Jill. *Lesbian Nation: The Feminist Solution.* New York: Simon & Schuster, 1974.

Kleindienst, Kris, ed. *This Is What a Lesbian Looks Like.* Ithaca, N.Y.: Firebrand Books, 1999.

Koedt, Ann. "The Myth of the Vaginal Orgasm." *Notes from the Second Year: Women's Liberation—Major Writings of the Radical Feminists,* April 1970. Available at many Web sites, including www.uic.edu/orgs/cwluherstory/CWLUArchive/vaginalmyth.html.

Laner, M. R., and R. H. Laner. "Sexual Preference or Personal Style? Why Lesbians Are Disliked." *Journal of Homosexuality* 5, no. 4 (1980): 339–356.

Law, Sylvia. "Homosexuality and the Social Meaning of Gender." *Wisconsin Law Review* 2 (1988): 187–235.

Mohin, Lilian, ed. *An Intimacy of Equals: Lesbian Feminist Ethics.* New York: Harrington Park Press, 1996.

Morland, Iain, and Annabelle Willox, eds. *Queer Theory.* Houndmills, Basingstoke, Hampshire [England]; New York: Palgrave Macmillan, 2005.

Nestle, Joan. *Persistent Desire: A Butch-Femme Reader.* Boston: Alyson Publications, 1992.

Phelan, Shane. *Identity Politics: Lesbian Feminism and the Limits of Community.* Philadelphia: Temple University Press, 1989.

Redstockings Manifesto. In *Sisterhood Is Powerful,* ed. Robin Morgan. New York: Random House, 1970.

Rich, Adrienne. "Compulsory Heterosexuality and Lesbian Existence." In *Living with Contradictions: Controversies in Feminist Social Ethics,* ed. Alison M. Jaggar. Boulder, Colo.: Westview Press, 1994.

Rule, Jane. *Lesbian Images.* Trumansburg, N.Y.: Crossing Press, 1982.

Samois. *Coming to Power: Writings and Graphics on Lesbian S/M.* Palo Alto: Up Press, 1981.

Shugar, Dana R. *Separatism and Women's Community.* Lincoln: University of Nebraska Press, 1995.

Stein, Arlene, ed. *Sisters, Sexperts, Queers: Beyond the Lesbian Nation.* New York: Plume, 1993.

———. *Shameless: Sexual Dissidence in American Culture.* New York: New York University Press, 2006.

Tanner, Donna K. *The Lesbian Couple.* Lexington, Mass.: Lexington Books, 1978.

Valk, Anne M. "Living a Feminist Lifestyle: The Intersection of Theory and Action in a Lesbian Feminist Collective." *Feminist Studies* 28, no. 2 (2002): 303.

Weed, Elizabeth, and Naomi Schor, eds. *Feminism Meets Queer Theory.* Bloomington: Indiana University Press, 1997.

Weise, Elizabeth Reba, ed. *Closer to Home: Bisexuality & Feminism.* Seattle: Seal Press, 1992.

Radical-Libertarian and Radical-Cultural Feminists:
On Reproduction and Mothering

Adams, Alice. *Reproducing the Womb: Images of Childbirth in Science, Feminist Theory, and Literature.* Ithaca and London: Cornell University Press, 1994.

Allen, Jeffner. "Motherhood: The Annihilation of Women." In *Women and Values: Readings in Recent Feminist Philosophy,* ed. Marilyn Pearsall. Belmont, Calif.: Wadsworth, 1986.

Alpert, Jane. "Mother Right: A New Feminist Theory." *Ms.,* August 1973.

Atwood, Margaret. *The Handmaid's Tale.* New York: Fawcett Crest Books, 1985.

Baruch, Elaine, Amadeo D'Adamo, and Joni Seager, eds. *Embryos, Ethics and Women's Rights: Exploring the New Reproductive Technologies.* New York: Harrington Park Press, 1988.

Blank, Robert H. *Mother and Fetus: Changing Notions of Maternal Responsibility.* New York: Greenwood Press, 1992.

Brakman, Sarah-Vaughan, and Sally J. Scholz. "Adoption, ART, and a Re-Conception of the Maternal Body: Toward Embodied Maternity." *Hypatia* 21, no. 1 (winter 2006): 54–77.

Brison, Susan J. "Contentious Freedom: Sex Work and Social Construction." *Hypatia* 21, no. 4 (fall 2006): 192–200.

Brown, Ivana. "Mommy Memoirs: Feminism, Gender and Motherhood in Popular Literature." *Journal of the Association for Research on Mothering* 8, nos. 1 and 2 (September 2006).

Cahill, Susan, ed. *Motherhood.* New York: Avon Books, 1982.

Chesler, Phyllis. *Sacred Bond: The Legacy of Baby M.* New York: Times Books, 1988.

Chodorow, Nancy. *The Reproduction of Mothering.* Berkeley: University of California Press, 1978.

Cohen, Cynthia B. "'Give Me Children or I Shall Die!' New Reproductive Technologies and Harm to Children." *The Hastings Center Report* 26 (1996).

Colb, Sherry F. *When Sex Counts: Making Babies and Making Law.* Lanham, Md.: Rowman & Littlefield Publishers, 2007.

Corea, Gena. "Egg Snatchers." In *Test-Tube Women: What Future for Motherhood?* ed. Rita Arditti, Renate Duelli Klein, and Shelley Minden. London: Pandora Press, 1984.

_____. *The Mother Machine: Reproduction Technologies from Artificial Insemination to Artificial Wombs.* New York: Harper & Row, 1985.

Crittenden, Anne. *The Price of Motherhood: Why the Most Important Job in the World Is the Least Valued.* London: Metropolitan Books, 2001.

Crossley, Mary. "Dimensions of Equality in Regulating Assisted Reproductive Technologies." *Journal of Gender, Race, and Justice* 9, no. 2 (winter 2005): 273.

DiQuinzio, Patrice. *The Impossibility of Motherhood: Feminism, Individualism, and the Problem of Mothering*. New York: Routledge, 1999.

_____. "The Politics of the Mothers' Movement in the United States: Possibilities and Pitfalls." *Journal of the Association for Research on Mothering* 8, nos. 1 and 2 (September 2006).

_____. "Reconceiving Pregnancy and Childcare: Ethics, Experience, and Reproductive Labor." *Hypatia* 22, no. 3 (summer 2007): 204.

Donchin, Anne. "The Future of Mothering: Reproductive Technology and Feminist Theory." *Hypatia* 1, no. 2 (fall 1986): 131.

Dresser, Rebecca. "Regulating Assisted Reproduction." *The Hastings Center Report* 30 (2000).

Dworkin, Andrea. *Right-Wing Women*. New York: Coward-McCann, 1983.

Ehrenreich, Barbara, and Deirdre English. *For Her Own Good*. New York: Anchor/Doubleday, 1979.

Ferguson, Ann. "Motherhood and Sexuality: Some Feminist Questions." *Hypatia* 1, no. 2 (fall 1986): 3–22.

_____. *Blood at the Root: Motherhood, Sexuality, and Male Dominance*. London: Pandora Press, 1989.

Folbre, Nancy. *The Invisible Heart: Economics and Family Values*. New York: New Press, 2001.

Goodwin, Michele. "Assisted Reproductive Technology and the Double Bind: The Illusory Choice of Motherhood." *Journal of Gender, Race, and Justice* 9, no. 1 (fall 2005): 1–55.

Goslinga-Roy, Gillian M. "Body Boundaries, Fiction of the Female Self: An Ethnographic Perspective on Power, Feminism, and the Reproductive Technologies." *Feminist Studies* 26, no. 1 (spring 2000): 113–141.

Green, Fiona Joy. "Developing a Feminist Motherline: Reflections on a Decade of Feminist Parenting." *Journal of the Association for Research on Mothering* 8, nos. 1 and 2 (September 2006).

Hattery, Angela. *Women, Work and Family: Balancing and Weaving*. Thousand Oaks, Calif.: Sage Publications, 2001.

Hewett, Heather. "Talkin' 'Bout a Revolution: Building a Mothers' Movement in the Third World." *Journal of the Association for Research on Mothering* 8, nos. 1 and 2 (September 2006).

Jaggar, Alison M. *Feminist Politics and Human Nature*. Totowa, N.J.: Rowman & Allanheld, 1983.

Ketchum, Sara Ann. "Selling Babies and Selling Bodies." In Helen Holmes and Laura M. Purdy, eds., *Feminist Perspectives in Medical Ethics*. Bloomington: Indiana University Press, 1992.

Mahowald, Mary Briody. *Women and Children in Health Care: An Unequal Majority*. New York: Oxford University Press, 1993.

Makus, Ingrid. *Women, Politics, and Reproduction: The Liberal Legacy.* Toronto: University of Toronto Press, 1996.

Mellown, Mary Ruth. "An Incomplete Picture: The Debate About Surrogate Motherhood." *Harvard Women's Law Journal* 8 (spring 1985): 231–246.

Mendell, Betty Reid. *Where Are the Children? A Close Analysis of Foster Care and Adoption.* Lexington, Mass.: Lexington Books, 1973.

Middleton, Amy. "Mothering under Duress: Examining the Inclusiveness of Feminist Mothering Theory." *The Journal of the Association for Research on Mothering* 8, nos. 1 and 2 (September 2006).

Mundy, Liza. *Everything Conceivable: How Assisted Reproduction Is Changing Men, Women, and the World.* New York: Alfred Knopf, 2007.

Naff, Clay Farris, ed. *Reproductive Technology.* Farmington Hills, Mich.: Greenhaven Press, 2006.

Oakley, Ann. *Woman's Work: The Housewife, Past and Present.* New York: Pantheon Books, 1974.

O'Brien, Mary. *The Politics of Reproduction.* Boston: Routledge & Kegan Paul, 1981.

Overall, Christine. *Ethics and Human Reproduction: A Feminist Analysis.* Boston: Allen & Unwin, 1987.

_____. *Feminist Perspectives: Philosophical Essays on Method and Morals.* Toronto: University of Toronto Press, 1988.

_____. *Human Reproduction: Principles, Practices, Policies.* New York: Oxford University Press, 1993.

"The Pathogenic Commune." *Science News* 122, no. 76 (July 3, 1982): 76.

Piercy, Marge. *Woman on the Edge of Time.* New York: Fawcett Crest Books, 1976.

Purdy, Laura. *In Their Best Interest? The Case Against Equal Rights for Children.* Ithaca, N.Y.: Cornell University Press, 1992.

_____. *Reproducing Persons: Issues in Feminist Bioethics.* Ithaca, N.Y.: Cornell University Press, 1996.

Raymond, Janice. *Women As Wombs: Reproductive Technologies and the Battle over Women's Freedom.* San Francisco: Harper & Row, 1993.

Rich, Adrienne. *Of Woman Born.* New York: W. W. Norton, 1979.

Rodin, Judith, and Aila Collins, eds. *Women and New Reproductive Technologies: Medical, Psychosocial, Legal and Ethical Dilemmas.* Hillside, N.J.: Lawrence Erlbaum Associates, 1991.

Rowland, Robyn. "Reproductive Technologies: The Final Solution to the Woman Question." In *Test-Tube Women: What Future for Motherhood?* ed. Rita Arditti, Renate Duelli Klein, and Shelley Minden. London: Pandora Press, 1984.

Ruddick, Sara. "Maternal Thinking." In *Mothering,* ed. Joyce Trebilcot. Totowa, N.J.: Rowman & Allanheld, 1984.

Sherwin, Susan. *No Longer Patient: Feminist Ethics and Health Care.* Philadelphia: Temple University Press, 1992.

"A Surrogate's Story of Loving and Losing." *U.S. News & World Report,* June 6, 1983, p. 12.

Tong, Rosemarie. *Feminist Approaches to Bioethics.* Boulder, Colo.: Westview Press, 1997.

Trebilcot, Joyce, ed. *Mothering: Essays in Feminist Theory.* Totowa, N.J.: Rowman & Allanheld, 1984.

Wilson, Leslie, et al. "'She Could Be Anything She Wants to Be': Mothers and Daughters and Feminist Theory." *Journal of the Association for Research on Mothering* 8, nos. 1 and 2 (September 2006).

Wolf, Susan, ed. *Feminism and Bioethics: Beyond Reproduction.* Oxford: Oxford University Press, 1996.

Critiques of Radical-Libertarian and Radical-Cultural Feminism

Beard, Mary R. *Woman As Force in History.* New York: Collier Books, 1972.

Cocks, Joan. "Wordless Emotions: Some Critical Reflections on Radical Feminism." *Politics and Society* 13, no. 1 (1984): 27–58.

Corrin, Chris. *Desperately Seeking Sisterhood: Still Challenging and Building.* Oxford: Taylor & Francis, 1997.

Coulter, Anne. *Godless: The Church of Liberalism.* New York: Three Rivers Press, 2007.

Elshtain, Jean Bethke. *Public Man, Private Woman.* Princeton, N.J.: Princeton University Press, 1981.

Ferguson, Ann. "The Sex Debate in the Women's Movement: A Socialist-Feminist View." *Against the Current* (September/October 1983).

_____. "Sex War: The Debate Between Radical and Libertarian Feminists." *Signs: Journal of Women in Culture and Society* 10, no. 1 (autumn 1984): 106–112.

Friedan, Betty. *The Second Stage: With a New Introduction.* Boston: Harvard University Press, 1998.

Hirsch, Marianne, and Evelyn Fox Keller. *Conflicts in Feminism.* New York: Routledge, 1990.

Hoff-Sommers, Christina. *Who Stole Feminism? How Women Have Betrayed Women.* New York: Simon & Schuster, 1995.

_____. *The War Against Boys: How Misguided Feminism Is Harming Our Young Men.* New York: Simon & Schuster, 2001.

Jaggar, Alison M. *Feminist Politics and Human Nature.* Totowa, N.J.: Rowman & Allanheld, 1983.

Kassian, Mary A. *The Feminist Mistake: The Radical Impact of Feminism on Church and Culture.* Wheaton, Ill.: Crossway Books, 2005.

Lorde, Audre. "An Open Letter to Mary Daly." In *This Bridge Called My Back,* ed. Cherríe Moraga and Gloria Anzaldúa. Watertown, Mass.: Persephone Press, 1981.

Miriam, Kathy. "Re-thinking Radical Feminism: Opposition, Utopianism and the Moral Imagination of Feminist Theory." *Dissertation Abstracts International. Section A: Humanities and Social Sciences* 59, no. 2 (August 1998): 636.

O'Beirne, Kate. *Women Who Make the World Worse: And How Their Radical Feminist Assault Is Ruining Our Families, Military, Schools, and Sports.* New York: Sentinel, 2006.

Roiphe, Katie. *The Morning After: Sex, Fear and Feminism.* Boston: Back Bay Books, 1994.

Rowbotham, Sheila. *Women, Resistance and Revolution.* New York: Vintage Books, 1972.

Rowland, Robyn, and Renate D. Klcin. "Radical Feminism: Critique and Construct." In *Feminist Knowledge: Critique and Construct,* ed. Sneja Guner. New York: Routledge, 1990.

Siegel, Deborah. *Sisterhood, Interrupted: From Radical Women to Grrls Gone Wild.* Houndsmill, Hampshire, England: Palgrave Macmillan, 2007.

Smith, Craig R. "Multiperspectival Feminist Critiques and Their Implications for Rhetorical Theory." *American Communication Journal* 4, no. 3 (spring 2001): 26–42.

Chapter Three

The Marxist Concept of Human Nature

Buchanan, Allen. *Marx and Justice: The Radical Critique of Liberalism.* Totowa, N.J.: Littlefield, Adams, 1972.

Harding, Sandra. "Two Influential Theories of Ignorance and Philosophy's Interests in Ignoring Them." *Hypatia* 21, no. 3 (summer 2006): 20–36.

Holmstrom, Nancy. "A Marxist Theory of Women's Nature." *Ethics* 94, no. 1 (April 1984): 464.

Marx, Karl. *Capital.* Vol. 3. New York: International Publishers, 1967.

_____. *A Contribution to the Critique of Political Economy.* New York: International Publishers, 1972.

Schmitt, Richard. *Introduction to Marx and Engels.* Boulder, Colo.: Westview Press, 1987.

Slaughter, Cliff. *Marx and Marxism: An Introduction.* New York: Longman, 1985.

Vogel, Lise. *Marxism and the Oppression of Women: Towards a Unitary Theory.* New Brunswick, N.J.: Rutgers University Press, 1983.

The Marxist Theory of Economics

Acton, Henry Burrows. *What Marx Really Said.* London: MacDonald, 1967.

Benston, Margaret. "The Political Economy of Women's Liberation." *Monthly Review* 21, no. 4 (September 1969): 13–27.

Heilbroner, Robert L. *Marxism: For and Against.* New York: W. W. Norton, 1980.

Kuhn, Annette, and Ann Marie Wolpe, eds. *Feminism and Materialism: Women and Modes of Production.* Boston: Routledge & Kegan Paul, 1978.

Mandel, Ernest. *An Introduction to Marxist Economic Theory.* New York: Pathfinder Press, 1970.

Marx, Karl. *Grundrisse: Foundations of the Critique of Political Economy,* trans. and ed. T. B. Bottomore. New York: Vintage Books, 1973.

Suchting, Wallis Arthur. *Marx: An Introduction.* New York: New York University Press, 1983.

The Marxist Theory of Society

Foreman, Ann. *Femininity As Alienation: Women and the Family in Marxism and Psychoanalysis.* London: Pluto Press, 1977.

Marx, Karl. "Economic and Philosophic Manuscripts." In *Early Writings,* trans. and ed. T. B. Bottomore. New York: McGraw-Hill, 1964.

_____. *The 18th Brumaire of Louis Bonaparte.* New York: International Publishers, 1968.

Quick, Paddy. "The Class Nature of Women's Oppression." *Review of Radical Political Economics* 9, no. 3 (winter 1977): 42–53.

Saffiote, Heleieth I. B. *Women in Class Society,* trans. Michael Vale. New York: Monthly Review Press, 1978.

Wood, Allen W. *Karl Marx.* London: Routledge & Kegan Paul, 1981.

The Marxist Theory of Politics

Marx, Karl, and Friedrich Engels. *The German Ideology.* In *The Marx-Engels Reader,* trans. and ed. Robert C. Tucker. New York: W. W. Norton, 1978.

McLellan, David. *Karl Marx.* New York: Penguin Books, 1975.

Friedrich Engels: The Origin of the Family, Private Property and the State

Engels, Friedrich. *The Origin of the Family, Private Property and the State.* New York: International Publishers, 1972.

Flax, Jane. "Do Feminists Need Marxism?" In *Building Feminist Theory: Essays from "Quest," A Feminist Quarterly.* New York: Longman, 1981.

Kruks, Sonia. *Situation and Human Existence: Freedom, Subjectivity and Society.* New York: Routledge, 1990.

Lane, Ann J. "Woman in Society: A Critique of Friedrich Engels." In *Liberating Women's History,* ed. Bernice A. Carroll. Champaign: University of Illinois Press, 1976.

Millett, Kate. *Sexual Politics.* New York: Ballantine Books, 1969.

Oakley, Ann. *Sex, Gender, and Society.* London: Temple Smith, 1972.

Reed, Evelyn. *Problems of Woman's Liberation.* New York: Pathfinder Press, 1970.

Sacks, Karen. "Engels Revisited: Women, the Organization of Production and Private Property." In *Toward an Anthropology of Women,* ed. Rayna R. Reiter. New York: Monthly Review Press, 1975.

Classical Marxist Feminism, and General Reflections on Women's Wage Labor and Domestic Labor

Benston, Margaret. "The Political Economy of Women's Liberation." *Monthly Review* 21, no. 4 (September 1969): 16.

Bergmann, Barbara. *The Economic Emergence of Women.* New York: Basic Books, 1986: p. 212.

Boserup, Esther. *Women's Role in Economic Development.* London: George Allen and Unwin, 1970.

Boxer, Marilyn J. "Rethinking the Socialist Construction and International Career of the Concept 'Bourgeois Feminism.'" *American Historical Review* 112, no. 1 (February 2007): 131–158.

Braudel, Fernand. *Capitalism and Material Life 1400–1800,* trans. Miriam Kochan. New York: Harper & Row, 1973.

Bridenthal, Renate. "The Dialectics of Production and Reproduction in History." *Radical America* 10, no. 2 (March–April 1976): 3–11.

Caulfield, Mina Davis. "Imperialism, the Family, and Cultures of Resistance." *Socialist Revolution* 20, no. 4 (October 1974): 67–85.

Cowan, Ruth Schwartz. "The 'Industrial Revolution' in the Home: Household Technology and Social Change in the Twentieth Century." *Technology and Culture* 17, no. 1 (1976): 1–23.

Ferguson, Ann. "The Che-Lumumba School: Creating a Revolutionary Family-Community." *Quest* 5, no. 3 (February–March 1980).

Freedman, Estelle. *No Turning Back: The History of Feminism and the Future of Women.* New York: Ballantine Books, 2002.

Gottfried, Paul Edward. *The Strange Death of Marxism.* Columbia: University of Missouri Press, 2005.

Guettel, Charnie. *Marxism and Feminism.* Toronto: Women's Education Press, 1974.

Humphries, Jane. "The Working Class Family, Women's Liberation and Class Struggle: The Case of Nineteenth Century British History." *Review of Radical Political Economics* 9, no. 3 (fall 1977): 25–41.

Landes, Joan B. "Women, Labor and Family Life: A Theoretical Perspective." *Science and Society* 41, no. 1 (spring 1977): 386–409.

Lenin, V. I. *The Emancipation of Women: From the Writings of V. I. Lenin.* New York: International Publishers, 1934.

Levine, Rhonda, ed. *Social Class and Stratification: Classic Statements and Theoretical Debates.* Lanham, Md.: Rowman and Littlefield Publishers, 2006.

MacKinnon, Catharine A. "Feminism, Marxism, Method, and the State: An Agenda for Theory." *Signs: Journal of Women in Culture and Society* 7, no. 3 (spring 1982): 515–545.

_____. "Feminism, Marxism, Method and the State: An Agenda for Theory." *Signs: Journal of Women in Culture and Society* 7, no. 3 (spring 1982): 515–544.

Mitterauer, Michael, and Reinhard Sieder. *The European Family: Patriarchy to Partnership from the Middle Ages to the Present,* trans. Karla Oosterveen and Manfred Horzinger. Oxford: Blackwell, 1982.

Rosenberg, Charles E., ed. *The Family in History.* Philadelphia: University of Pennsylvania Press, 1975.

Scott, Linda M. "Market Feminism: The Case for a Paradigm Shift." *Advertising & Society Review* 7, no. 2 (2006).

Tilly, Louise A., and Joan W. Scott. *Women, Work, and Family.* New York: Holt, Rinehart and Winston, 1978.

U.S. Department of Labor. *Employment Standards Administration Wage and Hour Division.* January 1, 2007. Available at www.dol.gov/esa/minwage/america.htm#content.

Waters, Mary-Alice. *Feminism and the Marxist Movement.* New York: Pathfinder Press, 1994.

Webster, Bruce H. Jr., and Alemayehu Bishaw. *Income, Earnings, and Poverty Data from the 2005 American Community Survey: American Community Survey Reports.* U.S. Census Bureau, American Community Survey Reports, ACS–02. Washington, D.C.: U.S. Government Printing Office, August 2006. Available at www.census.gov/prod/2006pubs/acs–02.pdf, p. 7.

Weigand, Kate. *Red Feminism: American Communism and the Making of Women's Liberation.* Baltimore: Johns Hopkins University Press, 2001.

Weinbaum, Batya, and Amy Bridges. "The Other Side of the Paycheck: Monopoly Capital and the Structure of Conscription." *Monthly Review* 28, no. 3 (July–August 1976): 88–103.

Wolton, Suke, ed. *Marxism, Mysticism, and Modern Theory.* New York: St. Martin's Press, 1996.

Wright, Erik Olin. "Explanation and Emancipation in Marxism and Feminism." *Sociological Theory* 11, no. 1 (March 1993): 39–54.

Zarestsky, Eli. "Capitalism, the Family, and Personal Life." *Socialist Revolution* 3, nos. 1–2 (January–April 1973): 69–125.

The Wages-for-Housework Campaign

Barrett, Michèle, and Mary McIntosh. "The Family Wage: Some Problems for Socialists and Feminists." *Capital and Class* 2 (1980): 51–57.

Beechey, Veronica. "Some Notes on Female Wage Labour in Capitalist Production." *Capital and Class* 3 (autumn 1977): 45–66.

Brenner, Johanna, and Nancy Holmstrom. "Women's Self-Organization: Theory and Strategy." *Monthly Review* 34, no. 11 (April 1983): 40.

Brenner, Johanna, and Maria Ramas. "Rethinking Women's Oppression." *New Left Review* 144 (March–April 1984): 71.

Coulson, Margaret, Branka Magas, and Hilary Wainwright. "'The Housewife and Her Labour Under Capitalism': A Critique." *New Left Review* 89 (January–February 1975): 59–71.

Dalla Costa, Mariarosa. "A General Strike." In *All Work and No Pay*, ed. Wendy Edmond and Suzie Fleming. London: Power of Women Collective and Falling Wall Press, 1975.

Dalla Costa, Mariarosa, and Selma James. *The Power of Women and the Subversion of Community*. Bristol, England: Falling Wall Press, 1972.

Davin, Delia. *Woman-Work: Women and the Party in Revolutionary China*. Oxford: Clarendon Press, 1976.

Edmond, Wendy, and Suzie Fleming. "If Women Were Paid for All They Do." In *All Work and No Pay*, ed. Wendy Edmond and Suzie Fleming. London: Power of Women Collective and Falling Wall Press, 1975.

Gardiner, Susan. "Women's Domestic Labour." *New Left Review* 89 (January–February 1975): 47–58.

Garson, Barbara. *All the Livelong Day: The Meaning and Demeaning of Routine Work*. New York: Penguin Books, 1975.

Gerstein, Ira. "Domestic Work and Capitalism." *Radical America* 7, nos. 4–5 (July–October 1973): 101–128.

Glazer-Malbin, Nona. "Housework." *Signs: Journal of Women in Culture and Society* 1, no. 4 (1976): 905–922.

Gordon, David M., Richard Edwards, and Michael Reich. *Segmented Work, Divided Workers*. New York: Cambridge University Press, 1982.

Hartmann, Heidi I. "The Family As the Locus of Gender, Class, and Political Struggle: The Example of Housework." *Signs: Journal of Women in Culture and Society* 6, no. 3 (1981): 366–394.

Holmstrom, Nancy. "'Women's Work,' the Family and Capitalism." *Science and Society* 45, no. 1 (spring 1981): 208.

Jackson, Stevi. "Towards a Historical Sociology of Housework." *Women's Studies International Forum* 15, no. 2 (1992): 153–172.

_____. "Marxism and Feminism," in *Marxism and Social Science,* ed. Andrew Gamble, David Marsh, and Tony Tant. Champaign: University of Illinois Press, 1999: p. 17.

Kaluzynska, Eva. "Wiping the Floor with Theory: A Survey of Writings on Housework." *Feminist Review* 6 (1980): 27–54.

Lopate, Carol. "Pay for Housework?" *Social Policy* 5, no. 3 (September–October 1974): 28.

Malos, Ellen, ed. *The Politics of Housework.* London: Allison & Busby, 1980.

Molyneux, Maxine. "Beyond the Domestic Labour Debate." *New Left Review* 116 (July–August 1979): 3–27.

Nicholson, Linda J. *Gender and History: The Limits of Social Theory in the Age of the Family.* New York: Columbia University Press, 1986.

Scott, Anne Crittenden. "The Value of Housework for Love or Money?" *Ms.*, June 1972, pp. 56–58.

Secombe, Wally. "The Housewife and Her Labour Under Capitalism." *New Left Review* 83 (January–February 1973): 3–24.

Walby, Sylvia. *Patriarchy at Work.* Cambridge: Polity Press, 1986.

_____. "Policy Developments for Workplace Gender Equity in a Global Era: The Importance of the EU in the UK." *Review of Policy Research* 20, no. 1 (spring 2003): 45.

Contemporary Socialist Feminism: Focus on Classism and Sexism, and General Reflections on Relationship Between Capitalism and Patriarchy

Beneria, Lourdes. "Capitalism and Socialism: Some Feminist Questions." In *The Women, Gender, and Development Reader,* ed. Visanthan Nalini et al.. Atlantic Highlands, N.J.: ZED Books, 1997.

Bureau of Labor Statistics, U.S. Department of Labor. "Median Weekly Earnings of Full-Time Wage and Salary Workers by Detailed Occupation and Sex." January 2006. Available at ftp://ftp.bls.gov/pub/special.requests/lf/aat39.txt.

Delphy, Christine. *Close to Home: A Materialist Analysis of Women's Oppression,* trans. and ed. Diana Leonard. Amherst: University of Massachusetts Press, 1984.

Easton, Barbara. "Socialism and Feminism I: Toward a Unified Movement." *Socialist Revolution* 4, no. 1 (January–March 1974): 59–67.

Ehrenreich, Barbara. "Life Without Father: Reconsidering Socialist-Feminist Theory." *Socialist Review* 14, no. 1 (January–March 1974): 59–67.

_____. "What Is Socialist Feminism?" *Win,* June 3, 1976, pp. 4–7.

Eisenstein, Zillah, ed. *Capitalist Patriarchy and the Case for Socialist Feminism.* New York: Monthly Review Press, 1979.

Ferree, Myra Marx. "Patriarchies and Feminisms: Two Women's Movements in Post-Unification Germany." *Social Politics* (spring 1995): 10–24.

Friedman, Marilyn. "Nancy J. Hirschmann on the Social Construction of Women's Freedom." *Hypatia* 21, no. 4 (fall 2006): 182–191.

Graff, E. J. "The Opt-Out Myth." *Columbia Journalism Review* (March/April 2007). Available at www.cjr.org/issuess/2007/2/Graff.asp.

Guenther, Katja M. "'A Bastion of Sanity in a Crazy World:' A Local Feminist Movement and the Reconstitution of Scale, Space, and Place in an Eastern German City." *Advance Access* (winter 2006): 551–575.

Hartmann, Heidi I. "The Unhappy Marriage of Marxism and Feminism: Towards a More Progressive Union." In *Women and Revolution: A Discussion of the Unhappy Marriage of Marxism and Feminism,* ed. Lydia Sargent. Boston: South End Press, 1981.

_____. "Capitalism, Patriarchy, and Job Segregation by Sex." In *Capitalist Patriarchy and the Case for Socialist Feminism,* ed. Zillah Eisenstein. New York: Monthly Review Press, 1979.

_____. "The Unhappy Marriage of Marxism and Feminism: Towards a More Progressive Union." In *Women and Revolution: A Discussion of the Unhappy Marriage of Marxism and Feminism,* ed. Lydia Sargent. Boston: South End Press, 1981.

Holmstrom, Nancy, ed. *The Socialist Feminist Project: A Contemporary Reader in Theory and Politics.* New York: Monthly Review Press, 2002.

Jaggar, Alison. *Feminist Politics and Human Nature.* Totowa, N.J.: Rowman & Allanheld, 1983.

_____. "Prostitution." In *Women and Values: Readings in Recent Feminist Philosophy,* ed. Marilyn Pearsall. Belmont, Calif.: Wadsworth, 1986.

Mitchell, Juliet. *Psychoanalysis and Feminism.* New York: Vintage Books, 1974.

_____. *Woman's Estate.* New York: Pantheon Books, 1971.

_____. "Women: The Longest Revolution." *New Left Review* 40 (November–December 1966): 11–37.

Nicholson, Linda J. *Gender and History: The Limits of Social Theory in the Age of the Family.* New York: Columbia University Press, 1986.

Page, Margaret. "Socialist Feminism: A Political Alternative." *m/f* 2 (1978).

"Part-Time Programs Do Help Firms Hold on to Women Lawyers." *Law Office Management & Administration Report* 7, no. 5 (May 2007): 3.

Phelps, Linda. "Patriarchy and Capitalism." *Quest* 2, no. 2 (fall 1975): 35–48.

Radical Women's 23rd Anniversary Conference General Membership. *The Radical Women Manifesto: Socialist Feminist Theory, Program and Organizational Structure.* Seattle: Red Letter Press, 2001.

Rowbotham, Sheila, Lynne Segal, and Hilary Wainwright. *Beyond the Fragments: Feminism and the Making of Socialism.* London: Merlin Press, 1979.

Smith, Sharon. *Women and Socialism: Essays on Women's Liberation.* Chicago: Haymarket Books, 2005.

Weinbaum, Batya. *The Curious Courtship of Women's Liberation and Socialism.* Boston: South End Press, 1978.

Young, Iris. "The Ideal of Community and the Politics of Difference." In *Feminism/ Postmodernism,* ed. Linda J. Nicholson. New York: Routledge, 1990.

_____. "Socialist Feminism and the Limits of Dual Systems Theory." *Socialist Review* 10, nos. 2–3 (March–June 1980): 174.

_____. "Beyond the Unhappy Marriage: A Critique of the Dual Systems Theory," in *Women and Revolution: A Discussion of the Unhappy Marriage of Marxism and Feminism,* ed. Lydia Sargent. Boston: South End Press, 1981, p. 428.

Women's Labor Issues:
Pay Gap

Bar-Lev, Abby. "Equal Pay Still Unequal." *Minnesota Daily,* November 30, 2006. Available at www.mndaily.com/articles/2006/11/30/70093.

Bergmann, Barbara. *The Economic Emergence of Women.* New York: Basic Books, 1986.

Bowers, Katherine. "Ruling OKs Class Action Suit Against Wal-Mart." *WWD: Women's Wear Daily* 193, no. 29 (February 7, 2007): 39.

Equal Pay Act of 1963 (Pub. L. 88–93) (EPA), as amended, as it appears in volume 29 of the United States Code, at section 206(d).

Scott, Hilda. *Working Your Way to the Bottom.* London: Pandora Press, 1984.

Thomas, G. Scott. "Where the Men, and Women, Work." *American City Business Journals,* April 19, 2004. Available at www.bizjournals.com/edit_special/12/html.

Women's Labor Issues:
Comparable Worth

Amott, Teresa, and Julie Matthaei. "Comparable Worth, Incomparable Pay." *Radical America* 18, no. 5 (September–October 1984): 25.

Feldberg, Roslyn L. "Comparable Worth: Toward Theory and Practice in the United States." *Signs: Journal of Women in Culture and Society,* 10, no. 2 (winter 1984): 311–313.

Hennessy-Fiske, Molly. "Gender Pay Gap Narrows—for Unexpected Reasons." *Los Angeles Times,* December 3, 2006, A23.

Lamar, Jake. "A Worthy but Knotty Question." *Time,* February 6, 1984, p. 30.

Nussbaum, Karen. "Women Clerical Workers." *Socialist Review* 10, no. 1 (January –February 1980): 151–159.

"Paying Women What They're Worth." *QQ Report from the Center for Philosophy and Public Policy* 3, no. 2 (spring 1983).

Pfister, Bonnie. "It's National Equal Pay Day—and U.S. Women Earn 77 Cents to a Man's Dollar." *San Antonia Express-News,* April 20, 2004.

Remick, Helen. "Major Issues in A Priori Applications." In *Comparable Worth and Wage Discrimination: Technical Possibilities and Political Realities,* ed. Helen Remick. Philadelphia: Temple University Press, 1984.

Sixel, L. M. "EEOC Alleges Unequal Pay for Same Work." *Houston Chronicle,* August 23, 2005, p. 94.

Women's Labor Issues:
Global Market

Burn, Shawn Meghan. *Women Across Cultures: A Global Perspective.* Mountain View, Calif.: Mayfield Publishing Company, 2000.

Clarke, Simon. *Keynesianism, Monetarism and the Crisis of the State.* Aldershot: Edward Elgar, 1988, p. 177.

Friedman, Jonathan. "Global System, Globalization and the Parameters of Modernity." In *Global Modernities,* ed. Mike Featherstone et al. London: Sage, 1995, p. 77.

Giddens, Anthony. *Consequences of Modernity.* Cambridge: Polity Press, 1990, p. 64.

Lash, Scott, and John Urry, *Economies of Signs and Space.* London: Sage, 1994.

Luxemburg, Rosa. "The National Question and Autonomy." In *The National Question: Selected Writings by Rosa Luxemburg,* ed. Horace B. Davis. New York: Monthly Review Press, 1976.

Robertson, Roland. *Globalization.* London: Sage, 1992.

_____. "Globalization: Time-Space and Homogeneity-Heterogeneity." In *Global Modernities,* ed. Mike Featherstone et al. London: Sage, 1995, p. 27.

Rosenberg, Justin. *The Empire of Civil Society.* London: Verso, 1994.

Scott, Linda M. "Market Feminism: The Case for a Paradigm Shift." *Advertising and Society Review* 7, no. 2 (2006).

Shaw, Martin. *Global Society and International Relations.* Cambridge: Polity Press, 1994.

Smart, Barry. *Postmodernism.* London: Routledge, 1993, p. 173.

Tsutsui, Kiyoteru. "Redressing Past Human Rights Violations: Global Dimensions of Contemporary Social Movements." *Social Forces* 85, no. 1 (2006): 331–354.

Wallerstein, Immanuel. *The Modern World System I: Capitalist Agriculture and the Origins of the European World-Economy in the Sixteenth Century.* New York: Academic Press, 1974.

_____. *The Modern World System II: Mercantilism and the Consolidation of the European World-Economy, 1600–1750.* New York: Academic Press, 1980.

_____. *The Modern World System III: The Second Era of Great Expansion of the Capitalist World-Economy, 1730–1840s.* New York: Academic Press, 1989.

World Bank Group. "Globalization." Web page of World Bank Group, 2001. Available at www.worldbank.org/globalization+globalization&hl=en&clnk&cd=3&gl=us.

Critiques of Classical Marxist and Contemporary Socialist Feminism

Adams, Parveen, Beverly Brown, and Elizabeth Cowie. "Editorial." *m/f* 1 (1978): 3–5.

Anyon, Jean. "The Retread of Marxism and Socialist Feminism: Postmodern and Poststructural Theories in Education." *Curriculum Inquiry* 24, no. 2 (summer 1994): 115–133.

Barrett, Michèle. *Women's Oppression Today: Problems in Marxist Feminist Analysis.* London: Verso and New Left Books, 1980.

———. "Words and Things: Materialism and Method in Contemporary Feminist Analysis." In *Destabilizing Theory: Contemporary Feminist Debates,* ed. Michèle Barrett and Anne Phillips. Oxford: Polity Press, 1992.

Bartky, Sandra L. *Femininity and Domination.* New York: Routledge, 1990.

———. "Narcissism, Femininity and Alienation." *Social Theory and Practice* 8, no. 2 (summer 1982): 127–144.

———. "On Psychological Oppression." In *Philosophy and Women,* ed. Sharon Bishop and Marjorie Weinzweig. Belmont, Calif.: Wadsworth, 1979.

Beasley, Chris. *What Is Feminism?* London: Sage Publications, 1999, pp. 62–64.

Berch, Bettina. *The Endless Day: The Political Economy of Women and Work.* New York: Harcourt Brace Jovanovich, 1982.

Carby, Hazel. "White Women Listen! Black Feminism and the Boundaries of Sisterhood." In *The Empire Strikes Back: Race and Racism in 70s Britain,* ed. Centre for Contemporary Cultural Studies. London: Hutchinson, 1982.

Coward, Rosalind, and John Ellis. *Language and Materialism.* London: Routledge & Kegan Paul, 1977.

Crowley, Helen. "Women's Studies: Between a Rock and a Hard Place or Just Another Cell in the Beehive?" *Feminism Review: Snakes and Ladders: Reviewing Feminisms at Century's End* (spring 1999): 131–150.

Delphy, Christine. *Close to Home: A Materialist Analysis of Women's Oppression,* trans. and ed. Diana Leonard. London: Hutchinson, 1984.

Delphy, Christine, and Diana Leonard. *Familiar Exploitation: A New Analysis of Marriage in Contemporary Western Societies.* Cambridge: Polity Press, 1992.

Dietz, Mary G. "Current Controversies in Feminist Theory." *Annual Review* (2003): 399–421.

Elshtain, Jean Bethke. *Public Man, Private Woman.* Princeton: N.J.: Princeton University Press, 1981.

Ferree, Myra Marx. "The Rise of 'Mommy Politics': Feminism and Unification in (East) Germany." *Feminist Studies* 19 (1993): 89–115.

Flax, Jane, "Postmodernism and Gender in Feminist Theory." In *Feminism/Postmodernism,* ed. Linda J. Nicholson. New York: Routledge, 1990.

Fraser, Nancy, and Linda J. Nicholson. "Social Criticism Without Philosophy: An Encounter Between Feminism and Postmodernism." In *Feminism/Postmodernism,* ed. Linda J. Nicholson. New York: Routledge, 1990.

Friedman, Marilyn. "Nancy J. Hirschmann on the Social Construction of Women's Freedom." *Hypatia* 21, no. 4 (fall 2006): 182–183.

Funk, Nanette, and Magda Mueller, eds. *Gender Politics and Post Communism.* New York: Routledge, 1993.

Gal, Susan, and Gail, Kligman. *The Politics of Gender after Socialism.* Princeton, N.J.: Princeton University Press, 2000.

_____, eds. *Reproducing Gender: Politics, Publics, and Everyday Life After Socialism.* Princeton, N.J.: Princeton University Press, 2000.

Gimenez, Martha E. "What's Material About Materialist Feminism? A Marxist Feminist Critique." *Radical Philosophy* (May 1–June 2000).

Groenhout, Ruth E. *Philosophy, Feminism, and Faith.* Bloomington: Indiana University Press, 2003.

Harding, Sandra. "The Instability of the Analytical Categories of Feminist Theory." *Signs: Journal of Women and Culture and Society* 11, no. 4 (1987): 645–665.

_____. "Two Influential Theories of Ignorance and Philosophy's Interests in Ignoring Them." *Hypatia* 21, no. 3 (summer 2006): 20–36.

Hartmann, Heidi, and Ann R. Markusen. "Contemporary Marxist Theory and Practice: A Feminist Critique." *Review of Radical Political Economics* 12, no. 2 (summer 1980): 87–93.

Martin, Gloria. *Socialist Feminism: The First Decade, 1966–1976.* Seattle: Freedom Socialist Publications, 1978.

Mitchell, Juliet. *Psychoanalysis and Feminism.* Harmondsworth: Penguin, 1975.

Modleski, Tania. *Feminism Without Women.* New York: Routledge, 1991.

Questions Féministes Collective. "Variations on a Common Theme" (editorial to *Questions Féministes* 1). Reprinted in *New French Feminisms,* ed. Elaine Marks and Isabelle de Courtivron. Brighton, U.K.: Harvester, 1981.

Rosaldo, Marilyn. "Women, Culture, and Society: A Theoretical Overview." In *Women, Culture, and Society,* ed. Marilyn Rosaldo and Louise Lamphere. Stanford, Calif.: Stanford University Press, 1974.

Rowbotham, Sheila. *Woman's Consciousness, Man's World.* Baltimore: Penguin Books, 1973.

Sargent, Lydia, ed. *Women and Revolution: A Discussion of the Unhappy Marriage of Marxism and Feminism.* Boston: South End Press, 1981.

Spivak, Gayatri Chakravorty. *In Other Worlds.* New York: Routledge, 1988.

Taylor, Barbara. "Lords of Creation: Marxism, Feminism and 'Utopian Socialism.'" In *Reader in Feminist Knowledge,* ed. Sneja Gunew. New York: Routledge, 1991, pp. 360–365.

Voronina, Olga. "Soviet Patriarchy: Past and Present." *Hypatia* 8, no. 4 (fall 1993): 107.

West Coast Poverty Center. "Poor Families with Children, 2005." Chart in "Poverty and the American Family," Web page of West Coast Poverty Center, University of Washington, Seattle. U.S. Census Bureau, Current Population Survey, 2005, West Coast Poverty Center. Available at http://wcpc.washington.edu/basics/family.shtml.

Chapter Four

Sigmund Freud

Bernstein, Anne E., and Gloria Marmar Warna. *An Introduction to Contemporary Psychoanalysis.* New York: J. Aronson, 1981.

Cohen, Ira H. *Ideology and Unconscious: Reich, Freud, and Marx.* New York: New York University Press, 1982.

Erdelyi, Matthew Hugh. *Psychoanalysis: Freud's Cognitive Psychology.* New York: W. H. Freeman, 1984.

Freud, Sigmund. *Civilization and Its Discontents,* trans. James Strachey. New York: W. W. Norton, 1962.

_____. "Femininity." In Sigmund Freud, *The Complete Introductory Lectures on Psychoanalysis,* , trans. and ed. James Strachey. New York: W. W. Norton, 1966.

_____. *Sexuality and the Psychology of Love.* New York: Collier Books, 1968.

_____. *The Standard Edition of the Complete Psychological Works of Sigmund Freud.* Vol. 12. London: Hogarth Press, 1971.

_____. "Totem and Taboo." In *The Standard Edition of the Complete Psychological Works of Sigmund Freud,* trans. and ed. James Strachey. New York: W. W. Norton, 1966.

Gay, Peter. *Freud: A Life for Our Time.* New York: W. W. Norton, 1988.

Hall, Calvin Springer. *A Primer of Freudian Psychology.* New York: New American Library, 1954.

Joes, Ernest. *The Life and Work of Sigmund Freud.* New York: Basic Books, 1961.

Laplanche, Jean. *The Language of Psychoanalysis.* New York: W. W. Norton, 1973.

Lichtman, Richard. *The Production of Desire: The Integration of Psychoanalysis into Marxist Theory.* New York: Free Press, 1982.

Reppen, Joseph, ed. *Beyond Freud: A Study of Modern Psychoanalytic Theorists.* Hillsdale, N.J.: Analytic Press, 1985.

Roazen, Paul. *Freud: Political and Social Thought.* New York: Alfred A. Knopf, 1968.

Feminist Critiques of Freud

Adler, Alfred. *Understanding Human Nature.* New York: Greenberg, 1927.

Beauvoir, Simone de. *The Second Sex,* trans. and ed. H. M. Parshley. New York: Vintage Books, 1974.

Firestone, Shulamith. *The Dialectic of Sex.* New York: Bantam Books, 1970.

Freud, Sigmund. *Dora: An Analysis of a Case of Hysteria,* ed. Philip Rieff. New York: Collier Books, 1963.

Friedan, Betty. *The Feminine Mystique.* New York: Dell, 1974.

Izenberg, Gerald N. *The Existentialist Critique of Freud: The Crisis of Autonomy.* Princeton, N.J.:. Princeton University Press, 1976.

Klein, Viola. *The Feminine Character.* London: Routledge & Kegan Paul, 1971.

Millett, Kate. *Sexual Politics.* New York: Ballantine Books, 1969.

Van Herik, Judith. *Freud on Femininity and Faith.* Berkeley: University of California Press, 1982.

Voloshinov, V. N. *Freudianism: A Marxist Critique.* New York: Academic Press, 1976.

Early Feminist Appropriations of Freud's Thought

Adler, Alfred. *Understanding Human Nature.* New York: Greenberg, 1927.

Deutsch, Helene. *The Psychology of Women: A Psychoanalytic Interpretation.* New York: Grune & Stratten, 1944.

Garrison, Dee. "Karen Horney and Feminism." *Signs: Journal of Women in Culture and Society* 6, no. 4 (1981): 672–691.

Horney, Karen. "The Flight from Womanhood." In *Feminine Psychology.* New York: W. W. Norton, 1973.

Kofman, Sarah. *The Enigma of Woman: Woman in Freud's Writings.* Ithaca, N.Y.: Cornell University Press, 1985.

Miller, Jean Baker, ed. *Psychoanalysis and Women.* Baltimore: Penguin Books, 1974.

Rudnick Jacobsohn, Susan. "An Ambiguous Legacy." *Women's Review of Books* 5, no. 4 (January 1988): 22.

Thompson, Clara. "Problems of Womanhood." In *Interpersonal Psychoanalysis: The Selected Papers of Clara Thompson,* ed. M. P. Green. New York: Basic Books, 1964.

Later Feminist Appropriations of Freud's Thought

Chodorow, Nancy. *The Reproduction of Mothering: Psychoanalysis and the Sociology of Gender.* Berkeley: University of California Press, 1978.

Dinnerstein, Dorothy. *The Mermaid and the Minotaur: Sexual Arrangements and Human Malaise.* New York: Harper Colophon Books, 1977.

Elshtain, Jean Bethke. *Public Man, Private Woman.* Princeton, N.J.: Princeton University Press, 1981.

Mitchell, Juliet. *Psychoanalysis and Feminism.* New York: Vintage Books, 1974.

————. *Women's Estate.* New York: Pantheon Books, 1971.

Ortner, Sherry B. "Oedipal Father, Mother's Brother, and the Penis: A Review of Juliet Mitchell's *Psychoanalysis and Feminism.*" *Feminist Studies* 2, no. 2–3 (1975): 179.

Piercy, Marge. *Woman on the Edge of Time.* New York: Fawcett Crest, 1976.

Rich, Adrienne. "Compulsory Heterosexuality and Lesbian Existence." In *The Signs Reader: Women, Gender, and Scholarship,* ed. Elizabeth Abel and Emily K. Abel. Chicago: University of Chicago Press, 1983, p. 182.

Vetterling-Braggin, Mary, ed. *"Femininity," "Masculinity," and "Androgyny."* Totowa, N.J.: Rowman & Littlefield, 1982.

Williams, Juanita. *Psychology of Women: Behavior in a Biosocial Context.* New York: W. W. Norton, 1977.

Jacques Lacan's Thought

Derrida, Jacques. "The Ends of Man." In *Margins of Philosophy,* trans. Alan Bass. Sussex: Harvester, 1982.

Duchen, Claire. *Feminism in France: From May '68 to Mitterrand.* London: Routledge & Kegan Paul, 1986.

Lacan, Jacques. *Écrits: A Selection,* trans. Alan Sheridan. New York: W. W. Norton, 1977.

_____. *The Language of the Self.* Baltimore: Johns Hopkins University Press, 1968.

Mitchell, Juliet, and Jacqueline Rose. *Feminine Sexuality: Jacques Lacan and the Ècole Freudienne.* New York: W.W. Norton, 1983.

Ragland-Sullivan, Ellie. *Jacques Lacan and the Philosophy of Psychoanalyses.* Chicago: University of Illinois Press, 1986.

Ragland-Sullivan, Ellie, and Mark Bracher. *Lacan and the Subject of Language.* New York: Routledge, 1991.

Roudinesco, Elisabeth. *Jacques Lacan,* trans. Barbara Bray. New York: Columbia University Press, 1999.

Weedon, Chris. *Feminist Practice & Poststructuralist Theory.* New York: Basil Blackwell, 1987.

Feminist Appropriations of Lacan's Thought: Luce Irigary and Julia Kristeva

Beardsworth, Sara. "Freud's Oedipus and Kristeva's Narcissus: Three Heterogeneities." *Hypatia* 20, no. 1 (winter 2005): 54–77.

_____. *Julia Kristeva: Psychoanalyses and Modernity.* Albany: SUNY Press, 2004.

Brennan, Teresa, ed. *Between Feminism and Psychoanalyses.* New York: Routledge, 1989.

Burke, Carolyn, et al., eds. *Engaging with Irigaray: Feminist Philosophy and Modern European Thought.* New York: Columbus University Press, 1995.

Butler, Judith. "The Body Politics of Julia Kristeva." In *Revaluing French Feminism,* ed. Nancy Fraser and Sandra Lee Bartky. Bloomington: Indiana University Press, 1992.

Chanter, Tina. *Ethics of Eros: Irigaray's Re-Writing of the Philosophers.* New York: Routledge, 1995.

Chodorow, Nancy. "Toward a Relational Individualism: The Mediation of Self Through Psychoanalysis." In *Reconstructing Individualism: Autonomy, Individual-*

ity, and the Self in Western Thought, ed. Thomas C. Heller, Morton Sosna, and David E. Wellbury. Stanford, Calif.: Stanford University Press, 1986.

Engel, Stephanie. "Femininity As Tragedy: Re-examining the 'New Narcissism.'" *Socialist Review* 10, no. 5 (September–October 1980): 77–104.

Fuss, Diana J. "'Essentially Speaking": Luce Irigaray's Language of Essence.' In *Revaluing French Feminism,* ed. Nancy Fraser and Sandra Lee Bartky. Bloomington: Indiana University Press, 1992, pp. 94–112.

Gallap, Jane. *Reading Lacan.* Ithaca, N.Y., and London: Cornell University Press, 1985.

Irigaray, Luce. *Speculum of the Other Woman,* trans. Gillian C. Gill. Ithaca, N.Y.: Cornell University Press, 1985.

_____. *This Sex Which Is Not One,* trans. Catherine Porter. Ithaca, N.Y.: Cornell University Press, 1985.

_____. "Is the Subject of Science Sexed?" trans. Carol Mastrangelo Bové. *Hypatia* 2, no. 3 (fall 1987): 65–87.

_____. "Sorcerer Love: A Reading of Plato's Symposium, Diotima's Speech." In *Revaluing French Feminism,* ed. Nancy Fraser and Sandra Lee Bartky. Bloomington: Indiana University Press, 1992): 64–76.

Kozel, Susan. "The Diabolical Strategy of Mimesis: Luce Irigaray Reading of Maurice Merleau-Ponty," *Hypatia* 11, no. 3 (summer 1996): 114–129.

Kristeva, Julia. "Cillation du 'Pouvoir' au Refus." Interview by Xavière Gauthier for *Tel Quel* 58 (summer 1974). In *New French Feminisms,* ed. Elaine Marks and Isabelle de Courtivron. New York: Schocken Classics, 1981.

_____. "The Novel As Polylogue." In *Desire in Language,* trans. Leon S. Roudiez, and ed. Thomas Gora, Alice Jardine, and Leon S. Roudiez. New York: Columbia University Press, 1990.

_____. *Powers of Horror,* trans. Leon Roudiez. New York: Columbia University Press, 1982.

_____. *The Sense and Non-Sense of Revolt: The Powers and Limitations of Psychoanalysis.* Vol. 1, trans. Janine Herman. New York: Columbia University Press, 2000.

_____. *In the Beginning Was Love: Psychoanalysis and Faith.* New York: Columbia University Press, 1987.

Kuykendall, Eleanor H. "Introduction to *Sorcerer Love* by Luce Irigaray." In *Revaluing French Feminism,* ed. Nancy Fraser and Sandra Lee Bartky. Bloomington: Indiana University Press, 1992): 60–63.

Leland, Dorothy. "Lacanian Psychoanalysis and French Feminism: Toward an Adequate Political Psychology," *Hypatia* 3, no. 3 (winter 1989).

Margaroni, Maria. "The Lost Foundation": Kristeva's Semiotic Chora and Its Ambiguous Legacy." *Hypatia,* 20, no. 1 (winter 2005): 78–98.

Meyers, Diana T. "The Subversion of Women's Agency in Psychoanalytic Feminism: Chodorow, Flox, Kristeva." In *Revaluing French Feminism,* ed. Nancy Fraser and Sandra Lee Bartky. Bloomington: Indiana University Press, 1992, pp. 136–161.

Mitchell, Juliet and Jacqueline Rose. *Feminine Sexuality: Jacques Lacan and the École Freudienne.* New York: W.W. Norton and Company, 1982.

Moi, Toril. *Sexual/Textual Politics: Feminist Literary Theory.* New York: Methuen, 1985.

Nye, Andrea. "The Hidden Host: Irigaray and Diotima at Plato's Symposium." In *Revaluing French Feminism,* ed. Nancy Fraser and Sandra Lee Bartky. Bloomington: Indiana University Press, 1992, 77–93.

Oliver, Kelly. "Julia Kristeva's Feminist Revolutions," *Hypatia* 8, no. 3 (summer 1993): 94–114.

Schmitz, Bettina. "Homelessness or Symbolic Castration? Subjectivity, Language Acquisition, and Sociality in Julia Kristeva and Jacques Lacan," trans. Julia Jansen. *Hypatia* 20, no. 2 (spring 2005): 69–87.

Udovicki, Jasminka. "Justice and Care in Close Associations," *Hypatia* 8, no. 3 (summer 1993): 48–60.

Whitford, Margaret. *Luce Irigaray: Philosophy in the Feminine.* New York and London: Routledge, 1991.

Wiseman, Mary. "Renaissance Madonna and the Fantasies of Freud," *Hypatia* 8, no. 3 (summer 1993): 115–135.

Conclusion

Bordo, Susan. "Feminism, Postmodernism, and Gender-Scepticism." In *Feminism/ Postmodernism,* ed. Linda J. Nicholson. New York: Routledge, 1990.

Butler, Judith. *Gender Trouble: Feminism and the Subversion of Identity.* New York: Routledge, 1990.

Chesler, Phyllis. *Women and Madness.* Garden City, N.Y.: Doubleday, 1972.

Cockburn, David. *Other Human Beings.* New York: St. Martin's Press, 1992.

Cott, Nancy. *The Grounding of Modern Feminism.* New Haven, Conn.: Yale University Press, 1987.

Eisenstein, Hester. *Contemporary Feminist Thought.* Boston: G. K. Hall, 1983.

Gallop, Jane. *The Daughter's Seduction: Feminism and Psychoanalysis.* Ithaca, N.Y.: Cornell University Press, 1982.

Grimshaw, Jean. *Philosophy and Feminist Thinking.* Minneapolis: University of Minnesota Press, 1986.

Harding, Sandra. "Two Influential Theories of Ignorance and Philosophy's Interests in Ignoring Them." *Hypatia* 21, no. 3 (summer 2006): 20–36.

Chapter Five

The Roots of Care-Focused Feminism: Carol Gilligan and Nel Noddings

Bowden, Peta. *Caring: Gender Sensitive Ethics.* London: Routledge, 1997.

Bubeck, Diemut. *Care, Gender, and Justice.* Oxford: Claredon Press, 1995.

Clement, Grace. *Care, Autonomy and Justice: Feminism and the Ethic of Care.* Boulder, Colo.: Westview Press, 1996.

Dinnerstein, Dorothy. *The Mermaid and the Minotaur: Sexual Arrangements and Human Malaise.* New York: Harper and Row, 1977.

Fisher, Berenice, and Joan Tronto. "Toward a Feminist Theory of Caring." In *Circles of Care,* ed. Emily Abel and Margaret Nelson. Albany: SUNY Press, 1990.

Friedman, Marilyn. *Autonomy, Gender, Politics.* New York: Oxford University Press, 2003.

Gilligan, Carol. *In a Different Voice.* Cambridge: Harvard University Press, 1982.

_____. "Adolescent Development Reconsidered." In *Mapping the Moral Domain,* ed. Carol Gilligan, Janie Victoria Ward, and Jill McLean Taylor. Cambridge: Harvard University Press, 1988, p. xxii.

_____. "Moral Orientation and Moral Development." In *Women and Moral Theory,* ed. Eva Feder Kittay and Diana T. Meyers. Totowa, N.J.: Roman & Littlefield, 1987): 25–26.

Gilligan, Carol, and Grant Wiggins. "The Origins of Morality in Early Childhood Relationships." In *The Emergence of Morality in Young Children,* ed. Jerome Kagan and Sharon Lamb. Chicago: University of Chicago Press, 1987, p. 279.

Gordon, Suzanne, Patricia Benner, and Nel Nodding, eds. *Caregiving: Readings in Knowledge, Practice, Ethics, and Politics.* Philadelphia: University of Pennsylvania Press, 1996.

Halwani, Raja. "Care Ethics and Virtue Ethics." *Hypatia* 18, no. 3 (fall 2003): 161–192.

Jaggar, Alison M. "Caring As a Feminist Practice of Moral Reason." In *Justice and Care: Essential Readings in Feminist Ethics,* ed. Virginia Held. Boulder, Colo.: Westview Press, 1995.

Koehn, Daryl. *Rethinking Feminist Ethics: Care, Trust, and Empathy.* London: Routledge, 1998.

Kohlberg, Lawrence. "From Is to Ought: How to Commit the Naturalistic Fallacy and Get Away with It in the Study of Moral Development." In *Cognitive Development and Epistemology,* ed. Theodore Mischel. New York: Academic Press, 1971, pp. 164–165.

Kroeger-Mappes, Joy. "The Ethic of Care vis-à-vis the Ethic of Rights: A Problem for Contemporary Moral Theory." *Hypatia* 9, no. 3 (summer 1994): 108–131.

Larrabee, Mary Jeanne, ed. *An Ethic of Care: Feminist and Interdisciplinary Perspectives.* New York: Routledge, 1993.

Li, Chenyang. "The Confucian Concepts of *Jen* and the Feminist Ethics of Care: A Comparative Study." *Hypatia* 9, no. 1 (1994): 70–89.

_____. "Revisiting Confucian *Jen* Ethics and Feminist Care Ethics: A Reply to Daniel Star and Lijun Yuan." *Hypatia* 17, no. 1 (2002): 130–140.

Little, Margaret. "Seeing and Caring: The Role of Affect in Feminist Moral Epistemology." *Hypatia* 10, no. 3 (1995): 117–137.

McLaren, Margaret A. "Feminist Ethics: Care As a Virtue." In *Feminists Doing Ethics,* ed. Peggy DesAutels and Joanne Waugh. Lanham, Md.: Rowman & Littlefield, 2001.

Noddings, Nel, ed. *Educating Citizens for Global Awareness.* New York: Teachers College Press, 2005.

_____. *Starting at Home: Caring and Social Policy.* Berkeley: University of California Press, 2002.

_____. *Happiness and Education.* New York: Cambridge University Press, 2003.

_____. *Caring: A Feminine Approach to Ethics and Moral Education.* Berkeley: University of California Press, 1984, p. 3.

_____. *Women and Evil.* Berkeley: University of California Press, 1989, p. 91.

_____. *Starting at Home: Caring and Social Policy.* Berkeley: University of California Press, 2002.

Sander-Staudt, Maureen. "The Unhappy Marriage of Care Ethics and Virtue Ethics." *Hypatia* 21, no. 4 (fall 2006): 21–39.

Star, Daniel. "Do Confucians Really Care? A Defense of the Distinctiveness of Care Ethics: A Reply to Chenyang Li." *Hypatia* 17, no. 1 (2002): 77–106.

Yuan, Lijun. "Ethics of Care and Concept of *Jen:* A Reply to Chenyang Li." *Hypatia* 17, no. 1 (2002): 107–129.

Critiques of Gilligan's and Noddings's Ethics of Care

Baier, Annette C. "Caring About Caring." In *Postures of the Mind: Essays on Mind and Morals.* Minneapolis: University of Minnesota Press, 1985.

Bartky, Sandra Lee. *Femininity and Domination.* New York: Routledge, 1990, p. 105.

_____. "Feeding Egos and Tending Wounds: Deference and Disaffection in Women's Emotional Labor." In *Femininity and Domination,* ed. Sandra Lee Bartky. New York: Routledge, 1990, pp. 99–119.

Benhabib, Seyla. "The Generalized and Concrete Other: The Kohlberg-Gilligan Controversy and Moral Theory." In *Women and Moral Theory,* ed. Eva Feder Kittay and Diana T. Meyers. Totowa, N.J.: Roman & Littlefield, 1987.

Card, Claudia. "Caring and Evil." *Hypatia* 5, no. 1 (spring 1990, p. 106.

Davis, Kathy. "Toward a Feminist Rhetoric: The Gilligan Debate Revisited." *Women's Studies International Forum* 15, no. 2 (1992): 219–231.

Faludi, Susan. *Caregiving: Readings in Knowledge, Practice, Ethics, and Politics.* Philadelphia: University of Pennsylvania Press, 1996, p. 276.

Friedman, Marilyn. "Beyond Caring: The De-Moralization of Gender." In *Science, Morality and Feminist Theory,* ed. Marsha Hanen and Kai Nielsen. Calgary: University of Calgary Press, 1987, p. 100.

Frye, Marilyn. *The Politics of Reality.* Trumansburg, N.Y.: Crossing Press, 1983, p. 9.

Hekman, Susan J. *Moral Voices, Moral Selves: Carol Gilligan and Feminist Moral Theory.* University Park: Pennsylvania State University Press, 1995.

Hoagland, Sarah Lucia. "Some Concerns About Nel Noddings' *Caring.*" *Hypatia* 5, no. 1 (spring 1990): 114.

_____. "Some Thoughts About *Caring.*" In *Feminist Ethics,* ed. Claudia Card. Lawrence: University Press of Kansas, 1991, p. 250.

Miller, Sarah Clark. "A Kantian Ethic of Care?" In *Feminist Interventions in Ethics and Politics: Feminist Ethics and Social Theory,* ed. Barbara S. Andrew. Lanham, Md.: Rowman & Littlefield, 2005, pp. 111–127.

Moody-Adams, Michele M. "Gender and the Complexity of Moral Voices." In *Feminist Ethics,* ed. Claudia Card. Kansas: University Press of Kansas, 1991, pp. 193–198.

_____. "The Social Construction and Reconstruction of Care." In *Sex, Preference, and Family: Essays on Law and Nature,* ed. David Estlund and Martha Nussbaum. New York: Oxford University Press, 1997, pp. 3–17.

Puka, Bill. "The Liberation of Caring: A Different Voice for Gilligan's 'Different Voice.'" *Hypatia* 5, no. 1 (spring 1990): 59.

Scher, George. "Other Voices, Other Rooms? Women's Psychology and Moral Theory." In *Women and Moral Theory,* ed. Eva Feder Kittay and Diana T. Meyers,. Totowa, N.J.: Roman & Littlefield, 1987, p. 188.

Simons, Margaret A. "Two Interviews with Simone de Beauvoir." *Hypatia* 3, no. 3 (winter 1989): 11–27.

Simson, Rosalind S. "Feminine Thinking." *Social Theory & Practice* 31, no. 1 (January 2005): 1–26.

Slicer, Deborah. "Teaching with a Different Ear: Teaching Ethics after Reading Carol Gilligan." *Journal of Value Inquiry* 24 (1990): 55–65.

Slote, Michael. "Caring in the Balance." In *Norms and Values,* ed. Joram G. Haber and Mark S. Hatfon. Lanham, Md.: Rowman & Littlefield, 1998.

Stack, Carol. "The Culture of Gender: Women and Men of Color." *Signs: Journal of Women in Culture and Society* 11, no. 2 (winter 1986): 322–323.

Maternal Ethics and the Practice of Care:
Sara Ruddick, Virginia Held, and Eva Feder Kittay

Aronow, Ina. "Doulas Step in When Mothers Need a Hand." *New York Times,* August 1, 1993, p. 1, Westchester Section.

Badinter, Elisabeth. *Mother Love: Myth and Reality.* New York: Macmillan, 1980.

Bart, Pauline. "Review of Chodorow's *The Reproduction of Mothering.*" In *Mothering Essays in Feminist Theory,* ed. Joyce Treblicot. Totowa, N.J.: Rowman & Allanheld, 1983, pp. 147–152.

Blustein, Jeffrey. *Care and Commitment.* Oxford: Oxford University Press, 1991.

Chodorow, Nancy. *The Reproduction of Mothering: Psychoanalysis and the Sociology of Gender.* Berkeley: University of California, 1978.

Daniel, Norman. *Am I My Parents' Keeper? An Essay on Justice Between the Younger and the Older.* New York: Oxford University Press, 1988.

Ferguson, Ann. "Motherhood and Sexuality: Some Feminist Questions." *Hypatia* 1, no. 2 (fall 1986): 3–22.

Goodin, Robert. *Protecting the Vulnerable*. Chicago: University of Chicago Press, 1985.

Halfon, Mark S., and Joram C. Haber, eds. *Norms and Values: Essays on the Work of Virginia Held*. Lanham, Md.: Rowman & Littlefield, 1998.

Hanisberg, Julia, and Sara Ruddick, eds. *On Behalf of Mothers: Legal Theorists, Philosophers, and Theologians Reflect on Dilemmas of Parenting*. New York: Beacon Press, 1999.

———, eds. *Mother Troubles: Rethinking Contemporary Maternal Dilemmas*. Boston: Beacon Press, 1999.

Harrington, Mona. *Care and Equality: Inventing a New Family Politics*. New York: Knopf, 1999.

Held, Virginia. "The Obligation of Mothers and Fathers." In *Mothering: Essays in Feminist Theory*, ed. Joyce Trebilcot. Totowa, N.J.: Rowman & Allanheld, 1984, p. 1.

———. "Feminism and Moral Theory." In *Women and Moral Theory*, ed. Eva Feder Kittay and Diana Meyers. Savage, Md.: Rowman & Littlefield, 1987, p. 112.

———. "The Meshing of Care and Justice." *Hypatia* 10, no. 2 (spring 1995): 128–132.

Held, Virginia. *Feminist Morality: Transforming Culture, Society, and Politics*. Chicago: University of Chicago Press, 1993.

Held, Virginia, and Alison Jaggar, eds. *Justice and Care: Essential Readings in Feminist Ethics*. Boulder, Colo.: Westview, 1995.

Kittay, Eva Feder. *Love's Labor: Essays on Women, Equality and Dependency*. New York: Routledge, 1999, p. 19.

———. "At the Margins of Moral Personhood." *Ethics* 116 (October 2005): 100–131.

———. "Human Dependency and Rawlsian Equality." In *Feminists Rethink the Self*, ed. Diana T. Meyers. Boulder, Colo.: Westview Press, 1996.

———. "Taking Dependency Seriously." *Hypatia* 10 (winter 1995): 29.

Kittay, Eva Feder, and Diana T. Meyers, eds. *Women and Moral Theory*. Totowa, N.J.: Roman & Littlefield, 1987.

Kramer, Betty J., and Edward H. Thompson, Jr. *Men As Caregivers: Theory, Research, and Service Implications*. New York: Springer, 2002.

Lorber, Judith. "On *The Reproduction of Mothering*: A Methodological Debate." *Signs: Journal of Women in Culture and Society* 6, no. 3 (spring 1981): 482–486.

MacIntyre, Alasdair. *After Virtue*. Notre Dame, Ind.: University of Notre Dame Press, 1981, p. 177.

Manning, Rita C. *Speaking from the Heart: A Feminist Perspective on Ethics*. Lanham, Md.: Rowman & Littlefield , Inc., 1992.

Raymond, Janice. "Female Friendship: Contra Chodorow and Dinnerstein." *Hypatia* 1, no. 2 (fall 1986): 44–45.

Rich, Adrienne. *Of Woman Born*. New York: W.W. Norton, 1979, p. 174.

Romero, Mary. "Who's Taking Care of the Maid's Children?" In *Feminism and Families*, ed. Hilde Lind. New York: Routledge, 1997.

Rossi, Alice. "On *The Reproduction of Mothering*: A Methodological Debate." *Signs: Journal of Women in Culture and Society* 6, no. 3 (spring 1981): 497–500.

Ruddick, Sara. "Maternal Thinking." In *Mothering: Essays in Feminist Theory*, ed. Joyce Trebilcot. Totowa, N.J.: Rowman & Allanheld, 1984, p. 214.

_____. *Maternal Thinking: Toward a Politics of Peace*. Boston: Beacon Press, 1989, p. 17.

_____. "Injustice in Families: Assault and Domination." In *Justice and Care: Essential Readings in Feminist Ethics*, ed. Virginia Held. Boulder, Colo.: Westview Press, 1995): 203–223.

_____. "Care As Labor and Relationship." In *Norms and Values: Essays on the Work of Virginia Held*, ed. Mark S. Halfon and Joram C. Haber. Lanham, Md.: Rowman & Littlefield, 1998.

Ruddick, William. "Parenthood: Three Concepts and a Principle." In *Family Values: Issues in Ethics, Society and the Family*, ed. Laurence D. Houlgate. Belmont, Calif.: Wadsworth, 1998.

Sommers, Christina Hoff. "Filial Morality." In *Women and Moral Theory*, ed. Eva F. Kittay and Diana T. Meyers. Totowa, N.J.: Rowman & Littlefield Publishers, 1987.

Treblicot, Joyce, ed. *Mothering: New Essays in Feminist Theory*. Totowa, N.J.: Rowman & Littlefield, 1987.

Tronto, Joan. *Moral Boundaries: A Political Argument for an Ethic of Care*. London: Routledge, 1993.

_____. "Woman and Caring: What Can Feminists Learn about Morality from Caring?" In *Justice and Care: Essential Readings in Feminist Ethics*, ed. Virginia Held. Boulder, Colo.: Westview Press, 1995): 101–115.

Willett, Cynthia. *Maternal Ethics and Other Slave Moralities*. New York: Routledge, 1995.

Wong, Sau-ling C. "Diverted Mothering: Representations of Caregivers of Color in the Age of Multiculturalism." In *Mothering: Ideology, Experience and Agency*, ed. Evelyn Nakano Glenn, Grace Chang, and Linda Rennie Forcey. New York: Routledge, 1994.

Public and Global Issues

Allmark, Peter. "Is Caring a Virtue?" *Journal of Advanced Nursing* 28, no. 3 (1998): 466–472.

Behuniak, Susan M. *A Caring Jurisprudence*. Lanham, Md.: Rowman & Littlefield, 1999.

Botes, Annatjie. "A Comparison between the Ethics of Justice and the Ethics of Care." *Journal of Advanced Nursing* 32, no. 5 (2000): 1071–1075.

Brender, Natalie. "Political Care and Humanitarian Response." In *Feminists Doing Ethics,* ed. Peggy DesAutels and Joanne Waugh. Lanham, Md.: Rowman & Littlefield, 2001.

Clement, Grace. *Care, Autonomy, and Justice: Feminism and the Ethic of Care.* Boulder, Colo.: Westview, 1996.

Davion, Victoria. "Pacifism and Care." *Hypatia* 5 (1990): 90–100.

Deveaux, Monique. "Shifting Paradigms: Theorizing Care and Justice in Political Theory." *Hypatia* 10, no. 2 (spring 1995): 115–119.

England, Paula, and Nancy Folbre. "The Cost of Caring." *Annals of the American Academy of Political and Social Science* 561 (January 1999): 39–51.

Engster, Daniel. "Rethinking Care Theory: The Practice of Caring and the Obligation to Care." *Hypatia* 20, no. 3 (summer 2005): 51–74.

————. "Care Ethics and Natural Law Theory: Toward an Institutional Political Theory of Caring." *Journal of Politics* 66, no. 1 (February 2004): 113–135.

Gottlieb, Roger S. "The Tasks of Embodied Love: Moral Problems in Caring for Children with Disabilities." *Hypatia* 17, no. 3 (summer 2002): 225–236.

Gould, Carol, ed. *Beyond Domination: New Perspectives on Women and Philosophy.* Totowa, N.J.: Rowman & Allanheld, 1983.

Hankivsky, Olena. "Imagining Ethical Globalization: The Contributions of a Care Ethics." *Hypatia* 2, no. 1 (June 2006): 91–110.

Held, Virginia. "Care and the Extension of Markets." *Hypatia* 17, no. 2 (spring 2002): 19–33.

Kittay, Eva Feder. "A Feminist Public Ethic of Care Meets the New Communitarian Family Policy." *Ethics* 111 (April 2001): 523–547.

Kuhse, Helga. *Caring: Nurses, Women and Ethics.* Oxford: Blackwell, 1997.

Morris, Jenny. "Impairment and Disability: Constructing an Ethics of Care That Promotes Human Rights." *Hypatia* 16, no. 4 (fall 2001): 1–16.

Mullett, Sheila. "Shifting Perspectives: A New Approach to Ethics." In *Feminist Perspectives,* ed. Lorraine Code, Sheila Mullett, and Christine Overall. Toronto: University of Toronto Press, 1989.

Nagel, Thomas. *The View from Nowhere.* Oxford: Oxford University Press, 1986.

Nicholson, Linda J. *Gender and History: The Limits of Social Theory in the Age of the Family.* New York: Columbia University Press, 1986.

Nietzsche, Friedrich. *On the Genealogy of Morals,* trans. Walter Kaufmann and R. Hollingdale. New York: Vintage, 1969.

Okin, Susan. *Justice, Gender and the Family.* New York: Basic Books, 1989.

Porter, Elisabeth. "Can Politics Practice Compassion?" *Hypatia* 21, no. 4 (fall 2006): 97–123.

Purdy, Laura M. *Reproducing Persons: Issues in Feminist Bioethics.* Ithaca, N.Y.: Cornell University Press, 1996.

Reverby, Susan. *Ordered to Care.* Cambridge: Cambridge University Press, 1987.

Robinson, Fiona. *Globalizing Care: Ethics, Feminist Theory, and International Relations.* Boulder, Colo.: Westview, 1999.

———. "Care, Gender and Global Social Justice: Rethinking 'Ethical Globalization.'" *Hypatia* 2, no. 1 (June 2006): 5–25.

Sevenhuijsen, Selma. "Feminist Ethics and Public Health Care Policies." In *Feminist Ethics and Social Policy,* ed. Patrice DiQuinzio and Iris Marion Young. Bloomington: Indiana University Press, 1996.

———. *Citizenship and the Ethics of Care: Feminist Considerations on Justice, Morality and Politics.* London: Routledge, 1998.

Shanley, Mary Lyndon. "Public Policy and the Ethics of Care." *Hypatia* 16, no. 3 (summer 2001):157–160.

Sherwin, Susan. *No Longer Patient: Feminist Ethics and Health Care.* Philadelphia: Temple University Press, 1992.

Stone, Deborah. "Why We Need a Care Movement." *The Nation,* March 12, 2000, pp. 13–15.

Tong, Rosemarie. *Feminine and Feminist Ethics.* Belmont, Calif.: Wadsworth, 1993.

Tronto, Joan C. "The 'Nanny' Question in Feminism." *Hypatia* 17, no. 2 (spring 2002): 34–51.

———. "Care As a Political Concept." In *Revisioning the Political: Feminist Reconstructions of Traditional Concepts in Western Political Theory,* ed. Nancy J. Hirschmann and Christine Di Stefano. New York: Free Press, 1996.

Walker, Margaret Urban, ed. *Mother Time: Women, Aging, and Ethics.* Lanham, Md.: Rowman & Littlefield, 1998.

West, Robin. "The Right to Care." In *The Subject of Care: Feminist Perspectives on Dependency,* ed. Eva Feder Kittay and Ellen Feder. Lanham, Md.: Rowman & Littlefield, 2002.

White, Julie Anne. *Democracy, Justice, and The Welfare State: Reconstructing Public Care.* University Park: Pennsylvania State Press, 2000.

Chapter Six

General Readings

Albrecht, Lisa, and Rose M. Brewer, eds. *Bridges of Power: Women's Multicultural Alliances.* Philadelphia: New Society Publishers, 1990.

Alcoff, Linda Martín. *Visible Identities: Race, Gender, and the Self.* Oxford: Oxford University Press, 2006.

Beemyn, Brett, and Mickey Eliason, eds. *Queer Studies: A Lesbian, Gay, Bisexual and Transgender Anthology.* New York and London: New York University Press, 1996.

Bulkin, Elly, Minnie Bruce Pratt, and Barbara Smith, eds. *Yours in Struggle: Three Feminist Perspectives on Anti-Semitism and Racism.* Ithaca, N.Y.: Firebrand Books, 1984.

Chock, Phyllis Pease. "Culturalism: Pluralism, Culture, and Race in the *Harvard Encyclopedia of American Ethnic Groups.*" In *(Multi)Culturalism and the Baggage of "Race."* Special Issue. *Identities: Global Studies in Culture and Power* 1, no. 4 (April 1985): 301–24.

Crenshaw, Kimberle, Neil Gotanda, and Gary Peller, eds. *Critical Race Theory: The Key Writings That Formed the Movement.* New York: New Press, 1996.

Davies, Miranda. *Third World-Second Sex.* London: Zed Books, 1983.

Davis, Angela Y. *Angela Davis: An Autobiography.* New York: International Publishers, 1988.

_____. *Women, Culture, and Politics.* New York: Vintage Books, 1990.

_____. *Women, Race, and Class.* New York: Vintage Books/Random House, 1981.

Dicker, Susan. *Languages in America: A Pluralist View.* Philadelphia; Multilingual Matters Limited, 1966.

DuBois, Ellen Carol, and Vicki L. Ruiz, eds. *Unequal Sisters: A Multicultural Reader in U.S. Women's History.* New York: Routledge, 1990.

Eisenstein, Zillah R. *Hatreds: Racialized and Sexualized Conflicts in the 21st Century.* New York: Routledge, 1996.

Essed, Philomena, and Rita Gircour. *Diversity: Gender, Color, and Culture.* Amherst: University of Massachusetts Press, 1996.

Eze, Emmanuel Chukwudi. *Achieving Our Humanity: The Idea of a Postracial Future.* New York: Routledge, 2001.

Ferguson, Russell, et al., eds. *Out There: Marginalizations and Contemporary Cultures.* New York: New Museum of Contemporary Art; Cambridge, Mass.: MIT Press, 1991.

Fernandez, Carlos. "La Raza and the Melting Pot: A Comparative Look at Multiethnicity." In *Racially Mixed People in America,* ed. Maria P. P. Root. Newbury Park, Calif.: Sage, 1992.

Fowers, Blaine J., and Frank C. Richardson. "Why Is Multiculturalism Good?" *American Psychologist* 51, no. 6 (June 1996): 609.

Fraser, Nancy, and Axel Honneth. *Redistribution or Recognition? A Political-Philosophical Exchange,* trans. Joel Golb, James Ingram, and Christiane Wilke. London: Verso, 2003.

Fusco, Coco. *English Is Broken Here: Notes on Cultural Fusion in the Americas.* New York: New Press, 1995.

Glazer, Nathan, and Daniel Patrick Moynihan. *Beyond the Melting Pot: The Negroes, Puerto Ricans, Jews, Italian, and Irish of New York City.* 2nd ed. Cambridge, Mass.: MIT Press, 1970.

Gunew, Sneja, and Anna Yeatman. *Feminism and the Politics of Difference.* St. Leonards, New South Wales: Allen and Unwin, 1993.

Haraway, Donna J. *Private Visions: Gender, Race, and Nature in the World of Modern Science.* New York: Routledge, 1989.

Hardin, C. L. "A New Look at Color." *American Philosophical Quarterly* 21, no. 2 (April 1984): 125–34.

Herr, Ranjoo Seodu. "A Third World Feminist Defense of Multiculturalism." *Social Theory and Practice* 30, no. 1 (January 2004): 73–103.

Hochschild, Jennifer. *Facing Up to the American Dream: Race, Class and the Soul of the Nation.* Princeton, N.J.: Princeton University Press, 1995.

Hollinger, David A. *Post-ethnic America: Beyond Multiculturalism.* New York: Harper Collins, 1995.

Holmstrom, Nancy. "Human Nature." In *A Comparison to Feminist Philosophy,* ed. Alison M. Jaggar and Iris Marion Young. Oxford, : Blackwell, 1998.

Hull, Gloria T., Patricia Bell Scott, and Barbara Smith, eds. *All the Women Are White, All the Blacks Are Men, But Some of Us Are Brave.* New York: Feminist Press at the City University of New York, 1982.

King, Katie. *Theory in Its Feminist Travels: Conversations in U.S. Women's Movements.* Indianapolis: Indiana University Press, 1994.

Lamphere, Louise, Helena Ragoné, and Patricia Zavella, eds. *Situated Lives: Gender and Culture in Everyday Life.* New York and London: Routledge, 1997.

Lee, Jung Young. *Marginality: The Key to Multicultural Theology.* Minneapolis: Fortress Press, 1995.

Lourde, Audre. "Age, Race, Class, and Sex." In *Sister Outsider,* ed. Audre Lourde. Trumansberg, N.Y.: Crossing Press, 1984.

Matisons, Michelle Renee. "Feminism and Multiculturalism: The Dialogue Continues." *Social Theory and Practice* 29, no. 4 (October 2003): 655–664.

Mookherjee, Monica. "Review Article: Feminism and Multiculturalism—Putting Okin and Shachar in Question." *Journal of Moral Philosophy* 2, no. 2 (2005): 237–41.

Moraga, Cherríe, and Gloria Anzaldúa, eds. *This Bridge Called My Back: Writings by Radical Women of Color.* Latham, N.Y.: Kitchen Table/Women of Color Press, 1981.

Moya, Paula M. L. *Learning from Experience: Minority Identities, Multicultural Struggles.* Berkeley: University of California Press, 2002.

Okin, Susan M. *Is Multiculturalism Bad for Women?* Princeton, N.J.: Princeton University Press, 1999.

Phillips, Anne. "Multiculturalism, Universalism, and the Claims of Democracy." In *Gender, Justice, Development, and Rights,* ed. Maxine Molyneux and Shahra Razavi. Oxford: Oxford University Press, 2002.

Powell, Timothy B. "All Colors Flow into Rainbows and Nooses: The Struggle to Define Academic Multiculturalism." *Cultural Critique* 55 (fall 2003): 152–181.

Ramazanoglu, Caroline. *Feminism and the Contradictions of Oppression.* London and New York: Routledge, 1989.

Raz, Joseph. "Multiculturalism: A Liberal Perspective." *Dissent* (winter 1994): 74.

Rich, Adrienne. "Compulsory Heterosexuality and Lesbian Existence (1980)." In *Blood, Bread, and Poetry: Selected Prose 1979–1985.* New York: W.W. Norton, 1986.

Scheman, Naomi. *Engendering: Construction of Knowledge, Authority, and Privilege.* New York: Routledge, 1993.

Schlesinger, Arthur M. Jr. *The Disuniting of America.* Knoxville, Tenn.: Whittle Books, 1990.

Shachar, Ayelet. *Multicultural Jurisdictions: Cultural Differences and Women's Rights.* Cambridge: Cambridge University Press, 2001.

Shohat, Ella, ed. *Talking Visions: Multicultural Feminism in a Transitional Age.* Cambridge, Mass.: MIT Press, 1998).

———. "Area Studies, Transnationalism, and the Feminist Production of Knowledge." *Signs: Journal of Women in Culture and Society* 26, no. 4 (2001): 1269–1272.

Spelman, Elizabeth V. *Inessential Woman: Problems of Exclusion in Feminist Thought.* Boston: Beacon Press, 1988.

Spillers, Hortense J. *Comparative American Identities: Race, Sex and Nationality in Modern Text.* New York: Routledge, 1991.

Spinner-Halev, Jeff. "Feminism, Multiculturalism, Oppression, and the State." *Ethics* 112 (October 2001): 84–113.

Takaki, Ronald. *Iron Cages: Race and Culture in 19th Century America.* New York: Oxford University Press, 1990.

———. *A Different Mirror: A History of Multicultural America.* New York: Oxford University Press, 1993.

———. *From Different Shores: Perspectives on Race and Ethnicity in America.* 2nd ed. New York: Oxford University Press, 1994.

Warnke, Georgia. "Race, Gender, and Antiessentialist Politics." *Signs: Journal of Women in Culture and Society* 31, no. 1 (autumn 2005): 93–116.

Wiegman, Robyn. *American Anatomies: Theorizing Race and Gender.* Durham, N.C.: Duke University Press, 1995.

Wing, Adrien Katherine, ed. *Critical Race Feminism: A Reader.* New York and London: New York University Press, 1997.

Zack, Naomi. "Mixed Black and White Race and Public Policy." *Hypatia* 10, no. 1 (winter 1995): 120–132.

Zinn, Maxine Baca, and Bonnie Thornton Dill, eds. *Women of Color in U.S. Society.* Philadelphia: Temple University Press, 1994.

Caucasian/White Issues

Alcoff, Linda Martín. "What Should White People Do?" *Hypatia* 13, no. 3 (summer 1998): 6–26.

Bailey, Alison, and Jacquelyn Zita. "The Reproduction of Whiteness: Race and the Regulation of the Gendered Body." *Hypatia* 22, no. 2 (spring 2007): vii–xv.

Frankenberg, Ruth. *White Women, Race Matters.* Minneapolis: University of Minnesota Press, 1993.

Gallagher, Charles. "White Reconstruction in the University." *Socialist Review* 94, nos. 1 and 2 (1994): 165–88.

Haney López, Ian F. *White by Law: The Legal Construction of Race.* New York: New York University Press, 1996.

Harris, Cheryl I. "Whiteness As Property." In *Critical Race Theory: The Key Writings That Formed the Movement,* ed. Kimberlé Crenshaw et al. New York: New Press, 1995.

Katz, Judith. *White Awareness: Handbook for Anti-racism Training.* Norman: University of Oklahoma Press, 1978.

McDonald, Steven J. "How Whites Explain Black and Hispanic Inequality." *Public Opinion Quarterly* 65 (2001): 562–573.

Olsen, Joel. "The Democratic Problem of the White Citizen." *Constellations* 8, no. 2 (June 2001): 163–83.

Parker, Pat. "For the White Person Who Wants to Know How to Be My Friend." In *An Expanded Edition of Movement in Black, 99.* Ithaca, N.Y.: Firebrand Books, 1999.

Schueller, Malini Johar. "Analogy and (White) Feminist Theory: Thinking Race and the Color of the Cyborg Body." *Signs: Journal of Women in Culture and Society* 31, no. 1 (autumn 2005): 63–92.

Ware, Vron. *Beyond the Pale: White Women, Racism and History.* New York and London: Verso, 1992.

Zack, Naomi. "Mixed Black and White Race and Public Policy." *Hypatia* 10, no. 1 (winter 1995): 123–124.

African American Issues

Bobo, Jacquelin. *Black Women As Cultural Readers.* New York: Columbia University Press, 1995.

Carby, Hazel. *Reconstructing Womanhood: The Emergence of the Afro-American Woman Novelist.* New York: Oxford University Press, 1987.

Collins, Patricia Hill. *Black Feminist Thought: Knowledge, Consciousness, and the Politics of Empowerment.* Boston: Unwin and Hyman, 1990.

_____. "Learning from the Outsider Within: The Sociological Significance of Black Feminist Thought." In *Feminist Approaches to Theory and Methodology: An Interdisciplinary Reader,* ed. Sharlene Hesse-Biber, Christina Gilmartin, and Robin Lydenberg. New York: Oxford, 1999.

Combahee River Collective. "A Black Feminist Statement." In *Capitalist Patriarchy and the Case for Socialist Feminism,* ed. Zillah R. Eisenstein. New York: Monthly Review Press, 1979.

Davis, Angela Y. "Gender, Class, and Multiculturalism: Rethinking 'Race' Politics." In *Mapping Multiculturalism,* ed. Avery R. Gorden and Christopher Newfield. Minneapolis: University of Minnesota Press, 1996): 40–48.

DuBois, W. E. B. *Black Reconstruction in America 1860–1880*. New York: Free Press, 1999.

Giddings, Paula. *When and Where I Enter: The Impact of Black Women on Race and Sex in America*. New York: Bantam Books, 1984.

hooks, bell. *Yearning: Race, Gender and Cultural Politics*. Boston: South End Press, 1990.

_____. "Naked Without Shame: A Counter-Hegemonic Body Politic." In *Talking Visions: Multicultural Feminism in a Transnational Age,* ed. Ella Shohat. Cambridge, Mass.: The MIT Press, 1998.

_____. *Ain't I a Woman: Black Women and Feminism*. Boston: South End Press, 1984.

_____. *Black Looks: Race and Representation*. Boston: South End Press, 1992.

_____. *Feminist Theory: From Margin to Center*. Boston: South End Press, 1984.

_____. *Talking Back: Thinking Feminist, Thinking Black*. Boston: South End Press, 1989.

James, Stanlie M., and Abena P. A. Busia, eds. *Theorizing Black Feminisms: The Visionary Pragmatism of Black Women*. New York and London: Routledge, 1993.

King, Deborah. "Multiple Jeopardy: The Context of a Black Feminist Ideology." In *Feminist Frameworks,* ed. Alison M. Jaggar and Paula S. Rothenberg. 3rd edition. New York: McGraw-Hill, 1993.

Lorde, Audre. "Age, Race, Class, and Sex: Women Redefining Difference." In *Race, Class, and Gender,* ed. Margaret L. Andersen and Patricia Hill Collins. 2nd edition. Belmont, Calif.: Wadsworth, 1995.

_____. *The Cancer Journals*. San Francisco: Spinster/Aunt Lute, 1980.

_____. *I Am Your Sister: Black Women Organizing Across Sexualities*. New York: Kitchen Table/Women of Color Press, 1985.

_____. *Sister Outsider*. Freedom, Calif.: Crossing Press, 1984.

_____. *Zami, A New Spelling of My Name: A Biomythography*. Freedom, Calif.: The Crossing Press, 1982.

Mosley, Albert G. "Negritude, Nationalism, and Nativism: Racists or Racialists?" In *Racism,* ed. Leonard Harris. Amherst, N.Y.: Humanity Books, 1999.

Pearson, Jonna Lian. "Multicultural Feminism and Sisterhood among Women of Color in Social Change Dialogue." *Howard Journal of Communications* 18 (2007): 88.

Piper, Adrian. "Passing for White, Passing for Black." In *Talking Visions: Multicultural Feminism in a Transitional Age,* ed. Ella Shohat. Cambridge, Mass.: MIT Press, 1998.

Smith, Barbara, ed. *Home Girls: A Black Feminist Anthology*. Lantham, N.Y.: Kitchen Table/Women of Color Press, 1983.

Latin American/Hispanic Issues

Alcoff, Linda Martin. *Visible Identities: Race, Gender, and the Self*. New York: Oxford University Press, 2006.

Anzaldùa, Gloria. *Borderlands/La Frontera: The New Mestiza.* San Francisco: Spinsters/Aunt Lute, 1987.

_____, ed. *Making Face, Making Soul/Haciendo Caras: Creative and Critical Perspectives by Women of Color.* San Francisco: Aunt Lute Books, 1990.

Asencio, Marysol, and Katie Acosta. "Macho Men and Passive Women." *Conscience: The News Journal of Catholic Opinion* 28, no. 2 (summer 2007).

Blea, Irene I. *La Chicana and the Intersection of Race, Class, and Gender.* Westport, Conn., and London: Praeger, 1992.

Dávila, Arlene. *Latinos, Inc.: The Marketing and Making of a People.* Berkeley: University of California Press, 2001.

Flores, William V., and Rina Benmayor. *Latino Cultural Citizenship: Claiming Identity, Space and Rights.* Boston: Beacon Press, 1997.

Haney López, Ian F. "Race and Erasure: The Salience of Race to Latinos/as." In *The Latino Condition,* ed. Richard Delgado and Jean Stefancic. New York: New York University Press, 1998.

Lugones, Maria, and Elisabeth Spelman. "Have We Got a Theory for You! Feminist Theory, Cultural Imperialism, and the Demand for the Woman's Voice." In *Feminist Philosophies,* ed. Janet A. Kourany, James P. Sterba, and Rosemarie Tong. Englewood Cliffs, N.J.: Prentice-Hall, 1992.

Moraga, Cherríe. *Loving in the War Years: Lo Que Nunca Paso Por Sus Labios.* Boston: South End Press, 1983.

_____. "La Guerra." In *This Bridge Called My Back: Writings by Radical Women of Color,* ed. Cherríe Moraga and Gloria Anzaldùa. New York: Kitchen Table Press, 1983.

Oboler, Suzanne. *Ethnic Labels, Latino Lives: Identity and the Politics of (Re)Presentation in the United States.* Minneapolis: University of Minnesota Press, 1995.

Ramirez, Deborah A. "It's Not just Black and White Anymore." In *The Latino Condition,* ed. Richard Delgado and Jean Stefancic. New York: New York University Press, 1998.

Ramos, Juanita, ed. *Compañeras: Latina Lesbians.* New York: Latina Lesbian History Project, 1987.

_____. "Latin American Lesbians Speak on Black Identity: Violeta Garro, Minerva Rosa Pérez Digna, and Juanita C. Magdalena." In *Black Women's Diasporas,* vol. 2 of *Moving Beyond Boundaries,* ed. Carole Boyce Davies. New York: New York University Press, 1995.

Rosaldo, Renato. "Identity Politics: An Ethnography by a Participant." In *Identity Politics Reconsidered,* ed. Linda M. Alcoff et al. New York: Palgrave Macmillan, 2006.

Schutte, Ofelia. *Cultural Identity and Social Liberation in Latin American Thought.* Albany: State University of New York Press, 1993.

_____. "Cultural Alterity: Cross-Cultural Communication and Feminist Theory in North-South Contexts." In *Decentering the Center: Philosophy for a Multicultural, Postcolonial, and Feminist World,* ed. Uma Narayan and Sandra Harding. Bloomington: Indiana University Press, 2000. First published in *Hypatia* 13, no. 2 (spring 1998).

Trujillo, Carla, ed. *Chicana Lesbians: The Girls Our Mothers Warned Us About.* Berkeley: Third Woman Press, 1991.

Zea, Leopoldo. "Identity: A Latin American Philosophical Problem." *Philosophical Forum* 20 (fall–winter 1988–1989): 33–42.

Native American Issues

Allen, Paula Gunn. *The Sacred Hoop: Recovering the Feminine in American Indian Traditions.* Boston: Beacon Press, 1986.

_____, ed. *Spider Woman's Granddaughters: Traditional Tales and Contemporary Writing by Native American Women.* Boston: Beacon Press, 1986.

Betaille, Gretchen, and Kathleen Mullen Sands. *American Indian Women: Telling Their Lives.* Lincoln: University of Nebraska Press, 1984.

Dearborn, Mary V. *Pocahontas's Daughters: Gender and Ethnicity in American Culture.* New York: Oxford University Press, 1986.

Green, Rayna. *Native American Women: A Contextual Bibliography.* Bloomington: Indiana University Press, 1983.

_____. *Indians of North America: Women in American Indian Society.* New York and Philadelphia: Chelsea House Publishers, 1992.

Jaimes, Annette M., ed. *The State of Native America: Genocide, Colonization and Resistance.* Boston: South End Press, 1992.

Lawrence, Bonita. "Gender, Race, and the Regulation of Native Identity in Canada and the United States: An Overview. *Hypatia: A Journal of Feminist Philosophy* 18, no. 2 (spring 2003): 3–31.

Pillow, Wanda. "Searching for Sacajawea: Whitened Reproductions and Endarkened Representations." *Hypatia* 22, no. 2 (spring 2007): 1–19.

Poupart, Lisa. "The Familiar Face of Genocide: Internalized Oppression among American Indians." *Hypatia* 18, no. 2 (spring 2003): 86–100.

Sarris, Greg. *Keeping Slug Women Alive: A Holistic Approach to American Indian Texts.* Berkeley, Los Angeles, and Oxford: University of California Press, 1993.

Silko, Leslie Marmon. *Yellow Woman and a Beauty of Spirit: Essays on Native American Life Today.* New York: Touchstone/Simon & Schuster, 1997.

Smith, Andy. "Not an Indian Tradition: The Sexual Colonization of Native Peoples." *Hypatia* 18, no. 2 (spring 2003): 70–85.

Waters, Ann. "Introduction: Indigenous Women in the Americas." *Hypatia* 18, no. 2 (spring 2003): ix–xx.

Asian American Issues

Asian Women United of California, eds. *Making Waves: An Anthology of Writings by and About Asian American Women.* Boston: Beacon Press, 1989.

Cha, Theresa Hak Kyung. *Dictée.* New York: Tanam Press, 1982.

Hongo, Garrett, ed. *Under Western Eyes: Personal Essays from Asian-Americans.* New York: Anchor Books, 1995.

Kim, Elaine H. *Asian American Literature: An Introduction to the Writings and Their Social Context.* Philadelphia: Temple University Press, 1984.

_____. "Between Black and White: An Interview with Bong Hwan Kim" In *The State of Asian America: Activism and Resistance in the 1990s,* ed. Karin Aguilar-San Juan. Boston: South End Press, 1993.

Kim, Elaine H., and Lilia V. Villanueva, eds. *Making More Waves: New Asian American Writing by Asian Women.* Boston: Beacon Press, 1997.

Kim, Elaine H., and Eui-Young Yu. *East to America: Korean American Life Stories.* New York: New Press, 1995.

Klasen, Stephan, and Claudia Wink. "A Turning Point in Gender Bias in Mortality? An Update on the Number of Missing Women." *Population and Development Review* 28, no. 2 (January, 2002): 285–312.

Lowe, Lisa. "Heterogeneity, Hybridity, Multiplicity: Making Asian American Difference." *Diaspora* 1 (1991): 24–44.

Marchetti, Gina. *Romance and the 'Yellow Peril': Race, Sex, and Discursive Strategies in Hollywood Fiction.* Los Angeles and Berkeley: University of California Press, 1994.

Okihiro, Gary. *Margins to Mainstreams: Asians in American History and Culture.* Seattle: University of Washington Press, 1994.

Sen, Amartya. "More than 100 Million Women are Missing." *The New York Review of Books* 37, no. 20 (December 20, 1990).

Takagi, Dana Y. *The Retreat from Race: Asian-American Admissions and Racial Politics.* New Brunswick, N.J.: Rutgers University Press, 1992.

Wong, Diane Yen-Mei. *Dear Diane: Letters from Our Daughters.* San Francisco: San Francisco Study Center, 1983.

Wu, Frank. *Yellow: Race in America beyond Black and White.* New York: Basic Books, 2002.

Global Feminism

Barber, Benjamin. *Jihad vs. McWorld: How Globalism and Tribalism Are Reshaping the World.* New York: Ballantine, 1995.

Barry, Kathleen. *The Prostitution of Sexuality: The Global Exploitation of Women.* New York and London: New York University Press, 1995.

Benhabib, Seyla. *Claims of Culture: Equality and Diversity in the Global Era.* Princeton, N.J.: Princeton University Press, 2002.

Cohen, Colleen Ballerino, Richard Wilk, and Beverly Stoeltje. *Beauty Queens on the Global Stage: Gender, Contests, and Power.* New York and London: Routledge, 1996.

Crystal, David. *English As a Global Language.* Cambridge: Cambridge University Press, 1997.

Ehrenrich, Barbara, and Annette Fuentes. *Women in Global Factory.* Boston: South End Press, 1983.

Enloe, Cynthia. *Bananas, Beaches, and Bases: Making Feminist Sense of International Politics.* Berkeley: University of California Press, 1989.

Ferguson, Ann. "Resisting the Veil of Privilege: Building Bridge Identities As an Ethico-Politics of Global Feminisms." *Hypatia* 13, no. 3 (summer 1998): 95–113.

Ginsburg, Faye, and Rayna Rapp, eds. *Conceiving the New World Order: The Global Politics of Reproduction.* Berkeley, Los Angeles, and London: University of California Press, 1995.

Hellsten, Sirrku Kristiina. "From Human Wrongs to Universal Rights: Communication and Feminist Challenges for the Promotion of Women's Health in the Third World." *Developing World Bioethics* 1, no. 2 (2001): 108–109.

Jabri, Vivienne. "Feminist Ethics and Hegemonic Global Politics." *Alternatives* 29 (2004): 275.

Jaggar, Alison. "Globalizing Feminist Ethics." *Hypatia* 13 (1998): 7–31.

King, Anthony D., ed. *Culture, Globalization and the World-System: Contemporary Conditions for the Representation of Identity.* Minneapolis: University of Minnesota Press, 2000.

Mohanty, Chandra Talpade, Ann Russo, and Lourdes Torres, eds. *Third World Women and the Politics of Feminism.* Bloomington and Indianapolis: Indiana University Press, 1991.

Nah, June, and Maria Patricia Fernandez-Kelly. *Women, Men, and the International Division of Labor.* Albany: State University of New York Press, 1983.

Nussbaum, Martha. "Women's Capabilities and Social Justice." In *Gender, Justice, Development, and Rights,* ed. Maxine Molyneux and Shahra Razavi. Oxford: Oxford University Press, 2002.

Okin, Susan Moller. "Inequalities Between Sexes in Different Cultural Contexts." In *Women, Culture, and Development,* ed. Martha Nussbaum and Jonathan Glover. Oxford: Clarendon Press, 1995, p. 294.

_____. Feminism, Women's Human Rights, and Cultural Differences." *Hypatia* 13, no. 2 (1998): 42.

_____. "Recognizing Women's Rights As Human Rights." *APA Newsletters* 97, no. 2 (spring 1998).

Peterson, Spike V., and Laura Parisi. "Are Women Human? It's not an Academic Question." In *Human Rights Fifty Years On: A Radical Reappraisal,* ed. Tony Evans. Manchester: Manchester University Press, 1998.

Sinclair, M. Thea, ed. *Gender, Work, and Tourism.* London and New York: Routledge, 1997.

United Nations Declaration on the Elimination of Violence against Women. 85th Plenary Meeting. December 20, 1993. A/RES/48/104. Available at http://www .un.org/documents/ga/res/48/a48r104.htm.

Postcolonial Feminism

Abu-Lughod, Lila. *Writing Women's Worlds: Bedouin Stories.* Berkeley and Los Angeles: University of California Press, 1993.

Afkhami, Mahnaz. *Women in Exile.* Charlottesville and London: University Press of Virginia, 1994.

Ahmed, Leila. *Women and Gender in Islam: Historical Roots of a Modern Debate.* New Haven, Conn.: Yale University Press, 1992.

_____. "Western Ethnocentrism and Perceptions of the Harem." *Feminist Studies* 8 (1982): 521–534.

Alexander, M. Jacqui, and Chandra Talpade Mohanty, eds. *Feminist Genealogies, Colonial Legacies, Democratic Futures.* New York: Routledge, 1996.

Alexander, Meena. *The Shock of Arrival: Reflections on Postcolonial Experience.* Boston: South End Press, 1996.

Alloula, Malek. *The Colonial Harem.* Minneapolis: University of Minnesota Press, 1986.

Bartkowski, Frances. *Travelers, Immigrants, Inmates: Essays in Estrangement.* Minneapolis: University of Minnesota Press, 1995.

Bulbeck, Chila. *Re-Orienting Western Feminisms: Women's Diversity in a Postcolonial World.* Cambridge: Cambridge University Press, 1998.

Chaudhury, Nupur, and Margaret Strobel, eds. *Western Women and Imperialism: Complicity and Resistance.* Bloomington and Indianapolis: Indiana University Press, 1992.

Donaldson, Laura E. *Decolonizing Feminisms: Race, Gender and Empire Building.* Chapel Hill: University of North Carolina Press, 1992.

Etienne, Mona, ed. *Women and Colonization: Anthropological Perspectives.* New York: Bergin & Garvey Publishers, 1980.

Green, Mary Jean, et al., eds. *Post-Colonial Subjects: Francophone Women Writers.* Minneapolis and London: University of Minnesota press, 1996.

Guerrero, M. A. Jaimes. "'Patriarchal Colonialism' and Indigenism: Implications for Native Feminist Spirituality and Native Womanism." *Hypatia* 18, no. 2 (spring 2003): 58–69.

Jayawardena, Kumari. *Feminism and Nationalism in the Third World.* London and New Jersey: Zed Books, 1986.

Loomba, Ania. *Colonialism/Postcolonialism.* London: Routledge, 1998.

McClintock, Anne. *Imperial Leather: Race, Gender and Sexuality in the Colonial Contest.* New York and London: Routledge, 1995.

McClintock, Anne, Aamir Mufti, and Ella Shohat, eds. *Dangerous Liaisons: Gender, Nation, and Post-Colonial Perspectives.* Minneapolis: University of Minnesota Press, 1997.

Mohanty, Chandra Talpade. "Under Western Eyes Revisited: Feminist Solidarity through Anticapitalist Struggles." *Signs: Journal of Women in Culture and Society* 28, no. 2 (2003): 499–535.

Narayan, Uma. *Dislocating Cultures: Identities, Traditions, and Third-World Feminisms.* New York: Routledge, 1997.

Narayan, Uma, and Sandra Harding. "Introduction. Border Crossings: Multicultural and Postcolonial Feminist Challenges to Philosophy (Part I)." *Hypatia* 13, no. 2 (spring 1998): 86–106.

_____. "Introduction. Border Crossings: Multicultural and Postcolonial Feminist Challenges to Philosophy (Part II)." *Hypatia* 13, no. 3 (summer 1998): 1–5.

Ong, Aihwa. "Colonialism and Modernity: Feminist Re-presentations of Women in Non-Western Societies." *Inscriptions* 3 (1988): 79–93.

Seshadri-Crooks, Kalpana. "At the Margins of Postcolonial Studies." In *The Pre-Occupation of Postcolonial Studies,* ed. Fawzia Azfal-Khan and Kalpana Seshadri-Crooks. Durham, N.C.: Duke University Press, 2000.

Sharpe, Jenny. *Allegories of Empire: The Figure of Woman in the Colonial Text.* Minneapolis: University of Minnesota Press, 1993.

Spivak, Gayatri. *A Critique of Postcolonial Reason: Toward a History of the Vanishing Present.* Cambridge, Mass.: Harvard University Press, 1999.

Chapter Seven

Some Roots of Ecofeminism

Adorno, Theodor W. *Minima Moralia: Reflections from Damaged Life,* trans. E. F. M. Jephcott. London: New Left Books, 1974.

Aiken, William. "Non-Anthropocentric Ethical Challenges." In *Earthbound: New Introductory Essays in Environmental Ethics,* ed. Tom Regan. New York: Random House, 1984.

Caldecott, Leonie, and Stephanie Leland, eds. *Reclaim the Earth.* London: Women's Press, 1983.

Callicott, J. Baird. "Do Deconstructive Ecology and Sociobiology Undermine Leopold's Land Ethic?" In *Environmental Philosophy,* ed. Michael E. Zimmerman et al. 2nd ed. Upper Saddle River, N.J.: Prentice-Hall, 1998, pp. 145–164.

Carson, Rachel. *Silent Spring.* Boston: Houghton Mifflin, 1962.

Cheney, Jim. "Ecofeminism and Deep Ecology." *Environmental Ethics* 9, no. 2 (1987): 115–145.

_____. "The Neo-Stoicism of Radical Environmentalism." *Environmental Ethics* 11, no. 4 (1989): 293–326.

_____. "Postmodern Environmental Ethics: Ethics As Bioregional Narrative." *Environmental Ethics* 11, no. 2 (1989): 117–134.

Code, Lorraine. *Epistemic Responsibility.* Hanover, N.H.: University Press of New England, 1987.

Collard, Andree, with Joyce Contrucci. *Rape of the Wild: Man's Violence Against Animals and the Earth.* Bloomington: Indiana University Press, 1988.

Devall, Bill, and George Sessions. *Deep Ecology: Living As If Nature Mattered.* Salt Lake City: Peregrine Smith Books, 1985.

Ferry, Luc. *The New Ecological Order,* trans. Carol Volk. Chicago: University of Chicago Press, 1992.

Gebara, Ivone. *Longing for Running Water: Ecofeminism and Liberation.* Minneapolis: Fortress Press, 1999.

Harding, Sandra. *The Science Question in Feminism.* Ithaca, N.Y.: Cornell University Press, 1986.

Leopold, Aldo. "The Land Ethic." In *Sand County Almanac.* New York: Oxford University Press, 1987.

McDaniel, Jay B. *Earth, Sky, God, and Mortals: Developing an Ecological Spirituality.* Mystic, Conn.: Twenty-Third Publications, 1990.

Naess, Arne. "The Deep Ecological Movement: Some Philosophical Aspects." *Philosophical Inquiry* 8 (1986): 10–13.

_____. "The Shallow and the Deep, Long-range Ecology Movement: A Summary." *Inquiry* 16 (1973): 95–100.

Salleh, Ariel Kay. "Deeper Than Deep Ecology: The Ecofeminist Connection." *Environmental Ethics* 6, no. 1 (1984): 339.

Sessions, George. "The Deep Ecology Movement: A Review." *Environmental Review* 9, no. 1 (spring 1987): 115.

Wenz, Peter S. "Ecology and Morality." In *Ethics and Animals,* ed. Harlan B. Miller and William H. Williams. Clifton, N.J.: Humana Press, 1983.

Ecofeminism: New Philosophy or Ancient Wisdom?

Alaimo, Stacy. "Cyborg and Ecofeminist Interventions: Challenges for an Environmental Feminism." *Feminist Studies* 20, no. 1 (spring 1994): 133–152.

Allen, Paula Gunn. "The Woman I Love Is a Planet; the Planet I Love Is a Tree." In *Reweaving the World: The Emergence of Ecofeminism,* ed. Irene Diamond and Gloria Feman Orenstein. San Francisco: Sierra Club Books, 1990.

Auerbach, Judith. "The Intersection of Feminism and the Environmental Movement, or What Is Feminist About the Feminist Perspective on the Environment?" *American Behavioral Scientist* 37, no. 8 (August 1994): 1095.

Beauvoir, Simone de. *The Second Sex,* trans. and ed. H. M. Parshley. New York: Vintage Books, 1952.

Biehl, Janet. *Rethinking Feminist Politics.* Boston: South End Press, 1991.

Buege, Douglas. "Epistemic Responsibility to the Nature: Toward a Feminist Epistemology for Environmental Ethics." *American Philosophical Association Newsletter on Feminism and Philosophy* 91 (spring 1991): 73–78.

Cook, Julie. "The Philosophical Colonization of Ecofeminism." *Environmental Ethics* 20, no. 3 (fall, 1998): 227–246.

Crittenden, Chris. "Subordinate and Oppressive Conceptual Frameworks: A Defense of Ecofeminist Perspectives." *Environmental Ethics* 20, no. 3 (fall, 1998): 247–263.

Cuomo, Christine. "Toward Thoughtful Ecofeminist Activism." In *Ecological Feminist Philosophies,* ed. Karen J. Warren. Bloomington: Indiana University Press, 1996, pp. 42–51.

Diamond, Irene, and Gloria Feman Orenstein, eds. *Reweaving the World: The Emergence of Ecofeminism.* San Francisco: Sierra Club Books, 1990.

Fox, Warwick. "The Deep Ecology-Ecofeminism Debate and Its Parallels." *Environmental Ethics* 11, no. 1 (1989): 5–25.

Gaard, Greta. *Ecological Politics; Ecofeminists and the Greens.* Philadelphia: Temple University Press, 1993.

Gebara, Ivone. *Longing for Running Water: Ecofeminism and Liberation.* Minneapolis: Fortress Press, 1999.

Gruen, Lori. "Toward an Ecofeminist Moral Epistemology." In *Ecological Feminism,* ed. Karen J. Warren. New York: Routledge, 1994, pp. 120–138.

King, Roger J. H. "Caring About Nature: Feminist Ethics and the Environment." In *Ecological Feminist Philosophies,* ed. Karen J. Warren. Bloomington: Indiana University Press, 1996, pp. 82–96.

King, Ynestra. "The Ecology of Feminism and the Feminism of Ecology." In *Healing the Wounds: The Promise of Ecofeminism,* ed. Judith Plant. Santa Cruz, Calif.: New Society Publishers, 1989.

———. "Engendering a Peaceful Planet: Ecology, Economy, and Ecofeminism in Contemporary Context." *Women's Studies Quarterly* 23 (fall–winter 1995): 19.

Lahar, Stephanie. "Ecofeminist Theory and Grassroots Politics." In *Ecological Feminist Philosophies,* ed. Karen J. Warren. Bloomington: Indiana University Press, 1996, pp. 1–18.

Mellor, Mary. *Feminism and Ecology.* New York: New York University Press, 1997.

Merchant, Carolyn. *The Death of Nature: Women, Ecology, and the Scientific Revolution.* San Francisco: Harper & Row, 1980.

Mills, Patricia Jagentowicz. "Feminism and Ecology: On the Domination of Nature." In *Ecological Feminist Philosophies,* ed. Karen J. Warren. Bloomington: Indiana University Press, 1996, pp. 211–227.

Murphy, Patrick D. "Ground, Pivot, Motion: Ecofeminist Theory, Dialogics, and Literary Practice." In *Ecological Feminist Philosophies,* ed. Karen J. Warren. Bloomington: Indiana University Press, 1996, pp. 228–243.

Nordquist, Joan. "Ecofeminist Theory: A Bibliography." In *Social Theory: A Bibliographic Series* 36. Santa Cruz, Calif.: Reference and Research Services, 1994.

Ortner, Sherry B. "Is Female to Male As Nature Is to Culture?" In *Readings in Ecology and Feminist Theory,* ed. Mary Heather MacKinnon and Marie McIntyre. Kansas City, Kans.: Sheed and Ward, 1995.

Plumwood, Val. "Ecofeminism: An Overview and Discussion of Positions and Arguments." *Australian Journal of Philosophy* 64, supplement (June 1986): 135.

Roach, Catherine. "Loving Your Mother: On the Woman-Nature Connection." In *Ecological Feminist Philosophies,* ed. Karen J. Warren. Bloomington: Indiana University Press, 1996, pp. 52–65.

Salleh, Ariel Kay. *Ecofeminism As Politics: Nature, Marx and the Postmodern.* New York: Zed Books, 1997.

Sandilands, Catriona. *The Good-Natured Feminist: Ecofeminism and the Quest for Democracy.* Minneapolis: University of Minnesota Press, 1999.

Spretnak, Charlene. "Feminism and Ecology: Making Connections." In *Readings in Ecology and Feminist Theology,* ed. Mary Heather MacKinnon and Marie McIntyre. Kansas City, Kans.: Sheed and Ward, 1995.

_____. "Feminism and the Environment: An Overview of the Issues." *APA Newsletter on Feminism and Philosophy* 90, no. 3 (fall 1991): 110–111.

_____. "The Power and the Promise of Ecological Feminism." In *Ecological Feminist Philosophies,* ed. Karen J. Warren. Bloomington: Indiana University Press, 1996.

Sturgeon, Noël. *Ecofeminist Natures: Race, Gender, Feminist Theory and Political Action.* New York: Routledge, 1997.

Tuana, Nancy, and Karen J. Warren, eds. Special issues on Feminism and the Environment, *American Philosophical Association Newsletter on Feminism and Philosophy* 90, no. 3 (fall 1991), and 91, no. 1 (winter 1992).

Warren, Karen J. "Care-Sensitive Ethics and Situated Universalism." In *Global Environmental Ethics,* ed. Nicholas Low. London: Routledge, 1999, pp. 131–145.

_____. "Deep Ecology and Ecofeminism." In *Philosophical Dialogues: Arne Naess and the Progress of Ecophilosophy,* ed. Nina Witoszek and Andrew Brennan. Lanham, Md.: Rowman & Littlefield, 1999, pp. 255–269.

_____. "Feminism and Ecology." *Environmental Review* 9, no. 1 (spring 1987): 3–20.

_____. *Ecofeminist Philosophy: A Western Perspective on What It Is and Why It Matters.* Lanham, Md.: Rowman & Littlefield, 2000, p. 970.

Zabinski, Catherine. "Scientific Ecology and Ecological Feminism: The Potential for Dialogue." In *Ecofeminism: Women, Culture, Nature,* ed. Karen J. Warren. Bloomington: Indiana University Press, 1997, pp. 314–324.

Arguments for Severing, Reaffirming or Transforming Woman-Nature Connection

Adams, Carol J., ed. *Ecofeminism and the Sacred.* New York: Continuum, 1994.

Christ, Carol. *She Who Changes: Re-imagining the Divine in the World.* New York: Macmillan Palgrave, 2003.

Corrigan, Theresa, and Stephanie T. Hoppe. *With a Fly's Eye, Whale's Wit, and Woman's Heart: Animals and Women.* Pittsburgh: Cleis Press, 1989.

Cuomo, Christine. "Unravelling the Problems in Ecofeminism." *Environmental Ethics* 14, no. 4 (winter 1992): 351–363.

Curtin, Deane. "Toward an Ecological Ethic of Care." In *Ecological Feminist Philosophies,* ed. Karen J. Warren. Bloomington: Indiana University Press, 1996, pp. 129–143.

Daly, Mary. *Gyn/Ecology.* Boston: Beacon Press, 1978.

_____. *Pure Lust.* Boston: Beacon Press, 1984.

Dinnerstein, Dorothy. "Survival on Earth: The Meaning of Feminism." In *Healing the Wounds: The Promise of Ecofeminism,* ed. Judith Plant. Santa Cruz, Calif.: New Society Publishers, 1989.

Eaton, Heather, and Lois Ann Lorentzen. *Ecofeminism and Globalization: Exploring Culture, Context and Religion.* Lanham, Md.: Rowman & Littlefield, 2003.

Eisler, Riane. "The Gaia Tradition and the Partnership Future: An Ecofeminist Manifesto." In *Reweaving the World: The Emergence of Ecofeminism,* ed. Irene Diamond and Gloria Feman Orenstein. San Francisco: Sierra Club Books, 1990.

Gray, Elizabeth Dodson. *Green Paradise Lost.* Wellesley, Mass.: Roundtable Press, 1981.

_____. *Sacred Dimensions of Women's Experience.* Wellesley, Mass.: Roundtable Press, 1988.

Griffin, Susan. *Pornography and Silence: Culture's Revenge Against Nature.* New York: Harper & Row, 1981.

_____. *Woman and Nature: The Roaring Inside Her.* New York: Harper & Row, 1978.

Kheel, Marti. "The Liberation of Nature: A Circular Affair." *Environmental Ethics* 7, no. 2 (1985): 135–149.

Maccauley, David. "On Women, Animals and Nature: An Interview with Eco-feminist Susan Griffin." *APA Newsletter on Feminism and Philosophy* 90, no. 3 (fall 1991): 118.

McDaniel, Jay B. *Of God and Pelicans: A Theology of Reverence for Life.* Louisville, Ky.: Westminster/John Knox Press, 1989.

Merchant, Carolyn. *Reinventing Eden: The Fate of Nature in Western Culture.* New York: Routledge, 2003.

Piercy, Marge. *Woman on the Edge of Time.* New York: Fawcett Crest Books, 1976.

Plant, Judith, ed. *Healing the Wounds: The Promise of Ecofeminism.* Santa Cruz, Calif.: New Society Publishers, 1989.

Ruether, Rosemary Radford. *New Woman/New Earth: Sexist Ideologies and Human Liberation.* New York: Seabury Press, 1975.

_____. *Ecofeminism: Symbolic and Social Connections Between the Oppression of Women and the Domination of Nature.* Charlotte: University of North Carolina, 1991.

_____, ed. *Women Healing Earth: Third World Women on Ecology, Feminism and Religion.* Maryknoll, N.Y.: Orbis Books, 1996.

Spretnak, Charlene. "Toward an Ecofeminist Spirituality." In Judith Plant, ed., *Healing the Wounds: The Promise of Ecofeminism.* Philadelphia, PA: New Society Publishers, 1989.

_____, ed. *The Politics of Women's Spirituality.* Garden City, N.Y.: Anchor, 1982.

_____. "Earthbody and Personal Body As Sacred." In *Ecofeminism and the Sacred,* ed. Carol J. Adams. New York: Continuum, 1994, pp. 261–80.

Starhawk. *The Spiral Dance: A Rebirth of the Ancient Religion of the Great Goddess.* San Francisco: HarperSanFrancisco, 1979.

_____. *Dreaming in the Dark: Magic, Sex and Politics.* Boston: Beacon, 1982.

_____. *Truth or Dare: Encounters with Power, Authority and Mystery.* San Francisco: Harper and Row, 1987.

_____. "Feminist, Earth-based Spirituality and Ecofeminism." In *Healing the Wounds: The Promise of Ecofeminism,* ed. Judith Plant. Philadelphia: New Society Publishers, 1989.

_____. "A Story of Beginnings." In *Healing the Wounds: The Promise of Ecofeminism,* ed. Judith Plant. Philadelphia: New Society Publishers, 1989, p. 115.

_____. "Power, Authority, and Mystery: Ecofeminism and Earth-based Spirituality." In *Reweaving the World: The Emergence of Ecofeminism,* ed. Irene Diamond and Gloria Orenstein. San Francisco: Sierra Club Books, 1990.

_____. *Rebirth of the Goddess: Finding Meaning in Feminist Spirituality.* New York: Routledge, 1997.

_____. *She Who Changes: Re-imagining the Divine in the World.* New York: Macmillan Palgrave, 2003.

Global Ecofeminism

Chua, Amy. *World on Fire: How Exploring Free Market Democracy Breeds Ethnic Hatred and Global Instability.* New York: Anchor, 2003, pp. 123–45; 163–75.

Cuomo, Christine. "Ecofeminism, Deep Ecology, and Human Population." In *Ecological Feminism,* ed. Karen J. Warren. New York: Routledge, 1994, pp. 88–105.

Eaton, Heather, and Lois Ann Lorentzen. *Ecofeminism and Globalization: Exploring Culture, Context and Religion.* Lanham, Md.: Rowman & Littlefield, 2003.

"From Bretton Woods to Alternatives." In *Alternatives to Economic Globalization,* ed. International Forum on Globalization. San Francisco: Berrett-Koehler, 2002, pp. 228–238.

LaChapelle, Dolores. *Earth Wisdom.* Silverton, Colo.: Way of the Mountain Learning Center and International College, 1978.

Mellor, Mary. *Feminism and Ecology.* New York: New York University Press, 1997.

Merchant, Carolyn. *Radical Ecology: The Search for a Livable World.* New York: Routledge, 1992.

Mies, Maria, and Vandana Shiva. *Ecofeminism.* London: Zed, 1993.

Mies, Maria. "White Man's Dilemma: His Search for What He Has Destroyed." In *Ecofeminism,* ed. Maria Mies and Vandana Shiva. London: Zed, 1993, pp. 132–163.

———. "The Need for a New Vision: The Subsistence Perspective." In *Ecofeminism,* ed. Maria Mies and Vandana Shiva. London: Zed, 1993, pp. 319–322.

Moe-Lobeda, Cynthia. *Globalization and God: Healing a Broken World.* Minneapolis: Fortress Press, 2002.

Nader, Ralph, et al. *The Case against 'Free Trade': GATT, NAFTA, and the Globalization of Corporate Power.* San Francisco: Earth Island Press, 1993.

Rich, Bruce. *Mortgaging the Earth: The World Bank, Environmental Impoverishment and the Crisis of Development.* Boston: Beacon, 1994, pp. 49–106.

Rocheleau, Dianne, Barbara Thomas-Slayter, and Esther Wangari, eds. *Feminist Political Ecology: Global Issues and Local Experiences.* New York: Routledge, 1996.

Ruether, Rosemary Radford. "Culture and Women's Rights." *Conscience* 16, no. 4 (winter, 1995–96): 13–15.

———, ed. *Women Healing Earth: Third World Women on Ecology, Feminism and Religion.* Maryknoll, N.Y.: Orbis Books, 1996.

Seager, Joni. *Earth Follies: Coming to Feminist Terms with the Global Environmental Crisis.* New York: Routledge, 1993.

Shiva, Vandana. "Taking Empirical Data Seriously: An Ecofeminist Philosophy Perspective." In *Living with Contradictions: Controversies in Feminist Social Ethics,* ed. Alison M. Jaggar. Boulder, Colo.: Westview Press, 1994, pp. 642–643.

———. "The Chipko-Women's Concept of Freedom." In *Ecofeminism,* ed. Maria Mies and Vandana Shiva. London: Zed, 1993, p. 247.

———. *Biopiracy: The Plunder of Nature and Knowledge.* Boston: South End Press, 1997.

Starhawk. *Webs of Power: Notes from the Global Uprising.* Gabriola Island, British Columbia: New Society Publishers, 2002, pp. 244–45.

———. *Webs of Power: Notes from the Global Uprising.* Gabriola Island, British Columbia: New Society Publishers, 2002.

Sutcliffe, Bob. *100 Ways of Seeing an Unequal World.* London: Zed, 2001, sections 23, 33.

Chapter Eight

Postmodern Influences on Postmodern Feminism

Brennan, Teresa, ed. *History after Lacan.* London: Routledge, 1993.

Clement, Catherine. *The Lives and Legends of Jacques Lacan.* New York: Columbia University Press, 1983.

Grosz, Elizabeth. *Jacques Lacan: A Feminist Introduction.* New York: Routledge, 1990.

Hicks, Stephen R. C. *Exploring Postmodernism: Skepticism and Socialism from Rousseau to Foucault.* Tempe, Ariz.: Scholarly Publishing, 2004.

Lacan, Jacques. *Écrits: A Selection,* trans. Alan Sheridan. New York: W. W. Norton, 1977.
_____. "The Meaning of the Phallus." In *Feminine Sexuality,* ed. J. Mitchell and J. Rose. New York: W. W. Norton, 1982.
Lyotard, Jean-François. *The Postmodern Condition: A Report on Knowledge.* Minneapolis: University of Minnesota Press, 1984.
Rosenau, Pauline Marie. *Post-Modernism and the Social Sciences: Insights, Inroads, and Intrusions.* Princeton, N.J.: Princeton University Press, 1992.
_____. *Post-Modernism and the Social Sciences: Insights, Inroads, and Intrusions.* Princeton, N.J.: Princeton University Press, 1992.
Smart, Barry. *Postmodernity: Key Ideas.* New York: Routledge, 1993.
Sturrock, John. Introduction to *Structuralism and Since: From Lévi-Strauss to Derrida.* New York: Oxford University Press, 1979.
Wolin, Sheldon. "Modernism vs. Postmodernism." *Telos* 62 (1984–1985): 9–29.
Zerilli, Linda M. G. "A Process Without a Subject: Simone de Beauvoir and Julia Kristeva on Maternity." *Signs: Journal of Women in Culture and Society* 8, no. 1 (1982): 111–135.

Focus on Jacques Derrida

Derrida, Jacques. *Speech and Phenomena and Other Essays on Husserl's Theory of Signs,* trans. David B. Allison. Evanston, Ill.: Northwestern University Press, 1973.
_____. *Of Grammatology,* trans. Gayatri Chakravorty Spivak. Baltimore: Johns Hopkins University Press, 1974.
_____. "Cogito and the History of Madness." In *Writing and Difference,* trans. Alan Bass. Chicago: Chicago University Press, 1978, pp. 31–63.
_____. *Writing and Difference,* trans. Alan Bass. Chicago: University of Chicago Press, 1978.
_____. *Spurs: Nietzsche's Styles,* trans. Barbara Harlow. Chicago: University of Chicago Press, 1978.
_____. *Margins of Philosophy,* trans. Alan Bass. Chicago: University of Chicago Press, 1982.
_____. *Positions,* trans. Alan Bass. Chicago: University of Chicago Press, 1982.
_____. *The Ear of the Other: Otobiography, Transference, Translation: Texts and Discussions with Jacques Derrida,* trans. Avital Ronell and Peggy Kamuf. New York: Schocken Books, 1985.
_____. *The Post Card: From Socrates to Freud and Beyond,* trans. Alan Bass. Chicago: University of Chicago Press, 1987.
_____. *The Truth in Painting,* trans. Geoff Bennington and Ian McLeod. Chicago: Chicago University Press, 1987.
_____. *Of Spirit: Heidegger and the Question,* trans. Geoffrey Bennington and Rachel Bowlby. Chicago: University of Chicago Press, 1989.

_____. *Gift of Death,* trans. David Wills. Chicago: University of Chicago Press, 1995.

_____. *On the Name.* Stanford: Stanford University Press, 1995.

_____. *Politics of Friendship,* trans. George Collins. London: Verso Books, 1997.

_____. *A Taste for the Secret,* trans. Giacomo Donis. Cambridge: Cambridge University Press, 2001.

Elam, Diane. *Feminism and Deconstructionism: Ms. En Abyme.* New York: Routledge, 1994.

Feder, Ellen K., Mary C. Rawlinson, and Emily Zakin, eds. *Derrida and Feminism.* New York: Routledge, 1997.

Kamuf, Peggy, ed. *Between the Blinds.* New York: Columbia University Press, 1991.

Focus on Michel Foucault

Christmas, Simon. "Michel Foucault." In *An Introduction to Modern European Philosophy,* ed. Jenny Teichman and Graham White. New York: Palgrave MacMillan, 1995.

Connolly, William. "Taylor, Foucault, and Otherness." *Political Theory* 13, no. 3 (1985): 365–376.

Diamond, Irene, and Lee Quinby, eds. *Feminism and Foucault: Reflections on Resistance.* Boston: Northeastern University Press, 1988.

Dudrick, David. "Foucault, Butler, and the Body." *European Journal of Philosophy* 13, no. 2 (2005): 226–246.

Eribon, Didier. *Michel Foucault.* Cambridge, Mass.: Harvard University Press, 1991.

Foucault, Michel. *Madness and Civilization,* trans. Richard Howard. New York: Pantheon, 1965.

_____. *Archeology of Knowledge,* trans. A. Sheridan Smith. New York: Harper & Row, 1972.

_____. *The Birth of the Clinic,* trans. A. Sheridan Smith. New York: Pantheon, 1973.

_____. *The Order of Things.* New York: Vintage, 1973.

_____. *Discipline and Punish: The Birth of the Prison.* London: Allen Lane, 1977.

_____. *Language, Counter-Memory, Practice: Selected Essays and Interviews,* trans. Donald F. Bouchard. Ithaca: Cornell University Press, 1977.

_____. *Power/Knowledge,* ed. Colin Gordon. New York: Random House, 1981.

_____. *The History of Sexuality.* Vol. 1, *An Introduction.* London: Penguin, 1984.

_____. *The History of Sexuality.* Volumes 1–3, *Introduction, The Uses of Pleasure, and Care of the Self,* trans. Robert Hurley. New York: Vintage, 1988–1990.

McHoul, Alec, and Wendy Grace. *A Foucault Primer: Discourse, Power and the Subject.* New York: New York University Press, 1993.

McNay, Lois. *Foucault and Feminism and the Self.* Boston: Northeastern University Press, 1993.

Mitchell, Juliet, and Jacqueline Rose, eds. *Feminine Sexuality: Jacques Lacan and the École Freudienne,* trans. Jacqueline Rose. New York: W. W. Norton, 1982.

Ramazanoglu, Caroline, ed. *Up Against Foucault: Exploration of Some Tensions Between Foucault and Feminism.* New York: Routledge, 1993.

Sawicki, Jana. *Disciplining Foucault: Feminism, Power, and the Body.* New York: Routledge, 1991.

Taylor, Dianna, and Karen Vintges. *Feminism and the Final Foucault.* Urbana: University of Illinois Press, 2004.

Postmodern Feminism in General

Agger, Ben. *Gender, Culture, and Power: Toward a Feminist Postmodern Critical Theory.* New York: Praeger Publishers, 1993.

Alcoff, Linda Martín. "Cultural Feminism Versus Post-Structuralism: The Identity Crisis in Feminist Theory." In *Feminism and Philosophy: Essential Readings,* ed. Nancy Tuana and Rosemarie Tong. Boulder, Colo.: Westview Press, 1995.

_____. "Philosophy Matters: A Review of Recent Work in Feminist Philosophy." *Signs: Journal of Women in Culture and Society* 25 (2000): 841–882.

Assiter, Alison. *Enlightened Women: Modernist Feminism in a Postmodern Age.* London: Routledge, 1996.

Benhabib, Seyla. *Situating the Self: Gender, Community, and Postmodernism in Contemporary Ethics.* London: Routledge, 1992.

_____. "Feminism and Postmodernism." In *Feminist Contentions: A Philosophical Exchange,* ed. Seyla Benhabib et al. New York and London: Routledge, 1994, pp. 17–34.

Bordo, Susan. "Feminism, Postmodernism, and Gender-Scepticism." In *Feminism/Postmodernism,* ed. Linda J. Nicholson. New York: Routledge, 1990, pp. 133–156.

Bree, Germaine. *Women Writers in France.* New Brunswick, N.J.: Rutgers University Press, 1973.

Brown, Wendy. "Feminist Hesitations, Postmodern Exposures." *Differences* 3, no. 1 (1991): 63–84.

Burke, Carolyn Greenstein. "Report from Paris: Women's Writing and the Women's Movement." *Signs: Journal of Women in Culture and Society* 4, no. 4 (summer 1978): 843–854.

Butler, Judith. "The Body Politics of Julia Kristeva." *Hypatia* 3, no. 3 (winter 1989): 104–118.

Cahill, Ann J., and Jennifer Hansen. *Continental Feminism Reader.* Lanham, Md.: Rowman & Littlefield, 2003.

Chanter, Tina. *Ethics of Eros: Irigaray's Rewriting of the Philosophers.* New York: Routledge, 1995.

Code, Lorraine. "Feminist Epistemology." In *A Companion to Epistemology,* ed. Jonathan Dancy and Ernst Sosa. Oxford: Blackwell, 1992, pp. 138–142.

Cornell, Drucilla. *Beyond Accommodation: Ethical Feminism, Deconstruction, and the Law.* New York: Routledge, 1991.

Di Stefano, Christine. "Dilemmas of Difference." In *Feminism/Postmodernism,* ed. Linda J. Nicholson. New York: Routledge, 1990, pp. 63–82.

Faure, Christine. "Absent from History." *Signs: Journal of Women in Culture and Society* 7, no. 1 (1981): 71–80.

Flax, Jane. *Thinking Fragments: Psychoanalysis, Feminism, and Postmodernism in the Contemporary West.* Berkeley: University of California Press, 1989.

_____. "Postmodernism and Gender Relations in Feminist Theory." In *Feminism/Postmodernism,* ed. Linda J. Nicholson. New York: Routledge, 1990.

Fraser, Nancy. *Unruly Practices: Power, Gender and Discourse in Contemporary Critical Theory.* Minneapolis: University of Minnesota Press, 1989.

Fraser, Nancy, and Linda J. Nicholson. "Social Criticism Without Philosophy: An Encounter Between Feminism and Postmodernism." In *Feminism/Postmodernism,* ed. Linda J. Nicholson. New York: Routledge, 1990.

Grosz, Elizabeth. *Sexual Subversions: Three French Feminists.* Sydney: Allen & Unwin, 1989.

Grosz, Elizabeth, with Pheng Cheah. *Irigary and the Political Future of Sexual Difference.* Baltimore: Johns Hopkins University Press, 1998.

Hekman, Susan. *Gender and Knowledge: Elements of a Postmodern Feminism.* Cambridge: Polity Press, 1990.

Irigaray, Luce. "Is the Subject of Science Sexed?" Carol Mastrangelo Bové. *Hypatia* 2, no. 3 (fall 1987): 66.

_____. *Speculum of the Other Woman,* trans. Gillian C. Gill. Ithaca, N.Y.: Cornell University Press, 1985.

_____. *This Sex Which Is Not One,* trans. Catherine Porter. Ithaca, N.Y.: Cornell University Press, 1985.

_____. *An Ethics of Difference,* trans. Carolyn Burke and Gillian Gill. Ithaca, N.Y.: Cornell University Press, 1993.

Jardine, Alice and Hester Eisenstein, eds. *The Future of Difference.* New Brunswick, N.J.: Rutgers University, Press, 1985.

Jones, Ann Rosalind. "Writing the Body: Toward an Understanding of *l'Écriture Féminine.*" *Feminist Studies* 7, no. 1 (summer 1981): 248.

Kolmar, Wendy, and Frances Bartkowski, eds. *Feminist Theory: A Reader.* New York: Routledge, 2000.

Kristeva, Julia. *About Chinese Women,* trans. Anita Barrows. New York: Marion Boyars, 1977.

_____. "Women's Time." *Signs: Journal of Women in Culture and Society* 7, no. 1 (summer 1981): 13–35.

_____. *Desire in Language,* trans. Leon Roudiez. New York: Columbia University Press, 1982.

_____. *Powers of Horror,* trans. Leon Roudiez. New York: Columbia University Press, 1982.

Kuykendall, Eléanor H. "Toward an Ethic of Nurturance: Luce Irigaray on Mothering and Power." In *Mothering: Essays in Feminist Theory,* ed. Joyce Trebilcot. Totowa, N.J.: Rowman & Allanheld, 1984.

Marchand, Marianne H., and Jane Parpart, eds. *Feminism/Postmodernism/Development.* New York: Routledge, 1994.

Marks, Elaine. "Review Essay: Women and Literature in France." *Signs: Journal of Women in Culture and Society* 3, no. 4 (summer 1978): 832–842.

Messer-Davidow, Ellen. *Disciplining Feminism: From Social Activism to Academic Discourse.* Durham, N.C.: Duke University Press, 2002.

Moi, Toril. *Sexual/Textual Politics: Feminist Literary Theory.* New York: Methuen, 1985.

_____. *The Kristeva Reader.* New York: Columbia University Press, 1986.

Nicholson, Linda, ed. *Feminism/Postmodernism.* London: Routledge, 1989.

Oliver, Kelly. "Julia Kristeva's Feminist Revolutions." *Hypatia* 8, no. 3 (summer 1993).

_____, ed. *French Feminist Thought: A Reader.* New York: Blackwell, 1987.

_____. *French Feminism Reader.* Lanham, Md.: Rowman & Littlefield, 2000.

_____. *Witnessing: Beyond Recognition.* Minneapolis: University of Minnesota Press, 2001.

Oliver, Kelly, with Lisa Walsh, eds. *Contemporary French Feminism.* New York: Oxford University Press, 2005.

Shildrick, Margrit. *Leaky Bodies and Boundaries: Feminism, Postmodernism and (Bio)Ethics.* New York: Routledge, 1997.

Spivak, Gayatri Chakravorty. *In Other Words: Essays in Cultural Politics.* New York: Routledge, 1987.

_____. *Identity: Further Essays on Culture As Politics.* New York: Routledge, 2000.

Steward, Danièle. "The Women's Movement in France." *Signs: Journal of Women in Culture and Society* 6, no. 2 (winter 1980): 353.

Weedon, Chris. *Feminist Practice and Poststructuralist Theory.* Cambridge: Blackwell, 1987.

Whitford, Margaret. "Luce Irigaray and the Female Imaginary: Speaking As a Woman." *Radical Philosophy* 43 (summer 1986): 7.

_____. *Luce Irigaray: Philosophy in the Feminine.* New York: Routledge, 1991.

_____, ed. *The Irigaray Reader.* Cambridge: Blackwell, 1991.

Wittig, Monique. *The Opoponax.* New York: Simon & Schuster, 1966.

_____. *The Lesbian Body.* New York: William Morrow, 1975.

_____. *Les Guérillères.* New York: Viking, 1971.

_____. *The Straight Mind and Other Essays.* Boston: Beacon Press, 1992.

Focus on Hélène Cixous

Cixous, Hélène. "Castration or Decapitation?" *Signs: Journal of Women in Culture and Society* 7, no. 1 (summer 1981a): 41–55.

———. "The Laugh of the Medusa." In *New French Feminisms,* ed. Elaine Marks and Isabelle de Courtivron. New York: Schocken Books, 1981.

———. *Inside,* trans. Carol Barko. New York: Schocken Books, 1986.

———. *Reading with Clarice Lispector,* trans. Verena Adermatt Conley. Minneapolis: Minnesota University Press, 1990.

———. *The Book of Promethea,* trans. Betsy Wing. Lincoln: University of Nebraska Press, 1991.

———. *"Coming to Writing" and Other Essays,* trans. Sarah Cornell et al. Cambridge, Mass.: Harvard University Press, 1991.

———. *Three Steps on the Ladder of Writing,* trans. Sarah Cornell and Susan Sellers. New York: Columbia University Press, 1993.

Cixous, Hélène, and Catherine Clément. "Sorties." In *The Newly Born Woman,* trans. Betsy Wing. Minneapolis: University of Minnesota Press, 1986.

Cixous, Hélène, with Mirelle Calle-Gruber. *Hélène Cixous, Rootprints: Memory and Life Writings,* trans. Eric Prenowitz. New York: Routledge, 1997.

Duchen, Claire. *Feminism in France: From May '68 to Mitterrand.* London: Routledge & Kegan Paul, 1986.

Sellers, Susan, ed. *The Hélène Cixous Reader.* New York: Routledge, 1994.

Focus on Judith Butler

Allen, Amy. "Dependency, Subordination, and Recognition: On Judith Butler's Theory of Subjection." *Continental Philosophy Review* 38 (2006): 199–222.

Butler, Judith. *Subjects of Desire: Hegelian Reflections in Twentieth Century France.* New York: Columbia University Press, 1987.

———. *Gender Trouble: Feminism and the Subversion of Identity.* New York: Routledge, 1990.

———. *Bodies That Matter: On the Discursive Limits of "Sex."* New York: Routledge, 1993.

———. *Excitable Speech: A Politics of the Performative.* New York: Routledge, 1997.

———. *The Psychic Life of Power: Theories in Subjection.* Stanford, Calif.: Stanford University Press, 1997.

———. *Undoing Gender.* New York: Routledge, 2004.

Butler, Judith, Elisabeth Beck-Gernsheim, and Lidia Puigvert. *Women and Social Transformation.* New York: Routledge, 2003.

Disch, Lisa. "Judith Butler and the Politics of the Performative." Book review in *Social Theory* 27, no. 4 (August 1999): 545–559.

Magnus, Kathy Dow. "The Unaccountable Subject: Judith Butler and the Social Conditions of Intersubjective Agency." *Hypatia* 21, no. 2 (spring, 2006): 81–103.

McNay, Lois. "Subject, Psyche, and Agency: The Work of Judith Butler." *Theory, Culture & Society* 16, no. 2 (1999): 175–193.

Mills, Catherine. "Efficacy and Vulnerability: Judith Butler on Reiteration and Resistance." *Australian Feminist Studies* 159, no. 32 (2000): 265–279.

_____. "Contesting the Political: Butler and Foucault on Power and Resistance." *Journal of Political Philosophy* 11, no. 3 (2003): 253–272.

Nussbaum, Martha C. "The Professor of Parody: The Hip Defeatism of Judith Butler." *The New Republic,* February 22, 1999, pp. 37–45.

Salih, Sara. *Judith Butler.* New York: Routledge, 2002.

Webster, Fiona. "The Politics of Sex and Gender: Benhabib and Butler Debate Subjectivity." *Hypatia* 15, no. 1 (winter 2000): 1–22.

Third-Wave Feminism

Alfonso, Rita, and Jo Trigilio. "Surfing the Third Wave: A Dialogue Between Two Third Wave Feminists." *Hypatia* 12, no. 3 (summer 1997): 8–16.

Baumgardner, Jennifer, and Amy Richards. *Manifesta: Young Women, Feminism, and the Future.* New York: Farrar, Straus, and Giroux, 2000.

_____. *Grassroots: A Field Guide for Feminist Activism.* New York: Farrar, Straus, and Giroux, 2005.

Breines, Wini. "What's Love Got to Do with It? White Women, Black Women, and Feminism in the Movement Years." *Signs: Journal of Women in Culture and Society* 27, no. 4 (summer 2002): 1096–1133.

Bruns, Cindy M., and Colleen Trimble. "Rising Tide: Taking Our Place As Young Feminist Psychologists." In *The Newest Generation: Third Wave Psychotherapy,* ed. Ellen Kaschak. Binghamton, N.Y.: Haworth Press, 2001): 19–36.

Cashen, Jeanne. "The Revolution Is Mine: Grrrl Resistance in a Commodity Culture." Unpublished manuscript, University of New Orleans, 2002.

Dicker, Rory, and Alison Piepmeier, eds. *Catching a Wave: Reclaiming Feminism for the 21st Century.* Boston: Northeastern University Press, 2003.

Edut, Ophira, ed. *Adios Barbie: Young Women Write about Body Image and Identity.* Seattle: Seal Press, 1998.

Ensler, Eve. *The Vagina Monologues.* London: Virigo Press, 2001.

Findlen, Barbara, ed. *Listen Up! Voices from the Next Feminist Generations.* Berkeley, Calif.: Seal Press, 1995.

Gillis, Stacy, Gillian Howie, and Rebecca Munford. *Third Wave Feminism: A Critical Exploration.* New York: Palgrave, 2007.

Halstead, Ted. "A Politics for Generation X." *Atlantic Monthly* 284, no. 2 (August 1999): 33–42.

Henry, Astrid. "Feminism's Family Problem: Feminist Generations and the Mother-Daughter Trope." In *Catching a Wave: Reclaiming Feminism for the 21st Century*, ed. Rory Dicker and Alison Piepmeier. Boston: Northeastern University Press, 2003, pp. 209–231.

_____. *Not My Mother's Sister: Generational Conflict and Third-Wave Feminism*. Bloomington: Indiana University Press, 2004.

Hernandez, Daisy, and Bushra Reman. *Colonize This! Young Women of Color and Today's Feminism*. Berkeley, Calif.: Seal Press, 2002.

Heywood, Leslie, and Jennifer Drake, eds. *Third Wave Agenda: Being Feminist, Doing Feminism*. Minneapolis: University of Minnesota Press, 1997.

Huffman, D. J. "Making Sense of Third Wave Feminism." MA thesis, University of New Orleans, 2002.

Jervis, Lisa, and Andi Zeisler, eds. *Bitchfest*. New York: Farrar, Straus, and Giroux, 2006.

Kaminer, Wendy. "Feminism's Third Wave: What Do Young Women Want?" *New York Times Book Review*, June 4, pp. 8–9.

Kinser, Amber. "Negotiating Space For/Through Third-Wave Feminism." *NWSA Journal* 16, no. 3 (2005): 124–153.

Koyama, Emi. "The Transfeminist Manifesto." In *Catching a Wave: Reclaiming Feminism for the 21st Century*, ed. Rory Dicker and Alison Piepmeier. Boston: Northeastern University Press, 2003, pp. 244–259.

Martin, Susan. "Keep Us on the Pedestal: Women Against Feminism in Twentieth-Century America." In *Women: A Feminist Perspective*, ed. Jo Freeman. Mountain View, Calif.: Mayfield, 1989.

Musico, Inga. *Cunt: A Declaration of Independence*. Berkeley, Calif.: Seal Press, 2002.

Quinn, Rebecca. "An Open Letter to Institutional Mothers." In *Generations: Academic Feminists in Dialogue*, ed. Devoney Looser and Ann Kaplan. Minneapolis: University of Minnesota Press, 1997.

Rowe-Finkbeiner, Kristin. *The F-Word*. New York: Avalon Publishing Group, 2004.

Siegel, Deborah L. "The Legacy of the Personal: Generating Theory in Feminism's Third Wave." *Hypatia* 12, no. 3 (1997): 46–75.

Springer, Kimberly. "Third Wave Black Feminism?" *Signs: Journal of Women in Culture and Society* 27, no. 4 (2002): 1059–1082.

Walker, Rebecca, ed. *To Be Real: Telling the Truth and Changing the Face of Feminism*. New York: Anchor Books, 1995.

Whittier, Nancy. *Feminist Generations: The Persistence of the Radical Women's Movement*. Philadelphia: Temple University Press, 1995.

Index

radical feminist view of critiqued, 91–92

as symbiotic with capitalism, 5

women's bodies and, 60–61

women's oppression and, 51, 52–54, 115–118

Patrilineage, 105–106

Peace, 186–188, 196

Penis, 136, 137

Penis envy, 131, 132, 134, 144

Performativity, 282

Perlocutionary acts, 282

Personal Responsibility Act of 1996, 197–198

Personality, 103

Personhood, 16, 34

Phallic feminine, 314n70

Phallic stage, 130

Phallic symbol, 126

Phillips, Anne, 231

Philosophy, 38

Phoneme, 274–275

Piercy, Marge, 75–78, 257–258

Pill, the, 220

Piper, Adrian, 209–210

Plastic passions, 65

Plato, 41, 249–250

Pleasure, 58

Plumwood, Val, 244–245

Political lesbianism, 72

Political skepticism, 38, 39

Political solipsism, 38–39

Politics

linking women and peace, 187–188

Marxist theory of, 102–104

of resistance, 187

Polyandrogyny, 37

"Polymorphous perverse" sexuality, 129–130

Pornography, 53, 68–71, 251

Possessiveness, 75

Postcolonial feminism

alternative terms for "feminist," 215–216

on economic development programs, 225–228

focus of, 200–201, 215

friendship and sisterhood, 233–236

global production issues, 223–224

global reproductive issues, 218–223

issues of universalism *versus* relativism, 228–233

long-term goals, 216

perspectives within, 7–8

recognizing and addressing differences, 217–218

Postcolonial feminists, 8

Postgate, John, 81–82

Postmodern feminism

Judith Butler, 272, 280–283

Hélène Cixous, 275–277

critique of, 283–284

Jacques Derrida, 274–275

Michel Foucault, 277–280

French feminists, 329–330n6

overview of, 270

perspectives within, 8–9

postmodernism and, 270, 273–274

rise of, 126

second-wave feminism and, 272

shared tendencies with third-wave feminism, 290

Postmodernism, 270, 273–274

Potted passions, 65

Pour-soi-en-soi dialectic, 244

Poverty, 170–171

Power and Power relations

capitalism and, 99

formulations of, 58–59, 62, 278–280

masculine and feminine versions of, 58–59

modernist notion of, 273

sexuality and, 52, 278–280

Practices, 182–183. See also Maternal practice

Preferential treatment, 35–36

Pregnancy, 79